THE GRAND STRATEGY
OF THE HABSBURG EMPIRE

The Grand Strategy
of the Habsburg Empire

A. WESS MITCHELL

PRINCETON UNIVERSITY PRESS
PRINCETON & OXFORD

Published by Princeton University Press,
41 William Street, Princeton, New Jersey 08540

In the United Kingdom: Princeton University Press,
6 Oxford Street, Woodstock, Oxfordshire OX20 1TR

press.princeton.edu

Cover art: Jacob van Schuppen, *Portrait of Prince Eugene of Savoy*, 1718.
Oil on canvas. Rijksmuseum, Amsterdam

LCCN 2017964042
First paperback printing, 2019
Paperback ISBN 978-0-691-19644-2
Cloth ISBN 978-0-691-17670-3

British Library Cataloging-in-Publication Data is available

This book has been composed in Arno Pro

Printed on acid-free paper. ∞

Printed in the United States of America

For Kent Ellis, an old Texan who loved history and learned from it

CONTENTS

THIS BOOK BEGAN with a question: How does a Great Power with limited military resources manage strategic competition against multiple rivals simultaneously? All states face constraints in their ability to project power; most face threats that, if effectively combined, would overwhelm their capacity for self-defense. But for certain types of state, the gap between threats and resources is especially wide. Great Powers that occupy interstitial geography—that is, states of major military potential inhabiting the space between other large power centers—must anticipate existential threats from more than one direction. Even if their enemies do not actively conspire and combine against them, the mere presence of competitors at opposite points on the compass stretches attention and resources. If war comes, they must assume that unless carefully managed, any conflict could spread to include several theaters. For such powers, exposure to the chaos of geopolitics is greater, reprieves from the strains of war are fewer, and bondage to financial, human, and moral trade-offs in the quest for an affordable safety is sharper than for states that enjoy more protective geography.

Interstitial powers in history have often had short and turbulent lives. The classical empires between the Mediterranean and Persian seas rose and fell in astonishing rapidity—Babylonians eclipsed Akkadians, and in turn, Assyrians and Persians overtook Babylonians. The rulers of the Achaemenid Empire had to contend with problems on a dizzying array of frontiers, only one of which eventually brought the conquests of Alexander with whom Western audiences are so familiar. The Eastern Roman Empire, from its perch in Constantinople at the crossroads of Europe and Asia Minor, achieved a longer run of success than most, but was plagued by omnidirectional threats in the years leading up to its collapse. The Polish-Lithuanian Commonwealth was just one in a long procession of empires that flourished for a season only to founder in the violent soil between the Baltic and Black Seas. And even the powerful German Empire built by Otto von Bismarck (1815–98), buoyed by offensive warfighting qualities par excellence, endured in various forms for less than a century before succumbing to the encircling *cauchemars des coalition*.

The problem facing interstitial powers is time. Unable to secure all of their frontiers with equal strength, they must choose where to concentrate precious diplomatic and military resources, and in the process, inevitably incur vulnerabilities elsewhere. The modern solution to the problem of time in strategy is offensive technology. The Clausewitzian idée fixe of a decisive battle, harnessed to new technologies propelling lethality across large distances, has seemed to offer the possibility of quickly defeating multiple opponents in turn. The picture of German generals in 1914 using railway timetables to shuffle armies from east to west, and in 1940 using tank armies to neutralize flanking opponents at leisure, is firmly entrenched in the Western imagination, despite the disastrous outcomes of German strategy in both wars. Above all, the American experience in the Second World War, when vast fleets and armies delivered knockout blows to peer competitors in opposite directions from the US mainland, appeared to confirm technology's triumph over geography. The end of the Cold War only heightened the effect; so confident was the United States of the space-conquering attributes of offensive technology that it envisioned defeating continent-sized rivals in Europe and Asia while handling a third, smaller crisis elsewhere without even mobilizing its full warfighting capabilities.

The pages that follow examine how one Great Power, far less gifted materially than twentieth-century Germany or twenty-first-century United States, dealt with the problem of *tous azimuts* strategic danger. Few empires in history better exemplify the unforgiving nature of interstitial geography than the Habsburg Monarchy. From its emergence as a stand-alone entity in the early eighteenth century until its collapse after the First World War, the Danubian realm of the Austrian Habsburgs was engaged in uninterrupted military competition across a space extending from the warm waters of the Adriatic to the snowy crests of the Carpathians and from the Balkans to the Alps. This book's immediate interest lies in the debates that took place among small groups of Habsburg soldiers, rulers, and diplomats whose lives were spread across perhaps six or seven generations, but all of whom were bound together by the shared experience of contemplating strategic statecraft in the vortex of the "lands between."

A grand strategic account of the Habsburgs is overdue. Such a subject holds intrinsic merit. But it is also worth studying for our own benefit today. In a century that seems well on track to delivering a scale of geopolitical turmoil that no one could have imagined in the heady days after 1989, the experiences of an empire that weathered centuries of change, and in whose soil the strategic issues of our own time are irrevocably intertwined, seem more relevant than ever. Such lessons as can be gleaned from Habsburg Austria's successes and failures hold, if anything, heightened value at a time when the effects of traditional geopolitical competition are being rendered no less severe by distance, technology, and the passage of time. This book is offered in hopes of managing, though perhaps never fully mastering, these challenges in order to preserve America's global leadership and extend the genial effects that skillful tenancy of the geographic position between the Eurasian rimlands has brought to humankind over the past seventy years to future generations.

In attempting such a task, I have incurred many debts. Eberhard Sand-schneider was the first to see merit in the idea of mining Habsburg history for the present. My mentor and former boss Larry Hirsch supported the project from the outset, and urged me to see it through to completion despite the demands of work, family, and life. Nadia Schadlow and Marin Strmecki at the Smith Richardson Foundation provided the grant that allowed me to complete research at the Austrian state archives. Andrew May encouraged me to seek strategic wisdom amid the fragments and ruins of the past. Colin Dueck, Jakub Grygiel, Ingo Peters, Thomas Mahnken, Brian Hook, and Eliot Cohen all pro-vided helpful comments as the manuscript evolved. Eric Crahan at Princeton University Press saw promise, both in the topic of grand strategy as a field and in the Habsburg Monarchy as a neglected chapter in this canon. The Press's Sara Lerner showed great skill in keeping the book on schedule, and I am grateful to the talented Cindy Milstein and David Luljak for patiently copyediting and reviewing a long text filled with archaic terminology about an illogical empire.

I would be remiss not to acknowledge my former colleagues at the Center for European Policy Analysis, without whose help an undertaking of this scale would not have been possible. Peter Doran and Ilona Teleki stepped in to lead the institute so that I could take a sabbatical in the book's final phases; Milda Boyce and Marta Sikorski Martin quietly took up the slack to allow me to be out of the office for an extended period. I am especially grateful to Matthew Brown, chief research assistant on the project, who skillfully led a battalion of junior staff in locating and collating large amounts of arcane in-formation, often under difficult circumstances and at short notice. Daniel Richards helped me grasp the complexities of Habsburg finance and brought a discerning eye to chapter drafts. Michal Harmata showed technical versatil-ity and clairvoyance in designing, from scratch, the detailed maps without which large portions of the text would simply not make sense to the reader. Tobias Schneider, Anna Grimminger, and Jessica Niebler helped with deci-phering difficult German-language passages. Carsten Schmiedl assisted with nineteenth-century Austrian diplomatic sources and German translations, and spent long hours slogging through documents at the Library of Congress. Tjasa Fejer brought grace and perspective, rooted in family history, to re-search on the Habsburg Military Border, and together with Maria Benes, sup-plied helpful translations from Hungarian and Croatian. Piotr Włodkowski and Lidia Gibadlo sifted through documents on the Habsburg kingdom of Galicia and Lodomeria, and translated Polish-language texts. Sebastiano Dina was an indefatigable resource, not only in collecting and translating Italian-language materials, but in explaining the complex terrain of Lombardy and conducting correspondence with Italian scholars on the technical details of the quadrilateral forts. Eric Jones and Bryan Rosenthal helped with economic statistics, and Stephanie Peng, Marushia Li Gislen, Jackie Mahler, Bart Bachman, Joshua Longaria, Corbett Manders, Jacob Hart, Drake Thomas, and Nick Pope tracked down obscure sources, military figures, and other data.

I am also grateful to the patient staff of the Austrian state archives for helping to locate hard-to-find research material. Stefan Mach provided advice on navigating the Kriegsarchiv, Mag Röhsner and Metin Yilmaz helped me decipher difficult entries at the Haus-, Hof- und Staatsarchiv, and Michael Hochedlinger offered insights in response to e-mail queries about the eighteenth-century Austrian Army. Reinfrid Vergeiner from the Österreichische Gesellschaft für Festungsforschung sent me valuable archival material and sharpened my understanding of Habsburg thinking on fortifications. Czech researchers Roman Gazsi and Petr Capek from Pevnost Terezín aided in my search for material on Bohemian fortresses, and Jaroslav Zajicech assisted in locating Czech historians and material. In the United States, I am indebted to David Morris from the European Division of the Library of Congress for helping me navigate that institution's substantial German-language and Habsburg resources, and Mark Dincecco at the University of Michigan for assistance in untangling the complicated public revenues of nineteenth-century Austria.

I would especially like to thank my young family, who have watched this book project evolve from conception to completion. For longer than I can remember, my long-suffering wife, Elizabeth, has tolerated the presence of an unseemly host of periwigged and mustachioed dramatis personae in our marriage. She has patiently endured the frustrations and triumphs of chapter drafts, lengthy overseas trips, and early morning writing sessions amid the demands of two jobs and the arrival of two babies. I am grateful to Elizabeth's grandmother, Diana Kruse ("grandma Duck"), proud descendant of a general from the Croatian Military Border, for permitting me the use of a writer's cottage in Santa Barbara, California. Finally, I am thankful to my small children, Wesley and Charlotte, whose entire lives to date have occurred within the time frame of this project, and who have spent countless weekend mornings asking why daddy is in his study again, writing about the "housebirds." It is with their futures in mind that this book was written.

Finally, let me add a word about the timing of this book. Shortly after it was completed, I was offered the opportunity to serve my country as an official at the US Department of State. While the historical topics addressed in this book hold lessons for geopolitical competition in our own day, any observations for the present are offered only in the most general sense, and are not intended as a commentary on specific US policies of the past, present, or future.

THE HABSBURG MONARCHY notoriously defies attempts at a standardized nomenclature. The Habsburg Austrian Empire went by a number of appellations at different moments in its history, corresponding to the shifting constellation of lands under the Habsburg family's dominion. Compounding the problem is the fact that the empire underwent a series of incremental but significant changes in constitutional and administrative formats in the time period covered by this book, from being simply the easternmost possessions of a family that saw itself as a Monarchia Universalis, to a conventional though still far from monolithic Monarchia Austriaca, to being a more recognizable "Austrian Empire" after changes forced by Napoleon Bonaparte (1769–1821) in 1806, to finally becoming the convoluted confection of Austria-Hungary following the Ausgleich of 1867. In addition, there is the problem of the Habsburg emperor's status inside the German Reich, or Holy Roman Empire, entailing elective leadership of the lands west and north of Austria in present-day Germany. By contrast, in Hungary, the ruler in Vienna was not emperor at all but king, requiring a separate coronation in Pressburg.

In sorting through the welter of terms required for such a polity, I have erred on the side of simplicity and consistency, choosing, when forced, clarity over pedantry. I use "Habsburg Monarchy" and "Habsburg Empire" to refer to the lands of the Danube that comprised the dynasty's principal resource base from the early eighteenth century forward. As shorthand, I frequently call these lands "Austria," "the monarchy," or "the empire," reserving the term "Reich" specifically for the mainly German and extra-Danubian Holy Roman Empire. I refer to the Habsburg line generic by its main name and spare the reader the distinctions among its various branches.

I take a similar approach to place-names. Across the many centuries of Habsburg rule, most cities and towns of the empire developed more than one name, almost always including one (for the Habsburgs, official) designation in German, and another in one or more local languages. The period since the end of the empire brought further political, linguistic, and ethnic redesignations. For simplicity's sake, I have chosen to stick to the German name in most instances. Hence, I use Pressburg rather than Bratislava (in Slovak) or Pozsony (in Magyar), Theresienstadt rather than Terezín (in Czech), and

Hermannstadt rather than Sibiu (in Romanian) or Nagyszeben (in Magyar), and so on. In a few notable cases, I deviate from this practice when the city or place in question is so well established in the English reader's mind that alteration would add unnecessary confusion. Thus, I use Prague and not Prag, Cracow and not Krakau, Budapest and not Ofen, Vienna and not Wien, and Danube and not Donau. I also try where possible to stick with German for technical or military terms, using *Tschardaks* (a type of watchtower) instead of *çardak, ardaci, eardaci,* or *Chartaque,* and *Grenzers* (Balkan soldier-settlers) instead of what in British English would translate as "borderers."

I am aware that using German place-names in regions with so much tragic and ethnically fraught history as central Europe and the Balkans runs the risk of offending national sensibilities and resurrecting bitter memories for those families for whom such places carry deep personal meaning. The alternative, though, would have been to use terms that however correct on today's map, would defy attempts at consistency, change from one century or even decade to the next, and not correspond to the period-specific maps that are often referenced in the book. While cognizant of the perils of taking this German-centric approach, I have deliberately chosen to view the places of the Habsburg Monarchy as its own rulers, diplomats, and generals did rather than through the lens of today. Any errors that occurred along the way are mine entirely.

THE GRAND STRATEGY
OF THE HABSBURG EMPIRE

1

The Habsburg Puzzle

Take care, Sire.... Your Monarchy is a little straggling: it connects itself with the North, the South, and the East. It is also in the center of Europe. Your Majesty must give them law.

—PRINCE EUGENE OF SAVOY

If that ... empire is to be considered the greatest and most powerful which has the most secure borders and the least to fear from its neighbors, then Austria is to be counted among the weak, despite its size and inner resources.

—WENZEL ANTON VON KAUNITZ

ON NOVEMBER 1, 1700, Charles "the Bewitched," great-grandson of Phillip II and last Habsburg king of Spain, died, childless. With his death, a dynasty that had ruled over much of the known world, from Peru to Prague, was shorn of its largest western possessions and relegated to the back corner of Europe. The new cockpit of the Habsburg imperium was a ragged cluster of duchies and kingdoms a thousand miles to the east, in the violent borderlands between Christendom and the empire of the Turk. Its capital was Vienna, seat of the eastern Habsburg archdukes who for nearly half a millennium had ruled over much of middle Europe, first as march lords, and then as emperors of the German Reich and kings of Bohemia and Hungary.

The eastern realm of the Austrian Habsburgs was different, not only from the dynasty's western holdings, but from the other European Great Powers forming around it. Amassed over several centuries by marriage, war, diplomacy, and luck, it was an *omnium gatherum* of tribes and languages—German, Magyar, Slav, Jew, and Romanian—bound together by geographic happenstance, legal entailment, and the person of the emperor who ruled them. The lands inhabited by this multiethnic menagerie were a place of war. Formed around the banks of the Danube, its tributaries and outlying plateaus, the

Habsburg Monarchy sat in one of the world's great interstitial geopolitical zones—a triangle-shaped delta at the base of the isthmus formed by the Baltic, Black, and Adriatic Seas. An invasion route for millennia, the lands of the Danube represented both a civilizational and military frontier—the collision point of the Christian, Orthodox, and Muslim worlds converging at Europe's turbulent southeastern corner.

In every direction, the Austrian Habsburgs faced enemies. To the south lay the ancient menace of the Ottoman Empire. For centuries, the lands of the Marca Orientalis or "Austria" had formed a Christian rampart against the banners of militant Islam, shouldering a burden of frontier defense bequeathed by Byzantium along with the medieval kingdoms of Serbia and Hungary, which had fallen in rapid succession to the advancing Ottoman armies. To the east sprawled the tractless Great Hungarian Plain, whose wild expanses had only recently been freed from the Turks and whose truculent Protestant princes still resisted rule from Catholic Vienna. Beyond Hungary loomed the colossus of the Russian Empire, whose armies were just embarking on the concentric expansions that would eventually bring them to the banks of the Danube and shores of the Black Sea. To the north lay the still-expanding empire of Sweden and its Baltic neighbors, the precocious military kingdom of Brandenburg-Prussia and the Polish-Lithuanian Commonwealth, a decaying giant that attracted predation from stronger neighbors. And to the west were scattered the wealthy but fractious vassal states of the German Reich and northern Italy, and beyond them, the military superstate of Bourbon France, dynastic *Erbfeind* to the Habsburgs and centuries-long aspirant to west-central European primacy.

As long as Spain had remained in the hands of the Habsburg family's senior branch, the multidirectional pressures bearing down on the eastern half of the empire had been manageable. Although not administered as a unified whole, the Habsburg domains had tended to support and succor one another in war. At least until Spanish power began to wane in the seventeenth century, Austria could count on Spain to divert French attention and resources, and thus avert the danger of *double guerre*—a two-front war. But with Charles's death and the accession of a Bourbon prince to the Spanish throne, Austria's western line of support vanished (see figure 1.1).

The resulting assortment of dangers was beyond the ability of the Danubian empire to handle through military strength alone. Earlier generations of Habsburg dynasts had occasionally been capable of fielding powerful offensive armies, reaching the cusp of military hegemony under Charles V and the imperial armies of Tilly and Wallenstein. By contrast, the eastern Habsburgs were a relatively impoverished line, hampered in the quest for a large standing army by the continual fiscal and constitutional constraints of their motley realm.

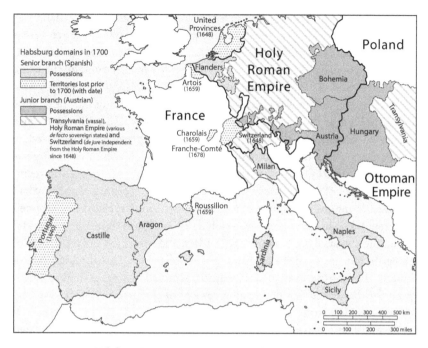

Just how severe a predicament the threats facing Austria could produce became apparent in the war that now broke out following Charles's death. The so-called War of the Spanish Succession (1701–14) brought a Bourbon bid for the Spanish throne that pitted the military machine of the French king Louis XIV against the Holy Roman emperor, Leopold I, whose Austrian armies were a tenth the size of his opponent's. Stripped of their accustomed Spanish support base, the Austrian Habsburgs became enmeshed in a desperate multifront war against five enemies. In Italy, Leopold and his son Joseph I, who succeeded the throne in 1705, faced the combined armies of France and Spain, which sought to retain the rich Italian territories possessed by the Spanish Habsburgs. In Germany, they were confronted with a joint French and Bavarian assault on Habsburg primacy in the German Reich. In the south, the renegade prince Francis II Rakoczi stirred the Magyars to revolt while border tensions flared with an Ottoman Empire that longed to regain lands only recently lost to Austria. And in the north, the powerful armies of Sweden's Charles XII threatened to invade Bohemia in support of Austria's Protestant minorities.

As a rite of passage, the Spanish war previewed in vivid and violent form the difficulties that Austria would face as an encircled power in the topsy-turvy

European balance of power. By the war's climax, the Austrian heartland was threatened by invading armies from both west and east, as French forces marched down the Danube and Hungarian *kuruc* raiders scourged the outskirts of Vienna. By its end, Austria was militarily exhausted and on the brink of financial ruin. As the Emperor Joseph I lamented, "[My allies] know how divided my military power is, scattered about every corner of Europe ... how I stand in Hungary and Transylvania, how difficult it would be for me to raise a force to protect myself should a threat suddenly emerge from Sweden, which still must be reckoned with, how weak I am ... in the Reich where as head I should certainly be the strongest."[1] Yet somehow, despite the seemingly insurmountable threats arrayed against it, the Habsburg Monarchy had survived. Summoning resources far beyond their own, the Habsburgs stopped the French invasion at Blenheim, evicted the Bourbons from Lombardy, deterred the threats from Sweden and Turkey, and resecured the territories of renegade Hungary and the loyalties of its nobles. In the concluding peace at Rastatt, the Habsburgs reaped a territorial windfall that more than compensated for the loss of Spain, bringing control of resource-rich northern Italy and new holdings as far afield as the Low Countries.

Austria's experience in the Spanish succession struggle would be repeated in the decades that followed. Time and again, new wars would erupt around the monarchy's far-flung frontiers. Just two years after Rastatt, Austria was at war with the Turks; nineteen years later—less than the amount of time that elapsed between the first and second world wars—it was embroiled in a new 5-year war with France. Three years later it was invaded on three sides and brought to the brink of extinction by the armies of Frederick the Great, who would subject the monarchy to almost three decades of continuous warfare and crisis. After a brief pause and yet another war with Turkey, Austria was thrown into a 23-years-long contest with France that would see its capital occupied, territories cut down to a rump, and ancient dynasty denigrated to the status of second-rate supplicants and in-laws to Napoleon. Altogether, in the 183 years from 1683 to 1866, Austria was involved in conflict for all but perhaps 75 (see figure 1.2).

Rarely in these military contests was Austria dealt a strong hand. It entered most of its wars with an army of middling quality led by indifferent generals and backed by shaky finances; it ended most of them bankrupt. It routinely faced enemies more numerous or technologically advanced than itself, occasionally commanded by the great captains of history. At all times the threat of a multifront war loomed. And yet time after time, the Habsburg Monarchy survived. It outlasted Ottoman sieges, Bourbon quests for continental hegemony, repeated efforts at dismemberment by Frederick the Great, and no fewer than four failed attempts to defeat Napoleon. Each time, it weathered

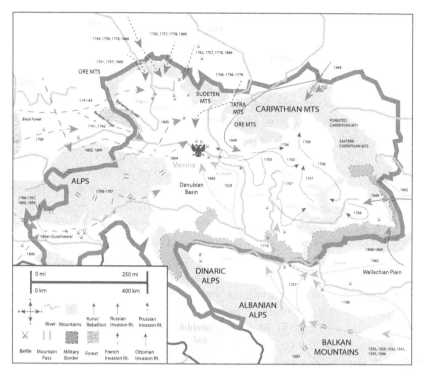

FIG. 1.2. Major Battles and Invasions of the Habsburg Empire, 1680–1866.
Source: Center for European Policy Analysis, 2017.

the threat at hand and more often than not emerged on the winning side. Despite losing most of its battles, it won most of its wars and continued to add territorial holdings long after it was considered a spent force. At times it even came to dominate European diplomacy, exercising a degree of influence over its external environment out of all proportion to its resources. Altogether, the dynasty endured for more than half a millennium, from the Middle Ages to the age of the airplane and automobile. By virtually any standard measure— longevity, wars won, alliances maintained, or influence exerted—the Habsburg Empire must be judged a geopolitical success.

The Habsburg Puzzle

How do we explain this unlikely success? How did an externally encircled, internally fractious, and financially weak state survive and even thrive for so long in Europe's most dangerous neighborhood? Had the Habsburgs possessed the attributes normally associated with successful empires, there would be little to explain. But they did not. Geographically, Austria lacked the natural advantages of many other European Great Powers. Unlike Britain and Russia, Austria had no ocean moats or vast steppes to shelter it from threats. As we will see, its mountains afforded some protection, but these only partially mitigated the multifront dilemma. Where France or Prussia might be confronted, in the severest of emergencies, with a two-front war, Austria faced threats at every point on the compass. At four thousand miles, the Habsburg security perimeter brought the monarchy into contact with enemies of widely differing fighting techniques, from conventional European armies to Tatar raiders and the semi-Asiatic armies of the Ottoman Empire, any one of which could attack with little warning. Coping with them required the Austrian Army to be prepared for combat in military theaters as diverse as the rugged Balkans, snowy Alps, and malarial floodplains of the Danube Delta.

The Habsburgs did not possess a military instrument capable of subduing this forbidding landscape. While more effective than many modern critics have alleged, the Austrian imperial army never attained the fighting qualities of the armies possessed by other large land powers like France, Russia, or Prussia.[2] One historian notes of the Austrians a "cultural disinclination toward wars of conquest," another that their commanders lacked a "killer instinct."[3] Loyal and frequently resilient in defense, the Habsburg Army was not in itself a tool with which to overmaster or consistently overpower or deter the empire's numerous rivals.

Nor can the Habsburgs be said to have possessed the characteristics of an economically domineering state. To be sure, the monarchy had the physical makings of a strong economy. It was large—around 260,000 square miles at its height, or about the size of Texas—rich in natural resources and maintained a population roughly comparable in size to some of its western rivals.[4] But this paper strength was misleading; throughout its history, the Habsburg Monarchy was plagued by a degree of constitutional and administrative complexity that hampered the systematic mobilization of resources. Successive monarchs would labor to impose greater efficiency and uniformity on the state, occasionally bringing the monarchy within reach of its major competitors. Nevertheless, Austria would never be able to achieve a sustained position in the top ranks of European economic powers or realize the vast power potential suggested by the empire's size.

In none of these categories—geography, military, or economic—can the House of Austria be said to have enjoyed a decisive advantage sufficiently pronounced to secure its position against the number of potential enemies arrayed against it. The outside environment placed Austria in a position of continual danger while the political and economic structure of the empire narrowed the range of viable tools for responding effectively to external threats and putting it on a secure long-term footing. Summing up Austria's predicament, Prince Kaunitz, the leading Habsburg statesman of the late eighteenth century wrote, "If that … empire is to be considered the greatest and most powerful which has the most secure borders and the least to fear from its neighbors, then Austria is to be counted among the weak, *despite its size and inner resources*. It is surrounded by three very dangerous neighbors, in part more powerful and in part equally powerful [as itself]."[5]

One common explanation offered for the Habsburg Monarchy's longevity is that it was a "necessity"—a construction whose continued existence in the troubled lands between the East and West provided a public good so valuable to Europe that its neighbors and even rivals dared not demolish it. In this view, the empire survived for so long, not because of any decisions Habsburg statesmen made, but because other Great Powers *wanted* Austria to survive. Thus, Austria's fellow Great Powers made a calculation, not just once, but repeatedly over several centuries, to prop it up, lest its collapse generate problems beyond their ability to solve.

As we will see, Austria was indeed frequently able to rally coalitions composed of allies motivated, at least in part, by the desire to retain the Habsburg Monarchy, first as a Christian glacis against the advancing Turks and later as a stabilizing ballast to the balance of power. But the idea of Austria as a necessity is, on its own, insufficient to explain its success. On more than one occasion, Austria was invaded by aggressive neighbors who viewed it not as a necessity but rather an anachronistic hindrance to their own aggrandizement and prize to be carved up. In the War of the Austrian Succession (1740–48), to take the most prominent example, Austria would face no fewer than five opponents determined to divvy up its richest territories between them. With the monarchy seemingly on the verge of collapse, neither Austria's enemies nor its traditional allies were particularly disturbed by the possibility of its territorial truncation or even extinction. "Fuck the Austrians" was Frederick the Great's succinct sentiment; "the House of Austria has ceased to exist!" was the exaltation of the French cardinal Fleury.[6] In London, Lord Newcastle said bluntly to the House of Lords, "The preservation of the balance of power and liberties of Europe does not … depend upon preserving entire the dominions of the House of Austria."[7]

While an extreme example, this episode demonstrated two salient geopolitical facts of life for the Habsburg Monarchy. First, Austria's status in the eyes of other powers could change rapidly for the worse if it came to be seen as overly weak—indeed, its polyglot composition made it the *most natural* target on the European chessboard for predatory revisionists. Second, the assumption that the balance of power would operate as a kind of geopolitical "invisible hand" was not something that Habsburg statesmen could take for granted; like all states in history, insecurity was a perpetual reality for Austria, and security too precious a commodity to be vouchsafed to abstract notions of geopolitical surrogacy. Whatever benefit Austria rendered to the balance of power—and as we will see, Habsburg statesmen were very much aware that it did—the mere fact of being a necessity was not in itself a solid enough foundation on which to gamble the monarchy's existence.

The Missing Link: Strategy

Inherent in the idea of Austria as a necessity is that the monarchy was, to some extent, a ward of the international system, which in turn implies a degree of helplessness on the part of its leaders for guiding, much less controlling, security outcomes. Perhaps it is therefore unsurprising that the question of how the Habsburg Monarchy conceived of and conducted strategy has not received the degree of attention accorded to other large empires in history. At most, there is the vague image of Austria succeeding in its early days through marriage, summed up in the often-repeated expression *Bella gerant alii, tu felix Austria nube / Nam quae Mars aliis, dat tibi regna Venus* (Let others wage war, but thou, happy Austria, marry; for those kingdoms that Mars gives to others, Venus gives to thee). To be sure, there have been many serious and detailed accounts of Habsburg foreign policy in the century since the monarchy's demise.[8] But virtually nothing has been written about Habsburg grand strategy per se.[9] To the extent that historians have considered the question, they have cast doubts on Austria's capacity to conduct strategy in any meaningful sense of the term. Historian Charles Ingrao writes that "it would be erroneous to suggest that [Austria's] statesmen consciously conceived of a comprehensive and well-coordinated program" for dealing with the challenges around their borders; instead, they "invariably concentrated on responding to individual crises as they arose in a particular theater." There is "no evidence," he continues, "that the emperor and his ministers ever conceived or clearly elucidated a strategy for the maintenance of secure buffers beyond the monarchy's borders. Nor are there more than a few instances when they expressed an appreciation of the multiple strategic difficulties that were occasioned by Austria's exposed position in the heart of East-Central Europe."[10] Michael Hochedlinger argues that Austria "had to content itself mostly with preserving the status quo and, if this failed, with last-minute defensive reactions against acute foreign threats."[11] And Manfried Rauchensteiner notes an almost-total absence of the indigenous military-theoretical predilections that normally accompany the development of strategy in major land powers.[12]

Perhaps one reason the question of Austrian grand strategy has not received more attention is that the Habsburg Monarchy does not fit the stereotype of a successful empire. In the standard account, Great Powers win in geopolitics by amassing a preponderance of material resources, which they then translate into armies and fleets capable of territorial expansion.[13] Inherent to this model is the capacity for offensive military action. Indeed, the very idea of strategy in the Western mind is tightly interwoven with the offensive in general and Napoleonic ideal in particular, enhanced by Carl von Clausewitz's later writings, of victory through bold thrusts, maneuver, and speed.[14] Not surprisingly, military historians are drawn to states that succeeded through conquest—Sparta, Macedon, the Roman Empire at its height, Napoleonic France, and above all Prussia. By contrast, the idea of defensive strategy evokes images of passivity, reaction, and even folly—Achaemenid Persia buckling before the armies of Alexander, or the French Fourth Republic sheltering behind the Maginot Line. The result is an offensive bias in the study of war that leads us to look for evidence of strategy where expansion occurred, and impute wisdom to audacity and unwisdom to caution.[15]

In Austria's case, the effect is perhaps reinforced by the unfavorable appraisals of Habsburg behavior left to us by so many of the empire's enemies. Napoleon's alleged comment to Austrian envoys during negotiations for the Peace of Campo Formio that the Habsburg Monarchy was "nothing but an old maidservant, accustomed to being raped by everyone," is about as flattering as Bismarck's comparison of Austria to "a worm-eaten old galleon," anchored at bay, and rotting from within and without.[16] Prussian officers after the Napoleonic Wars cast aspersions on the dilatory methods of their Austrian counterparts, the most damning of which were Clausewitz's acerbic observations about the Archduke Charles's (1771–1847) stubborn adherence to outmoded eighteenth-century attritional warfare. In a similar vein, German officers and military writers after the First World War reflected scathingly on the military-strategic performance of Austrian allies on whose shoulders they placed part of the blame for Germany losing the war.[17] Together with Clausewitz's disapproval, such commentary from the German military professional class—the ultimate font of authority for Anglo-American strategists—cast a pall over the House of Habsburg Monarchy in modern strategic studies.

The fact that the empire in question did not survive only underscored the point; Austria's demise seemed to be written into the Habsburg genetic code, rooted as much in strategic failure as geopolitical inevitability. Thus we are left with the picture of a bumbling empire that was equal parts miracle and albatross—an anachronism that survived for centuries amid the most contested geography without much effort beyond ad hoc reaction to crises as they arose and was, in the long run, doomed to extinction.[18] To the extent that strategy played a part in Austria's perpetuation, it was in the use of well-timed marriages at some misty early moment of history; subsequent survival was the by-product more of the strategizing done by *other* powers, which possessed the long-term clairvoyance to see the need to keep Austria intact, or even luck, than strategic decisions taken by Austria's own leaders.

The Necessity of Strategy

The relative absence of Habsburg Austria from the Western strategic imagination is to be regretted. For while perhaps less warlike than other European powers, the Habsburgs were, if anything, more successful for much of their history in staving off defeat and achieving the ultimate goal for any state in geopolitics: survival. In the words of Metternich, Habsburg methods were "not heroic, but [they] saved an empire."[19] With meager resources and abundant threats, the Austrians managed to erect a sustainable and ultimately affordable safety for the lands of the Danube that would only be replicated with the expansion of Western military and political institutions in the late twentieth century.

This book argues that this track record cannot be explained without understanding the strategies that the Habsburgs devised for coping with their difficult environment.[20] All states need strategy to survive. Great Powers in particular must develop higher or grand strategy if they are to endure in the world of competition with other large states.[21] The term "grand strategy" has been used in many ways in the century since its introduction.[22] For the purposes of this book, it is useful to think of it as consisting of three dimensions: a "what," "how," and "when."[23] The first of these, the functional aspect, is best described by the international relations scholar John Lewis Gaddis, who defined grand strategy as "the calculated matching of means to large ends."[24] Because the matching of means and ends is not a onetime act but instead occurs repeatedly across the life cycle of a Great Power, it must also be thought of as encompassing a structural component, or a how—a method by which means-ends calculations are transmitted within and between generations. Perhaps the best handling of this dimension of grand strategy is that by the diplomatic historian Hal Brands, who describes it as a "conceptual framework," or "intellectual architecture that lends structure to foreign policy; the logic that helps states navigate a complex and dangerous world."[25]

Finally, there is a when of grand strategy—a time frame in the life of a nation or empire in which its leaders are most prompted to confront means-ends trade-offs.[26] While it may be true that states devise grand strategies in times of both peace and war, it is in war, amid the exigencies and dangers that armed conflict presents to a society, that the need for grand strategy becomes urgent. War is a clarifying moment for states; it is a tutorial by which they come to identify gaps between the means at their disposal and ends they wish to pursue. War, especially if it is intense or prolonged, has the effect of focusing the attention of policy makers' means-ends calculations beyond the imperium of the now and toward the future state, forcing them, as the historian Williamson Murray has written, to "act beyond the demands of the present" and "think about the future in terms of the goals of the political entity."[27]

States develop a grand strategy not because they are wise but because without one they will die. The urge to react to crises as they emerge is a constant for policy makers in any era. But geostrategic threats tend to be a corrective to this urge, forcing states to equip themselves for competition, both mentally and materially, in order to avoid extinction.[28] A state may pursue a particular grand strategy in a given war, but it is through the accumulated experiences of multiple wars, on the basis of trial and error by numerous successive generations of statesmen attempting to square means and ends within the constraints of geography, that the contours of a broader grand strategic framework or logic emerges, unique to that state and corresponding to its peculiar circumstances and geography. In this sense, grand strategy bears a resemblance to learned behaviors in nature; it is to a great state what instinct is to an animal: a set of rules, formed in response to its surroundings, that guides behavior by rewarding certain actions and punishing others. Deviation from this rule set is possible, in the same way that mutations occur in genetics, but it is limited by the constraints imposed by the available resources and geography.

Some states need grand strategy more than others. The necessity of making means-ends calculations frequently and accurately increases in proportion to the demands of the competitive environment in which the state finds itself. A Great Power that enjoys congenial geography or few looming threats has a greater margin of error for putting off the task of bringing order to the array of competing priorities in its foreign policy. True policies of drift— neglecting active diplomacy and military preparation—tend to be found, if at all, in maritime powers with a high degree of insulation from the constant pressure of geopolitics. Thus, nineteenth-century Britain was supposedly able to manage problems remotely through a combination of finance and naval supremacy—in Lord Salisbury's memorable phrase, to "float lazily downstream, occasionally putting out a diplomatic boat-hook to avoid collisions."[29] By contrast, Great Powers that face an imminent threat or possess a naturally weak basis for security have a pressing need to think about how they will match means to ends, and on that basis, set priorities for the state.[30] Vulnerable powers *need* strategy in its purest sense, as a set of stratagems or artifices to compensate for gaps in physical capabilities. For them, strategy is an offset or "substitute" (*Aushilfe*), in the words of the German general Helmuth von Moltke (1800–1891), or a supplement of knowledge and reasoning with which to replace missing aspects of physical power.[31] The greater the gap to be filled, the greater the need for strategy.[32]

The Case for Habsburg Grand Strategy

This book argues that the Habsburg Empire engaged in the pursuit of grand strategy on all of the levels outlined above, and that the stratagems its leaders devised, more than the strength of their armies or charity of their neighbors, was the primary reason for its longevity as a Great Power. I make four main claims. First, I maintain that the Habsburg Monarchy's geography as an interstitial Great Power necessitated the pursuit of higher-level strategy, not as a means of enhancing territorial power, a dubious enterprise in Austria's case, but a prerequisite for existence altogether.[33] The sheer number of threats penalized reactive crisis management; "collisions," to use Salisbury's term, tended to seek out the boat. While geography did not determine the content of Austrian grand strategy, it did provide powerful cues, which if ignored, would lead to catastrophe. I contend that these cues were already present at the time of the Spanish succession war, but were obscured by the military successes of Prince Eugene of Savoy (1663–1736). The string of defeats following Eugene's death jolted Austria's rulers into the business of strategy, not as an act of wisdom, but as a necessity for survival. Uninterrupted warfare in the decades that followed ensured that the lessons, mind-sets, and formal structures needed to support this grand strategy did not evaporate but rather become ingrained components of the Habsburg Monarchy's DNA as a Great Power.

Second, I argue that the Habsburg Monarchy's internal makeup dictated the kinds of grand strategy that Austria could realistically expect to pursue. Specifically, the lack of abundant and effective offensive military tools, a function of the monarchy's financial constraints and internal composition, effectively ruled out the most obvious and efficacious means by which a land empire in Austria's position would have responded to the cues of its geography. That is not to say that the Habsburgs nursed a philosophical attachment to nonaggression; to the contrary, the dynasty had begun its tenancy of the lands between as frontier warlords, and war was written into the fabric of the Danubian empire from its infancy.[34] Instead, the claim here is that such military force as Austria had on offer, *even at its moments of highest resource mobilization*, was woefully inadequate to the task of achieving security for the state through military means. This central reality reinforced the impetus toward grand strategy as a tool to plug the gap between means and ends while guaranteeing that military force would inevitably be of secondary importance alongside other, nonmilitary tools in any strategies Austria pursued.

Third, from this combination of geographic and internal constraints, I argue that a coherent intellectual framework emerged that was primarily defensive in nature and preoccupied with conserving Austria's fragile position by avoiding tests of strength beyond its ability to bear. For all its vulnerabilities, the

Habsburg Monarchy did possess natural advantages—mountainous frontiers, a loyal army, and the spiritual superiority of Austria as a force for order and legitimacy in the European balance of power. While none was sufficient in itself to endow the monarchy with a basis for policies *de l'audace*, in tandem they provided a means of resisting the audacity of others. I hold that these three toolboxes—terrain, technology, and treaty rights—were employed by the Habsburgs, first on an ad hoc basis and then more synchronously, to bridge the gap between available means and foreseeable ends. Together, they comprised a framework or system of strategy unique to Austria among Europe's continental powers—the pieces of which worked interdependently to reinforce one another's effects.

While important aspects of this system would change over time, I trace three central themes of Habsburg strategy across the period covered by this book:

1. The maintenance of secure buffers around each of the monarchy's frontiers. Intermediary bodies in Germany, Italy, Poland, and the Balkans offset Austria's military vulnerability by interposing defensible spaces between its heartland and rivals while providing a medium—semi-independent client states—by which to extend Habsburg influence without the concomitant costs of formal empire.

2. The preservation of an army-in-being, supported by networks of frontier forts. Lacking in the offensive traits of other large land powers, Austria instead developed the army as a dynastic tool, loyal to the emperor and predominantly Catholic, whose main role was to stay alive and thus underwrite the existence of the monarchy. From this imperative emerged a general aversion to risk taking and the extensive use of props, including most notably terrain-based defensive tactics and fortifications, to achieve economy of force and make maximal use of the empire's internal lines of communication.

3. Allied coalitions. The sine qua non of Habsburg statecraft was a proactive and flexible diplomacy aimed at enmeshing both allies and would-be rivals into relieving the pressure on Austria's vulnerable position. Through confederations of weaker states, Austria sought the benefits of client armies and tutelary fortresses. Through defensive alliances, grouping coalitions, and appeasement, it tried to first channel and later transcend the balance of power in order to suppress attempts at hegemony and cultivate an independent European center under Habsburg leadership.

In employing these tools, I argue, fourth, that Habsburg grand strategy developed a preoccupation with the element of time in strategic competition.[35]

Coping with the danger of multifront war amid resource scarcity demanded the ability to achieve a concentration of force at a particular time and place without incurring unacceptably high risks on other frontiers. This in turn required Austria's leaders to devise tools for manipulating time on two levels— sequencing (which contests occur when) and duration (how long a contest lasts). I argue that the need to contemplate the time factor was muted during Austria's seventeenth-century wars against the Ottomans and French by Spanish help, and again during the early eighteenth century by Eugene's offensives, which allowed Austria to pursue a "radial" strategy of shifting attention from one theater to another.[36] Later wars spurred the development of more formal structures to deal with the problem, first on individual frontiers and then on an empire-wide basis. By manipulating the time dimension in strategy, Austria was able, for the most part successfully so, to alleviate the pressure of multifront war without incurring the full costs of tous azimuts defense preparation. When it lost the ability to strike this balance, through changes beyond its control, but also, crucially, by shifting to a more military-centric and offensive security policy that abnegated key tenets of its traditional grand strategy, Austria lost the ability to decisively influence time and suffered catastrophic defeats that sealed its fate as a Great Power.

Evidence and Approach

The frame of this book is limited to Austria's life span as a stand-alone Great Power and the principle cockpit of Habsburg power in Europe between the loss of Spain at the beginning of the eighteenth century and the military loss to Prussia in 1866. The preceding period, in which the dynasty's interests encompassed a far broader array of issues including Spain and its overseas colonies, entailed qualitatively different grand strategic calculations and a much wider power base for Habsburg decision-making.[37] The period after 1866 and in particular the final years leading up to World War I, heavily covered by historians, were characterized by a degree of truncation in Habsburg power in Europe, through the loss of the monarchy's principle buffers and concomitant constraining of its grand strategic options, so severe as to call into question Austria's real independence as a strategic actor.[38]

In addressing the period between 1700 and 1866, my interest is in understanding how Habsburg leaders approached the task of grand strategy as well as the content of the strategies they pursued. Habsburg grand strategy was not written down in one place in the form of a single, unifying document. Extensive evidence of it nevertheless exists in documentary, institutional, and behavioral form. The ultimate bureaucratic empire, the Habsburg Monarchy was the forerunner of the modern state in producing paper trails of even the most mundane aspects of power. Austrian military men wrote about strategy and warfare, developed maps to picture the monarchy as a defensive whole, and studied Austria's past wars to learn lessons about their own and enemies' behavior for future conflicts. Habsburg diplomats and monarchs conducted extensive correspondence and wrote memorandums outlining their thoughts on Austria's strategic options in both war and peacetime.

Habsburg grand strategy is also reflected in the institutions that Austria developed for conceiving of and implementing decisions about means and ends in both their conceptual and material dimensions.[39] These included a court war council with specialized roles to prepare for war on a standing basis, a professional and highly competent diplomatic corps, an intelligence bureau, and a general staff. As in modern bureaucratic states, influence over strategic decision-making was fluid in Habsburg Austria, floating between various governmental bodies and individual ministers from one emperor to the next. But to perhaps an even greater extent than today, the person of the emperor and his immediate circles formed a central locus of power that gave continuity of grand strategic perspective, if not necessarily policy priorities, from one generation to the next. Informing their deliberations was a coherent sense of mission as a Great Power, rooted in the monarchy's Catholic disposition and the dynasty's historic roles as emperors of the German Reich and guardians of Christendom against the Turks.

Finally, this book looks for evidence of Austrian strategy in the Habsburg military behavior and physical structures the monarchy left behind. The conduct of the Austrian Army in major wars shows considerable elements of similarity from the beginning of the period following Eugene's death until the beginning of the reign of Francis Joseph. Further evidence can be seen in the extensive fortifications that the Habsburgs built across their realm, eventually including more than twenty major fortresses and scores of smaller forts, towers, and blockhouses strewn across the empire's mountain passes, plains, and coastlines. An equivalent, in expense and symbolism of power, would be today's aircraft carriers. By their physical location and evolution, first on the Balkan frontier, then the Rhine, then Bohemia, then Italy, and finally Poland, we can see what the Habsburgs were most worried about, when and where.

Purpose

In sifting through these various forms of evidence, my objective is not to expand our knowledge of the basic facts or chronologies of the Habsburg Monarchy. A large number of fine books exist on Habsburg Austria in both English and German.[40] Many provide a high degree of detail about its political and economic development, the accomplishments and follies of its rulers, and theories about why it rose and fell. In German, a small but valuable literature exists on the subject of nineteenth-century Austrian military and strategic thinking.[41] As noted above, many excellent sources exist in English on the Habsburg Army and the empire's security and foreign policy at various moments in its history.

Instead of trying to replicate these approaches, this study seeks to examine the Habsburg state as a security actor in much the same way that one would look at the drivers and actions of a modern state. It is offered as a contribution to the growing literature on grand strategy, and seeks to highlight patterns and analyze them rather than merely chronicle and describe. The aim is not to contribute to knowledge of history per se but instead explore the application of history to the present. As such, the undertaking is explicitly didactic in nature: to gain a better understanding of how a now-dead Great Power succeeded and failed in navigating security challenges, and thus render insights for modern statecraft. It does not pretend that the Habsburgs were consistently wise or that historical analogies work in every instance. But nor does it view history as an impenetrable mass of facts or deny that the challenges confronted by states of the past are similar to those of the present.[42]

Indeed, the experiences of the Habsburgs are not as distant from the dilemmas of our own time as they may at first seem. The twenty-first-century West faces a twofold strategic problem of proliferating threats and constrained resources. Today's threats are multidirectional in nature and encompass an array of challengers, from religiously motivated radicals who wish to attack the West at its civilizational core to large industrialized powers determined to revise the existing balance of power to their advantage. In countering these dangers, the West is increasingly unable to rely on military predominance to sustain its primacy. Battlefield victory is becoming harder to attain, the nature of threats more nebulous, and the quest for short wars more elusive, in ways that call into question the applicability of the classic Clausewitzian model, with its emphasis on full national mobilization to achieve decisive results in war. Perhaps most important, the West increasingly finds that the security problems it faces cannot be defeated or solved outright; rather, they must be managed as open-ended pressures for which a satisfying solution is likely to remain elusive for the foreseeable future. This is a task for which the contemporary strategic mind-set is not well suited, requiring both an acceptance of limits and weary resolve that were the stamps of Habsburg statecraft.

In telling how the Habsburgs approached the task of strategic statecraft in their time, I am aware that many details of history will be overlooked. While writing the book, I have been forced, as a concession to space, to leave out significant aspects, personalities, and events that while interesting or important in their own right, I judged to not add substantially to the central point of the text. The book is no doubt poorer for these omissions, but hopefully, what is lost in complexity and nuance will be gained in clarity of argument. As a rule, I have tried to be cognizant of important historiographical debates, make note of these in the footnotes, and where they bear on the main thesis, mention them in the text itself. But I have also kept in mind that this material is well covered elsewhere, and not the main aim or contribution of the text.

The book is divided into three sections. The first (chapters 2–4) examines the constraints on Habsburg power, both external and internal, and the effect that they had on Austrian thinking about strategy. Within this section, chapter 2 describes the monarchy's physical environment, how it influenced Habsburg perceptions of space, and the vulnerabilities and advantages that it created in competition with other major powers. Chapter 3 looks at the constitutional makeup of the Habsburg state and limitations it placed on the mobilization of resources. And chapter 4 explores the outworkings of geography and administrative complexity on Habsburg conceptions of military force and political power more broadly.

The second section (chapters 5–7) assesses the evolution of Habsburg grand strategy on the level of individual frontiers. It is roughly chronological, reflecting the order in which major threats to the monarchy unfolded. Within this section, chapter 5 looks at the competition with the Ottoman Empire and Russia from the reconquest of Hungary to Joseph II's (1741–90) final Turkish war. Chapter 6 examines the struggle with Prussia from Frederick the Great's first invasion of Silesia to the stalemate of the War of the Bavarian Succession (1778–79). And chapter 7 traces the contest with France, from the wars of Louis XIV to the bitter life-or-death struggle with the revolution and Napoleon.

The third section (chapters 8–10) brings the frontiers together in a panoramic view of Habsburg grand strategy in the Metternichian and Francis Joseph eras. Within this section, chapter 8 examines Austria at its post-Napoleonic peak, assessing congress diplomacy and the pecuniary, forts-based system that undergirded it. Chapter 9 traces the breakdown of the Metternichian system from the time of the revolution of 1848 and Crimean War to the debilitating defeats by Italy in 1859 and Prussia in 1866. Finally, chapter 10 provides general reflections and an epilogue offers observations for geopolitics in our own time.

PART I

Strategic Characteristics of the Habsburg Empire

2

Empire of the Danube

THE GEOGRAPHY OF HABSBURG POWER

No other part of Europe faces as many enemies.

—COUNT RAIMONDO MONTECUCCOLI

Austria should, by the dictates of reason, possess all of the Danube region, from the river's source to the Black Sea.

—DIETRICH HEINRICH VON BÜLOW

LIKE ALL STATES, the Habsburg Monarchy depended for its survival on the ability to exercise undisputed control over a clearly defined territorial space.[1] This in turn involved two tasks: building a sound political and economic base, and providing security against internal or external attack.[2] In the first task, the Habsburgs enjoyed the advantage of a compact, riparian heartland bounded on most sides by mountains. The second task was made difficult in the extreme by the empire's wider east-central European security environment. This combination of defensible local terrain and geopolitical vulnerability influenced how Habsburg leaders thought about and conducted strategy by encouraging the development of strategic forms of knowledge to conceptualize space for defensive purposes, and pulling attention outward to the frontiers, while demanding the maintenance of a "big picture" capable of taking in the security position of the empire as a whole.

The Habsburg Heartland

The geographic space over which the Austrian Habsburgs presided was a wild expanse of territories on Europe's eastern edge, the effective defense of which required mastery of enormous distances and an array of climates and terrains.

While the political boundaries of the Habsburg Monarchy would change over time, its epicenter corresponded to the heart of the Danubian-Pontic zone of European geography, consisting of the Danube River Basin and its outlying plateaus.[3] Geologically, this region is the meeting point of three of the world's great geographic formations: the Eurasian steppe, extending westward from Mongolia to Hungary; the dense river network of middle Europe; and the line of mountain chains that run from the Pyrenees to Asia Minor.[4]

The contours of this space are recognizable on a physical map of Europe as the hermit crab–shaped recess between the Balkan Peninsula and north-central European plain (see figure 2.1). Its heartland is the drainage basin of the Danube and its three subregions: the mainly mountainous zone of Alpine Austria, semi-enclosed highlands of the Bohemian Massif, and Great Hungarian Plain, or Nagy Alföld—a vast tableland marking the westernmost extension of the Eurasian steppe. Together, these plateaus form a distinctive subregion of continental Europe that is bounded on every side by mountains and rivers: in the west, the Alps; in the east, the Carpathians; in the north, the Sudetens and Tatras; and in the south, the Sava River to its junction with the Danube at the Iron Gates.[5]

Viewed geostrategically, as a space to be unified, governed, and defended from attack, the first significant feature of the Danubian Basin is its interstitial quality, forming the "lands between" two seas (the Baltic and Black) and major geographic zones (the western Europe peninsula and Eurasia plains).[6] A second is its sheer size. At its height, the Habsburg Monarchy covered more than 260,000 square miles—ten degrees of latitude and eighteen degrees of longitude—making it the largest continental European power and second only to the Russian Empire in total landmass. Its west-east length, from Italy to eastern Transylvania, was about 860 miles, and its north-south length, from Bohemia to Croatia, was about 500 miles (excluding Dalmatia).[7] Measured end to end, its frontiers were more than 4,000 miles by the end of the eighteenth century—about the width of the Atlantic Ocean.

The Habsburg Power Gradient

Large distances impeded strategic mobility between the Habsburg heartland and periphery. Depending on weather and road conditions, an infantry regiment could expect to march for three weeks from the imperial capital to the Ottoman frontier, two weeks to forward positions in Moravia, a month to the Italian frontier, and about as long to outposts in Poland (see figures 2.2–2.3).[8]

A further complication was the topographic variety of the empire's lands. Straddling the transition zone between western Europe and both Eurasia and

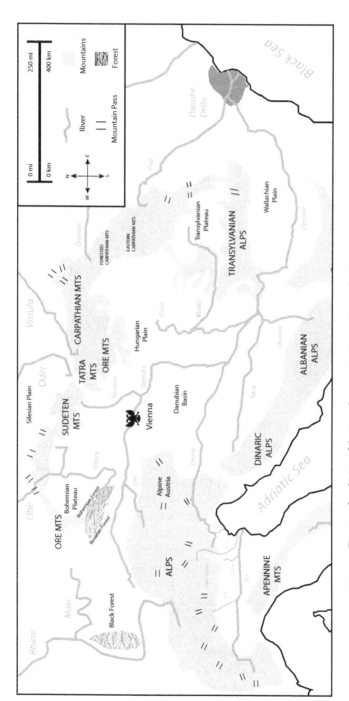

FIG. 2.1. Topographical Map of the Danubian Basin. *Source:* Center for European Policy Analysis, 2017.

Vienna to:	Belgrade	619km / 24 Days
	Bucharest	1070km / 42 Days
	Essegg	478km / 25 Days
	Gradisca	535km / 21 Days
	Karlsburg	752km / 30 Days
	Olmütz	201km / 8 Days
	Theresienstadt	360km / 14 Days
	Unghvar	645km / 25 Days
	Verona	809km / 31 Days

FIG. 2.2. March Times in the Habsburg Empire, ca. 1800. *Source:* Base calculations taken from *U.S. Army Field Manual 21–18*, modified to reflect Austrian equipment, roads, and terrain gradients, and cross-referenced with contemporary accounts.

Asia Minor, the Habsburg state encompassed several topographically dissimilar subregions. Where most western armies could expect to fight their wars in the rich agricultural lands of middle Europe, with its established seasons of campaigning, foraging, and wintering, Habsburg armies had to be prepared for operations in theaters as diverse as the flooded plains of Walachia, rugged hills of the Balkans, where summertime conditions approximated those of the American Southwest, and snow-bound passes of the Alps and Carpathians. This represented a wider range of terrain and climate conditions than anything confronting other European powers. Only the global empires of Britain,

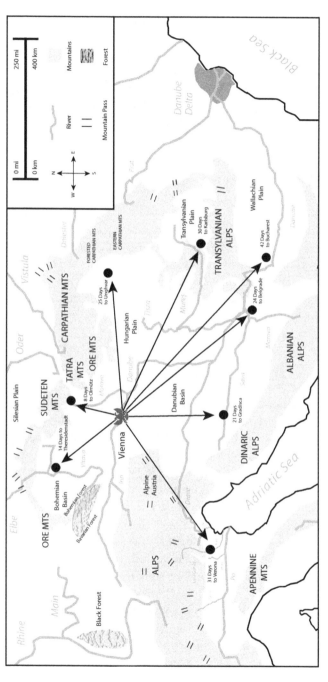

FIG. 2.3. March Times between Major Points in the Habsburg Empire, ca. 1815. *Source:* Center for European Policy Analysis, 2017.

Russia, and the United States had to contend with a greater variety of physical geography in their possessions.

The size and complexity of the empire's physical geography presented the Habsburgs with a power gradient problem familiar to all large empires. Space and terrain consume power as it is projected, with the result that "effective power declines in proportion to distance."[9] Large distances from the empire's center to its periphery complicated the task of asserting political dominance over a contiguous space that is a prerequisite to collecting revenue and building a sound economic base. Militarily, distance and the abundance of rough terrain slowed the movement of armies to confront internal and external enemies.

Austria was similar to other large land powers in these regards. Yet in confronting this challenge, it enjoyed two significant geographic advantages that would aid the task of empire building in both its political and military dimensions. One was the abundant rivers that knit together its territories, and sped the projection of political influence, culture, and military force; a second was the fact that its extensive mountain ranges were concentrated primarily at the empire's frontiers separating the empire from its neighbors and gave it breathing space to focus on creating an integrated polity.

The Danube: "Spinal Column" of Empire

The unifying physical feature of the Habsburg Monarchy was the Danube River. In geopolitics, rivers play two main roles: barriers and highways. Historically, the Danube has performed both functions, being, in the words of Hugh Seton-Watson, "a line of invasion, a commercial thoroughfare and a frontier line."[10] Pliny the Elder traveled the river and counted sixty tributaries, half of which were already navigable in his time.[11] The Roman Empire used the Danube as a fortified boundary, part of the extensive, eastward-facing defensive lines known as the Limes Germanicus that blocked the path of advancing Germanic and Hunnic tribes. The medieval kingdoms of central Europe used it as a commercial thoroughfare, centered on the bend in the river at Visegrád, as well as a frontier separating Catholic Hungary and Orthodox Serbia. With the eruption of Ottoman military expansion in southeastern Europe in the sixteenth century, most of the middle and all of the lower Danube fell under Turkish rule while the upper Danube formed the main dividing line between Christendom and Islam.

With the expulsion of Ottoman power from Hungary in 1699, the Danube reverted to its historic role as an artery tying together neighboring lands. From this point forward, the Danube would form both the central axis of

Habsburg political power and basis for a common middle European civilization centered on Vienna. The Danube's predominant role in the life of the empire is comparable to those of other river-based empires, such as the Nile, Euphrates, or Indus. As for these empires, the footprint of Habsburg power in both a political and cultural sense traced the contours of the river at its core. As one eighteenth-century German writer observed about the Danube,

> A river valley forms a whole. The water course offers transportation facilities and thus unites both halves of the valley—the inhabitants of both sides having the same interests. The great river is like a spinal column, and its tributary waters to the right and left are like the two sides of the human body. It is, therefore, natural that such a riverine domain should either form a state apart or the integral part of a state.[12]

The distinctiveness of the Danube as a "spinal column" for Habsburg power lay mainly in the direction of its current. Where other German rivers such as the Elbe or Rhine flow toward the Baltic and North Sea, the Danube's easterly watershed helped to demarcate a separate and distinctively east-central European geopolitical space.[13]

Conquering Distance

The Habsburg Monarchy's central river systems helped it mitigate the effects of the power gradient in several ways. Historically, the surface area across which a state's center can collect revenue has defined the reach of its power. The further and more complicated the distances to outlying lands, the harsher the effects of the power gradient, and the weaker the levels of political control and smaller the revenue base, the weaker the empire. Hence, the ability to overcome distance (that is, to shorten travel times), whether by natural or synthetic means, is a prerequisite for the success of empires, whether the spaces they cover are primarily sea or land.[14] Overcoming distance requires a capital-intensive effort—for sea powers, the construction of expensive merchant and naval fleets; for land powers, the construction of roads, infrastructure, and armies.

Habsburg rivers helped to address this problem by providing a ready-made communication network that facilitated efforts to extend political control over a large expanse of territory. Possessing abundant natural arteries at the center of the Habsburg holdings was a major advantage in the era before railroads. Like the empires that formed on the basins of the Indus, Tigris, and Nile, the Danube provided a connective tissue for a common political civilization. Wide, long, and in many places navigable, the region's rivers cut the travel time to some parts of the empire by more than half. Its 315,445-square-mile drainage basin is the largest of any European river, with 300 tributaries stretching into every corner of southeastern Europe, linking both of the region's major plateaus, the Bohemian and Transylvanian, to the basin's central plain.[15]

In every direction around the Habsburg core, rivers provided highways for collecting taxes, promulgating laws, spreading culture, and imposing military rule. The Danube glued together the Habsburg heartland territories of Austria, Bohemia, and royal Hungary; the Elbe, Vltava, Morava, and Iser linked the Czech lands; the Po unified the territories of northern Italy; and the Drava, Sava, and Tisza tied in Hungary and portions of the Balkan peripheries.

The same communication networks that sped the movement of armies and tax collectors also facilitated commercial exchange. The numerous navigable arms of the Danube allowed for the cheaper movement of goods, services, and labor. Combined with the Habsburg heartland's mild winters and mid-latitude temperate climate, the presence of a large freshwater drainage basin created an arable landmass capable of supporting a large population. Well-watered plains generated rich soils capable of supporting extensive agriculture.[16] Nearby mountain ranges provided timber, minerals, and ore for metallurgy and early industry. These attributes gave the Danubian lands a degree of internal economic complementarity (metals from Bohemia, grain from Hungary, and timber from Transylvania) that made them a natural economic space and strong material base on which to build an empire.

Rivers aided in the integration of an otherwise mostly landlocked economic space with wider European and global markets. Europe's second-longest river, the Danube runs almost two thousand miles from its source in the Black Forest to its exit into the Black Sea. Its long length and easterly flow supported the movement of commerce and technology from the western European interior to the eastern European periphery that would otherwise have required passage through the Alps. With headwaters and tributaries located near the Rhine and Oder, which connected to the Atlantic and Baltic, respectively, the Danube could with overland portage (and later, canals) link up with European and international trade routes. Without the river, the empire would have been primarily reliant on its handful of ports on the Adriatic for this function. The fact that the Danube's exit occurs at a point well beyond the empire's natural borders meant that it lacked assured access to the sea, depriving it of the full strategic and economic benefits of a river connecting western Europe with the Black Sea. This reality would become a significant factor in Habsburg geopolitical history.

Together, the Danube's political and economic roles not only aided but also made altogether possible the knitting together of the Habsburg territories as a coherent polity and its vocation as a European Great Power. The Danube's drainage basin furnished a geopolitical heartland sufficiently large, well resourced, and interconnected to provide the foundation for a large state with a material base transferrable into military power. The orientation of this resource base to the larger European landmass provided the benefits of Western cultural and economic exchange while setting it apart sufficiently from other western European power centers to form a politically coherent and militarily defensible space. Although the empire's peripheries would shift over the centuries, at moments encompassing points as far-flung as the Netherlands and Sicily, its heartland would remain centered on the lands lining the banks of the Danube and tracing that river's major tributaries. However Habsburg fortunes might rise or fall elsewhere, as long as its position here was secure, it remained a Great Power.

The Habsburg Monarchy's rivers did present some challenges. The upper Danube was not amenable to navigation until its conjunction with other rivers in southern Germany near Ulm; in its middle course, it contained navigation hazards from Pest to Baja in Serbia and was blocked by cataracts at the Iron Gates. On the Great Hungarian Plain, the river was flanked in spring by swamps, which in flood season impeded access to the river and produced silt that formed into sandbanks, and the river's swift current made movement downriver easier than upriver.[17] Overcoming these obstacles would be a major focus of Austrian infrastructure development over the centuries. Even with these important exceptions, however, the wider river systems of the Danubian Basin were an unmistakable advantage compared to the exertions that would have been needed to conquer distance in a comparably sized landmass lacking rivers. As a frame of reference, the large land empires of Rome, the Incas, and Persia all required the construction of vast networks of roads, undertaken at vast public expense, as a precondition for the imperial center's ability to exert power and collect taxes across the periphery. The difficulties encountered by the Austrians in the dredging and canalization of rivers were by comparison relatively modest. For all the other obstacles the Habsburgs may have faced, rivers represented a major leg up in the game of empire building.

Rivers and Time

Habsburg leaders were aware of the geopolitical importance of the Danube, and viewed it as key to building and maintaining an empire. Central to its role in this regard was the river's ability to aid in the management of time. It did this, first, by providing a central axis around which to rally Habsburg strength. In warfare, mastery of time begins with the ability to concentrate force—the collection of force in denser forms in a specific space. The Danube helped in this task by forming an internal network around which to assemble military forces. As Count Joseph Radetzky von Radetz (1766–1858), one of Austria's leading generals of the nineteenth century, described it:

> The great artery of the Monarchy and the basis, not only of its combined military system but also its political system, is the Danube. Our forces must be assembled along the Danube at all times, and the necessary resources be prepared at once there. . . . The maneuverability and security of our forces hinges upon the number and strength of our defensive works along the Danube.[18]

Force concentrations along the Danube allowed for the swift movement of armies not only by water itself but also along the natural highways of river valleys, both within the Habsburg core and to threatened points on the periphery. A defender occupying the stretch of Danube from the Bavarian frontier to Budapest could maximize the empire's main strategic advantage, its central location, and move across internal lines of communication without bearing the full logistical and time costs to defend such a large space. In the southeast, the Danube's current allowed for the transfer of large armies and supplies to project power beyond the Carpathians into the Wallachian Plain. In the west, the Danube valley's extrusion into Germany allowed for offensive operations, via land, up the Rhine and into France and the Austrian Netherlands—a route that Habsburg armies would use repeatedly in wars against the French.

These same routes also allowed outside invaders to bypass mountain defenses and attack the empire's heartland. Successive generations of Habsburg leaders would view the inability to control the entirety of the river, from the headwaters at Donaueschingen to the river's estuary at the Black Sea, as an organizing strategic problem. In the words of Radetzky, "As long as we do not control the entirety of the river, we stand at risk of embarrassing ourselves at one place or another."[19] The gap that the Danube cuts between Bohemia and the Alps was one such place; another was the Danube's exit between the Carpathian and Balkan Mountains. Nevertheless, the known existence of these points made them predictable as invasion routes, thereby allowing Habsburg military planners to concentrate force. This too saved time, in obviating the need to spread forces across an entire frontier and only converge on a threat once it materialized.

Should an attacker pierce Austrian defenses at the frontier, the Danube and other rivers performed another, time-related strategic role: forming obstacles that could be used as secondary lines of defense. As Clausewitz noted, rivers favor a defender by requiring an invader to break a preferred front:

> River defense can often gain considerable time—and time, after all, is what the defender is likely to need. It takes time to assemble the means of cross-

ing. If several attempts at crossing fail, even more time will have been gained. If the enemy changes his direction because of the river, still other benefits will no doubt fall to the defense.[20]

Abundant internal rivers, many of which lay just inside and parallel to the monarchy's frontiers, allowed Habsburg armies to form defensive positions reinforcing the first, natural line formed by mountains. As Austria's Archduke Charles, the foremost Habsburg commander and war theorizer of the Napoleonic era, wrote,

> In the defense of rivers, as nature indicates the places where crossings are possible, it follows that entrenchments can have, in this case usefulness for covering from the fire of the enemy the cannon of the batteries that it is necessary to rest, to flank the crossing area. These areas are those where the bank on which one finds oneself dominates the bank of the enemy, or the bank is concave upon the side of the enemy.[21]

Numerous natural defensive sites existed along the banks of the empire's major rivers. In the north, the Elbe and Iser formed an inverted U behind which Habsburg armies could entrench (and later fortify) lines facing both of the main Prussian invasion routes into Bohemia. In Italy, the Mincio and Po Rivers and numerous left-bank tributaries formed a defensive glacis against eastward thrusts toward the Alpine passes entering Upper and Lower Austria via the Tyrol and Carinthia. In both cases, rivers bought time for Habsburg forces in the interior to mobilize. Deeper inside the empire's territory, rivers provided opportunities for its armies to rally against a successful invader. At its moments of greatest emergency, the empire's rivers repeatedly afforded its forces the ability to conduct strategies of Fabian delay and harassment against militarily stronger opponents.

The Alps: Ramparts of Empire

The second dominant feature of Habsburg geography was mountains. On almost every side, the Danubian heartland is fenced by mountain ranges. The most formidable of these were the Alps, which extend for 746 miles across south-central Europe and reach heights of thirteen thousand feet, splitting into dependent branches across Habsburg territory. In the west, the Alps run in three chains from Piedmont to the outskirts of Vienna, at least partially blocking the westward approaches. In the north, the Ore, Sudeten, and Tatra Mountains separate the Bohemian highlands from the surrounding Thuringian and Silesian plains. In the east, the Carpathians form a vast, scimitar-shaped, eight-thousand-foot-high barrier from the Vistula River in Poland to the Dobruja, coming within two hundred miles of the Black Sea. In the southeast, the

Transylvanian Alps extend to the Iron Gates, where the Danube cuts a canyon on its way to the sea. In the south, a continuous curtain of mountains stretching from the Serbian Mountains across the northern face of the Balkans and into the Dinaric Alps, which hug the coastline the full length of the Adriatic Sea and merge with the Julian Alps in the north, complete the circle.

Placed end to end, the mountains of the Habsburg Empire ran for more than three thousand miles. The prevalence of this rugged terrain would exercise a dominating influence on the empire's military options and strategic culture. In geopolitics, mountains divide rather than unite territories. Where rivers facilitate contact and communication, mountains delay them. Excelled only by oceans in their ability to impede movement, the primary political value of mountains lies in the clarity with which they demarcate a state's territory from that of a neighbor. For this reason, the benefit of mountains generally increases in proportion to how near they lie to a state's frontiers. States without mountains or other obstacles on their borders are susceptible to invasion; those with mountainous interiors, such as classical Persia or modern-day Mexico, face severe challenges in achieving internal unity. Thus the mountainous Balkans would become the antithesis of a unified geopolitical space, defying efforts at integration and remaining politically fragmented to the present day.

In the Habsburg Empire's case, the possession of frontier mountain ranges was arguably a precondition for any meaningful degree of political integration occurring within the Danube River Basin at all. The fact that the empire's mountains were concentrated primarily at the edge rather than interior of the realm gave the monarchy terrain that combined the best features of the two neighboring eastern European subregions: the integrative qualities of the well-watered central European plain to the north and defensive qualities of the Balkans to the south. Without mountainous frontiers, the region's rivers, rather than unifying a coherent economic space, could just as easily have made the region an extension of neighboring geographic zones. As two mid-nineteenth-century geographers noted, of the two empire's two main mountain ranges, the Alps and Carpathians, "The first divides the region of the German ocean and Baltic from those of the Black Sea and Mediterranean. The second mountain range, which has much more elevated summits, and covers a larger tract of country, divides the region of the Mediterranean from that of the Black Sea."[22]

An absence of mountains in the north would have rendered the empire's territories a southern extension of the Polish plain—an indefensible and therefore politically chaotic invasion route subject to incorporation in whatever stronger entity existed around it. In the east, where the Carpathians mark the only significant obstacle between the Danube and Urals, an absence of mountains would have made the Great Hungarian Plain a de facto extension of the Volhynian-Podolian Plateau and thus subject to domination by whatever force was strong enough to possess Ukraine and Russia. Instead, the presence of extensive mountains on all sides made the Danubian Basin an eddy in the turbulent currents of east-central European geopolitics—a sustainable middle zone where an independent civilization of some kind could form and resist the tug of both the European rimland and Eurasian heartland.

Mountains and Time

As with rivers, the principal contribution of mountains to Habsburg empire building stemmed from their role in conquering space and time. Where rivers speed up movement, mountains slow it down. Even when undefended, they impede the transit of armies, complicating travel across even short distances and entailing significantly greater logistical difficulties than flat land, much less water. In the Habsburg Monarchy's case, the time advantages provided by mountains were significant, given the high proportion of defensive perimeter that could be considered "unpassable" in the age before airpower. Seeing mountain ranges like the Alps on paper gives an imperfect impression of their actual formidability; as an early chronicler wrote, "It is difficult to compass the Alps and all the mountains on a map, for one gets false ideas of the distances that are reduced to scale."[23] Movement through the Alps is funneled to a handful of dependable passes, most of which are narrow, long, and winding; all but a few are blocked by snow in winter, and can become blocked during warm months with mud or debris.

For armies that choose to pass through the mountains, these factors impose a significant time cost and restrict logistics as well as tactical options when entering, transiting, and exiting the passes. In the eighteenth century, the French Army calculated that it could move about forty-eight hundred soldiers per day through some of the defiles of the Western Alps; the numbers for longer or more complicated passes were lower.[24]

Armies that try to pass through mountains are forced to split their forces, and once transited, run the risk of leaving a major obstacle in their rear. As Clausewitz noted,

> Where a province is protected by a mountain range, no matter how lightly the range is defended, the defense will at any rate suffice to prevent enemy raids and other plundering expeditions.... No ... attacker likes to march across a mountain massif like the Alps and to leave it in his rear.... The higher and less accessible the mountains, the more the forces may be split: indeed, the more they *must be split*, because the smaller the area that can be

secured by the combinations based on movement, the more its security must be taken care of by direct coverage.[25]

Trying to go around mountains also cost time, since the attacker was forced to take a more circuitous and thus longer route to its target.

In addition to imposing time costs, mountains increase the effects of attrition on invading armies. Passing through mountains exacts a toll in lives and the amount of supplies used; perforce, an army crossing a mountain range will be weaker when it exits than when it entered—as Hannibal discovered during his Alpine descent into Italy. Austria's Archduke Charles noted this effect in his military writings; in "rugged and rocky mountain chains," he observed,

> there is no means of replenishing supplies.... One must either use the few and arduous connections and passages which nature provides or has to make one's own path with much a lot of troublesome effort and time loss [*Zeitverlust*]. Marches and supplies can only be performed by long, constricted, and thus slow columns. In any case the course of operations is slow and jerky ... and supremacy over physical elements rather than man becomes the primary obstacle to victory.[26]

From the defender's standpoint, mountains provide advantages proportional to the disadvantages inflicted on attackers. By slowing the offensive army, mountainous terrain gives the defender time to organize a defense; time and again in Habsburg military history, mountains would supply a first line of defense behind which Vienna could muster its forces and transfer troops from quieter frontiers more quickly than its opponent could achieve deep penetration of imperial territory. By magnifying the defensive fighting power of even small numbers of troops, they allowed the Habsburgs to achieve a greater economy of force than would have been possible in open terrain. Because mountains funnel attackers to predictable invasion routes, they helped make Austria less susceptible to surprise, allowing a defender to hold down one attacker with minimum force and concentrate elsewhere without inordinate fear of losing on the weaker front.

Together, Austria's possession of mountainous frontiers and extensive internal rivers helped to mitigate its power gradient problem, aiding in the task of holding together a large geopolitical space. What the Danube and its tributaries integrated by easing movement and cutting internal travel time, the Alps and Carpathians protected by impeding external attacks. Such a combination is rare in geopolitical history. Most mountainous states, like Switzerland, Andora, or Tibet, are small and embedded within a single mountain chain. Most large powers possessing a mountainous border, such as France or

Germany, have them on one or two sides, or have mountain ranges embedded well within the political frontiers of the state in ways that separate the state from itself, like the Rockies in the United States or Urals in Russia.

Habsburg Periphery

The Habsburg Monarchy would need such topographic advantages as it possessed to cope with the dangers of its east-central European security environment. For millennia, the thousand-mile stretch of territory between the Baltic and Black Seas has formed a funnel for westward migration and invasion from the Eurasian steppe to the European peninsula as well as the eastward expansion of western military empires. In southeastern Europe, there was the added pressure of the states and empires of the eastern Mediterranean and Asia Minor expanding northward into Europe. Together, these forces created what the early twentieth-century British geopolitical writer James Fargrieve called a "Crush Zone"—a contested space in political geography in which empires collide and all but the toughest polities find it hard to endure for long periods of time.[27]

The Danubian Basin sits in the epicenter of this Crush Zone, astride both the main east-west and north-south axes of the European continent. This interstitial position gave the Habsburg state strategic and economic interests in multiple regions while exposing it to various enemies rather than one primary security theater. From the time of its emergence as a mainly Danubian state, the empire was flanked by aggressive rivals along the entire length of its security perimeter except the Adriatic Sea. In each direction, the empire faced a combination of an established or expanding power center separated from its frontiers by a belt of weaker ethnicities or states. These comprised four distinct security frontiers, each representing a separate security complex with its own geographic constraints, opportunities, and threat vectors.

The Southeastern Frontier: Adriatic to Black Sea Delta

The southeastern frontier of the Habsburg Empire extended from the Dalmatian coastline of the Adriatic along the Sava River to the Transylvanian Alps. As a security space, it encompassed the better part of the Balkan Peninsula, from Croatia through the southern portion of the Great Hungarian and Wallachian Plains to the Dniester River. A combination of arid uplands and flooded plains transitioning to rugged hills in the south, the geography of this region was inhospitable to prolonged military operations for much of the year. Defensive keys included possession of strongpoints along the middle and lower Danube, control of strategic passes in the Carpathians, control or denial of the economically important Danube Delta, and the ability to define a line of sustainable expansion in the unhindered but largely featureless southern approaches to Hungary.

From antiquity, the southeastern corner of Europe has been a collision point of empires. By the early modern period, the eastern portion of this region was dominated by the Republic of Venice, which entered into a period of decline roughly coinciding with the ascendancy of the Austrian Habsburgs, but represented a source of residual commercial and political competition in Dalmatia along with portions of northern Italy. The primary strategic rival on this frontier for much of Habsburg history was the Ottoman Empire, a large, aggressive, and militarily and religiously expansionist power with a geopolitical heartland in Anatolia and outlying lands in Egypt and Persia. Expanding on a northerly axis, the Ottomans exerted unceasing pressure on the Habsburg frontier from the sixteenth to the mid-eighteenth centuries. For much of this period, they would represent perhaps the greatest strategic threat to the empire, invading the Austrian heartland and besieging Vienna in 1529 and 1683.

The military contest for this region initially revolved around Turkish-occupied Hungary. With the ejection of Ottoman influence in the late seventeenth century, the locus of conflict shifted to the Habsburg acquisition and consolidation of a substantial hinterland centered on the Tisza and Danube Rivers, and extending through Transylvania to the Carpathians. Thereafter, Austria and Turkey would engage in a protracted struggle across the rugged and underdeveloped lands between the Habsburg and Ottoman heartlands—first Hungary itself, and later the territories of Banat and Bosnia, and in the east, the Turkish-dominated principalities of Moldavia and Wallachia as well as the territory of Bukovina. Ethnic fragments from the Christian kingdoms that had fallen to the Turks populated this intermediary zone: Hungarians, Romanians, Orthodox Serbs, Croats, and various smaller groups. Here, Austria squared off across the Balkans with a steadily declining Ottoman state in Croatia, the lower Danube (where both empires maintained lines of fortresses), and the Black Sea littoral.

From the mid-eighteenth century, a third empire, Russia, would become an active and eventually domineering presence across much of the Wallachian and Balkan marchlands. Its expansion on a southerly axis from the Dniester and Bug Rivers in the quest to build a Black Sea littoral extension of the Russian Eurasian Empire would collide repeatedly with remaining Ottoman footholds in Europe while presenting challenges for the defense of Habsburg interests in the wider Balkans. Russia's ejection of Ottoman influence from the north shore of the Black Sea and Crimea would precipitate a two-century-long contest in which Russian influence would eventually expand through Dobruzha, then into the Balkans proper, and finally the Bosporus itself. The combination of accelerating Ottoman decrepitude and Russian ascendancy would threaten to place many of the strategic keys to the geography of this frontier under the sway or control of a stronger rival power. To this mix would be added from the mid-nineteenth century, with backing from the western powers Britain and France, the coalescence of the Danubian Principalities into an embryonic Romanian independent state.

The Northeastern Frontier: Carpathians to Oder

The northeastern frontier of the Habsburg Empire historically traced the full length of the Carpathian Mountains extending from their intersection with the Oder River to their ninety-degree westward turn near the Oituz Pass. The region beyond this line of mountains formed a large downward-facing triangle anchored on the hinge between the Sudeten and Tatras Mountains in the south, Pomeranian coastline in the northwest, and Kaliningrad in the northeast. A flat, featureless tableland punctuated only by rivers and bordered by marshes, this region was a natural expansion zone for land warfare. Defensive keys in this theater included control of the numerous passes through the Carpathians, possession of the populated and mineral-rich Silesian Plateau, and securing the largely defenseless forward slopes of the Carpathians south of the Vistula and Dniester Rivers.

The pivot of this frontier, the line of the Vistula River, formed a natural conversion point for the westward advance of Eurasian power, southward expansion of Baltic empires, and eastward jut of German colonization. To the west lay the northern states of the German Reich, Saxony, and the small but formidable military kingdom of Brandenburg-Prussia; to the north the cold-water maritime empire of Sweden; and to the east the ancient kingdom of Poland and trackless borderlands of czarist Russia. By the eighteenth century, the main military threat facing Austria on this frontier was Prussia, which seized the Habsburg province of Silesia and waged a two-decades-long war against the monarchy. To this pressure would be added the growing attention and activities of Russia, which following its eviction of Sweden from the east Baltic littoral would press forward on a vast western frontier stretching across the Ponto-Baltic Isthmus.

Strategic competition in this region revolved primarily around the fate of Poland, which for more than two centuries formed a large intermediary body between the stronger neighboring empires around its flanks. Feuds within the Polish elite generated power vacuums and a resulting degree of instability that by the late seventeenth century, offered abundant opportunities for foreign intervention. Nominal Saxon kingship gave way to Great Power jostling, with major European states advancing the claims of various powerful Polish families for the hereditary throne. With the gradual decline of the Polish state, Austria faced the threat of losing this buffer altogether, either through chaos inviting invasion or foreign-backed state capture. A series of partitions in the late eighteenth century ended Polish independence and brought large portions of territory into Habsburg possession north of the defensive Carpathian line, centered on the lower Vistula around Cracow. From this point until the early twentieth century, the empire would face the challenge of managing a vast frontier directly abutting the territories of powerful rival empires Prussia (later Germany) and Russia.

The Southwestern Frontier: Adriatic to Alps

The southwestern frontier of the Habsburg Empire ran in a line from the northern end of the Adriatic near Trieste up the Isonzo River valley to the spine of the Alps. As a wider strategic theater, it included most of the Italian Peninsula above the Apennines, extending across the Lombardy plain from the Julian Alps to the Western Alps and French border. A region of fertile valleys shielded by mountains to the north, this theater was capable of supporting large-scale agriculture and population, and therefore sustaining lengthy high-intensity military campaigning. It presented a combination of rivers that were difficult to ford, cities that were costly to besiege, and passes for rapid retreat and resupply. Defensive keys included securing the Alpine passes that proliferate east of Lake Garda and denying the Piave River valley as a *point d'appui* for enemy armies seeking to debouch onto Carinthia and the Austrian heartland.

Strategic competition on this frontier centered on the Po River valley and Lombardy (initially more a geographic rather than political term denoting the space between the Po and Alps). The region's economic resources made it attractive to the major powers of the Mediterranean—first Spain and later France, which used it as a military corridor for attacking Austria under the Bourbon kings, Napoleon I and his nephew, Napoleon III. Throughout the eighteenth century, the region's primary strategic value was mainly linked to the modalities of dynastic warfare, while in the nineteenth century its value became more economic, as a resource base and supplier of tax revenues. A key barrier against French designs, in tandem with the Danubian Valley, Lombardy allowed the possibility of forestalling marches on Vienna from a reasonable distance and military glacis for forward fortifications.

As on other Habsburg frontiers, the geography immediately abutting its southwestern periphery was populated by weak polities. From the Middle Ages through the mid-nineteenth century, this region was filled with a kaleidoscope of small Italian duchies and kingdoms, none possessing sufficient strength to dominate the others. As in Poland, the primary geopolitical threat facing the empire was the potential for a hostile power to occupy or control what amounted to a geopolitical fracture zone, which in this case directly bordered the imperial heartland. Habsburg possessions in this space from the early eighteenth century included the duchies of Milan and Mantua; traditional allies included Venice, Piedmont-Sardinia, which guarded the strategic passes from France into Lombardy, and Tuscany; while Genoa and Parma/Piacenza were typically in Bourbon hands, and so often allied to the French or Spanish. From 1815, Habsburg possession of an enlarged Kingdom of Lombardy-Venetia would bring the empire into direct competition with growing forces of Italian nationalism, fostered by Piedmont with French backing.

The Northwestern Frontier: Inn to Oder

The northwestern frontier of the Habsburg Empire stretched from the northern face of the Bavarian Alps along the line of the River Inn through the Bavarian and Bohemian Forests, and along the western escarpment of Bohemia to its apex between the rivers Elbe and Oder. As a strategic theater of operations, this area encompassed the whole of the Rhine and Elbe watersheds, from the headwaters of the Danube up the Rhine Valley to Alsace. Fat, flat, and fertile, the German plains were capable of supporting large armies through long campaigning seasons. The central military axis of this region was the Danube River valley, which narrows between the Bavarian Forest and Alps to enter Habsburg lands unimpeded. Defensive keys on this frontier included possession or denial of the entry points to the upper Danube and Inn River valleys as invasion routes, including possession or control of the area around the Black Forest, and ability to project power up the Rhine Valley to the frontiers of France.

The primary focus of military competition on this frontier was southern Germany, which for centuries was a cockpit of competition among the large power centers of western Europe. For centuries the German lands were organized under the auspices of a succession of increasingly loose imperial configurations—first the Holy Roman Empire, or German Reich, and later the German Confederation. Austria's historic rivals for hegemony in Germany from the late Middle Ages were the dynasties of France, which by the early eighteenth century constituted a large and centralized military superstate capable of challenging Habsburg primacy in both Italy and Germany. Periodic French bids for European hegemony, first under the Bourbon kings and later under Napoleon, were typically accompanied by military advances on southern Germany and an attempted invasion of the Danubian lands. From the mid-eighteenth century, the empire found itself under growing pressure from Prussia, a Sparta-like military kingdom whose century-long rise and quest for leadership of Germany would gradually eclipse France and the Ottoman Empire as the main military-political threat facing the Habsburg Empire.

As in Poland and Italy, the political geography of Germany was made up of numerous small and midsize states, and as in those other regions, the primary strategic contest revolved around the geopolitical orientation of states occupying the territory between the empire and its rivals. As the elective leaders of the Holy Roman Empire and later German Confederation, the Habsburg dynasty held nominal sway, but in practice competed with rival powers for influence, allies, and on rare occasions, the emperor's seat itself. The main threat in this theater was twofold: militarily, the ease of rapid movement for enemy armies down the region's large river valleys both into and out of Habsburg territory; and politically, the potential for a rival power to organize these states into an anti-Habsburg constellation, either from within (Prussia) or without (France). The most industrially advanced of Austria's frontiers, Germany would from the eighteenth century to the empire's end represent the source of its greatest military challenges.

Effects of Geography on Strategy

In sum, the Habsburg Monarchy's frontiers embroiled it in four separate, continually evolving security competitions across a space that stretched from the Rhine to the Black Sea and from the Vistula to the Adriatic. No other continental European power faced such a set of challenges except perhaps Russia, which was insulated by larger spaces and usually able to count on at least one or more secure flanks. The possession of a mountain-enclosed riverine heartland helped to mitigate the pressures emanating from this Habsburg periphery. While not insulating the monarchy from the effects of its neighborhood altogether, the empire's defensive terrain gave it a wider margin of error in geopolitics than an interstitial power of its size and location would have possessed in the absence of abundant mountains, as the short and violent histories of states on the featureless Polish plain to Austria's immediate north demonstrate.

The combination of vulnerability and defensibility in Habsburg geography influenced how the monarchy's leaders approached strategy. Grand strategy is a by-product of geography.[28] The physical location of a state, its size, orientation to land and sea, and position in relation to other powers are important factors in the behavior and performance of a state in security competition. While geography does not determine policy, it does limit choices. It also determines the kinds of tools that a state will need to cope with its surrounding environment and reveals gaps in national power capabilities that will need to be filled through some other means. By rewarding some behaviors and penalizing others, it builds up a knowledge base over time about what will and will not work in the quest for survival.

Habsburg geography made Austria an almost exclusively continental power, largely insulated from the direct effects of competition at sea. At the same time, the presence of multidirectional threats placed more severe limitations on Habsburg strategic options than most continental empires have faced. As we will see in chapter 4, these limitations would be reflected in how the Habsburgs thought about and conducted war, contributing to the development of a largely defensive and risk-averse military culture that placed a greater emphasis on terrain than perhaps any major army in European history. More broadly, the effects of geography on Habsburg strategy can be seen in how it conditioned the monarchy's leaders to think about physical space, in several ways, by encouraging the development of strategic forms of knowledge, including maps and other tools, to visualize and conceptualize space for defensive purposes; pulling attention outward, to the frontiers; and demanding the maintenance of a "big picture" capable of taking in the security position of the empire as a whole.

Conceptualizing Space

Austria's difficult location necessitated attention to the spatial dimensions of power both topographically, for the defense of the empire's main territories, and geopolitically, for the management of its security position in the wider European balance of power. While this is true in a general sense for all empires, the ability to conceptualize space is more important for some than others. In the case of Russia, to use one notable example, the possession of wide expanses of largely featureless terrain meant that accurate maps, while desirable, were less essential to the conduct of effective military operations or diplomacy. In this regard, Russia and other large steppe empires such as those found in Central Asia and Mesopotamia were perhaps more comparable to sea powers in their relationship to space, with plains that resembled oceans in their unbroken vastness and armies that needed to navigate like fleets.

By comparison, Habsburg rulers had compelling military and strategic reasons to accurately map and thus visualize the shape and extent of their realm. Historically, states have made maps for many reasons—to legitimize claims to territory, then measure and assess, and hence tax, the lands under their rule, so as to create visual symbols of their power. Prior to the eighteenth century, the Habsburgs had occasionally produced maps for all these reasons. The composite nature of the monarchy, involving historically distinct kingdoms and provinces tied together by dynastic reach, made maps important for establishing claims to individual territories. Habsburg maps of this period reflect this emphasis, usually depicting stand-alone possessions with little topographic accuracy, military value, or effort at depicting the Danubian empire as a whole.[29]

But the geopolitical turbulence of the eighteenth century gave Austria another, different reason to make and use maps: as aids to the defense and security of the realm. An example of this transition can be seen as early as 1705, when at the high point of the War of the Spanish Succession, Prince Eugene of Savoy, Austria's most successful commander, commissioned a detailed map of the main theater of war in northern Italy. Titled *Le Grand Théâtre de la Guerre en Italie*, the map marked a significant departure from Habsburg maps of the previous century.[30] Produced on four sheets of 2 by 1.5 feet each, the map was explicitly intended as a tool to assist in military campaign and battle. Illustrations in the corner of the map, typical for the period, show Eugene's armies carrying the double-headed standard of the emperor through the Alps, with mechanical hoists lifting cannons over the mountains. The message—mastery of the monarchy's geography using the scientific means of the day—is reinforced by the details of the map itself. Where previous maps had often been artistic in nature, emphasizing towns and scenery, and not drawn to scale, Eugene's map used the latest cartographic tools to depict topographic and artificial features with a high degree of accuracy. Roads, rivers, forts, and other military sites are shown in great detail.

Subsequent wars would prompt ever more elaborate attempts at mapping the Habsburg Monarchy. Conflict with the Ottomans spurred bouts of periodic surveying in the south, while border disputes in Italy and the Netherlands required accurate maps to establish the monarchy's claims in the west. It would ultimately be the wars with Prussia, however, that do the most to catalyze Habsburg seriousness about cartography. Between 1740, when Frederick the Great launched his first invasion of Austrian Silesia, and 1790, Habsburg leaders would undertake mapmaking on a vast scale, laying the foundations for what would become the most advanced strategic cartographic culture in Europe. In 1747, the newly created Habsburg corps of engineers created *The General Map of All Imperial and Hereditary Lands*—the first attempt at depicting the empire as a geographic whole. Illustrations in the margin of *The General Map* underscore its geopolitical rather than artistic purpose, with the Empress Maria Theresa (1717–80) shown, amid various mapmaking instruments and cannonballs, pointing her scepter at France (*Galiae pars*), Austria's historic rival.[31]

The decades that followed brought an explosion of Habsburg mapmaking. Building on the *The General Map*, in 1764 Vienna launched what would become the first in a series of highly detailed, comprehensive military surveys of the Habsburg Empire. Known as *The Great Military Map*, or *Josephinische Aufnahme* (Josephine survey), it represented the most advanced cartographic instrument of its time, requiring an astonishing 22 separate surveys and showing more than 220,000 square miles of territory on 3,500 sheets.[32] This effort was accompanied by scores of smaller projects focused on specific regions and objects: *The Great Military Map of Transylvania*, the so-called *Ferraris Map of Belgium* (named after its creator), maps of Lombardy and other provinces, and extensive surveys of outside territories directly abutting the borders of the monarchy and countless small maps of individual strategic sites, such as fortresses, mountain passes, and individual frontiers—altogether amounting to more than 16,000 maps.[33]

Habsburg maps were made with a strategic as opposed to merely commercial or artistic purpose in mind. Several characteristics of Habsburg cartography demonstrate this point. One is that the effort to produce them was driven from the top, with an overtly military goal in mind. The principal drivers were Empress Maria Theresa and her coregent and successor Emperor Joseph II as well as their senior advisers, State Chancellor Kaunitz and Field Marshal Count Franz von Lacy. Motivated by the long and bitter wars with Frederick, these and other Austrian leaders sought to harness the conceptual and scientific tools of the Enlightenment to reform the state on all levels—in Maria Theresa's words, to "organize and put [it] on a firm footing."[34]

The aim of these efforts was to make the empire a unified polity, thereby leveraging its combined means in natural and human resources toward the political end of victory over revisionist Prussia. Maps were an important tool for achieving this goal, since they helped the empire's leaders picture, and thus calculate, the range of resources at their disposal as well as fight battles more effectively and reach more favorable territorial deals in postwar negotiations. To this end, Habsburg leaders of the late eighteenth century devoted large-scale resources in money and intellectual power to the creation not only of maps but also the institutional and scientific infrastructure needed to support an advanced, modern cartography. The aim was not momentary but long term: to cultivate spatial knowledge as a competitive advantage for the monarchy in competitions with rivals.

The fact that strategy was the motivating force behind these efforts can also be seen in the content of Habsburg maps. The level of detail in Habsburg maps of this period far exceeds the maps of the monarchy's major adversaries. When *The Great Military Map* was commissioned, the most accurate map in Europe was the Cassini map of France, which was drawn at a 1:86,400 scale.

By contrast, Austria's military surveys were conducted at a 1:28,800 scale, with 275 of the 3,500 sheets produced at an astonishing 1:11,520 scale—or more than seven times more detailed than the maps of their rivals.[35] This is roughly the difference between looking at the earth from the window of a low-flying aircraft and looking at it from a high-altitude jetliner.

As notable as the level of detail are the objects of emphasis in Habsburg maps—that is, what their makers chose to depict. Comprehensive in nature, they took into account both natural and artificial features. Elevation was shaded in gradients, with even small degrees of change indicated. Various kinds of forests and fields were clearly demarcated, while mountain passes received particular attention, with narrow defiles and defensible points highlighted. Rivers were marked to show widths, curves, islands, fords, and the directions of currents as well as the locations of floodplains and marshy areas. Existing structures, particularly those with potential military value, were illustrated carefully and precisely. Towns and farms were sketched to show their exact layout, with everything from mills and forges to orchards shown true to form. Roads were depicted in exact detail, from major highways and boulevards, to the smallest and most remote footpaths. Fortifications were shown down to the layout of individual ramparts and battlements, and the locations of arsenals were marked in every province. On the frontiers, even the smallest military posts and blockhouses were included, to the point where on the southern borders, individual frontier watchtowers, each roughly the size of a large deer blind, were depicted and clearly labeled at intervals every few thousand yards.

Further indication of the strategic purpose of Habsburg maps is the manner in which they were handled. Where most other European powers made their maps available to the public for commercial and other uses, the Habsburg Monarchy treated them as sensitive state material, restricting the means by which they were produced, viewed, and circulated. This tradition of secrecy had a long history in Austria, beginning with the strict intelligence controls introduced by Raimondo Montecuccoli, Hofkriegsrat president, in the 1670s. As cartographic efforts expanded in the late eighteenth century, these controls intensified. Habsburg maps were treated as what would today be called "top secret" classified information. Each section of map produced for the military survey was made in triplicate form, with copies going respectively to the emperor and president of the Hofkriegsrat.[36] Outside a small senior military and diplomatic circle, anyone wishing to view a map had to receive explicit, written permission from the monarch.[37] Cartographers, many of whom were inevitably drawn from outside the empire, were vetted for reliability. Kaunitz offered payment for a large mapping project in Italy on the condition that a foreign power not recruit the mapmaker, and Maria Theresa delayed a similar effort on the grounds that it needed to be conducted "without needing to hire foreigners."[38] So strict were the classifications on Habsburg maps that when an imperial officer possessing classified cartographic information or tools died, the state moved swiftly to seize these materials before they could fall into foreign hands, even if they were killed in a combat zone.[39]

The lengths to which the Austrians went to control their maps, together with the amount of state resources that went into their construction and high degree of military relevance of their contents, demonstrate that the Habsburg Monarchy's leaders saw them as a form of strategic knowledge to be cultivated and protected in order to gain a competitive advantage in geopolitics. Under Maria Theresa and Joseph II, Austria created the institutional infrastructure for generating this intelligence on a systematic rather than ad hoc basis. Vienna devoted large shares of the defense budget not only to maps but also the development of the scientific support structures needed to sustain mapmaking on a long-term basis, including observatories, collections of the most modern astronomical and geodetic tools, a professional military corps of engineers, map archives, and detailed protocols for mapping practices, surveys, and border demarcations.[40]

In today's terms, Habsburg cartography represented what would be called "geospatial intelligence"—the systematic development of visual aids, used in combination with other intelligence-gathering tools, for the explicit purpose of aiding the state in war and diplomacy. Indeed, there was a symbiotic relationship between intelligence and maps in the Habsburg Monarchy. During military campaigns, engineers accompanied the troops and made extensive maps of the local terrain. Likewise, teams of military officers accompanied surveying teams and took careful notes on the defensive features of anything of potential military value, marking the exact location of everything from morasses to orchards and cemeteries. These notes were attached to the corresponding section of a map with a legend, thus providing a detailed intelligence guide that could be readily referenced by senior commanders and the Hofkriegsrat in wartime (see figure 2.4). The emphasis in these notes is on assessing the monarchy's lands as a potential future battlespace, as this example shows:

> The town is a solidly built affair, with a large military barracks and stables on the edge. Principal buildings are the town hall, a convent, a church, and a large parish house. Outlying buildings are well constructed, especially those near the mill on the banks of the Crems river. That river joins the Danube just below the town, and at that point the Danube makes the area something of an island. The terrain is generally flat but dominated by the hill rising behind the town.[41]

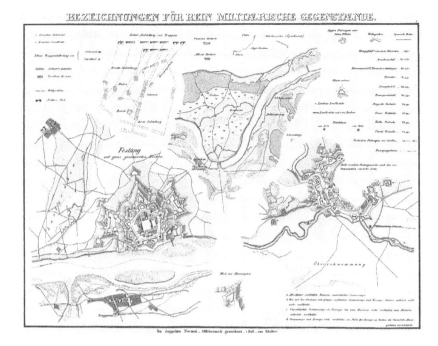

FIG. 2.4. Example of Austrian Military Survey Key. *Source:* Gabor Timar, Gabor Molnar, Balazs Szekely, Sandor Biszak, Jozsef Varga, and Annamaria Janko, *The Map Sheets of the Second Military Survey and their Georeferenced Version* (Budapest: Arcanum, 2006).

The Pull of Frontiers

In addition to encouraging conceptualizations of space generally, the Habsburg Monarchy's geography and geopolitical position focused the attention of its leaders on specific points in space that were tied to its security and survival as a state. As for states in today's world, this was first and foremost about those places where problems were most likely to emerge: the frontier. It was here, at the outer reaches of Habsburg power, that Austria's interests were bound to come into conflict with those of a neighboring state, where the monarchy would first encounter an attack, and where it would either expand or concede space after war.

The presence of numerous outside dangers around Austria's borders exerted what historian Owen Lattimore, in his work on the Ch'in Empire, called the "pull" of frontiers: a continual demand for attention and resources that draws the imperial center's focus outward, toward the point of contact with the enemy.[42] In Austria's case, this pull was especially strong due to the number of active military fronts and overall length of frontiers, across more than four thousand miles. Pressure from the frontier—pressure to react, but also to plan, prepare, and act proactively—would be a constant throughout Habsburg history, often transcending the dynastic preoccupations and predilections or rivalries of individual emperors.

Habsburg maps reflect this strategic emphasis on frontiers. Its roots lie in military competition with the Turks. At the Treaty of Karlowitz in 1699, Vienna ordered its commissioners to conduct a survey in order to move beyond interminable debates over "ancient" or "natural" frontiers, and establish the exact location of the Sava-Maros Line that would form the new frontier between the two empires.[43] An expedition by the Austrian military engineer Johann Christoph Müller would establish cartographic parameters to support what would eventually become the famous Military Border (see chapter 5). In subsequent wars, the first act after acquiring new territory would be to order a comprehensive survey and census.[44]

This stress on frontiers formed a pattern that would persist into the late eighteenth century. Frontiers routinely received the closest attention in military-topographic surveys. Sections of *The Great Military Map* dealing with front-line territories were often produced at 1:11,520 and 1:17,200 scales rather than the usual 1:28,800.[45] *The Great Military Map of Transylvania* produced follow-on maps of the neighboring non-Habsburg frontier territories of Moldavia and Wallachia, which as we will see figured prominently in Austrian military strategy in the southeast.[46] Similarly, maps of the Austrian Netherlands and Lombardy gave special emphasis to identifying defensive features of the borderlands.

The degree to which Habsburg strategic attention was centered on frontiers can also be seen in numbers: according to calculations by the Romanian researcher Madalina Valeria Veres, by the late eighteenth century, around 79 percent of the monarchy's maps devoted to its own territories depicted frontier provinces; of the 252 maps covering outside powers, 227 were of states sharing a frontier with the monarchy.[47]

Over time, these mapping efforts formed a repository that was actively used by Austrian rulers, statesmen, and generals to support the conduct of Habsburg strategy. Detailed knowledge of frontiers helped Austria address the ubiquitous border disputes afflicting a state of its central location, such as after the 1737–39 Turkish War, to resolve a 1743 disagreement with Venice, and delimit the frontiers of the Austrian Netherlands and river boundary of Lombardy. Maria Theresa and Kaunitz spent hours pouring over maps of the western frontiers in the lead-up to the War of the Bavarian Succession, the diplomatic resolution of which revolved around the ability to ascertain small but important physical characteristics (salt mines, population counts, and locations of rivers) reflected in the empire's maps.[48] The ensuing negotiations of the Polish partition hinged on similar details, though on a larger scale, while Metternich's famous diplomacy at the Vienna Congress involved cartographic assessments of the strategic value of frontier regions in Poland and Saxony in which successful diplomacy depended on the ability to accurately tally "a certain measure of territory, count of population, and stock of resources."[49]

Extensive frontier maps also had military application. Possession of such a database allowed Austrian commanders of the late eighteenth and early nineteenth centuries to avoid Eugene's improvisations, and instead rely on an established database of knowledge, both for prewar defense planning and conducting military campaigns. Austrian expeditions into the Balkans in the 1716–18 and 1727–39 wars benefited from access to the work of Müller and other earlier border-surveying missions. When Joseph II's legions marched south in 1788, its officers from the General Staff down to the level of individual regimental commanders would be carrying some 150 engraved copies of sections from *The Great Military Map* and *The Great Hungarian Map* (*Die große ungarische Karte*) for Croatia, Slavonia, Banat of Temesvár, Transylvania, and Galicia.[50] By the late phases of the Prussian wars, Habsburg field commanders had access to vastly improved maps compared to what had been available in the first disastrous encounters in Silesia. As we will see in chapter 6, Joseph II and his generals would use these maps to plan fortifications, painstakingly cited in Bohemian topography, during the 1760s and 1770s. And when the monarchy went to war with revolutionary France, the Hofkriegsrat would possess a cartographic library sufficiently well evolved to support a twenty-year struggle in the west as well as extensive, subsequent rounds of frontier fortification construction.

The Big Picture

The pull of frontiers exercised a prevailing influence on Habsburg strategic thinking. As we will see in chapter 4, the pressures that frontiers exerted would decisively shape the empire's military planning and diplomatic concepts well into the nineteenth century. Because dynamics at the frontier, particularly for a relatively weak power, tend to be driven by an external source (the rival), they generate problems that require crisis management, which in turn implies a high degree of reaction on the part of the defender. This would appear to be especially true for a power like Austria, which was enclosed on four sides by frontiers and would seem to be a victim of *perpetual* reaction to external engines of crisis beyond its ability to anticipate, much less control.

But precisely because it had so many frontiers, Hapsburg leaders could not afford to be purely reactive; they needed the ability to get ahead of escalatory dynamics and picture their realm as a defensive whole, for at least two reasons.

First, the empire's geography penalized concentration on any one frontier at the expense of others for very long. "Take care," as Eugene of Savoy warned the emperor. "Your Monarchy is a little straggling: it connects itself with the north, the south, and the east. It is also in the center of Europe."[51] Such a state could not afford to prioritize a threat du jour to such an extent that it neglected preparations for attack from other directions. Being prepared required its leaders to be able to visualize the juxtaposition of frontiers, study the distances and times between them, and conceptualize the means of balancing among their threats. Second, Austria's central position and frequent military weakness meant there was a good chance its armies would be involved in fighting in the interior of the empire itself. By the second half of the eighteenth century, this had already happened in three wars—1701–14, 1740–48, and 1757–63. In such cases, the ability to conceptualize defensive measures integrating the monarchy's heartland and periphery was crucial for survival.

Habsburg maps reflected both realities. The explicit purpose of large-scale mapping efforts in the second half of the eighteenth century had been to create tools for allowing Habsburg monarchs and their advisers to make strategic appraisals about the realm as a unified whole. As Joseph II wrote to the Austrian ambassador to France in 1781, "We must do what we can to acquire the necessary notions about the general situation of the monarchy."[52] Both *The General Map of All Imperial and Hereditary Lands* and *The Great Military Map* were attempts to achieve precisely that: a picture of the empire as a whole. The first fulfilled this goal inaccurately; the second failed, not for effort, but for technical reasons, because the surveys were begun before the astronomical measurements had been made, creating misalignments between the individual map sheets that prevented them from being assembled as a whole. In subsequent decades, the goal would be realized.

The ability to piece together a big picture was important for defensive reasons. The fact that Austria's leaders devoted so much time and resources to developing an ability to visualize their *own* spaces suggests that they anticipated often having to fight future wars on Habsburg rather than foreign soil. Altogether, 65 percent of the maps in the Hofkriegsrat archives are focused on Habsburg territory, with much of the remaining 35 percent concentrated on directly adjacent lands.[53] The point is further reinforced by the degree of attention given to depicting the kinds of artificial and natural features that would be used to fight a defensive war, with militarily relevant points noted well into the empire's interior and travel times marked between key points— ostensibly to aid in postal deliveries, but with obvious military application.

Taken together, these characteristics of Austrian maps show that Habsburg monarchs both wished to be able to form a big picture of their state and developed the means to do so. While their frontiers may have been a source of constant friction and attention, they were conscious of the need to avoid a perpetual state of reaction to the problems generated there. They sought to equip themselves with spatial tools to support the matching of means (defense resources) to ends (countering multiple threats), and do so on a forward-looking basis—that is, for the purposes of strategy.

The location of a state determines what its leaders care about, what they fear and prioritize, and how they picture themselves in relation to the outside world. Soviet maps during the Cold War, as the geostrategist Zbigniew Brzezinski noted, were centered on Moscow, with an optically smaller United States divided into Atlantic and Pacific halves, while the United States used North American–centric maps that split the Eurasian landmass in two and exaggerated the size of North America in relation to the rest of the world.[54] Soviet maps conveyed the preponderance of the Eurasian landmass and suggested preoccupation with the maintenance of long land borders; US maps depicted America as a continent-sized island and highlighted the need to manage two great oceans and their coastal rimlands.

Similarly, Habsburg cartography tells a great deal, both about how its rulers viewed the vulnerabilities of their geography and how they thought about managing those vulnerabilities. Above all they show a preoccupation with frontiers and the numerous threats that lined the empire's lengthy perimeter. Frontiers represented a continual source of danger that drew Austrian attention outward at the same time that the empire's large distances imposed power gradients on its ability to effectively manage all four frontiers simultaneously. Together, these represented severe constraints on Habsburg power. Where Russia was afflicted with steeper power gradients across its much larger territories, it was able to find security in these vast spaces. Austria, by contrast, had the logistical difficulties of managing large space while possessing a larger number of physically closer foes.

Habsburg geography also offered some advantages to offset the difficulties of its geopolitical position. Chief among these were the internal lines of a central position. The unusual length and integrating properties of the Danube River system helped to soften the power gradient for Austria, aiding in both defense and the construction of a secure resource base. The presence of defensive boundaries in the form of enclosing mountain ranges provided a degree of separation and protection favorable to the tasks of empire building. The contrast to the lands north of Austria is striking in this regard; where the north-central European plain was naked to attack, the Danubian Basin's encircling mountains created a cradle capable of sustaining a riparian heartland. In the words of Claudio Margris, this provided the ingredients for a "great civilization of defensiveness, of barriers thrown up to protect oneself from outside attack ... a fortress which offers excellent shelter against the threat of the world."[55]

This combination of vulnerability and defensibility lies at the heart of Habsburg strategy. Austria's geopolitical environment made the development of strategies for coping with perennial danger necessary; its immediate geography and topography made the implementation of strategy possible. This distinguishes the Habsburg Monarchy from some other interstitial states in history. Vulnerability without defensibility would have produced a larger, southern version of eighteenth-century Poland: a state that was physically indefensible and showed the traits of that indefensibility in a strategic culture of offensive-minded resignation to fate. Conversely, defensibility without vulnerability would have made Austria a larger version of Switzerland—a state for which security is near total, and with a corresponding strategic outlook that is retiring, insular, and able to assume that problems are distant and will dissipate with time.

It is in the Austrians' quest to manage their obvious vulnerabilities by leveraging their empire's advantages, however modest, that we see the stirrings of strategy in the Habsburg Monarchy. Austrian maps and attempts at constructing geospatial intelligence show that the Habsburgs studied their physical setting, noted its vulnerabilities, and sought to systematically address them with the tools available. One need only look at a map to grasp the scale of threats arrayed against the monarchy. But one need only look at the Alps or Carpathians, standing on the ground, to grasp the immense defensive potential that such features imprinted on the minds of their owners. Surveying the empire's mountains and rivers, Austrian rulers, soldiers, and diplomats could imagine not just survival but also the prospect of bringing safety to the cluster of territories under their dominion—building a durable order, anchored in Catholicism, and buttressed by nature, tradition, and ingenuity against the forces of chaos. As we will see in chapter 4, the result was a conservative and defensive strategic mind-set motivated by danger, but buoyed by the rational quest for an attainable security. Habsburg geography thus helped to create a sense of strategic viability—a perception that however numerous the threats arrayed against it, the empire could, with the application of reason, endure.

3

Damnosa Hereditas

HABSBURG PEOPLE AND STATE

The Austrian monarchy is composed of five or six ... different constitutions.
What a variety, in culture, in population and in credit! The title of emperor
does not bring with it a single man nor a Kreutzer. He must even negotiate
with his empire.

—PRINCE EUGENE OF SAVOY

The spirit of this country is so bad ... that while our troops are engaged abroad
we may face a more dangerous enemy at home.

—ARCHDUKE JOSEPH

IN CONTRAST TO its physical geography, the political geography of the Danubian Basin greatly complicated the task of Habsburg empire building. Accumulated in a pell-mell fashion over several centuries, the territorial holdings of the Austrian Habsburgs formed a composite state made up of multiple, historically separate polities, each with its own separate constitutional arrangement with the ruling dynasty. Its human population consisted of more than a dozen ethnic groups, none of which was strong enough to dominate the others. This internal makeup impeded the monarchy's evolution as a modern state in two ways: by hindering the development of a centralized, efficient state administration and implanting sources of domestic conflict into the social fabric of the state. Both factors shaped Austria's behavior as a strategic actor, placing it at a disadvantage in competition with more centralized and unified Great Power rivals. Ultimately, these characteristics prevented the monarchy from mobilizing its full power potential, effectively removed territorial expansion as an option for increasing state security, and presented internal vulnerabilities for enemies to exploit in wartime.

Habsburg Political Geography

The Habsburg Monarchy was a layer cake of lands that by the eighteenth century, consisted of seventeen historically separate polities and more than a dozen ethnic groups. The empire's political geography was the by-product of a series of territorial acquisitions that occurred in a sedimentary fashion over more than five centuries, but had its roots in the much older human history of the Danubian Basin. The Ponto-Baltic Isthmus on which the basin sits is an ancient highway of migration—the point at which the Eurasian landmass narrows into the western European peninsula. Within this funnel, the basin acted as a sieve, collecting and retaining fragments of passing tribes. The same abundant rivers and protective mountains that made the basin so amenable to later empire building had, at a much earlier point in its history, attracted waves of human settlement. Eastern tribes entered through the Carpathian passes; horse people of the steppe came through the Panonian Plain, and Roman settlers ventured beyond the Limes Germanicus in search of farmland.

By the tenth century, three main ethnic groups had established themselves as the basin's most numerous and entrenched residents: the Slavs, Magyars, and Vlachs, ancestors of modern Romanians.[1] Over the centuries, each group built kingdoms and statelets of varying sizes and duration, some of which would grow into substantial holdings by the Middle Ages.

The subsequent political dynamics of the Habsburg Monarchy were an outworking of the centuries-long collision of these preexisting settlement patterns with the eastward march of the medieval German Reich. This process began in earnest in the eighth century, with efforts to extend Frankish rule into the chaotic eastern marchlands of Charlemagne's empire. By the late 700s, the Reich had incorporated a strip of eastern territory from the Elbe through modern-day Austria to the Istrian Peninsula and across the northern half of Italy. Frankish primacy would reach its furthest extent in the southeast, stretching from the Bavarian Alps as far as the midway points of the Sava and Drava Rivers. A major factor behind this eastward jut of German influence and subsequent Habsburg expansion was the Danube itself, which propelled German political and commercial activity along the spine of the Alps on an easterly axis, from the Black Forest toward the Black Sea. By the mid-tenth century, this movement had crystallized into a series of German-administered borderlands—the Eastern, Styrian, Carinthian, and Carniolan "Marches"— that would form the nucleus of Austria. Beyond these territories, the Danube watershed set the path for subsequent expansion.[2]

It was in the context of the quest by the German Reich to stabilize and govern its eastern frontier that the Habsburgs emerged into central European politics in the mid-thirteenth century from their family strongholds of

Switzerland and Swabia. Under Rudolph I, the family acquired a series of titles and territories that would form the font of their legitimacy in subsequent
centuries, beginning with election to the seat of the Holy Roman Empire after
the death of the last Hohenstaufen emperor in 1254, and the acquisition of the
duchies of Styria and Austria after the defeat of the Premyslid king Ottokar of
Bohemia at the Battle on the Marchfeld in 1282. In the centuries that followed,
the Habsburgs enlarged their central European holdings by marriage, war, and
diplomacy. In the fourteenth century, they consolidated their core Austrian
lands with the acquisition of Tyrol, Carinthia, and Carnolia. The sixteenth
century brought a burst of expansion to the east with the incorporation of
Bohemia, Moravia, Upper and Lower Silesia, and Royal Hungary into the
Habsburg domains by inheritance following the death of King Louis II of
Hungary at the Battle of Mohács against the Turks.

This period also saw the growth of Habsburg influence in western Europe,
with Burgundy and Spain coming into the family's possession. By the mid-
sixteenth century, Habsburg power had reached its apogee in Europe, forming
a continental Catholic empire that encompassed a vast swath of the central
portion of the European landmass from the Atlantic lands of Spain and Low
Countries, through northern Italy and the German Reich to the middle Danube, and eventually controlling outlying territories as far afield as the East
Indies and Mexico.

From this apex, Habsburg holdings would devolve into their eventual
Danube-centric shape through a series of events in the final decades of the
seventeenth century. The first was the end of the Thirty Years' War (1618–48),
by which Habsburg Catholic dominance of Germany was decisively weakened and the dynasty was pushed to look eastward, to the Danube valley, for
compensation.[3] The second was the prosecution of a successful war of expansion following the repulsion of the Turkish siege of Vienna in 1683, by which
the monarchy absorbed a wide tract of territory in Hungary, formerly a contested borderland between itself and the Ottoman Empire. The third event,
the death of the final Spanish Habsburg king, Charles II, in 1700, would bring
the western branch of the Habsburgs to extinction, making its eastern, junior
line the locus of all subsequent dynastic growth.

This rapid sequence of changes would give the Habsburg realm the character of a principally east-central European geopolitical enterprise that it would
retain until its demise after the First World War. Essential to the monarchy's
strategic reorientation was the enclosure of Greater Hungary, with its broad
expanses, alongside the Danubian possessions of Bohemia, Moravia, and the
Austrias to form a territorially contiguous mass capable of furnishing the
Habsburg state with the resource base and strategic depth necessary to be-

come a Great Power. While the dynasty retained the title of Holy Roman emperor, and would continue to command military resources and political influence in Germany for another century and a half, this function would become increasingly symbolic with the growing autonomy of the German states and consolidation of Habsburg east of the Alps. And although the monarchy would acquire extensive extra-Danubian appendages over time, eventually amassing territories as far afield as the Netherlands and Sicily, its geopolitical heartland would remain centered on the three sets of territories clustered around the Danube: the Austrian Hereditary Lands, or Erblände, the Lands of the Bohemian Crown, and the Kingdom of Hungary.

The Erblände: Cockpit of Empire

At the heart of the Habsburg possessions lay the Erblände. Held since the Middle Ages, these included the Archduchies of Upper and Lower Austria with the capital of Vienna, Inner Austria (the duchies of Styria, Carinthia, and Carniola), the Adriatic principalities (Gorizia, Istria, and Trieste), the Tyrol, and the Vorlände (Anterior Austria, Swabian Austria, and the Voralberg). Geographically, these lands form a backward L extending eastward along the Danube and Mur Rivers from Switzerland to the Great Hungarian Plain, and northward along the eastern face of the Alps to the Bohemian Plateau. The human composition of the Erblände was primarily German, but with large enclaves of Croats, Hungarians, Slovenes, and Italians in the south and east. By the mid-eighteenth century, Habsburg rulers would often refer to Bohemia and Moravia as being part of the Erblände, yet for the sake of clarity the term here will be used to describe the Austrian lands alone.

As the dynasty's original territorial possessions, the Erblände were the taproot of Habsburg political legitimacy in central Europe, the seat of its capital, and a major contributor of war resources to the dynasty. Together with the neighboring Czech lands, they comprised the most populous and economically productive provinces of the monarchy. Styria, Upper Austria, and Carinthia were major sites of metallurgy mining and later industry, producing 75 percent of the empire's pig iron by the late eighteenth century (and more than all of Britain in Styria alone).[4] Vienna and the Voralberg were sites of significant textile enterprises, with paper, glass, and agriculture dominating elsewhere. In 1790, Lower Austria alone accounted for 50 percent of the empire's manufacturing firms.[5] Commercially, Outer Austria acted as a bridge to the nearby Swabian and Alsatian economies as well as the wider western European markets. The proximity of Upper and Lower Austria to the Danube and its tributaries naturally integrated these provinces into the Bohemian and

Hungarian trade networks at the empire's center, while Inner Austria's trade network connected it to northern Italy, and the ports of Trieste and Fiume provided access to Mediterranean trade routes.[6]

As a launchpad for empire building, the Erblände possessed certain advantages: being partly mountainous, these territories were naturally defensible; being compact, ethnically homogeneous, and largely Catholic, they were a usually reliable source of political support to the dynasty. But viewed as a cockpit from which to manage a large and complex empire, the Erblände had limitations. Most notably, its territories were small—perhaps a fifth of the empire's overall landmass. While the local terrain was advantageous, the overall location of the Erblände subjected it to the pressures of east-central European geopolitics. The territories were within easy striking distance of enemies in the south, where the Turks could reach Vienna with little warning, and in the north, where Prussia had a fast route through Bohemia to Vienna. This combination—a microcosm of the wider empire's mixture of defensive terrain and geopolitical vulnerability—made the possession of adequate buffer zones a prerequisite for Habsburg security.

Lands of the Bohemian Crown: Habsburg Coffer

To the north of the Erblände lay the Bohemian Crownlands, a grouping of medieval provinces acquired by the Habsburgs through marriage amid the political vacuum created by the defeat of the indigenous kingdoms at the hands of the Turks in the first quarter of the sixteenth century. These lands were centered on the Kingdom of Bohemia, ancient stronghold of the Czech kings, and included its historic appendages: the Margraviate of Moravia, Duchy of Silesia, and for a period, Margraviates of Upper and Lower Lusatia. Together, these territories formed a bell-shaped outcropping of highlands above Upper and Lower Austria along the parallel axis of the Vltava and Morava Rivers, flanked by thick forests to the west and mountains to the north and east. Most of these lands were contained within the Bohemian Massif. An important outlier was Silesia, which lay beyond the Ore Mountains in the exposed Silesian plain.

In geopolitical terms, the Bohemian Crownlands can be viewed as an extension of the Habsburg heartland, and indeed they were commonly treated as such politically throughout the eighteenth century.[7] They were the most thickly peopled territories of the monarchy, containing twice the population of the Erblände.[8] By Habsburg standards, they were relatively homogeneous; except for Silesia, ethnic Czechs and Slovaks dominated the region, with large concentrations of ethnic Germans and Jews in the towns. Grafting foreign (mainly German) nobility into the mix reinforced this in the seventeenth century.[9] Unlike in the Austrian Erblände, confessional conflict had been a political leitmotif of history in the Czech provinces, although by the eighteenth century the vigorous Counter-Reformation had rendered religious separatism a spent force, and the territories well-integrated and predominantly Catholic constituents into the Habsburg polity. They were henceforth a major provider, both of soldiery and of dynastically loyal officials for service in Habsburg bureaucracy.

Economically, the Bohemian Crownlands were the strongest sources of export and other revenue for the Habsburg Empire. Rich in minerals (iron, silver, and tin), they were natural sites for the development of industry—glass in Bohemia, wool in Moravia, and textiles around Prague and Brünn.[10] The reign of Maria Theresa brought a boom in mills and manufacturing that would result in about a third of all Habsburg manufacturing firms being located in the region.[11] Eventually, cotton textiles and iron emerged as the principal industries. The contribution of tax revenue from the Czech lands exceeded that of other parts of the monarchy by a considerable margin.[12] Silesia alone accounted for a quarter of Habsburg tax revenue—some 3.5 million florins per year by the early 1740s, making it, in the words of statesman and diplomat Baron von Bartenstein, "the true jewel of the house of Austria."[13] Even after the definitive loss of Silesia to Prussia in 1745, the remaining Bohemian Crownlands were providing many times the revenue of the Erblände (6 million florins by the 1750s compared to 1 million florins each for Inner Austria and the archduchies, respectively, and no revenue at all from Tyrol and Outer Austria).[14]

Strategically, the Czech lands performed several important functions for the Habsburg Empire. At thirty thousand square miles and a fifth of the monarchy's overall population, they acted as a much-needed annex to the otherwise-small Austrian Erblände and a politically reliable counterweight to the territorially large and often-obstreperous Lands of the Hungarian Crown. In military terms, the possession of extensive northern territories rich in defensive rivers provided much-needed strategic depth vis-à-vis Prussia. Economically, the merging of the Czech and Austrian lands into a developed industrial region, when combined with the territorially large but economically backward agricultural hinterland of Hungary, provided a high degree of economic complementarity.[15]

Other features of the Czech lands presented challenges. Strategically, the loss of Silesia would deprive the northwestern Habsburg frontier of a substantial buffer, presenting Prussia with easy access to Vienna via invasion routes that led through the empire's richest territories.[16] Economically, the close proximity of Czech rivers to the Elbe facilitated commercial exchanges with the German territories, luring the region's trade toward the markets of western

Europe.[17] Demographically, despite the relative degree of integration in the early modern period, the presence of a large ethnic non-German population with a history of political independence would become a source of tension in the nineteenth century.

Kingdom of Hungary: Breadbasket of Empire

To the east of the Erblände lay the vast Kingdom of Hungary, comprising both the rump of territory north of the Danube that had avoided incorporation into the Ottoman Empire in the seventeenth century (so-called Royal Hungary) and the large tablelands of the Great Hungarian Plain and Transylvania that stretched beyond it to the Carpathian Mountains. Remnants of a medieval kingdom that had once encompassed most of the Danubian Basin outside Alpine Austria, Hungary included a number of distinct territories, including modern-day Croatia, Slovakia, and a large portion of Romania. Together these lands marked the transition point between the forested landscape of central Europe and grasslands of the Eurasian steppe. They extended along the north-south column of the parallel Danube and Tisza Rivers, bordered by the Czech highlands in the north, Sava and lower Danube in the south, and elongated elbow of Transylvanian Alps in the east.

Geopolitically, Hungary played two roles in the Habsburg Monarchy. Its northern and central territories were a de facto extension of the Habsburg heartland, being well watered, populous, and the center of Hungarian industry. Its eastern approaches formed a large hinterland that had been useful as a buffer zone between Austria and the Turks in previous centuries, and would continue to be treated as a kind of internalized buffer long after it had been formally incorporated into the monarchy.

The Hungarian economy was primarily agrarian. Despite comprising almost 38 percent of the monarchy's total population by the late eighteenth century, the Hungarian lands were economically backward, both as a result of long wars with the Turks and archaic social structures. Industry was underdeveloped. Although Budapest, with its large population of urban Germans and Jews, was a significant source of commerce, Hungary made up a much smaller proportion of Habsburg industry than the smaller Austrian or Czech lands. Northern portions of Hungary in modern-day Slovakia were an important center of mining, and the ports of the Croatian coast held some commercial significance through long exposure to Mediterranean trade. But as a whole, Hungary's main economic contribution to the Habsburg economy was agricultural, providing large volumes of grain, livestock, and other commodities from inner Hungary.

Politically, the Hungarian lands were late and reluctant participants in Habsburg empire building. A long history of Magyar independence and strong sense of ethnic identity had created an entrenched political class with a powerful attachment to accumulated freedoms. These inherited privileges derived from the so-called Tripartitum, a legal arrangement from 1514 whereby the Hungarian nobility was largely exempted from taxation. Due to this arrangement, an unusual amount of wealth was concentrated in a narrow slice of the nobility, with around a hundred families controlling about a third of Hungary's land. Renegotiation of the terms of this exemption and other vestigial Magyar rights would be a source of perennial friction. The resulting feuds impeded the economic development of Hungary, slowing the removal of internal trade barriers, and stunting investment and public works on the scale needed to improve river transport in Hungary's central region.[18] Attempts at removing these privileges tended to be predictable triggers for conflict.

The strength of the Habsburg heartland in geopolitical terms was the relatively compact and complementary nature of its core territories. The proximity of a small but wealthy and populous Austria and Bohemia to a large, resource-rich Hungary, all tied together by riverine networks, created the natural conditions for a common market. What one historian called a "marriage of textiles and wheat" when referring to the internal economic exchange of the Austrian and Hungarian lands at a later date in the empire's history was in reality a marriage of Austrian (and Czech) textiles, Hungarian wheat, and Bohemian coin.[19]

The Price of Complexity

The ability of the Habsburg state to realize the full potential of these core territories would be a major determinant of its performance as a Great Power. Historically, the success of states in strategic competition has been a by-product of the extent to which they can achieve mastery over the internal resources at their disposal.[20] This in turn has depended on two things: the ability of a state's central government to dominate its constituent parts and efficiently organize their capacity for war, and the ability of a state's population to provide a sufficient degree of unity to support the state's political aims. Beginning in the eighteenth century, major European states had started to develop both features, placing them on a track to become the centralized nation-states that formed the basis for the large Great Powers of the nineteenth century.

On paper, the Habsburg Monarchy possessed many of the traits necessary to become a modern Great Power. Its combined landmass was larger than any

European power except Russia. Its population, while smaller than France's, was on par with other large powers. Its physical resources, stemming from fertile soils, metal-rich mountains, and abundant rivers, gave it one of the greatest potential power bases of any state in the European states system. And the configuration of the Habsburg lands, combining a developed industrial core with an agricultural hinterland, made the monarchy a good candidate for the mercantilist policies that most European powers would use to achieve aggressive centralization as modern military states in the eighteenth century.[21]

But in reality, the empire was never able to realize this full power potential. The monarchy's unique political geography made it different from emerging nation-states in two important ways: by imposing residually feudal forms of government that impeded the quest for administrative efficiency, and imparting a degree of ethnic complexity that hindered internal unity. These factors obstructed the mobilization of Austria's nominally large power base, while complicating its use of those resources that it did mobilize. Together, they made it harder for the empire to adapt to match the strength and efficiency of its rivals, thus placing it at a disadvantage in geopolitical competition.

Administrative Inefficiency

Although geographically contiguous, the territories that made up the Habsburg Monarchy's geopolitical base were semi-independent polities with little in the way of a common political character.[22] Until the mid-eighteenth century, the Danubian territories, including not only the Czech and Hungarian lands but even the original possessions in Austria itself, were a "conglomerate," in the words of one history, which "even lacked a political identity":

> [They were] a collection of duchies and kingdoms, each with its own historical tradition, constitutional structure, economic framework and ethnic peculiarity. The only common denominator was the dynasty itself, and the political power of the dynasty was so feeble as to render the significance of this shared identity negligible. In each province or kingdom, the ruler's role was mediated by a powerful aristocratic oligarchy, which wielded effective political power through its respective provincial Estates. These Estates needed not only to consent to taxation, but were the agents of collection as well.... What central government existed took the form of provincial chancelleries, the crown's household administration and the co-ordination of diplomatic and military decision-making.[23]

More an archipelago than a unified polity, the constituent parts of the monarchy resembled separate islands, each with their own separate arrangements with the Habsburg family that entailed different obligations on the part of the territories and corresponding responsibilities and limitations on the part of the ruler.[24]

The resulting jumble—a "mildly centripetal agglutination of bewilderingly heterogeneous elements," as R. J. W. Evans described it—was the result of centuries of gradual territorial accumulation.[25] The process of organizing resources for war inside such an entity was contested and chaotic. Back to the late Middle Ages, the Habsburgs had in their relative penury struggled, more than their French counterparts, to secure funds from the aristocracy to support the running expenses of a court and army. By the eighteenth century, they were still hobbled by the intricacies of perennial horse-trading between the dynast and estates, which eventually settled into an annual process whereby the provincial assemblies, or diets, would vote to sustain a certain level of support for the imperial center through taxes. As part of this dynamic, an annual allotment, or *Kontribution*, was raised to fund the army. In exchange, the Habsburgs made certain political concessions to each estate, which became the basis for a governing consensus with the various local nobilities of the monarchy.[26] In these arrangements, the estates held the power of the purse and operated most of the machinery for collecting taxes—a portion of which they withheld for themselves. As Prince Eugene bemoaned, "The title of emperor does not bring with it a single man nor Kreutzer. He must even negotiate with his empire."[27]

These constraints gave Habsburg power a "mediated" character, in which the ruler negotiated with subjects to obtain the implements of state power.[28] This was true to varying degrees of most European states of the early modern period. Yet where other states gradually and purposefully shed these vestiges of feudalism—breaking the corporate privileges of the nobility, church, and other bodies to centralize the power of the state for war—the Habsburgs retained many of these features well into the eighteenth century. In addition to influencing the degree and character of Austria's performance in its wars of emergence, this slower pace in the monarchy's political evolution stunted its development as a geopolitical actor at a critical moment when continental powers like France and Prussia were achieving greater efficiency in matters of state and war. Other states of this period that failed to evolve these functions at a brisk pace—most notably, eighteenth-century Poland—quickly fell behind in military competition and ceased to exist as independent polities. A similar fate for Austria would perhaps have occurred were it not for the more protective geography and sheer size of the state.

While spared Poland's fate, the persistence of residual feudalism in Habsburg governance nevertheless decisively affected Austrian strategic capabilities, ensuring that its potential power routinely outstripped its strength in actual power attributes. The most important constraint in this regard was financial, in the extent of available monetary resources with which to field armies. The Habsburg state found it harder than its western rivals to predictably fund military endeavors. Even when the estates-centric funding system operated smoothly, revenues routinely fell short of what was needed to sustain Habsburg forces through the crises that frequently beset the monarchy. Amounts raised by the Kontribution were almost always wildly exceeded by military needs, generally amounting to between a third and half of what was actually required in the late seventeenth and eighteenth centuries.[29] In the War of the Spanish Succession, the monarchy was only able to raise about a quarter of the funds it needed, fielding an army and budget about one-tenth the size of France's.[30] At the outset of the wars with Frederick II (1712–86) a few decades later, the Austrian state was on the verge of bankruptcy, with an army of barely thirty thousand men; Prussia, by contrast went into the war with a budget surplus and an army nearly triple that of Austria's, despite possessing only a fraction of the Habsburg Monarchy's size and an eighth its population.[31] In the Seven Years' War, the Kontribution provided less than a third (114.3 million) of the 391.8 million florins ultimately needed for the war effort, with most of the balance coming from loans and taxes.[32]

So severe were the financial constraints on the Habsburg state that Count Friedrich Wilhelm von Haugwitz (1702–65), supreme chancellor and a driver of attempts at reform under Maria Theresa, called its convoluted revenue system an "internal enemy fully as dangerous to the Crown as the more obvious enemies without."[33] Tackling this "enemy" would motivate Habsburg reform efforts from the early eighteenth to the twentieth century. The impetus to do so, as with the development of more accurate cartography, was geopolitical in nature, arising from the pressure of the French and later Prussian military threats.[34] Beginning in doses under Joseph I and gaining force from 1748 onward under Maria Theresa, the monarchy implemented measures to strengthen the central power of the state and keep pace with an ever-evolving competitive landscape populated by strong foes. By the final quarter of the eighteenth century these efforts had broken the power of the estates, and would continue to bear considerable fruit into the nineteenth century in rationalizing imperial administration, increasing state revenues from domestic sources, and fielding ever-larger armies.

Even with these reforms, the Habsburg Monarchy would only rarely realize its full military potential—and then, only for short stretches usually coinciding with times of great crisis.[35] While Maria Theresa would succeed in rationalizing government structures and subordinating the Austrian and Bohemian estates to central rule, the monarchy would struggle for decades, unsuccessfully, to find a way of realizing the financial and military potential of its largest territory, Hungary. After a brief period of abrogation under Leopold I

TABLE 3.1. Size and Contribution of Major Habsburg Territories, circa 1780s

Habsburg region	Proportion of population	Proportion of landmass	Contribution to army
Erblände	18.9% (4.3 million)	17.8% (43,110 square miles)	Approx. 70.2% (153,864 men)
Lands of the Bohemian Crown	19.3% (4.4 million)	12.7% (30,533 square miles)	
Hungary	37.4% (8.5 million)	51.8% (125,402 square miles)	Approx. 20.5% (44,936 men)

Sources: Michael Hochedlinger, *Austria's Wars of Emergence* (New York: Routledge, 2013); P. G. M. Dickson 1987, *Finance and Government under Maria Theresa, 1740–1780,* 2 vols. (Oxford: Clarendon Press, 1987). Army calculations are author's own.

following Hungary's reconquest from the Turks, the Magyars managed with only occasional interruptions to protect their historic tax exemptions until the mid-nineteenth century. As a result, for most of the monarchy's history, a large portion of what would have been a fundamental pillar of state power and resource base was at best only partially contributing directly to the state's revenue stream.

Nowhere is this absence more visible than in the composition of the Habsburg Army. Overreliance on recruitment from Austria and Bohemia, a consequence of Hungarian constitutional exceptionalism, persisted for much of the monarchy's history. Between 1706 and 1742, Hungarians (including Magyars and subject ethnicities of the Hungarian Crown) consistently made up between 2 and 6 percent of the army, while from 1743 to 1794, their numbers hovered between 15 and 20 percent—startling percentages, considering that Hungary accounted for around a half of the empire's total landmass and more than a third of its population (see table 3.1). These proportions changed little in the nineteenth century; in 1865, Magyars still made up around 6 percent of the army, compared to 26 percent for ethnic Germans (slightly more than their population strength) and percentages for smaller ethnicities often well in excess of their population.[36]

While the degree of special treatment accorded to Hungary was unique, vestigial arrangements of this kind—for the estates, church segments of the nobility, and later, other so-called master nationalities—would constrain the power of the monarchy throughout its lifetime. Where the dynasty had begged the estates for money in the first half of the eighteenth century, later in the nineteenth century it would face a less formally constrained but still unpredictable and conflict-prone process of negotiating an annual military budget in two separate parliaments. These dynamics made Habsburg war funding a hand-to-mouth exercise at a time when the monarchy's rivals were

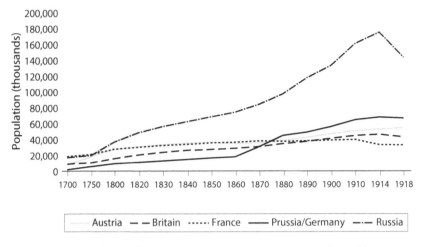

FIG. 3.1. Population of European Powers, 1700–1918. *Sources:* Data derived from
J. David Singer, Stuart Bremer, and John Stuckey, "Capability Distribution, Uncertainty,
and Major Power War, 1820–1965," in *Peace, War, and Numbers*, ed. Bruce Russett (Beverly
Hills: Sage, 1972), 19–48; Paul M. Kennedy, *The Rise and Fall of Great Powers: Economic
Change and Military Conflict from 1500 to 2000* (New York: Random House, 1987).
Graph: Center for European Policy Analysis, 2017.

regularizing their defense budgets on a fixed basis. While frequently fielding
large armies in times of war, Austria nonetheless consistently ranked near the
bottom of Europe's Great Powers in military spending and personnel (see figures 3.1–3.3).

REVENUE AND FINANCE

Difficulty organizing resources for war led Austria to look for other means to
support its foreign policy and military goals. In peacetime, gaps between revenue and spending could usually be covered from special taxes or other measures. In wartime, however, spending mushroomed, pressuring the monarchy
to find money from other sources. The main recourse was to loans, both from
domestic and foreign sources. Throughout its lifetime, the monarchy engaged
in borrowing on a fairly large scale. At the end of the French and Ottoman
wars of the 1680s, the Habsburg debt stood at around 10 million florins—a
figure that had grown to 25 million by 1700, and by 1740 was 100 million, for
a 900 percent increase in a little over fifty years.[37] Even with the introduction
of reforms to streamline administration and expand revenue, the stock of
Habsburg debt continued to increase, reaching 542 million florins by the end
of the century.[38]

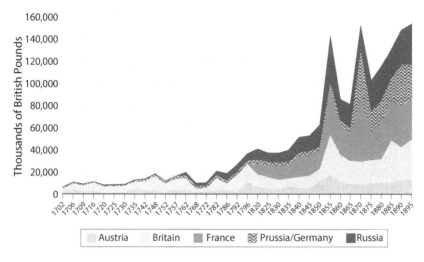

FIG. 3.2. Proportion of Military Expenditure of European Powers, 1702–1895. *Sources:* Data derived from J. David Singer, Stuart Bremer, and John Stuckey, "Capability Distribution, Uncertainty, and Major Power War, 1820–1965," in *Peace, War, and Numbers*, ed. Bruce Russett (Beverly Hills: Sage, 1972), 19–48; Paul Kennedy, *The Rise and Fall of Great Powers: Economic Change and Military Conflict from 1500 to 2000* (New York: Random House, 1987); Janet M. Hartley, *Russia, 1762–1825: Military Power, the State, and the People*. (Westport, CT: Praeger, 2008); Gunther E. Rothenberg, *The Army of Francis Joseph* (West Lafayette, IN: Purdue University Press, 1976); A. C. Macartney, *The Habsburg Empire, 1790–1918* (New York: Macmillan, 1969); J. J. Sanchez, "Military Expenditure, Spending Capacity, and Budget Constraint in Eighteenth-Century Spain and Britain," *Revista De Historia Economica: Journal of Iberian and Latin American Economic History* 27, no. 1 (2009): 141–74. Graph: Center for European Policy Analysis, 2017.

A large amount of this borrowing—about three-quarters in the first half of the century—was from internal sources. The Habsburgs generally preferred domestic credit in peacetime, but would aggressively tap foreign sources when hostilities broke out.[39] The creation of the Vienna City Bank in 1706 allowed for the retirement of a portion of the state's seventeenth-century debt as well as a widening of the empire's domestic and foreign base of private lenders. Additional borrowing took place among the estates, with Vienna occasionally resorting to mortgaging estate-based revenues to secure financing. The burden shifted gradually toward overseas borrowing from the mid-eighteenth century onward, first in Amsterdam and London, and then to the growing capital markets in Brussels, Genoa, and Milan.[40] In wartime, the monarchy was usually kept afloat by financial aid from allies, which often took the form of guarantees for borrowing on foreign money markets.[41] So decisive was British monetary help in the War of the Spanish Succession that Prince Eugene

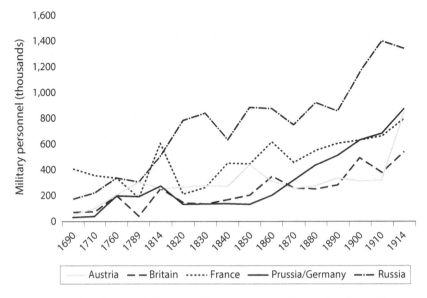

FIG. 3.3. Military Personnel of European Powers, 1690–1914. *Sources:* Data derived from
J. David Singer, Stuart Bremer, and John Stuckey, "Capability Distribution, Uncertainty,
and Major Power War, 1820–1965," in *Peace, War, and Numbers,* ed. Bruce Russett
(Beverly Hills: Sage, 1987), 19–48; Paul Kennedy, *The Rise and Fall of Great Powers:
Economic Change and Military Conflict from 1500 to 2000* (New York: Random House, 1987);
Michael Hochedlinger, *Austria's Wars of Emergence, 1683–1797* (New York: Routledge, 2013);
Catherine Casson, "European State Finance Database: An Introduction," European
State Finance Database, http://www.esfdb.org/table.aspx?resourceid=11342.
Graph: Center for European Policy Analysis, 2017.

wrote to the emperor, somewhat sarcastically, that war for Austria was "impossible without the money of England," and Frederick II would complain
that Britain was "the mainspring of the Austrian machine."[42]

The basic contours of Habsburg military funding continued into the nineteenth century, albeit with more predictable revenue streams and expenditure
patterns along with a large legacy deficit.[43] In the immediate post-Napoleonic,
or *Vormärz,* period, indirect taxation came to comprise a large portion of
revenue (especially customs and excise, plus salt and tobacco monopolies).
From the mid-nineteenth century on, the burden would tilt toward direct
taxation (especially on land), and by 1854, a third of all revenue was going
toward the servicing of the public debt.[44] With the resumption of military
crises in this period, Vienna's fiscal position deteriorated, and the 1850s saw an
explosion of military expenditure, state debt, and the issuance of bank paper,
with a corresponding increase in tax revenues (achieved in large part by ending Hungary's tax privileges in 1849 and introducing wider systems of direct

taxation). Eventually, the monarchy had to resort to transferring responsibility for outstanding paper currency to the National Bank, alongside mortgaging the proceeds from salt mines, state monopolies, and entire classes of tax revenue.[45]

HABSBURG DEBT

War is expensive. For the Habsburgs, the costs of warfare grew steadily over the monarchy's lifetime. The 1716–18 Turkish War cost 43 million florins—almost double the military budget for that period.[46] The War of the Polish Succession (1733–38) cost 73 million florins, only 14 million of which could be afforded out of pocket. The Turkish War of 1737–39 cost 146 million florins, the War of the Austrian Succession about 185.85 million florins, and the Seven Years' War 392 million.[47] The five-year War of the First Coalition (1792–97) against Napoleon cost about 500 million florins.[48] Even wars against a nominally weaker rival could rapidly deplete the state's resources. The three campaigns of the 1788–91 Turkish War, to cite one example, cost more than 70 million florins apiece (214–23 million total), at a time when the annual revenue was about 80 million.[49]

The costs of war represent a burden to any state. The Habsburg Empire's rivals also spent vigorously on the military and frequently went into debt to fund their wars. Britain borrowed on a prodigious scale throughout the eighteenth and nineteenth centuries, but maintained a debt-servicing capacity that was among the highest of Europe's Great Powers. France borrowed often, while Prussia was known for an efficient tax system (though also frequently dependent on subsidies), and Russia possessed an underdeveloped financial system backed by prodigious, if inefficiently organized, internal resources.[50]

What set Austria apart in its geopolitical relationship with money was its combination of a weak economic base and exposure to four-sided security competition. Habsburg geography subjected the monarchy to greater military challenges than its limited resource-mobilization capabilities could support. This created more numerous triggers for debt growth than most states face, and ensured that once incurred, debt would form recurrent overhangs to burden the economy in peacetime. By contrast, Habsburg rivals could usually find some form of alleviation from these pressures. Prussia, for instance, shared Austria's multisided security position but possessed a stronger economic base that helped to ameliorate debt burdens. Russia, though possessing a relatively weak economic base, occupied a more insulated geopolitical position facing less security pressure.

Once at war, or even in the prelude to war, the money crunch began to be felt quickly, limiting the monarchy's geopolitical options. An indication of how sharply these pressures could be felt can be seen in the correspondence of Habsburg monarchs and ministers. As Maria Theresa wrote to Joseph II about mounting costs in the early phase of the War of the Bavarian Succession,

> You are going to feel the consequences [of spending] later. The monthly accounts are arriving in complete disorder. I fear chaos; such financial sums can have dire consequences. Eventually, one surrenders and simply goes for a cut-off.... Over the past four months we spent at least six million in excess of the monthly sum set by yourself, while in July there was already an advance of 1.8 million fl. for the coming year, only to be followed by another demand for 600,000 fl. in August. If things continue on this path, no imaginable order/system can be maintained. Time is needed. Our losses worsen available credit rates abroad, and the depredations of the private sectors those at home....
>
> I only dive into these details in response to your remarks calling for the mobilization of all [national] strength in the war. I cannot see how that would be possible. We ought to be weaker by 30 to 40,000 men, whereas it will be impossible to maintain an army stronger than this year. We should be happy if we are able to sustain our current force level.[51]

The longer a war lasted, the greater the likelihood that the costs incurred would outstrip the state's limited resources. While this rule generally applies for any state, it was a particular concern for the Habsburgs, partly because the empire's baseline financial position was usually one of indebtedness and partly because its vulnerable geography penalized lengthy distractions. The advent of war against one rival could set in motion potentially exponential borrowing, at the same time that the monarchy needed to remain on guard against other rivals, and be prepared to see even small and initially limited conflicts spiral into broader (and therefore longer and more expensive) crises.

The methods used to cover the gaps between the state's resource base and military needs also brought disadvantages that grew more acute the longer a war lasted. Subsidies came with expectations among Austria's allies that they could, on some level, influence its foreign policy and even military objectives on the battlefield. As a conflict dragged on and new fronts required attention, this could become a source of intra-alliance friction, as Habsburg efforts to address threatened fronts not aligning with the ally's interests opened up divergences in war strategy, as occurred in both the War of the Spanish Succession and War of the Austrian Succession. Eugene's complaint that allies "are often very inconvenient and become a sort of tutors" is echoed in Maria Theresa's advice to Kaunitz on the eve of negotiations at the end of the Austrian succession struggle in 1748 to find ways of relying on Austria's own cunning "rather than to beg for foreign money and thereby remain in subordination."[52]

For obvious reasons, borrowing could sour relations with allies after a war. In the 1820s, the inability to pay debts from the 1790s (with interest, around £20 million) strained links between Vienna and London at a pivotal moment in the Eastern Question, arguably becoming one of many contributing factors to the eventual collapse of Metternich's congress system.[53]

Large-scale external borrowing created debt overhangs that could constrain strategic options and require military retrenchment in the postwar period. During the eighteenth century, debt servicing typically accounted for a volume of state expenditure (about 30 percent) second only to the army.[54] By comparison, debt servicing for the United States today usually stands at about 6 percent of annual spending. The years following the Seven Years' War, Napoleonic Wars, and the 1850s to 1860s are all prime illustrations of the strictures that could result from periods of substantial borrowing.

And while internal borrowing was more reliable as a source of funding than loans from external sources, extraordinary domestic collections could also be problematic. Printing money ran the risk of triggering runaway inflation, which only added to economic instability at moments when the monarchy could ill afford it (even if high inflation in practice was one way to liquidate debts). This dynamic could be encouraged by foreign powers, too, as France did by attempting to flood Austria with forged currency during the Napoleonic Wars. At moments of great crisis, complete shortages of money could lead the state to extreme measures, including redenomination, write-downs of paper currency, and even rounding up bullion and silver plate.[55] Emergency levies or increased taxation could have ripples within the monarchy's unusual domestic fabric, and strain Vienna's relationship with key constituencies, especially the Magyar nobility.

MONEY AND TIME

All this translated into pressure for short wars. Habsburg rulers and their ministers were keenly aware of the fiscal burdens brought by war, and frequently advocated military restraint or even avoiding war altogether in order to offset these risks. Maria Theresa's letters to Joseph II in the War of the Bavarian Succession, itself more a game of maneuvers than a shooting war, abound with warnings about the state of the monarchy's finances and the need to be a "cheap-minded" ruler and avoid a prolonged crisis.[56] In the aftermath of Joseph II's Turkish war, the monarchy's supreme chancellor, Count Leopold Kolowrat, used grim reports outlining the inexorable growth in military spending to counsel against a new war.[57] In a similar vein, Habsburg finance minister Count Michael Wallis warned amid the wars with Napoleon that "no war could be undertaken by Austria for at least ten, perhaps another thirty years."[58] These constraints carried over into the early nineteenth century, sometimes limiting Austria's options for handling even small crises. An 1821 uprising in northern Italy could only be undertaken with a loan from the Rothschilds, prompting the finance minister to ask Metternich, "For the love of God, how is this to be paid for?" and joke that the empire was "armed for perpetual peace."[59] In 1827, Emperor Francis was constrained from his preferred response to aggressive Russian moves in the Balkans of sending an observation corps of a hundred thousand into Hungary by economic concerns, and again in 1831 financial problems curtailed Austrian options for handling crises in Italy.[60] Even at the height of the 1848 revolution, a moment of existential peril for the monarchy, Treasury officials argued for a diplomatic rather than military solution to the problems in Italy on the grounds that "ever-continuing" reinforcements would have disastrous ripple effects for Austria's credit and financial solvency.[61]

Austrian military commanders also felt fiscal constraints once the monarchy was at war. The field correspondence of Prince Eugene is filled with lamentations about the inability to carry out war "without troops or money," with the prince eventually threatening to resign more than once in protest over the inability to pay his regiments.[62] A lack of funding gutted the Habsburg Army in the lead-up to the First Silesian War, resulting in northern fortresses so weak that one only contained a single, leather cannon dating from the previous century. Even after years of fighting in the Napoleonic Wars, Archduke Charles would nervously ask, on the eve of the 1805 campaign, "What would be the financial consequences of war? While such would ordinarily be [the] purview of the Fiscal Administration, anyone who would wish to make pronouncements on the possibilities in military operations must make some account of the money necessary."[63] And Count Radetzky, Austria's foremost commander of the post-Napoleonic period, would repeatedly find the size of his armies and range of logistical options curtailed by, in his words, the "immense financial pressures" facing the monarchy, prompting him to write lengthy memorandums filled with ideas on how to sustain operational efficiency amid conditions of budget austerity, with titles like "How to Maintain Good and Large Armies at Little Cost."[64]

In addition to placing limits on the empire's own range of options, the monarchy's usually impecunious state presented an opportunity for its rivals to pursue what today would be called "cost-imposition" strategies—the practice of using sustained military expenditures or the development of new technologies to force a rival into a scale of exertions beyond its ability to sustain. The combination of internal weakness and encirclement made Austria unusually susceptible to such strategies, allowing opponents on one frontier to undertake local military buildups in the knowledge that matching these moves while maintaining other frontiers would place financial and military strains on Austria. This in turn allowed rivals to attempt to force diplomatic concessions that would have been harder to extract from a stronger opponent.

Ethnic Complexity

The second feature of Habsburg political geography that distinguished the monarchy from its rivals was its ethnic composition. For any state, building a strong material base requires a foundation of internal unity. Historically, most have derived this unity from shared ethnic or religious commonalities among the population. Even multiethnic empires have been preceded by and built around an earlier, successful attempt at forging a homogeneous group that provides a sufficiently numerous and loyal core from which to exert political rule to the heterogeneous periphery.

For the Habsburg Monarchy, much of the "glue" for internal unity existed in the form of religion. Devout adherence to Catholicism animated the otherwise ethnically or constitutionally disparate populations of the empire's heartland and set them apart, both from the northern lands in which the Reformation had taken root and those to the south and east where Orthodoxy and Islam held sway. Throughout the eighteenth and nineteenth centuries, more than three-quarters of the Habsburg population was Catholic, with proportions as high as 90 percent in the western portions of the empire. An important exception was Hungary, where the Counter-Reformation made limited progress and the persistence of strong pockets of Calvinism formed the monarchy's "only large populations of non-Catholics."[65]

This relatively high degree of religious homogeneity notwithstanding, the Habsburg lands lacked the ethnic foundations for state building on the traditional European model. Where Austria's western rivals possessed the building blocks to become large nation-states, and its eastern rivals were able to forge empires led by a single dominant nationality, Austria was characterized by a bewildering degree of ethnic complexity over which the imperial center was never able to achieve more than partial dominance. This reality would place limitations on Austria's performance, both in the task of empire building and how it competed geopolitically with major rivals.

ETHNICITIES AND EMPIRE BUILDING

Mile for mile, the Danubian Basin is home to one of the densest concentrations of ethnic diversity of any comparably sized space in the world. Major groups populating the Habsburg lands included Germans, Hungarians, Italians, Czechs, Poles, Slovaks, Croats, Serbs, Slovenes, and Romanians, with

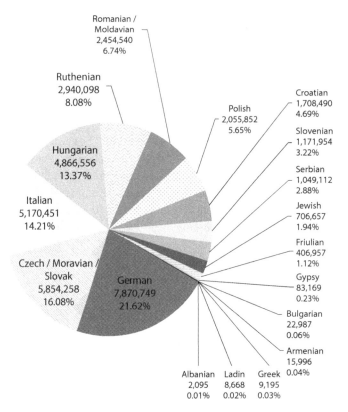

FIG. 3.4. Ethnic Breakdown of the Austrian Empire, ca. 1851.
Source: Center for European Policy Analysis, 2016.

smaller numbers of Jews, Gypsies, Greeks, Bosnians, Szeklers, and Ruthenians. Altogether at its high point in the nineteenth century, the monarchy was home to no fewer than fourteen ethnic groups speaking seventeen languages and practicing three religions—all in a physical space 260,000 square miles in size (see figure 3.4). By comparison, the Ottoman Empire of the same period contained a similar number of ethnicities spread across a landmass of about 700,000 square miles—more than double that of the Habsburg Monarchy.

From a geopolitical perspective, the crucial aspect of the empire's ethnic makeup not its diversity per se; other European empires, most notably Russia, but also to a certain extent Prussia, were made up of more than one ethnic group. It bears pointing out that the problems that would later emerge as a result of Austria's ethnic complexity should not be projected onto the eighteenth century. Indeed, well into the prenationalist era, ethnic homogeneity was neither a prerequisite to effective state building nor was it particularly prevalent among the major powers of Europe.

What made the Habsburg monarchy different was the absence of a dominant ethnic group sufficiently numerous to subjugate the others under a unified language and culture. Statistically, ethnic Germans made up about a
quarter of the population, Magyars another quarter, and Slavs of various
types a little less than half.[66] In the Russian Empire, by comparison, ethnic
Russians made up just under half the population (44 percent)—a proportion
that was considerably higher at earlier stages of the state-formation process,
before the czar's armies had acquired new territories. If culturally similar
groups such as Ukrainians and the Baltic Germans who maintained a symbiotic relationship with the ethnic Russian elite are added to the equation, the
percentage is even higher—around 67 percent. In Prussia, ethnic Germans
made up an even higher proportion: more than 80 percent, out of a mixed
population that included Poles, Lithuanians, Czechs, and other minorities. In
both Prussia and Russia, the presence of a numerous and dominant ethnic
provided a basis for unifying political elites and to a large extent also the population behind a common foreign policy.

By contrast, the 25 percent of ethnic Germans in the Austrian Empire,
while comprising a majority in Habsburg political and military institutions,
were too weak to overawe, let alone assimilate, the other nationalities along
ethnic or cultural lines. Among the Habsburg Monarchy's non-German ethnic groups, the most populous were the Magyars and Czechs, both of which
had histories of protonational development stretching into the early Middle
Ages and therefore had prior claims to primacy over large portions of the
Danubian Basin. The Czech lands had formed an indigenous Slavic empire
in the ninth century that later became the nucleus for a Bohemian-Moravian
state under the Přemysl kings well into the fifteenth century.

The Magyars had formed a large kingdom under the Arpads in the tenth
century that would endure under various dynasties and act as the principal
eastern bastion of Christendom until military defeat at the hands of the Turks
at Mohács in 1526. At its zenith in the fifteenth century, Hungary would include most of modern-day Croatia, Bosnia, and Slovakia as well as Transylvania and a large portion of Serbia south of the Danube. The kingdom offered
military resistance to both the northward expansion of Islam and eastward
expansion of the Habsburg-led Counter-Reformation. Unlike the Czechs, the
Magyars retained an unusually large and politically active indigenous nobility, acutely aware both of their kingdom's past geopolitical role and the over-
lordship that their families had enjoyed over neighboring lands.

More than any other Habsburg minority, the Magyars possessed the req-
uisite traits—a landed patrician class, culture of political independence, and
recent history of regional paramountcy—to become sources of resistance to
Habsburg rule. This was especially true in the traditionally recalcitrant territories of Transylvania, where Protestant princes had long formed alliances

with the Ottoman Turks to check Habsburg advances. The presence of a group with these characteristics in such large numbers, both inside the Habsburg heartland and along the strategically important southern frontier, represented a strategic disadvantage for the Habsburgs in their quest to build a unified Great Power. The search for a formula to both contain the often-truculent Magyar nobility and offer adequate incentives to recruit their help in empire building would become a recurrent pattern of Habsburg history from the early eighteenth century until the monarchy's final days.

ETHNICITIES AND SPACE

An important factor in how the Habsburgs managed these dynamics was the spatial arrangement of the empire's major ethnic groups. The wavelike arrival of groups in the Danubian Basin created laminous rather than linear settlement patterns, with the densest population clusters appearing near rivers and other major arteries. The Slavs congregated around the Vlatava and Vistula in the north, and Sava and Drava in the south; the Magyars between the two, along the double axis of the Tisza and middle Danube; Vlachs between the lower Danube and Prut; and Germans primarily along the River Inn and upper Danube. The crucial point is that none of these groups were settled in entirely contiguous geographic spaces, but rather interspersed among one another. While concentrated mainly in the Erblände, ethnic Germans were found in pockets across the Czech and Hungarian lands; Croats, Serbs, and Romanians were found in significant numbers across Hungary, both in the border areas and interior; Hungarians, Italians, and Croats could be found in southern portions of the Erblände; and so on.

The Danubian Basin's helter-skelter demographic footprint influenced how the Habsburgs approached the task of empire building. On the one hand, the monarchy's dispersed tribal layout aided in the task of multinational statecraft. No single minority, especially the Hungarians, were so concentrated in one place as to amass the characteristics of a geographically compact and ethnically homogeneous internal "state" within the empire's borders. The fact that numerous smaller nationalities, each with a history of subjugation under the Magyars, existed in pell-mell pockets within and around both the major Magyar footprints—the middle Danube and Transylvania—presented abundant opportunities for containing the Hungarian problem. In a classic pattern of geopolitics, weak groups often seek patronage from a stronger yet still-distant source to counterbalance a historic rival. For the empire's weaker minorities, this just-strong-enough force was the Habsburg dynasty. Being small made them the chief beneficiaries of Vienna's regional primacy, since they would lose out disproportionately in any scheme to reorganize the basin along ethnic (and therefore likely Magyar-dominant) lines. These fears gave the Habsburgs a ready source of strategically located, highly motivated allies to assist in the task of containing their chief internal rivals.

Various Habsburg monarchs indirectly reinforced this pattern by resettling Catholic German colonists in the eastern lands from which the Ottomans had been expelled. This process began after Austria's victory in the Great Turkish War (1683–99) and continued through the reign of Maria Theresa. Lacking an overt ethnic motivation, these efforts were instead driven by the mercantilist and dynastic aim of harnessing the resource potential of the monarchy's newly acquired territories to the political and strategic objectives of the state. As William McNeil notes,

> This program was supplemented by efforts to recruit settlers from German lands outside Austrian borders. Transportation, land, initial capital, and tax exemption for a period of years were offered such immigrants. These inducements were such that between 1762 and 1772, when the program was in full operation, a total of about 11,000 German families were settled in the Banat under official, government aegis. Others came from Lorraine, Belgium, Italy and elsewhere, but the German immigration far outweighed all the other strands and sufficed to establish a fairly numerous "Swabian" population along the Danube from its junction with the Sava as far as the Iron Gates.[67]

Such practices achieved a small but measurable impact in reaching the development ceiling of some portions of the underdeveloped Hungarian periphery.[68] As we will see in chapter 5, the Habsburgs undertook a longer-lasting and more ambitious attempt at geopolitical engineering in the creation of the famous Military Border along the southern border, where Vienna would systematically resettle thousands of Serb, Croatian, and later Romanian soldier-settlers in a series of semiautonomous, centrally managed administrative districts running from the Adriatic to the Carpathians from the late seventeenth to mid-nineteenth centuries.

These efforts notwithstanding, the political geography of the Danubian Basin remained by and large an obstacle to be overcome rather than an advantage to be harnessed in the process of empire building. The physical distribution of Habsburg ethnicities posed significant and recurrent challenges of frontier statecraft. One dimension of the problem was that only a handful of the region's indigenous ethnicities existed entirely within the confines of the Danubian Basin. Of these, the largest (the Magyars) were never fully reconciled to Habsburg dynastic supremacy. Hungarian history and social structure inhibited the degree of outside engagement and economic development that would have been required for full incorporation into the monarchy. As late as the end of the eighteenth century, after more than a century under Habsburg rule, large swaths of Hungary remained economically underdeveloped.[69] The outlook of the Hungarian elite tended to alternate between seasons of support for the monarchy as a vehicle of conservative political continuity and protection of historic land and tax rights, and resistance to bureaucratic rule from Vienna in search of independence.

EQUIVOCAL LOYALTIES

Magyar mood swings were typical of what the historian Owen Lattimore called "equivocal loyalty"—the tension often found in frontier peoples of supporting the state as a source of stability while continuing to seek cultural and political autonomy. The nineteenth century would see the development of this phenomenon in Habsburg nationalities. Among non-Magyar groups, the problem would be exacerbated by the fact that all but a few were parts of larger ethnic footprints that overlapped the territories of neighboring states. On almost every frontier, Habsburg local communities directly abutted ethnic kin across the border: in Alpine Austria, the south German states; in Trieste, the fellow Latins of northern Italy; in Transylvania, Romanians living in nearby Wallachia/Moldavia; in the Balkans, Serbs and Croats under Ottoman and later national rule; and in Poland, ethnic Poles and Ruthenes living under Prussian and Russian rule. This made the Habsburg Empire a frontier state in the truest sense—an interstitial polity astride separate civilizational spaces. As Lattimore wrote of such empires,

> [There is an] "axiom of frontier administration that a tribe or group of tribes situated between two comparatively powerful States must be under the influence of one or other of these"—for where the sense of kinship does not operate, other forces—such as military power, class interest, or the opportunity for an individual career act all the more strongly.[70]

A large portion of the Habsburg population fell under Lattimore's axiom. More than half its ethnic groups were geopolitical "straddlers," inhabiting the space between larger or more homogeneous entities. Under the right conditions, the presence of such a large number of frontier groups, with divergent histories and separate languages, could undermine the sense of shared identity that for most states has provided the foundation of political order. The largest of these groups, the Hungarians, would mount persistent attempts to enhance political autonomy at the expense of the larger polity—a pattern that would intensify among other ethnicities with the advent of modern nationalism in the mid-nineteenth century. These dynamics would distract the attention of the state in the quest for new templates of compromise and multinational governance from the Treaty of Szatmar in 1711 to the Austro-Hungarian Ausgleich of 1867.

Ethnicities and Geopolitical Competition

In addition to shaping how the Habsburgs conducted empire building, the monarchy's ethnic composition affected how Austria behaved in military competition with major rivals. The effects can be seen both in the constraints that internal dynamics placed on Austria's strategic options and the opportunities these factors created for competitors.

First, on a fundamental level, domestic complexity exacerbated the difficulties of mobilizing Habsburg power. For most Great Powers in history, the path to survival and security has been through "internal balancing"—that is, through increasing the capabilities at the state's disposal, either by maximizing the efficiency of the resources that it already possesses or growing the overall size of the resource base through physical expansion. The Habsburg Monarchy's makeup complicated both options. The presence of numerous groups with different forms of social and political organization across subregions with often widely differing levels of economic advancement contributed to uneven development patterns. While this could be a spur to growth, it also required that a considerable amount of energy be spent in aiding the "catching up" process of backward regions. As a result, the monarchy did not possess the degree of economic strength or overall advancement that a European state of similar size and population would likely have possessed with a more ethnically and economically homogeneous human base. Together with the empire's administrative inefficiency, this uneven composition would prove to be an obstacle—perhaps not insuperable, but real and persistent—to realizing the monarchy's full power potential.

Nor could the monarchy escape its problems through the second traditional form of internal balancing: territorial growth. Historically, land powers have been able to enhance their security by expanding the surface area over which the state can collect revenue and raise armies. For the Habsburgs, this was a tricky proposition; the monarchy's complex internal ethnic balances, together with its layered and contested mechanisms of governance, meant that additions of space were likely to increase the commitments of the state without necessarily increasing its actual power. New lands brought new problems. Whether acquired through war or diplomacy, they brought new groups that would have to be incorporated alongside other, preexisting ethnicities. They carried new security liabilities and exposure to new sources of friction on the frontiers, too, stretching the responsibilities of the military and increasing the demands on state finances. Even in the era before modern nationalism, such acquisitions brought inevitable geopolitical complications with Austria's neighbors demanding "compensation," potentially in more places more valuable to Austria than the spaces acquired. More dangerously, with expansion would come questions about the constitutional status of new territories, bringing population shifts that could upset the empire's increasingly delicate ethnic balances. As a result, unlike in many other empires in history, expansion usually brought less security for Austria, not more.

Second, Habsburg ethnic complexity created opportunities for the monarchy's rivals, *even in the era before modern nationalism.* Austria's opponents were aware of the monarchy's fissures and frequently sought to exploit them as a source of strategic advantage in wartime. While the full force of equivocal loyalty would not be felt until late in Habsburg history, after the emergence of nationalism as a major political force, its effects were seen in geopolitics long before then. The Magyars in particular represented a sufficiently large and determined source of opposition—a Habsburg *Fronde*, in the words of one historian—to attract the political and military courtship of foreign powers.[71] The Bourbon kings of France provided arms and encouragement to successive Rakoczi uprisings; the Swedes threatened to link up with Hungarian Protestants during the War of the Spanish Succession; Russia promoted defection and emigration among the Orthodox Slav inhabitants of the Military Border in the mid-1700s; Prussia incited unrest among the Poles of Austrian Galicia at inopportune moments; Napoleon III stoked the embers of Kossuth's insurrections; and Bismarck tried to stir up problems in Hungary, Serbia, and Romania during the war of 1866—to name just a few instances.

The value of such tactics to rivals was twofold: creating an internal distraction that siphoned off Habsburg military resources, and leveraging Hungarian political grievances to such a degree that they might lead to a splintering of the empire's territories after war. The former was especially valuable to rivals attacking a frontier in the west, in creating conditions for a multifront war. To this manipulation by Great Powers would be added, in the nationalist era, the efforts by newly emerged abutting nation-states (Italy, Romania, and Serbia) and eventually also allied governments to incite separatism among ethnic groups living in Austrian territory. While other Great Powers occasionally dealt with problems of rivals inflaming internal "fifth columns" in wartime— France's courtship of Britain's Scots and Irish is one such example—none faced this challenge on the scale that Austria did. Although rarely successful, the potential for enemies to attempt such tactics always had to be factored into Habsburg military strategy. As we will see in later chapters, this sharpened the time pressures on Austria in wartime, essentially creating an additional, internal front that required troops and attention to manage.

Finally and relatedly, it is worth noting the effects that equivocal loyalty had on the Habsburg concepts of power. The continual encounter with ethnic complexity and the constraints it placed on Austrian economic and geopolitical options profoundly shaped the possibilities of Habsburg governance across the empire's lifetime. Claudio Magris's characterization, while perhaps more appropriate for a later phase of the empire's history, bears some truth for the empire's history in general that ethnic complexity forced Vienna away from true bureaucratic centralism whenever it was tried, and instead required a reliance on "flexible prudence, on wary carelessness ... not the levelling, centralist despotism of Louis XIV, Frederick the Great or Napoleon, but ... more to administer the resistance which universalism and medieval particularism put up in opposition to the modern state."[72]

Constrained by a constitutional and financial straitjacket, Habsburg rulers developed an approach to power that more often than not, did not try to "overcome contradictions, but [instead] cover[ed] and compos[ed] them in an ever-provisional equilibrium, allowing them substantially to go on as they are and, if anything, playing them off against one another."[73] This preference for *fortwursteln* (muddling through), as with so many other features of Habsburg behavior closer to the geopolitical traits of maritime than a classic land power, evolved not from principled restraint but rather necessity, as the only sustainable method of governance for such a complicated realm. Surprisingly resilient and durable, it nevertheless can be seen as a concession to complexity and constraint that tacitly acknowledged a permanent inability to perform at the level indicated by Austria's apparent strength.

The Habsburg Monarchy was not, and could never become, a normal Great Power.[74] Its internal machinery of government was more complicated, its processes of tax and administration subject to greater interruption and constraint, and its human population less unified than contemporary nation-states. As a result, while capable of surprising feats of resilience in the mobilization of resources, such as in the Seven Years' War and 1809 campaign against Napoleon, for most of its existence the monarchy struggled unsuccessfully to express its full potential as a Great Power.

The large nominal surface area and population base that its territories represented on paper were misleading; in real terms, on any sustainable basis involving economic or military power, the monarchy was a fettered giant. Is it conceivable that the nominal and latent, as opposed to actual and expressed, potential of the monarchy occasionally guided the behavior of its more ambitious statesmen? Perhaps. What is certain is that the monarchy's complicated constitutional order and the contested nature that it gave to Habsburg domestic power placed constraints on the empire's range of strategic maneuvers—constraints that tended to express themselves as a "ticking clock" of time pressure in the monarchy's geopolitical contests. The historical record leaves no doubt that the Habsburg leaders, even at relative apogees in Austrian strength such as the late eighteenth century or immediate post-Napoleonic period, felt these constraints acutely when attempting to wield diplomatic or military power.

Important corollaries followed from these constraints for Austria's behavior as a player in European geopolitics. The most obvious was that the Habsburg Empire could not grow or reform its way out of its security problems.[75] Where most western states have or at least perceive themselves to have the option of mastering strategic challenges over time through the enhancement (quantitative or qualitative) of internal strengths, this was at best a partial option for the Habsburg Monarchy. On a short-term basis, it could not spend sufficiently to overmaster its security competitors on all four frontiers; financial limitations simply did not allow this. On a long-term basis, attempts to create a centralized bureaucratic state capable of maximizing tax yields to support the growth of the military-industrial base in support of a sustained technological edge to mitigate geographic vulnerability were virtually guaranteed to run afoul of the web of complex constitutional bargains that upheld the empire's fragile internal order. Attempts to develop the economic potential of the territories possessed by the monarchy were also problematic. Realizing the full transport potential of the Danube, to take one prominent illustration, would have required a degree of mobilization of the Hungarian tax base that the Magyar nobility would not have allowed without a protracted political fight. Without such resource mobilization, the expense of such large-scale projects for economic development that the monarchy needed to realize its potential as a Great Power was constrained by the sheer scale of expenditures on the military in the imperial budget.

In addition to complicating the quest for security outright, Austria's internal complexities brought another, less tangible geopolitical disadvantage: the time and opportunity costs of dealing with them. Attempts at tackling the empire's administrative and ethnic challenges, irrespective of how successful they were in outcomes, were intensely difficult and draining. They required that a certain amount of effort, attention, and resources be directed inward rather than outward.

To some extent this is true for any state, particularly in the era of the eighteenth century, when most European powers turned their thoughts to mastering the residua of feudalism to produce a more efficient military machine. In

Austria's case, however, this process was open-ended, playing out throughout the empire's lifetime and never being fully resolved. Even in a static environment, without determined competitors looking for ways to exploit the empire's competitive disadvantages, the formidable internal challenges would have represented a drain on the activity and attention of the state. But Austria's geographic position meant that it never had the luxury of such an environment; rivals were aware of its complexities and willing to use them as a tool against it. In this sense, foreign and domestic policy were always linked for the Habsburg Monarchy. The distraction effect of dealing with recurrent attempts to modernize the state, tame the estates, tweak the constitutional and later ethnic formulas, and most of all renegotiate compromises with the Hungarian nobility represented a kind of invisible "tax" on Habsburg power that impeded even the most enlightened efforts at leveraging the monarchy's nominal resources—a tax that tended to rise in proportion with the instability of outside geopolitics.

In sum, Austria was a Great Power, but a constrained one. The quests for external security and a stable and productive internal political order and resource base that together comprise the central tasks for any state were to some degree mutually contradictory for the Habsburg Monarchy. Pursuing one tended to complicate the other. Achieving greater security through the means normally used in geopolitical history—centralization, larger territory, and economic development—were not as readily available for Austria, at least without bringing significant internal repercussions that would have to be dealt with to the detriment of strategic competitiveness. Nowhere were the effects of these constraints more keenly reflected than in the effort to mobilize and conceptualize military power—the subject of the next chapter.

4

"Si Vis Pacem"

HABSBURG WAR AND STRATEGY

Your army, Sire, is your monarchy; without that, it will revert to the Turks, to the French or perhaps, one day or other to the Hungarians.

—PRINCE EUGENE OF SAVOY

Better a mediocre peace than a successful war.

—EMPRESS MARIA THERESA

THE HABSBURG MONARCHY'S physical and political geography shaped how its leaders thought about war. Austria's position at the heart of Europe dictated that it would be a continental power and thus need large land armies to achieve security. But encirclement by powerful rivals meant that Austria could not defend all of its frontiers simultaneously using military force alone. Internal complexities placed further limitations on the size and capabilities of Habsburg armies, curtailing their utility as offensive instruments. Together, these constraints influenced Habsburg strategic behavior by encouraging the development of defensive conceptions of force that sought to avoid risk when possible, highlighting gaps that would need to be filled to augment the monarchy's weak military capabilities, and prompting the systematic development of strategy as a tool for coping with Austria's difficult environment, with a particular emphasis on managing the time parameters of competition and avoiding the full impact of the virtually limitless threats facing the monarchy.

The Limits of Force

A state's physical and political geography influence how it behaves and performs in war.[1] On the most basic level, where a state sits determines what it fears and what tools it will need for self-protection. Historically, most Great

Powers have tilted toward either a primarily continental or maritime orientation in their strategic outlook. Thus Russia, surrounded by plains, developed large land armies while Britain, surrounded by oceans, concentrated on building naval fleets.

Habsburg geography dictated that it would be a principally land power; the monarchy's position as a mostly landlocked state in east-central Europe largely insulated it from the effects of competition at sea. Such exposure as Austria faced from maritime pressure was mitigated by the presence of large mountains (the Dinaric Alps), and the fact that the adjacent sea—the Adriatic—was a sideshow to the world's main theaters of oceanic competition in the Atlantic and, to a secondary extent, the Mediterranean. As a result, for most of its history Austria would have, at best, a second-rate fleet whose operations had little bearing on its prospects in war.

By contrast, the monarchy's four landward frontiers exposed it to the heaviest areas of military-strategic competition of the European and west Eurasian landmasses. This location at one of history's great crossroads of conflict demanded the development of a large land army while requiring that it be capable of waging warfare against widely varying types of enemies in dissimilar terrains and climates. By the eighteenth century, these included not only the conventional armies of western Europe but also semi-Asiatic Ottoman forces, incursions by mounted Tatar irregulars through the Carpathian passes, and the backward but mobile and adaptive armies of the Russian Empire. In addition, they would need to be able to counter low-intensity threats and border raids along the empire's southern border and conduct gendarmerie functions among unruly territories of the monarchy itself, if called on.

While defining the scope of Austria's military needs, Habsburg physical and political geography also placed constraints on its ability, using its own power, to meet those needs. The number and variety of potential enemies facing the monarchy meant that it could never hope to produce an army large enough to subdue all four frontiers simultaneously through military means alone; the task was simply too great. Even if the Habsburgs had wanted to take on this task through predominantly military means, financial reality placed effective limits on the size of armies and how long they could be maintained in the field. Prince Kaunitz noted this problem in words that would hold equal validity for later decades:

> Nobody can have any reasonable doubt about the necessity of a large, powerful and well prepared army. Still, there are two principles that should never be forgotten:
>
> 1—That no [Austrian] army, however strong in numbers, can stand against all possible foes [at once].

2—That, at least in peacetime, any army's strength needs be in proportion to that of the state.[2]

This basic tension—between needing an army to fend off numerous land rivals but lacking the means to indefinitely sustain the size of force required for Austria's threat environment—would persist until the end of the empire in 1918. While capable of impressive feats of mobilization in an emergency, Austria's defense establishment was rarely able to match the size of armies deployed by even one of its major foes for a protracted conflict, much less meet the challenges of all four of its main security frontiers. To be sure, the army maintained a high degree of professionalism, was led by a loyal officer corps, and would display marked cohesion and resiliency as a fighting force throughout its history.[3] But the army's resources and makeup inevitably affected the ways in which it could be used as a tool. Even in the age before ethnic nationalism, the infantry that made up the bulk of Habsburg military strength tended to take longer to train, introduce to new technology, and master complex maneuvers than their counterparts in more homogeneous western armies.[4]

In both size and quality, Habsburg military force fell short of the array of tasks that it would have needed to accomplish to meet Austria's 360-degree security needs. These limitations set Austria apart from most other large continental powers. While land power would always have first call on the monarchy's military priorities, Austria could not produce standing armies on the scale of Bourbon France without encountering significant financial strains. Unlike Prussia, Austria could not expect to fashion even a subset of its forces into a tool of national excellence through focused military spending and bonds of ethnic homogeneity. Nor could it expect to employ its armies in large-scale offensive operations like Russia, which while ethnically polyglot like Austria, enjoyed far larger manpower reserves and fewer peer competitors around its borders.

For Austria, the military instrument was inherently weaker than in these other continental powers while the military dangers facing the state were more numerous. This gap between capabilities and threats, or means and ends, shaped how Habsburg leaders pursued the goal of security, on several levels. For one, the relative scarcity of military capabilities in proportion to threats required that force be husbanded and used sparingly, primarily as a defensive tool that could not be subjected to undue risk. Second, the inadequacies of Habsburg military power highlighted which additional tools the monarchy would need to possess to bridge performance gaps. And finally, the extent of the gulf between limited military means and virtually limitless ends encouraged the development of strategy as a tool to offset burdens, and set priorities about which threats should receive the greatest attention and when. Together, these factors helped to shape a conservative approach to war and strategy that was distinctive to Austria, and corresponded to the needs of managing its severe environment.

Conserving Force

Conservation of force was a foundational principle for the Habsburg Empire. All Great Powers need to avoid exertions capable of exhausting their military capabilities. But the danger of doing so was particularly great for Austria, given its location and composition as a state. War has the potential to be a more destructive force for an encircled and artificial power, which by definition possesses a narrower margin of survival. Even initially limited conflicts run the risk of spreading into multifront crises that outstrip the state's military resources. For an internally weak power, virtually any war, for any length of time, brings dangerous economic strains.

The Habsburgs had an additional reason to preserve the army: their monarchy needed it to exist at all. If France lost the bulk of its army in a crushing defeat, it might lose territory or even its ruling dynasty, but France itself would continue to exist as a state. To varying degrees, the same could be said of Prussia and Russia. In all three, the existence of the state was rooted in something permanent—an ethnically and territorially linked polity, or sense of nation, which would eventually become the modern nation-state. The Habsburg Empire was different. A dynasty ruling over multiple polities not tied together by blood or language, it depended on the army to underwrite not only the legitimacy of its rule but its very existence as a state, too. The fates of the dynasty and army were inextricably intertwined; as long as an armed force remained in the field under independent Habsburg command, the dynasty stood a good chance of outliving even the worst defeats. The moment the army was gone, all bets were off for the dynasty—it, and the artificial state it embodied, could easily be replaced, either by some other family of warlords or else the numerous polities composing the realm.

Warfare therefore carried unusually high stakes for the Habsburg Monarchy. War is of course dangerous and potentially destabilizing for any state. But for certain Great Powers—Sparta or Prussia, for example—offensive war can bring an opportunity, such as gaining territory or preemptively neutralizing a foe, thereby contributing to the safety of the state. For Austria, the inherent fragility of the polity made war of almost any kind an inherently risky proposition. Even if victorious, the state would face immense strains, and at best add new territories that would be difficult to integrate and manage; if defeated, the results were potentially catastrophic, not only in lives and resources, but in blows to the internal stability of the empire—in the worst case, resulting in the state's extinction.

TAMING BELLONA

Beyond being a practical drain and danger, war represented for the lands of the Danube a form of moral chaos—an eruption of disorder capable of threatening the underlying order and civilization embodied by the state. A major pillar of the Habsburg claim to legitimacy as a supranational ruling dynasty was the ability to shelter its dominions against the cyclonic forces of the wider region. Inherent in this role was the belief, deeply felt by many Habsburg rulers, in the dynasty's mission as an agent ordained by God to protect otherwise-fragmented peoples from predation. The monarchy's identity as a defender of the faith was heightened by its status, first as a bulwark against Ottoman invasions and later, from the late seventeenth century onward, as an outpost of Western Catholicism confronting the forces of Reformation to the north.

The dynasty's apostolic mission imbued early Habsburg warfare with a moral component that exceeded that of any other European state and found a parallel only in czarist Russia. Archduke Charles's *Principles of War*, the most famous and influential Habsburg military pamphlet of the nineteenth century, begins with the statement that "war is the greatest evil that can happen to a state or nation."[5] In a similar vein, a contemporary of Charles, Austrian staff officer Karl Friedrich von Lindenau, wrote, "Among all the physical and moral evils that penetrate the true good of life, war stands out as the one greatest disaster, and a bad war the greatest calamity that could befall a state."[6] For Charles, a deeply religious man who wrote extensively on theological subjects, the subjects of morality and war were interconnected. His foundation was the injunction in Matthew 22:35–46 to "love the Lord thy God with all thy heart, and with all thy soul, and with all thy mind," and "love thy neighbor as thyself."[7]

Drawing on scripture and the writings of Saint Augustine, Charles saw a universe governed by eternal law. Abiding by this law entailed certain constraints on all human activity but especially war. It meant eschewing the temptation to all-out war as an overstepping of ethical boundaries as much as a practical imposition on the state's abilities. By extension, those individuals or states that gave into unbridled ambition were acting in opposition to moral laws that would eventually rein them back in. Thus Maria Theresa saw in Frederick II not only a mortal military threat but also an inherently untrustworthy and unpredictable opponent—a "monster" determined to terrorize her Christian realm and carry it into the "abyss."[8] A generation later, Archduke Charles would write of Napoleon, another rationalist claimant to central European hegemony, that he "was everything except a human being.... [He] was to his contemporaries what our ancestors would have called the devil, and all peoples consider the basis of evil: the extraordinary confluence of power, spirit and wickedness."[9]

Charles and earlier Austrian military thinkers grounded such beliefs in the Christian just war tradition, which entailed two propositions. First, war was to be pursued as a last resort. A state that views war as evil does not seek to employ it gratuitously and does not move toward offensive war under any but the direst circumstances. Instead, it takes up a defensive position, buttressed by its God-given legitimacy, and tries when possible to avert disruptions to the political order. In addition to the Christian tradition of *jus ad bellum*, Austrian military writers found support for this attitude of restraint in secular, classical history. From the late seventeenth century onward, numerous studies appeared in Vienna examining the campaigns of Greek and Roman generals. Especially popular were writers such as Polybius and Vegetius, both of whom emphasized self-mastery as the path to victory.[10] Illustrative of this trend was a 390-page translation in 1777 by an Austrian cavalry officer of the writings of the tenth-century Byzantine emperor Leo VI ("the Strategist"), a ruler noted more for his mastery of opponents through cunning and deception than for his offensive spirit.[11]

A similar appeal drew the Habsburgs to earlier Italian writers and, in particular, the work of Niccolò Machiavelli, whose firsthand observation of the feuds of the Italian city-states had bred sensitivity to the costs of war. Machiavelli counseled states to "temporize with [a threat] rather than to strike at it" and only enter into war when other options have been exhausted.[12] The self-restraint and proportion in this and other Renaissance thinkers exerted a strong influence on Habsburg views of war. "In reading Machiavelli's treatises on warfare," Charles wrote, "one is impressed by the importance and depth of the Florentine's thinking. His propositions on how to view, prepare, and prosecute wars are timeless. They will further remain relevant, for they are derived from the calculations of composition and balance of forces and relations, meaning from the subject matter in and of itself."[13] The fascination with such texts stemmed from the restraint that they embodied in avoiding conflict until the odds were favorable, thereby limiting the physical and moral evils of war.

A second tenet of just war was that if conflict could not be avoided altogether, it should be fought in a way that avoids exhaustion, and maintains a degree of control over the material and spiritual factors of the contest. In addition to the *jus in bello* tradition, an important foundation for this approach was the work of Lazarus von Schwendi, a sixteenth-century military commander in the service of Charles V whose treatises emphasized the advantages of a defensive style of warfare centered on denying crucial advantages to the enemy rather than seeking victory through risky gambles. A more significant influence was the work of Count Raimondo Montecuccoli, a seventeenth-century Neopolitan nobleman who served the monarchy as a field commander and first president of the Hofkriegsrat. Montecuccoli's views on war were formed amid the excesses of the Thirty Years' War. His *Sulle Battaglie* (Concerning battle) outlines a cautious approach to war in which commanders eschew the temptation to fight offensively, and instead use self-control and judicious planning to outwit the enemy, prevent it from fighting on its preferred terms, and thus deprive it of victory.[14]

Sulle Bataglie would exercise considerable influence over subsequent Habsburg military thinking and warfare. At its heart was a sense of proportion and moderation, or *metodizmus*, in which commanders seek not so much to win wars as not to lose them, keeping their armies alive and holding onto whatever modest gains they can acquire to gain an advantage at the concluding peace treaty. In this kind of warfare, the job of the commander is not to seize opportunities but rather manage risk in order to limit the amount of evil that the war produces. Archduke Charles would later capture the essence of this mind-set when he observed that "the object of all war must be an advantageous peace, because only an advantageous peace lasts, and it is only a lasting peace that can, by making nations happy, accomplish the ends of governments."[15]

The restraint inherent in this approach to war was a by-product of the positional and maneuver-based warfare of the seventeenth and eighteenth centuries, in which human conflict came to be viewed as a mathematical science, and victory went to those most skilled in the habits of reasoned observation, exact measurement, and defense of key geographic positions. While such concepts were present in most European armies of the period, they found a particular resonance in the Habsburg Monarchy, as offering the means to curbing the destructive effects of war or "taming Bellona" through the pursuit of limited war.[16] From this mind-set stemmed certain principles about how military force should be used in the field. Foremost of these was the preservation of the army itself. Since the very existence of the state rested on its shoulders, it was imperative that the main army be intact at war's end.

The goal of military self-preservation is a constant theme in Habsburg history. Montecuccoli's maxim "Never risk the main army" is echoed in Prince Eugene's warning to Joseph I during the Spanish succession war, "Your army, Sire, is your monarchy," Archduke Charles's comment a century later, "If the army is defeated there is no salvation," and Gillparzer's famous accolade to General Radetzky amid the tumult of the 1848 revolution, "In thy camp is Austria."[17]

Preserving the army meant not exposing it to undue risk. The goal is not to annihilate the enemy but instead to deprive him of victory, which means not fighting on his terms. As Johann Burcell, a Habsburg officer and veteran of the Prussian wars, put it,

> War arranges things in such a fashion that anything that benefits us, proves necessarily detrimental to the enemy, and anything that benefits him we should resent.... [We must] pursue solely that which benefits ourselves.... It is preferable to defeat the enemy through hunger, cunning and perpetual harassment than in open battle, where luck often ends up playing a greater role than valor.... One ought to never dare, unless the potential advantages of victory far outweighed the horrible consequences one would have to suffer in defeat."[18]

On this calculus, Austrian commanders were to avoid bold strokes, gambles, and above all, committing a disproportionately large portion of the army to one big decisive battle that, if lost, would deprive it of the means for sustaining the wider conflict.

Inherent in "never daring" is the proposition that victory can be attained by not offering or accepting battle until highly favorable conditions are present. The idea of avoiding battle as a means of gaining an advantage over an enemy shows up repeatedly in Austrian military thought and practice. At the tactical level, it involved the deceptive use of terrain and securing flanks and lines of communication. One early nineteenth-century military pamphlet provided a compilation of ways to avoid battle, gleaned from ancient warfare, and was supplied, rather hopefully, in paperback form for easy reference in the field.[19] At the strategic level, Austrian generals devoted as much attention to avoiding decisive combat as offensive generals devote to seeking it out. Maria Theresa's ablest field marshals—Count Ferdinand von Abensberg und Traun (1677–1748) and his protégé, Count Leopold Joseph von Daun (1705–66)—elevated combat avoidance to an art form, waging campaigns of attrition against Frederick the Great that were modeled on the methods used by the Roman general Quintus Fabius Maximus against Hannibal. Daun summed up his approach in layman's terms to the empress:

> People talk about exterminating all and sundry, about attacking and fighting every day, about being everywhere at once and anticipating the enemy. Nobody desires this more than I do.... God knows that I am no coward, but I will never set my hand to anything which I judge impossible, or to the disadvantage of Your Majesty's service."[20]

Years later Maria Theresa warned her son Joseph II to avoid coming to blows with Frederick II because "a battle is not advisable for you as it is for him in the same degree."[21] Best, if possible, to deny the enemy a fight altogether since

> we have quite only to lose and nothing to gain [through battle]. Our whole force is concentrated in one point; if we meet with misfortune, it's all over and we are left with no support. It would be a disaster if this happened.... So I ... must see if you cannot find the means to prevent all of this great evil that occurs once the sword is drawn.... The well-being of thousands and thousands, the existence of the monarchy and the preservation of our house depend on it.[22]

This reasoning would continue to exert an influence on Habsburg military thinking after the emergence of more offensive forms of warfare in the nineteenth century. In 1823, an Austrian general wrote in terms reminiscent of Daun:

> Impartial history would confer great glory on he who could win without fighting, over he who surrendered the well-being of the army. As a shining star and role model for all commanders, Fabius Cunctator triumphantly took his place in world history, as he who defeated Hannibal, because he knew to avoid battles. Wellington, through his marvelous campaign on the Iberian Peninsula, gained eternal glory through steadfast observation of a nonconfrontational approach and avoidance of every battle, taking every opportunity for victory from his opponent, whose entire plan was based on offensive operations.... This type of thinking about security, this rejection of force for any purpose, speaks also to the value he places on diversion, the demonstration of its use in finessing the enemy. The enemy should become tempted to do what is useful according to his own calculations. Through that, one wins time and initiative.[23]

Habsburg military thought throughout the eighteenth and early nineteenth centuries consistently emphasized the importance of not getting carried away in pursuit of victory. Commanders were to prioritize the safety of their own forces above speed or initiative. If a battle was lost, the army had to have access to carefully prepared avenues of retreat to allow it to live and fight another day. If a battle was won, pursuit of the enemy must not be undertaken if it exposes the army to risks. "Let us not get carried away by zeal or lust for vengeance [Rachelust]," as Maria Theresa wrote, "but rather seek to retain our army for our realm."[24]

The potential uses for the army almost always exceeded its available strength, while the risks of catastrophe if it overcommitted itself and lost were greater than the benefits of even the most spectacular success. Thus, whatever other political ends might present themselves as a potential object of war, they were secondary to preserving the army, which meant preserving the dynasty and state. This supreme political imperative transcended other strategic and tactical considerations. It ensured that the preoccupation with the conservation of force would endure even as the passage of time rendered the original Christian and Renaissance foundations for this kind of warfare less relevant. While Austrian military writers would gradually jettison the moral view of war as an "evil," the emphasis on limited aims, proportionality, and preservation of the army would continue well into the nineteenth century.

These characteristics distinguished the Habsburg approach to war from its continental rivals. Where most European armies evolved over time along the lines of the Napoleonic and Prussian models of warfare, in which military force is used to seek out and annihilate the enemy army, the Habsburg Army retained an attachment to positional warfare and produced commanders who tended to be risk averse on the battlefield. Clausewitz would later criticize Austria's conservative warcraft, viewing Montecuccoli in particular as excessively cautious about pushing war to its fullest extent.[25] Reflecting on one of Archduke Charles's campaigns, Clausewitz puzzled over why someone would fight "for no other reason than to facilitate his own retreat," concluding that he "never entirely understood the reasoning of the famous general and writer."[26]

The reason, to answer Clausewitz's question, is that unlike in Prussia, the loss of the army in Austria could result in the extinction of the state. The development of more restrained and defensive forms of warfare in the Habsburg lands has to be understood in the context of both the inherent limitations of Austria's military instrument and unusual political needs of the Habsburg state.[27] Far from being an instrument to achieve gains for the state through the pursuit and destruction of enemy forces on the Prussian mold, war for Austria was "not a grand strategic option under all but the most desperate circumstances."[28] In many ways this made the Habsburg land army more comparable to what in naval terms is called a "fleet in being"—a force that achieves its purpose by existing rather than fighting. Understood in this way, the Habsburg Army bears comparison to George Washington's Continental Army or Robert E. Lee's Army of Northern Virginia in its later phases, in that it was a force to be conserved, and when employed, used in moderation.[29] A conservative institution with a conservative role, its first job was to preserve the political order of which it was a creature by preserving itself in the field.

Filling Capability Gaps

As a result of these limitations, Austria possessed an army that while politically loyal and capable of resilience in emergencies, could not be solely entrusted with the task of ensuring the monarchy's existence. To survive, Habsburg leaders would have to find ways to bridge the gap between these limited military capabilities and the enormous demands of their security environment. For all states, geography constrains choices, highlighting what tools a Great Power needs most to respond to the threats and opportunities around it. Such choices inevitably come at the expense of other kinds of capabilities that the state could have chosen, and hence point to gaps that it will need to fill in wartime from internal or external sources.[30] Thus Britain's naval concentration implied the need for land allies to contain and defeat continental rivals. France and later Germany, as states invested primarily in land power, would in a war with Britain either need to divert some of their resources to building fleets or recruit (or capture) the fleets of other sea powers to move their land armies across the English Channel.

Austria's exposed geography and internal weakness cast light on the power assets it would need to complement its field army. Primarily landlocked, it did not need the help of a sea power, at least for the purposes of projecting power against an enemy; rather, Austria needed ways to enhance its ability to compete effectively on land. As for other states, finding these tools was important for augmenting and completing their own power capabilities. But for Austria, such tools were also needed to shelter the army from the risks of attempting to manage its exposed position unaided. The Habsburg Monarchy sought to fill the gaps in its power capabilities through a combination of internal and external means. The tools that it used for this task can be grouped into three categories: terrain, technology, and treaty allies.

TERRAIN

The most natural asset at Austria's disposal for enhancing its power capabilities was the physical form of the empire itself. The monarchy possessed a plentitude of defensive topographic features in its mountainous frontiers and extensive internal rivers. The very existence of these terrain attributes encouraged defensive thinking. As discussed in chapter 2, one by-product was the development, from the mid-eighteenth century onward, of extensive cartographic capabilities. Another, which went hand in hand with maps, was a heavy emphasis on the use of defensive terrain in Habsburg tactical and strategic thinking.

Over the course of the eighteenth and nineteenth centuries, the Habsburg Army developed perhaps the greatest concentration on terrain of any army in European history. Terrain helped to fill the gaps in Austria's power portfolio in several ways. On the most basic level, it aided in the effort to avoid or delay battle. As discussed in chapter 2, mountains buy time. At the start of a war, they give a defender breathing space to rally armies and shift forces from one frontier to another. Together with rivers, they aid in stalling attackers until the defending power is ready to fight on its terms. Montecuccoli laid the foundation for Austrian thinking about how to use terrain in this fashion in *Sulle Battaglie*, where he encouraged commanders to look for defensive sites "favored by a river, forest mountain, lake or city, by the sea, swamps, precipices or something of like nature."[31] The writings of eighteenth-century Austrian officers abound with similar references. Henry Lloyd, a Welshman who served as adjutant to Field Marshal Lacy in the Seven Years' War and whose writing was popular in Austria, wrote in 1783, "Smart generals will rather base themselves on the study of terrain, than stake everything on the uncertain outcome of a battle. Those who master this discipline will be able to ... prosecute [wars] perpetually without ever being obliged to battle."[32]

Another military writer who expounded on the benefits of terrain was Johann Georg Julius Venturini. An engineer officer from Braunschweig who died at thirty and dedicated portions of his writing to Archduke Charles, Venturini wrote extensively on the use of terrain at both tactical and strategic levels in warfare. In his chief work, *The Teaching of Applied Tactics or Real Military Science: Adapted from the Foremost Authorities and with Examples Using Real Terrain*, Venturini advanced the thesis that the proper employment of terrain can, in and of itself, bring success in war. Building on Burcell's maxim that "anything that benefits us, proves necessarily detrimental to the enemy, and anything that benefits him we should resent," Venturini argued that "a given piece of terrain has military advantages if, when occupied it increases the security and effectiveness of our troops' combat style while weakening the combat style of the enemy and making him insecure."[33]

The view of terrain as the key variable in war was deeply ingrained in the Habsburg military. "The terrain advantage," Venturini wrote, "varies with the general abilities of humans and horses, in accordance with the combat style of the three arms (infantry, cavalry, and artillery)."[34] The curriculum at Vienna's Neustadt military academy devoted extensive attention to how to use topography to maximize the effectiveness of each of these unit types. Joseph Auracher von Aurach, a Neustadt professor, expanded on many of Venturini's concepts, writing that "the application of armaments appropriate to the type of terrain aids in the defense or capture of that terrain. Thus the science of war consists in the advantageous allocation of various arms on different types of terrain in the pursuit of military objectives."[35]

Venturini devoted substantial effort to replicating the effects of terrain, designing a game to simulate its effects on war (see figure 4.1). The game used thirty-six hundred colored terrain squares marked to show changes in elevation and differentiate between mountains, rivers, and other features, with playing turns that represented three months. Venturini's goal was to use terrain

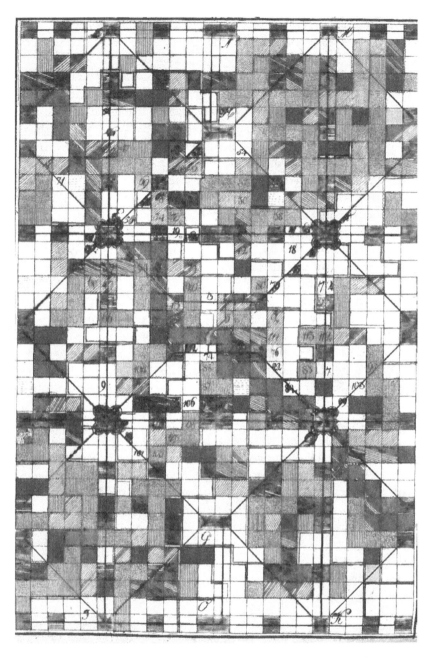

FIG. 4.1. Venturini's War Game. *Source:* G. Venturini, *Beschreibung und Regeln eines neuen Krieges-Spiels, zum Nutzen und Vergnügen, besonders aber zum Gebrauch in Militär-Schulen.* Schleswig: Bey J. G. Röhß, 1797). With thanks to the staff of the Forsvarets Bibliotekscenter for the high-quality scan.

simulations to support scenario planning, and help "the future warrior" be able to "capture at a single glance the relationship between cause and effect in the great events of war and through experience on a small scale deduce the possible consequences from first causes on the world's big scene." By doing so, he hoped to use "mental games ... and the study of history, in combination with geography," to help players grasp "the master plan of a war and the connection of all its components."[36]

The grand scale of Venturini's game is a reflection of the value that he and other contemporary writers attached not just tactically but at the strategic level as well, as an object in itself that informs the aim and definition of war. "The main and all-subordinate purposes of war," Auracher wrote, "is either to hold a certain terrain against the enemy, or evict him from an area and occupy it for oneself. Terrain is thus the decisive factor of battle."[37] "Terrain is everything," he noted elsewhere—a conviction echoed in Archduke Charles's writing many decades later, in 1826: "War is terrain ... and the constitution of the surface has supreme impact on the effectiveness of the forces."[38]

This outlook produced a belief that the very fact of controlling certain pieces of terrain will lead to success in war. While emphasis on retaining important nodes—magazines, fortified passes, and other critical infrastructure—was prevalent in the eighteenth century, this would reach its apogee in the Habsburg military. As Auracher wrote,

> The entire internal defensive structure, which was built by artisans on natural foundations and on which the outer protective shell rests, has strong and also weak sides to it, both when it comes to breaches as well as exploiting internal lines that connect the whole structure. The latter spots [are] key to the entire defensive structure [and can] bring about the fall of the entire defensive position.[39]

Archduke Charles later expanded on this concept:

> In a given theater, there are certain points, the possession of which exercises a predominant influence over outcomes, either by facilitating one's own efforts or paralyzing those of the enemy. This is called the decisive point. For a point to be decisive, its possession must allow the side that holds it to dominate the space around it in such an overwhelming manner as to either deny the enemy the ability to control it by gaining ground unpunished or by being able to bypass it.[40]

Given the importance of such points, strategy became, by definition, an exercise in defending or capturing them. "If one applies the rules of pure tactics," Venturini asserted, "the art of protecting land as well as that of reaching the goals of the war itself, strategy—or the science of generalship—comes about."

And elsewhere: "Strategy is the situational application of position, maneuver, and battle in war for land."[41]

Study of terrain would be the primary focus of the Austrian military until the mid-nineteenth century. Mastery of basic cartographic skills was a required competence for Austrian staff officers. As with maps generally, this requirement was driven by experience in war. Where no more than a handful of senior Austrian officers had been familiar with basic mapmaking skills at the start of the Seven Years' War, by 1766, more than half of staff officers had training in basic cartography, and by 1786, 100 percent of them did.[42] The extent of focus on topography as a strategic domain can be seen in the fact that the General Quartermaster, the cerebrum of Austrian military planning, would evolve over time into the department responsible for surveying terrain with the explicit aim of identifying advantages and disadvantages in operations and battle.

Preoccupation with terrain on this scale—as not just as a tool of war but indeed as war's very purpose—was distinctive to Austria.[43] While all armies historically have paid close attention to terrain, the Austrians brought its study as a capability enhancer to a level that would not have been needed in a state with weaker terrain properties, such as Poland, or one that possessed extensive offensive warfighting abilities, such as Russia. At the tactical level, terrain helped to fill gaps in capabilities by increasing the fighting effectiveness of Austria's often numerically or qualitatively limited armies. The parallel at the strategic level was that it came to be seen as offering the means of closing the gaps on the empire's lengthy frontiers and securing the realm as a whole.

TECHNOLOGY

Austria also used technology to bridge gaps in military capabilities and responsibilities. Recourse to technology, whether from internal or external sources, is a frequent means of compensating for a state's limitations. Thus Rome deliberately sought out allies possessing skilled archers, slingers, and light cavalry to make up for its overconcentration on heavy infantry, and Germany developed U-boats in both world wars to make up for its weakness at sea.

Similarly, Austria needed to extend its military capabilities on land. The monarchy's economically advanced western territories (the Austrias and Bohemia) enabled it to keep pace with the military technology of western rivals for most of its history. As we will see in chapter 5, such technologies often allowed Austrian armies to achieve escalation dominance against less advanced enemies. The empire's physical and political geography, however, placed constraints on the ability to field technology offensively on a scale that would have been required to subdue the surrounding environment.

The primary technological means by which Austria sought to address its military gaps was fortresses. Historically, most major land powers have employed fixed defenses to augment their field armies. But forts held an unusually strong attraction for the Habsburgs, for two reasons. First, the sheer extent of the imperial security perimeter lent value to structures that allowed forces to safely remain in theater. Second, the monarchy's terrain, as we have seen, invited technological augmentation. As discussed above, the ready availability of mountains encouraged thinking about how to improve on its defensive properties through, in Auracher's words, "the application of armaments appropriate to the type of terrain."[44]

Over the course of the eighteenth and early nineteenth centuries, the Habsburg Monarchy invested significant energy and resources into the development of forts around its frontiers. In modern US military thinking, the term "fort" conjures images of primitive structures defended by a handful of soldiers against poorly armed aboriginal attackers. But the Vauban fortresses of the eighteenth century were large, expensive, and technologically sophisticated structures requiring many years of effort along with advanced engineering tools to construct. As weapons platforms, they were the rough equivalent in capital investment of the dreadnought in the early twentieth century or today's aircraft carriers.

At its zenith, the Habsburg Empire would possess more than twenty such major fortresses and hundreds of smaller installations. Like maps, the skills and techniques required for making fortresses was treated as sensitive state information. As early as the 1670s, Montecuccoli, as Hofkriegsrat president, had placed the army engineers working on forts under the war council's direct authority and subjected their blueprints to "top-secret" controls, requiring that two copies of each be made and placed, respectively, in the hands of the Hofkriegsrat and local commanding general.[45] The similarity in treatment accorded to maps and fortification blueprints is evidence that they formed a symbiotic relationship in Habsburg strategic thinking. "The main purpose of studying military plans and maps," as one eighteenth-century Austrian text on fortifications stated, "is the considered thought on the placement of fortifications."[46]

Not surprisingly given this linkage, the importance of forts for Austria grew in tandem with the growth of professional cartography, which as we have seen in the previous chapter was driven by warfare. In the early eighteenth century, the Austrian Habsburgs possessed few fortresses, prompting Eugene's doleful observation to the emperor, "Your capital is a frontier town; your Majesty has no fortress on any side."[47] The Turkish wars and expansion into Hungary brought Austria into possession of numerous riverine fortresses that had developed over the course of preceding centuries by the medieval Kingdom of

Hungary. The wars with Bourbon France led the Habsburgs to extensively use the forts of the German Reich along the Rhine and eventually beef up their own defenses in the west. But as with maps and military strategy more generally, it was the wars of the late eighteenth century, first against Prussia and then against France, that would inaugurate the greatest expansion in Habsburg fortification technology.

Fortifications performed several functions for the Habsburgs. A 1790 manual on fortifications published by Franz Kinsky at the Wiener Neustadt military academy spelled out two broad purposes: "the defense of an area against enemy intrusion," and "providing support for one's own operations against the enemy," while noting that the best forts are those that "fulfill both offensive and defensive purposes at once." It went on to outline four criteria that terrain should meet to support such a dual-use fort:

1. That it controls land
2. That it hinders, or at least impedes, enemy operations
3. That it facilitates one's own operations against the enemy
4. To make it difficult to be besieged or blockaded through the use of terrain and situations as well as force the enemy into a disadvantageous fighting position.[48]

These functions pointed to a foundational role for Habsburg forts: deterrence. A major objective of the Habsburg Army, as noted earlier, was often to avoid conflict. A powerful fortress helped to accomplish this goal by forcing an offensive-minded enemy to pause and count the costs of assaulting an obstacle that would be hard to overcome and was capable of launching raids into his own heartland. As Archduke Charles wrote,

> In every state that has a war system it should be [the] principle of the state to set such points in defense alert and preserve them even during profound peace, be able to maintain them for a long time with little effort, and discourage every enemy from war by the belief in the difficulty of its conquest.[49]

Similarly, Radetzky noted that forts were meant, if possible, to "avert entirely the danger posed by the opponent."[50] Such deterrents were especially useful in the west, against militarily powerful European states. Complaining about the lack of even an "entrenched camp" here, Prince Eugene implored the economy-minded Charles VI to build fortresses "not so much to make war, as to form a barrier against France, which might deter her from attacking us."[51] Later, Austrian fortification networks in Bohemia and Italy would be constructed with precisely this goal in mind.

Once war started, forts bought time for the defender by delaying attackers and forcing them to split their forces. "If a defensive fort's purpose," the fortification manual noted,

> is to block the entrances to the lands behind it, [then] it follows that an enemy should not be able to just pass it by. Even if a fort does not directly cut the enemy's supply lines, it impedes him by forcing him off the main routes and developed roads, onto side paths.... [If he gets] far enough from his depots and magazines ... the fort would effectively cut off his supply line. He would either have to station a corps [of observation], thus dividing his forces, or start running armed convoys, a difficult enterprise in war.

In short, Kinsky concluded, forts are "physical obstacles that hold up the attacker, that make him waste time."[52] In a similar vein, Charles would write,

> The task of the defensive is to gain time; that consideration must never be lost sight of in the choice of emplacing fortresses to defend a country. They will thus be placed in such a manner that the enemy cannot easily leave them behind him without risking all for his communications and his convoys, and that by this he is obliged to leave in his rear a considerable force to observe them, blockade them, or besiege them, which will weaken his army and make it incapable of an ulterior offensive.[53]

Because of their delaying abilities, forts also helped the Habsburgs achieve economy of force. In the era before railways and the telegraph, there was significant strategic value to having troops in situ near the likely site of conflict. This was especially true for large land empires, for which distance imposed steep power gradients. Forts helped address this by facilitating concentration and allowing the defender to, in Kinsky's words, ensure that the "few can hold out against many," or as Radetzky would later observe, "make defense of the few against an attack by the many possible."[54]

In all these roles—defense, deterrence, and economy of force—the forts that were most valuable to Austria were the ones located near the frontier. "Fortresses situated upon the frontiers," Charles wrote, "change all conditions of war."[55] They strengthen deterrence by putting military hardware where the enemy can see it; they strengthen defense by promising to stop an enemy at the furthest point from the capital. Montecuccoli had advocated their placement on the frontier when he contended,

> Frontier posts, especially those where hostilities may be expected first, are provided with victuals, munitions, and full garrisons in order that the men

will not be intimidated by the sight of the victorious enemy. The majority of the infantry can be thrown into these places in order to absorb the initial impact of the attacking forces. The reason for doing this is that a fortress which resists for a certain length of time and detains the foe affords great relief to the defeated party.[56]

Habsburg military men from Eugene onward regarded the absence of frontier fortresses as a contributing factor to Austria's difficulties in the wars of the early 1700s. "Due to a lack of these [forward fortifications]," Joseph II lamented in 1766, "we rely on the establishment of rearward strongholds and magazines, which make the transport of supplies difficult, costly, and burdensome for the country while precluding any swift forward movement and ensuring that the army remains split into small groups that must move to defend the strongholds at every sign of danger."[57]

The question of where exactly to place fortifications on frontiers was a major preoccupation for Austrian military writers. Venturini, Auracher, Charles, and Radetzky all devoted substantial portions of text to debating the finer points of how forts should be incorporated into the local terrain. Kinsky's manual lists nine factors that should be taken into account, ranging from "unimpeded field of vision" to "avoiding indentations" and "wide and secure lines of communication." As a general rule, it was agreed that frontier fortresses should be placed in locations that made use of the defensive aspects of rivers and mountains. "A fort positioned near a river," Kinsky wrote,

> will have all the more advantages if it is located near the confluence of two or more waterways, thus cutting off even more land and valleys. A fort on a river fork, especially when in control of floodgates, will leave only one side from which to be attacked, allowing the defenders to reinforce the fort's natural defenses by placing obstacles and mines.

As we will see, a large number of forts can be found in such positions on every Habsburg major frontier. Regarding mountains, Kinsky advised that forts be placed

> at the foot of a mountain range, reachable only via cumbersome terrain or roads and passages. There they are more useful than on the mountain itself, even though forts may be useful to cover mountain passes. These so-called *Bicoques* cannot be cleared without heavy artillery, and thus enemy operations will be significantly impeded, to the point where overcoming them together may prove more difficult than the main fort itself. These positions are very useful to scare and annoy the enemy periphery and create diversions against an enemy.[58]

Also debated was the question of how to arrange series of forts across a broad area. Venturini devoted particularly close attention to the attributes of Austria's Italian and German frontiers and the optimal fortification systems for guarding each. In looking for where to put forts in relation to one another, he developed postulates such as "the lateral boundaries of the terrain have to perpendicularly meet the war frontier," and "if this is not the case, the tapering state suffers from the disadvantage."[59]

Venturini advocated against cordons of posts "unconnected by a formal defensive structure and located on the forward front" of the frontier since they "do not cause a sufficiently large gap in the advancing hostile force." Instead, he argued for what would today be called defense-in-depth, writing that to "avoid the disadvantages of forward fronts," the army should develop "mutual operation plans" in which buffer states absorbed the first blow of an attack while Austria "pull[ed] the defense force back" to form a "formal, fortified, double-fronted defensive structure" along the Main-Lech-Danube-Adda-Po line.[60] As we will see in subsequent chapters, such questions and the debates they fueled would take on great significance in Habsburg strategy.

TREATY DIPLOMACY

A third way that Austria sought to bridge the capability-threat gap was through the recruitment of treaty allies with which to share the burdens of defense. Historically, a state's geography determines not only how badly it needs allies but *what kinds* of allies it needs. Britain's ocean moats allowed it to forego extensive formal alliances while dictating that it would need security ties with smaller continental states to complement the maritime capabilities of the Royal Navy against major foes. While Russia's steppe environment gave it a similar freedom of maneuver, the need to govern vast spaces led it to prefer a combination of direct rule over its neighboring territories and client state relationships with potential rivals beyond the western periphery.

By contrast, Austria needed allies in order to exist at all. Of particular value were alliances with large powers capable of harassing the rearward frontiers of an enemy and drawing offensive military attention away from the Erblände, or providing financial or military support to supplement Austria's land army. The powers that Austria courted for these purposes shifted over time, from the maritime powers (England and Holland) against Louis XIV, to France against Prussia, Prussia against Napoleonic France, and perhaps most consistently, Russia to free up attention from the eastern frontier.

Another focal point of Habsburg diplomacy was the smaller states around Austria's borders. As the twentieth-century geopolitical writer Nicholas John

Spykman has argued, maritime powers have tended historically to prefer buffer zones as solutions to frontiers while large continental powers have tended to favor spheres of interest or partitions, on the calculation that outright ingestion of neighboring spaces is better than seeing them fragment and be recruited into a rival's orbit.[61]

As discussed in chapter 3, expansion of this latter variety was problematic for Austria, which was too weak to extend formal empire over its neighbors. Instead, for most of its history the monarchy sought to promote the existence of buffer zones composed of numerous smaller polities in the spaces around its borders. The bond linking these states as clients to Vienna was one of indirect patronage rather than direct rule: protection from Austria in exchange for fealty and mutual defense against stronger and more dangerous outside foes.

The benefit of buffers to Austria was partly spatial: by helping to avoid direct border-on-border contact with powerful neighbors, they lessened the sources of friction for war. Hence Prince Kaunitz, in tutoring the future Leopold II on geopolitics, wrote in a memo of 1789 that it was the presence of buffer spaces in the east that provided a basis for stability and friendship in relations with Russia, which "possesses all the characteristic traits of a natural ally" because "it is not directly adjacent [*unmittelbar nicht benachbart*] and thus capable of undertaking territorial enlargements" without necessarily threatening Austria.[62]

Should a war break out, buffer states helped buy time for Austria to organize its own defenses while providing financial aid, client armies to assist Austria in the field, and tutelary fortresses to extend its reach beyond the frontier. Eugene ranked the support supplied by "a kind of subscription by all the petty Italian princes" as second in strategic importance only to the subsidies of England and Holland.[63] Venturini extolled the importance of using the states of Germany and Italy as "a means for weakening the hostile force" and "making [the states of] Germany unconquerable" by a policy of encouraging each one to "cover itself as a separate state."[64]

Prompting Strategy

Terrain, forts, and allies were all tools that the Habsburg Monarchy cultivated over its lifetime to extend the often-slender military resources at its disposal while shielding the Habsburg Army from the full brunt of geopolitical competition. In addition, Austria's harsh environment prompted its leaders to develop conceptual tools, or strategy, to enhance the monarchy's competitive position as a Great Power. Strategy takes different forms in peace- and wartime. In the former, it is primarily concerned with rationality—with matching means to ends as they are likely to exist tomorrow. In wartime it is concerned mainly with interaction, or attempting to pursue a chosen set of ends against the determined opposition of an enemy.[65] The first is proactive and anticipatory of future events that have not occurred. The second is fluid and frequently reactive, involving crisis management and continual rearrangements of the state's means to confront shifting threats. The Habsburg Monarchy's environment required its leaders to develop both.

THE PAIN OF INTERACTION

The doorway through which Austria entered the path to grand strategy was managing interaction dynamics. This level of strategy involves matching ends and means after a military contest has already begun, amid the counteractions of adversaries. If the central question of strategic rationality is, "Can we achieve the political objective with the tools available?" the question that interaction poses is, "Can we do so despite the enemy's reaction?"[66] The problem of interaction is the inherent difficulty that unexpected enemy moves create for attempts at rationality. They do this either by triggering unforeseen consequences that exceed the defender's ability to manage or raising the overall costs of war to a point that "ceases to be commensurate with ends," thereby creating economic or domestic problems that force the weaker side to de-escalate. "The very nature of interaction is bound to make it unpredictable," in the words of Clausewitz. "The effect that any measure will have on the enemy is the most singular factor among all the particulars of action."[67]

Strategy at the level of managing interaction comes more naturally to states than futuristic planning, for the obvious reason that it requires little prior effort, and is about adjusting day-to-day plans to account for the latest battlefield or diplomatic developments. But it is also the most dangerous level of strategy, since by the time competition reaches the point of war, the stakes are high and can involve the survival of the state itself. It is especially dangerous for an interstitial power, for which even initially limited conflicts can quickly widen as rivals move cooperatively or opportunistically to take advantage of the defender's plight. Once ignited, multifront wars generate a high degree of complexity, spawning interaction dynamics that have to be managed in numerous places simultaneously. This is especially difficult when the defender is militarily weak, since the burdens on the state can quickly grow beyond its ability to bear, requiring emergency fixes that bring knock-on effects internally.

Austria learned just how dangerous these interaction dynamics could be in the War of the Spanish Succession. It entered the war without much in the way of a preconceived strategy other than the desire to protect wealthy possessions, particularly in Italy, from Bourbon control. It had few frontier forts or forward magazines, few useful maps, little in the way of preparatory diplomacy, and disordered finances.[68] Its one asset was a veteran army with experience from recent combat with the Turks and a commander, Eugene, skilled in audacious battle tactics. As Eugene described the chaotic environment at the start of the war,

> War being upon the point of breaking out, on account of the Spanish succession, a grand council of conference was held. My advice was, that the archduke should be sent into Spain immediately, to lead an army into Lombardy; but it was rejected by the wise counsellors of Leopold. They were offended at it. Prince Louis was appointed commander in the Empire and I in Italy.[69]

The ensuing thirteen-year struggle was an extended introduction to the severity of interaction dynamics for an interstitial empire. At its high point, Austria was beset by Spanish and French armies advancing across Italy, French and Bavarian armies marching down the Danube, kuruc rebels raiding from Hungary, a Swedish army menacing Bohemia, and the danger of border disputes erupting with the Turks. Handling these threats through sheer reaction required the juggling of scarce resources between frontiers *during the heat of battle*, which in turn required Habsburg leaders to confront strategic opportunity costs. Being strong in one theater implied being weak somewhere else.[70] If Vienna chose to place its troops in Italy, it had to find something to take up the slack in Germany; if it wanted to deter a threat from Sweden, it would have to draw down forces somewhere else and be prepared for the repercussions; and so on.

As we will see in subsequent chapters, the war produced awareness that the threats of the monarchy's environment outstripped its capabilities, but this failed to take deep root in the Habsburg strategic consciousness, primarily because of the continued presence of Eugene and the victories that he brought on the battlefield. For not the last time in history, victory lulled a Great Power into not absorbing the lessons of a conflict. With Eugene's death in 1736, Austria would be confronted with a series of military defeats. Lacking Eugene's military talents and starting as before from a position of unpreparedness, the monarchy barely navigated the War of the Austrian Succession, fending off invasions from the north, west, and southwest.

STRATEGIC RATIONALITY

Together, the experiences of the Spanish and Austrian succession wars drove home a point that Habsburg leaders could no longer ignore: multifront dynamics were too lethal to handle on a purely reactive basis. The pain of interaction dynamics necessitated that Austria be more conscientious about squaring limited means with the abundant threats around it. This required attempts at strategic rationality, or systematically preparing the state for future conflicts.

Rationality in strategy involves leaders asking whether the tools that they have can be used, in isolation or combination, in such a way as to achieve security. It asks, "Can we do it?"[71] If the answer is "yes," then they must count, in Clausewitz's words, "the sacrifices to be made in *magnitude* and also in *duration*"; if the answer is "no," then leaders must determine how they will augment their tools at hand to counter the threats they face.[72] Austria's experiences in the Spanish and Austrian succession wars suggested that the answer was "no": the tools that it possessed were insufficient for the task of achieving security on anything like a predictable basis. Moreover, where the effort at rationality in strategy is for most states usually intruded on by the chaos of war, in Austria's situation it was impeded long before the point of war, in peacetime, as a result of the fabric of the state itself. Beginning with the reign of Maria, Austria's leaders intensified the quest for strategic rationality as a means of avoiding a state of perpetual reaction. This quest took several forms: institutional, material, and conceptual.

STRATEGIC INSTITUTIONS

The development of Austrian strategic institutions can be traced to the Middle Ages and status of Habsburg monarchs as emperors of the German Reich.[73] As in most other European states, foreign and security policy was traditionally the preserve of the ruler along with a small circle of advisers, but required the development of more formal bodies with the territorial and administrative growth of the state. In the 1520s, a Privy Council (Geheimrat) was created to counsel the monarch on "confidential great matters" of the Danubian lands as a distinct sphere from the wider German Reich, whose affairs were handled in the Imperial Aulic Council (Reichshofrat).[74] The expansion of the Privy Council to an unmanageably large size (150 members by 1700) led Leopold I to create, at the end of the Great Turkish War, a second, smaller advisory body, the Privy Conference (Geheimkonferenz), to improve the efficiency of higher-level decisions in both foreign and domestic policy.

Austria's diplomatic corps evolved in similar doppelgänger fashion, with the Imperial Chancellery (Reichskanzlei) vying, from 1620 on, with the Austrian Court Chancellery (Österreichische Hofkanzlei) for the prize of authority over diplomatic correspondence. This tension was resolved in 1706, amid the Spanish succession war, through an imperial order granting the latter full authority over the functions of foreign policy and thus its head, the Austrian court chancellor, the status of de facto foreign minister. The appointment in 1726 of Johann Christoph von Bartenstein (1689–1767) to the new post of secretary of state in the chancellery brought new seriousness of purpose and a larger staff. From here, a Chancellery of State (Staatskanzlei) emerged, first as the foreign affairs department of the Austrian Court Chancellery and then, in 1742, during the first Silesian War, as a stand-alone institution. The arrival in 1753 of Wenzel Anton von Kaunitz-Rietberg as chancellor of state, the second in a series of three dominating figures beginning with Bartenstein and culminating in Metternich, would firmly establish the Chancellery of State's status as the locus of Habsburg foreign policy. Under the prompting of the Prussian wars and Maria Theresa's wider reforms, Kaunitz would professionalize the Chancellery of State and sharpen the competencies of the diplomatic corps, incorporating lessons from the French Foreign Ministry's *premiers commis* and effectively halting the practice of end runs by diplomats to the Privy Conference.[75]

In parallel with these institutions, the Habsburg Monarchy developed a court war council, or Hofkriegsrat, whose origins lay in the need to support a standing army during the sixteenth-century wars with the Turks. The mandate of the Hofkriegsrat revolved primarily around the logistical and material dimensions of war planning, without which, as Habsburg officials argued to the emperor in 1556, "too many provisions will be purchased, which will go bad if not consumed."[76] Its core responsibilities included recruitment, procurement, victualing, the maintenance of capital equipment, especially artillery and fortifications, and administration of the Military Border in Croatia as well as responsibility for diplomatic relations with Turkey and Russia (until 1742 and 1753, respectively).[77] Barred initially from making any but the most trivial of financial decisions without approval from the Hofkammer, the Hofkriegsrat was eventually given greater spending powers and oversight of military campaigns.[78]

The Hofkriegsrat was a complicated institution. In its time, it encompassed the functions of War Ministry, General Staff, and Military Chancellery.[79] In today's terms, it would be akin to combining the US National Security Council, Defense Policy Board, and Pentagon's Office of Acquisition and Logistics into one institution. At its helm was a president, often a former field commander, supported by a mixed military and civilian staff divided into functional departments.[80] The war council's wide-ranging mandate and complicated structure impeded quick, efficient decision-making.[81] Compounding the problem was the complexity of the surrounding bureaucratic environment in which it existed, which frequently brought overlap and conflict with other agencies.[82] As with other Habsburg strategic institutions, times of war tended to bring focused attempts to improve the Hofkriegsrat's operational effectiveness. Most notably, after the cataclysmic first encounters with Frederick, Maria Theresa streamlined the body, cutting the number of military advisers from 144 to 36, and relocating quartermaster and judicial functions to specialized bodies.[83]

Despite its often-cited flaws, the Hofkriegsrat did have some positive attributes. Most obviously, it represented, in institutional form, an attempt at planning for war in the future tense. For all the factionalisms it housed, the Hofkriegsrat's existence ensured routine interaction between a cross-section of senior military and civilian elite that encouraged a culture of strategic planning and forethought for the matching of means to large ends. It placed under one roof those tools most essential for the preservation of the dynasty— especially army loyalty, through control over appointments and pay along with the means of escalation dominance (artillery and fortresses) against internal and external enemies. The frequent dominance of civilian bureaucrats in the Hofkriegsrat's structures so frequently decried by the military was not altogether undesirable for an empire that could not afford to venture the army on gambles, and in which military subordination to political objectives was necessary to survival. It is impossible to imagine the Hofkriegsrat producing the kind of political dominance by generals that occurred in Prussia.

Habsburg intelligence capabilities, too, increased as a result of exposure to the interaction dynamics of eighteenth-century warfare.[84] The Habsburg Monarchy was the first European Great Power to establish a formal intelligence service. The tradition had its roots in the culture of cartography, census taking, and communication in an ethnically diverse but compact land area. An Austria-wide mail system, formed in the late fifteenth century, gave birth during the Spanish succession war to deciphering and other intelligence functions, first in the Office of Inspections and Interceptions, and later the Secret Service of the Cabinet.[85] As with court, diplomatic, and war institutions, intelligence capabilities increased in both formality and competence as a result of the wars of the eighteenth century. Under Maria Theresa, the "Black Cabinet" conducted counterespionage activities, and military intelligence activities were expanded and centralized to go beyond mere battlefield reconnaissance.[86] Joseph II and Leopold II continued this process with the creation of the Secret Police, which held wide-ranging powers to monitor and manage public opinion, and keep tabs not only on foreign officials and diplomats posted in Vienna but even clergy—functions that, as we will see, Metternich expanded on both vertically, with deeper surveillance networks inside the monarchy, and horizontally, with the spread of Habsburg spies throughout neighboring buffer states and foreign powers.[87]

MATERIAL PLANNING

Both the War of the Spanish Succession and War of the Austrian Succession had found the monarchy lacking in adequate forces, provisions, forts, and forward magazines. A major lesson from both wars had been that such materiel was difficult to organize once a war was under way, with enemy armies occupying provinces and depriving the state of their resources. To survive, Austria needed to take better stock of the "means" at its disposal and place them on a war footing before conflicts broke out. Early on, Eugene had seen the need to take these precautions. In 1724, he wrote,

> I applied myself greatly to the concerns of the [empire].... I said to our generals, Could we not ... raise regiments.... Have large garrisons at Vienna, Presbourg, Olmütz, Gratz, Lintz, Brussels, Luxembourg and Milan? Make an entrenched camp upon each frontier, since fortresses cost too much? Establish and keep up studs, that money may not go out of the kingdom?

Again, shortly before his death, he warned about the consequences of unpreparedness:

> If I were still to interfere with affairs, I should say to the Emperor, "Take every precaution for your succession: it will be devilishly embroiled. Two or three different powers will support their pretensions. Prevent it while you are alive.... The army and the artillery are falling into decay. They will not be in a state to resist if they do not arrange together to prevent all that will happen; and if, on the death of Charles VI, they do not refuse to go to war with the Turks. I wish great good fortune to the house of Austria ... and I hope that she will extricate herself."[88]

Failure to heed these warnings had contributed to the monarchy's plight in 1740–48. Afterward, as we will see in chapter 6, Maria Theresa undertook large-scale efforts to reorganize the empire's military resources, enlarging and reforming the army, and forming military commissions to ensure that the empire would be able to more quickly mobilize resources at the start of the next war.

When the Seven Years' War ended, Joseph II expanded on this process. "Recent experience," he explained, "has proved quite clearly the necessity of preparing sound arrangements for the future."[89] To create a basis for such arrangements, he asked the Hofkriegsrat to provide a detailed (*mit vollster Genauigkeit*) appraisal of the military resources available to the monarchy.[90] After reviewing their findings, he wrote a long memorandum arguing that Austria needed to make material preparations well ahead of the next war and outlining what steps specifically it should take. The opening lines of the memo read,

> We require peace, so we must prepare for war. Yet how far are we from being prepared.... The time when this important question was first raised I now see as like a vision that God presents to sinners, but from which they do not profit at all, remaining ever more incapable of conversion. Your majesty spent 17,500,000 francs on the army ... and yet we are not at all in a state to defend against our attacks by our neighbors. What a prospect for a man who adores his monarch and treasures his country.... To this state of affairs, ill effects have been quite demonstrated, I can propose no other remedies except to surrender ourselves to Providence, or forecast with certainty that there will be no more war ever again, or address the situation's challenges through feasible and necessary actions. All that this comes down to is the conviction of the necessity of these changes and a firm resolve to bring them about.[91]

Titled "Si vis pacem para bellum" (If you want peace, prepare for war), the memorandum was a clarion articulation of the insufficiency of crisis management for a state in Austria's position, and the need to engage in the systematic weighing of means and ends in order to act beyond the demands of the present. Its emphasis is firmly on the future tense; as the first axiom states,

> It is probable that the monarchy will, before the end of time, once again be at war, and that in consequence, we are obliged to make arrangements so that we—even our great-grandchildren—can defend ourselves with dignity. To this end we must choose now the most appropriate sites for fortresses, prepare men to replace the dead, increase the number of service horses, ... acquire firearms, and finally be assured of having bread for our men and oats for our horses.

Inherent in the preparations suggested in "Si vis pacem para bellum" is the goal of breaking out of the reactive mode that had plagued Austria in earlier wars. The second axiom maintains that

> it is possible to forecast that the next war will be incredibly bloody and vigorous.... What we are unable to defend and hold ... during the first two campaigns we will neither recover nor take even if we were to fight ten [campaigns], because outlays of money and men made in the initial moments will not necessarily support us for the duration [*on finit par l'inaction*]. It follows that if one will be attacked, then one *must already be in a state of defense* [emphasis added] ... that we must not wait until they start to prepare ourselves, when it will be too late, but rather we should

have our resources ready during peacetime, so as to be able to act at the first signal.[92]

Joseph's stress on material preparation shows the influence of earlier writers like Montecuccoli and Machiavelli, the latter of whom had underscored preparation of depots before a conflict: "Whoever has not taken proper care to furnish himself with a sufficient stock of provisions and ammunition bids fair to be vanquished without striking a stroke."[93] It also echoes Eugene's earlier, practical emphasis on the need for reliable sources of manpower, money for fortresses, and systematic horse breeding.

In other memorandums, Joseph would elaborate on the provisions that Austria should institute to be war ready on a standing basis.[94] These included a permanently enlarged land army, transitioning to a canton system, developing magazines and depots, and creating defense infrastructure on the northern frontier. Not all of these would prove practicable, due to the financial constraints facing the monarchy. But many would be implemented, shifting Austria toward a numerically larger army and large-scale defensive construction projects. These changes and the culture of planning they instituted ensured that Austria would never again find itself as militarily unprepared as it had at the start of the wars of the first half of the eighteenth century.

CONCEPTUAL PLANNING

The material preparations prompted by the wars with Frederick went hand in hand with increased attention to the conceptual dimensions of strategy. As we have seen above, this was reflected in the work of late eighteenth-century Austrian military writers such as Venturini and Auracher. But it was also apparent at the official level, in the formal war plans developed by the Habsburg General Staff.

One early example can be seen in the planning that was set in motion by Joseph's "Si vis pacem para bellum" memorandum, which was circulated among senior generals and members of the Hofkriegsrat and used as the basis for a conference to debate its contents.[95] At the end of the meetings, which ran for three days, three of the officials present—Field Marshal Lacy, State Minister Count Heinrich von Blümegen, and Count Johann Georg Adam von Starhemberg—were tasked with drafting a white paper. The resulting document, titled "Organization of a Reliable Defensive Strategy," presented the findings from the conference and outlined recommendations for future policy.

In today's terms, the contents of "Organization of a Reliable Defensive Strategy" reads like a combination of the US Quadrilateral Defense Review and US National Security Strategy. It analyzes military threats facing Austria, ranks them in level of priority, and proposes solutions for addressing them that are within the means of the state. "For some time now," it begins, "there has been discussion about the necessity to create reliable defensive systems to be better prepared for a breach of the peace." It then conducts what today would be called an exercise in contingency planning:

> How many enemies could we afford to counter under current circumstances and ... must we focus on one or multiple armies? ... An eruption by the King of Prussia alone would seem the most likely, whereas an attack from the Turkish side would not be as easy, at least while the current mood at the Porte prevails. The Austrian provinces ... would be covered to the point that, if a crisis were to break out somewhere else, troops could be shifted from them according to need. At the same time, considering conditions may always change, it would be smart to prepare with whatever resources the monarchy has available for the case of a war on two fronts.

Surveying the threats facing the state, the paper analyzes which is the gravest:

> We know from experience, as well as from the state of its lands, that the Porte is in no position to mount any surprise attacks. In any case, we would have several months to contain the situation and prepare ourselves. Prussia however, in its bellicose constitution, is capable of rapidly assembling its forces to realize its hostile intentions at a moment's notice. Consequently, we must focus our attention and consider putting our defenses on an equal footing to theirs.

On the basis of this threat assessment, the white paper asks, "What assistance could be expected from our allies?" "What armies [could] the various enemy powers field against us?" and "How do our forces measure up against these requirements?" In counting necessary resources, the paper takes account of the interaction dynamics that the army had learned could arise in war, including "the possibility of a two-front war," allies reneging on promises, and the "contingency of an ever costly insurrection in Hungary."[96] The paper concludes with recommendations that include the construction of forts in Bohemia, with cost estimates provided, and where to move army units when war breaks out.

Together, the "Si vis pacem para bellum" memorandum and "Organization of a Reliable Defense Strategy" white paper mark an important watershed in the formulation of Habsburg grand strategy. On the most basic level, they represent a formal, deliberative attempt at calculating relationships between means and large ends. Coming after a period of sustained crisis, their explicit aim was to ensure the state's ability to act "beyond the demands of the present." As we will see, many of the recommendations developed in these documents were implemented in subsequent years, laying the foundation for an offensive war against the Turks and defensive operations in Bohemia, and setting a standard for war planning that would be replicated in the development of detailed war contingencies for the eventual collision with France.[97]

Beyond the immediate recommendations they contained, Joseph II's planning efforts were also important for elucidating what Hal Brands calls "the intellectual architecture" to Habsburg grand strategy—a "logic" by which, on the basis of recent experience and an anticipated future, Austria would seek to "navigate a complex and dangerous world." The logic the Habsburgs sought was one that could deal with the fundamental problem facing Austria as a geopolitical actor: the mismatch between its internally constrained resources and abundance of enemies around its borders. Joseph II's preferred solution was primarily military, envisioning a comprehensive reorganization of war-making resources to enable Austria to put more troops in the field, earlier in a conflict. In his responses to Joseph II's 1766 memo, Kaunitz doubted Austria's ability to imitate Prussia's war machine, casting doubt on the idea that Austrian armies, however large, could ever handle all of her enemies, and that it would be able to sustain such an effort without overtaxing its long-term economic capabilities and the morale of its people.[98]

These debates can be seen as a working out of the logic of Habsburg grand strategy, and by extension, an attempt at defining the limits of the options at its disposal for security. Inherent in Joseph II's ideas is a rationalist attempt to view the monarchy as a mechanism not unlike other states in Europe and thus look for ways to systematically increase its material capabilities. By contrast, Kaunitz viewed Austria as constrained by internal limitations; for him, Prussia's recent successes pointed above all to the need for improved strategy on the premise that, as his biographer put it, "the outcome of a war depended less on the readiness for the decisive first campaign than on the ability to endure for an extended period of time."[99] Both paths involved trade-offs— Joseph's approach, maximizing capabilities at the cost of economic strength and possibly domestic stability; and Kaunitz's approach, tending the bases of long-term strength at the expense of vulnerability and future losses in the opening campaigns, as had occurred in Austria's past wars. The tension between these approaches would replay in various forms in the Habsburg grand strategy of later decades.

Time and "Systems"

The exchanges between Joseph II and Kaunitz underscore the extent to which, in grappling with grand strategy, Habsburg leaders were forced to perhaps a greater extent than their competitors to come to grips with the factor of time. Time in strategy is mainly about two things: duration (how long a contest lasts) and sequencing (which contests occur when). Clausewitz places duration at the heart of the problem of interaction, posing it as the central impediment to strategic rationality in pursuit of a political object.[100] For Austria, duration mattered enormously, since the longer a war lasted, the more likely it was to create dynamics beyond the army's ability to manage. Conversely, when facing a militarily stronger foe, Austria might need to be able to draw out the contest until alliances could come into play. Above all, the Spanish and Austrian succession wars showed that Vienna needed to be able to sequence its wars—to have some means of prioritizing which rival to face when, well before war ever began.

Time figures prominently in Habsburg strategic behavior. Charles's *Principles of War* identifies it as the central concern facing Austrian commanders, noting that "the principal tasks of defensive [war] are to gain time," "time is often times more valuable than even intrinsically precious human blood," and "the principal need of a sovereign or a general-in-chief will be to ... employ [forces] in such a way that the war lasts as shortly as possible."[101] The problem of time is frequently discussed in imperial memorandums and letters. "Time itself is against us," wrote Maria Theresa when Austria was diplomatically isolated. "The longer war drags on the more new enemies we have to fight.... [We] have to seek to gain time." When facing a stronger foe, she pines for "types of warfare that grant time to recover," and the ability to "gain time and not rush." Joseph II's memorandums worry about a *double guerre* producing enemies beyond Austria's ability to sequence, and the 1767 white paper centers on the need to "buy us enough time in case of a sudden breach of peace."[102]

It is in wrestling with issues of time that Habsburg strategy takes on its defining quality. In both a military and diplomatic sense, the heart of the strategic problem facing Austria had to do with how power is arranged in space. As Metternich said, "Power distributed is no longer power."[103] For true power to exist at all for any state, it must be concentrated in a specific location. This implies the need for concentration, which is about space and therefore time. For an encircled and weak state, concentration is hard to achieve because the commodity of power is, in the natural state of things, diffuse. It is stretched geographically, by the "pull" of frontiers and need to guard against threats on every side; politically, by the drain of constitutional constraints and ethnic quarrels; and financially, by the scarcity of resources for tous azimuts security readiness. The moves of rivals only complicate concentration further.

The need to deal with the time factor pointed Austria's leaders toward the creative and integrated use of the tools that it possessed to ensure survival. Anything that they came up with strategically would have to compensate for the inadequacies of military power to cope with the state's 360-degree threat environment. One by-product was a search for systems to provide security without overstretching resources. In strategy, the term "systems" usually refers to the employment of tools in an interdependent fashion to achieve sustainable security.[104] As Luttwak used the term in the context of the Roman Empire, it refers to: "integrated diplomacy, military forces, road networks, and fortifications to serve a single objective [in which] the design of each element reflected the logic of the whole."[105]

The idea of systems in strategy, as expressed in systems theory, is a tricky one, involving as it does the implicit proposition that statesmen are capable of imposing instrumental rationality in a complex form, on the basis of some agreed-on plan, over a long period of time. Nevertheless, a systems construct does provide a useful way to think about how the Habsburgs approached the task of security, for a couple of reasons. First, a systematic approach to war and strategy were logical outworkings of Austrian strategic and political culture. The historical foundations of Habsburg military science, with its Catholic emphasis on striving for a just order along with the late Renaissance and Enlightenment preoccupation with using reason and mathematics to master human passions as much as physical environments, lent itself to such an approach. The central concept of *metodizmus* from Montecuccoli is built around the view of war as a type of chaos (Charles's "evil" of war) that can be managed with rational systems of thought and behavior. For the Habsburg field marshal, "strategy and perspective are those of the Cabinet room.... [H]is art of war consists in ... measured geometric order, carefully weighed-up knowledge of circumstances and rules, a tranquil 'thinking things over'; without [which] there is little use in being acquainted with that 'infinity of situations' in which a soldier finds himself."[106]

Second, this is how the Austrians themselves talked about strategy. The search for an optimal *Verteidigungssystem* (defensive system) is pervasive in Habsburg military writing from the reign of Maria Theresa to Francis Joseph. Such terminology was in widespread use by the time of Joseph's postwar planning exercises. The 1767 white paper seeks to "create reliable defensive systems" combining troops, forts, terrain, and allies. Venturini, with his Enlightenment belief that geometry can guarantee success, advocates "general defense systems" and a "mutual operation plan" integrating terrain, buffer states, and fortresses. Auracher thinks in terms of systems as well, stressing the interaction of field armies and forts to secure key nodes on the terrain. J. W. Bourscheid admonishes his contemporaries to emulate Byzantine "tactical systems," allowing military force to be "opened and folded like a fan to any side ... for the ultimate purpose of winning time and territory" against enemies on multiple sides.[107] In a similar vein, Archduke Charles writes about developing *Kriegssysteme* and *Verteidigungssysteme* to seal off Austria's frontiers in a systematic, almost geometric manner.[108] Even Radetzky, who tended to think not in systems but rather in terms of seeking and destroying enemy armies, writes about the need for a "defense system," composed of "internal and external" strongholds to secure multiple war theaters at an affordable cost.[109]

References to systems were frequently vague, appearing to mean something like a methodology of war.[110] But more often it was a shorthand for some combination of tools—usually a mixture of defensive terrain, perimeter forts (whether in rows or cordon), and allies (whether large or buffer states) to extend the army's abilities. Perhaps the term's meaning can best be described by what it was not: pure crisis management. The lesson from Austria's early eighteenth-century wars had been that relying on improvised reaction to events was not a viable option for a state in Austria's position. The unpredictable and escalatory nature of interaction dynamics for an interstitial state penalized this unpreparedness financially, logistically, and militarily. Thus Joseph worried, "We at present have made no arrangements or preparations; neither to be able to act immediately, nor to create a system that will allow us to operate ... in a coming war."[111] As Archduke Charles wrote, "[The state needs] a system that directs the proceedings into prepared structures, and unburdens the mind of having to make decisions under pressure, and constantly adjust and modify them. [One that brings consistency to the art of war], which is as incompatible with constant excitement as it is with strict principles."[112]

Systems, in other words, were an attempt to free decision-makers from the straitjacket of constant reaction. In this sense, the search for them was a function of dealing with the time problem. Since the army could not, in Daun's words, be "everywhere at once," Austria needed things that could be in these places on its behalf.[113] As we will see, the various permutations of Kaunitz's *Allianzsystem* were about enabling Austria's military to safely deprioritize some frontiers and focus on others. Similarly, the forts in Charles's defensive systems were aimed at enabling concentration (prioritization) against a main threat by putting objects in place elsewhere so that the army would not have to "occupy all the other frontiers of the state save with the absolutely necessary number of troops."[114]

Systems thinking was inherently defensive, representing a search for means to cope with the reality of an army that was weak relative to the challenges it faced, and whose retention was necessary for the survival of the state. The offensive armies of eighteenth-century France or Prussia would not have needed such systems, since their essence was to seek out opportunities on foreign soil. It is for this reason that the handful of instinctively offensive Austrian sources—Burcell, Laudon, and Radetzky—did not gravitate toward systems thinking, and as we will see, why it was relinquished amid the move toward more offensive warfighting concepts in the Habsburg Army of Francis Joseph. At the same time, systems thinking reflected Habsburg geography. It is hard to imagine generals in eighteenth- or nineteenth-century Russia wrestling with pseudomathematical systems of warfare in their use of deep strikes to conquer the endless spaces of the Eurasian heartland. For Austria, systems were an attempt at amplifying the defensive traits of abundant mountains and internal lines. In this sense, the method of thought that they reflected was inherently optimistic—an expression of the quest for order and an attainable security that was encouraged by Danubian topography.

Habsburg physical and political geography significantly influenced Austria's behavior as a strategic actor. Surrounding threats required a large land army while placing effective limitations on what that army could accomplish. Domestic complexity amplified these constraints. The composite nature of the state made such military power as existed precious, for reasons that went beyond the normal security responsibilities held by most armies and had to do with the dynasty's survival—and thus the state itself.

Habsburg grand strategy can be understood as the search for expedients to husband this weak but valuable tool, and hence the state, against the chaos of geopolitics and war. Terrain, technology, and treaties were the foremost ways for doing so. Used in combination, they offered an affordable means of offsetting strategic burdens and avoiding a coalescence of unmanageable threats. The search for these combinations fueled the development of Habsburg strategy. Strategy as a conscious exercise therefore arose for Austria as an expedient, the need for which was driven home by the painful consequences of trying to survive without it, through ad hoc reactions to invasion. These experiences created incentives to try to transcend pure crisis management and be deliberate about matching means to ends—to prepare materially ahead of conflicts and think conceptually about threats before they emerged. Coming at a moment when the Enlightenment seemed to offer rational processes to tackle even the most vexing state challenges, the pressures on Austria encouraged attempts at creating methodical systems to fend off the chaos intruding from its strategic environment.

The result was a defensive grand strategy, the essence of which was to use an army in being, frontier forts, buffer states, and a flexible system of alliances to mitigate and deflect the strains of external encirclement and internal weakness. Like the development of accurate maps and attempts at reforming state administration and finance, Austrian efforts to formulate grand strategy were spurred by war and geopolitical necessity. Periods of reflection, planning, and fortress construction tended to occur in the wake of conflicts, which in

Austria's case were an almost-permanent occurrence. These wars took place at the frontier—first against the Turks, then the French, and then the Prussians. As we will see in the next three chapters, it was here, at the outer reaches of imperial power, that Habsburg grand strategy would be prompted, shaped, and tested most.

PART II

Habsburg Frontier Defense "Systems"

5

Harvest of Briars

I do not find that Your Majesty would be well-served by the possession of these faraway places.

—PRINCE EUGENE OF SAVOY

Russia is almost useless as a friend, but could cause us considerable damage as an enemy.

—WENZEL ANTON VON KAUNITZ

ON ITS SOUTHERN and eastern frontiers, the Habsburg Monarchy contended with two large land empires: a decaying Ottoman Empire, and a rising Russia determined to extend its influence on the Black Sea littorals and Balkan Peninsula. In balancing these forces, Austria faced two interrelated dangers: the possibility of Russia filling Ottoman power vacuums that Austria itself could not fill, and the potential for crises here, if improperly managed, to fetter Austria's options for handling graver threats in the west. In dealing with these challenges, Austria deployed a range of tools over the course of the eighteenth century. In the first phase (1690s–1730s), it deployed mobile field armies to alleviate Turkish pressure on the Habsburg heartland before the arrival of significant Russian influence. In the second phase (1740s–70s), Austria used appeasement and militarized borders to ensure quiet in the south while focusing on the life-or-death struggles with Frederick the Great. In the third phase (1770s–90s), it used alliances of restraint to check and keep pace with Russian expansion, and recruit its help in comanaging problems to the north. Together, these techniques provided for a slow but largely effective recessional, in which the House of Austria used cost-effective methods to manage Turkish decline and avoid collisions that would have complicated its more important western struggles.

Eastern Dilemmas

The end of the Great Turkish War in 1699 brought the Habsburg Monarchy into possession of a vast span of territories to the south and east of its historic heartland in Upper and Lower Austria. Under the terms of the Treaty of Karlowitz, the monarchy gained nearly sixty thousand square miles of land, effectively doubling the size of the empire. The new territories stretched to the Sava River in the south and the Carpathians in the east, bringing Slavonia, Croatia, and most of Hungary, including Transylvania but without the Banat, under Habsburg rule (see figure 5.1).[1]

Acquisition of these new lands greatly alleviated the ancient security problem in the south, where since the sixteenth century an expansionist Ottoman Empire had placed unrelenting pressure on the Habsburg core, rendering Royal Hungary and Styria as buffer territories. With the Ottoman frontier so far north, Turkish armies had been able to maraud the borderlands and invade the Erblände itself with little warning. Twice in previous centuries—once in 1529 and again in 1683—large Ottoman siege trains had moved through the gap in the Šar Mountains up the Maritsa, Morava, and Sava River valleys

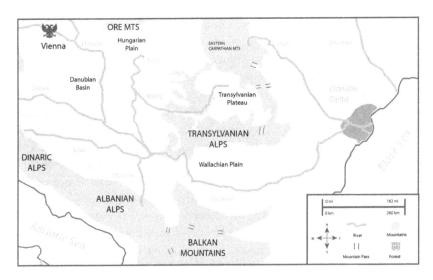

FIG. 5.1. Southeastern Frontier of the Habsburg Empire.
Source: Center for European Policy Analysis, 2017.

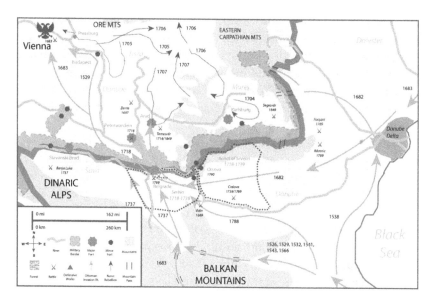

FIG. 5.2. Ottoman Invasions of the Habsburg Heartland.
Source: Center for European Policy Analysis, 2017.

to invest Vienna itself (see figure 5.2).[2] Only with great effort and the help of allied armies from across Europe had these attacks been repelled. By placing a generous layer of territory under Habsburg control, Karlowitz effectively removed this problem of surprise invasions while furnishing the monarchy with the nominal size and strategic depth of a first-rank power. Expansion in the southeast, however, created two sets of problems for the Habsburg state—one administrative in nature, and the other geopolitical.

The Eastern Power Gradient

First, Austria faced the question in the Balkans, encountered by most land empires at their height, of where to draw the line of conquest. As noted in chapter 2, the power of an empire can be assessed according to the surface area over which it can exercise control and collect taxes. The frontier historian Lattimore Owen has surmised that historically, land empires eventually hit an "outer limit of desirable expansion," at which the ability to bring new territories under civil administration is undercut by the costs of projecting military power. Beyond this point, the power gradient, or rate at which military power is eroded by distance, becomes too steep, and the empire faces a "zone of diminishing returns," where additional gains, rather than strengthening the empire, weaken it. Not expanding to this point deprives an empire of resources and safety, as was the case for Austria in the period before Karlowitz. But going beyond it leads to overstretch and increases the state's vulnerability. The ability to accurately identify the point of maximal expansion is therefore an important objective for successful empires. Only by doing so can they establish the parameters of an *orbis terrarium*—what the Chinese called *t'ien hsia*—that can be sustainably administered through the construction of a defensive perimeter.[3]

Finding the point of maximal expansion is easier when geographic features demarcate the space in question, and herein lay much of the problem for Austria in the southeast. The Balkans were the only Habsburg frontier to possess relatively weak natural borders. Major mountain ranges lie several hundred miles south of the rivers Sava and Drava, which allowed substantial fluctuation of formal borders according to military realities. To the east, the map would seem to indicate the possibility for expansion to the Black Sea, but the interposition of the Carpathians some 270 miles before the river delta and malarial flood zones on the Wallachian Plain placed obstacles to such enlargement.

The nature of the terrain in the southeast also worsened the effects of the power gradient. At almost 800 miles in length, this was the monarchy's largest frontier. Unless properly managed, it could easily require large forces to hold down far-flung sectors often separated by rugged terrain with few roads. Units deployed to the south were harder to reposition than in other frontiers. The travel distances from the Balkans to the monarchy's other frontiers was further and more complicated than movement between the other three. Once deployed, troops were more likely to get bogged down: in the Serbian sector, by seasonal rains, and in Wallachia, by floodplains and fever. The longer a war lasted here, the more troops it was likely to suck in, thereby embroiling the monarchy in protracted fighting. These factors impacted military range, not only by making the radius of effective operations shorter than in more congenial territories of western Europe, but also by creating logistical incentives for Habsburg commanders to tether forces here to predictable supply depots and avenues of retreat.

A further complication was the human makeup of the southeastern territories. The territories that Austria acquired at Karlowitz possessed social, political, and economic traits very different from the rest of the monarchy. Such formal economy as existed bore the stamp of a century and a half of Ottoman rule—artisanal and agricultural, kept local by the underdeveloped infrastructure, and not easily incorporated into the western Habsburg lands.[4] As in neighboring frontier spaces under Ottoman and Russian rule, social organization in Hungary was archaic and rustically agrarian, with only five towns with populations greater than twenty thousand.[5] Further south, frontier cultures of tribalism and raiding did not readily lend themselves to assimilation by bureaucratic empire. In the eyes of much of the Orthodox population, the Habsburg soldiers and administrators who arrived after Karlowitz brought a liberating but new and alien form of rule; to the Magyar nobility, they had the appearance of foreign interlopers.

In both territorial and human terms, Austrian expansion in the southeast, while necessary for keeping neighboring empires at bay, tended to not significantly add to the monarchy's economic resource base. Indeed, expansion here brought problems. On the border itself, the long-standing *Ghazi* tradition of incessant raiding brought low-intensity attacks on a more or less permanent basis, creating a "constant state of emergency" that made "official boundary marks worthless."[6] The presence of a large and churlish Magyar nobility in the historically secessionist territory of Transylvania near the Ottoman border created a continual danger of revolt. These factors amplified the geopolitical "pull" on the monarchy's southeastern flank, requiring frequent military intervention and ensuring that the army's attention here would be directed inward as much as outward.

Together, this mixture of large distances, internal difficulties, and low returns on investment made the south a nettlesome place for the exercise of Habsburg power. Despite their formal incorporation into the monarchy from the early eighteenth century onward, it is more accurate to think of these lands as a kind of internalized buffer zone, militarily valuable as a shock absorber but not a net contribution to Habsburg power in anything other than status terms. As Prince Eugene mused to the emperor in the midst of one of his Balkan campaigns, "I do not believe that Your Majesty would be well served by these wretched, distant places, many of which, without lines of communication to the others or revenue, are expensive to maintain and more trouble than they are worth. Potential liabilities, Your Majesty, need not insist on their retention."[7]

Balancing Turks and Russians

A second problem for Austria in the southeast was geopolitical in nature: the need to manage relations with two large, neighboring empires, the Ottoman Empire and Russia. Each posed a distinct challenge to the Habsburgs.

In spite of their recent defeat, the Turks remained a potent military force committed to projecting power in, if not pursuing outright mastery of, their northern frontiers. With a heartland in Anatolia, and outlying provinces in Persia, the Balkans, and Northern Africa, the Ottoman Empire enjoyed a significant degree of insulation in the era before modern air and naval power. While they would eventually lag behind the West technologically, the Ottomans at this stage still possessed military capabilities roughly equivalent to their Habsburg and Russian neighbors, with large stores of gunpowder, small arms, and field and siege artillery.[8] The decentralized Ottoman military system, or *seyfiye*, consisted of local forces supplied by fiefdoms backed by a professional army centered on the famous Janissary corps. Rich in cavalry, their armies employed a combination of conventional and irregular battle techniques reflecting their partly Asiatic composition. Through centuries of Balkan warfare they had amassed numerous fortresses along the lower Danube and Black Sea. Slow to mobilize in wartime, the Ottomans suffered from inefficient administration, and were already showing signs of the political instability and court intrigue that would later paralyze the empire and trigger outside intervention. At the time of Karlowitz, however, they remained a resilient and aggressive power capable of fielding large armies and inflicting defeats on western opponents.

As the Turks began their long decline, Russia was emerging as a regional military power. The late seventeenth century saw Russia initiate the concentric expansion from the Muscovy heartland that would eventually make it one of the largest land empires in history.[9] As Russian settlers and soldiers pushed east and south into the steppe, they also moved west toward the Baltic-Carpathian-Pontic line.[10] At the time of Karlowitz, Russian attention was primarily focused on competition with Sweden over the Baltic and decaying Polish-Lithuanian Commonwealth. But the Russians looked south as well. Just three years earlier, the czar's armies had expelled the Turks from the fortress of Azov, signaling Russia's appearance as a serious military presence on the north shore of the Black Sea. In the years that followed, Russian czar Peter I systematically reformed the Russian state, establishing a modern fleet and professional army on the Western model. Coinciding with a period of population growth and territorial expansion, Peter's reforms set Russia on the path to deep offensive strikes that would become the defining features of Russian military strategy well into the nineteenth century.[11]

The combination of Ottoman decline and Russian expansion represented both an opportunity and challenge for Austria. On the one hand, the diminishing strength of the Turks relieved much of the traditional source of security pressure that had existed here prior to 1699. It also created room for a Habsburg territorial enlargement that Russia, a fellow Christian power, could help exploit. At the same time, this process created vacuums that Russia itself might eventually be able to fill.

At the heart of this problem was the growing physical reality of Russian military strength in the region. After defeating Charles XII of Sweden and consolidating Russia's position in the north, Peter I diverted the bulk of the army to a southerly axis. Following an unsuccessful campaign in 1710–11, Russian forces launched a series of offensive wars that expelled the Turks from their fortresses on the northern rim of the Black Sea, seized Crimea, and began pressing down the sea's western coastline to Ottoman positions on the Danube. Already by the early eighteenth century, these exploits showed Russia's potential to conduct large, well-organized expeditions using Western military technology well beyond its traditional periphery and eventually become an ordering presence in Austria's backyard.

The fact of Russian strength constrained Habsburg strategic options for managing the southeast. The monarchy's own military limitations and diminishing returns of Balkan conquest meant that Austria was unlikely to be able to fill emerging Turkish vacuums to such an extent as to bar Russia's expansion, much less win in a sustained contest against Russia. At the same time, Austria could not simply let regional voids be filled by Russia alone. The speed of Russian conquests, if unchecked, could conceivably create a mammoth competitor bordering Austria from Poland to Serbia, thereby blocking future Austrian expansion to the mouth of the Danube. Sustained Russian proximity to the culturally and religiously similar Slavic population of Austria's Balkan territories was likely to present a greater challenge to Habsburg authority than the common enemy of Islam.[12] Should these factors lead to a diminution or ejection of Habsburg strength in the east, it could negatively affect the monarchy's prestige and strategic depth for dealing with problems in the west.

Eastern Strategies

Habsburg rulers recognized this dilemma. A meeting of the Privy Conference in 1711 concluded that "if the tsar is victorious he could throw himself into Turkish territory as far as the Danube and possibly force his way to Constantinople, an outcome much more menacing in its long-term consequences for Austria than even the most far-reaching Turkish victory."[13] From the early eighteenth century onward, the Habsburgs would debate three broad options for how to deal with this problem: unilateral extension of Habsburg power; cooperation with Russia to eject and supplant the Turks, and comanage the remnants of their rule; and support for the status quo and resistance to Russian encroachments.[14] Over the century that followed, all three alternatives would be attempted in different forms and combinations. The viability of each option at given moments in time would be a function of Austria's power position relative to that of its two eastern neighbors, and how they judged developments on this frontier to rank alongside priorities on the monarchy's frontiers in the west and north.

The Era of Mobile Field Armies: 1690s–1730s

In the opening decades of the eighteenth century, local conditions favored the first option: seeking to militarily shape the southeastern security environment to Austria's advantage. At this early stage, Ottoman weakness, as demonstrated by the scale of Habsburg territorial gains in the previous war and recent Turkish defeats at the hands of the Russians, presented an opportunity to consolidate the monarchy's enlarged position in the southeast. The prospects of gain seemed to outweigh the risks, either from the Ottoman military itself or Russian interference, which was foreseen but still on the horizon, and mainly restricted to the Sea of Azov and Dniester.

The strategy that evolved in response to this environment was shaped primarily by the desire to exploit areas of military advantage that Austria possessed as a result of the previous Turkish war along with its recent contests with Spain and France. Experiences in combat had revealed a considerable Habsburg tactical-technological edge over Turkish forces, rooted in the development of modern Austrian armies using Western equipment and fighting methods. As recently as 1697, Prince Eugene had demonstrated the decisive results that such forces could have against traditionally deployed Ottoman armies by inflicting a crushing defeat on the Turks at the Battle of Zenta that resulted in more than thirty thousand Ottoman casualties.

The early decades of the eighteenth century offered opportunities to repeat this victory. Ottoman forces of this period were equipped in similar fashion to their European rivals; indeed, Ottoman muskets and artillery were in some cases qualitatively superior to those found on the Habsburg side.[15] The Habsburg edge lay in the quantity of such weapons and how they were employed tactically. The first was a by-product of advantages in the Austrian system for procuring military technology. Traditionally, the Ottoman Empire had financed its wars through plunder—a system that required continual conquest to support the growth of the military establishment. While possessing the core of a standing army, the system supporting it was unstable and contingent on victory. The development of munitions in the Ottoman Empire was tightly controlled by government, and depended on a combination of arsenals and networks of skilled artisans, the latter of which were organized by guild and dominated by the Janissary corps, an elite but conservative military body that frequently opposed innovation.[16]

In Austria, by contrast, procurement was tied more heavily to military contractors, who had at their disposal a larger reservoir of artisanal talent, and access to the techniques and resources not only of the Erblände but also neighboring Bohemia and Italy. To this must be added the advantage of greater resources for war in Habsburg lands, which while deficient alongside many western rivals, compared favorably with the Turks. Efforts at bureaucratic centralization, and from 1714 onward, by the monarchy's acquisition of the Italian and Dutch lands, enabled a larger tax base and more powerful standing army. By the early 1700s, Habsburg revenue was already at least double that of the Ottoman Empire, where an astonishing 80 percent of revenues collected failed to ever reach the Treasury as a result of corruption and rent seeking.[17] Of those Ottoman funds raised for defense, a large portion went to the navy, while in Austria virtually all could be concentrated on the upgrading and up-keep of the army.

One result of these financial disparities was that while the quality of Turk-ish weapons may have been comparable or occasionally superior, Habsburg forces tended to go to war with both more numerous and higher-quality weap-ons. By the time of the Turkish wars of the early eighteenth century, Habsburg units had transitioned to the flintlock musket (*Flinte*), which fired faster and more reliably than previous matchlock and wheel lock pieces. The newer muskets also allowed for the widespread use of bayonets, which would not be widely used in Turkish armies for many decades.[18] By contrast, Ottoman armies were equipped with a mixture of European and traditional weapons. The total proportion of their armies equipped with modern firearms—the Janissaries, *sipahis* cavalry regiments, and artillery corps—typically made up only a third of the forces available for a campaign.[19] The bulk of the army would consist of private troops raised by the local governor and volunteer forces—both of which bore arms of varied make and quality.[20] Although re-forms in the late eighteenth century would raise these proportions and stan-dardize weaponry, for most of this period Habsburg forces were proportion-ally stronger in regular troops, with Janissaries still making up less than a third of the Ottoman Army at Peterwardein in 1716. Those Turkish units that did carry muskets were equipped with an array of different types. "Their weap-ons," an Austrian military memo noted, "lack a uniform caliber, causing balls to often get stuck in the breach; as a result, their supply is slow and their fire never lively."[21]

Another Austrian advantage was tactical, in how their weapons were used on the battlefield. Individually, Ottoman troops tended to be formidable fight-ers. As Archduke Charles wrote, "The Turk has a strongly constituted body: he is courageous and bold, and possesses a particular ability in the handling of his own arms. The horses of the Turkish cavalry are good; they possess a particular agility and rapidity."[22] Numerically, they tended to field larger armies than the Habsburgs, composed of different troop types from across the Ottoman Empire, and including everything from stock Anatolians to Persians, Egyptians, and Tatars. Their favored method of war was offensive, forming dense masses that charged headlong with Islamic banners waving and screaming, as Eugene put it, "their cursed yells of Allah! Allah! Allah!"[23] Austrian eyewitnesses frequently commented on the unnerving effects that such chants, coming from tens of thousands of advancing Ottoman soldiers, could have on their opponents.[24]

Despite such ferocity, Turkish armies suffered from a lack of discipline, which in turn undermined tactical handling and fire control. Ottoman attacks, though large, tended to be pell-mell and poorly coordinated. As Eugene said of the chaos in Turkish formations, "The second line [is] in the intervals of the first, and others in the third line [are] in the intervals of the second, and then, also, reserves [are thrown in] and their *saphis* on the wings."[25] A later Austrian source characterized these assaults as proceeding "without rule or order" (*ohne Regel, ohne Ordnung*), comparing them to the "pigs-head" (*Schweinskopf*) formations described in antiquity, in which the bravest fighters inevitably push to the forefront while the mass lingered behind them.[26] In a similar vein, Archduke Charles wrote that the Turks "attack in mixed groups of all types of troops, and each isolated man abandons himself to the sentiment of his force."[27]

By contrast, by the early eighteenth century, Habsburg armies were drilled to fight based on the western European model, in synchronized fashion by unit. From long experience on European battlefields, the infantry was trained to deliver controlled volleys on command. The resulting discipline translated into a tactical advantage that allowed Austrian armies, if well handled, to sustain rates of fire capable of repelling or even massacring massed charges of the kind favored by the Turks. "As the effort of several Turks acts neither to the same end, nor in the same manner," Charles noted, "they always fall against an enemy who opposes against them a unified mass acting cohesively. They rout with the same disorder and the same rapidity as they came up."[28]

The question of how to maximize these advantages against the Turks was intensely studied by Habsburg military men. In *Sulle Battaglie*, Montecuccoli advised Austrian commanders to abandon the defensive methods used on western battlefields and adopt an aggressive, tactically offensive mind-set. "If one had to do battle with the Turk," he wrote,

1. Pike battalions have to be extended frontally, more than has ever been the case before, so that the enemy cannot easily enclose them with his half-moon order.
2. Cavalry is intermingled with the infantry behind and opposite the intervals so that the foe ... would be exposed on both sides to the salvoes of the musketry.
3. One should advance directly against the Turk with one's line of battle, and one should not expect him to attack because, not being well-furnished with short-rage, defensive weapons, he does not

readily involve himself in a melee or willingly collide with his adversary.... Using the wings of his half-moon formation, it is also easy for him to approach and retire laterally....

4. Squadrons are constituted more massively than is ordinarily the case.

5. One stations a certain number of battalions and squadrons along the flanks of the battle line in order to guarantee security.[29]

Prince Eugene would adopt and expand on this template in later years, systematizing fire control, introducing uniform regimental drill, placing greater emphasis on the speed of deployment for plains warfare, and adopting defensive formations to allow small units greater flexibility in movement across broken terrain.[30]

The overarching goal of Austrian tactics in the south was to bring their greater firepower to bear while making provisions for the safety of flanks, which Turkish cavalry were expert at attacking. To account for Ottoman speed, Austrian commanders were to form their units in square formations not unlike those later used by colonial European forces against indigenous armies in Africa. As Charles observed,

The suppleness and rapidity of their horses permit their cavalry to profit from all openings in front or in flank and penetrate there. To give them no chance of doing it, one should thus form the infantry in square ... and not to put into lines anything save the cavalry which is equally rapid as their cavalry.... [Commanders should] form several squares, each one of two or three battalions strength at most. These squares constitute lines of battle as much in march as in position. One forms in the end some of these squares in checkerboard fashion, and from it one derives the great benefit of being able to mutually defend and support each other.[31]

So great was the risk of Turkish cavalry penetrating the flanks of these squares that Austrian units were to "camp and march always in squares," and when possible, protect these formations with *chevaux-de-frises* or so-called Spanish Riders—lances several yards long fitted with boar spears—to provide a thick hedge and keep irregular cavalry at bay while reloading.[32] As a further precaution, Austrian forces in the south were typically given a higher complement of cavalry (at times approaching 50 percent of field armies).

EUGENE'S OFFENSIVES

It was with these techniques that Habsburg forces took the field against the Turks in 1716. Leading them was the fifty-two-year-old Prince Eugene of Savoy. Raised among the French nobility and court of Louis XIV, Eugene had been rejected from the French Army and forced to leave Paris after a romantic controversy involving his mother and the king. Small in stature, he was a tenacious, creative, and offensive-minded general whose motto in war was "seize who can."[33] A veteran of the Turkish wars, Eugene's first combat experience had been as a twenty-year-old volunteer pursuing the Turks alongside the Polish hussars at the siege of Vienna in 1683, for which Leopold I had awarded him a regiment of dragoons. By the time of the 1716 war, Eugene was a seasoned senior field commander who had successfully led the armies of Austria and the Holy Roman Empire in three wars and more than a dozen major battles.

The immediate cause of the war was a conflict between the Ottoman Empire and Venice, the latter of which was bound by defensive alliance to Austria. Strategically, however, the incident offered a rare opportunity to strengthen Habsburg security in the southeast at a moment when Austria's armies were not tied up in fighting in western theaters. Eugene's war aims, as outlined by the Privy Conference, were twofold. First, he was to secure Habsburg control of the Danube down to Vidin, thus closing the Banat salient and restricting the Turks to a second line of fortresses at Giurgiu-Babadag-Ismail, and by doing so, impose a diplomatic settlement making Wallachia and Moldavia de facto buffer states. As the emperor communicated to him, it was critical to establish these provinces as client states (*unser tributär erhalten*).[34]

While tactically offensive, Eugene's overarching strategic objective was defensive: to round off and buy breathing room for the territories acquired in the previous war. This was particularly important with regard to the final, as-yet-unconquered part of Hungary, the Banat, without which strategic communications between Habsburg possessions in Croatia and Transylvania were severed. In the ensuing campaign, Eugene inflicted crushing defeats on the Turks. Going into the war less than two years after the conclusion of the Spanish succession struggle, he was able to draw on a large reservoir of seasoned veterans from campaigns in Italy and Germany. Using the Danube as a supply artery, he bypassed Belgrade, a major Ottoman fortress holding the key to southeastern lines of communication, and instead chose to seek out and destroy the main Ottoman army. This he intercepted in late summer at Peterwardein under the personal command of the grand vizier, and despite possessing numerically inferior forces, inflicted a decisive defeat from which barely a third of the Turkish Army escaped.[35] In the months that followed, he consolidated this victory by taking Ottoman fortresses at Timisoara, in the Banat, and most notably, in Belgrade.

Eugene's military victories would not have been possible without prior Habsburg diplomacy. The key to his victories was the ability to concentrate Austria's limited military forces, which had only occurred because Austria did not have to worry about maintaining large troop concentrations on other frontiers while fighting in the south. This was made possible by preparatory diplomacy, which had begun years before the war, when Habsburg diplomats worked to ensure that a war in this theater would not occur until the timing was militarily favorable to the monarchy.

The foundation to this diplomacy had been efforts to prevent the breakout of conflict too early—most notably, at the high point of the Spanish succession war, when Charles XII invaded Saxony with forty thousand troops, raising the threat of intervention to support Silesian Protestants or even alongside Protestant Hungarian rebels against Vienna. With the Erblände naked to attack from this quarter, Joseph I used what amounted to preemptive appeasement at Altranstädt to buy peace with Charles by recognizing Sweden's candidate to the Polish throne, ceding German land and even making concessions to the Protestants in Silesia in exchange for avoiding Austrian entanglement in the Great Northern War.[36] The following year a similar problem loomed in the south, when tensions with the Porte threatened to open a new front in the war after several Ottoman merchants were killed in a border incident at Kecskemet. Faced with the prospect of a Turkish declaration of war at a moment when Habsburg forces were pinned down on the Po and Rhine, Joseph I used a combination of bribery at the sultan's court and compensation for Turkish damages to buy peace.[37] Again in 1709, the passage of Sweden's Charles XII into Ottoman protection following his defeat by the Russians threatened to bring the Turks into the war. This time Austria responded by rallying its western allies against the Swedes, issuing a war threat to Turkey and creating a new northern corps under Eugene to deter attack.[38] In both instances, the Habsburgs were able to avoid war with the Ottomans at an inconvenient moment for their broader strategic interests.

A similar mixture of accommodation and force had been used to ensure that Eugene would not have to worry during his campaigns about problems from the Hungarians. From 1703 to 1711, Magyar kuruc raiders under the rebel prince Rákóczi had waged a relentless irregular war against Austrian positions in Hungary, momentarily even threatening the Habsburg capital.[39] In order to concentrate force in the western theater, Austrian diplomats in 1706 brokered a temporary armistice that allowed Eugene to focus attention on his operations in Italy, without granting the scale of constitutional concessions sought by the rebels.[40] After achieving victory in the west, the Habsburgs were able to use a "surge" of cavalry into Hungary to defeat the rebels and force a favorable peace. The resulting Treaty of Szatmar (1711) was a showpiece of Habsburg diplomacy, mixing threats (as Joseph I said when threatened by a resumption of kuruc raids, "tell them bluntly that we 'could do even worse'") and magnanimity with pardons for rebel leaders and a guarantee of Hungary's historic liberties.[41] This peace proved durable. As a result, by the time Eugene began preparing for military operations four years later, he was not troubled by the prospect of Hungarian uprisings along his lines of communication and was even able to employ former kuruc rebels in his army.

These earlier preparations helped make possible a sharp, successful war. Charles VI had explicitly requested that the campaign be short, instructing Eugene to achieve a "quick and glorious peace"—partly to avoid creating an opening for crises (*große Unruhen*) on other frontiers, and partly to ensure that any lands won could be secured rapidly and without foreign interference (*ohne Mediation*).[42] The need for a speedy outcome was heightened by growing signs of conflict in Italy, where Spain's Philip V sought to take advantage of Austria's distraction in the Balkans to launch an attack on Sicily. As the Turkish war drew to a close, the Spanish challenge was forcing Eugene to siphon off regiments from the Balkans, leading him to lament that "two wars cannot be waged with one army."[43] While Eugene used the opening of negotiations with the Turks at Passarowitz to consolidate Austria's new gains in the southeast and free up military resources for the west, Charles struck an agreement with Britain and France renouncing his claims to the Spanish throne in exchange for military cooperation against Philip. These measures helped to avoid a protracted two-front emergency. As negotiations wrapped up with the Ottomans, Charles rejoiced to Eugene that "our hands are now free to deal with those who want to chew on us [elsewhere]."[44]

The physical scale of Eugene's victory over the Turks was immense. In the concluding Peace of Passarowitz, Austria absorbed, *uti possidetis*, all the ground that its armies held at the time that hostilities ceased, or a total of some thirty thousand square miles of new territory. The addition of these large spaces bolstered Habsburg security in the southeast. Per Eugene's advice to "expand following the lay of the land," Austria absorbed the Banat, closing the gap between its defenses in Croatia-Slavonia and Transylvania. The war also enhanced the size and status of the monarchy's regional buffers, placing northern Serbia and Little Wallachia under Habsburg rule, while designating Wallachia, Moldavia, and Poland under Article I as intermediary bodies: "Distinguished and separated as anciently by the Mountains, in such manner that the Limits of the ancient Confines may be unchangeably observed on all sides."[45]

Passarowitz was a high-water mark for Habsburg power in the Balkans. But it would not last. In the years that followed, Austria's ability to shape the southern frontier through unilateral military action evaporated as a result of two changes—one military in nature, the other geopolitical.

First, Eugene died. The extent to which Austria's spectacular battlefield victories had been the result of the prince's talents became dramatically apparent when the next Austro-Turkish war broke out in 1737–39.[46] The parallels with the 1716–18 war are striking. As before, Habsburg officials favored the timing for military action because of the recent end of a conflict in the west (the Polish succession war) and thus recent relative quiescence on other fronts.[47]

As their predecessors had done prior to 1716, Habsburg diplomats successfully labored to create the conditions for an exclusive focus on the Balkan frontier before going to war. Also like the previous war, Habsburg forces set out to win a short war using mobile field armies. Echoing its earlier instructions to Eugene, the Privy Conference insisted that "the war last but one campaigning season."[48] And as before, the strategic goal was largely defensive: to consolidate and round off Austria's holdings along the central Danube axis while expanding Austrian influence in the buffer territories of Wallachia and Moldavia.

Without Eugene at the helm, though, Austria quickly found that it was no longer able to rely on rapid strikes to secure its security objectives in the southeast. Poorly led and suffering from the years of neglected military spending that Eugene had so often predicted would lead to catastrophe, Habsburg forces suffered defeats at Banja Luka and Belgrade. In the ensuing Treaty of Belgrade (1739), Austria was forced to disgorge most of its gains from Passarowitz. While using many of the same tactics as in the previous war, Habsburg generalship was weaker, the army had lost its fighting edge, and the Ottomans themselves had incorporated lessons from past wars, adopting improved technology in both small arms and artillery with the help of foreign military advisers.

The second, far-larger change to conditions in the southeast, however, came as a result of geopolitical developments elsewhere. In the year after the war ended, Austria was invaded from the north by the armies of Frederick II of Prussia, setting off what would become an almost forty-year life-or-death struggle for the Habsburg Monarchy.

The Era of Appeasement: 1740s–70s

With virtually all its military resources pulled northward, Austria would not be able to devote the attention to the Balkans that it had in prior decades. But this did not mean that it had no strategic needs in the southeast or could ignore this frontier. Border raiding continued, and the possibility of a Turkish renewal of hostilities to expand on its recent victories had to be taken into account. Russia, too, continued its expansion down the Black Sea coastline. However bad things might get in the north, these dynamics would have to be monitored—and managed. Above all, Austria needed to avoid a Turkish invasion from the south while its armies were detained in Bohemia. And if possible, it needed to recruit Russia's active help against Prussia.

For these purposes, the Habsburg Monarchy developed a strategy quite different, but no less effective, than the one it had used to expand offensively under Eugene. Instead of mobile field armies, it would rely on appeasement to engage and placate eastern enemies, undergirded by frontier defenses to deter conflict and keep the Balkan frontier quiet without sacrificing ground in its longer-term regional position.

As we will see in chapter 6, Austria's fight with Prussia in the years between 1740 and 1779 was a bitter contest that would at one point threaten the very life of the monarchy. The severity and length of these wars not only demanded that Austria deprioritize its southern flank but also be able to redirect as many resources as possible from this sector without compromising security there. To support these goals, Vienna pursued policies of proactive engagement with its rivals in this theater throughout the middle years of the eighteenth century. Collectively, these efforts would amount to an almost forty-year strategy of détente in the Balkans, the key pillars of which were appeasement with the Turks, accommodation with the Hungarians, and a defensive alliance with Russia.

The first of these was especially important. The end to hostilities in the 1739 Turkish war, coming barely a year before Frederick II's invasion of Silesia, left open the possibility of renewed hostilities with the Porte. Given the recent poor performance of Austrian forces and the lingering tension in many sectors of the border, it was not inconceivable that the Turks, emboldened by their recent recapture of Belgrade, would use Austria's plight in the north as an opening to seize territory—a prospect that Austria's enemies, particularly France, actively encouraged through aggressive diplomacy inciting the Turks to attack.

The Habsburg response to this threat was a diplomatic offensive as determined and creative in its use of the arts of persuasion as Eugene's campaigns had been in the art of force. At the official level, Austrian diplomats worked to remove sources of friction, taking less than two years—an astonishingly short period by Balkan standards—to resolve disputes left over from the previous war. Much as Austrian diplomats had massaged Turkish court politics to keep the Ottomans from entering the Spanish succession war, their successors now used similar techniques on a larger scale to deactivate tensions over a period that would stretch from the first clashes of the War of the Austrian Succession in 1740 to the end of the Seven Years' War in 1763.

The architects of these successes were now-forgotten Austrian diplomats stationed in Constantinople. One was Heinrich Christoph Penkler, who assiduously manipulated court dynamics to avoid war. Acting on Vienna's admonition that a war with the Turks "would be the worst thing that could happen to our court and therefore we must do all we can to turn aside this misfortune," Penkler outmaneuvered his French and Prussian counterparts, using intrigue, bribery, and propaganda to discourage Ottoman alignments with Austria's enemies.[49] One example of his techniques was the well-timed leaking of the details of the latest Austro-Russian treaty to defuse the threat of Turkey turning its attention north after putting down a rebellion in its Persian provinces.[50] Through these efforts, Penkler was able to not only project a greater image of Austrian strength than actually existed but also successfully solicit an Ottoman condemnation of Frederick II's invasion and extension of the conditions of peace under the Treaty of Belgrade.[51] In a subsequent contest with Prussian diplomats from 1756 to 1762, Penkler's successor, Josef Peter von Schwachheim, used similar methods to forestall a concerted Prussian attempt at enticing the Turks into a formal alliance.

Austria's success in Ottoman internal diplomacy was the result of centuries of experience navigating the complex politics of the sultan's court. Key to this mastery was the cultivation, through bribery and favors, of local intelligence through which to not only divine the sultan's intentions but assess and manipulate the factions among his chief ministers, too. Using these knowledge networks, Austria was able to construct a kind of "early warning system" that told it when rival diplomats' efforts at agitation were succeeding, and just as important, when the Ottomans were more concerned with problems on their other frontiers. The ultimate testimony to the success of this diplomacy came from Austria's archenemy, Frederick, who commented that "the Viennese court knows the Turks better" than their adversaries.[52]

HUNGARIAN ACCOMMODATION

A renewal of Ottoman hostilities was only one of the ways that Austria's southeastern frontier could complicate its focus on the north in the wars with Prussia; another was an eruption of problems in Hungary. The destructive impact that Magyar uprisings could have on wider Habsburg interests at times of emergency had been shown in the Spanish succession war, when raids by Rákóczi's kuruc cavalry had forced the Austrians to construct fortified lines and entrenchments on the outskirts of Vienna and siphon off troops from other fronts to protect the Erblände.[53]

Conditions were ripe for a repeat of such disturbances at the outset of the War of the Austrian Succession, as Austria faced attacks from Prussia, France, and Bavaria. Her susceptibility to Hungarian trouble on this occasion was arguably even greater than in the Spanish war, since Britain's initial refusal to provide subsidies and Russia's distraction with a Swedish war deprived Austria of the extent of allied help that it had enjoyed before.[54] The war also came at a sensitive political moment with Maria Theresa's accession to the throne, which would require ratification and coronation by the Hungarian Diet. The Magyar nobility frequently used such moments of transition to register new demands on and extract fresh concessions from a new monarch. These dynamics gave Hungarians the upper hand at the same time that the external situation created a greater strategic need not only for the Habsburgs to ensure tranquil conditions in Hungary but also to find military resources here to contribute to aid in the overall struggle.

Maria Theresa's approach to dealing with this dynamic replicated the tactics of earlier Habsburg monarchs in their use of accommodation to dampen the embers of separatism and motivate voluntary Hungarian support. While her armies waged war in Bohemia and her diplomats sought to appease the Turks, Maria Theresa engaged in a personal charm offensive with the Hungarian Diet. In exchange for affirming Hungary's historic rights and reconfirming Hungary's separate administrative status within the monarchy, the empress was able to not only secure Hungarian support for succession but also extract promises of four million florins and thirty thousand Hungarian troops under the *generalis insurrectio* (general levee).

Like her forebears Leopold I and Joseph I, Maria Theresa was careful in these barters not to give away too much constitutional ground, restricting her concessions to provisions that could be rescinded to Hungary's disadvantage if future circumstances dictated. Through these efforts, she was able to "flip" Hungary from a source of potential military concern to an active contributor to the monarchy's defense. While a portion of the diet's troop pledges were never fulfilled, the far more important gain from Maria Theresa's efforts, from an Austrian strategic perspective, was the successful avoidance of what could have become an *additional*, internal military front at a time when all of the monarchy's resources needed to be focused on a supreme crisis elsewhere.

RESTRAINING RUSSIA

While appeasing Turkey and accommodating the Hungarians, Austria needed to find a way to deal with its other potential problem in the east: Russia. Here, it had something to build on. As with the Hungarians and Turks, Austria had worked to lay a foundation for future détentes with Russia in earlier years, forming a bilateral anti-Turkish alliance in 1697 and toying with the idea again in 1710 on the suggestion of Eugene as an expedient for forestalling Swedish-Hungarian flirtations. A new pact was formed in 1726, which led to Habsburg participation in the Austro-Turkish War of 1737–39.

As Austria struggled against Prussia, it now needed such an alliance not to check the Swedes or widen gains against the Turks but rather to prevent Russia from stirring up conflicts in the south that would derail Austria's overall strategy. More than that, it needed to mobilize Russia as an *active* military partner against Prussia. This goal was forestalled at the start of the Austrian succession war by conflicts in the Baltic with Sweden that prevented Russia from providing meaningful aid to its ally at the height of crisis.

As we will see, the effort to ensure greater Russian involvement against Prussia would become a driving force for Habsburg diplomacy under Kaunitz, second in importance only to recruiting France out of Frederick's orbit. The centerpiece was a defensive alliance, constructed by Kaunitz, committing the two empires to mutual aid against attacks by Prussia or Turkey, with a secret clause to repatriate Silesia and territorially weaken Prussia. In the ensuing Seven Years' War, Russia acted as a reliable Habsburg ally, sending a relief army to link up with Habsburg forces at Kunersdorf in a battle that would set a precedent for later, numerous Russian military interventions on Austria's behalf, including most notably in 1805 and 1849.

FRONTIER DEFENSES

As impressive as Habsburg diplomacy was at appeasing eastern rivals, the monarchy still needed to be able to show military strength on its southeastern frontier. Even amid the wars of the north, internecine border raids, an ancient feature of the Balkans, continued. More important, the placatory diplomacy that Austria used with neighboring rivals depended for its effectiveness on the assumption that the distracted monarchy was still a military factor in the region. To succeed in its overall strategy of deprioritizing the Balkan frontier, Austria therefore needed to be able to maintain baseline security here, and if diplomacy failed, have the means to deter or defeat attacks.

In both tasks, the Habsburgs were aided by the presence of extensive and well-planned defenses along their empire's southern and eastern approaches. Their backbone was the Militärgrenze, or Military Border, an integrated defensive system that would eventually stretch across the full length of the frontier, from the Adriatic to the Carpathians. The Military Border had its roots in the medieval Kingdom of Hungary, which from the fourteenth century onward had organized the Croatian-Slavonian frontier (the Vojna Krajina) into a series of interdependent forts, supported by a *militia portalis* under the control of the Ban of Croatia, a Hungarian client.[55] As the Ottomans penetrated northward, nearby Austrian lands became comanagers of these defenses, supplying money and troops to ensure their maintenance as Hungary gradually collapsed.

By the late sixteenth century, with most of Hungary in Turkish hands, the remnants of the Military Border formed a ragged bulwark protecting the southern approaches to the Erblände and city of Vienna. "Th[is] system of fortresses," a military appraisal in 1577 told the emperor, "is the only means by which your Majesty will be able to contain the power and the advance of the enemy, and behind which Your countries and peoples will be secure."[56] Keeping these defenses in good working order was therefore a high priority for the Habsburg state, and the origins of the Hofkriegsrat lay in the need to create an institution capable of ensuring their proper supply and administration.

To defend the Military Border, the Habsburgs continued the practice, begun by the Hungarians, of recruiting soldier-settlers from the displaced Christian populations of nearby Ottoman territories.[57] To attract these colonists, the Habsburg Monarchy offered incentives that included land, arms, tax exemptions, and religious tolerance in exchange for military service and loyalty to the emperor. Using these allurements, the Austrians were able to attract large numbers of Orthodox Serbs, Croats, Szeklers, and Wallachs to permanently resettle their families in fortified villages, known as *zadruga*, on the frontier. Administered directly from the Hofkriegsrat, the zadruga were encouraged to maintain high birth rates and operated according to a strict frontier legal. Self-selecting, motivated, and martial, the Balkan colonists provided a cheap and abundant source of military manpower well versed in the irregular "small war" (*Kleinkrieg*) techniques of the Balkans. "The *Grenzer* [are] a warlike people," one Austrian military observer wrote, "so proud of [their] military status that the men retain their muskets and side arms even when they are attending Holy Mass."[58]

Following the acquisition of new lands in 1699, the Habsburgs expanded the Military Border southward to the new frontier on the Sava, Danube, Tisza, and Maros Rivers. They reorganized it into two main geographic clusters: one along the Slavonian border and centered on the fortresses at Brod and Esseg, and a second along the boundary with Serbia, centered on fortresses at Szeged and Arad on the Tisza-Maros line. In later years, the border would be pushed further eastward into Transylvania following the acquisition of the Banat (see figures 5.3–5.4).[59] It would eventually form one of the densest concentrations of military personnel in Europe, with one in ten males under arms by the late seventeenth century, and one in three by the later eighteenth century.[60]

The enlarged Military Border had three main components (see figure 5.5).

Fortresses. At the outer edge stood a line of large fortresses, with a second row some 150 to 200 miles behind them in the interior. The forward fortresses included both updated medieval forts and newer structures, and were usually located at strategic sites on the terrain, such as bends in the river, known invasion routes, or commanding heights above the frontier. They were equipped with heavy artillery capable of dominating the nearby countryside and staffed not by Grenzers but rather German regulars.

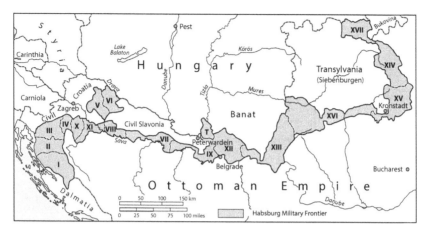

FIG. 5.3. Map of the Habsburg Military Border, ca. 1780.
Source: Center for European Policy Analysis, 2017.

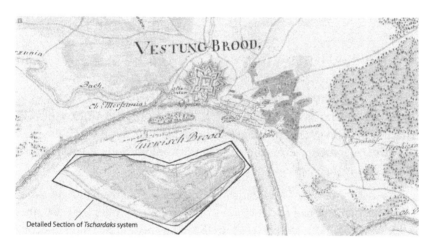

FIG. 5.4. Detailed Section of Military Frontier. *Source:* Gabor Timar, Gabor Molnar, Balazs
Szekely, Sandor Biszak, Jozsef Varga, and Annamaria Janko, *The Map Sheets of the Second
Military Survey and their Georeferenced Version* (Budapest: Arcanum, 2006).

Watchtowers. Between the forward row of fortresses stood a network of
watchtowers, placed at intervals of about a mile and a half. Known as
Tschardaks—also called *çardaks, ardaci, eardaci,* or *chartaques*—these were
two-stories-high wooden huts, usually accompanied by a small trench or pal-
isade to obstruct access to its base. Towers of this kind had a long history as
frontier posts going back to antiquity and were not unlike the wooden structures placed at intervals along the Roman *limes*.[61] The Habsburgs had used

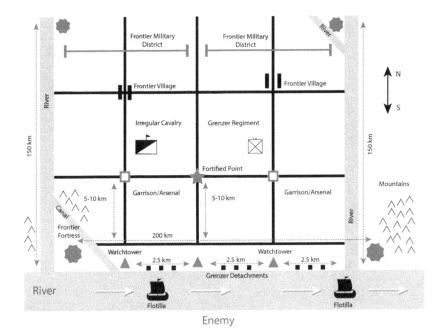

FIG. 5.5. Diagram of the Habsburg Military Border, ca. 1780.
Source: Center for European Policy Analysis, 2017.

these for centuries, not only in the south, but occasionally in the west.[62] The Tschardaks of the Military Border were guarded at all hours by Grenzer detachments that rotated every few days. A nineteenth-century English traveler described one such post and its guards as follows:

> The sentry-house or Tschardak stood on the height immediately overlooking the sands. It had two divisions, one for the watch-fire, and the other for the soldiers to sleep in. Before this little shed, under the projecting roof, the men had piled their arms. There were six or seven soldiers at the Tschardak, and their dress like their political constitution was half military and half peasant-like. Over the usual peasant's frock they wore knapsacks, fastened to a leathern strap. Their legs were wrapped in linen or woolen cloths, and their feet covered with those sandals . . . common to most Eastern Slavonian nations. . . . No soldiers remain more than seven days together at a sentry post; they are then relieved by six or seven others, who likewise remain a week. Every soldier spends ninety days of the year on guard at these places.[63]

The spacing of the Tschardaks, never more than a thirty- or forty-five-minute walk apart, meant that if assaulted, a post could depend on rapid support from nearby towers.[64] This spacing also allowed for visual communication, mainly through the use of signal fires, which when lit in succession down the length of the frontier could be used to rapidly alert nearby fortresses to an approaching attack.

Logistical infrastructure. A carefully planned support network sustained the Military Border. Connecting the Tschardaks and fortresses were communication roads that ran adjacent to the river and into the interior. Behind the frontier, at intervals of five or ten miles, were strategically located depots and magazines as well as the various zadrugas, sited in easy reach of the border to respond to a crisis. Maintenance of this infrastructure was a high priority well into the nineteenth century. "It is a no less agreeable surprise to the traveler coming from Hungary, or still more from Turkey," the English traveler wrote, "to observe the good state of the roads and bridges in the Military Frontier."[65]

All three components—forts, watchtowers, and infrastructure—were organized into separate districts, each corresponding to a Grenzer regiment, which in turn was split between piquet troops assigned to Tschardaks, and a reserve of infantry and irregular cavalry assembled into mobile frontier units. These were augmented by flotillas of gunboats that patrolled the river between the fortresses.

DETERRENCE AND DEFENSE

The Military Border supported Austria's goal of safely deprioritizing the southern frontier during the Prussian wars in several ways. First, it dealt effectively with raiding. A permanent feature of Balkan life, border raids varied in scale, and usually involved nighttime attacks across the river to steal livestock, other valuables, and women. These raids were more than simply an irritant. Unchecked, they could pull in army units desperately needed in the north. As both the War of the Spanish Succession and War of the Polish Succession had shown, border incidents could escalate to major crises that threatened to inflame Austro-Turkish relations. By stationing local troops familiar with raiding techniques directly on the frontier, the Military Border provided an effective, inexpensive means of repelling these low-intensity attacks and launching counterraids. Indeed, as late as 1764, the Hofkriegsrat considered 7,000 of such troops to be more than adequate for dealing with "Tatar adventurism" at a moment when it was preparing to deploy 130,000 against Prussia.[66]

Second, the network of large fortresses around which the border was built helped to deter larger attacks by the main Ottoman army. To be sure, for much of the period of Austria's wars with Frederick II, the Turks were uninterested in launching an invasion, being detained by internal crises in other parts of their far-flung empire. Habsburg diplomats like Penkler were able to monitor these developments through their intelligence networks. At the same time, attempts by rival diplomats to incite the Turks to open a second front were determined and ongoing. While well informed, Habsburg diplomats could never be sure of the extent to which these efforts were succeeding. The ability to point to Austria's well-planned and provisioned southern fortresses provided a valuable counterweight to their bribes and blandishments.

Relatedly, the Military Border helped to discourage mischief by the Hungarians. Already in 1672 and 1678, the Grenzers had shown their value in suppressing kuruc revolts.[67] In reorganizing the border after Karlowitz, Emperor Leopold had sought to strengthen this function, barring the Magyars from oversight of or participation in border units.[68] In the Spanish succession war, the Grenzer had helped to deal with Hungarian insurrections—a role they would play again in 1848–49.[69] The presence of loyal troops in situ on the frontier demonstrated that the monarchy had options, even amid the wars in the north, for dealing with local uprisings, thereby placing a stick alongside the carrots that Maria Theresa used to entice the Magyar nobility into helping against Prussia.

The third and perhaps greatest contribution of the border in this era was the aid that it provided to the Habsburg war effort in the north. While holding down the frontier with minimal force, the Grenzers were able to feed large numbers of troops into the battles raging in Bohemia and Moravia for a fraction of the cost that would have been required to field this number of regular units.[70] As we will see in chapter 6, the Kleinkrieg raiding techniques of Grenzer troops would prove a crucial component in Austrian military strategy against the Prussians.

The Era of Alliances of Restraint: 1770s–1800s

Austria's policies of appeasement and accommodation, backed by the defenses of the Military Border, allowed it to manage the southeastern frontier at minimal cost and stay focused on northern crises from the time of Frederick's first invasion in 1740 until the last standoff with his armies in 1778–79. This approach succeeded in both its principal aims, avoiding the opening of a second front and roping Russia into efforts against Prussia.

During this period, however, geopolitical dynamics in the south had evolved in other ways that were not favorable to Habsburg interests. Most important, Russia continued to grow in strength as a Balkan power. As Austria dealt with Prussia, Russian armies continued their encroachments into Ottoman positions along the coasts of the Black Sea. In 1768, a new czarina, Catherine II, launched Russia's most ambitious southeastern gambit to date, sending offensive armies across the Dniester that crushed the primary Ottoman fortress at Kotyn and clawed their way down the Moldavian Plain. Within a few months they had captured the capitals of both Moldavia (Jassy) and Wallachia (Bucharest). From here, they then penetrated even deeper into Ottoman territory, eventually reaching positions that were 373 miles from their starting points.

The scale of Russian successes showed the extent of the Ottoman Empire's decline as well as Russia's ability to devour large swaths of Balkan territory without Habsburg help. At the war's end, Austria faced a radically altered situation on its southeastern flank. In place of the old landscape of rickety Ottoman outposts with diminishing military potential and decentralized local rule, there now stood a well-armed and acquisitive Russia, backed by a large military force on the River Bug and fleets at Azov and Crimea, capable of projecting power throughout the Black Sea region. Where Russia had previously been constrained mainly to the northern coastlines of this sea, its offensives down the coastline placed it near the mouth of the Danube and thus astride the main axis of Austria's traditional path of eastern expansion.

This new reality posed two serious problems for Austria. First, Russian advances threatened the continued existence of regional buffer zones. From the beginning of the century, the maintenance of these intermediary bodies—in the north, Poland, and in the south, Wallachia and Moldavia, or the so-called Danubian Principalities—had been a central objective of Habsburg strategy. Ensuring the independent status of the latter two provinces had been an explicit goal of both Eugene's 1716 campaign and the unsuccessful 1737 war. The treaties that followed both wars had dealt with the question of their status in their opening paragraphs, with the Karlowitz text stipulating that Wallachia, Moldavia, and nearby Podolia be preserved intact "by observing the ancient boundaries of both sides, [which] shall not be extended on either side."[71]

The existence of these buffer territories produced significant strategic advantages for Austria. By ensuring, as Kaunitz later wrote, that Habsburg territories were "not directly adjacent" to the territories of large military rivals, they helped to avoid disagreements that could escalate into war.[72] This in turn relieved part of the burden of frontier defense, obviating the need for a large, standing security presence on long stretches of the eastern periphery. As a result, the monarchy could safely concentrate its scarce military resources elsewhere, which as recent events with Prussia had shown was a vital necessity in wartime.

By endangering these spaces, Russian expansion therefore undermined a keystone of Austria's entire southeastern strategy. While the 1768 war had left the Danubian Principalities nominally intact under Turkish rule, the terms of the concluding treaty (Küçük Kaynarca) granted Russia the ability in the future to intervene here and elsewhere as "protector" to all Christians living in Ottoman territories. Concurrently, Russian inroads in Poland, now in a state of growing internal chaos, were growing.

Second, Russia's aggressive moves in the east complicated Habsburg strategy at the European level. Austria needed to maintain viable buffers, which meant resisting Russian moves. But it also needed Russia to participate as an active ally against Austria's archenemy Prussia in the west. The two goals were incompatible. If it chose the latter—the natural choice given the degree of threat posed by Prussia—it would come at the expense of the buffers, which over time could create sources of tension in Austro-Russian relations that could either lead to the loss of Russia as an ally against Prussia or war with Russia itself over the east.

COURTING TURKEY, SPLITTING POLAND

Austria's initial approach to handling this dilemma was to try to balance against and thus check Russian expansion through alignment with the Ottomans. The fact that Habsburg diplomats were willing to contemplate such a move with the monarchy's historic Muslim archenemy shows the degree to which they were concerned about Russia's growing strength as the organizing security problem on the southern frontier. "To save our archenemy," Kaunitz wrote, "is rather extraordinary, and such decisions can be justified only in truly critical situations, such as self-preservation."[73] While admitting that Habsburg policy would have to strike a careful balance between the two powers, Maria Theresa was unhappy at the thought of striking a deal with a non-Christian state, noting in January 1771,

> I have determined that the situation is that the Turks are the aggressors, that the Russians have always demonstrated the greatest respect for us, that they are Christians, that they must deal with an unjust war, all while we are now considering supporting the Turks. All of this and other reasons have convinced me not to engage the Russians.... I must add that I would be even less capable of siding with the Russians in expelling and exterminating the Turks. Both of these points are non-negotiable and, accordingly, one must determine the necessary disciplinary measures [against Russia].[74]

Tilting toward the Turks to contain the growth of Russian influence, Vienna entered into the so-called Austro-Turkish alliance of July 6, 1771, promising to resist further Russian aggression against the sultan in exchange for monetary and territorial remuneration.[75] Much like Kaunitz's earlier alignment with archenemy France to contain Prussia, the move represented a reversal of long-standing Habsburg policy in order to deal with a near-term threat. To give substance to the new posture, the monarchy deployed forces to the eastern frontier, shifting troops from Italy and the Netherlands to Transylvania, directly across the border from the Russian forces staged in Wallachia.

These moves were ultimately a calculated bluff: Austria had neither the financial nor military strength to sustain a conflict with Russia. Nor, in contrast to its earlier alliance with France, could it hope to obtain much in the way of a lasting strategic benefit from partnership with the teetering Ottoman state against a Russia whose friendship the monarchy needed for sustaining the military competition with Prussia. Within less than a year after it was formed, the Austro-Ottoman treaty was jettisoned as Vienna's attention turned from the principalities to the adjacent territories of Poland, where by 1771 both Prussia and Russia were actively looking to gain new advantages and territory. To a certain extent, the firmer stance adopted by Austria over the Danubian Principalities, by heightening the danger of a wider European crisis, had contributed to the reorientation of attention northward.

Unlike the principalities, Poland did not involve Ottoman interests, and represented a potential locus for at least short-term cooperation between the Russian, Prussian, and Austrian empires. But the prospect of partitioning the giant territories of the long crisis-plagued commonwealth, by now a subject of active discussion between Frederick II and Catherine II, presented a significant strategic problem for Austria.[76] For decades, Austria had sought to maintain the Polish Commonwealth as a buffer state to absorb and reduce conflict on its eastern borders. Over a century earlier, in 1656, it had successfully resisted an attempt by Sweden and Brandenburg as well as Lithuanian and Ukrainian separatists to partition the already internally tumultuous giant.[77] Continuing this policy, in the War of the Polish Succession, Austria had worked to prevent the insertion of a Bourbon-backed candidate for the Polish throne and thus forestall the spread of French influence in the region. Throughout these contests, the Habsburg aim was to preserve an eastern glacis in which Austria maintained a vital influence alongside other competing powers while avoiding the extremes of domination by a hostile power, or increased direct responsibility that would be the result of state failure and collapse.

This delicate balancing act, long a mainstay of Austria's eastern policies, was now threatened by the grim prospect of a partition in which peer competitors Prussia and Russia would obtain not only large swaths of Polish territory and resources but also a more commanding strategic position from which to threaten the monarchy's northern and eastern frontiers. From a Habsburg perspective, partition was the "least favorable" outcome—a view that Maria Theresa in particular, but initially Joseph II and to a somewhat lesser extent Kaunitz, all shared.[78] But the alternatives of either a major European war or Russo-Prussian partition excluding Austria were even more problematic, especially given the monarchy's financial position. Choosing the least-bad option, in 1772 Austria joined in what would ultimately be the first of three Polish partitions between the three eastern empires. In the first of these, she acquired some 31,600 square miles of territory and 2.65 million inhabitants in the palatinates of Rus, Sandomierz, and Cracow (except for the city itself), which were collectively renamed the Kingdom of Galicia-Lodomeria in commemoration of their earlier, sixteenth-century title and status under the Hungarian Crown.[79] In addition, Austria received a portion of the Bukovina—a small but strategic territory that provided a land bridge between Galicia and Transylvania and a promontory from which to monitor future Russian moves on Moldavia.

Once it became clear that Austria would participate in the partition, Habsburg leaders faced the question of how and to what extent to integrate the Polish territories into the monarchy. In keeping with past Austrian practice, Kaunitz preferred to avoid the full incorporation and thus full cost of managing Galicia. Instead, he envisioned the new territory becoming a semi-independent appendage, whose subjects retained a high degree of autonomy and were permitted to show at least nominal obedience in domestic matters to the Polish Diets. Such a Poland would act as both a glacis to future Russian or Prussian expansion and an entry point through which to funnel Austrian influence into the rest of Poland. As a model, Kaunitz looked to the Austrian Netherlands and Duchy of Milan, both of which were administered by the foreign ministry, and neither of which "had any 'existential' significance for the Monarchy."[80] By contrast, Joseph II argued forcefully that Galicia should be fully incorporated into Austria's core territories as an integral component of the Habsburg state.

The disagreement between Kaunitz and Joseph about Galicia's fate was reflective of the larger debate in Habsburg grand strategy after the end of the Prussian wars—between the desire to maximize security through the maintenance of an expanded army, backed by the resources of a large, consolidated state whose resources were calculatingly leveraged for war, and a more traditionally Habsburg reliance on buffer states, allies, and carefully regulated balances abroad. It also reflected a tension, inherent in the monarchy's composition, of requiring space, and hence expansion, to be able to keep pace with expanding rivals, but facing steep internal obstacles to fully ingesting and benefiting from the resources obtained through expansion. As we will see, this tension would only grow stronger in later decades with the emergence of nationalism, and the debate between Kaunitz and Joseph about Galicia would play out in more dramatic form in debates between Metternich and Francis I about the fate of Austrian possessions in Italy.

RESTRAINING RUSSIA

The First Polish Partition demonstrated the growing dilemma facing Austria in the east. It could not merely concede ground to what was becoming an inexorable process of Russian expansion. Yet nor could it resist Russia outright and expect to succeed, given this state's growing power capabilities and Austria's critical need for Russian support to deal with the far graver threat of Prussia. In response to this dilemma, Austria's strategy of the 1770s embraced a third option: to restrain its large eastern neighbor by drawing closer to it.

Elements of such an approach had been present in Austria's eastern diplomacy for decades; as early as the reign of Joseph I, Habsburg diplomats had seen the idea of allying with Russia in order to monitor and keep pace with its expansion as a core tenet of eastern strategy. The difference, by the reign of Russia's Catherine II, was the accelerating pace of this expansion and sheer scale of Russian ambitions in regions of strategic interest to Austria.[81] The dangers that this expansion could pose, both for Austrian security in the southeast and its broader position in the European balance of power, was made clear by a period of turmoil that ensued after the "unraveling" of its old alliance and the emergence of strained relations with the Russians from 1761 onward.[82] In a long memorandum in 1771, Kaunitz weighed the options for how Austria could respond strategically to the steady growth of Russian strength at Turkey's expense. The document is worth quoting at length:

> The main purpose of a solid judgment of important state affairs consists of essentially a true and pure conception of the end purpose, because one must imagine the means that lead to this end purpose. In order to apply this general rule to the current political situation, and to properly judge it from our side, we observed in the war between Russia and the Porte that nothing else is needed, other than the end purpose that we are seeking to achieve, with the means that we have seized thus far, to maintain the status quo against one another, and to find out whether the ultimate purpose we seek would be best for our welfare, and the means that we employed thus far are likewise reasonable for that purpose.
>
> On the one hand, the unpredictable war preparations of the Porte and on the other hand the blind luck of Russian arms have dramatically changed the previous situation and given the Russians such superiority over the Turks that by all accounts is dangerous and must make us think carefully. In this critical situation, we had four potential paths before us:
>
> *The first* is to put to use the weakness of the Porte and to act against them jointly with Russia.

The second is to take the side of the Porte.

The third is inaction.

The fourth is to attack neither Russia nor the Turks, and instead, as the circumstances permit, to act against both, and thereby to seek to achieve our end goal.

Regarding the last option, merely conceiving of it is sufficient proof of its wrongness. Our hard-won trust and the thereupon grounded solid political credit would be lost at once. We would ruin it for all sides, miss the targeted end goal completely, the threat would increase, and leave us insurmountable consequences.

The third option would leave everything to fate, neither propagating the good nor preventing the terrible, but rather generally the prevailing idea in Europe would be that we, because of Russia's overpowering strength and unmistakable threat, acted out of fear and hypocrisy. We, at the right time, left behind abandoned our passive behavior, in order to remove the impression of foreboding, which already had started taking root. Nothing remained but to take the Turkish or Russian side. To establish a grounded judgment, obtained from both parties, depends upon an assessment of the following gradations of our own true national interest.

First gradation: ending the current war without both parties maintaining an advantage, although we will keep a few ancillary advantages.

Second gradation: ending the current war on the condition of ancillary advantages for us, established so that Russia has as few advantages as possible.

Third gradation: ending the war such that Russia achieves some vague goals, but simultaneously that we also achieve some of our goals.

If we therefore had, in siding with the Russians, decided against the Porte at the beginning, the immediate consequences thereof would have persisted.[83]

Kaunitz's conclusion was that Austria would have been better off "siding with the Russians from the beginning," as much because of the positive gains it could achieve as from the negative consequences it could avoid. These included both a regional danger—the prospect of Russia achieving a dominant position over the Ottoman Empire—and a broader, European danger—the possibility of heightened Russo-Prussian cooperation at Austria's expense. The potential for the former was illustrated by the successes scored by Russian armies against Ottoman forces and would be most vividly shown a few years later by the 1774 Treaty of Küçük Kaynarca, under which Russia ejected the Turks from their remnant positions on the north coast of the Black Sea and Crimea, and achieved rights of commercial penetration while laying the groundwork for future intervention in Ottoman internal affairs. The Russo-Prussian Treaty of 1764 and coordination between Berlin and Saint Petersburg in the lead-up to the Polish partition both exemplified the latter.

As the 1770s drew to a close, Kaunitz determined that Austria's best, and indeed only, hope for success was to forge a close and enduring strategic partnership with Russia, and that this should henceforth be a foundational component of Habsburg grand strategy broadly struck. The centerpiece would be a new treaty—the Austro-Russian Treaty of 1781—built around three principle aims.

For starters, Kaunitz wanted to obtain a means by which to monitor, and if possible, restrain and channel, Russian moves in the Balkans. In this, he sought a classic alliance of restraint aimed not primarily at aggregating capabilities, as is the case with traditional defensive alliances, but rather constraining the other partner in the alliance.[84] Austria's earlier 1726 alliance with Russia had to a large extent been pursued with this in mind. In the war that followed, Habsburg commanders had used the alliance primarily to push the main burden of fighting to the Russians and learn more about their ally's military capabilities. The 1781 alliance deepened this cooperation, committing the two states to mutual military support within three months of any conflict initiated by the Ottomans.[85] Implicit in Austria's approach was the belief that the greatest benefit of having the alliance was avoiding the dangers of *not* having it. As Kaunitz would reflect many years later,

> Every system of alliance, and also ours with Russia, is made advisable, useful, and necessary based on two major considerations—one being the real benefits, which can be extracted from its existence, and the other being the drawbacks ... if the alliance did not exist.... If the real [benefit] that we derive from [the alliance with Russia] seems accidental, then the real harm that would arise from the alliance not existing is inevitable, imminent, and highly worrying.[86]

Second, Kaunitz wanted to use the alliance to ensure that in those instances when Russia could not be constrained, Austria would at a minimum have the ability to keep pace with its territorial gains. Sitting out the war in 1768–74 had almost resulted in Austria being left empty-handed in the peace —an outcome averted through last-minute maneuvers in Poland. Staying in sync with Russian moves, Kaunitz wrote, "has enabled significant benefits for us and can do so in the future." While Austria's preference would have been to maintain a weak Ottoman presence, supported by smaller buffer states, it could not afford to see Russia grow steadily larger and thus more powerful against it without attempting to gain commensurately. Instead, Kaunitz was forced to accept, as one historian wrote, the "lesser evil" of an alliance with

Russia "geared to the extinction of the weak," lest it suffer the greater evil of "the absorption of a strategic chunk of Turkey by Russia alone, with the potentially disastrous consequences for Austria of a Russo-Prussian condominium or Russian hegemony in Eastern Europe."[87]

A third, vital aim of the new alliance was to ensure Russian support for Austria in its contest with Prussia. Experience in the Partition of Poland had shown that when Austria sat still or resisted Russia in the east, it tended to result in closer Russo-Prussian ties. This was existentially dangerous for Austria. In the brief War of the Bavarian Succession, the absence of a close link between Austria and Russia had threatened to bring it into the war on Prussia's side. By shoring up their eastern alliance, the Austrians sought to prevent opportunities for Prussia of this kind from recurring. Kaunitz later wrote,

> If we refuse the renewal of the alliance today, the Russian empress will be welcomed with open arms by Prussia and England immediately. The certain consequence would be the creation of an alignment against us by Russia, Prussia, and [other powers]. In doing so, we would become completely isolated.... In this isolated position, to the excess of all misfortune, we would not even be able to make peace with the Ottomans.... [It is therefore] beyond a shadow of doubt that the renewal and continuous cultivation of our system of alliance with Russia is all the more advisable, useful, and necessary the more its destruction is at least desired and sought by our most dangerous enemy, the court in Berlin.[88]

Even if Austria wanted to preserve buffers like Poland, the policies of resistance or inaction that this would have required carried far higher costs. Flanked in the east by a Russia bent on offensive war against the Turks and in the north by a bellicose Prussia determined to expand at Austria's expense, the one course not available to the Habsburg Monarchy was fence-sitting. While Austria had aligned with Russia intermittently for decades, Habsburg strategy from this point forward would place the goal of alliance with its large eastern power at the heart of its entire security policy. This would continue to be the case through the Napoleonic Wars and into the time of Metternich, and fall apart only under Francis Joseph, with disastrous consequences for the monarchy.

AUSTRIA'S FINAL TURKISH WAR

The first major test of Austria's deepened alliance with Russia came almost immediately after it was signed. Beginning in 1781, a series of uprisings against Turkish rule in the Crimea seemed likely to provoke a new Russo-Turkish war. The danger for Austria was that these tensions would boil over into the

Balkans and Danubian Principalities. Mobilizing its forces and using the improved channels provided by the alliance, Austria was able to contain the crisis to the Black Sea coast and avert a wider conflagration.

Yet this only delayed the inevitable confrontation between a now-emboldened Russia and the faltering Ottoman state. Under a grandiose plan presented to Joseph II years earlier, Catherine II proposed to extend Russian power to dismember the Ottoman Empire altogether and replace it with a resurrected Byzantine Empire, which inter alia, would replace Wallachia and Moldavia with a new "Kingdom of Dacia" under Russian tutelage. For Austria, such an outcome was highly undesirable. As Maria Theresa had written before her death, in words that echo Eugene's concerns about overextension in the Balkans decades earlier,

> The partition of the empire of the Turks is of all enterprises most hazardous and most dangerous, the consequences of which we have the most to fear. What do we gain from conquests, even all the way to the gates of Constantinople? The territories are unhealthy, without culture, depopulated or inhabited by treacherous and ill-intentioned Greeks [*des Grecs perfidies*]; they are not capable of strengthening the monarchy but may rather weaken us. Moreover, the esteem that my house has always been eager to preserve [of not being a partitioning power] would be lost forever and this would be irreparable ... even worse than our partition of Poland.... I hope that our descendants will never see [the Ottomans] expelled from Europe.[89]

The threat of a Russian invasion and partition of Turkey would persist well into the nineteenth century. The scale of Russian ambitions ensured that when war finally came in 1787, Austria could not sit on the sidelines. Doing so in the previous crisis had allowed Russia to annex Crimea while Austria gained nothing and bore the expense of mobilization.

In going to war, Joseph II enjoyed a better range of strategic tools for managing the terms of the conflict than his predecessors had possessed.[90] As a result of its wars against Prussia, Austria had a quarter of a million troops under arms. Its armies were battle tested, with a large cavalry complement and the latest artillery. This was backed by extensive fortresses, and due to recent territorial gains in Bukovina and Galicia, could bring pressure to bear more quickly in the main military theaters.

Like earlier Habsburg rulers, Joseph was concerned by the time factor of a war in the south. As in the past, Austria could only safely concentrate forces here if it did not face pressing threats on other frontiers. Prussia represented a greater problem in this regard than France had been in Eugene's 1716 war, possessing as it did a large army in striking range of the Habsburg border. The danger was that it would use the war as an opportunity to attack in Bohemia or take some portion of Poland. There was also the possibility that France, despite its recent alliance with Austria, could be tempted into an opportunistic grab at the Austrian Netherlands, then in a state of unrest, or even join with Prussia for an attack on the Erblände, as it had done in 1741.

To counter these eventualities, Kaunitz renewed the Austro-French alliance of 1756, thereby enabling Austria to shift forces from its western frontier, and create a deterrent force in Bohemia and Moravia totaling fifty-eighty infantry battalions and thirty-five cavalry.[91] In addition, unlike in previous wars, it now possessed a line of northern fortresses that could be used to deter Prussian moves while its main armies were preoccupied in the south. As in 1716 and 1737, the aim was to achieve a short war, partly to avoid prolonged stress on the monarchy's finances, partly to deny an opening for Prussian mischief, and partly to keep domestic difficulties in the monarchy, including especially in Belgium and Hungary, from getting out of hand.[92]

These preparations allowed for a higher degree of Habsburg force to be concentrated in the south than would otherwise have been possible. Austria's generals were also able to draw on detailed plans for a war in the south that had been created much earlier, anticipating the contingencies that they now faced. In a series of memos in 1769, senior Austrian commanders had contemplated contingencies for how such a war should be fought.[93] Taking account of the latest intelligence, the memos assessed the organization, weapons, and tactics of Turkish armies. Like previous generations of Habsburg soldiers contemplating a Balkan war, they were struck most by the lack of innovation in Turkish methods. While capable of rapid and violent attacks in which "many people are lost ... the conventional methods of coordinated [tactical] movements remain unknown to the Turks, who are attached to their peculiar fighting methods, in keeping with their forebears, whether from nature or some other motivation."[94] In light of this stasis, they recommended that the army employ the disciplined firepower it had honed against Prussian opponents while making only limited accommodations for local topographic conditions. Drawing on lessons from Eugene's campaigns, they advocated what would today be called seek-and-destroy missions combining small unit flexibility and security of flanks through square formations and fortified camps.[95]

BALKAN ATTRITION

Despite this extensive planning, several factors worked against the goal of a short war. Unlike in 1716, Austria's 1787 positions included territories that had now been settled for several decades and were therefore more vulnerable to economic devastation at the hands of the enemy. The need to guard these far-flung possessions led Joseph II to spread out his forces across a wide area and thus lose the focused punching power that Eugene had been able to achieve at the start of his campaign.[96]

From the war's outset, the time pressure was sharply felt in Habsburg military and diplomatic calculations. The longer Austrian units remained in their positions, the more subject they were to the attritional factors of Balkan warfare. From their fortress at Orsova, the Ottomans could strike either in the direction of the Banat and Transylvania, or into Serbia, forcing the Austrians to further split their forces. Through past experience, the Turks also understood the Austrian habit of seeking short wars against them, and had learned to stretch out the fighting in order to increase the time and money costs facing the monarchy. "Turkish obstinacy and attempts to prolong the war," Kaunitz lamented in one memo to the emperor, meant that "our expenses and sacrifices continue to grow."[97] Such pressures were hard to mitigate in southern campaigns unless either the main Ottoman force was shattered or an enemy managed to threaten Constantinople—the latter being an unlikely scenario in wars with Austria as long as the Turks retained their second, southerly line of Romanian fortresses.[98]

The Russian alliance also tended to prolong the war. Where Austria's interstitial position demanded that it avoid prolonged Balkan entanglements to be able to focus on other frontiers, Russia faced no such constraint, at least in this instance. Indeed, since Russia's goal was to gain territory, and if possible, break the Turks, it had an incentive to draw out the conflict as long as necessary in the knowledge that it was stronger than its enemy. Austria, by contrast, was unlikely to gain significantly from such acquisitions. This created a paradox, inherent in the structure of the Austro-Russian alliance, whereby the very edifice that the monarchy needed to ensure its overall security—a close relationship with Russia—had the potential to drag it into long conflicts that undercut that security.

The chief beneficiary of the time pressures facing Austria was Prussia. Repeating French tactics from the Spanish succession war, Berlin fomented unrest in Galicia and Hungary, offering to back a Magyar declaration of independence. While the scheme miscarried, Prussia's machinations served to complicate the Habsburg domestic position.[99] As the war progressed, Hungary became more reluctant to provide troops and supplies, and opposition in the Netherlands to bearing the tax burdens of the war stiffened. This required Austria to divert a growing trickle of forces away from the war zone, eventually siphoning off 117,000 troops, compared to 194,000 in the south.[100]

Berlin's renewed mischief also distracted Austrian military and diplomatic resources. With Prussian troops amassing in the north, the old threat of *double guerre* loomed once again, prompting Kaunitz to warn Joseph, "I would not be fulfilling my duties … if I failed to tell you that to resist two enemies at the same time such as the Porte and the King of Prussia, which surround the whole monarchy, is an impossible task."[101] Such fears, together with the pressure of prolonged military spending, eventually forced Vienna to exit the conflict earlier than Russia.

At the war's end, Habsburg forces occupied a greater extent of territory than Eugene had in 1718. They had accomplished their main war aims, ejecting the Turks from the Banat and most of Wallachia, bringing a large portion of Serbia under Austrian control, and reaching as far south as Bucharest. Under the concluding Treaty of Sistova, Austria relinquished many of these territories, not least because it could not afford to administer them. It retained the fortress at Orsova, closing off the invasion route into the Banat, the vulnerability of which had been a major reason for going to war. Building on the traditions of Karlowitz and Passarowitz, Habsburg diplomats used the postwar negotiations to try to gain long-term advantages, reinforcing Austrian navigation rights on the Danube as well as strengthening the independence of the buffers of Wallachia and Moldavia.

While the outcomes of Austria's final Turkish war were mixed, the Russian alliance that formed the heart of Joseph's foreign policy had served its purpose. Austro-Russian cooperation deterred Prussia and had forced the Turks to divide their forces, thereby reducing the overall military pressure on Austria. Habsburg participation in the war was costly, but it foiled the grander Russian schemes of an Ottoman partition as Austria's blocking moves in Wallachia forced Russia to concentrate on new acquisitions east of the Dniester and abandon the idea of a Russian-dominated Kingdom of Dacia.[102] It would take another sixty years to bring about the permanent loss of Wallachia and Moldavia as Habsburg buffers in a crisis that would have very different outcomes for Austria.

Austria possessed few good strategic options on its southeastern frontier. To achieve security here, it needed to manage two very different competitors— one weaker than itself, and the other stronger—across an eight-hundred-mile border on which the range of its army was restricted, the landscape inhospitable, and much of the local population unfriendly. In this environment, Austria needed to accomplish two contradictory objectives: benefit from Turkey's weakness without losing it as a factor of stability, and enlist Russia's help in the west without allowing it to dominate the east. Even if it succeeded unambiguously in both tasks, the local rewards were likely to be minimal. Yet if it failed, the risks to its overall position were high.

Assessing the success of Austrian strategies on this frontier is therefore not a straightforward exercise; it is less about how many wars the monarchy won or lost, or how much territory it gained, and more about how well Austria avoided the worst-possible outcomes (Ottoman collapse and Russian dominance) while realizing the best-possible ones (maintenance of buffers and mobilizing Russian help against Prussia).

Viewed through this lens, Austria's southeastern strategies were largely successful. By the end of the eighteenth century, Austria possessed a beneficial, if increasingly uneven, security alliance with Russia through which it had achieved the single most important goal for its survival: containing Prussia. It retained stable buffers to the east, where Russia was still not in possession of the Danubian Principalities. While it is true that Austria permanently lost much of Eugene's earlier conquests, it nevertheless held a large, contiguous, and consolidated line of possessions that included not only Hungary but also the Banat, Bukovina, and Galicia. Its Hungarian population, while equivocally loyal in many regards, was a much more politically and economically integrated part of the monarchy than it had been in 1699. As a frontier empire, Austria had succeeded in finding a maximal range of expansion that while not as great as its rulers had hoped, was territorially intact and viable.

Perhaps the best measure of Austria's accomplishment in the southeast, however, can be seen not in what it achieved but rather in what it avoided. Not once in the eighteenth century did the Habsburg Monarchy fight a war against a western rival in which either of its two eastern rivals was also fighting against it. In the defining struggles of the century—the War of the Spanish Succession, War of the Austrian Succession, and Seven Years' War—the Ottomans did enter on the sides of Austria's enemies, and in all but the first of these the Hungarians did not rebel. On the three occasions when Austria launched wars on this frontier, it avoided open-ended quagmires. Neither the 1716 war nor 1737 war lasted more than two campaigning seasons. While Joseph II's Turkish war was longer than expected, it was because of a calculated decision to prioritize a more valuable objective: safety against Prussia. When the wider strategic environment ceased to make concentration in the south possible, Vienna ended the war.

Austria also avoided unbearable costs in the southeast. Empires that reach their maximal line of expansion in hostile environments yet try to keep going often incur high financial outlays.[103] Austria moderated the expenses of managing the Balkans, its harshest and least rewarding frontier, by avoiding a rigid *limes* and relying on more flexible defensive systems. It benefited from the extensive prior construction of forts along this frontier, and in the Military Border, developed an effective expedient, the costs of which were largely self-supporting. In exchange for a few wooden palisades and some tax incentives, by 1780 it was receiving the manpower equivalent of seventeen infantry regiments—so many soldiers that the border became a net exporter to its other wars.

Buffer states also offset the costs of frontier security; as troublesome as Wallachia and Moldavia frequently were, they would have been far costlier as attempted experiments under direct Habsburg rule. Similarly, the money spent on bribery at the sultan's court was a fraction of what would have been required to sustain military buildups on the frontier. The Russian alliance helped to lower frontier costs, too, by both freeing up resources needed elsewhere and allowing Austrian commanders to "buck pass" in field operations. At a strategic level, even after the Partition of Poland, this alliance would enable Austria to effectively avoid permanent, large-scale defenses and troop presence across virtually the entire length of its northeastern frontier until well into the nineteenth century. For an empire whose greatest geopolitical handicap was encirclement, this de facto demilitarization of an entire frontier represented a not-inconsiderable gain from the Russian alliance.

As we will see, the challenges involved in managing the Balkans would only intensify in the following century, while Austria's viable options for managing them narrowed. In the meantime, the monarchy's greatest task would lie not in quelling a turbulent backyard but instead in managing far graver dangers to the north and west—the subject of the next two chapters.

6

"The Monster"

PRUSSIA AND THE NORTHWESTERN FRONTIER

The king of France only gnaws at the edges of those countries that border on
it.... [T]he king of Prussia proceeds directly to the heart.

—PRINCE SALM

Fuck the Austrians.

—KING FREDERICK II OF PRUSSIA

ON ITS NORTHWESTERN FRONTIER, the Habsburg Monarchy contended
for most of its history with the military Kingdom of Prussia. Though a member of the German Reich and titular supplicant to the Habsburg Holy Roman
emperor, Prussia possessed predatory ambitions and a military machine with
which to realize them. Under Frederick II ("the Great"), Prussia launched a
series of wars against the Habsburg lands that would span four decades and
bring the monarchy to the brink of collapse. Though physically larger than
Prussia, Austria was rarely able to defeat Frederick's armies in the field. Instead, it used strategies of attrition, centered on terrain and time management,
to draw out the contests and mobilize advantages in population, resources,
and allies. First, in the period of greatest crisis, 1740–48, Austria used tactics
of delay to separate, wear down, and repel the numerically superior armies of
Frederick and his allies. Second, from 1748 to 1763, Austria engineered allied
coalitions and reorganized its field army to offset Prussian advantages and
force Frederick onto the strategic defensive. Third, from 1764 to 1779, it built
fortifications to deter Prussia and finally seal off the northern frontier. Together, these techniques enabled Austria to survive repeated invasions, contain the threat from Prussia, and reincorporate it into the Habsburg-led German system.

Northern Dilemmas

At the same time that the Habsburgs were expanding eastward under the Treaty of Karlowitz, they were in the midst of a period of retrenchment in the west. For centuries, the foundation of Habsburg power had been the dynasty's status as elective leaders of the Holy Roman Empire, or German Reich—an amalgam of kingdoms, principalities, and bishoprics that had endured since its creation by Charlemagne in the eighth century. Since the mid-fifteenth century, the Habsburgs had maintained primacy among the princes of the Reich as their elective emperor, using German resources to extend their power and influence across Europe. In the Thirty Years' War, imperial armies had fought the combined forces of northern Europe to a standstill, bleeding Germany white and exhausting Habsburg resources.

The end of the war diminished Habsburg power in Germany. The concluding Treaty of Westphalia recognized French and Swedish influence in the affairs of the Reich, and strengthened the sovereignty of its members. More important, the war demonstrated the dynasty's inability to dominate Germany by force of arms. Afterward, the Habsburgs retained their status as emperors. But the body over which they presided was much changed from its earlier medieval form, now containing wealthy and willful states less constrained than before by German patriotism or loyalty to the emperor, and more conscious of their prerogatives and interests as separate states.

Among the Protestant states that emerged from the Thirty Years' War was the northern German electorate of Brandenburg-Prussia. Formed through a series of mergers between the Margraviate of Brandenburg, historic seat of the Hohenzollerns, and Duchy of Prussia, former Teutonic vassal to the Kingdom of Poland, the electorate had emerged by the late seventeenth century as the leader of the group of Protestant states, or *corpus evangelicorum*, within the Reich.[1] At face value, Prussia was unimpressive, with a population of 2.25 million in 1740 compared to more than 20 million for Austria. No more prosperous in commerce than its neighbors, it was, if anything, less well endowed for agriculture as a result of the sandy soils of the Baltic region. Indeed, entering the eighteenth century, Prussia possessed few of the attributes that normally explain the rise of a state to Great Power status.

Sparta of the Baltic

What set Prussia apart was its army. To mobilize resources for the incessant warfare engulfing their realm, the electors broke the power of the estates, effectively destroying constitutionalism and laying the foundation for a military-bureaucratic state at an earlier point than any European power except France.[2] Under Frederick William I, the "Great Elector," Prussia spent the middle decades of the seventeenth century creating a strong central government and standing army. In 1701, Frederick William's son, Elector Frederick III, was able to leverage these strengths to extract consent from Habsburg emperor Leopold I for Prussia to attain the status of a kingdom and its rulers the title of "kings in Prussia." Under his son, Frederick William I, Prussia became the militarized state with which its name would later become synonymous.

Known as the "Soldier King," the dour and frugal Frederick William worked to systematically harness the energies of the Prussian state to the task of future war.[3] A conservative Junker class provided the substrate for a loyal Officer Corps. A small and scattered but largely homogeneous population, bolstered by immigration from other Protestant states and additional military recruits from abroad, provided the basis for an efficient professional army. In the twenty-seven years of Frederick William's reign, the Prussian Army would double in size from 40,000 to 80,000 troops, eventually absorbing 1 in 28 male subjects and an estimated 90 percent of the Prussian nobility.[4] Maintenance of such a large force required that a high proportion of the state budget (about three-quarters of yearly revenue) be devoted to war. The result was a disproportionate degree of resource mobilization for a country Prussia's size, with the army as a proportion of the population eventually hitting 7.2 percent compared to 1.2 to 1.6 percent for Austria.[5] "It has been calculated," as Rodney Gothelf writes, "that if other European powers had structured their military along the same lines as Prussia in 1740, then Austria would have an army of 600,000 men and France an army of 750,000."[6]

Compared to larger states like France or Austria, Prussia faced the significant geographic disadvantage of being an archipelago of disconnected lands. The territories comprising the Prussian state—what Voltaire called the "border strips"—stretched from the Rhineland in the west through the main Elbe possessions of Brandenburg and Pomerania to the Polish lands in the east. "The consequent problems of self-defense," writes H. M. Scott, "in the face of hostile and predatory neighbors, were considerable: the furthermost border of East Prussia lay some 750 miles from the Rhineland possessions."[7] In earlier times, Prussia's central position had made it a highway for invading armies and would again become a significant military liability later in its history. But by the mid-eighteenth century, as Prussia's military capabilities peaked, the kingdom's surrounding geography presented it with a target-rich environment for expansion: to the west and south lay a mosaic of weaker German states— Hanover, Braunschweig, Münster, and Saxony; to the east the inert giant of the Polish-Lithuanian Commonwealth. A garrison state surrounded by less warlike polities, Prussia was poised to expand. The military machine assembled by Frederick William represented a powerful and largely unchecked tool for shaping the kingdom's surrounding landscape, should a leader emerge who was inclined to use it for this purpose.

Naked Frontier

One potential target was the Habsburg Monarchy. Though physically larger and more populous than Prussia, Austria's circumstances in the mid-eighteenth century could hardly have been less favorable for dealing with a major military threat from this direction. Of all Austria's frontiers, Bohemia was at this time the weakest (see figure 6.1). Unlike in the south, where large expanses of poor territory gave Austria time to prepare for an attack, in the north the threat was a stone's throw from its richest territories. Unlike in Italy and southern Germany, where numerous buffer states separated Austria from France, in the north there was only one—Saxony—whose coverage of the frontier was partial. To the east, the Oder River valley provided a direct route deep into Habsburg territory. And while mountains sheltered most of the Czech lands, the territory of Silesia, one of the monarchy's wealthiest provinces, sat exposed on a plain north of the mountains. Once in Silesia, an enemy would have little difficulty transiting the numerous, well-marked mountain passes to strike at the heart of the Erblände, feeding off the fattest Habsburg lands along the way (see figure 6.2).

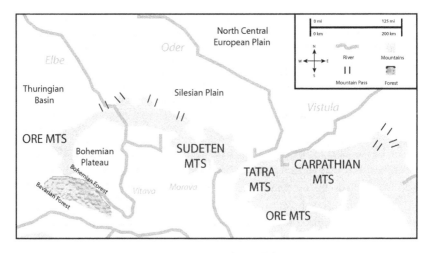

FIG. 6.1. Northern Frontier of the Habsburg Empire.
Source: Center for European Policy Analysis, 2017.

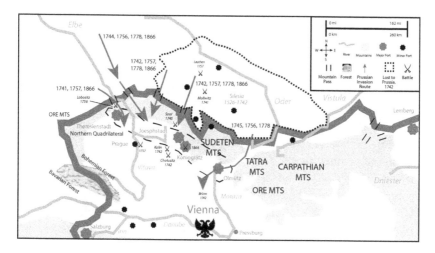

FIG. 6.2. Prussian Invasions of the Habsburg Empire.
Source: Center for European Policy Analysis, 2017.

Austria had weak military options for dealing with a threat from the north. Following the death of Eugene, its army had fallen into neglect, suffering defeats in the War of the Polish Succession and then the catastrophic Turkish War of 1737–39. At the end of these wars, Habsburg finances were depleted, and its army was at half strength and scattered across the empire.[8] Unlike in the south, Austria's defenses were virtually naked in the north. The four forts in Silesia at Glogau, Brieg, Breslau, and Glatz were aging and dilapidated.[9] The passes were unguarded, Bohemia and Moravia lacked major fortresses, and there were few depots or magazines. A 1736 review of defenses in the area noted these inadequacies but was ignored.[10] Nor were Austria's alliances in good repair. Britain was distracted and weary from its recent war with Spain. Russia was consumed by internal turmoil following the death of czarina Anna.[11]

Then there was the succession problem. Habsburg relations with allies and foes alike were dominated by the question of the Pragmatic Sanction, a legal instrument created by Emperor Charles VI to ensure the eventual succession of his daughter, Maria Theresa. Under Salic law, the code that had determined European rights of succession since the sixth century, women were barred from princely inheritance. Without male heirs, Charles VI needed to engineer an agreement from other courts to respect the coronation of his daughter when he died and not launch a succession struggle of the kind that perennially wracked Europe. For more than two decades, Habsburg diplomacy was consumed by this quest. Led by Bartenstein, Charles VI's chief diplomat, these efforts succeeded in winning acceptance from all the major powers of Europe including, notably, Frederick I of Prussia.

Despite Bartenstein's success, the matter of the succession hung in the air in the years leading up to Charles VI's death. It was especially problematic within the German Reich, where two members—Saxony and Bavaria—had been the only states in Europe that did not consent to the Pragmatic Sanction. Saxony's elector, Frederick Augustus II, was married to one of the daughters of Charles VI's elder brother, Joseph I, and the Bavarian elector, Charles, was married to another. On this basis, both saw for their offspring claims to the Habsburg lands. With the Bavarians, there was the added dimension of a centuries-long rivalry between their ruling house, the Witelsbachs, and the Habsburgs for the title of emperor. Elective rather than hereditary, this title was not covered by the Pragmatic Sanction and therefore vulnerable to contestation after the succession.

These dynamics weakened Austria's ability to use the Reich as a political tool. Under normal circumstances, it would have provided a natural mechanism to aid in the task of containing Prussian ambition. A federative body in which Prussia was a vassal to the emperor, the Reich offered the Habsburg monarchs levers for influencing and disciplining wayward princelings. One was the Reichshofrat, or Aulic Council, a judicial body through which the emperor could bribe and cajole members involved in territorial feuds.[12] The Reich also supplied some military tools. By declaring a Reichskrieg, a collective defense provision not unlike the North Atlantic Treaty Organization's (NATO) Article 5, the Habsburg emperor could call on the German states to provide military contingents and fulfill financial quotas in support of a war effort. Even in the Reich's reduced post-Westphalian state, it had proven useful in this role, offering a major addition to Habsburg military power in the war against Bourbon France earlier in the century. Such arrangements, however, were designed to counter threats from outside powers, not from a fellow German power. Such influence as Austria possessed for rallying the military aid of Reich states would be impeded by the inevitable struggles over the title of emperor.

Frederick Strikes

It was in this volatile climate that a new Prussian king came to the throne in 1740. Frederick II was twenty-eight when he succeeded his father. As a youth, there was little to indicate the military prowess of the future Frederick the Great. Frederick's bent was philosophical and musical; he played the flute, wrote poetry, and corresponded with Voltaire. But his nature was stamped for war. Frederick's Enlightenment proclivities masked a militaristic, caustic, and controlling personality; he worked feverishly, wrote vulgar doggerel to mock his enemies, and carried a vial of poison around his neck in case he failed in battle.[13] Misogynistic and atheistic, he referred to Christianity as an "old metaphysical fiction" and preferred the company of men.[14] It would be hard to imagine a ruler more different from the conservative, pious, and often-temporizing monarchs of the Habsburg Empire.

From his father, Frederick inherited a well-drilled army of ninety thousand and budget surplus of eight million taler.[15] In Silesia, he saw a vulnerable and valuable prize that, if taken, would enrich his small kingdom and round off its southern frontiers. Rich in metals, and home to a third of Habsburg industry and annual tax revenue, Silesia was one of the richest territories in Europe. Frederick was scornful of the Habsburg Army's ability to hold these territories. As a younger man he had accompanied Eugene of Savoy to the siege of Phillipsburg and been appalled by the laggardly comportment of Austrian troops. Contemptuous of the Habsburgs as a dynasty and eager to expand his realm, he had no compunctions about seizing their lands or even, if circumstances permitted, dismembering their realm altogether.

When Charles VI died on October 20, 1740, Frederick was ready to strike. In addition to a march-ready army, the Prussian king had made secret overtures to France to arrange the opening of a second front against Austria in the west once the war begun. On December 16, without a declaration of war and disregarding his father's consent to the Pragmatic Sanction, Frederick led twenty-seven thousand troops across the Austrian frontier into Silesia. The invasion marked the beginning of nearly forty years of running conflict and crisis that would see the Habsburg heartland repeatedly invaded, involve fighting on every Habsburg frontier except the Balkans, and eventually engulf all of Europe and much of the known world. For the House of Habsburg, these wars would be as desperate as the Turkish invasion of the previous century, longer than all of Austria's previous eighteenth-century wars combined, and more threatening to its existence than anything it would face until the revolutions of the mid-nineteenth century.

Survival and Strategy

The Habsburg ruler who bore the brunt of these wars was Maria Theresa.[16] The dynasty's only female monarch, she was twenty-three years old when her father died in winter 1740. Like Frederick, Maria Theresa had little prior experience in affairs of state and even less exposure to the military. Also like Frederick, she was drawn to the rationalist ideas of the Enlightenment, and would become perhaps the boldest and most successful state reformer in Habsburg history. But unlike Frederick, Maria Theresa was deeply religious and familial, eventually producing eleven children. Intelligent, resolute, and hearty in physical constitution, she later described the daunting scene she found on taking the throne, "without money, without credit, without army, without experience … without counsel."[17] In the years that followed she would be animated by a hatred of Frederick, whom she called "the Monster," and as determined to retake Silesia as he was to keep it.

From the outset, the main problem facing Maria Theresa was the military superiority of her enemy. A revisionist-minded ruler with a powerful army, Frederick possessed the advantage of the strategic initiative and, it quickly became apparent, tactical dominance on the battlefield as well. His forces, and in particular his infantry, outmatched hers in almost every regard—leadership, logistics, discipline, speed, and offensive spirit. Under Frederick's gifted command, Prussian armies were virtually unbeatable in the early phases of the conflict. And while Habsburg fighting skills would improve substantially over time, eventually surpassing the Prussians in cavalry and especially artillery, Frederick would prove capable of inflicting defeats on larger Austrian armies all the way into the 1760s.

In formulating a response to the Prussian challenge, Maria Theresa did not have the benefit of a sustained period of reflection or preexisting strategic framework of the kind that her predecessors had in dealing with the Turks. The enemy was present, active, and powerful; the threat was existential. The methods that Maria Theresa and her advisers developed for handling this problem were initially reactive, aimed purely at survival. Yet they would congeal over time into a coherent set of strategies specifically tailored to the Prussian threat. Viewed collectively, they were rooted in the premise, familiar to weak states throughout history, that the best way to defeat an unbeatable enemy is to avoid fighting on their terms. Unable to overpower Frederick on the battlefield, Maria Theresa would try to outlast him. The essence of her approach was the defensive use of time, both on the battlefield, by employing terrain to deny combat until conditions were favorable, and in diplomacy, to avoid bearing the full brunt of war until Austria's alliances and military manpower could be mobilized.

This basic template would endure throughout the long contest with Prussia and can be broken into three phases. In the first war (1740–48), Austria fought to preserve itself using delay, sequencing, and harassment. In the second war (1748–63), Austria sought to recuperate and retake Silesia using restructured alliances and a reformed army. And in the third war (1764–79), Austria used preventive strategies to seal off the frontier and deter future attacks.

Preservative Strategies: Stagger and Delay (1740–48)

In the opening phases of the War of the Austrian Succession, Habsburg strategy was defined less by what could be achieved than by what must be avoided.[18] Maria Theresa's aims can be understood as the inverse of Frederick's. Opportunistically revisionist, Frederick sought a short and decisive conquest of Silesia, fought on his terms, and concluded by diplomatic ratification, and to support this goal, a wider conflict that by bringing other invaders into Austria, would increase his bargaining position and the pressure to cede Silesia. Maria Theresa needed the opposite: time to mobilize her resources and "turn off" other threats to focus on her greatest threat. Over the course of the eight-year conflict, Maria Theresa crafted strategic tools, some rough and ready, and others derived from prior Habsburg military and diplomatic culture and prior experience, to achieve both goals and manipulate the timing of the contest to its advantage.

BUYING TIME TO MOBILIZE

Austria's opening moves were dictated by the imperative of warding off existential threats to the Erblände while setting in motion a mobilization of resources that would take time to bear results. By 1741, four invading armies sat on Austrian soil and the situation was desperate; as one minister wrote, "The Turks seemed ... already in Hungary, the Hungarians already in arms, the Saxons in Bohemia and the Bavarians approaching the gates of Vienna" (see figure 6.3)[19]

While dispatching armies to the north, Maria Theresa reached out to traditional allies—England, Holland, and Russia—to organize military pressure on Frederick's flanks, and get subsidies flowing to fund the scale of mobilization that would be needed to get Austria's scattered and poorly equipped regiments onto the field. In rallying this coalition, the empress concentrated on those powers that had reasons to fear Prussian ambition. This included in particular the states closest to the revisionist powers: Hannover, and through it, its patron Britain; Saxony, Prussia's weaker southern neighbor; the Dutch, sandwiched between France and Prussia; and Piedmont, vulnerable to both Spain and France. Such a collection of states, like all coalitions in war, would be difficult to coordinate and hold together. But much as Austrian diplomats had used fear of French hegemony to align otherwise status quo–minded states behind the monarchy in the wars with Louis XIV, fear of Prussian strength now provided a powerful glue for a defensive coalition.

As she rallied allies, Maria Theresa also moved in the opening stages of the war to mobilize the monarchy's own armies and resources. Because the

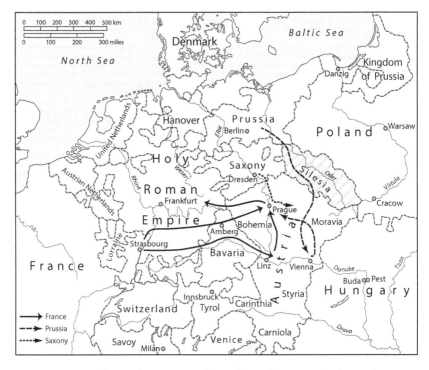

FIG. 6.3. Austria under Attack, ca. 1741–42. *Source:* Center for European Policy Analysis, 2017.

enemy occupied Silesia along with most of Bohemia and Moravia, these efforts would need to be focused on Austria proper and the territories to the south and east. That meant Hungary. This was a challenge, given the dynasty's long-standing difficulties organizing regiments and munitions from the Magyar nobility. In addition, Maria Theresa still needed to win the formal ratification of her succession from the Hungarian Diet. But above all, it was imperative that Austria avoid a Hungarian uprising so as to take advantage of the crisis in the west—a crisis of the kind that had distracted Habsburg attention and resources during the Spanish succession war.

Against the odds, Maria Theresa accomplished all these goals. Weak as the monarch may have been amid the Prussian invasion, she still had two levers with the Hungarians: constitutional concessions and Magyar pride. Traveling to Pressburg, Maria Theresa appealed directly to the Hungarian Diet. From start to finish, the trip was a public relations coup. Arriving by the Danube on a boat festooned in Hungarian red, white, and green, the young empress used her presumed frailty to charm the Magyar magnates and excite their sense of duty. For months prior to the trip, and though pregnant, Maria Theresa had practiced her equestrian skills in anticipation of the coronation ceremony, which required her to ride to the top of a hill to receive the Crown of Saint Stephen. She also brought constitutional concessions, widening the kingdom's tax exemptions and confirming Hungary's separate administrative treatment in Habsburg government.[20] Her methods worked.[21] The Hungarians not only approved her succession but also called a *generalis insurrectio*, promising more than thirty thousand troops, mostly cavalry, and four million florins for the war effort. While many of these pledges would never be met in full, Maria Theresa's diplomacy had accomplished something more valuable: prevention of a Magyar revolt through the duration of the Prussian wars.

More effective for Habsburg needs was Maria Theresa's mobilization of the hardy regiments of the Military Border. As we have seen, the Grenzers were not conventional soldiers in the European mold but rather irregular fighters trained in the methods of Kleinkrieg—raiding, harassment, and guerrilla hit-and-run tactics. Use of such soldiers on western battlefields had not been attempted on a large scale. But for Maria Theresa, these troops represented an untapped manpower pool that was numerous, loyal, and as events would prove, terrifyingly skillful. In the years that followed, the Military Border would contribute large numbers of troops to the Austrian armies in the west: 45,000 in the Austrian succession war (out of a total Habsburg Army of 140,000), and 50,000 in the Seven Years' War, all for about a fifth of the cost that would have been required to field similar numbers of regular units.[22]

DIVIDING ENEMIES

Maria Theresa also employed what would become a signature Habsburg technique of the wars with Prussia: sequencing the conflict to avoid fighting all her enemies at once. Austria had used such methods to juggle between fronts in Italy, the Netherlands, Germany, and Hungary in the War of the Spanish Succession (see chapter 7). In the opening war with Frederick, it faced a similarly dispersed set of challenges. In addition to France, Prussia was joined in its invasion by the armies of Bavaria and Saxony. As the conflict widened, Spain became involved as an enemy of Austria as well as smaller Italian players, Genoa and Naples. Altogether, before the war ended, Austria faced active fronts in Bohemia, Moravia, Upper Austria, the Rhine, and Italy.

If Austria tried to fight all these enemies simultaneously, it would lose. The monarchy was particularly susceptible to exhaustion in the early phases of the conflict, when its allies had not yet taken the field and its own forces were still assembling. To survive, it needed to find ways to concentrate scarce resources until the balance of power had begun to swing in its favor. Maria Theresa did this in several ways.

First, she worked to prevent new enemies from coming into the war. One technique that Austria had learned in the Spanish succession war, as discussed in chapter 5, was to proactively appease threats that had not yet entered an existing conflict. Engagement with the Hungarians was done with this in mind. Similarly, Maria Theresa worked to ensure quiet relations with the Ottoman Empire. Repeating methods used earlier in the century by Joseph I, Maria Theresa sought to tamp down tensions with the Turks, ordering her diplomats to wrap up outstanding issues from the recent war and employing bribery in the sultan's court to ensure that the Porte did not enter the war on Prussia's side.

Second, Maria Theresa sought to prioritize among the various enemies that had already entered the war. Among these, Prussia represented the ultimate danger, but also the one that Austria was least prepared to fight at this stage. Maria Theresa therefore sought a temporary peace, or *recueillement*, to recover strength and concentrate elsewhere. Early on in the conflict, she had instructed her diplomats to seek a cease-fire with the Prussians for precisely this purpose. Frederick himself, who wanted a short war to grab Silesia, eventually provided the opening. Using this urge to their advantage, Austrian diplomats brokered the Convention of Kleinschnellendorf, a temporary peace that allowed their armies to disengage in the north. That their purpose was to concentrate against other foes can be seen in the fact that Maria Theresa rejected Frederick's offer of a "general pacification" in the conflict.[23] The Austrian Empress *wanted* the war to go on, only on her and not her enemies' terms. That she intended to resume the contest with Frederick once she had dealt with other foes is illustrated by the fact that her diplomats would not cede permanent ground to the Prussians in the convention, ultimately only consenting to a loss of parts of Silesia, and vaguely.

Third, with this cease-fire in place, Maria Theresa prioritized the gravest danger: a Franco-Bavarian threat to Upper Austria and the capital. In the Spanish succession war, Austria had been able to safely deprioritize the Erblände when threatened by kuruc forces from the east, relying on hastily erected defenses to keep the raiders at bay while focusing on economically valuable lands in Italy.[24] But a threat from conventional European armies was a different matter. In late 1741, such a threat existed in the form of a Franco-Bavarian army that had moved in force into Upper Austria and captured Linz. With the north quieted by the cease-fire, Maria Theresa massed Austria's forces against this threat, sending reinforcements from Hungary while shifting troops from Silesia and Italy. Launching a winter offensive unusual for Austrian armies in the eighteenth century, the monarch took the enemy off guard, pushing them out of Austria and across the Bavarian frontier.[25] While the move came at the expense of temporarily ceding Silesia to Prussia and weakened Austrian positions in Italy, it consolidated Austria's position on home territory and instilled confidence in the monarchy's foreign allies.

With her concentration of force in Upper Austria, the empress had placed Bavaria, the smallest member of Frederick's coalition, on the defensive, forcing its units to return home from their deployments in Bohemia. She now moved Austrian forces into Bavaria, including large numbers of Croats and other Military Border units, which savaged not only the enemy army but the civilian population, too. Militarily, the move chiseled off a target that the Habsburg Army could handle, depriving Frederick of an ally once the war in the north was resumed. Politically, it dealt a severe blow to the home base of the elector of Bavaria, the Habsburgs' main rival in Germany who became Holy Roman emperor following the succession. By making this move early in the conflict, Maria Theresa sent a message to the other Reich states about Austria's continued military potency, increasing the likelihood that they would side with her as the war progressed.

GUERRILLA WAR

Maria Theresa's effort to sequence the war to Austria's advantage was made possible not just by diplomatic cease-fires but also by guerrilla war. While concentrating against the Bavarians, the empress had to find ways of ensuring that the large enemy forces still in Bohemia and Moravia were not neglected altogether. The main method that she used to preoccupy them was Kleinkrieg, the practice of irregular warfare imported from Austria's southern frontier. Maria Theresa had a wild assortment of troops available for this task that included Hungarian hussars and other frontier light cavalry as well as large numbers of Croat, Serb, and Hajduk irregular infantry. Known collectively as Pandurs, these forces comprised not only regimented Grenzers of the kind organized in the Military Border's administrative districts but also numerous free corps raised specifically for the war. The latter often consisted of rogue elements—bandits, criminals, and adventurers—assembled from the hardscrabble Balkan countryside.[26]

The fighting techniques used by these troops were quite different from the linear warfare of the period on which Frederick had based his military machine. Kleinkrieg was a savage form of warfare similar to that practiced by the Cossacks, Comanches, and other tribal irregulars found in the world's frontier regions. A contemporary observer described them as

> fierce to the highest degree; they live among mountains and forests, are inured to hardships from their infancy, and live more by hunting and fishing than by the milder arts of manufacture and cultivating the ground.

Every enemy with whom they are at war, have complained of their want of generosity after a battle, and of their rapine and barbarity when stationed in a country with whom their Sovereign is at war.[27]

The Prussians feared the Pandurs. As one of Frederick's officers wrote, "They are always hidden behind trees like thieves and robbers and never show themselves in the open field, as is proper for brave soldiers"[28] Frederick told his generals that they could do little to harm Prussian units in the field, but that "it is a different question in the woods and mountains. In that kind of terrain the Croats throw themselves to the ground and hide behind the rocks and trees. This means that you cannot see where they are firing from, and you have no means of of repaying them for the casualties they inflict on you."[29]

Deployed against the Prussians and French in Bohemia, the Pandurs targeted supply lines, depots, baggage trains, and isolated detachments. Such methods hit the weak spot of eighteenth-century armies: the logistical arteries supporting armies in the field. Their raids were especially effective against Frederick's army in Moravia in winter, when the Prussians needed to forage for provisions. Pandur units mercilessly stalked Prussian detachments in the countryside, wearing down their numbers, munitions, and morale. Frederick complained, "We are going to be flooded with Hungarians, and with the most cursed brood that God has created."[30]

Resistance by the local population augmented Pandur raiding. Resentful of the heavy-handed Prussian occupation, Moravian peasants were encouraged by Vienna to fight, and in turn, equipped with weapons and instructors from the Austrian Army.[31] Together, the Pandurs and local insurgents harassed the Prussians, allowing Austria to concentrate the bulk of its regular army elsewhere. When Frederick finally left Moravia, his forces were weakened and demoralized for the next phase of the conflict.

When Austria did engage the Prussians on a large scale, it looked for ways to magnify the strategic effects of its irregular forces on the enemy. The moment came in 1744, when Frederick ended the temporary peace and invaded Bohemia yet again with eighty thousand troops. This time he quickly took Prague and penetrated south to threaten Vienna while the main Habsburg Army was deployed on the Rhine against the French. Redirecting her forces, Maria Theresa now had much larger and more experienced armies than earlier in the war. Prince Charles of Lorraine and his lieutenant, Field Marshal Count Traun, commanded these forces.

Traun was a capable officer who had won distinction in the War of the Polish Succession at the siege of Capua, where he held out for seven months with six thousand troops against a Franco-Spanish force of twenty thousand.[32] The strategy that Lorraine and Traun employed against Frederick sought to deplete Prussian strength rather than confront it directly. With Bavaria neu-tralized and French armies pushed back into Germany, Austria would be able to concentrate significant numbers against Frederick in Bohemia once its forces had been collected from their far-flung stations. Learning from its ear-lier guerrilla methods in Moravia, Austria's commanders believed that if they could deny Frederick the possibility of provisioning from the countryside, he would have to quit Habsburg territory. As Lorraine wrote to his brother, if Frederick persisted in driving so hard into the province, it would be easy to starve him out; "I believe God has blinded him, because his movements are those of a madman."[33] Frederick himself quickly saw the difficulty of his posi-tion, finding that despite the strength of his armies, he was unable to subdue the land, whose entire population "from the high nobility, to the city mayors and general public spirit are devoted to the House of Austria."[34]

With the populace on their side and reinforcements converging from the west, the Austrians played for time, harrying and exhausting Frederick's forces. Exploiting Frederick's weaknesses, they avoided pitched battle and made careful use of the terrain, skirting enemy columns along major rivers and se-lecting strong defensive locations for encampment. In these movements, Traun reflected Montecuccoli's admonition that "even limited battle should be sought only when one has superior numbers and troops of better quality."[35] In today's terms, Traun's methods resembled what would be called a "logisti-cal persisting" defense—the practice of creating an inhospitable environment in which an invader can neither sustainably victual themselves nor bring the defender to decisive engagement.[36] Accompanied by swarms of Pandurs, Traun's forces chipped away at Frederick's rearguards and flanks until Lor-raine arrived with the main army, by which point the Prussians had been sufficiently depleted and were able to be driven out of the province without a major battle.

Recuperative Strategies: Allies, Artillery, and Revenge (1748–63)

Austria survived the war of succession but at an enormous cost, spending eight times its annual revenue on the war, losing hundreds of thousands of lives, and seeing its richest province consumed by Prussia.[37] As the war drew to a close, the writing was on the wall: if the House of Habsburg wanted to endure, it would need to be better prepared for the next phase of the war. Even before hostilities ended, Maria Theresa had already begun to make pro-visions for the future. She was assisted in these tasks by Kaunitz, who would come to exercise a dominating influence over Habsburg diplomacy for al-most forty years from the time of his appointment as state chancellor in 1753 until the start of the French wars at century's end.[38] A member of the old

Moravian nobility, Kaunitz had served during the previous war as an envoy in Italy and the Austrian Netherlands, and later as the chief Habsburg representative at the concluding peace of Aix-la-Chapelle. Eccentrically brilliant— "individualist, hedonist, humanist, and hypochondriac," as Franz A. J. Szabo describes him—Kaunitz brought talents to Habsburg statecraft not seen since Bartenstein that would only be surpassed decades later, perhaps, by Metternich.[39] He formed a close bond with Maria Theresa similar in some ways to the relationship between Disraeli and Queen Victoria, holding, as one historian put it, "power like that of a demonic seducer" in matters big and small.[40]

Using this influence, Kaunitz would decisively shape Habsburg diplomatic and military strategy as the monarchy prepared for the inevitable renewal of hostilities with Frederick II. His signature contribution was to engineer a seismic shift in Austria's alliances, away from the centuries-old enmity toward France and dependence on England, the latter of which had proven to be a demanding and not altogether reliable paymaster in the previous war, toward closer ties with France and Russia. As early as 1749, Kaunitz had begun to argue for a move in this direction on the premise that Prussia was likely to remain the greatest security threat facing the monarchy for the foreseeable future. In France, Kaunitz saw a power that shared Austria's status quo orientation and was likely to feel threatened by Frederick's restless territorial ambitions.

Together with the continent's other large land power, Russia, Kaunitz correctly identified France as the state that, unlike sea-bound Britain, would be best positioned to help Austria militarily in a future crisis. At Aix-la-Chapelle, he laid the foundation for this landward reorientation of Habsburg diplomacy by deprioritizing the Austrian Netherlands in favor of a strengthened position in Italy, thus reducing Austria's reliance on the Royal Navy.[41] As ambassador to France from 1750 to 1752, he labored to engineer a rapprochement with Versailles, which finally bore fruit in the so-called Diplomatic Revolution of 1756—a defensive alliance providing mutual aid against Prussia. As a makeweight to these arrangements, he brokered a renewal of the 1746 treaty with Russia " 'to make war against the King of Prussia' in order to reconquer Silesia and Glatz and place him in a position whereby he could no longer disturb the peace."[42]

At the same time, Kaunitz worked to restore confidence in Habsburg power among the Reich states. Maria Theresa had this goal in mind in the late phases of the succession struggle when she treated generously with those members that had sided against Austria. At the Treaty of Füssen in 1745, she had given the Bavarians, still recovering from despoliation by the Pandurs, new territory while occupying key towns as "hostages" to guarantee their support for the reelection of a Habsburg as Holy Roman emperor.[43] By dealing with Bavaria and Saxony magnanimously, Maria Theresa had strengthened Reich support for the monarchy as, in the words of one Austrian memo, "neither an all-powerful nor an all-too-powerful" hegemon.[44]

Maria Theresa also worked systematically to strengthen Austrian domestic capabilities for war.[45] Acting under the dictum that "it is better to rely on one's own strength than to beg for foreign money and thereby remain in eternal subordination," Maria Theresa and her advisers, above all Kaunitz and the able Count Haugwitz, undertook a wholesale reorganization of the Habsburg state and economy. In 1748, the year the war ended, she succeeded in the long-running battle to curb the Estates' power, introducing requirements for higher and more predictable contributions to the budget.[46] She launched a comprehensive census, tallying the properties of rich and poor alike, and streamlining tax collection. Maria Theresa also slimmed government to cut waste, eliminating redundant institutions and subjugating provincial bodies to Vienna. To staff this rationalized bureaucracy, she expanded the political elite, issuing new patents of nobility and pardoning nobles who had been disloyal in the war. She worked to abolish remaining vestiges of feudalism, reducing the work obligations of the peasantry and transferring their regular labor quota—the hated *Robot*—into fixed cash payments.[47] These changes not only made revenue flows larger and more predictable in wartime but also increased the loyalty of the populace to the Crown. These reforms had a grand strategic purpose: to bring greater military capabilities to bear, on a more durable and predictable basis, for sustaining the contest with Frederick the Great and ensuring that Austria would be more likely to succeed in its next installment. The result, as one historian has written, was a "revolutionary metamorphosis" in the Habsburg Monarchy—brought about by "a coherent masterplan" executed over the span of nearly fifty years—that was aimed at "increase[ing] the state's authority, resources and organizational capacity."[48]

Inevitably, Maria Theresa's reforms also reached deeply into the Habsburg military, beginning at the level of command and control.[49] The Hofkriegsrat was overhauled in an effort to create a leaner institution focused on its core function of war planning. The number of staff members was cut, and the functions for military law and logistics were decoupled into separate institutions. The latter became the function of a new military commissariat, charged with bringing order to the chaotic supply system that had crippled Austrian forces in the early stages of the last war, alongside the new Corps of Engineers.[50] A new military academy was created at Wiener Neustadt as well as a finishing school for officers and revamped engineering academy. At the rank-and-file level, the army was expanded to create the basis for a standing force of 108,000 troops. Maria Theresa worked to increase Hungarian military contributions, merging Magyar and non-Magyar units, and making the army an outlet for Hungarian social mobility.[51] She also sought to more systematically leverage the full manpower potential of the Military Border. The previous war had shown the enormous potential that the Grenzers held for warfare in places other than the frontier. Halfway through it, Vienna had begun to look for ways to maximize its contributions. Under Prince Joseph Sachsen-Hildburghausen, a new military code was introduced, and the unpredictable free corps was replaced by larger and more standardized formations.[52] Importantly, these organizational changes were made without attempting to alter the indigenous warfare methods of the Grenzers.

While expanding the size of the army, Maria Theresa also sought to improve its quality. Recent battlefield experiences offered abundant lessons in tactics and technology. To absorb these, the Military Reform Commission was created and given the task of systematically preparing the forces for future conflict.[53] Chaired by Lorraine, it was composed of officers with combat experience from the recent war, including Field Marshal Daun, a talented disciple of Traun who had assisted in the successful relocation of the army from the Rhine in the 1744 campaign, and Prince Joseph Wenzel von Liechtenstein, who had led Austrian forces to victory in Italy. Within a year of its creation the commission produced a standardized drill manual. The first of its kind for Austrian forces, the new *Regulament* simplified infantry movements and tactics on the Prussian model, implementing changes that would remain in place until 1805.[54] To learn the *Regulament* and improve tactics, the army formed large exercise camps in Bohemia to retrain, drill, and equip large formations.[55]

In the technological realm, the Austrians devoted particular attention and resources to improving the artillery. For armies of this period, the artillery represented the most labor- and capital-intensive weaponry to develop, requiring large-scale state investment, advanced metallurgy, and industry to produce. In their collisions with Prussian forces in the 1740s, Austrian armies had found that they lagged dangerously behind in this technology. Overcoming this disadvantage became the focus of a major modernization effort after the war. Achieving "catch-up" in artillery was not a quick or easy task, requiring not only the development of the weapons themselves but also the cultivation of specialized technical skills and a supporting military body to sustain them.

The effort to improve the artillery was led by Prince Liechtenstein. A member of one of the wealthiest families in Europe, Liechtenstein had almost been killed by Prussian artillery at the Battle of Chotusitz in 1742. Drawing heavily on his own wealth, the prince funded ballistic experiments and created a new artillery corps headquarters in Bohemia.[56] Altogether, Liechtenstein spent ten million florins on the project, eventually producing a new class of improved guns in 1753.[57] His efforts essentially comprised a private research and development facility that moved more quickly than would otherwise have likely been possible. A measure of Liechtenstein's success can be seen by comparing Austria's artillery in its first and second wars with Frederick's. In the first, it possessed 800 artillerists. In the second, it had 3,100 men servicing 768 guns, supported by specialized fusilier, munitions, and mining detachments.[58] From one of the Habsburg Army's most neglected elements, the artillery would become its corps d'elite with a claim to being "18th-century Austria's major contribution to the art of war."[59]

By reforming alliances and expanding the army, Maria Theresa and Kaunitz sought to position the Habsburg Monarchy for renewed war with Prussia. The goal was partly offensive in the sense that they were preparing to initiate a conflict to retake Silesia. Like Carthage after the loss of Spain to Rome and France after Prussia's seizure of Alsace-Lorraine, Austria's leaders were animated by the desire to repatriate a province that was not only economically valuable but symbolized their monarchy's strength and influence in the balance of power as well. Viewed more broadly, however, her efforts were based on the correct assumption that Frederick would continue to launch revisionist wars in search of more territory. While the immediate aim was to take back Silesia, Austria's leaders wished to substantially reduce Prussia's potential as a long-term threat to their state. Kaunitz envisioned "a post-war environment without the evil of 'remaining armed beyond our means and burdening loyal subjects with still more taxes rather than granting relief from their burdens.' "[60] In this sense, Maria Theresa's aims were preventive in nature, intended to restore lost balance and preclude future disruptions on the scale that Austria had narrowly survived in the 1740s.

To achieve this goal, Maria Theresa and Kaunitz pursued a strategy of two parts. First, they would seek to field a larger number of allies than Austria had possessed in the previous war to take the offensive against Frederick. By allying with France and Russia, Austria would be able to exploit Prussia's own interstitial geography, thus shifting the economic burden of war away from the Habsburg home territories and onto Prussia itself. In addition to Russia and France, Austrian diplomacy succeeded in bringing Saxony, which had changed sides in the previous war, and traditional enemy Bavaria on board as allies. Second, as a by-product of these alliances, Austria's leaders sought to achieve a greater concentration of force for the Habsburg Army than it had in the previous war. The absence of threats from France and Bavaria would enable Austrian forces to concentrate on one unified front against Prussia. Prewar treaties aimed at pacifying the Ottoman and Italian fronts further supported this goal. Paradoxically, the loss of Silesia allowed the army to develop improved forward positions on the defensive terrain around Bohemia's rivers. Here, Austrian commanders planned to concentrate the monarchy's now-enlarged forces.[61]

FREDERICK STRIKES AGAIN

Anticipating Maria Theresa's intentions, Frederick launched a preemptive strike into Bohemia in August 1756.[62] Frederick's war aims were similar in some ways to those of the previous war, except that now he had to anticipate moves by the two large powers to Prussia's east and west—Russia and France—that Kaunitz had recruited as Austrian allies. To avoid subjecting Prussia to a multi-front war of the kind he had previously inflicted on Austria, Frederick needed to achieve a fast knockout punch against his chief adversary, thereby discouraging French and Russian action altogether, or if this failed, be in a position to pivot his forces against the other two armies from a central position.[63] To this end, he envisioned a fall campaign in 1756 to neutralize the Habsburg buffer state of Saxony, followed by a penetration into Bohemia the following year, where his forces would be provisioned at his hosts' expense in order to "disorder the finances of Vienna and perhaps render that court more reasonable."[64]

After a rapid conquest of Saxony, Frederick crossed the frontier into Austria in April 1757. As in the last war, he entered through the familiar mountain passes, this time bringing seventy thousand troops, more than double the size of his first invasion. As in the last war, he advanced on a line offering multiple objectives in order to pin down Austrian forces in the empire's richest province, Bohemia, while threatening to raid Moravia or move in force against Vienna. And as in the last war, Frederick scored early successes against the Habsburg forces that he encountered, foiling an attempted linkup of Austrian and Saxon forces at Lobowitz in 1756, and defeating the Austrian Army outside Prague under its commander in chief, Lorraine, who despite numerous defeats at Prussian hands in the previous war retained a prominent political place in the Habsburg Army as Maria Theresa's brother-in-law.

Notwithstanding these similarities with the previous war, Frederick quickly saw that he was dealing with a very different Austrian Army than the one he had encountered in the past. From the outset, Habsburg forces managed to use enhanced logistics and planning to achieve higher force concentrations in forward theaters than in the previous war, with thirty-two thousand troops in Bohemia and twenty-two thousand in Moravia by the time the Prussians entered Austrian territory. This positioning allowed Austria to contest Frederick more effectively from an earlier point in the campaign, preventing both the easy utilization of Habsburg resources and speedy knockout punch that Frederick depended on for his overall strategy.

At the tactical level, too, Austrian forces showed the benefits of Maria Theresa's reforms, inflicting higher costs on Prussian forces even in battles where they were forced to retire from the field. In his initial encounter with Austrian forces near the border at Lobowitz, Frederick was intercepted by a large force under Field Marshal Maximilian Ulysses Browne, who had commanded Austria's Silesia garrisons in the first invasion of 1740. In a foretaste of coming battles, Frederick found that Browne had positioned his army behind defensive terrain at a bend in the Elbe with his flanks anchored on mountains and marshes. While eventually yielding ground, Browne mauled the Prussian invaders and gave pause to their king. As one Prussian officer noted afterward, "Frederick did not come up against the same kind of Austrians he had beaten in four battles in a row.... He faced an army which during ten years of peace had attained a greater mastery of the arts of war."[65]

In the campaigns that followed, Austrian forces deployed tools and techniques that equalized or negated many of the advantages the Prussians had become accustomed to enjoying in the previous war. The Habsburg infantry was steadier and better drilled, and did not break as easily when pressed. The Croat irregulars still harassed the Prussian flanks and supply lines in the old style, but in addition were now more numerous and better integrated into the Austrian battle order during pitched combat, inflicting casualties on advancing Prussian units before they could make contact with the main Austrian lines. Perhaps most noticeably, the Austrian artillery was more abundant, better handled, and technically superior to that of the Prussians. "Your Majesty himself is willing to concede," one of Frederick's lieutenants wrote to the king, "that the Austrian artillery is superior to ours, that their heavy guns are better served, and that they are more effective at long range—both from the quality of their powder and the weight of their charges."[66] As the late nineteenth-century German military writer Hans Delbrück, certainly no fan of the Austrians, later conceded,

> The principal change in this arm—that is, the huge increase of heavy artillery—originated not with the Prussians but with the Austrians, who sought and found in these heavy guns their protection against the aggressive spirit of the Prussians. Frederick then reluctantly agreed with the necessity of following the Austrians along this path. At Mollwitz [in 1740] the Austrian Army had 19 cannon, one to every thousand men, while the Prussians had 53, or 2–1/2 for every thousand men. At Torgau [in 1760] the Austrians had 360 cannon, or 7 for every thousand men, and the Prussians had 276, or 6 per thousand men.[67]

Improved artillery tilted the advantage to the defensive, in Austria's favor. Where Prussian offensive tactics required light, mobile guns that sacrificed range in order to keep pace with advancing units, Austria's investments had gone in the opposite direction, developing heavier, longer-range pieces that could hit the Prussians' main advantage—the infantry—at a greater distance than Prussian artillery could return fire. By placing large batteries of these heavier guns behind defensive terrain, the Austrians forced Frederick to fight on unfavorable terms in one encounter after another, subjecting his army to attrition on the battlefield while Austrian irregulars subjected it to logistical attrition off the battlefield. Frederick acknowledged the change in Austrian fighting capabilities, noting that his adversaries had become "masters of the defensive as a result of their campcraft, their march tactics, and their artillery fire."[68]

Habsburg command and control had improved as well. In 1756, a new ministerial council was created to coordinate Austrian strategy in the conflict. This "war cabinet" operated in parallel with the Privy Conference and a third conference concerned with purely military matters.[69] While these bodies inevitably had some degree of overlap, the creation of the war cabinet enhanced the monarchy's ability to conceive and pursue a coherent grand strategy by combining in one place the components necessary for considering means and ends in all aspects of Habsburg power—military, diplomatic, and economic. The effect was heightened by the dominating presence of Kaunitz, who maintained close correspondence with Austria's field commanders, and often intervened in military deliberations about when and where to offer battle.[70]

Reversals at the start of the war also prompted refinements in Habsburg planning at the operational level. In 1757, the foundation was laid for a professional General Staff, with a separate reporting structure from that of the civilian-dominated Hofkriegsrat.[71] These changes, together with the improved education for military officers and heightened emphasis on maps and planning, had an unmistakable effect on the army's performance in the field. Perhaps the highest praise came from Frederick himself, who commented positively on the altered behavior of Austrian generals and, in particular, their enhanced application of terrain-based defensive planning. "The changes in procedure of the Austrian generals," he wrote, resulted in defensive positions with "flanks like a citadel, ... protected from the front by swamps and impassible ground—in short, by every conceivable obstacle terrain could afford," which made the act of attack "almost the same as storming a fortress."[72]

KOLIN

Few officers in the Austrian Army better personified Habsburg military improvements than Count Daun, a subordinate to Lorraine who would later become senior commander of the Austrian forces in the war.[73] An understudy of Field Marshal Traun, Daun had come of age in the army of Prince Eugene, under whom he had served at Peterwardin and, as one contemporary wrote, "learned the first rudiments of the art of war." Drawn from the impoverished German nobility of Bohemia, Daun had a stolid and cerebral person-

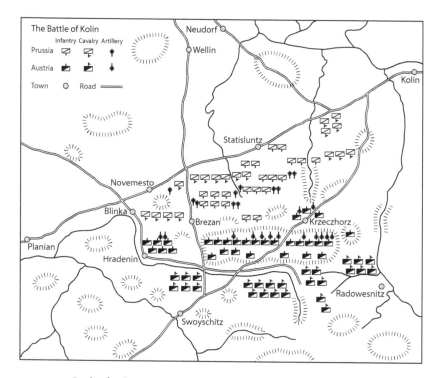

FIG. 6.4. Battle of Kolin, June 18, 1757. *Source:* Center for European Policy Analysis, 2017.

ality well matched to the culture of the Habsburg military, being "so conversant in maps ... [that] there was not a village either in Germany, Hungary, [or] Bohemia ... but he knew its longitude and latitude."[74] In the period between the wars, Daun had put these skills to good use as a member of the Military Reform Commission that had systematically studied the Austrian Army's failures in an attempt to improve its future performance.

At Kolin in June 1757, Daun handed Frederick the first major defeat of his career.[75] Unable to reach Lorraine's main force at Prague, Daun collected Austrian remnants from the battle, amassing a force of forty-four thousand troops east of the city that forced Frederick to split his army and move out against him with thirty-two thousand. Like Browne at Lobowitz, Daun took up a strong defensive position that made maximum use of the local terrain. Placing his main force south of the village of Kolin, he anchored its rear and flanks on nearby rivers and forests (see figure 6.4). Advancing up the slopes at the Austrian lines, Frederick's forces found themselves confronted by massed Austrian infantry and the concentrated fire of Daun's entrenched artillery. Thrown into retreat, they were harrassed by large bodies of Croat infantry and hussars, and driven from the field.

So severe was Frederick's loss at Kolin that he was forced to lift the siege of Prague, give up his invasion of Bohemia, and retreat back across the border. At this stage in the war, Austria was able to finally contemplate a major offensive campaign, pushing Prussian forces back into Saxony and Silesia with a view to moving the war onto Frederick's home territory. At the same time, many of the fruits of Kaunitz's earlier alliance diplomacy were beginning to materialize. In the north, Russian forces invaded East Prussia; in the west, a Reichsarmee composed of units from the smaller German states, which had unanimously declared war on Prussia earlier that year, linked up with French forces to threaten Frederick's position in southern Germany.

It would be hard to imagine a fuller reversal of Austria's earlier military fortunes or more dramatically different strategic state of affairs to that which had confronted the monarchy at an analogous point in the earlier succession war than in the months after Kolin. It was at this moment, when Prussian fortunes seemed at their nadir, that Frederick pulled off a string of stunning battlefield victories transforming the strategic situation to his advantage. At Rossbach in Saxony in November 1757, the Prussian king inflicted a crushing defeat on the Franco-German army, which outnumbered him two to one, effectively forcing France out of the war as an Austrian military ally. A month later at Leuthen, he decimated the main force that Lorraine and Daun had led into Silesia after the successful operations following Kolin, wiping out the gains of earlier Austrian victories and forcing a Habsburg retreat into Bohemia.

FABIUS AND HANNIBAL

After the catastrophe of Leuthen, Maria Theresa replaced Lorraine, who by now had suffered repeated defeats at Frederick's hands, with the younger and more talented Daun. As the war progressed, however, Habsburg grand strategy was handicapped by a mismatch between the ends that Austria sought to accomplish and the means at its disposal. Even in its enhanced state, the Habsburg Army remained an essentially defensive tool being harnessed to a strategic objective—the reduction of Prussia—that was ultimately offensive. Austria could use its reformed armies to go beyond the mainly reactive "preservative" strategies of the previous war and frequently defeat Frederick in battle. But the makeup of its forces and mind-set of its top generals did not naturally lend themselves to carrying an aggressive war beyond Habsburg territory, into the Prussia heartland, on the scale that would be required for achieving Vienna's full strategic aims of recovering Silesia and diminishing Prussia's position in Germany.

This tension in Habsburg strategy became more apparent from 1758 onward, as Daun and Frederick maneuvered their armies along the monarchy's northern frontiers. At Hochkirch in October, Daun defeated Frederick's forces in a surprise attack that cost the Prussian king a third of his forces, several generals, and most of his artillery. After the battle, though, Daun refused to capitalize on his victory by pursuing Frederick, preferring instead to keep his army in place to recuperate its strength. Similar caution had prevented Austrian forces from reaping the full benefits of the victory at Kolin the previous year, followed by a daring but small hussar raid on Berlin that while psychologically satisfying, had done nothing to improve Austria's overall strategic position. After Hochkirch, Kaunitz implored Daun to move boldly and seize the rest of Saxony in order to place Frederick at a disadvantage at the start of the following year's campaigning season.[76] Despite this pressure, Daun remained cautious, thus giving Frederick the breathing space to rebuild his forces over the winter.

Daun's dilatory behavior was rooted in an inherently defensive philosophy of war pervasive among Habsburg commanders of the period. In words that Montecuccoli would have recognized, Daun believed that Austrian generals "should offer battle [only] when you find that the advantage you gain from victory will be greater, in proportion, than the damage you will sustain if you retreat or are beaten."[77] And elsewhere he wrote, "God knows that I am no coward, but I will never set my hand to anything which I judge impossible, or to the disadvantage of Your Majesty's service."[78] Modeling himself on the Roman general Quintus Fabius Maximus, who had hounded the stronger armies of Hannibal while avoiding battle, Daun believed that Austria's chief advantages lay in terrain-based delay and denial. Rather than risking the army in head-on attacks against Frederick, he preferred to shadow the enemy and take up defensive positions that, if attacked, would place Prussian forces at a disadvantage.

Daun persisted in these methods despite intense pressure from the Hofkriegsrat. As a result, Frederick was able to remain active in the field and continue to wage war largely on his terms even after absorbing large losses in troops and resources. Repeated ideas and plans for offensive thrusts or moving against Berlin were rejected.[79] While Daun would be subjected to criticism, the reality was that the Habsburg Army as an institution remained a defensive tool, with a cautious culture and conservative leadership that could not easily be brought to bolder uses. As Frederick had commented about himself many years earlier, "A Fabius can always turn into a Hannibal; but I do not believe that a Hannibal is capable of following the conduct of a Fabius."[80] Daun's behavior showed that the opposite was also true: a Fabius such as himself could not so easily turn into a Hannibal, even when the political object of war demanded it. Even in victory, more often than not Austria's commanders reverted to what they knew best: self-conservation through deliberation and maneuver.

The mismatch between Austrian means and ends was also visible in the diplomatic realm in Kaunitz's attempts to corral and motivate an effective international coalition against Frederick. Defensive alliances are easier to organize and sustain than offensive ones. Where Austria had been successful in marshaling friends among the numerous states that felt threatened by Prussia's growing power and ambition, it was a different matter entirely to hold this group together and keep its members focused on common strategic objectives through what turned out to be many years of bitter warfare marked by frequent defeats and setbacks.

Historically, Austrian efforts at *managing* groups of allies had usually involved the states of the German Reich, which were both smaller than the monarchy and bound to a certain extent to Austrian leadership by historical custom and established structures. In large wars, Austria was more often a subordinate and financial supplicant to another Great Power—usually England. In assuming the role of offensive alliance manager therefore, Austria, for all of Kaunitz's immense talent, was attempting an enterprise in many ways beyond its means as a state. Austria lacked the financial heft to provide the subsidies that were essential to keeping allies in play through a long war, and lacked the offensive army to keep allies inspired by a vision of imminent victory. As with its military reforms, Austria's ability to fully realize the advantages gained by its alliance formulations before the war was to a certain degree hobbled by its composition as a Great Power. In both the military and diplomatic realms, the monarchy's geopolitical position necessitated the development of strategy for security and survival while placing natural limits on how far such strategies could be taken in practice.

CAGING FREDERICK

Even with these limitations, Austria's army and allies eventually brought Frederick to heel. Converging Habsburg, Russian, and Swedish armies forced the Prussians onto the defensive in their own territory. While Frederick still retained much of the initiative through his characteristic daring and genius, the multidirectional pressures bearing down on his small kingdom effectively negated the strategic effects of even large Prussian victories. Unlike in the previous war, Austrian strategy succeeded in forcing Frederick to do less fighting on Austrian soil and more on his own. When in 1758 he had attempted to revert to his preferred strategy of predation on the Habsburg lands, the presence of active enemies on his flanks prevented a long stay; bogged down by the Habsburg fortress at Olmütz and with his supply columns hounded by Croats, he was forced to withdraw—this time, never to return. Within a year, Daun's talented lieutenant, Ernst Gideon von Laudon, achieved the long-sought strategic convergence with the Russian Army at Kunersdorf in 1759, where the two empires combined forces to beat Frederick in a battle that almost destroyed the Prussian Army as a fighting force.

While the war continued on for a little more than three additional years, both Austria and Prussia were materially exhausted. By 1763, the military situation in central Europe was at a virtual stalemate, with Prussia in possession of the northern portions of Saxony and Silesia, and Austria holding the south, including the Saxon capital of Dresden and Silesian county of Glatz, the latter forming a small but crucial toehold in the lands lost to Frederick. The concluding Treaty of Hubertusburg, signed in February 1763 by Austria, Prussia, and Saxony, largely reinstated the status quo ante bellum. Under the treaty, a more or less even swap was agreed on: Prussia gave up Saxony and Austria gave up Glatz.

Assessed according to Maria Theresa's central aim—regaining Silesia—the war must be judged a failure. But as an installment in the wider contest with Frederick that had begun in 1740, the balance sheet of Austrian grand strategy is more positive. Seen in this light, Austria's overarching need was to stabilize its position as a central European power broadly and put a stop specifically to the periodic Frederickian bursts of predatory revisionism targeting the Habsburg lands. In this goal, Maria Theresa largely succeeded. Her reformed armies not only fought the theretofore-undefeated Prussian "monster" to a standstill but together with Kaunitz's alliances, drained the lifeblood of his kingdom. While Silesia was lost for good, the loss of Saxony, a crucial and indeed the only northern Habsburg buffer state whose absorption by Prussia would have converted Frederick's kingdom into a more formidable state, thereby holding profoundly negative long-term implications for Austria's security, was prevented.

As important, Austria emerged from the conflict with its prestige as a Great Power restored. Within the European balance of power, Austria had restored its status as a powerful and permanent player capable of assembling coalitions to safeguard continental stability. In Germany, Frederick reaffirmed Prussia's status as a vassal to the Habsburg emperors—a symbolic but nevertheless significant concession for shoring up Habsburg influence in Germany. Compared to Austria's desperate circumstances in 1740, at the start of Frederick's ravaging reign, its situation in 1763 could not have been more different. The turnaround in the monarchy's fortunes was the result of the determined efforts that Maria Theresa and her subordinates—above all, Kaunitz—had made to fully organize and leverage Austria's capabilities as a Great Power, and harness them to a set of political objectives for the renewed security of the state—in short, because they had pursued an effective grand strategy.

Preventive Strategies: Forts, Rivers, and Deterrence (1764–79)

After the Seven Years' War, Austria's rulers again turned their attention to contemplations of future strategy. Twenty-three years of almost-continuous warfare had taken a toll on the monarchy. The latest installment alone had cost more than three hundred thousand Austrian casualties, the state was burdened by heavy debts, and large swaths of the northern countryside were still recovering from years of occupation, pillage, and depleted labor at harvest time. The question facing Austria's leaders was how to avoid all this happening again.

The man who would grapple with this question more than any other was Joseph II, Holy Roman emperor and coregent alongside his mother, Maria Theresa, in 1765, and sole monarch from 1780 on.[81] Joseph was a creature of the Prussian wars. Maria Theresa had been pregnant with him while she practiced horse riding ahead of her trip to the Hungarian Diet at the start of the first Silesian War. Raised amid the turmoil of constant invasion, Joseph took an interest in military affairs from a young age and was enamored with Frederick. Like the Prussian king, he was an absolutist monarch committed to building a strong central state grounded in toleration and enlightened administration. Intelligent and impulsive, he chafed at his mother's baroque religiosity and continuing control in matters of state.

Joseph believed that Habsburg security could be put on a stronger long-term footing by applying the tools of reason: logic, deliberation, and planning. He took long rides across the monarchy's frontiers, accompanied by his generals, examining every detail of topography. In the north, Joseph visited the battlefields of the recent wars with Frederick, and devoted close study to the hills and rivers of northern Bohemia that with Silesia gone, now made up the northern frontier. In Vienna, he composed countless memorandums and commissions to debate the question of how the frontier should be secured against yet another Prussian invasion.

Joseph's collaborator in these exercises was Field Marshal Count Franz Moritz von Lacy (1725–1801), a talented protégé of Field Marshal Daun who served as the first head of the Austrian General Staff and president of the Hofkriegsrat in the years after Daun's death. The central lesson that both Joseph and Lacy took from the Prussian wars was that a lack of preparation not only made Austria's defense more difficult but also invited such attacks to begin with. These wars, Joseph wrote, "proved quite clearly the necessity of preparing sound arrangements for the future."[82] One important ingredient in being better prepared was the deployment of a larger standing army. Maria Theresa's expansion of the military between the wars had helped to shorten Frederick's campaigns in Bohemia and prevent the loss of new territory. "During the previous campaign," a report by senior generals after the war argued, "it became clear that unless we maintain equally large bodies of troops at the border to what the enemy is able to deploy, the enemy can come and go without hindrance."[83]

To deal with the Prussian threat in the future, Austria's generals estimated they would need 140,000 troops—three times more than on the Turkish frontier, and not counting whatever troops would be needed in Italy, Germany, and Galicia. One report stated,

> The situation in Bohemia and Moravia requires that the King of Prussia be opposed by no fewer than his own numbers, meaning 130 to 140,000 men at any time. Against the Turks, at least 40 to 50,000 troops will need to be stationed in the Banat and positioned around the Danube.... In order to ensure just the *minimum* of defense against both sides, the War-President thus recommends at least 200,000 men to be kept in the field.... [But] one ought to then consider the aforementioned restrictions in the case of a two-front war which would require a force of 310,000 men, including garrisons.[84]

Meeting these demands on a standing basis would not be easy. At the time the estimates were produced, Austrian forces in the north already fell short of the desired number by sixty thousand men. Filling the gap would be expensive. Already in 1763, the military budget had been raised to seventeen million florins, and an additional five million was sought.[85] Joseph was an advocate of both a larger force and larger budget, but also understood the financial burdens that these preparations would bring. "We must try always to combine the necessary security with the country's welfare," he wrote to his brother, "and ensure that the former protects the latter as cheaply as possible."[86]

Even if it could afford a larger army, that alone would not buy security against Prussia. Larger forces in 1756 had not deterred Frederick's invasion, which had only been ejected with difficulty. Once deployed to the north, Austria's field armies had to worry about guarding multiple invasion routes while keeping an eye on other frontiers. As Maria Theresa observed,

> [Frederick] has the advantage of interior lines, while we need to cover double the distance to get into position. He owns forts, which we lack. We have to protect very large areas and are exposed to all manner of invasions and insurrections.... One knows the Prussian machinations ... that he leaves no means untried to rush us and fall upon our necks.[87]

With Silesia in Prussian hands, an invading force could enter through mountain passes from more than one direction, forcing Austrian commanders to parcel out their strength, as one general put it, without "the faintest idea of Prussian intentions."[88] Recent experience had shown that this could all happen at short notice, and by the time the army reacted, Frederick was already on the path to Vienna. Once lodged in Bohemia, he could linger while the army chased him, feeding his forces on Austria's fattest provinces; as Maria Theresa put it, "This monster stretches out his campaigns ... until everything is sorted and saved."[89]

THE ELBE FORTRESSES

To deter future Prussian invasions, Joseph and Lacy envisioned the construction of a series of fortresses across the northern half of Bohemia. "As a principle," Lacy explained, "fortifications are absolutely necessary for security of the country."[90] The absence of such defenses was believed to have encouraged Frederick's attacks, while forcing the army to "rely upon the establishment of rearward strongholds and magazines, which make the transport of supplies difficult, costly, and burdensome for the country."[91] As long as no such fortifications existed, Joseph and Lacy believed, Frederick would not be deterred from attacking. As Lacy worried in 1767, "Given that we did not commence construction [of forts] immediately after our most recent war, the King of Prussia [may not] wait for completion of such a project, [but rather] act on his aggressive intent before being faced with a new bulwark."[92]

The potential for well-sited fortresses to strengthen Bohemia's defenses had been demonstrated by the ease with which the entrenched camp at Olmütz had thwarted Frederick's last attempted invasion in 1758. Local terrain, too, favored such fixed defenses. As Daun and Lacy had found in recent campaigns, the shape of the Elbe River, with its numerous elbows and tributaries, was ideal for protecting the flanks of a prepared defensive position. The river's course just south of the base of the mountains, set back somewhat from the main ingresses, allowed a defender located at its center to quickly pivot eastward or westward, and thus cover a broad section of frontier.

To fortify the northern frontier, Joseph and Lacy solicited the advice of a team of French military engineers, eventually selecting sites to cover each of the main invasion routes—one at the west end of the Elbe, south of the Nachod Pass, and the other at the east end of the river, south of the gap leading from Dresden to Prague. At the former, the Austrians built a large fortress near the intersection of the Adler and Elbe at Königgrätz.[93] A few years later, a second fortress, Josephstadt, was built twelve miles upriver at Pless, where a large plain provided a space suitable for assembling large forces. Together, these two forts placed obstacles at the spot at which the Prussians normally formed up after exiting the Sudeten passes, or as Joseph II described it, "Naturally the weakest stretch of the Elbe."[94] To cover the eastern approach, a third fortress was built near the intersection of the Eger and Elbe, and named

Theresienstadt. More than 1.16 square miles in size, it was placed astride Frederick's 1741 and 1744 invasion routes, denying Prussian armies the advantage they had enjoyed of shipping forces down the Elbe to Leitmeritz.[95] In addition to these large structures, numerous smaller forts were built. A star-shaped earthwork was constructed near the pass at Jablunka, blockhouses and watchtowers were sprinkled in the mountain valleys, forward depots and arsenals were established, and the defenses of major cities were strengthened.

THE QUESTION OF CORDONS

Lacy's efforts to strengthen Habsburg defenses would later become associated with the idea of "cordons"—the practice of spreading forces evenly across wide distances to cover all possible points of attack.[96] Cordons often appeared in eighteenth- and early nineteenth-century military writings, and were usually prescribed as the best method for defending rugged terrain.[97] The Habsburg Army would use them in various forms over its life span, stretching division-sized units across the frontier in the opening phases of war to detect and intercept an invader whose exact location or strength was unknown. As we will see, doing so placed Habsburg forces at a disadvantage in the early days of the French revolutionary wars.

Later military writers would criticize Lacy for advocating dispersed positions that lent themselves to defeat by a concentrated opponent.[98] This is not an altogether-accurate characterization. First, while Lacy's plans for Bohemia did involve a string of forts at the frontier, their main purpose was not to disperse force but rather to concentrate it. As a pupil of Daun, he would have agreed with his mentor's comment that "you cannot defend everywhere at once"; as Lacy wrote, "The magnitude and quantity of the army is not the decisive factor in war, as experience has taught us," and warned against trying to "take too many objects together."[99] The question was how to achieve concentration in an empire where it was rendered inherently difficult by geopolitical encirclement and large distances. In the era before railways, the answer to this problem was to build forts to allow some forces to remain in the theater. Forts enabled a handful of troops to monitor an area that otherwise might have required an entire corps, allowing the rest to be pulled into the interior. When trouble arose, troops could coalesce to, as Lacy phrased it, do "surgery" at the threatened point:

> If a crisis were to break out somewhere else, troops could be shifted according to need.... [B]esides the necessity of being able to man all the forward positions with the garrisoned troops present, it may also be required that, in accordance with the demands of war and the movement of the enemy,

all forces can be deployed to a single fort. Thus, that all, however unevenly distributed, garrisons be at a readiness level that allows for alternative operations.[100]

Lacy's concept for northern defense was not that a single, exposed curtain of forts would intercept and defeat an invader. As an eighteenth-century military officer, he appreciated the importance of placing rows of forts in an echelon to ensure their mutual support in emergency. As an Austrian fortifications manual of the period described this practice,

> Protecting an entire country ... with just one fort would be as inadequate as having only one recruit for a position.... The obstacle to be overcome by an enemy trying to enter the country becomes formidable with two lines of fortifications, placed *en échiquier*, in a row. In the defense of a country without [these], the protection of depots and magazines would require the defender to always have these in his back. A chain of forts protects all magazines and protects the positions of operating corps or armies. They can reinforce and recover damages according to circumstances even to evade a major confrontation. Chains of fortifications protect the backs and flanks of our forces, so that they may position themselves and move freely between the forts, whereas the enemy will be hesitant to move between such positions.[101]

The value of arranging forts in this manner was well understood from antiquity. The fortifications of Austria's southern frontier sat in exactly such a pattern, with border fortresses supported by forts anywhere from a hundred to two hundred miles to the interior. By contrast, in the north, there were no forward posts (following the fall of the Silesian forts), meaning that the interior forts—Olmütz, Prague, and Brünn—had been forced to bear the brunt of defense in recent wars, with devastating consequences for the adjacent farmland and Habsburg economy. By constructing forts on the Elbe, Lacy was attempting to remedy this deficit; his aim was not to build an unsupported forward screen but rather to provide the missing pieces to a defense-in-depth posture that, with Silesia's loss, was now overreliant on its rearward elements.

In this and other regards, Lacy's defensive plans have to be understood in the context of a multifront war. "Considering that conditions may always change," as the 1767 white paper had argued, "it would be smart to prepare with whatever resources the Monarchy has available for the case of a war on two fronts."[102] In the event of such a war, Austria's forces would be stretched thin in an effort to juggle between fronts. Forts helped by allowing a small number of troops to hold down the enemy in one sector while concentrating its main strength against the other. In the 1760s, at a moment when Austria lacked forts in the north, its southern forts enabled Austria to shift the bulk of its field army to the north. By building similar fortifications in the north, Lacy wanted be able to do the reverse as well.

But nor did Lacy assume that forts alone would bring Austria protection; like earlier and later Habsburg military men, he viewed them as part of a wider system of layered defenses that extended well beyond the frontier. Before reaching Austrian soil, enemies would first have to contend with "assistance that could be expected from our allies," and the tutelary fortresses and client armies of Austria's buffer states. At the frontier itself, the invader would be intercepted by forward fortresses placed at natural points of entry, behind which lay a second line of interior magazines and fortresses, and finally, the main army. This layering of natural and artificial obstacles offered resiliency in a multifront crisis, but was especially helpful in the north, where Austria lacked extensive insulating space to buffer the Erblände from sudden attack.

LACY'S PLAN IN ACTION

The fact that Lacy sought concentration rather than dispersal can be seen when his plans were put to the test in 1778, in the short War of the Bavarian Succession. As they had done on so many previous occasions, the Prussians invaded through the mountain passes—Frederick with the main army through Nachod, and a second Prussian column southward from Lausitz. As in previous wars, Frederick's plan was to move these forces in a pincer, converging on the long-familiar portage near Leitmeritz, placing the Austrians on the horns of the same old dilemmas of choosing to guard Moravia or the capital, while his armies wrecked the provinces and lived off the land.

Instead of taking the bait, Lacy foiled the invasion through a defensive concentration on the Elbe. Though not all of Lacy's preparations had been completed, the fortress at Königgrätz had just undergone substantial improvement, and earthworks were in place at Theresienstadt.[103] Lacy spelled out Austrian strategy in a war plan titled "Combined Defense Plan for the Kingdom of Bohemia": "Since [Bohemia] is open on all sides ... [and] the approaching danger is therefore also multi-sided ... we must fix such a concentrated plan ... [whereby] our armies, which have not yet fully gathered, can ensure the ability to link up and at the same time keep the enemy columns separated from one another."[104] In earlier planning, Lacy had ensured that sufficient forces would be prepositioned in the theater to avoid the problems of surprise and weakness that had crippled Habsburg forces at the outset of the first Silesian War. Unlike in the past, Lacy's preparations confronted Frederick with a dense phalanx of defending corps in entrenchments behind the Elbe. Noting that "the river makes a bow in Bohemia, as the Upper Elbe runs from Arnau to

Königgrätz," Lacy's war plan concluded, "It is in this sector where our main defensive position should be developed."[105]

Lacy's chosen spot on the Elbe turned out to be exactly where Frederick had envisioned his own columns linking up. When the Prussians arrived they were surprised to find the Austrians present in strength. With the Austrian corps tightly spaced and supported by "numerous artillery of 15 guns per battalion," Frederick remained bottled up in Moravia and pitted against converging Austrian units while a smaller Prussian force petered out in the countryside near Prague.[106] Frederick declined to attack Lacy's position, loitering for three months before retreating back across the border. The short war was expensive. But its outcome had validated Lacy's strategy of developing the Elbe into a defensive barrier.[107] The war's nickname—"the potato war," from the potatoes that Prussian troops lived on—is a fitting end to the Prussian wars from an Austrian perspective insofar as the main objective of the post-1763 strategy had been to deprive Frederick of his accustomed habit of succoring his forces on the rich Bohemian countryside to the south. Lacy's defensive line had accomplished this goal, depriving the Prussians of supply and Frederick of the ability to squeeze Vienna economically for concessions. A different outcome would occur in the next century, when Austrian and Prussian armies squared off in the same place using similar strategies. For now, though, Lacy's efforts to close the monarchy's northern back door had succeeded.

The Prussian wars jolted Austria into the business of grand strategy on a standing basis. Unlike on its southeastern frontiers, where centuries of conflict spurred the evolution of defensive concepts and infrastructure, Austria had no significant history of conflict with Prussia prior to 1740. Aside from a few neglected garrisons and the rusty machinery of the German Reich, it entered the wars with Frederick possessing little in the way of a coherent strategy or theater-specific strategic tools. Three wars and thirty-nine years later, it emerged with a modernized army, the best artillery in Europe, a rationalized system of revenue and administration, and a sophisticated network of fortresses.

Habsburg strategic behavior matured over the course of the Prussian wars, from a reactive effort to stay alive and avoid defeat, to a recuperative strategy of retaking lost lands, to a preventive strategy to manage future conflict on Austria's terms. The goal in the first was survival, in the second renewal, and in the third, stability. Unlike in the south, where Austria sought to ensure short wars against a weaker opponent, in the north it drew out the conflict to mobilize internal resources and alliances against a militarily stronger opponent. In the War of the Austrian Succession, Habsburg diplomats used temporary treaties to stagger the conflict into manageable chunks, while Habsburg generals used terrain and irregulars to hound and hamper tactically superior enemy armies. In the Seven Years' War, Austria employed widened alliances to bring time pressure to bear against Frederick II, creating theretofore-unimaginable military opportunities that its armies were unable fully to exploit. In the War of the Bavarian Succession, Austrian military technology, effectively intertwined with defensive terrain, secured tactical advantages that denied the Prussians their preferred strategy.

Austria coped with Prussian pressure in part by shifting the burden of containing Frederick to other parties—first to the English and Dutch, and later, more efficiently, to the French, Russians, Swedes, and Saxons. The construction of fortresses aided this burden shifting, providing permanent structures that shielded the field army and made Austria less reliant on external aid for repelling Prussian strength. The success of this gradual evolution in mitigating enemy military pressure can be seen by the number of battles fought on Austrian soil in the three wars. The first saw extensive fighting across Bohemia and into Upper Austria along with lengthy Prussian and French occupations. The second saw Prussian incursions promptly ejected and most of the fighting on foreign territory. And the third ended without a single major battle or siege. Where the War of the Austrian Succession lasted eight years, the War of the Bavarian Succession, which opened with the same Prussian moves, lasted three months.

The Prussian wars produced lasting consequences for Habsburg strategy. Geopolitically, Austria momentarily settled the question of how central Europe would be managed—largely to Austria's advantage, not through opportunistic land grabs, but through a continuation of the methods of rules-based compromise that had long governed the Reich. In this sense, Kaunitz's objective of seeking a more stable postwar order had been achieved. Frederick's invasions forced Austria to think about and plan for war on a proactive rather than reactive basis. Military necessity dictated the rationalization of strategic institutions in the form of a more efficient government and General Staff. Postwar commissions habituated the army to absorbing lessons from war and thinking systematically about the future.

The precedents set by Lacy's and Joseph II's planning would become an ingrained part of Austrian military practice at the same time that Kaunitz's diplomatic revolution and intervention in wartime decision-making brought higher coordination in Habsburg military and diplomatic planning. The resulting concepts, centered on a defensive army, frontier fortifications, and antihegemonic coalitions, would form the backbone of Habsburg grand strategy for most of the monarchy's remaining history. It is with these techniques and the hard-learned skills of resilience against a predatory neighbor that Austria would enter its next contest against an even more powerful opponent—Napoleonic France.

7

Teufelfranzosen

FRANCE AND THE WESTERN FRONTIER

If we weigh the comparative strengths of Austria and France, we find on the one hand a population of 25 million, of which about half is paralyzed by differing constitutions and, on the other, a France with unhindered access to 40 million, over which it has imposed an iron conscription law ... that knows no exemptions—a system, in short, of the kind that Your Majesty would never be able to implement in our lands.

—ARCHDUKE CHARLES

Only one escape is left to us: to conserve our strength for better days, to work for our preservation with gentler means—and not to look back.

—METTERNICH

ALONG ITS WESTERN FRONTIERS, the Habsburg dynasty was locked for most of its existence in an unequal contest with the military superstate of France. More advanced than the Ottomans and bigger than Prussia, France was capable of fielding large modern armies and elaborate alliances to threaten the Erblände from multiple sides. In conflicts with France, Austria was not able to count on the military-technological advantage that it enjoyed against the Turks, or the greater size and resources that gave it an edge against Prussia. Instead, Austria learned over time to contain French power through the defensive use of space, building extensive buffer zones to offset France's advantages in offensive capabilities. Habsburg strategy on the western frontier evolved through three phases. In wars with the Bourbon kings, successive Habsburg monarchs cultivated the smaller states of the German Reich and northern Italy as clients, committed to sharing the burden of defense through local armies and tutelary fortresses in wartime. Against Napoleon, these buffers collapsed, forcing Austria to use strategies of delay and accommodation similar to those employed against Frederick II to wear down and outlast a stronger military opponent. And in the peace that followed, Austria restored and expanded its traditional western security system, using confederated buffers and frontier fortresses to deter renewed French revisionism.

Playground of Empires

The western frontier of the Habsburg Monarchy ran across the middle mass of the European continent from the English Channel to the Mediterranean (see figure 7.1). At its epicenter lay the lands directly above and below the Alps, including the states of southern Germany and northern Italy that had formed the ancient heartland of Charlemagne's empire. Despite their separation by mountains, these territories represented a more or less contiguous zone of agriculturally fertile, mineral-rich provinces capable of sustaining high population densities, tax revenue, and the early development of industry. From the Middle Ages on, the states of this region had shared the characteristic of political fragmentation, forming weakly organized clusters of small polities that were susceptible to domination and influence by outside powers.

The central location and political tractability of these lands endowed them with great geopolitical importance for neighboring Great Powers. By the fourteenth century, an intense competition had formed over control of them between the Habsburgs and the Capetian dynasty of France, with its Valois and

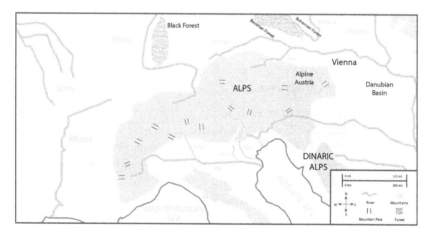

FIG. 7.1. Western Frontier of the Habsburg Empire.
Source: Center for European Policy Analysis, 2017.

Bourbon branches, that would persist for almost five centuries. Both dynasties sought to impose some degree of primacy over the weak polities of Germany and Italy, but in any event to prevent them from falling under the other's sway. The stakes for both empires were high. A France that could expand beyond the Rhine was capable of dominating Europe; one that could not face the prospect of confinement in the continent's westernmost corner and remaining perpetually on the defensive against the combined strength of Germany. An Austria that could retain a deciding influence over Germany and Italy could add depth and wealth to its small Alpine core; one that could not be reduced to the status of a marginal power and sequestered to Europe's eastern rim.

A Different Kind of Enemy

In this high-stakes competition, Austria faced a rival that was qualitatively different from its other competitors. France developed the resources and military-technological tools of a Great Power earlier than any Western state.[1] Its kings achieved early mastery over the nobility, building a centralized military state that was backed by the resources of a large, defensible, and well-proportioned landmass rich in natural wealth. To this was added a culturally and linguistically homogeneous population that numbered twenty million by 1700—larger than any other European power including Russia.[2] Drawing on these resources, France could assemble large, advanced armies, supported by an ample treasury and the latest Western warfare methods. Despite possessing a comparable landmass, Austria was usually unable to compete with France on equal military terms.[3]

One French advantage was geography. Located at the westernmost tip of the European peninsula, it was flanked by the sea on three sides and screened by mountains across its landward frontier. Combined with its numerous population, these physical traits presented a secure geopolitical base that gave France a natural offensive orientation in its behavior. As a nineteenth-century Austrian military appraisal put it,

> Bounded by oceans to its West and to its North.... [France] has but one defensive line and one direction of war. [It has] a coherent national identity—characteristics shared by no other major power, except Russia. This alone gives her position advantageous for war and lessens the pains of any potential defeat or setback. It is impossible to imagine breaking up France, even if it were defeated in an attempt to destroy and divide the rest of Europe.[4]

These characteristics represented a significant advantage in strategic competition. In wars with Austria, France's geography was conducive to launch-

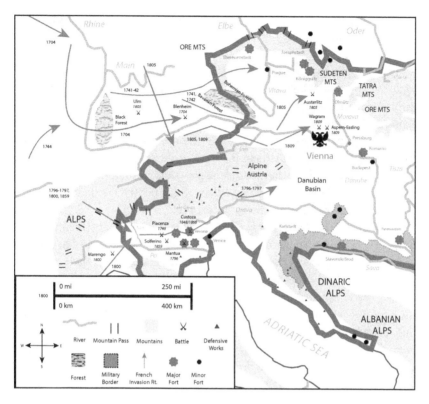

FIG. 7.2. French Invasions of Austria, Eighteenth and Nineteenth Centuries.
Source: Center for European Policy Analysis, 2017.

ing two-pronged offensives into the Danube River Basin. France benefited from the topographic arrangement of the Alps, whose east-west spine enabled an invader approaching from the west to enter the Erblände along two separate avenues while screening a substantial portion of its own forces—and ultimate intentions. Europe's rivers amplified this effect (see figure 7.2). North of the Alps, the Rhine Valley's near intersection with the Danube allowed for the swift eastward movement of troops from the French interior and supplies directly into the Habsburg heartland. As Venturini wrote of this section of frontier,

> The long border is throughout only beneficial for the French.... The assertion of mountains ... [means that] the French always have free rein there, a safe Rhine crossing, and the most commodious positions to attack the Austrian front on the right flank. They have the same advantages on the Upper Rhine through the formation of their power in Switzerland. Thus, the Austrian Army is in the highly disadvantageous position of defending

a completely surrounded unfortified border against a strong enemy, operating from an extremely strong eccentric base.[5]

To the south, France's Rhone River has a similar effect, aiding movement to the headwaters of Italy's River Po Valley, down which armies could march through fertile plains to the thirty-mile-wide "Ljubljana Gap" through the Karawanken Alps of modern-day Slovenia and an open road to Vienna.[6] These two paths—one through Germany and the other through Italy—created a Rhine-Po dilemma for Austria in the west, enabling invaders to approach on a dual axis in the assurance that defenders would not know until late in the game where their main blow would fall, by which point it would be too late to quickly shift forces from one front to the other.

Another French strength was alliances. As a state that combined the attributes of a maritime and continental power, France needed allies to support prolonged landward advances. An old dynasty, the Valois and their offshoots were skilled in collecting clients and advancing succession-based claims that formed the template for expansion until the late eighteenth century. Partly through this tradition, France developed a sophisticated diplomatic culture that treated alliances as an integral component of security policy. In the west, France's famous *Pactes de Familie* effectively sealed off its southern frontier and enlisted Spain as a virtual proxy in contests on the European mainland. In Germany, France cultivated those German states that chafed at Habsburg dominion, particularly Bavaria, but occasionally Brandenburg and Saxony. Further east, it organized military alliances with second-rank states located on the opposite side of its rivals—so-called *alliances de revers*. As early as the eighth century, the Carolingian kings had used such formulas to court the Abbasid Caliphate to harass the flanks of the Byzantine Empire. In the sixteenth century, it formed alliances with the still-extant kingdoms of Poland and Hungary, the latter of which would persist through patronage to renegade Magyar princes and offer France a ready base of opposition to the Habsburgs inside their own borders. Similar alliances would be nurtured with Sweden, Saxony-Poland, and the Ottoman Empire as counters to Russian expansion and tourniquets to Austria well into the eighteenth century.

France's combination of large armies, favorable geography, and alliances set it apart from other Habsburg rivals. Where the Ottomans often had numerical superiority and the Prussians frequently possessed a technological-tactical edge, France had both. Its facility with alliances differentiated it both from the Ottomans, who rarely attempted to coordinate with Western powers, and Prussia, which until Bismarck showed only a marginal aptitude for sustaining alliances. Where both the Ottoman Empire and Prussia had to use great exertions of diplomacy to trigger crises in theaters other than their own, France could pose threats to two separate frontiers merely by virtue of its geographic location. Together, these military, diplomatic, and geographic factors made it a full-spectrum peer competitor whose advantages were rendered all the more lethal by the fractious, harried, and resource-constrained state in which the Habsburg Monarchy usually found itself.

Building Blocks of Western Strategy

To understand the strategies that Austria developed to deal with the French threat, it is first necessary to understand what it could not do. The Bourbon wars made it plain that the monarchy could not dominate France militarily. Nor did it have the option of absorbing all or most of the territories to its west, as a more powerful empire might have attempted. France's alacrity as an offensive land power along with the high strategic-economic value of the German and Italian lands meant that Austria could not depend on a few fortresses and low-intensity border defenses of the kind it was able to employ across the barren expanses of the southeast. And while periods of détente and even alliance might be possible, conflicts between the two states often involved fundamental misalignments of strategic interest, foreclosing the option of a prolonged condominium of the kind that Austria developed with Russia.

Despite these limitations, Austria did possess certain advantages that over time would provide the building blocks for an effective strategy to counter French strength. Unlike on its northern or southern frontiers, Austria's western approaches were populated by scores of smaller and weaker states. Over previous centuries, the Habsburgs had amassed considerable influence over these states in their status as Holy Roman emperors. The Reich itself was not a powerful offensive military tool; as noted in chapter 6, by the eighteenth century it was a shadow of its former medieval glory. The Reich's influence in Italy was weak, with the region north of the Papal States existing under the nominal jurisdiction at best of the emperor.

Nevertheless, the Habsburgs' status in both sets of lands, seemingly irrelevant in hard-power terms, conveyed a moral authority and sets of levers for political influence among the small states of middle Europe that the Bourbon kings, for all their military strength, could not match.[7] This status provided a seemingly symbolic yet decisive edge in the battle for political influence among the smaller states of central Europe. Building on this foundation, the Habsburgs constructed a security system that by the early decades of the eighteenth century would consist of three interrelated pillars: a protective belt of buffer states, a network of fortresses, and antihegemonic coalitions.

WESTERN BUFFERS: THE *REICHSBARRIERE*

At the heart of Habsburg strategy in the west was the concept, initially inchoate but increasingly formal with the passage of time, of a series of obstacles—political, military, and spatial—to block eastward French expansion and organize the intervening territories under a Habsburg aegis. The overarching aim was to create a defensive bulwark, or *Reichsbarriere* as the Austrians called it, across the length of the western Habsburg frontier, from Switzerland to the English Channel. In the north this barrier was anchored on the Austrian Netherlands, which acted as a point d'appui for Austrian armies to threaten France in the rear, and in the south on the Alps, which provided a natural wall below the Rhine Valley.[8] Between these points, the Habsburgs organized a line of buffer states, under the auspices of the Reich, which continued in a more loosely organized format into the territories of northern Italy.

In engineering a Habsburg tilt among the states of this line, the Habsburgs enjoyed two advantages. One was fear. While German states were nominal vassals to the Habsburg throne, by the end of the Thirty Years' War this was no longer a sufficient force to congeal them into an anti-French bloc. What could unite them behind a common strategic purpose, at least for short periods, was the threat of attack by an outside, non-Germanic power. The acquisitive militarism of the French state under the Bourbon kings presented such a threat, made all the more adhesive by Louis XIV's habit of targeting weaker states for coercion.

Successive Habsburg monarchs harnessed German fears of the Bourbons to Austrian strategic needs, renovating the old collective defense mechanisms of the Reich for use against outside aggressors for the first time since before the Reformation.[9] They focused in particular on organizing defensive clusters among the small states that lined France's frontiers and principal invasion routes. In 1702, Leopold I worked with the princes of the Reich's most exposed members to form the Nördlingen Association, a subgrouping of states whose purpose was to defend against attack from the west (see table 7.1).[10] Within the Reich, the Nördlingen states helped to counterbalance opposition from northern or pro-French states to ensure the passage of a Reichskrieg—the equivalent of Article 5 in NATO—while lending credibility to Austria as a security patron in the eyes of its larger external allies.[11] Once war was declared, the group provided a mechanism for pooling defense resources well above the Reich average, often committing troops at triple the strength required by the diet while less exposed.

Similar though less formalized dynamics existed in Italy. Long a Habsburg stronghold, Italy's position in the wider Austrian orbit was reaffirmed in the Spanish succession war, with portions of Lombardy, including the duchies of

TABLE 7.1. The Nördlingen Association's
Military Manpower, circa 1702

Kreis	Contingent
Franconia	8,000
Swabia	10,800
Upper Rhine	3,000
Electoral Rhine	6,500
Austria	16,000
Westphalia	9,180
Total	53,480

Sources: Lünig, ed., *Corpus iuris militaris*, 1:402–7;
Hoffmann, ed., *Quellen zum Verfassungsorganismus*,
269–71.

Mantua and Milan, coming into Austrian possession in 1711. Between these territories and the Erblände sat Venetia, through which Austria brokered rights of passage for troops and supplies via the Brenner Pass in wartime. To the west lay the kingdom of Sardinia, an independent polity with a history of vassalage to Spain that shared the Nördlingen states' proximity to and therefore fear of stronger powers immediately beyond its borders. Straddling the mountains, Sardinia looked with apprehension on the expansion of Bourbon strength.[12] As in Germany, this anxiety provided an opening for Austria to cultivate close security links, and eventually, a glacis to French or Spanish re-entry into the peninsula.

Another factor that aided the Habsburg Monarchy's efforts to build a western buffer system, paradoxically, was its own weakness. Where early eighteenth-century France appeared strong and predatory to Europe's smaller states, Austria was already by this point widely seen as being unable to mount the attempts at continental primacy that it had attempted in its heyday of the sixteenth and seventeenth centuries. Capable of undertaking significant military efforts, it nevertheless posed no threat of hegemony. Indeed, its primary goal as an ancient, weak power was a stable territorial status quo. This aligned well with small states' interests in self-preservation. Not surprisingly, Austria's greatest base of support in the western buffers were those states that had the most to lose from revisionism: in Germany, the smaller principalities and archbishoprics—Salzburg, Passau, the imperial knights, and southern free cities; and in Italy, the small states of Lombardy and Sardinian satellite, which preferred a distant Viennese paternalism to centralized Bourbon rule.[13] In both sets of territories, a basic bargain presented itself: small-state fealty and contributions to collective defense in exchange for benign Habsburg domination and protection.

The Habsburgs actively promoted this bargain, using the largesse of the emperor's office—jobs in the imperial administration, bribes, and other favors—to reward loyal princes and punish disloyalty. At the same time, the Reich machinery limited imperial power through various checks and balances, including an electoral college that ratified major decisions and a diet that decided on declarations of Reichskrieg and, ultimately, electoral confirmation of new emperors. However formulaic, these rule sets helped to make Austrian hegemony more palatable to client states by wrapping it in the arcana of rules and procedures.

Habsburg monarchs were conscious of the strength that came from restraint in such a setting, and often cultivated a reputation for moderation in victory and leniency in dealings with wayward princes. An example, as we have seen, was Maria Theresa's extension of generous terms to the Bavarian Füssens in 1745. Such magnanimity could be alternated with acts of brutality. But ultimately, Habsburg rule was built on the foundation of a soft hegemony. This stemmed not from altruism but rather necessity; attempting a more coercive approach would simply not have worked given the often-tentative state of Habsburg military and financial power. In showing well-timed mercy, the dynasty was most likely to cultivate a voluntary willingness of states to remain loyal in future crises.

These measures did not make either Germany or Italy into uniformly pro-Habsburg domains. By definition, the nature of a buffer zone is that the states therein do not fall under the exclusive sway of either flanking power. Midsize members of the Reich frequently chafed at Habsburg dominance as a barrier to their own territorial growth and influence. Most notably, as we have seen, there was Bavaria, which in addition to bearing traces of the old Wittelsbach-Habsburg rivalry, was encircled by Habsburg possessions or allies, and therefore felt as much a menace from Austria as Sardinia or the Nördlingen states felt from France. Noting this dynamic, Eugene said of the Bavarians, "Geography prevented them from being men of honor."[14] Saxony too, while more consistently in the Habsburg orbit, often oscillated between Austria and its enemies. France encouraged these dynamics—in Italy, by playing Sardinian court politics and stoking discontent in Lombardy; and in Germany, by impeding efforts at a unified Reich military policy and fanning opposition to the emperor.[15] In both regions, Versailles dispensed bribes on a stupendous scale and exploited local factionalism. Above all it sought to nurture rival claimants to the imperial title, either by building German support for a Bourbon candidacy or backing that of a lesser German house hostile to the Habsburgs.

French efforts notwithstanding, armed opposition by the German princes to the Habsburgs was the exception rather than the rule. While French money could always find a fissure to exploit, more frequently than not, intrabuffer tensions were kept within bounds, taking the form of simmering discord rather than active revisionism. This was in part due to the fact that even the Habsburgs' German rivals derived a benefit from its weak hegemony, which was bearable, and in any event, usually preferable to a new and unknown foreign ascendancy. The Reich's rickety rule-making structures further channeled these currents into constitutional cul-de-sacs that tended to support continuation of the status quo. While Bavarian and certainly Prussian opposition could be formidable at times, the structures of the Reich gave Austrian diplomats options for managing these dynamics that they otherwise would have lacked. Even at the high point of its power, France never succeeded in building a permanent fifth column in Reich politics, and was only able to pull Sardinia fully into its sphere after the emergence of nationalist aspirations in the mid-nineteenth century.[16]

TUTELARY FORTRESSES

Habsburg success in organizing buffer regions enabled Austria to do something Great Powers are rarely able to do in such spaces: maintain a military presence on the territory of intermediary states. The Bourbon wars demonstrated the utility that forward force deployments, and particularly fortresses, could have in both Germany and Italy. In the Spanish succession war, France employed the Lines of Brabant, a 130-mile-long network of strongholds and entrenchments from Antwerp to Meuse, to slow the advance of allied forces under the command of John Churchill, First Duke of Marlborough (1650–1722) in the Low Countries. By contrast, Austria's fortifications in the west were initially meager, prompting Eugene to complain about the absence of even an "entrenched camp" here and make repeated pleas to build forts in the west "to form a barrier against France, which might deter her from attacking us."[17]

Through the Reich, however, Austria had access to the fortresses of fellow German states. Such defenses, particularly those along the Rhine that sat near the embarkation points of French armies, had proven effective at arresting the progress of French offensives early in their advance. Closer to Austria's borders, Ludwig of Baden's Stollhofen Line, while bypassed, fired imaginations about the potential for more fully developed defensive positions to block the gap between the Black Forest and Rhine that formed the favored entry point for French armies into Austria.[18] The rapid French reduction of Ulm, Regensburg, Menningen, and Neuburg, and subsequent enemy advance into the Tyrol, illustrated the dangers that could materialize for Austria when this crucial route through southern Germany was unhindered.[19]

Through the use of Reich forts during the Bourbon wars, the Habsburg Army gradually developed a concept of western security in which the ability

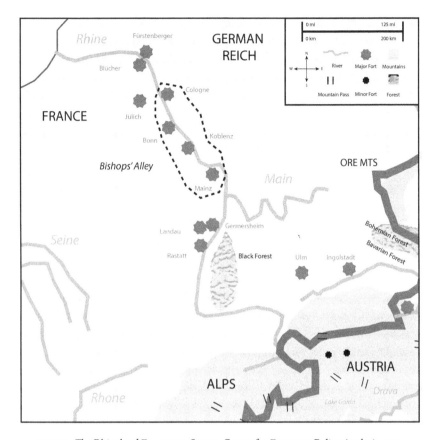

FIG. 7.3. The Rhineland Fortresses. *Source:* Center for European Policy Analysis, 2017.

to place force beyond Austria's borders, on the soil of acquired territories or friendly states, was seen as the key to the defense of the Erblände. Under the terms of a Reichskrieg, Austrian armies could transverse and operate from friendly Reich territory. When war was on the horizon, Vienna often negotiated terms with individual states allowing for sustained deployments or shared garrisoning of strategically important points on their territory. In Germany, these included the fortresses of Mannheim and Philipsburg on the Middle Rhine; Mainz, Coblenz, Bonn, and Cologne (the so-called Bishop's Alley) on the Lower Rhine; and Kehl, Villingen, Freudenstadt, Heidelberg, Mannheim, Frankenthal, and Freiburg on the Danube (see figure 7.3).[20]

Similarly, Austria had access to numerous frontier fortresses in Italy. Victory in the Spanish succession war brought possession of Fuentes, located near the mouth of the Adda; Pizzighettone, near Lake Garda; and the swamp fortress of Mantua guarding the Tyrolean passes.[21] Security arrangements with Venetia provided access to Peschiera, an island fortress at the intersection of the Mincio and Lake Garda, and to the west, the alliance with Sardinia informally incorporated the fortress at Turin and numerous smaller sites lining the Alpine passes.

While the main purpose of Habsburg buffer forts was defensive, their presence also expanded offensive options in wartime. Using the Rhine forts, Habsburg and Reich armies could converge on the Mosel Valley, the point of the French frontier with the fewest obstacles to Paris. Especially notable in this regard were the forts of Bishop's Alley and the strongholds at Mannheim and Philipsburg.[22] Used in conjunction with the Austrian Netherlands and Habsburg positions in Italy, these fortress networks provided a means of projecting power along the full length of the French frontier and achieving concentration early in a conflict.

Once an invader got beyond the intervening spaces of the Reich, an effective defense was harder to mount. As the Allied armies would find in World War II, the physical orientation of the Rhine tributaries tends to speed invading armies while complicating internal coordination between defending forces.[23] Using these rivers and picking off Reich members en route, a French invasion could penetrate southern Germany and swiftly reach Austrian soil. This reality intertwined the strategic fate of the Habsburg home territories with the territory of neighboring states, amplifying the importance of developing forward infrastructure on sites that were both militarily defensible and politically reliable.

ANTIHEGEMONIC COALITIONS

The same weakness that made Austria a tolerable patron to Europe's middle states aided its efforts to recruit Great Power allies against France. From the perspective of Europe's larger states, a France that was strong enough to break into the Netherlands and expand east of the Rhine and Alps was a France that would be hard to materially counterbalance on a long-term basis. The Habsburg Monarchy offered a force sufficiently strong to check this expansion without threatening to replace France as a danger to the European balance of power. In the east, Austria was an insurance policy against Ottoman decay devolving into vacuums that would invite predation by neighboring states. In the west, its client states and position in the Low Countries made it a natural barrier to French expansion on both a north-south and east-west axis.

In this combination of vulnerability and indispensability lay part of the origins of Austria's role as a geopolitical "necessity"—the "hinge upon which the fate of Europe must depend," as the British diplomat Castlereagh would later say.[24] In the age-old geopolitical pattern whereby large status quo powers support weaker states to guard against the rise of new hegemons, Austria was a hybrid, possessing the attributes of a Great Power, but through its internal complexities and exposed geography, the security dilemmas of a smaller state.

As an ally, Austria possessed certain attributes that stronger powers needed to manage the continent. One was location. Britain's wealth and naval power allowed it to provide subsidies, blockades, and small expeditionary forces, but it needed Austria as an onshore organizer of land armies. Russia was rich in military manpower yet distant from contests with western rivals, which unless impeded by Austria, would have the strength to contemplate eastward expansion. Another Habsburg strength, mentioned above, was legitimacy. Going back to the sixteenth century, Austrian diplomacy had developed a culture of playing to the dynasty's status as a bulwark against the Turks to enlist the help of other European states. After the Treaty of Westphalia, the Habsburgs built on this tradition, positioning themselves as the defender of the sanctity of European treaties. Invoking legitimacy, the monarchy became the guardian of treaty-based rights in the European states system. In the context of French military expansion, this positioned Austria to attract the patronage of other status quo–minded powers that stood to lose from force-based revisionism.

WESTERN TIME MANAGEMENT

The elements in Austria's western defenses worked together to give it greater control over sequencing in western conflicts. Buffer systems stalled invaders and won time to organize forces and recruit allies. Fortresses toughened middle-state terrain and ameliorated the Rhine-Po dilemma by enabling small forces on either side of the Alps to hold out until field armies could be shifted to the critical front. Allies heightened the effect by pressuring France's rearward approaches and providing relief armies to campaign on the Lower Rhine and Mosel—the points at which France was most vulnerable and the logistical reach of Austrian armies was most constrained. This in turn enabled Austria to safely deprioritize the front in Germany in the assurance that Reich armies (which faced jurisdictional obstacles to operating south of the Alps) and western allies could cover the north while it focused its own forces elsewhere. These various props allowed the monarchy to adopt an essentially "radial" approach to western crises, stripping to the bone Austrian deployments in the Rhine theater and concentrating troops elsewhere—sometimes in Hungary, but usually in Italy, where the richest territories were most likely to be won by Vienna in the war.[25]

This approach to managing the west could fail. In the War of the Polish Succession, Austria was shorn of support from England and Holland, and lost ground in Italy. In the War of the Austrian Succession, the Reich failed to rally, and allied help was weaker than in the Spanish succession war, forcing Austria to bear the brunt of multiple fronts on its own. Support from the maritime powers tended to focus on the Austrian Netherlands, but resist Habsburg expenditures of subsidies or effort on Hungary. Russian aid too, as we have seen, could be slow to materialize and often came at the cost of a pound of flesh in the east. Yet by and large, the system held, partly through Austrian diplomacy, but mainly because Europe's powers had few options but to sustain a central wedge to limit the growth of French strength, and Austria was the only game in town. From the beginning of Louis XIV's reign until the rise of Frederick the Great, Austria fought five wars against France, in all of which it was on the side with a greater number of allies, and in all but one of which it arguably came out on the better side of the ledger. In this period, Austria's western toolbox enabled it to offset most of France's offensive power advantages at a financial and human cost that was manageable for itself.

System Collapse: The Napoleonic Wars

As we saw in a previous chapter, the emergence of Prussia brought a coda to Austro-French rivalry in the middle decades of the eighteenth century, providing the basis for Kaunitz's successful courtship of Versailles. This interlude was shattered in 1789 with the outbreak of the French Revolution. Its aftermath marked the reactivation of France as a predatory power, igniting wars in which France would resume the multiaxis military expansion it had begun under Louis XIV.

In their first encounters with the new republic, the Austrians sought to use traditional methods to contain the threat. As in the past, Vienna rallied its buffer allies, mustering imperial forces and deploying the army to advanced posts on client state territory. It also enlisted extraregional allies, showing dexterity in the resumption of alliance ties with Britain after decades of lapse, and converting erstwhile enemy Prussia into a partner in a move as bold as Kaunitz's early French and Ottoman flips. As the diplomatic wheels turned to align the bulk of Europe in Austria's corner, the army prepared for an offensive use of Reich fortresses in a plan of operations that would have been recognizable to Eugene, amassing forces in forward positions at Coblenz for a concentric push from the Austrian Netherlands and Lower Rhine.

In the war that followed, Austria's plan and the century-old security system it embodied failed catastrophically. Ejecting allied armies from its frontiers, France invaded Austria's German and Italian buffers, imposing a peace at Campo Formio under which the monarchy ceded Belgium and lost control of large sections of northern Italy and the Rhineland.

The scale of Austria's defeat showed that the new French Republic was a more formidable threat than the Bourbons had been. Most noticeably, it was capable of generating larger armies. While France had always been able to sustain sizable forces, the republic's practice of placing all unmarried men eighteen to twenty-five under arms allowed it to put three-quarters of a million troops in the field—an astonishing half million of which were deployed for combat service.[26] In some early battles, Austrian forces faced opponents with a three-to-one numerical advantage. Animating French forces was an offensive *geist* very different from contemporary armies. Aggressive and mobile, they moved fast, unencumbered by supply trains. On the battlefield, they attacked in fat columns screened by skirmishers and supported by lighter, more maneuverable cannons, formed into large batteries.

THE NEW THREAT

Early campaigns against the French Republic were a foretaste of a new form of warfare for which Austria with its linear tactics and attritional approach to warfare was ill prepared. The man who would perfect these techniques was Napoleon. Born to parents of impoverished nobility on the island of Corsica, Napoleon was a junior artillery officer when the wars of the revolution broke out. After bold campaigns in Italy and Egypt, he was named consul in 1799, and in 1804, declared himself emperor of a new French Empire that would wage more than two decades of almost continual war against the armies of the Habsburg Monarchy.

In Napoleon, the Habsburgs were confronted with a very different kind of enemy than anything they had seen before. Unlike the Bourbon armies of the past, Napoleon formed his forces into large formations—divisions and corps rather than just regiments—that were able to operate as separate, self-contained armies in the field. Combining mass and mobility, the new French armies moved swiftly across Europe, ignoring many of the strategic and tactical considerations that had dominated warfare in the past. Where Louis XIV, Frederick, and the Turks had all to varying degrees relied on large supply trains that tied them to depots, Napoleon's armies lived off the land, marching as the crow flies. Where Frederick had prioritized the reduction of fortresses, Napoleon bypassed them, only besieging two in his entire career.[27] Where the Bourbons and Frederick had used attrition to achieve a peace on favorable terms, Napoleon sought the *destruction* of the enemy army.

Austrian strategy contributed indirectly to Napoleon's successes. Faced with the dilemma of French forces being able to approach from both north and south of the Alps, Habsburg commanders dispersed their armies at the frontier in hopes of detecting and intercepting the enemy before it could reach the Erblände. The early phases of the War of the First Coalition found the army strung across a three-hundred-mile front from Switzerland to the Rhine. Fast-moving French armies, to a greater degree than in the past, could exploit the Rhine-Po dilemma. In 1800, they moved in parallel down both river valleys, occupying the Swiss passes to block Austrian movement between the two fronts. While Austrian units struggled to concentrate, Napoleon delivered the decisive blow in Italy. From this experience, the Austrians concluded that they needed to prioritize Italy. In 1805, they placed the main army there, allowing Napoleon to blitz down the Danube while defeating weaker Austrian forces at Ulm and Austerlitz.

As dangerous as Napoleon's military behavior were his political moves. In his early campaigns in Italy and Germany, Napoleon revealed that he was motivated by a politically based strategy that targeted the weak spot of the enemy's underlying strategic or political system. In Austria's case, this weak spot, or "joint," as B. H. Liddell Hart called it, was the monarchy's numerous buffer states.[28] Segmenting client state armies from the Austrians and defeating them in detail, he then treated generously with their governments to undermine loyalty to Vienna. In doing so, Napoleon took what had previously been a basic strength of the Habsburgs—numerous small clients—and turned it into a weakness.[29] His aim was to permanently cleave these states from Austria and adhere them to France in a "rampart of republics" spanning Italy and Germany.[30] In 1806, Napoleon formalized this arrangement by abolishing the Holy Roman Empire, the linchpin of the Habsburg buffer system, and replacing it with the new, French-dominated Confederation of the Rhine. He outlined his strategic intentions for this new body in a conversation with Metternich shortly after its creation:

> I will tell you my secret. In Germany the small people want to be protected against the great people; the great wish to govern according to their own fancy; now, as I only want from the [German] federation men and money, and as it is the great and not the small who can provide me with both, I leave the former alone in peace, and the second have only to settle themselves as best they may![31]

Grasping the underlying logic of Austria's traditional client state model—guaranteeing the weak against the ambitions of the strong—Napoleon did the opposite, rewarding the strong at the expense of the weak to buy the former's loyalties, and armies, for France. Where the Bourbons had wanted merely to divide Germany and diminish its value as an Austrian glacis, Napoleon sought to undo the mechanics of Habsburg primacy and unite the remnants into an offensive tool.

The scale of Napoleon's ambitions made his threat to Austria not just territorial but also existential. Unlike in competitions against the Bourbons, Austria could not undo Napoleon's wartime gains at the peace table. Initially, Habsburg diplomats had tried to use Napoleon's defeats to continue the long practice of "rounding off" Austrian territories. But as the conflict widened, Napoleon cut more and more deeply into the political fabric of Austria's buffers—and eventually, its home territories. At Pressburg in 1805, Napoleon took Dalmatia, gave Istria to a new Kingdom of Italy, and ceded Tyrol and Voralberg to France's German clients, allowing the French Army to occupy bases directly overlooking Austrian territory.[32] At Tilsit in 1807, he went even further, forming a new Polish state, the Grand Duchy of Warsaw, and forcing Austrian recognition of an enlarged Kingdom of Westphalia.[33]

By 1808, France and its surrogates confronted the monarchy on three sides in Italy, Germany, and Poland. As Metternich commented, any war with France from this point on "would begin at the same time on the banks of the Inn and the Wieliczka"—frontier rivers some four hundred miles apart.[34] These changes spelled an end to the old Habsburg buffer system, and with it, the ability to conduct wars on Austria's terms. This in turn put stress on the remaining component of Austria's western system: extraregional allies. Successive military defeats undercut the logic of antihegemonic coalitions at the same time that they depleted Austrian resources for continued resistance. Prussia, an early and enthusiastic member of the anti-French coalitions, vacillated between policies of opposition and neutrality. Britain, though the most determined to outlast Napoleon, could do little to help Austria on land. As Archduke Charles wrote in 1804,

> Britain always needs to keep a part of its regular army at home. The past war proved that victory is not to be expected of English troops on the continent. The mercantilist England is further unlikely to consider continental politics as its true purpose. The history of the past 150 years has proved as much.... Except for Marlborough, no Englishman ever found a way to pursue their maritime superiority on the Danube.[35]

By contrast, Russia possessed the greatest land power reserves for sustaining a prolonged struggle. In 1800 and 1805, Austria replicated the pattern of military coordination from the Seven Years' War, at one point brokering the intervention of large Russian formations, under Suvorov as far west as Italy. The fundamental problem in such an arrangement was that as Napoleon pressed deep into the Habsburg home area, any Russian relief armies would place as great a burden on these lands as the enemy. As Charles noted, such allies

> are good for little more than diversions [and] are of no consequence to the defense of the core territory. Even if another power were to allow 100,000–120,000 men to operate on Austrian soil, it should be kept in mind that the

frontier provinces, Inner Austria and Tyrol, would not be able to sustain such a force. Importing such a mass of troops, if not entirely impossible, would be too expensive for Your Majesty's finances.[36]

Moreover, as in the wars against Frederick, large distances and conflicting military cultures beset Austro-Russian military cooperation. Where a linkup between the two armies at Kunersdorf in 1759 had given Frederick II a severe defeat, similar coordination at Austerlitz in 1805 ended in Napoleon's greatest victory. In all these alliances, the underlying challenge from an Austrian perspective was that its allies' money, ships, or armies were too far away to make a difference at a sufficiently early point in each new war, leaving it to bear the brunt and expense of French aggression.

While facing unprecedented new external challenges, Austria also had to contend with its old internal problems, which grew more pronounced as the wars with Napoleon dragged on. By the twelfth year of war, the monarchy was bankrupt, forcing the military budget to be cut by more than half.[37] Despite British subsidies, debts mounted, pressuring state finances and increasing the tax and inflationary burdens on the populace. Domestic strains emerged with a severity not seen since the early eighteenth century. As in the Austrian succession war, the Hungarian Diet voted a larger than usual revenue and military contribution for the war effort, which, as in that war, it failed to deliver. Previewing tactics they would employ again later, the Magyar nobility used the state of emergency to hand the dynasty a list of demands for fresh constitutional concessions. The diet refused conscription, and when the French attacked in 1805, commanders of the Magyar militia, or *insurrectio*, informed the invaders that Hungary "was neutral and would not fight."[38] Over time, the wars also steadily eroded the monarchy's material base for waging war, whittling away the troop reserves at the same time that France accumulated new territories and clients through conquest.

RESISTANCE AND RECUEILLEMENT: 1808–12

By 1808, little remained of the security system with which Austria had once managed its westward frontier. Its Italian and German buffers gone, the monarchy could no longer intercept French armies before they reached Austrian soil. Without the help of the Reichsarmee operating on the Rhine and Mosel, it could no longer outsource management of the German theater to allies while concentrating its own forces south of the Alps. With the Reich dissolved and the Italian states converted to French clients, the challenge of anticipating and countering dual-pronged enemy thrusts had become pronounced. Lacking their early warning system, Habsburg forces would in any future campaign be confined to a restricted space—the Austrian home area—on which a French attack could fall suddenly, from two directions.

Faced with these straitened circumstances, Habsburg leaders debated two strategic options: to adjust to the French hegemony by accommodating Napoleon or fight a new war. Archduke Charles favored the former course. The foreign minister, Count Johann Philipp von Stadion-Warthausen (1763–1824), advocated the latter, reasoning that Napoleon had "not changed his hostile sentiments toward us and is only awaiting the right moment to prove it by deeds."[39] In the period since Austria's last defeat, Stadion had pursued a policy of recueillement, avoiding any direct challenges to France in order to rebuild the monarchy's finances and army until an opportunity presented itself to use them to restore the monarchy's geopolitical position. By 1808, Stadion believed this opportunity had arrived and that Austria should "seek self-defense by taking the offensive" rather than letting the enemy attack on its terms, on the basis of its new advanced positions in Germany and Italy.[40]

The clenching argument for Austria to act at this particular moment was put forward by one of Stadion's subordinates, Count (later Prince) Klemens Wenzel von Metternich, then serving as ambassador to France. In a series of three memorandums, Metternich outlined the case for war. All three concentrated on the factor of timing. In the first, he argued that deteriorating French public support for Napoleon meant that in any new war, the French emperor would be distracted at home. The second asserted that Russia, despite its tacit 1807 alliance with France, would not attack Austria; "Alexander," Metternich wrote, "is not someone the French can enflame against us; to the contrary, he desires an intimate bond with us, which he believes we may yet reach through persistence."[41] In the third memo, Metternich made his strongest strategic argument: Napoleon's army was absorbed in and depleted by its attempt to subjugate Spain:

> The war against Spain divulges a great secret—namely, that Napoleon has but one army, his *Grande Armee*.... The questions to consider [are]:
>
> (1) What are the total forces of France and her allies at this present moment?
> (2) After deducting from the whole of these forces the number of men employed in the conquest of Spain, what number of effective troops could Napoleon bring against us?
> (3) What resources has Napoleon for carrying on the war against Spain and against us *at the same time*? [emphasis added] ...

The summary of the military position appears to me to be the following: (a) Napoleon can fight us now with 206,000 men, of whom 107,000 are French, 99,000 confederate and allies. (b) His reserves can after a time only be composed of conscripts below the age for service.... Thus the forces of Austria, so inferior to those of France before the insurrection in Spain, will be at least equal to them immediately after that event.[42]

Against France's divided forces, Austria's generals believed that through expanded conscription and the organization of militia units in politically reliable parts of the monarchy they could field the largest army in the monarchy's history—some 550,000 troops.[43] In addition, Stadion was convinced that the German popular sentiment recently stirred by Napoleon's conquest of Prussia could be harnessed to Austria's cause, and with early victories, Russia and Prussia might be convinced to enter as allies.

THE 1809 WAR

Given these favorable conditions, Stadion and the emperor, Francis II (I), judged that the moment for war was better than it would be again at any time in the foreseeable future. Leading Habsburg forces in the coming campaign was the emperor's younger brother, Archduke Charles. In 1809, Charles was thirty-seven years old and in the prime of his military career.[44] Unlike most of Austria's senior generals, he had shown the ability to hold his own against the French, delivering victories in Holland, Italy, and Switzerland. In 1805, he had been with the main army in Italy when Napoleon entered Austria through Germany. Epileptic and cerebral, Charles was a cautious commander who prioritized retention of key points of terrain and protection of communication lines over defeating the enemy (see chapter 4). Surveying Austria's financial and troop shortages, Charles had misgivings about the campaign's timing, which would later be validated.

When war was declared, Napoleon quickly shifted attention and resources from Spain to the Danube, while Austria mobilized fewer troops than expected.[45] Neither German popular sentiment nor Russian and Prussian help materialized. As in the past, the dilemmas of Austria's multivector geography hurt it. With part of the army deployed in Italy, the army had to choose between concentrating the main force in Bohemia, whence to strike into Germany, or the River Inn, to cover the capital. Ultimately choosing the latter, Charles also had to siphon off units to cover the Tyrol, Dalmatia, and Poland.[46]

When the French invaded, Charles adopted a strategy not unlike that used by Daun against Frederick. Rather than trying to intercept Napoleon outside Vienna and seek a decisive battle on the right side of the Danube, he used Austria's rivers to delay and wear down the stronger enemy forces. Charles's chief of staff, Maximilian Freiherr von Wimpffen, outlined the strategy in a memorandum of May 17:

> If the French lose the battle, ... they risk everything and us only a little. If we were to cross the Danube now, it would be the opposite: the Austrian emperor would not even be able to negotiate anymore before the monarchy were conquered. Fabius saved Rome, and Daun saved Austria not in haste, but through delay [*nicht durch Eile, sondern durch Zaudern*]. We must emulate their example and prosecute the war according to our patterns, befitting the state of our armed forces. Our supports are close, whereas the enemy is far from his. In holding the left bank of the Danube, we are defending the greater part of the monarchy. We would lose tremendously by crossing to the other side. Our army can reinforce itself from its depots, whereas Napoleon only expects another 12,000 Saxons.... We require the resources of the left Dabune bank for our armed forces, whereas the right side could not provide as such. If we make use of this quiet hour [*Schäferstunde*], we can prepare everything for quickly seizing the right moment.[47]

The ensuing campaign showed the influence of earlier Habsburg commanders in Charles's thinking. Preparing for a protracted war in the Austrian countryside like that which the Prussians had brought to Moravia a generation earlier, Charles anticipated the alienating effects that French requisitions of supply would have on the local population, instructing his own commanders to prevent similar behavior among their troops under threat of "severe punishments" (*strenge Strafen*).[48] Forming defensive positions behind the Danube, Charles emulated Prince Eugene at Zenta, destroying the enemy in detail as it attempted to cross and re-form ranks on the other side.[49] The strategy worked: with Austrian armies en route from Italy to threaten the French rear, and the danger of Russian or Prussian entry looming, Napoleon felt a time pressure not unlike that felt by Frederick in his Moravia campaigns. Attacking across the river, he suffered the first significant defeat of his career, at Aspern-Essling, on May 21–22. While Montecuccoli would have admired Charles's dispositions along the Danube, his attachment to the precepts of attritional warfare prevented the Austrian Army for not the last time in its history from capitalizing on victory.[50] After the battle, Napoleon quickly recovered his equilibrium to defeat the Austrians at Wagram and force the monarchy to sue for peace.

In the peace negotiations that followed, Austria lost a swath of valuable home territories to France and its allies: Salzburg to Bavaria, West Galicia to the Duchy of Warsaw, East Galicia to Russia, and southern Carinthia, Croatia, Istria, Dalmatia, and the port of Trieste to France. Altogether, the peace of

Schönbrünn carved 32,000 square miles and 3.5 million inhabitants out of the Habsburg Monarchy, while levying a large indemnity and restricting the Habsburg Army to 150,000 troops. Together with previous territorial losses, the new status quo sheared Austria of a substantial portion of its economic and manpower base for conducting future wars. Geopolitically, it was now encircled by Napoleon and his proxies in Italy, Germany, Poland, and Croatia, making France the only opponent in Austria's history to attain a standing military presence on four Habsburg frontiers simultaneously.

ACCOMMODATING NAPOLEON

After the 1809 war, Austria found itself in the position of a shrinking second-rate power wedged between the French and Russian empires. With Metternich at the helm, Austria now adopted a strategy of accommodation. The monarchy's only hope for survival, Metternich wrote, was "to tack, to efface ourselves, to come to terms with the Victor. Only thus may we perhaps preserve our existence till the day of general deliverance."[51]

A new policy along these lines would seem to be diametrically opposed to the course of isolated resistance that Austria had pursued in the lead-up to the 1809 campaign. But there was more continuity than change in Austrian strategy, for Metternich's goal, like that of Stadion, was to achieve a period of recueillement in which to play for time and gather strength. To do so he now embraced the first of the two strategic options that Vienna had been debating since Pressburg and Tilsit: cohabitation with the enemy. This was not the first time Austria had to accommodate a stronger foe to survive. Habsburg monarchs had long used temporary peace arrangements to improve the monarchy's circumstances before returning to deal with an enemy from a position of strength. One example was Joseph I's dealings with the Ottomans and Hungarians ahead of Eugene's campaigns, Maria Theresa's acquiescence to the Convention of Kleinschnellendorf another.

Metternich proceeded on a similar logic, but on a larger scale. Where Austria had often used tactical reprieves to gain positional advantages over enemies for short periods, Metternich faced the possibility of a long domination by a revolutionary opponent who had already demonstrated his capacity to dismantle the ancien régime. Where Stadion had aimed to break this hegemony and restore Austria's position in Germany and Italy, Metternich sought to come to terms with the hegemon in a prolonged marriage of convenience until a new day, however distant, dawned. If unsuccessful, Austria could face a gradual diminution between a Russian-dominated Balkans and French-dominated central Europe—in short, everything that its strategies had worked to avoid for more than a century. If Austria misplayed its hand, it was not unimaginable that it could be carved up among the mosaic of Napoleon's Germanic client kingdoms.

Austria needed to stave off extinction while keeping an eye on how its moves would position it after the war. To this end, Metternich became an obliging, if duplicitous, handmaiden to the new order. To bond the two states more closely together, he brokered the marriage of Marie Louise (1791–1847), Emperor Francis's eldest daughter by his second wife, to Napoleon. Coming less than a year after Austria's 1809 defeat, the move was humiliating for the Habsburgs, entailing the unification of an eight-hundred-year-old dynasty with a self-made general who represented the negation of the social order that the monarchy embodied. Nevertheless, the marriage served Metternich's goals, buying time by placating Napoleon and enhancing Austria's position relative to Russia.

In spring 1812, Metternich's policy reached its culmination when Austria entered into a formal military alliance with France, providing thirty thousand troops to assist, albeit indirectly, in Napoleon's invasion of Russia. The desperation of Austria's position is illustrated in the fact that Metternich was willing to bandwagon with a revisionist power, even if largely symbolically, in an attack on a power that represented the linchpin of Austria's long-term security interests. Joining in the invasion aided in Austria's game of keeping its head down as Napoleon's gambles exhausted French strength. In his diplomacy, Metternich was waging a larger geopolitical game of Fabian evasion and attrition like that which Charles and Daun had used on the battlefield, paralleling the moves of a stronger opponent and avoiding actions that would overplay Austria's hand.

System Restoration: 1813–14 and the Metternich System

With Napoleon's defeat in Russia, the opening for which Metternich had waited intermittently since 1805 appeared. Unlike in 1809, circumstances now overwhelmingly favored military action.[52] The scale of the disaster made France militarily weaker than it had been at any point since 1792. The series of recueillements undertaken by Stadion and Metternich had accomplished their purpose of giving Austria time to recuperate. As in the interlude between wars with Frederick II, Austria had used its post-1809 reprieve to mobilize internal capabilities, tending militia cadres and leveraging the resources of the Military Border. As a result, by the time war again broke out, the monarchy possessed a veteran core around which to quickly assemble armies that would number 160,000 by April 1813, 479,000 by August, and eventually reach 568,000.[53]

As in the Prussian wars, the Austrians had learned from their defeats at the hands of the French, forming postwar commissions to study lessons learned, and revamp tactics and doctrine—first in 1798–99, and again in 1801–4 and

1807. Also as in the Prussian wars, the responsibility for military strategy was centralized and eventually filled with better talent. Charles was given combined authority for the Hofkriegsrat and new Militär-Hof-Commission ahead of the 1805 and 1809 campaigns, and a young officer, Radetzky, was installed as chief of the quartermaster of the General Staff.[54] And as in previous wars, protracted emergency prompted a tighter interweaving of diplomatic and military goals, with Stadion and Metternich, like Kaunitz, exercising decisive influence on overall strategy.

External factors also favored action. Where Russia had been ponderous and distant in the earlier campaigns, and neutral when Austria was losing in 1809, it was now bringing its large resources fully into play. Prussia too was entering the scales with a rebuilt army backed by patriotic fervor. Britain, committed as always, now raked in a harvest of easy gains on French peripheries rendered vulnerable by Napoleon's eastern gambit. With this alignment of forces, Austria could now, after four years of self-abasement, reenter the military competition with prospects of success.

At the same time, with the other powers mobilized and Austria still occupying its truncated post-Schöbrunn form, the monarchy was in a weak position to shape the coming contest. In particular, the growth of Russia as a military factor in European affairs, both through its acquisitions at Tilsit and the steady westward trek of its enlarged land armies, threatened to supplant French hegemony with de facto Russian dominance. To counter this prospect, Metternich adopted a strategy centered on restraining the growth of Russian influence in Europe.[55] Its objectives were to retain France as a factor of balance against Russia, regain Austria's lost buffers, and engage the German states, most of which were now French allies, as factors of stability.

These goals, already coagulating before Napoleon's defeat, would guide Habsburg grand strategy throughout the coming 1813–14 campaign and well into the postwar period. Where Metternich had previously used accommodation to avoid unfavorable military outcomes, he now employed the army to avoid unfavorable diplomatic outcomes. He held two military cards with which to influence outcomes. One was control over the timing of when the Habsburg Army would enter the war. Rather than rushing into the conflict, Metternich delayed, remaining France's nominal ally and shifting to neutrality before entering the coalition. Withstanding pressure from the Russian and Prussian monarchs, he continued on this path until events on the battlefield ensured that Austria's entry would carry the greatest diplomatic impact. As Metternich later wrote,

> The Emperor left it to me to fix the moment which I thought most suitable to announce to the belligerent powers that Austria had given up her neutrality, and to invite them to recognize her armed mediation as the most

fitting attitude. Napoleon's victories at Lützen and Bautzen were the signs that told me that the hour had come.[56]

Metternich's characterizations of his actions and motivations as recounted in his memoirs have to be read cautiously, as these were written with the benefit of hindsight and desire to cast his own role in the most positive light. Paul Schroeder has convincingly argued that Metternich's real reason for delaying Austrian entry into the war was in fact to "give peace a chance" at a moment when Emperor Francis was averse to military action.[57]

Nevertheless, it is also clear that Metternich understood that delaying Austrian entry until Napoleon had won new battles would improve his negotiating position vis-à-vis Russian and Prussian allies who would now be less confident in their own margin of strength, and thus more keenly aware of their need for Austrian assistance. Delaying also helped to establish Austria as an independent force early in the campaign, wearing down both the French and Russian armies while leaving open as long as possible the potential for a negotiated peace in which Austria, as the mediating power, would have held the scales between the two forces.

Once committed to the war, Austria had a second card to play: determining where its army would be deployed. In this, Metternich benefited from his and Stadion's earlier policies of recueillement. Out of a total coalition force of 570,000, Austria's troops made up 300,000, rendering it the largest military force in the alliance and the essential factor for taking the fight against France, which was capable of fielding 410,000 troops.[58] On the reasoning that "the power placing 300,000 men in the field is the first power, the others are auxiliaries," Metternich insisted on an Austrian general, Prince Felix Schwarzenberg, being named commander in chief of the allied forces.

In the field, Metternich used Austria's alliance leadership to advance his goal of avoiding a weakening of France that could fuel the growth of Russian power. Rather than advancing directly across the Rhine to deliver a decisive defeat on the recoiling French, he sought to slow and redirect operations to Austria's advantage.[59] Prussian military writers would long criticize Schwarzenberg's attritional plans as laggardly. As Delbrück complained a century later, "The Austrians refused to move out and either intentionally or unintentionally clothed this reluctance with strategic considerations. They based their stand on the fact that neither Eugene nor Marlborough, both of whom were also great commanders, had ever directed their operations against Paris."[60]

From an Austrian strategic perspective, however, Schwarzenberg's actions conformed to Metternich's method of "always negotiating but negotiating only while advancing."[61] Militarily, they were a triumph of attritional warfare, using numerous allied armies to apply a tourniquet that steadily deprived Napoleon of the benefit of interior lines while denying him the opportunity for decisive battle that would have played to advantage. Politically, the campaign maximized Austria's opportunities to consolidate its old buffers and create openings for a negotiated settlement with France as a counterbalance to Russia. Had the armies moved more quickly into France and the disoriented French army capitulated in 1813, as was likely, Russian influence over the resulting political configuration would have been greater and the odds of a postwar equilibrium smaller. By buying Austrian diplomacy a few extra months, Schwarzenberg helped to ensure that Metternich would not only have a stronger position vis-à-vis the allies but would be able to count whatever new French government came into being as an Austrian ally, too.[62]

POST-NAPOLEONIC WESTERN SECURITY

Through his eleventh-hour maneuverings, Metternich positioned Austria to exercise a decisive influence over the postwar peace settlement. As we will see in the next chapter, the congress method he helped to engineer would mark the apogee of Habsburg diplomatic achievement. The fact that this system developed a pan-European character has tended to obscure its significance at the regional level vis-à-vis France specifically. For the purposes of this chapter, it is worth noting that the security system that Austria put in place after the Napoleonic Wars to secure the western frontier was a reinstatement of the basic principles that had guided Habsburg strategy against the Bourbons, but it was adapted to reflect the recent lessons.

As before, Austrian security in the west was rooted in the maintenance of buffers. The wars with Napoleon highlighted the importance of these intermediary bodies while revealing their susceptibility to subversion by an outside power. This problem had both a military and political dimension. Militarily, Napoleon's armies had pried apart the patron-client link at its vulnerable "joint" (the client); politically, he had been able to exploit internal dynamics in client state groupings by inverting the Habsburgs' traditional balancing of larger and smaller members while introducing a powerful new force of nationalism. Together, these methods represented a far more effective threat than anything the Bourbons had ever attempted through bribery and manipulation of middle-state courts. They had led to the death of the old German Reich; if used again in the future, such methods could conceivably lead to a lasting breakdown in Austria's western buffer-state system, placing the burden of security on the army alone.

In its postwar actions, Austria moved to address both dimensions of this problem. In Germany, Metternich worked to retain a confederated format, allowing the old Reich to remain dead, and devising in its place a reorganized and streamlined German Bund.[63] In Italy, he sought to inject a greater degree of confederation than had existed in the past by grouping Austria's territories into a new Italian League modeled on the Bund.[64] While the latter failed, in both cases Metternich's aim was to enhance the political viscosity of Austria's buffers and improve serviceability as a geopolitical hedge. The number of states in Germany was reduced from three hundred under the Reich to thirty-nine in the German Bund. The new Article 47 committing members, if attacked, to come to one another's aid replaced the messy Reichskrieg process. While shedding the title of Holy Roman emperor, Metternich ensured that Austria retained its leadership role as president of a new Federal Diet. Where Austria had cemented its primacy in the old Reich by being a protector of the smallest and most vulnerable states, it now was able, by championing sovereignty against not only France but Prussia and the force of nationalism as well, to expand its support base to include most of the new states in the German Bund, including old enemies like Bavaria. These changes allowed Austria to emerge from the war not only with its German buffer intact but also more geopolitically reliable than it had perhaps ever been.

Similarly, the Napoleonic Wars affected how the Austrian military thought about securing the western frontier. On a fundamental level, they reinforced the long-standing conviction that the monarchy's ability to defend itself here was inextricably linked to the fate of the intervening space between itself and France. The wars had shown more clearly than ever that Austria's western defense began on the Rhine and Po Rivers. By the time a foe reached the Habsburg border, the game was largely over. Should the territory of frontline states in these regions fall swiftly to an attacker, either because of their own underdeveloped defenses or because reinforcements could not reach them in time, the chances of waging a successful defensive campaign shrunk dramatically.

To address this problem, Vienna worked to enhance the ability of Austrian forces to maintain forward positions in Italy and Germany. Where past Habsburg defense policy had always been based to some extent on western networks of fortresses, it now sought to dramatically increase the size and number of fixed defenses in these territories while deepening their integration into the monarchy's defense policy. Altogether in the postwar period, Austria's military planners envisioned seventeen fortresses to ring-fence the French frontier. In Germany, they worked with the Bund to eventually develop five large forts—Mainz, Landau, and Luxemburg, and later, Ulm and Rastatt—tied together by smaller installations held by frontier member states and backed by an Austrian garrison in the federal city of Frankfurt.[65] In Italy, Austria expanded its old defensive positions near Lake Garda into a defensive complex—the famous "quadrilateral"—linking Mantua, Peschiera, Legnago, and Verona, while brokering rights to garrison the papal fortresses of Ferrara and Comacchio along with the Parmesan Piacenza.[66] Together, these defensive clusters were intended to alleviate the Po-Rhine dilemma by bogging down French offensives and buying time for reinforcement as needed, north or south of the Alps.

As important as the physical location and extent of these fortifications was the Austrian system for garrisoning and financing them. As in the past, the monarchy could not, in its parlous postwar financial position, afford to sustain extensive, permanent deployments and infrastructure in the west on its own. To defray the costs of the new defenses, Austria looked partly to its defeated foe, levying a seven-hundred-million-franc war indemnity, of which sixty million would go directly to the construction of the new Rhine fortresses. In addition, it looked to the buffer states themselves to share in the burden of defense, setting up a fund in the German Bund, endowed by member contributions, earmarked for the development and maintenance of western forts.[67] The burden of manning these posts would be spread among Bund members, which were now required to maintain, train, and outfit forces within the fortresses as well as a wider, revised Bund corps system on a fixed, proportional basis according to population.[68]

As a collective security infrastructure, the Bund's forts represented a considerable improvement over the old tutelary fortress model. Operationally, the standing military agreements of the new German Bund were more dependable than reliance on a Reichskrieg declaration, which even if successful, tended to place disproportionate risks and costs on the shoulders of the Reich's most exposed states. The Bund format provided the Austrian military with what, in today's terms, would be the equivalent of thirty-nine separate status of forces agreements (SOFAs) in one fell swoop. In essence, they transformed Germany into a giant-size version of the old Nördlingen Association, ensuring higher and more evenly spread defense contributions while committing even the least exposed members to the defense of the whole on a more predictable basis.

To underwrite Austria's expanded forward defenses, Metternich also updated the third pillar to its traditional western security system: Great Power alliances, brokering extensive new agreements committing other European powers to the maintenance of treaty rights, to be upheld through frequent conferences. For the western frontier specifically, he backed this with a formalized mechanism—the Quadruple Alliance—committing Britain, Prussia, and Russia to mutual defense in the event of a reemergence of the French military threat. As with changes to the Austrian buffer system, this grouping represented the continuation of a long-standing Habsburg policy approach while evolving it into a more predictable format.

The Quadruple Alliance represented an improvement on the method of recruiting outside powers into the comanagement of Austria's German position through ad hoc military expeditions to the Mosel Valley and a more stable security mechanism than periodic, Kaunitzian détentes at the bilateral level.

Rather than relying on last-minute antihegemonic groupings, the new setup made containment of France a systemwide responsibility, formally tying Austria's western security needs to the interests and resources of the Great Powers. While implicitly recognizing the public benefit that all states derived from prevention of hegemonic wars, the new alliance system disproportionately benefited the continent's central power, Austria, ensuring that the burdens for its maintenance would be borne by several powers and not just by itself.

Viewed panoramically, Austria's long competition with France is the story of a relatively weak power outmaneuvering and outlasting a stronger rival. At no point in these wars, with the debatable exception of the campaign of 1814, can Austria be said to have been a stronger military power than France. Its defense establishment was usually smaller, its internal composition always more fragile, and its finances more tentative. And yet Austria has to be judged the winner in the majority of these contests. In a period of about a century and a half, it checked the northward and eastward expansion of Louis XIV, recruited his successors into the joint containment of Prussia, staunched the Jacobin tide, and organized or participated in six military coalitions against the republic and Napoleon, emerging as the arbiter of the European balance and presiding over the dismemberment of a French Empire that stretched from the Atlantic to Poland.

Austria's greatest asset in these contests, paradoxically, was its own weakness. At face value, the sprawling nature of Habsburg western interests presented an unmanageable set of security liabilities. But France's comparative strength across this large space, by making it a threat to other states, presented a natural base of resistance to French expansion that with moderate effort, Austria could usually harness to its own security needs. The tools that Austria used for this purpose—the Reich, its Italian satellites, maritime alliances, and the anti-Napoleonic coalitions—varied in format, but all essentially involved the co-optation of other states on the basis of shared fear to manage a threat that while mutual, ultimately posed a disproportionate risk to the continent's central empire—Austria. In this sense, the monarchy's exposure to Europe's seismic core made it a surety on the stability of the continent.

The groupings that Austria organized gave it a reservoir of troops to even the odds against French military power. The wrinkle, so to speak, in all these arrangements was time. Contests on the western frontier ultimately came down to which could be brought to bear more quickly: France's advantage in offensive military capabilities or Austria's advantage in alliances. The latter are, by nature, slower to activate. For this reason, Austria usually lost the opening rounds of its wars with France, experiencing repeated losses in the Low Countries and seeing Rhine fortresses fall in the early stages of the Bourbon wars. Improvements in the speed of warfare brought by Napoleon were in this sense the culmination in a centuries-long arms race between offensive armies and defensive alliances.

It is in the mitigation of this French time advantage rather than efforts to equalize troop contests per se that Austria's western security system achieved its defining contribution. The recruitment of Italian and German buffer states, initially a purely dynastic impulse, provided a medium that, as competition evolved, became more crucial for survival. The addition of fortresses enhanced buffer-state value, interposing a series of longitudinal barriers that compensated for the latitudinal layout of the Alps. In the Bourbon wars, buffer fortress complexes allowed the monarchy to toggle its own forces between frontiers, offsetting France's advantage as a three-front aggressor. When this system broke down in the Napoleonic Wars, Austria developed a backup strategy that was, again, focused on time, alternating between seasons of accommodation and short bursts of resistance that avoided overwhelming it financially, while drawing out the wider contest until its core advantages in allies and legitimacy could be brought to bear. At the end of these wars, Austria invested its postwar windfall to lock in a lasting time advantage, effectively closing off southern Germany and northern Italy as French military highways.

This progression of Habsburg techniques underscores the political as opposed to military nature of Austria's overall western strategy. Arrangements with other states had a higher geopolitical value if already in place before a conflict began. The more regularized the grouping, the more effective, both in absorbing the initial French military advances and reducing the standing defense costs that Austria would have to bear. There is a clear evolution in Habsburg strategy of seeking increasingly regularized alliance formats, both with weaker clients and Great Powers, from Joseph I's renewal of the Reichskrieg format and Leopold's encouragement of the Nördlingen Association, to Thugut's and Stadion's coalitions, and ultimately, Metternich's Bund and congress system. In these groupings, the military value of buffers, measured in the predictability of Austrian forward military deployments, increased in proportion to the viscosity of the underlying political arrangements.

By the early decades of the nineteenth century, this evolution had placed the Habsburg Monarchy at the head of a large network of weaker states in central Europe, the geopolitical configuration and diplomatic effects of which disproportionately benefited Austria but the military costs of which were primarily borne by others. The resulting informal empire was in many ways as impressive as the Habsburg Monarchy itself. It is from this position of apparent strength, the culmination of two centuries of war and statecraft, that Austria would enter the maelstrom of European Great Power politics in the post-Napoleonic period.

PART III

Zenith, Decline, and Legacy

8

Barricades of Time

I have the feeling that I am in the middle of a web which I am spinning in the style of my friends the spiders, whom I like because I have admired them so often.... A net of this kind is good to behold, woven with artistry, and strong enough to withstand a light attack, even if it cannot survive a mighty gust of wind.

—METTERNICH

The Zeitgeist is a powerful stream. One cannot stay in front or behind it. Man is unable to accelerate or delay it. But by installing dams on its shores, one can neutralize it, and render it useful.

—ARCHDUKE CHARLES

THE HABSBURG MONARCHY emerged from the Napoleonic Wars in a position of unprecedented strength. In the postwar settlement at the Congress of Vienna, Austria regained lost territories to form an expanded empire whose possessions and dependencies stretched from Venice to Cracow. To protect these enlarged holdings, Habsburg leaders extrapolated on past frontier strategies to build a European-wide security system based on two broad components: a reorganized and fortified network of buffer territories integrating neighboring lands into Austrian defense; and elaborate diplomatic structures that mediated conflict and co-opted rivals into the joint management of Habsburg buffers. The resulting "Vienna system" mitigated the time pressure of managing multiple frontiers while converting long-standing enemies into participants in the maintenance of Austrian power. This in turn obviated the need for large standing military commitments on the scale that would have been demanded to manage Austria's sprawling position through force alone. The apogee of Habsburg strategic statecraft, this system of security endowed Austria with many of the attributes of hegemony at an affordable cost to itself, while creating conditions of European stability that lasted for half a century.

Pax Austraica

At the Congress of Vienna in 1814–15, the Habsburg Monarchy emerged as the most influential power in the European states system.[1] Of all Napoleon's enemies, Austria had endured the greatest financial and military strains, and suffered the largest territorial losses. In the postwar settlement, it received the greatest compensations in land and population, repatriating lost possessions and acquiring new ones on almost every frontier. In the west, the Habsburgs regained their hereditary holdings of Tyrol and Salzburg, and resecured leadership of the German Confederation. In the southwest, they regained northern Italy to form a new kingdom of Lombardy-Venetia while installing Habsburg rulers in Tuscany, Parma, and Modena. In the south, they reabsorbed the Illyrian Provinces and those portions of the Military Border lost to French rule as well as the Dalmatian port republic of Ragusa. In the east, they regained portions of Poland lost to the Duchy of Warsaw plus Tarnopol in modern-day Ukraine.

These acquisitions brought the Habsburg Monarchy to its greatest extent since Eugene's Turkish war and secured Austria's place as one of the largest land empires in Europe. With the Austrian Netherlands permanently ceded to form a new kingdom of Belgium, the Danubian state stood at its widest and territorially most compact configuration, with Habsburg rule extending from the shores of Lake Garda to Lemberg on the Russian border.

Problems of Postwar Order

At the Vienna Congress, Austria faced two main problems. The first was the growth of its flanking powers, Prussia and Russia, both of which had expanded in the course of the wars with Napoleon. While "all the powers that went to war with France exhausted themselves," Metternich later wrote, "Prussia alone" had drawn advantages from every turn in the conflict. "Every campaign gave her a pretext for extending her influence; every truce either confirmed an encroachment on a weak and timid neighbor, or contrived that such should voluntarily place itself under her banner; every peace brought her a reward for exertions which she had ... made only to serve her own purposes."[2] Russia too had found opportunities for growth during the wars, both through accommodation with Napoleon and counteroffensives following the 1812 campaign. At war's end, both states possessed large armies backed by growing demographic and economic bases. Both sought to formally acquire yet more territory—Prussia through absorption of Saxony, and Russia through annexation of Poland. With France forced back into its historic borders and the Austrian economy devastated from years of warfare, there was little to restrain these ambitions. Unless Austria could do so it faced the prospect of exchanging Napoleon's bid for hegemony in the west with a new era of intense military competition in the north and east.

A second danger confronting Austria in 1815 was the growth of nationalism as a force in European politics. The French Revolution's ideas had awakened across Europe a spirit of national fervor, grounded in the concept of the nation-state as the sole expression of political legitimacy. In Napoleon's satellite kingdoms, French clientage left behind the model of a rationalist public administration and activist citizenry; in the territories of Napoleon's victims, French occupation stoked a popular desire to eject the invader and salvage national pride. In both cases, the long wars left behind populations animated by the notion of unification on the basis of shared language, custom, and culture. And nowhere were these effects most intensely felt than in Austria's western buffers, Germany and Italy.

From a Habsburg security standpoint, these two problems—nationalism and expansionist rivals—were intertwined. German nationalism represented a potential vehicle whereby Prussia, as the largest of the Germanic states, could potentially harness its ambitions for military domination of central Europe to a popular spirit to which Austria, with its polyglot construction, could not appeal. Italian nationalism presented a similar, if less immediate, opportunity for France to eventually overturn Austrian primacy in Italy, while virtually any form of European nationalism presented an opening whereby an opportunistic Russia could undermine political order in its western rivals and use unrest as a pretext for armed intervention. Unless Austria could deal with this threat and delink nationalism from the geopolitical urges of its rivals, it faced the danger of engines of perpetual crisis capable of generating unified national masses on its frontiers and spreading revolution to the heart of the monarchy.

The Metternich System

The scale of problems facing Austria transcended its abilities as a Great Power to handle independently. Economically, the monarchy was bankrupt from more than two decades of conflict; militarily, the large field armies that had allowed the empire to exercise so much influence over the final peace settlements were unsustainable and required rapid dismantlement. To succeed,

Austria had to find ways of dealing with the post-Napoleonic landscape that were within the means of its constrained power capabilities.

The man to whom this task fell was Prince Metternich, Austria's foremost statesman of the postwar period.[3] By 1815, Metternich had been in continuous service to the monarchy for nearly fourteen years, serving Emperor Francis as minister to Paris and replacing Count Stadion as foreign minister after the 1809 defeat. Vain, worldly, and calculating, he possessed a sharp instinct for power that tended to be masked by an easy charm, dilatory style of diplomacy, and affinity for attractive women. A Rhinelander by birth, Metternich had witnessed firsthand the destructive effects of the revolution in the French confiscation of his family's hereditary estates in Germany. A product of the Enlightenment, he was an arch rationalist who distrusted the universal claims and crusading zeal of the Revolution and the nationalisms it birthed. In these forces he saw a chaos that threatened to unravel the fabric of the ancient Habsburg Empire and upend the foundations of European civilization.

To check this threat, Metternich sought to create a bulwark against both the destabilizing effects of rampant nationalism and renewed hegemonic warfare. Realizing that Austria did not possess the military strength to impose postwar stability, he sought instead to lay the foundation for a diplomatic-intensive security that would reduce the frequency and severity of tests of strength facing the monarchy. His overarching aim was to shape a stable, conservative order in which Austria could heal internally and position itself as a major player. In this he replicated the intentions, on a larger scale, of previous Habsburg statesmen. Where Kaunitz had tried to create an environment after the wars with Frederick "without the evil of 'remaining armed beyond our means,'" Metternich envisioned a "long general peace" for an "Austria [that] was enduring the after-pains of a two-and-twenty years' war."[4]

While militarily weak, the Habsburg state possessed certain advantages for achieving this aim. One, paradoxically, was its central position: long a disadvantage, being located in the middle of the chessboard now gave Austria the ability to adjudicate trade-offs between most of the major territorial questions facing postwar Europe. Another was Austria's unique position among the Great Powers as a defender of treaty rights. As the oldest empire in Europe and a state with domestic structures that gave it the most to lose from a period of renewed turmoil, Austria possessed a degree of moral credibility that allowed it to act as a conveyer of legitimacy in international disputes. A third advantage was Metternich himself. As we have seen, he was keenly aware of the power of time in negotiations and particularly the use of delay to gain advantages against a militarily stronger opponent. His "greatest art," French contemporary Charles-Maurice de Talleyrand-Périgord (1754–1838) once said, "is to make us waste our time, for he believes he gains by it."[5] Or as Metternich himself said, "I barricade myself with time and make patience my weapon," and on another occasion remarked, "I am bad at skirmishes but good at campaigns."[6] Much as Metternich had used periods of recueillement to improve Austria's fighting strength and delayed entry into the War of the Sixth Coalition to improve its diplomatic position, he now employed tactics of delay and sequencing to divide Austria's rivals at the peace table.

In the postwar settlement, Metternich sought the retention and strengthening of Austria's historic buffer zones, as previous Habsburg diplomats had so often done. But to a greater extent than his predecessors, he worked to achieve this aim through the recruitment of Europe's large powers, including Austria's rivals, into a formal system of collective security, anchored in international law and aimed at creating a stable European center free from renewed cycles of Great Power war. Together, these aims would become the twin pillars of Austrian grand strategy, with both diplomatic and military expression, for more than half a century.

METTERNICH'S BUFFERS

Metternich's system must be understood first and foremost as a set of measures to provide for Austrian security, devised for the protection and prolongation of the Habsburg Monarchy. As for previous generations of Austrian statesmen, Metternich's first objective in securing the monarchy was spatial in nature: to ensure geopolitical pluralism in the regions around its borders. In the immediate postwar period, this was a sizable task. Hemmed in on every side by the satellites of Napoleonic France, Austria had lost not only its historic German and Italian buffers but also substantial portions of its own frontier territories in the west, north, and south. Like his predecessors, Metternich saw the inherent danger of conflict that arises through direct physical contact between large states. Where Kaunitz had long sought to ensure that Austria remained "not directly adjacent" to its rivals, Metternich aspired "to remove our country from direct contact with France, and thus put an end to the wars which had been in consequence of this contact perpetually occurring between the two neighboring empires."[7]

Under Metternich's guidance, the Congress of Vienna "revived and developed the 18th century idea of intermediary bodies, independent smaller states and areas designed to buffer, separate, and link contending Great Powers."[8] The peace settlement dismantled Napoleon's "rampart of republics," evicting French influence from Germany, reinstalling the princely rulers of Italian states, and demolishing the Duchy of Warsaw. In the northwest, Metternich used the peace settlement as an opportunity to divest from the Austrian Netherlands on the logic that by providing direct physical contact of Habsburg territory with that of France, these lands increased the likelihood of future conflict between the two powers.[9] In this, he was following the practice of his eighteenth-century predecessors of "rounding off" Austrian territory into a more compact geopolitical unit.

Metternich's leadership would prove crucial for rebuilding buffers around Europe's center, as other continental powers would have preferred to absorb much of this territory for themselves. While France was for the time being at bay, Austria's flanking rivals were as yet satiated and bent on using the Congress of Vienna to expand their own frontiers. Prussia wanted to annex Saxony—the monarchy's sole buffer state in this theater—as compensation for Prussian military exertions and to punish the German kingdom for its spirited participation as a Napoleonic client state. Czar Alexander I sought to gain control of most of Poland, citing Slavic brotherhood but ultimately to increase Russia's strategic depth to the west.

If successful, Russian and Prussian expansion into central Europe would chip away at Austria's remaining buffer zones in the north and east, placing hostile armies in Dresden and Cracow, both within two hundred miles of Vienna. An independent Saxony in particular was vital to future Habsburg security—"as important to Austria as an intermediary body vis-à-vis Prussia," as Schroeder writes, "as Poland had been vis-à-vis Russia, and as the Ottoman Empire still was."[10] Rebuffing Prussian designs on Saxony, and with them the larger equation of Russo-Prussian cooperation, was therefore a principle focus of Metternich's diplomacy.

Metternich used tactics of delay to disaggregate his rivals. He feigned illnesses and long convalescences, kindled highly publicized love affairs, and otherwise appeared socially distracted to exploit his rivals' impatience and need for Austrian consent on other demands. Splintering off Berlin first, Metternich granted a partial acquisition of Saxony in exchange for Prussian support on the Polish question and an enhancement to Austria's western buffer through absorption of the fortress at Main into the southern defenses of the German Bund.[11] With Russia isolated, Metternich's first preference was to revert to the kind of full Polish buffer that Maria Theresa and Kaunitz had originally hoped for, but failed to retain. When his attempt at engineering an Austro-British-Prussian guarantee for an independent Poland failed, Metternich organized an alliance of Austria, Britain, and France, and threatened war, which frightened Alexander I into allowing the creation of buffer territories around Cracow and Posen.

The lengths to which Metternich was willing to go in the quest for buffers around Austria's frontiers underscores the foundational significance that they held for postwar Habsburg security. His first aim was simply to keep the territories in question from following under the direct control of Austria's rivals.

Having done so, he then worked through the Congress of Vienna to create elaborate international "rules and understandings for cooperation and concert" between Europe's states of all sizes.[12] The resulting framework gave the small states of Europe—the so-called *puissances intermediaires*—a greater degree of formalized influence and protection than they had perhaps ever enjoyed, or would again until the post–World War II period.

In fighting for space around Austria's borders that was independent and free from rival control, Metternich was pursuing a goal that Habsburg statesmen had long considered a prerequisite for the monarchy's survival. The longer-term task was to make sure that such spaces, once created, would be politically managed to Austria's advantage. This was particularly a challenge in Germany, where Napoleon had not only abolished Austria's traditional hegemonic position in the Reich but also pursued a policy of enlarging lesser states with territory in order to adhere them to France at the cost of loyalty to Austria. "How profoundly different," Metternich wrote of Germany in the postwar period, "were the situations of ... Austria, and of the Princes of the confederation of the Rhine, who owed all the growth of their power to the wars of Napoleon!"[13]

As discussed in the previous chapter, Metternich's solution to this problem was to build a new federalized German Bund consisting of larger and ultimately more tightly knit units than had existed in the old Reich. "Behind the quest for a viable organization for Germany," writes Schroeder, "lay concern for Austria's survival as a Great Power. This required two things above all: that Germany as a whole be tranquil, and that it support Austria where and when Austria needed that support."[14] To achieve these aims, Metternich utilized many of the same tools that past Austrian diplomats had used to cement loyalty to Vienna. Much as Joseph I and Maria Theresa had done in their time, Austria under Francis was careful not to punish and alienate those Germanic states that had fought against it in the previous war. Thus Bavaria, one of Napoleon's staunchest allies, was granted territory, and Saxony was spared the full wrath of Prussian ambition. Additional glue, as in the past, was the prospect of a soft Austrian hegemony less onerous than the alternatives presented by other powers. Metternich brought this formula to new heights, playing on small states' fear of Prussia to bind them to Austrian leadership while using Prussia's fear of nationalism to co-opt Berlin into joint management of the Bund.

The resulting structure offered a dual containment mechanism that kept Prussia's intra-Germanic ambitions in check while providing a joint defense for resisting encroachment by outside powers. Central to this design was Metternich's continued application of the bargain that lay at the heart of informal Habsburg empire in neighboring regions: relative political autonomy and protection by a weak hegemon in exchange for fealty and defensive security. Using this formula, Metternich positioned Austria as the voice of Germany's middle powers in the early decades of the nineteenth century.

Metternich's efforts to reconstitute the Habsburg Monarchy's buffers were intimately linked to his wider vision for how the European states system would function in the postwar period. Wrapped up in the individual issues of Saxony, Poland, and Italy was the fundamental question of whether the middle mass of the European continent, populated with mostly small states, could achieve a sufficient degree of strength to resist encroachments by stronger neighbors, without themselves combining to such a degree as to threaten the stability of Europe. The only way to achieve such an outcome, in Metternich's view, was to form a federated grouping of polities led by Austria that would be buttressed and guaranteed by other larger European powers—"an independent European center," grounded on "a broad political consensus in Europe, underpinned by law. The states in the center would have to unite against pressure from the too-powerful flanks; some outside states would have to support this unity and the flank powers themselves would have to accept it; and institutions would have to be constructed to sustain that independence, particularly a confederate organization for Germany."[15]

CO-OPTING RIVALS

To realize Metternich's vision, it was essential to find ways of enmeshing Austria's Great Power rivals in support of an independent European center, and thus the maintenance of Habsburg leadership, as representing a shared public good for the continent as a whole. The kernel of this concept was not altogether new to Habsburg diplomacy. Austrian statesmen before Metternich had worked to harness rivals to Austria's ends through legal arrangements trumping power politics and mitigating the monarchy's military weakness. Bartenstein's attempts at gaining the prior consent of Europe to a legal instrument, the Pragmatic Sanction, represented an affirmation of the primacy of law over force in international politics.

Above all, Metternich found a forerunner in Kaunitz, whose reversal of Austria's long-standing enmity with France to focus on competition with Prussia, later improvement of ties with Prussia to combine forces against revolutionary France, and momentary attempt at an alignment with Turkey against Russia were demonstrations of the understanding that as a centrally located state, it could not afford to permanently estrange former enemies. Viewed in toto, Kaunitz's diplomacy had come to rest on the organizing principle that Habsburg security ultimately rested on the construction of an ordered environment in which the balance of power, while a permanently operating force in the affairs of states, could be tamed and directed to favorable outcomes for both the security interests of the Habsburg Empire narrowly conceived and community of states as a whole. Late in life, Kaunitz encapsulated this line of reasoning in a memorandum reacting to the outbreak of the revolution in France:

> Any rational, fair and thinking being would agree that in order for a human society to be established and maintained, its first rule must be that no individual can ever attempt to take another's property. Thus follows: no state can infringe on any property gained legitimately, nor afford, without obvious injustice, to demand this of any other states, under any pretext, however special the circumstances.... What we refer to as the "balance" has always been found again, and will continue to be constantly found. It will be found in the protection that each individual state has to maintain for itself a large enough number of allies in Europe, to use in its own interest, in the face of an unfair aggressor. Therefore, it is very desirable that we let go once and for all of the concept of a so-called balance being a monster, and that we tell ourselves.... "Do unto others as you would have done unto you" [*Quod tibi non vis fieri alteri ne feceris*].[16]

Metternich, who incidentally married Kaunitz's granddaughter, thought along similar lines. Like Kaunitz, his desire was to transcend the balance of power, but on a grander and more formal scale through a "rejection of the system of conquest" altogether in favor of a collective security arrangement in which large and small powers alike resolved Europe's problems through regularized diplomatic coordination. In this conception, Metternich hoped to recruit not only Austria's natural allies but also its rivals into a standing league committed, in language reminiscent of Kaunitz, to the "principle of the solidarity of nations and of the balance of power" to employ their "combined endeavors against the temporary predominance of any one [power]."[17]

Metternich's desire for what amounted to a European collective security architecture, while rooted in earlier Habsburg diplomatic thinking, was greater in scale than anything that had preceded him. For the most part, previous Austrian attempts at co-opting rivals had usually focused on one power at a time and been temporary in nature, aimed at "turning off" one frontier to turn attention and resources elsewhere for a limited period of time. Efforts at building grouping coalitions had generally been task specific, intended to deal with a particular threat at a given point in time, after which allied cooperation dissipated. The intermittent alliances with the maritime powers to contain Louis XIV in the eighteenth century had been one set of examples;

Joseph I's attempt to build a neutrality league to keep Sweden and Turkey out of the War of the Spanish Succession was another; and Kaunitz's various alliances to box in Frederick II was another.

By contrast, Metternich envisioned a security system for Austria after the war that would encompass all of Austria's surrounding military theaters and involve open-ended time commitments. Confronted with the old, familiar dilemma of managing multiple vulnerable frontiers exposing Austria to perpetual military exertions beyond its ability to sustain, Metternich sought a means not of managing the latest crisis but rather transcending the cycle of crisis altogether. Where previous generations of Austrian statesmen had labored to improve Austria's position for the *next* war, Metternich sought to make war itself less likely by rendering attempts at European primacy by a Frederick or Napoleon impossible.

WAR AVOIDANCE

Such a system of coordination of large powers, if it could be achieved, would produce certain public goods that while benefiting Europe generally, would work disproportionately to Austria's advantage. The first and most obvious was war avoidance. By the early nineteenth century, all of Europe's states were exhausted from a century of continuous bids for primacy, beginning with Louis XIV, continuing through Frederick II, and culminating in Napoleon. Austria in particular had suffered from these contests. Its sprawling, multiregional posture meant that its frontiers touched most of Europe's major military flash points: Italy and Germany being the most recent, but in the late eighteenth century also Poland and the Balkans. By locking Europe's Great Powers into continual contact for the resolution of disputes, Austria sought to make it more likely that a settlement could be reached on future crises in these regions—crises that, should they escalate, would adversely affect Austria more than any other power.

Over time, Metternich reinforced the congress system with additional defensive alliances, each focused on constraining the powers most likely to disturb the peace—in the west, a Quadruple Alliance of Austria, Britain, Russia, and Prussia to contain France; in the east, a "Holy Alliance" of autocratic empires to restrain Russia; and in Germany, the new Bund to tie down Prussia. In these arrangements can be seen the first attempt at a European-wide collective security system, in which all lines lead back to the middle empire—Austria. By mitigating tensions on every frontier, these elaborate structures offered a means for Austria to relieve the unrelenting security pressures that sustained competition had brought to the Habsburg realm in the previous century.

Metternich's system was geared not only to restrain rivals but also to yoke them together in combating nationalist movements across the continent. Russia and Prussia proved especially helpful in this regard; much as Metternich had been able to use the fear of nationalist uprisings to strengthen Austria's moral leadership among the monarchical German states and keep Prussia in line, he was able to use fear to focus Russian statesmen on the shared goal of opposing nationalist uprisings. The ability to coordinate resources for the suppression of revolts provided a benefit to all these states, but it specifically benefited the continent's central empire, which relied for its security on buffer regions in Germany and Italy, where nationalism was most rampant. Metternich's arrangements gave the monarchy a ready tool of outside help in intervention that could be used not only to offset the security burden of managing its own buffers, but also in a worst-case scenario to provide a lifeline of military support for suppressing uprisings inside the monarchy itself.

In the years following the peace settlement, Metternich's collective security measures allowed Europe to navigate a series of crises without escalating into war. At Aix-la-Chapelle in 1818, the congress format enabled the powers to reach agreement on the removal of allied armies of occupation from France in a way that avoided an open breach between Russia and Britain. At Carlsbad a year later, Metternich coordinated a response to the first stirrings of German nationalism that deepened Prussia's commitment to the Austrian-led confederal architecture. At Troppau and Laibach in 1820 and 1821, respectively, Metternich succeeded in winning support from the continental powers for Austrian military intervention against nationalist uprisings in Naples and Piedmont while avoiding an Austro-French clash.[18] At Verona the following year, a similar formula was used to support a French suppression of nationalist uprisings in Spain. And at Münchengrätz in 1833, Austria, Prussia, and Russia agreed to mutual aid against revolution along with joint approaches for managing Poland and Turkey as buffer zones.

One advantage of the Vienna system was that it made security a shared task. When Austria needed to act militarily to secure its buffers, it was likely to have the prior political approval and backing of other powers. With the sanction of the congress, the Habsburg military undertook extensive gendarmerie functions in Naples and Piedmont in 1821, Rome in 1830, Parma in 1831, and Modena in 1847. For the Austrian intervention in Naples and Piedmont in 1821, Russia dispatched a corps of ninety thousand troops to the frontier to stand by as reinforcements. The czar offered troops again at the Verona conference for the intervention in Italy. In 1846, Russian troops coordinated with the Habsburg Army to jointly suppress an armed Polish uprising around Cracow.

The fact that Russia was willing to provide military support for Austrian actions as far afield as Italy and in the Danubian Basin itself underscored the practical security value that Metternich's arrangements held for an empire that maintained security commitments at all points of the compass, and yet possessed the smallest military establishment of any European Great Power. The very power whose armies had threatened to keep marching after the fall of France to upset the stability of post-1815 Europe now stood as a chief prop to continental stability.

The scale of support that Austria enjoyed from its rivals in the fight against revolution had an additional benefit, over and above the immediate problems that the various congresses were meant to solve: deterring traditional attempts at territorial revisionism. Russian military support for Austrian operations sent a signal that the monarchy was likely to enjoy powerful backing in any crisis that escalated into a major confrontation with another large power. Similarly, Austria's coordination with Prussia in German affairs, with Prussian and Habsburg troops conducting joint policing missions in the Bund, sent the message that the Germanic powers would resist encroachments as a defensive bloc. The result was a stable, if somewhat fragile, middle European order, internally unified, to a certain extent, under Habsburg leadership and with a considerable degree of voluntary support from Europe's flanking powers.

"Strategic Points" and Forward Defense

In describing the Metternichian order, Schroeder uses the metaphor of a catamaran—"a light, frail but mobile and buoyant vessel, its vulnerable center held above the waves by outriggers on both sides, needing constant attention and seamanship to keep it afloat."[19] In this "catamaran," congress diplomacy supplied the rivets and cords holding the vessel together; this was a diplomatically intensive rather than militarily intensive security system. Nevertheless, military power did play an important role. With Austria's territorial footprint effectively doubled from where it had stood following the truncations at Schöbrünn, the monarchy needed tools with which to reassert its dominance in regained territories. This could only be partially accomplished by diplomatic means; like any empire, Austria had to possess the ultima ratio of armed force to secure its position. With its army diminished in size by postwar austerity, the monarchy would have to find creative ways to signal its military capabilities to rivals, and when needed, use those capabilities. As in the past, this took two forms: the military use of terrain and ways in which the Habsburgs used military technology to secure its frontiers.

Terrain retained its central importance in post-1815 Austrian strategy in the quest for securing an intermediary zone between the monarchy's home terminal area and the territory of major rivals. As we have seen, ensuring the political independence of the mostly small states in these regions was a major objective of Metternich's diplomacy. In parallel, the Austrian military studied how to use the terrain on the monarchy's frontiers in the event of conflict. At the heart of post-Napoleonic Austrian military thinking was the idea that success in warfare could be achieved through the retention of certain key pieces of terrain or "strategic points," which held a disproportionate significance in deciding geopolitical results. As discussed in chapter 4, the main proponent of this view was Archduke Charles, whose writings on war would emerge, after some delay, as a foundation for Austrian military science in the decades after 1815. In his military writings after the war, Charles argued for an empire-wide defense system rooted in the retention and defense of these strategic points around the frontiers: "In every state that has a defensive system, it should be a maxim of the state to set such points in alert and preserve them in a high state of readiness even during peace, to be able to maintain them for a long time with little effort and discourage every enemy from war by the belief in the difficulty of their conquest."[20]

The operational questions facing the army were where these points were located, and how to defend them. On the first question, the view that emerged from the Napoleonic Wars was that the most important strategic points were located beyond the frontier, on the territory of Habsburg buffers or recently acquired territories. This was not altogether new. Habsburg military planning had long been wed to the concept that Austria's security began beyond the physical border. As we have seen, Austrian strategy in the west had made extensive use of forward Reich fortresses, and Lacy had advocated a layered concept of security encompassing external allies and rows of forts.

The wars with Napoleon, however, substantially strengthened this conviction by showing how quickly an enemy occupying strategic sites in the dominating terrain around the Alps and upper Danube could dominate the Austrian heartland. To varying degrees, the 1800, 1805, and 1809 campaigns had all demonstrated how improvements in the speed of armies, made possible by new ways of organizing force and managing logistics, had amplified French offensive advantages in this theater. As early as 1802, Venturini had argued for a "general defense system" to address this challenge in which double rows of military sites on the Rhine, Danube, and northern Italy would provide a defense-in-depth for Austria's western approaches.[21]

Radetzky was a close student of lessons from these campaigns. Descended from the same stock of German-Bohemian nobility that had produced Daun, Radetzky was a by-product of both the military system that Maria Theresa built in response to the Prussian threat and the bloody baptism that the army had received in the wars against Napoleon. Radetzky came of age as a cavalry trooper in Joseph II's Turkish war, where he absorbed crucial lessons on terrain and mobility. As an aide to Lacy, he watched Austria's aging generals grapple with the problems of war planning. As chief of staff to General Schwarzenberg, he had developed the allied war plan that blended Austria's traditional emphasis on attritional warfare with new Napoleonic methods of organization and tactics.

By the time of the Congress of Vienna, Radetzky had seen nearly three decades of almost-uninterrupted warfare and had served in every major theater of war around the empire's borders. A lifelong student of history, Radetzky believed in the importance of learning from the past, contributing to the establishment of the Kriegsarchiv, and commissioning military analyses of the campaigns of Eugene and the French wars.[22] Through this study of history and experience in the field, Radetzky developed a conviction that Austria's security began well beyond the political border, on the terrain of neighboring states and indeed, if possible, the enemy's soil.

For Radetzky, the main lesson from the wars with Napoleon had come from the 1809 war, which demonstrated in painful terms that if Austria could not stop an enemy beyond the frontier, it would be essentially incapable of waging an effective self-defense. As Radetzky wrote in a lengthy memo assessing Austria's strategic position,

> If the upper Danube is, as hitherto, neglected, and our defense solely based on the stretch of river downward from Vienna to Komarom [i.e., we are thrown back from the frontiers], at every sudden outbreak of war against an enemy approaching from the west, Upper Austria will have to be abandoned, Bohemia left to its own devices, and the German provinces, which were a bountiful auxiliary resource for the army, can be considered lost, because the enemy will be able to reach the imperial city faster than we can gather our forces.

In light of past experiences, Radetzky believed, like Venturini, that what Austria needed most was strategic depth—insulating space from which to both threaten enemies and, if necessary, conduct a stalling retreat. As Radetzky observed,

> All possible points of attack derive from a state's frontiers, and against each of these there exist defensive measures that—at the point of contact—can deter or deny the enemy assault. We protect against attacks by a neighboring power by seeking alliances with land and sea powers that may themselves be in a position to attack our neighbor, thus offering an external form of defensive, ... Just as we seek out states as means of defense, we can offer our services to other states in a similar fashion. Thus emerge alliance systems and power.[23]

At the furthest distance from Austria, the monarchy's big-power allies played the role of pinning down a peer competitor and dividing its forces in wartime. One square inward sat the monarchy's numerous small-state allies and buffer territories, which Radetzky saw as the key to its defense:

> Today, Austria borders the Papal States, Sardinia, Switzerland, the small states of Germany, ... and Turkey. The smaller states around us are too weak to attack us, either by themselves or united. They are similarly too impotent, however, to prevent movement through their lands by a Great Power. Now if Austria wishes some reassurance against such movements, it will need to behave in a fashion that will lead the minor states to consider blocking such maneuvers as being in their own national interest. These small states will seek protection from any possible future convulsions in our part of the world, and will accept safety wherever it is most securely offered.[24]

The military concepts of Venturini, Auracher, and Charles, with their stress on strategic points, dovetailed with Radetzky's emphasis on incorporating buffers into Austria's system of security. In Radetzky's view, Austria's previous wars had illuminated the "inner and outer" points where defensive arrangements were needed to secure its heartland. One of these was the stretch of Upper Rhine from Rastatt to Freiburg where French armies descended en route to the Austrian frontier.[25] A second was the upper Danube near Passau and adjacent Inn river where invaders could enter Habsburg territory unmolested.[26] Another was the four-sided stretch of land in central Lombardy between the Mincio and Po Rivers, centered on Verona, through which an invading army had to pass in order to threaten a two-pronged move on Austria through the Julian or Limestone Alps.[27] And yet another was the gap between Eperies (Prešov) and Czacza (Košice) in the foothills of the Carpathians along the main route for an eastern invader approaching Budapest.[28]

FORTIFICATIONS

To secure these strategic points, Radetzky advocated the extensive use of fortifications. For Radetzky, the fact that Austria faced foes on every side as well as potentially internally while possessing a relatively weak army gave forts greater utility than for most states. "Every war has a specific enemy, sometimes more than one," he marked, and

> every war has its own dangers. Each makes its own demands on fortresses.... Fortifications are means, defense is their purpose; their usefulness as a tool, however, can only be assessed by understanding the fortress's

purpose in a specific case.... What should be fortified? Why are these fortifications necessary? And why does one require such means? ... [Ulti-
mately] the defensive strength of a state consists in its monetary power,
the strength of its armed forces, and the power of its alliances. [In this con-
text] the purpose of fortifications is to make a defense of the few against
an attack by the many possible. Natural fortifications are provided by the
geographic shape of a country; through human skill, fortifications provide
a means of strengthening these traits, and addressing partial or large deficiencies of the terrain.[29]

As we have seen, forts had been growing steadily in prominence in Austrian military thinking since at least the end of the Prussian wars. By the post-
Napoleonic period, a firm orthodoxy had set in that fortresses, when sited
correctly in the surrounding terrain, could insulate, if not altogether inocu-
late, the monarchy against the threat of Napoleonic and Frederickian invasions. At first glance, this continued emphasis on fortresses is surprising given
the minor role that they had played in most of Napoleon's campaigns. But the
Austrians remained attached to them for several reasons. One was the out-
sized results that forts had achieved in a handful of cases. The most notable of
these was the small fortress of Bard, which with only twenty-two cannons had
held out for three weeks, complicating the movement of French heavy equipment in the exit from the Alps in the 1800 campaign, leading Napoleon to call
it "a more considerable obstacle to the army than the Great St. Bernard [Pass]
itself.[30]

More substantial was the impact that Austria's own forts had when used
against it. Napoleon's capture of the Sardinian fortresses provided the fulcrum
from which he had conducted his successful offensives into Austria. A French
garrison at Genoa held out for more than two months against a force five
times its size, preventing the Austrians from expelling French forces left behind in Italy by Napoleon. After the 1800 campaign, the French systematically
strengthened the defensive works of northern Italy into two lines of forts. In
1805, it was the presence of these works that allowed the French commander
Masséna, with a weak force, to pin down Charles's ninety thousand troops,
thereby sharpening Austria's Rhine-Po dilemma and enabling Napoleon's victory at Austerlitz. Ulm itself, once in French hands, had, in tandem with the
bases taken by France on other frontiers, enabled the buildup of strength on
Austria's borders in the lead-up to the 1809 campaign. It was because of the
possession of these defensive sites, in the eyes of Habsburg military men, that
France had been able to steadily tighten the tourniquet on Austria over its
various campaigns, eventually threatening the empire's existence.

This, rather than the disaster at Ulm or numerous examples of Napoleon bypassing fortresses, is what stood out in Austrian military minds as the monarchy entered the years of peace. Building on the earlier work of Venturini and others, Archduke Charles sought in the postwar period to rationalize and systematize the role of forts in Austrian military thinking. His central concept was that fortifications should be placed at strategic points where experience showed the local terrain was likely to have a disproportionate influence on the shape and outcomes of future wars. Among these he distinguished between inner and outer points that worked in tandem with the political leadership's goals of containing rivals while combating the forces of nationalism. In *Principles of War*, Archduke Charles outlined a rough framework whereby Austria would employ different kinds of fort for these different purposes:

> Fortresses are destined either to support the simple defense of a country or to serve to support offensive operations. . . . For fortresses destined to serve as supports for offensive operations it is necessary to have regard principally to the points upon which an offensive war could and should be conducted against the enemy; in consequence at the principal entries to his country, and upon communications with the same country. They should be able to contain important magazines, and be situated in such a way that in case of contrary events they cover the retreat of the army, and impede the progress of the enemy. They should be by this of a considerable size. There is a third sort of fortress, which is less for the defense of frontiers than for the security and retention of the whole country. These fortresses should be placed in the interior of provinces and are properly called "*places d'armes.*"[31]

Fortresses acted as a buttress to Austria's overall strategy in the postwar period. Those located in forward positions acted as a deterrent in dealings with large enemy powers. By maintaining a strong and visible security presence around the main arteries, forts, as Charles put it, "discourage the enemy from war by the belief in the difficulty of their conquest."[32] Should deterrence fail, forts assisted in the task of conducting a defense-in-depth. In Charles's words, "Fortresses situated upon the frontiers of warring powers change all conditions of war"; their purpose is "to gain time"—an objective that "must never be lost sight of in the choice of emplacing fortresses to defend a country."[33] To accomplish this purpose, frontier fortresses should be "placed in such a manner that the enemy cannot easily leave them behind him without risking all for his communications . . . and that by this he is obliged to leave in his rear a considerable force . . . which will weaken his army and make it incapable of an ulterior offensive."[34] In Radetzky's words, they "hinder the enemy from further advancement . . . secur[e] war munitions, shelter the army in case of defeat, [and] protect against hostile superiority until reinforcements arrive."[35]

In addition, forts played an increasingly offensive role in Austrian military thinking. As we have seen, there were some antecedents to this in earlier Habsburg wars with the Bourbons, which had shown that Austrian security began not at the frontier but instead on the banks of the Seine. What changed in the period after the Napoleonic Wars was the growing emphasis on the decisive battle as prime objective of warfare. Habsburg commanders, and in particular Radetzky, carried from the experiences in the 1813–14 campaign the central lesson that success in future wars would depend on the ability to take the fight into enemy territory. In juxtaposition with the 1809 campaign, which was fought almost entirely on Austrian soil, 1813 had seen allied armies remove the source of conflict at its source: Paris. Clam-Martinez, Metternich's chief military aide and architect of Austrian defense strategy at the high point of the congress system, saw the placement of fortresses at "the most useful points" on the frontier as a means of ensuring Austria's ability to deliver quick offensive strikes against enemies, thus effectively merging Charles's terrain-based attachment to strategic points and Radetzky's Napoleonic emphasis on seeking battle.[36] Forts located at the frontier provided a basis for both by allowing for a forward concentration of force, much like the forts of Bishop's Alley had long done on the Rhine, albeit now in a more systematic fashion and strung across the extent of the monarchy's frontiers with the notable exception of the border with Russia.

This use of frontier forts as a means of forward defense fulfilled not only military functions in relation to potential foes but also supported the key political aims of Metternich's wider diplomatic system. This was especially important vis-à-vis the neighboring buffer states on which the system depended for affordable safety. "The rapport of one state with another," Charles wrote, "and the measure of the influence it wishes to have on its neighbors or that its neighbors wish to have on it, determines the necessity and the importance of fortified points for the conservation of its proper independence."[37] In a similar vein, Radetzky observed that "in all border countries, the necessity of fortifications and the form they should take depends on on the political, geographic, and military relations that an empire has with those states with which these provinces form the actual border countries"; "every adjoining state" around the monarchy is itself "a potential enemy that awakens our anxiety, not only by sharing a border with us, but because its internal situation and relation to the wider state system may provide triggers for war."[38]

Forward defensive sites reinforced the efforts of Austrian diplomats to cement Vienna's ties with its tributaries. Embedded in this technique was an element of fear: communicating Austria's determination to hold the territories it had regained after 1815. But there was also an element of reassurance and benevolent paternalism. Ultimately, the more Austria helped the territories and states around its borders, the more it helped itself, since "these small states will seek protection from any possible future convulsions in our part of the world, and will accept safety wherever it is most securely offered."[39] By coordinating defense with these states, "Austria ... can be called the common haven of all the surrounding nations, for she is their common refuge in every need, their protecting wall against every attack."[40]

FORTRESS AUSTRIA

With these political and military objectives in mind, the Habsburg Army set about in the years following the Congress of Vienna to strengthen and refurbish the monarchy's fortresses. Much as the wars with Frederick had produced systematic postwar reviews that led to the placement of forts on the Elbe, the army after 1815 now studied on a much wider scale about how to devise a comprehensive defensive "system" to defend the monarchy as a whole.[41] Over the course of the first half of the nineteenth century, a series of military commissions took up this task, with varying degrees of success. In 1818, Archduke Johann made a tour of fortifications in other major European countries in his role as general director of engineers, and presented a draft plan that organized the monarchy's forts into three classes according to defensive value and proposed new works to guard the eastern and southwestern frontiers.[42]

The years that followed were filled with attempts at smaller upgrades, most of which were constrained by budgetary realities. In 1832, Johann and Radetzky presented joint plans for strengthening the defenses of northern Italy and placing barrier forts in the passes of the Alps and Carpathians.[43] Around the same time Archduke Maximilian, largely at his own expense, undertook the fortification of Linz using an experimental new tower system that was ultimately discontinued due to budgetary constraints. Field Marshal Franz von Scholl later oversaw improvements to the forts of northern Italy and the nearby Alps, including the Brenner Pass.[44] Plans of various shapes continued throughout the 1840s, with flurries of half-realized schemes and a continuous construction of countless small *sperre* (barrier forts) to guard the mountain passes and valleys in the Alps and Tatras. In 1850, jolted by the recent revolutions, an Imperial Forts Commission was established under the direction of Henrich Freiherr von Hess and given real money to work with.[45]

By midcentury, Austria possessed a large number of forts of varying degrees of quality. Scattered in clusters and networks along the empire's frontiers, internal river systems, and buffer territories, the shape and purpose of these defensive sites broadly trace the outlines of the categories that Charles,

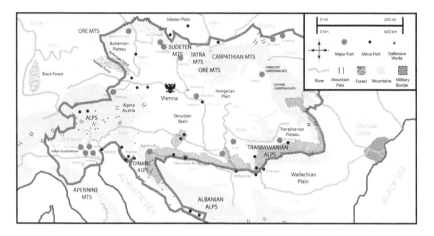

FIG. 8.1. Fortresses of the Habsburg Empire.
Source: Center for European Policy Analysis, 2017.

Radetzy, and other Austrian soldiers had envisioned (see figure 8.1). These included first-class fortresses in Mantua, Venice, and Brixen in Italy; Salzburg and Enns in Austria; Komorn in Hungary; Peterwardein (the so-called Gibraltar on the Danube) and Karlsburg on the Ottoman frontier; Prague, Olmütz, and Eperjes; and the older northern quadrilateral forts at Königgrätz, Theresienstadt, and Josephstadt. These complexes were supported by the large confederal fortresses in Mainz, Landau, Luxemburg, Ulm, and Rastatt, backed by a large Austrian garrison in Frankfurt, and in Italy, supporting networks of tutelary forts in adjacent territories under the rule of Habsburg family members or through agreed-on garrisoning rights, such as at the papal fortresses of Ferrara, Comacchio, and Piacenza.[46]

Perhaps the best illustration of the role forts played in this period in advancing Habsburg political and strategic goals can be seen in the famous quadrilateral fortresses of Italy (see figure 8.2). Long of importance in the wars of this region, the fortified towns of Verona, Peschiera, Mantua, and Legnano gained dramatically in significance with the extension of direct Austrian rule after 1815. To keep the French out and nationalists down, the monarchy needed to be able to project power beyond the Alps. Once there, Austrian forces found themselves on a flat plain, which as repeated wars had shown, were conducive to the movement of French armies, often enjoying numerical superiority, which unless intercepted, could quickly reach the Austrian frontier and use the numerous passes to threaten Vienna from both the north and south.

The Austrian solution to this problem was to construct a series of modern forts astride this military highway in the center of the Lombardy plain. The

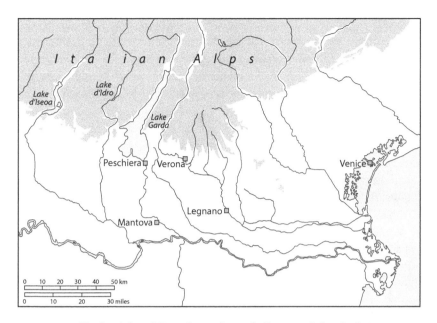

FIG. 8.2. The Quadrilateral Forts. *Source:* Center for European Policy Analysis, 2017.

citing of these fortresses was a masterpiece in the defensive use of terrain. In the north they were anchored on Lake Garda, in the south on the marshes of the River Po, and in the east and west on the rivers Micio and Adige. The Austrians placed forts at the four corners formed by these obstacles. Built with the most advanced fortification technlogy of the day, these structures included hydraulic engines and, eventually, rifled artillery capable of shelling the surrounding countryside at distances of 4.3 miles.[47] They were connected to one another and the distant Erblände by telegraph and rail track lines, and supported by lesser fortresses stretching back to the frontier as well as a gunboat flotilla on Lake Garda. The largest fort, Verona, was capable of sheltering big armies for long periods of time, thus enabling local forces to undertake offensive operations in neighboring states if needed. The forts presented a defensive complex that was virtually impenetrable to armies approaching from the west or south—in the words of one contemporary observer, they were "the most formidable military base we have, perhaps, ever known."[48]

PEACE ON THE CHEAP

Viewed as an integrated system, Austria's post-Napoleonic diplomacy and forts achieved security at an affordable cost during a vulnerable moment of recovery for the monarchy. The pieces worked in tandem: grouping coalitions coaxed rivals into joint stewardship of buffer regions; forts and tributary armies tethered these regions to Austrian leadership, and provided instruments for dealing with any problems that fell through the cracks in the diplomatic net. Together, these tools achieved a higher degree of success in addressing the problems of managing multiple frontiers than any previous Habsburg security system. While many historians have pointed to the setbacks that Metternich suffered in the post-1815 era, perhaps a better measure of the results of his system would be to compare the outcomes of this period with the goals that Metternich had set out to accomplish: a "long peace" in which Austria could recover internally from the "after pains" of twenty-two years of war, and a bulwark to suppress conflict and, specifically, address the twin dangers of Russian/Prussian expansion and nationalism.

The first of these goals was essentially economic in nature. Like most powers at the end of a major war, Austria therefore needed peace on the cheap. After the war, the monarchy carried substantial debt overhangs, mostly involving commitments to Britain, and other lingering effects of war—troop depletion, inflation, agricultural disruption, and loss of specie—which fueled conditions of economic depression into the 1820s.[49] Whatever arrangements Austria's diplomats and soldiers devised for navigating the new geopolitical setting would thus have to achieve imperial defense without worsening this economic situation. The components of the Vienna system worked in combination to achieve this goal. At the most fundamental level, the congress system and its supporting alliances helped to supply the recovery period needed by averting the one thing most likely to lead to economic collapse: renewed Great Power war.

The relative stability afforded by the first half of the century to Austria allowed it to maintain a substantially lower military footprint than would have been possible had Europe immediately reverted after 1815 to the power politics of the prewar period. As a result, the Habsburg state was able to drastically cut defense spending in the years following the peace. From a wartime environment in which Vienna had spent virtually all its available resources to military resistance to Napoleon, the portion of the budget devoted to the army was reduced to about half by 1817, 23 percent in 1830, and 20 percent in 1848.[50] The overall defense budget hovered around less than 100 million crowns throughout the 1820s, rose slightly in the 1830s, and dipped back to 1820s levels throughout the 1840s, making Austria one of the lowest defense spenders in the decades after 1815 (see figure 8.3).

Austrian military policies also helped to reinforce the economic effects of Metternich's diplomacy. From antiquity, empires have used forts to economize force. Walls require fewer troops to man than open country. Thus, the

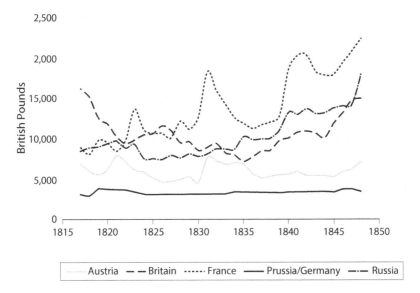

FIG. 8.3. Military Expenditure of Five European Great Powers, 1817–48. *Source:* J. David Singer, Stuart Bremer, and John Stuckey, "Capability Distribution, Uncertainty, and Major Power War, 1820–1965," in *Peace, War, and Numbers*, ed. Bruce Russett (Beverly Hills: Sage, 1972), 19–48; National Material Capabilities, Correlates of War Project, http://www.correlatesofwar.org/; Catherine Casson, "European State Finance Database: An Introduction," European State Finance Database, http://www.esfdb.org/table .aspx?resourceid=11342. Graph: Center for European Policy Analysis, 2017.

Romans employed modestly trained militia in forts to reduce the costs of frontier defense by substituting capital for labor.[51] Austria's use of forts like the quadrilateral offered to amplify the effects of such forces as it could deploy under reduced budgets. Because they increase force-space rations and entail a form of warfare—defense—that is simpler to conduct, and therefore train and arm for, than offense, fortifications amplify the fighting qualities of armies.[52] Their value tends to increase in inverse proportion to the quality of troops available to a state at a given moment. Hence, France used fortifications in the post–World War I era to augment the quality of conscript troops attached to defensive doctrines. In a similar way, Austria was able to use fixed defenses to compensate for its army's overall effectiveness at a time of stagnation in doctrine, training, and readiness.

Placing such forces in situ at the most likely site of disturbances further increased their effectiveness and lowered the transportation costs of shifting forces from frontier to frontier in response to crises. In Italy, for example, the army was able through the presence of a handful of forts and steadily smaller garrisons (from 104,000 troops in 1831, to 75,000 troops in 1833, to 49,000 in 1846) to hold a set of territories that provided more than a quarter of Austrian tax revenues.[53] The cost-effectiveness of these deployments was heightened by the fact that when uprisings occurred, the Italian states necessitating Austrian military intervention were ultimately required to bear the costs of the expeditions.[54] In the east, the close political relationship with Russia that was achieved through the Holy Alliance allowed the monarchy to almost entirely forego the task of fortresses and large-scale deployments on its longest frontier, while in Germany, as we have seen, the financial burden of maintaining numerous forts on the Rhine was carried to a large extent by the other German states. In addition, the decentralization of security in many parts of the Habsburg perimeter to buffer-state armies and the ability to rely on joint intervention by other Great Powers further defrayed the military costs of managing Austria's enlarged post-1815 territorial holdings.

ECONOMIC STABILIZATION

In part because of its reduced military expenditures, the Austrian economy was able to achieve a substantial recovery in the decades after 1815. Collectively known as the Vormärz, the years between the end of the Napoleonic Wars and the 1848 revolution were marked by significant and sustained growth. By the late 1820s, the monarchy had recovered from the sustained postwar depression. In Bohemia and Upper Austria, mechanization was beginning to occur, first in textiles, and then with increasing rapidity in other sectors. The result was a series of intermittent economic booms as markets stabilized and output increased after years of stagnation.

This process occurred in parallel with population growth, which by the middle decades of the century was averaging 1 percent (high by contemporary standards). Habsburg's large agricultural sector ensured that this expansion in population was internally sustainable, which in turn helped to fuel high economic growth rates. Supported by parallel revolutions in transportation (steam and rail), industrial output surged, with periods of growth as high as 2.5 to 3.3 percent, and overall per capita rates of industrial output somewhere between 1.8 and 2.6 percent (compared to 1.7 and 1.9 percent in France and England, respectively). Coal consumption—often used as a measure of growth and technology diffusion—increased 8.6 percent annually for two decades from the 1830s (eventually averaging almost 10 percent), compared to consumption rates of 7.5 and 5.8 percent, respectively. Overall, as David Good notes, "the behavior of population, output, and output per person in the Vormärz strongly indicates the emergence of modern economic growth."[55]

MILITARY SECURITY

Metternich's system also provided measurable security for Austria against the twin threats of rival expansion and nationalist uprisings. As outlined above, congress diplomacy supplied a template for navigating numerous crises in Italy in the 1830s and 1840s. In addition to dealing with the immediate problem, grouping coalitions allowed Metternich to avert escalation into Great Power confrontations. Austria's fortresses amplified the effects of its diplomacy by offering an extra element of deterrence. One example of this deterrent at work can be seen in 1840, when Austria's improved fortresses on the Rhine helped to dissuade French military adventurism in south Germany. Another illustration comes from 1850, when a combination of Russian backing, the mobilization of ninety thousand troops by Austria's Bund allies, and the reinforcement of the fortresses at Königgrätz, Josephstadt, and Theresienstadt helped to deter Prussia from launching a war to supplant Habsburg leadership of Germany.[56]

The greatest geopolitical success of the Metternich system came in 1848, however, when revolutions spread across Europe and into the Habsburg Monarchy, eventually engulfing Italy, Hungary, Bohemia, and Vienna itself (see figure 8.4). While involving armed insurgents rather than rival armies, Austria found itself facing many of the same challenges of balancing multiple theaters that it had in the Spanish and Austrian succession wars of the previous century. Like in these earlier contests, the monarchy needed to manage the sequencing of operations to avoid overwhelming its stretched military and the duration of the conflict to avoid unbearable strains on the Treasury.[57]

The task of time-management was aided under the Metternich system by the combination of by-then-tested tools at Austria's disposal. As in 1748, the monarchy in 1848 sought to separate its enemies, concentrating on the weakest and most immediate threats first, and then turning its attention to stronger foes as it combined the forces freed up on other fronts. In pursuit of this goal, the monarchy's earlier investments in forts was validated, as fortresses in Hungary and Italy allowed garrisons to preoccupy insurgents with sieges, thereby buying time for the army on other frontiers. In Hungary, the fortress of Arad held out for 270 days and that at Temesvar for 59. In Italy, the forts of the quadrilateral provided a shelter for Radetzky's beleaguered corps of twenty thousand after Milan fell and the towns of Lombardy-Venetia rose in arms around them.

The forts showed their full military value when Charles Albert (1798–1849) of Sardinia-Piedmont cast his lot into the struggle, amassing forces from most of the nearby Italian states to attempt an assault on Radetzky's position. Even

FIG. 8.4. Revolutions in Austria and Europe, ca. 1848–49.
Source: Center for European Policy Analysis, 2017.

with the fall of Peschiera, the other three forts were able to sustain one another and eventually allow Radetzky to launch a counteroffensive decisively defeating the numerically superior Sardinian nationalist forces at Custoza on July 24. Shortly before this battle, on June 12–17, General Windischgrätz put down the Prague uprising. Only when the crises in Italy and Bohemia had been dealt with did the army turn its full attention to the imperial capital, where it moved in force to suppress the revolution in October.

As in earlier wars, Austria's diplomats used well-timed appeasement, ranging from the granting of a new constitution to the emperor's abdication, to buy temporary reprieves and aid in military concentration. This allowed the army to defeat uprisings one theater at a time and eventually consolidate forces against its strongest opponent, the Hungarian army under Kossuth. As in the Prussian wars, Austria was able to draw on the enthusiastic troop pool of the Military Border, which performed its role of inward containment when

Croat forces under General Jellačić sortied northward to link up with the main force.

In this culminating act of the war, as in the wars against Frederick, Austria was able to bring its most powerful asset, the alliance with Russia, into play. Invoking the solidarity of the Holy Alliance, Czar Nicholas I sent an army of two hundred thousand troops into Hungary in three columns from the north, east, and south. By the time the Russians arrived, the Habsburg Army had largely defeated the revolution in Hungary.[58] Nevertheless, the Russian intervention showed continuity in Austrian grand strategy from previous wars as yet another example of the monarchy's eastern neighbor coming to its aid in an hour of emergency. It is in this final display of the Vienna system that the ultimate success of the arrangements that Metternich had made for more than three decades can be seen in furnishing the instruments that even if more symbolic than decisive, were ready to act in sustaining the existence of Austria against the forces of revolution.

At base, the Metternich system represented an attempt by a relatively weak power to shape a postwar order in which its abilities were outclassed by other powers. It succeeded in this regard, both in a narrow sense, in furnishing Austria with the breathing space needed for economic recovery, and more broadly, in giving Austria a degree of influence in European affairs out of all proportion to the monarchy's military capabilities.

The Metternich edifice compares favorably with the accomplishments of both previous and later attempts at engineering a postwar order. It lasted longer than the settlements of 1648, 1713–14, 1748, 1763, and 1801.[59] Compared to the post-1919 Versailles settlement, the decisions made at Vienna proved both more durable and successful in limiting the conditions for future conflict. Even in comparison to the post-1945 European settlement, the Vienna settlement was arguably more successful, at least for the first several decades, in lowering tensions between erstwhile antagonists and preventing a reversion to geopolitical crisis. As a war avoidance mechanism, the Metternich system was marked by moments of violence. But it avoided Great Power war for forty years and successfully averted a systemic upheaval involving all the major powers for a hundred years, from 1815 to 1914.

The success of Metternich's system is all the more impressive when Austria's relative weakness as an ordering power is taken into account. In 1815, Austria's strength in relation to its Great Power allies was smaller, on a proportional basis, than Britain's power relative to France and the United States in 1919, not to speak of the United States' strength vis-à-vis its allies in 1945. Yet unlike Britain after World War I, Austria ushered in a long peace that bought time for itself and the rest of Europe to recover without triggering a recurrence of general war. And in contrast to the British Empire in 1946, the system built by Metternich allowed Austria to avoid for many decades a shrinking, subordinate status in relation to its stronger partners; indeed, it positioned Austria to be a decisive shaper of the postwar environment to its own advantage.

It is the unavoidable reality of Austria's growing weakness in the first half of the nineteenth century that makes the monarchy's position at the heart of the Vienna system so arresting. At no point between 1815 and 1848 did the monarchy possess the ability to manage its extensive burdens using its own military power alone. To say that it succeeded by simply being a "necessity" to the rest of Europe is insufficient. The tools that Austria used to bridge the significant gap between capabilities and commitments—rings of forts, buffer-state clients, and above all, a system of collective security among Europe's Great Powers—required conceptualization and active maintenance by Habsburg diplomatic and military leaders. These were the by-products not of convalescence and dependency but instead a coherent grand strategy, consciously aimed at both mitigating and leveraging Austria's weakness as a Great Power.

In implementing this grand strategy, Metternich and his contemporaries were, as George Kennan once said, "gardeners and not mechanics"—tenders of an organic and, in their view, transcendent rules-based order in a world that they had put right, rather than tinkerers in a mechanistic balance of power that relied on exact weights and counterweights.[60] None was more a gardener than Metternich himself; the soil in which he dug was one of treaty rights between sovereign states, and the spade he used was the legitimacy that Austria held as an ancient civilization and empire. The army was there to pull the occasional weed, and its forts provided the picket fences separating the cultivated rows.

From a security perspective, the accomplishment of Metternich's system was that it gave Austria strategic choices that it would not have possessed in an environment of naked power politics, keeping major crises away from the Habsburg core. Metternich's diplomacy did this in a temporal sense by addressing problems at their source before they could metastasize into Europe-wide conflagrations; buffer zones and fortifications did so in a spatial sense by stopping threats well outside the Austrian home area. The result was a stable, if not altogether independent, European center buttressed by the continent's flanking powers. Austria's position at the core created the potential, arguably for the first time in Habsburg history, for a systematically "radial" strategy, allowing it deal with one problem and then pivot to another with a minimum of military risk or diplomatic cost to itself. By bringing Austria's multiple frontiers into one strategic frame, Metternich accomplished a mastery of the time problem at the heart of Austria's position that earlier Habsburg monarchs could only have dreamed of in their attempts to prop up one faltering front after another.

But perhaps the greatest measure of Metternich's legacy can be seen in what *did not* happen during this period. Austria did not sink into renewed economic depression under the weight of military spending and continued war. France and Austria did not come to blows over Italy for four decades. The monarchy did not succumb to the centrifugal forces that hit in 1848. And Prussia did not succeed in ejecting Austria from German affairs on its first attempt in 1850. Each of these events, when they finally occurred later in the century, would take on the appearance of inevitability.

In this sense, Metternich's system was truly a "barricade of time"—an edifice that held back the tide of events, and gave Austria room to breathe, rebuild, and amass influence when by the natural march of time it might well have been eclipsed by stronger forces. His goal was time management both in the narrow sense of seeking to juggle numerous frontiers and the wider, civilizational sense of seeking to extend the life span of an ancient empire beset by forces of radical change. As Henry Kissinger would later write, the success of the diplomatic system Metternich helped to construct should be measured "not by its ultimate failure, but by the length of time it staved off inevitable disaster."[61] Or as Metternich himself would say late in life, "The consideration may suffice that from the foundations of the political peace which has subsisted for eight-and-thirty years ... its most important decrees have been able not only to defy the storms which arose in the intermediate period, but even to survive the revolutions of the year 1848."[62] How well these foundations would stand up to the storms ahead is the subject of the next chapter.

9

Between Hammer and Anvil

ECLIPSE OF THE HABSBURG MONARCHY

Caught between a hammer and anvil, we are unable to attack in either
direction without fearing for our back.

—VON ARESIN

The time has come, not to fight the Turks and their allies, but to concentrate
all our efforts against perfidious Austria and to punish her severely for her
shameful ingratitude.

—CZAR NICHOLAS I

IN THE MIDDLE DECADES of the nineteenth century, the Habsburg Monarchy suffered defeats in a series of short, sharp wars that would bring an end to the Metternich system and pave the way for Austria's demise as a Great Power. This chapter argues that these changes occurred not primarily because of economic decay or the empire's internal complexity but instead because Austria lost the tools that it had used in the past to manage the sequencing and duration of its wars. This was the result of both structural changes beyond its leaders' control and avoidable errors and a deviation from the principles that had formerly shaped its past statecraft. Specifically, Austria's leaders abandoned the flexible statecraft that had allowed them to control conflict sequencing and avoid isolation; rivals adopted new technologies that denied the monarchy's armies the ability to use attrition and terrain to prolong conflict and outlast stronger militaries; and nationalism trumped treaty rights as a source of territorial legitimacy, allowing hostile polities to form in the areas that had previously served as the monarchy's buffer zones. Deprived of its traditional strategic toolbox, Austria was forced by its strongest rival to accept cohabitation with its strongest ethnic minority and for the first time had to absorb the full costs of managing a 360-degree defensive position.

The Puzzle of Austria's Eclipse

The Metternich era saw the high-water mark of Habsburg influence in Europe. It endowed Austria with more alliances than it had possessed at any prior point, ensconced it in buffer states secured by cooperative elites and client armies, and tilted the chessboard of geopolitical competition to Austria's advantage by making diplomacy rather than war the sine qua non of European politics. And yet within less than fifty years, the monarchy would find itself isolated in a series of disastrous wars in which it would fight alone against more than one enemy and gradually be pushed to the sidelines of European diplomacy. By the time these wars ended, Austria no longer possessed the position of influence it had enjoyed under Metternich and also would find its options for managing an independent foreign policy tightly constrained. Within another fifty years, and just a century after the apogee of Habsburg statecraft at the Congress of Vienna, Austria would fight a three-front war in which most of Europe would be aligned against it and subsequently disintegrate.

What happened? How in such a short period did Austria go from being an influential shaper of its environment to being a third-rate power whose demise would assume an aura of inevitability? Historically, the main reason that empires decline is that uneven economic growth rates cause them to fall behind their peers in power capabilities.[1] This was not entirely true for Austria; as we have seen, the Habsburg economy of the Vormärz period showed signs of dynamism and growth (see figure 9.1).[2] While in a state of relative economic decline, the degree of deterioration in the monarchy's power ranking was not terminal or even particularly precipitous; throughout the century it remained firmly anchored in the middle of the European development gradient, and indeed, in the final years of the nineteenth century would show signs of expansion.[3] Throughout this period, it would remain capable of fielding large land armies and sustaining defense budgets that were among the highest in Europe. There is therefore no reason on the basis of economic performance alone to assume that it should have fallen from the ranks of the Great Powers—much less dissolved as a state.

Nor can Austria's eclipse be explained entirely by its most obvious congenital flaw as a Great Power: the presence of ethnic diversity inside the state. Undoubtedly, the monarchy's internal complexion impeded its geopolitical performance.[4] As we will see in this chapter, the force of nationalism, especially in the lands immediately around Austria's borders, would become a major factor in its foreign policy predicaments. But from the vantage point of the midcentury mark, the monarchy seemed to have successfully weathered its severest storm. The uprisings of 1848–49 had been quelled and the dynasty reestablished on a firm footing. With the exception of Italy, large-scale unrest

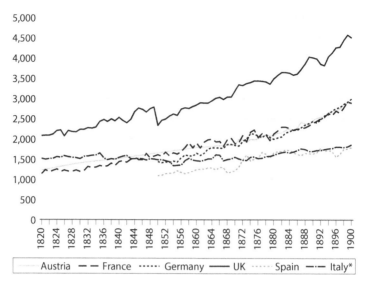

FIG. 9.1. Per Capita GDP of European Powers, 1820–1900. Notes: Italian figures are for center-northern Italy only, from 1820 to 1860. After 1861, the figures include the Kingdom of Italy. *Source:* The Maddison-Project, 2013, http://www.ggdc.net/maddison/maddison-project/home.htm. Graph: Center for European Policy Analysis, 2017.

was rare in the Habsburg lands in this period. Such tensions as existed did not constitute ingredients for civil war even, for the most part, in Italy.

Without doubt, both economic turmoil and ethnic tension would be ingredients in the empire's midcentury crisis. But neither alone can entirely explain the outcomes of that crisis.[5] Austria had faced economic problems off and on throughout its history, and not succumbed to them. Internal divisions had frequently beset Austria. And it had lost battles and even wars. Yet it had always survived. In moments of supreme emergency—1701–14, 1741–48, 1809, and 1848—it had always managed to avoid having to absorb the full burden of its predicament. This had usually boiled down to bringing some mixture of tools to bear to manipulate the timing of events so that Austria did not have to face its various external and internal problems simultaneously.

The first and most important of these tools was diplomacy. In life-or-death struggles, Austria had used a mixture of alliances, treaties, and appeasement to deactivate secondary threats (whether external or internal), and formed defensive alliances, even with rivals, to defray the burden of containing its most dangerous enemy, stagger its contests, and avoid multifront wars. A second tool was technology. When possible, Austria had often tried to avoid war entirely, and if that was not possible, avoid committing its loyal but frequently fragile army to contests it could not win. Instead, it had used force in combination with other aids—allies, client state armies, and defensive terrain. Above all it had maintained a largely defensive military outlook, seeking to hold and retain strategic ground, and never gambling, even in victory. This had helped allow Austria to conserve force and thereby exercise some influence over the length of wars, stringing out contests with stronger rivals until its deeper strengths—big armies, allied help, and so on—could be activated. Austria had often been able to use the postwar peace to regain lost ground and the intermediary status of the lands around its heartland as an insulating space to buy it time in future wars.

This combination had never been an exact science but rather a set of ad hoc tools that evolved to meet challenges. Habsburg statesmen abided by them with only rare deviations, which when made, were typically penalized by the hostile and constrained environment in which Austria lived. Metternich had brought these tools to their highest formal expression, creating structures that locked in certain geopolitical advantages. Using them, Austria had weathered numerous potentially severe crises in the early decades of the nineteenth century.

What made the crises that followed different is the conspicuous absence of these time management methods. In the space of about a decade and a half, from the end of the 1848 revolution to Austria's defeat by Prussia in 1866, a combination of structural changes beyond the monarchy's control and human errors would lead to the rapid erosion of Austria's traditional strategic toolbox. Together, these changes would bring about a dramatic deterioration in Austria's geopolitical position, subjecting it to forces beyond its ability to manage and ultimately leading to its failure as an empire.

Abandoning Flexible Statecraft

Flexible statecraft had always been foundational to Habsburg security. Because cleverness is cheaper than violence, diplomacy provided a prime means by which a weak and encircled state could survive when its environment produced threats too powerful for it to resist militarily. Diplomacy did this for Austria in two ways. First, defensive alliances acted as power aggregators to amass more military capabilities than the state possessed on its own—in Austria's case, often involving arrangements that brought allied armies onto Habsburg soil to rescue it from existential crisis. An important subcategory of alliance for Austria was the alliance of restraint, especially with its largest neighbor, Russia. As long as this held, Austria possessed a means by which to monitor and tame Russian moves, but also employ Russian help in the west, and—crucially—avoid military preparations on its longest and potentially most difficult frontier. A second kind of statecraft for Austria involved conflict avoidance with secondary threats. The monarchy had frequently used pre-emptive appeasement to placate a rival in order to concentrate attention on a greater threat. This applied not only to external actors like the Ottomans but internal groups, too—most notably the Hungarians—and putative client states that had opposed Austria's agenda in neighboring regions.

Both forms of statecraft had required a high degree of flexibility on Austria's part. Because enemies surrounded the monarchy, it needed to be able to have a full array of options for managing each new threat as it emerged, and therefore could never afford to permanently estrange even its bitterest rival from a previous war. The willingness to appease also required flexibility, since it often meant the deliberate deprioritization of an important issue with one threat in order to focus fully on another threat deemed more critical at that moment. With internal groups or client states, this usually required a degree of humility on the part of Habsburg dynasts to consciously forego prerogatives to which they were entitled or that would prevent the empire from mobilizing its full capabilities. Joseph I's handling of the Hungarians at Szatmar is one such example; Maria Theresa's leniency toward the Bavarians at Füssen and eschewal of increased demands on the Hungarians in the 1750s' war are two others.

Showing flexibility in both forms of statecraft had allowed Austria, more often than not, to concentrate resources and attention against the greatest challenge it faced at a given moment. Metternich's system represented the apogee of Austrian flexibility. It created standing arrangements that aligned the resources of Europe behind Austria in opposition to nationalism and hegemonic war. It also brought the big powers into coordinating formats that disproportionately played to Austria's strengths. This system of commitments and restraints helped to ensure that the monarchy would never find itself fully isolated in a time of crisis and would retain the maximum number of options for resolving the abundant problems of the spaces around its borders with diplomacy, which favored Austria, rather than military power, which did not.

As we have seen, Metternich's system successfully managed not only the challenges of the immediate post-1815 period but allowed Austria to pass the supreme test of the 1848 revolutions, too. It held together because other major powers perceived a greater gain to themselves through coordination than they did through independent action—as long, in other words, as they feared the consequences of going it alone (renewed war, exclusion, isolation, and defeat) more than they feared the loss of marginal gains through mediated outcomes.

This calculus eventually fell apart. Like all postwar orders, maintaining it became harder with time as memories of the horrors of war receded and a new generation of revisionist leaders emerged that saw prospects for territorial gain in their environment. France and Prussia in particular perceived advantages from a European territorial reorganization, and came to see Austria as an obstacle to their goals. Throughout the 1820s and 1830s, their resentment was kept in check by fear of revolution—a fear that Austria was adept at stoking—and most important, by Russia, whose support for Austria provided the ultimate deterrent to revisionism in Metternich's Europe. In the space of a few years after the 1848 revolutions, however, these restraints would disappear. Two specific flaws in the fabric of the Metternichian system—one involving Italy and the other the Balkans—made this happen when it did. Both had structural roots but were exacerbated by Austrian inflexibility.

THE ITALIAN STORM CENTER

The Achilles' heel of Austria's post-1815 security architecture was the overextension of its power in Italy.[6] Under the 1815 settlement, the monarchy had taken possession of the former Republic of Venice, which it had previously acquired in the 1797 Treaty of Campo Formio, and combined it with the Habsburg territory of Lombardy to form a new Kingdom of Lombardy-Venetia. The resulting entity represented a significant protrusion of Habsburg influence toward the southwest, encompassing a major portion of northern Italy.

At face value, this was an enhancement to Austrian security, providing both a thicker glacis between the Erblände and France, and an enlargement of the empire's western revenue base. But viewed from the standpoint of Austria's traditional approach to maintaining secure buffers around the monarchy's frontiers, the new situation in Italy was problematic. Geostrategically, the scale of Habsburg holdings made Austria, by a significant margin, the dominant security player in the peninsula without necessarily giving it the ability to perform this role. Possession of Lombardy-Venetia complicated relations with Austria's historic ally, Piedmont, while signaling a more or less permanent exclusion of France from major Italian affairs, and thus planting the seeds for future Franco-Austrian tension. As Schroeder writes,

> Austria's acquisition of Lombardy-Venetia created a deeper problem for the international system. It was defensible from a balance-of-power standpoint, as the only practical way to support and defend Piedmont and keep France out of Italy. But from the standpoint of Italy's general function as an intermediary body between France and Austria, Austria's acquisition of Lombardy-Venetia proved both too much and too little. It virtually forced Austria to lead and organize Italy, yet did not really empower her to do so. Lombardy-Venetia was not big enough as a power base to give Austria control of the whole peninsula, yet too big for the comfort of others, especially

Piedmont and the Papal State. Venetia alone might have been a province for Vienna to develop; Lombardy-Venetia became a cow for Vienna to milk, partly to cover the extra military obligations it involved. Owning Lombardy made Austria more rigid in its reaction to French efforts to regain a foothold in Italy. At the same time it enabled other Italian states, including Piedmont, to push onto Austria most of the burden of their own defense.[7]

Put differently, Lombardy-Venetia placed Austria in the position of managing not so much a buffer zone in Italy as a security liability and potential ulcer—a source of conflict rather than an intermediary body to act as a shock absorber in Great Power politics.

The root of the problem lay primarily in how Lombardy-Venetia would be governed. Until the end of the eighteenth century, Habsburg primacy on the Italian peninsula had been as much informal as formal. While Lombardy was ruled and administered directly from Vienna, it was only one part of a broader mosaic that included entities with less formal relationships to the Habsburg core. Venice retained considerable independence and held sway over the Adriatic; the pope exercised considerable influence; Naples and Sicily tended toward the Bourbon camp; and Piedmont, while tending to side with Austria out of fear of France, had nevertheless been a separate state, more client than constituent of the Habsburg imperium.[8] From a Habsburg perspective, this pattern was preferable to attempting to extend direct rule over the northern half of the peninsula; it heightened Italy's functionality as a buffer region by allowing Austria to bear only a portion of the costs of formal empire while enjoying the benefits of primacy in the form of patronage, revenues, and above all voluntary local resistance to outside encroachment.

Metternich's early preference had been to see some elements of this pattern continue after 1815. Most important, he wished for the new territory of Lombardy-Venetia to be governed less as a fully integrated unit of the monarchy and more as a semi-independent polity. In 1815, he wrote in a memorandum to Emperor Francis, "These lands must be governed here [in Italy], and the government here must then let themselves be represented in Vienna."[9] Under Metternich's formula, a large measure of autonomy would be granted to the kingdom in day-to-day matters, including a chancery and court of justice to represent Italian interests in Vienna. Echoing many of the arguments that Kaunitz had made to Joseph II about Poland more than four decades earlier, Metternich wished to offset the costs of empire building in Italy and avoid antagonizing the Italian populace by developing a benign Habsburg hegemony in the region. Ideally, this would have taken the form of a *Lega Italica*— "an Austria-led defensive league" roughly analogous to the German Bund.[10]

At first things seemed to be moving in a decentralized direction for Lombardy-Venetia. In 1817, a patent was issued incorporating many, if not all, of Metternich's proposals not only for Italy but also for a more decentralized structure in the monarchy as a whole. A separate chancery was created for the kingdom and placed under a Milanese count. But it quickly became apparent that Emperor Francis's intentions in Italy, like those of Emperor Joseph II in Poland before him, were to see the new kingdom fully incorporated into the central administrative apparatus of the monarchy, much as Lombardy had been in earlier decades.

The temptation toward centralization in Italy was an understandable and not altogether illogical course for Austria; for decades, Habsburg monarchs had pined to see their dominions expand in Italy—a region that unlike the German Reich or nettlesome lands to the east, seemed to offer the monarchy's only prospect for expansion into well-resourced territories at an affordable price in administration. This was, after all, the normal calculus for most empires throughout history: to achieve greater security and wealth through expansion. And indeed, the new arrangement seemed initially to bring benefits to both Vienna and its Italian subjects. Austrian investment brought economic growth and new jobs. Industrialization gathered pace, with expansion in the textile sector in particular. Habsburg administration introduced public works projects and infrastructure development. These changes seemed to bear out Metternich's conviction that Austria had "something to offer" in Italy: "orderly government and security in place of intrigue and revolutionary anarchy." Habsburg Italians were economically more prosperous than their counterparts in neighboring non-Habsburg regions. Austria, too, benefited from the region's wealth, and by the 1850s was able to collect a quarter of the empire's tax revenue from the Italian lands alone.[11]

But as the century progressed, strains in the Habsburg position in Italy began to appear, sowing the seeds for local and eventually international crises. Treating Lombardy-Venetia as a fully integrated administrative unit of the monarchy committed Austria to the defense of territories in which foreign oversight was virtually guaranteed to stoke resentment. Direct rule brought garrisons (numbering seventy thousand by midcentury), which in turn brought local taxes—and local animosities. This dynamic was heightened by the extensive Austrian employment of surveillance, aggressive policing, and spy networks to keep tabs on Italian revolutionary movements. Where previous generations of Italians had tended to view Vienna as a distant but benign force preferable to Bourbon control—to "hate France and fear the emperor," as the saying went—this equation was gradually reversed. Local populations and even normally supportive native princes came to view Austria as the occupier, and France, as a country of fellow Latins, as a source of sympathy and support for nationalist aspirations.

In 1831, the conservative king of Sardinia-Piedmont died and was succeeded by Charles Albert, a young king with liberal tendencies who yearned to become the champion of the burgeoning Italian nationalist movement. When revolution struck in Lombardy in 1848, Charles Albert cast his lot with the nationalists, providing armed support to the uprisings and encouraging other Italian princes to do the same.[12] That same year, France elected Louis-Napoleon Bonaparte (1808–73) as its president.[13] The nephew of Emperor Napoleon, the future Napoleon III, was, like Charles Albert, driven by messianic ambitions, albeit on a far grander scale, and dreamed of restoring France to imperial greatness. Unlike his immediate predecessors, he saw Metternich's system as an impediment to be discarded. In Italy's and Austria's resistance to centralized rule, he saw ready means for not only challenging this system but also conveying France with a moral cause as the renewed patron of European nationalism.

As the 1840s ended, the scene was therefore set for a sustained, Great Power–backed challenge to Austrian rule in Italy. An Austrian correspondent would later sum up the atmosphere of simmering anger that would build over the mid-nineteenth century and growing sense of futility among administrators in Vienna:

> I can illustrate the state of Central Italy and Italy generally with no expression other than: political Cholera. Rich and poor, ornate and modest, everything suffers.... My belief accordingly must involve armed force: The Italian obeys only overwhelming strength, he sees restraint as weakness, he knows not generosity, and his language even lacks a fitting word for "gratefulness." Have the millions, which the Archduke-Governor spent for the Lombards, been useful at all?[14]

Far from being a source of greater wealth and security for Austria as Metternich had envisioned, Italy would require an ever-larger share of Habsburg attention while creating a standing source of crisis, virtually guaranteeing that a conflict facing Austria in any other theater would, unless effectively managed, quickly spread into a second front.

THE EASTERN EXCEPTION

Revisionist ambitions of the sort harbored by Louis-Napoleon and Charles Albert were manageable for Austria as long as Russia remained a committed status quo power willing to uphold the monarchy's interests by force. At the same time that crisis was building in Italy, however, events on Austria's eastern frontier were threatening to remove this critical pillar of support to Habsburg security. The underlying problem, and second major flaw of the Metternich system, was the virtual exclusion of affairs in the east from the post-1815 congress framework. As a nonparticipant in the Napoleonic conflict, Turkey was not party to the Vienna peace settlement. This was problematic, since Austria maintained pressing security interests in the Balkans—in particular, as we have seen in a previous chapter, the need to maintain the existence of the Ottoman Empire as a check to Russian expansion. By the early nineteenth century this was becoming a more difficult task, as Turkish economic and political decay accelerated. Russia had possessed the territory of Bessarabia since 1812, and thus had a direct window onto the territories of Wallachia and Moldavia. Since Vienna viewed the continued functioning of these territories as a buffer zone to be a prerequisite for regional stability, the growth of Russian presence on the eastern frontier increased the potential for conflict between it and Austria.

The main rub for Austria lay in the interrelationship of events in the empire's eastern and western buffers. To manage the latter, Austria needed Russian support. This was especially true in Italy, where Russian military backing was required to keep a revisionist-minded France at bay, but also in Germany, where Russia acted as a restraint on Prussia. This was not a new dynamic for Austria; at least since the 1730s, it had balanced competing aims in the east and west. What *was* new was the scale of strategic commitments that Austria assumed after 1815, and especially the demands created by its attempt to exert centralized rule in Italy. If Lombardy-Venetia was going to be an integral part of the monarchy, then Austria was as committed to defending its interests there as it would be in core territories like Bohemia or Hungary. Hence Austria's commitments in Italy tied Vienna to something in the west that was immovable, and over which it could afford little flexibility, making Russian goodwill all the more essential and mandating Austrian flexibility in the east.

This complicated dynamic was manageable as long as Russia viewed the Balkans as an area of secondary rather than primary strategic interest, as it had done for much of the eighteenth century. But this would begin to change in the mid-nineteenth century as the center of gravity in Russian strategy shifted from the north to south. Prior to this moment, the main thrust of Russian strategy had been the Baltic, where abundant forests provided the lumber, pitch, and tar that, as staples for the world's navies, made up the czarist empire's main export.[15] But as fleets switched from sail to steam, Russia's exports shifted southward, to the wheat fields of Ukraine. This brought greater strategic focus to the nearest body of water that could serve as a highway for these exports, the Black Sea, and a heightened desire for dominance over the narrow passageways into the Mediterranean, where Russian ships needed to pass on the way to outside markets. At the same time, Turkey's accelerating internal decay presented opportunities for expanding Russian influence at the political core of the Ottoman Empire. With this came a change in the nature of Russian strategic objectives vis-à-vis Turkey. Instead of the acquisition of territory, Russia now came to focus on a far greater prize: the breakup of the Ottoman Empire or its outright subjugation as a Russian vassal.

As opportunities for Russian expansion grew, Austria found its own field of maneuver in the Balkans more constrained than ever. To be sure, territorial expansion had never been a particularly favorable alternative for the Danubian Monarchy on any of its frontiers, tending to bring problems in the form of new territories and changes to the empire's internal ethnic balances that outweighed whatever marginal gains it acquired in security. Nowhere was this truer than in the Balkans, where the lands in question tended to hold low intrinsic economic value. With the emergence of nineteenth-century nationalism, the cost-benefit ledger for expansion became even more lopsidedly negative. Many of the ethnic groups inhabiting the Balkan territories around the monarchy's southeastern borders, and indeed inside its borders, shared stronger cultural and linguistic commonalities with Slavic Russia than with the Habsburg Empire. As the Ottoman Empire declined, and its former Balkan possessions became more and more "at play" geopolitically, the fact of these territories' orientation toward Russia effectively foreclosed expansion as a viable Habsburg strategic option, since Russia would continue to hold immense influence inside these territories even if they were formally incorporated into the Habsburg imperium. As Schroeder notes,

> In Austria's case, the normal distinction between an internal threat of revolution and its external security dilemma was inapplicable; they were completely intertwined.... For most European great powers, Russia included, the acquisition of territory at this time usually meant gaining additional wealth, power, and security; once assimilated, the new territory would yield soldiers, revenues, and resources. Austria, because of its ethnic composition and geographic location, was already in the situation faced by all European powers and most states in the world today: territorial acquisitions would give Austria additional wealth, power, and security *if and only if* other powers, especially Russia, allowed them to. Other states, especially Russia, could if they wished render an Austrian territorial acquisition ungovernable, turning it into a burden rather than an advantage, by exploiting one or another of Austria's vulnerabilities.[16]

These vulnerabilities, congenital to Austria as a Great Power, placed tight constraints on its strategic options for dealing with the growth of Russian influence in the Balkans. As in Kaunitz's time, the monarchy could not forestall

Russia's expansion by attempting to grab these lands for itself, despite the allure that such various projects along these lines still occasionally held for Habsburg statesmen. Nor could it hope to resist this process by military force, given the extent of Habsburg security commitments in the Italian and German theaters, both of which, incidentally, depended on Russian support to manage. And yet at the same time, Austria could not merely consent to Russian expansion, lest it awaken to find a major military permanently blocking the monarchy's path to the Black Sea, and hemming in its southeastern frontiers with Russian-influenced or controlled clients, carved from the wreckage of Turkey's remaining European possessions.

Austria was thus confronted with a dilemma that represented, in heightened and steadily worsening form, the same basic issue that Kaunitz had confronted in the last quarter of the eighteenth century. Metternich's formula for dealing with the problem was, like Kaunitz, to avoid challenging Russia outright in the east, and instead attempt to channel its ambitions into outcomes that avoided permanent setbacks to Austrian interests or a destabilization of the wider balance of power. "The best way to check Russia," again quoting Schroeder, "perhaps the only feasible one—was the one which Austria had been advocating off and on ever since Kaunitz's time, and consistently since 1820: not challenging Russia directly or competing with it for influence at Constantinople, but grouping it, requiring Russia to act vis-à-vis Turkey only in concert with Europe."[17]

Channeling Russian ambitions in this way, when it could be achieved, benefited Austria because it allowed the monarchy to avoid the one thing that would most jeopardize its long-term security as a sandwiched, middle European power: having to make a choice between Russia and the west. Such a choice would entail only bad outcomes for Austria—on the one hand, an overly strong Russia that charged an exorbitant price (Balkan dominance) for its support of Austrian positions in the west, and on the other hand, an embittered Russia that would cease to backstop Habsburg security in Italy and Germany, and potentially become, in its own right, a revisionist rival to Austria along the lines of Napoleonic France or Frederickian Prussia.

For several years after the Vienna settlement, Austria was able to pursue its preferred course with Russia with a fair amount of success, and thus avoid having to choose decisively between Russia and the west. At Laibach in 1821, Metternich corralled the czar into suppressing an uprising in the principalities while simultaneously winning his support for Austrian military activities in Italy. In 1833 at Münchengrätz, he was able to plaster over the growing holes in the congress edifice by engineering a reaffirmation of the understanding between Austria, Russia, and Prussia under the aegis of the Holy Alliance— committing the three powers to joint policing of their neighborhood and guaranteeing Turkey's integrity. At the same time, Metternich succeeded in engineering a high degree of cooperation between Austria and Russia over Poland, where the two empires ran a virtual joint condominium over a large portion of the country, sharing intelligence and coordinating to suppress nationalist insurrections.

Metternich's balancing act enabled Austria to mask its growing weaknesses as a Great Power, and manage the inherent tension between its eastern and western security interests. This became harder to maintain, however, as the regional power balance shifted, and Russia turned more and more energy toward the south. In the 1820s, a new crisis erupted in which for the first time Europe's flanking powers, Britain and Russia, decided the outcome bilaterally, exposing the fragility of Metternich's eastern framework. In 1838, the pattern repeated itself, this time with Austria attempting to settle the matter via conference, with initial western backing, but being undercut by Russian defection and outreach to Britain.[18] With each new crisis, Austria's hand appeared weaker and the viability of Metternich's grouping formats for tying down Russian ambition less relevant. First sidelined by the western powers in an attempt to splinter the Holy Alliance, then sidelined by Russia in an effort to break out of the congress format, Austria was intermittently courted by both sides but was never in the driver's seat. And with each new crisis, the stakes grew higher, with Turkey's decay inviting progressively deeper Russian inroads and drawing the Great Powers—especially Russia and Britain—into confrontations that threatened to upend European stability.

THE CRIMEAN WAR

It was against this backdrop of escalating crisis and narrowing Habsburg options that in 1853, yet another eastern crisis broke out that would ultimately lead to the first Great Power war of the post-Napoleonic period. The immediate causes for the Crimea crisis were trivial, involving a Franco-Russian tussle over the status of Christians in the Ottoman-controlled Holy Land. The deeper cause was a Russian move—its most aggressive to date—to solidify the czar's status as a protector of Turkey's Orthodox subjects (more than two-fifths of the Ottoman population) and thus achieve uncontested primacy in Constantinople's internal affairs.[19] Britain aligned with France, seeking to use the crisis to force a climb down in Russia's elevated eastern position and, therewith, diminution in overall Russian power at the European level.

To an even greater extent than previous installments of the Eastern Question, the Crimea crisis carried heavy stakes for Austria. Most immediately, Russia's occupation of the Danubian Principalities in July 1853, undertaken to pressure the sultan, trod on a well-established Habsburg security interest and threatened to erode its sole remaining eastern buffer. More gravely, should Russia now achieve a commanding position in Turkish internal affairs or a partial breakup of the Ottoman Empire, Austria could find itself hemmed in by solidifying Russian pressure along a vast line stretching from Poland to the Adriatic. If Austria sided with Russia, it risked inviting a French attack against its positions in Italy, where tensions with Sardinia were near the boiling point. At the same time, if Austria aligned with Britain and France, it risked alienating Russia, the principal guarantor of its security against both the forces of revolution and French/Prussian revisionism in central Europe.

The task of handling this hornet's nest fell to Count Karl Ferdinand von Buol (1797–1865), a career diplomat who had previously served as envoy to Russia and succeeded to the post of foreign minister in 1852. In plotting a course for Habsburg diplomacy in the approaching crisis, Buol saw himself as adhering to the same principles that had been established by Metternich for Austria's eastern statecraft. Like Metternich, his overarching aim was to avoid war; like Metternich, he sought above all to avoid exclusive Russian primacy in the east generally and an occupation of the Danubian Principalities specifically; and like Metternich, he tried to solve the problem by using a grouping coalition to force Russia to accept "nominal satisfaction" from Turkey, and then, "having thrown a good fight into Turkey with its growls, now with honor return peacefully to its den."[20]

In pursuing this course, Buol faced serious opposition from within the Habsburg diplomatic and military establishments. Against him stood Baron Karl Ludwig von Bruck (1798–1860), Austria's ambassador to Turkey and a leading economist and statesman, as well as most of the senior commanders in the army. This "Russia faction" argued that Austria's best strategic option was to side with Saint Petersburg, on the grounds that in any ensuing war, Austria would absorb the brunt of the Russian attack while France and Britain were too far away to help. Further, the generals argued that the army was better prepared to meet a French attack on Italy, where it could count on the quadrilateral fortresses, than to meet a Russian attack in Galicia, where it possessed little in the way of fixed defenses.[21] Bruck went even further, maintaining that Austria should use the situation as an opportunity to conclude "a secret agreement with Russia ... [to] occupy Serbia, Bosnia and Herzegovina."[22]

As events unfolded, Buol quickly found himself in the same tightening vise that Metternich had faced in previous crises, as both the western allies and Russia looked to Austria to support their positions. Invoking the Holy Alliance, Russia requested Habsburg backing or, at a minimum, armed neutrality. Britain and France lobbied Buol to defect from the Holy Alliance, take a firm stance behind their position, and mobilize the Austrian Army to tie down as many Russian troops and resources as possible along the Danube. In keeping with Metternich's past practices, Buol tried to triangulate between the powers in hopes of striking a compromise and, above all, avoiding a war that would hold disproportionately negative implications for Austria.

When war broke out in fall 1853, Buol doubled down on this approach, encouraging bilateral talks between the Turks and Russians while seeking to arrange a four-power plan to mediate the conflict. As the war progressed, however, he tacked more and more toward the maritime powers in hopes of restraining Russia, which he correctly saw as the main aggressor and disturber of the peace. The conditions he presented to Saint Petersburg for Austrian neutrality were to commit Russia to "non-revolutionary conduct"—and specifically, "not to cross the Danube, not to raise the Balkan peoples in revolt and not to take any Turk territory"; failing such a promise, "Austria would have to join Turkey and the West, at least diplomatically, in order to check Russian expansion by forcing Russia out of the Danubian Principalities."[23] The breaking point came in January 1854, when the Russians rejected these conditions and, as a consequence, Buol committed Austria to cooperation with the western allies.

Austria's approach from this point forward, while steering clear of participation in hostilities, inevitably became more bellicose. In July, Buol issued an ultimatum demanding Russian evacuation of the principalities on threat of war, and to give credibility to the threat, undertook a buildup of military force on the empire's eastern territories.[24] To do so required mobilization and a wholesale shift of Habsburg units—altogether, eleven corps, or 327,000 troops—to Galicia and Transylvania, leaving only three corps to guard Italy and the western frontier.[25] In addition, the high command was asked to draw up plans for an offensive war against Russia using the Bug River as a center of operations.[26] This forward Austrian posture would prove decisive in determining the outcome of the war; while not entering combat, the sheer scale of Habsburg deployments on the Danube forced Russia to split its forces and therefore lack sufficient numbers to counter the Anglo-French operations on the Crimean peninsula. Buol's policy, in other words, had sealed Russia's fate in the conflict.

Buol was not unaware of the risks that the denuding of Austria's western frontiers might expose it to from France in Italy or Prussia in Germany. Much as Joseph II had done in the 1787–88 war, he addressed these vulnerabilities through preemptive treaties—one with France to safeguard the status quo in Lombardy-Venetia, and another with Prussia, with which he tried unsuccessfully to engineer pan-German backing to Austria's stance in the crisis.

In siding with the west, Buol hoped to achieve something of lasting strategic value to Austria in the east: a decisive rebuff to Russia's ambitions that would give its leaders pause when contemplating aggressive moves in the future. If, by siding unambiguously against Russia as the aggressor, Austria could not only stave off Turkey's collapse but also once and for all exclude Russia from the Danubian Principalities and perhaps even form its own military presence there, the monarchy would attain a more durable basis for security on its eastern and southern frontiers than it had possessed in more than a generation.

There is debate among historians about Buol's handling of the Crimea crisis.[27] What is clear is that Buol understood his approach to the crisis to be consistent with the tradition of Metternich and Kaunitz before him—that is, restraining Russia through coordination with the other Great Powers. Equally clear is that like Metternich, he identified the chief threat at hand to be Russia's turn toward increasingly revisionist aims and methods in the region. It is also worth remembering the extent to which Buol's strategic options in the crisis were constrained, corresponding to the resources of what was by then a power of middle standing in the European military hierarchy that was financially strapped after the exertions of 1848–49, and increasingly hard-pressed on its other security frontiers and especially Italy.

If there is a case to be made against Buol's handling of the Crimea crisis, it is simply that he overplayed Austria's hand. As F. R. Bridge puts it, Buol "embarked on an ambitious policy; but he was in no position to pursue it by military means."[28] Precisely because Austria was unprepared, both militarily and economically, to sustain participation in a major conflict, a stance of energetic armed neutrality seems in retrospect to have been an illogical course. While the broad contours of his approach, and certainly Buol's starting point in the crisis, may have been in keeping with Metternichian practice, the scale of militarization he undertook in Austrian policy was a break from previous practice. To be sure, previous Habsburg statesmen had on occasion used military posturing to back their diplomacy with Russia—Kaunitz, during the Austro-Turkish alliance of 1771, and Metternich during the 1820s' crisis, to name two examples. But the scale of military buildup and extent of war rhetoric used by Buol was of an entirely different magnitude, involving the bulk of the army (eleven out of fourteen corps), preparation of offensive war plans, and occupation of the principalities at Russia's expense.

In aligning so conspicuously against Russia, Buol did something that previous Habsburg statesmen had avoided in the east: he picked sides. Metternich had warned Buol from the outset of this danger and would criticize him later on these very grounds: that Austria must never be seen "either as the advance guard of the east against the west, or of the west against the east."[29] To the degree that Austria *had* made a choice in the past, there is a reasonable case to be made that it had tended to err on the side of avoiding moves that would embitter or estrange Russia. When the chips were down, Habsburg diplomats had tended, at least since the 1780s, to, in Kaunitz's words, "side with the Russians from the beginning."[30] Taking this approach to the extreme, as envisioned by Bruck, by participating in a partition of Turkey was of course no more realistic than it had been for Joseph II in his time. Rather, the viable alternative was simply to remain neutral—to "stay out of the war, defend her interests, and wait until war weariness on both sides enabled Austria to mediate a peace without victory."[31] This was how Metternich had handled the 1820s' crisis and what he advocated as an approach for Buol, and there is no obvious reason why it would not have worked.

Perhaps the main criticism of Buol's policy, though, is that it was unwise on geostrategic grounds because it exposed Austria to the greater of the two sets of then-visible dangers. To be sure, the prospect of an expansive Russia in the Balkans was not a positive one from a Habsburg security perspective. But Austria had been managing this danger for decades, and it is hard to argue that it represented a mortal threat to the monarchy on the scale of French and Prussian revisionism in Italy and Germany, respectively. Indeed, these latter two were by a wide margin the gravest threats facing Austria. Unlike Russia, these were two powers that had within recent history threatened the very existence of the Habsburg Monarchy. Both nurtured aspirations for pushing Austria out of regions in the west that on demographic, strategic, and economic bases, were of far greater long-term significance to Austrian interests than anything in the Balkans. By contrast, Russia had been the closest thing to an infallible ally that Austria possessed by this point in Austria's history, rallying to its defense in moments of supreme emergency—against Frederick, Napoleon, and most recently, in the revolution of 1848–49.

From a near-term military standpoint, the generals were right in their strategic calculation that Austria was in a far better position to side with Russia and weather a French attack against Italy than to hastily enforce the monarchy's naked eastern frontier and become the main battleground in a war against the larger Russian Army. From a broader, grand strategic standpoint, and this is the essential point, their argument was even more irrefutable: neither Britain nor France could provide as allies what Russia could and in fact had been supplying for decades on the things that mattered most for Austria's primary security interests: the maintenance of its position in Italy and Germany. Whatever temporary guarantees France might provide for Lombardy-Venetia, its interests here were fundamentally misaligned with Austria's. The same could be said for Prussia in Germany. If these powers attacked Austria in the west, as both shortly would, Russia was the only power on earth that would be able to help the monarchy. On this basis alone, it is reasonable to contend that Buol made the wrong choice.

Whatever the merits of his decisions at the time, one thing that is beyond dispute is that the outcomes of the Crimean War would have disastrous consequences for the Habsburg Monarchy. Initially the results seemed positive: under the concluding Treaty of Paris, Russia was forced away from its efforts at breaking up Turkey to instead accept the neutralization of the Black Sea and relinquish its protectorate over the Danubian Principalities.[32] Yet it quickly became apparent that whatever benefits Austria had gained would be ephemeral. Habsburg occupation of the principalities proved no more sustainable than it had in the time of Eugene, paving the way for their unification into a new, unified polity—Romania—that with Russian, French, Prussian, and Sardinian backing, would pose a far greater burden under Austria's blanket than had the presence of Moldavia and Wallachia.

Longer term, the war spawned a far-larger grand strategic problem for Austria: the emergence of Russia as an avowedly anti-Austria military power. Where Russia of the Metternich era and indeed as recently as the early 1850s had been "the chief supporter of the established order in Europe," henceforth it would be a determined revisionist power, and one that was motivated by a particularly acute animus toward the interests of the Habsburg Monarchy as both standard-bearer of the established order and architect, in Russia's eyes, of its humiliation in Crimea.[33]

The implications of this change for Habsburg defense policy could not have been more dramatic. Since the eighteenth century, Austria had been able, as a result of its alliances with Russia, to more or less neglect the securitization of an eastern frontier that from the Vistula to the Iron Gates was its longest border. This had amounted to a de facto Russian subsidization of Austrian security, allowing for limited defense resources to be concentrated primarily on the western frontiers.[34] With this alliance in tatters and Russia now militating against Austria, the vast eastern frontier would for the first time require an active defense. This meant not only the brick-and-mortar infrastructure of forts but garrisons, roads, and railways, too—in short, a whole, expensive apparatus necessary for round-the-clock defensive preparedness. Such investment was unlikely to be able to match Russian capabilities, and an arms race in the east was something that Austria could not hope to win. As one writer commented, "This tension with Russia can never become beneficial for Austria, as Russia is in the arena of an awe-striking advantage: every newly-constructed railroad track, every new wheel on newly-constructed machines awakens his latent strength; and if these strengths are in excess, on which side do you think the advantage will be?"[35]

For Habsburg diplomacy more broadly, the fallout from the war would effectively deprive Austria of meaningful Russian support where it was needed most in the years that followed. Since the mid-1700s, the pursuit of an alliance of some kind with Russia had been a constant in Austrian diplomacy, not only as a mechanism for restraining Russia in the east, but at least or more important, to ensure its *active* participation as a buttress to Habsburg aims in central European diplomacy. In the Metternich era, this alliance had become the keystone in the arch of Habsburg security, providing material backing against the forces of nationalism and Great Power revisionism that constituted the main threats to Austria. As long as it had held, even the worst blows to the edifice of Austrian security could be avoided or endured. Once it was gone, Austria was confronted with the possibility of the one thing that a militarily weak power in its central position could not afford: diplomatic isolation. As subsequent events would show, no other power could supply for Austria what Russia had done in maintaining Austria's buffers and indeed its overall position as a Great Power; if anything, most of them were eager to bring about the downgrading of Habsburg power and influence in Europe.

Offensive Technology Trumps Defensive Terrain

By undermining the Metternich treaty system, the Crimean War significantly eroded the foremost tool—alliances—by which the monarchy had traditionally influenced the time factor of its geopolitical competitions. From this point forward, Austria faced rivals on every side with little to protect it from a simultaneous, multifront crisis. The chief beneficiaries of this change were the powers that possessed the greatest ambitions for revising the European order. The most powerful and motivated of these was Prussia.

Since the time of Frederick II, Prussia had aspired to be the predominant power in Germany. Austro-Prussian competition had been temporarily suspended during the wars with Napoleon, but gradually reintensified again in the Vormärz period as Prussian growth accelerated and fissures began to appear in the Metternichian system. Like France, however, Prussia's ambitions throughout the Vormärz were kept in check by fear of revolution and Russian military support for Austria. The first of these restraints had already begun to break down by the time of the 1848 revolutions, which demonstrated the fragility of Austrian power as well as the latent demographic and economic potential of Germany. By harnessing these forces to its own strategic interests, Prussia's political and military leaders saw an opportunity to catapult Prussia into the status of central Europe's—and in fact Europe's—most powerful player.

The collapse of the Austro-Russian alliance over Crimea therefore presented an opportunity for Prussia to act on this goal. It nevertheless still faced a challenge. Physically, it was significantly smaller than the Habsburg Monar-chy, with a fraction of the population, surface area, and army. As previous standoffs had shown, Austria was capable of deploying a large army to the north while also mobilizing the client armies of its Bund allies, which in the 1850 crisis had produced a force of 130,000 to Prussia's 50,000.[36] To effectively challenge Austria, Prussia had to find a way to offset its rival's size and gain strategic advantages for itself. An answer presented itself in the emerging technologies of the Industrial Revolution.

DISRUPTIVE TECHNOLOGIES

In the early decades of the nineteenth century, a burst of technical break-throughs occurred that held revolutionary promise for any state capable of harnessing their military potential. Three in particular would give Prussia a competitive edge in its coming clash with Austria—one that made its armies more lethal, another that made them move faster, and a third that made them easier to control. The first came in the realm of ballistics. As is often the case after long wars, innovators applied the lessons of the recent conflict to the quest for more efficient ways to kill. The foundation for this revolution in small arms was laid in the late 1840s with the advent of the first modern bullet—the minié ball—a conical lead projectile that expanded after leaving the rifle's barrel. By easing the process of forcing bullets down a rifled barrel, the minié allowed rifles to be issued to entire armies rather than just a few elite units. At the same time, it vastly improved the effective range of infantry on the battlefield, from about seventy-five yards to between three hundred and a thousand yards.

Equipped with mass-produced rifled weapons, soldiers could shoot fur-ther, with greater precision and penetration. Soon they could shoot faster as well. In 1841, the Prussian Army adopted the world's first mass-issue breech-loading rifle. Developed by a Prussian inventor named Johann Nikolaus von Dreyse, the rifle was called the *Zündnadelgewehr* (needle-gun), after the pro-nounced firing pin (or needle) that was used to penetrate a percussion cap at the bottom of a self-contained paper cartridge, which was inserted into an open chamber near the trigger (the "breech") instead of with a ramrod down the barrel. The Dreyse allowed infantry to achieve unprecedented rates of fire—ten to twelve shots per minute compared to three to four for a muzzle-loader—while firing from prone positions that freed soldiers from the vulner-able standing and kneeling formations needed to operate muzzleloaders.

This period was also marked by improvements in the speed of communi-cation and travel. After the invention of the steam engine in Britain in the early

1800s, rail networks sprouted up across the continent. By the 1850s, trunk lines had appeared between major cities and the industrial hinterlands of Europe. These lines substantially cut travel time, propelling armies four to six times faster than they could achieve by road. At the same time, the development of the electric telegraph allowed for instantaneous communication across large swaths of Europe; by the early 1860s, most major powers had developed national telegraph systems. More than most European powers, Prussia would seek to develop these new technologies and harness them to its strategic interests. It embraced the breech-loading rifle a quarter century before its major rivals, promoted the introduction of the world's first steel guns, and devoted a large share of the national budget to the development of a rail grid that would become one of Europe's densest, with five lines to the eastern frontier and six to the western frontier by the late 1860s.

Several factors aided in this effort. An important one, noted above, was willpower: Prussia's leaders wanted to change Germany and were looking for the means to do so. To this can be added opportunity: unlike Austria or Prussia's other Bund neighbors, it possessed the political attributes of a large, homogeneous German state to organize the economies and national aspirations of the smaller polities around it. Prussia also had the means—the industrial area in the Ruhr, supported by a skilled workforce, with which to support the indigenous military plant. The state cultivated its potential, using protectionism and investments to spur growth. It encouraged native inventors, backing promising projects and giving medals to those who succeeded. But perhaps the biggest reason for Prussia's success in adapting new technologies lay in the Prussian Army and its relation to the state. Unlike its rivals, Prussia had the advantage of a military elite committed to studying the question of how technology—and for that matter, practically any other potential advantage—could be exploited to win future wars.

No one reflected this mind-set more than Moltke. Chief of the General Staff of the Prussian Army from 1857 to 1888, Moltke was the embodiment of a military intellectual: shy but strict, brainy but conservative, and devoted to his king and state.[37] Like Radetzky, he was inspired by history, translating Gibbon's *The History of the Decline and Fall of the Roman Empire* as a young man.[38] But unlike Radetzky, Moltke was a dedicated theorizer of war who devoted his energies to studying human conflict as an enterprise subject to mastery by a state willing to apply itself to the task. In developing the capacities of the Prussian Army, Moltke had the advantage of drawing on a coherent, homegrown framework that lent itself to the use of modern technology. He was a disciple of Clausewitz, a Prussian general and military writer who had served in the 1806 and 1813–14 campaigns. In his military treatise *Vom Kriege* (*On War*) written in 1831, Clausewitz embraced and expanded on the essentially political aims that Napoleon had brought to warfare, advocating "maximum use of force" to secure the state and advance its political interests. "War," he wrote,

> is an act of force to compel our enemy to do our will.... Force—that is, physical force, for moral force has no existence save as expressed in the state and the law—is thus the means of war; to impose our will on the enemy is its object. To secure that object we must render the enemy powerless; that, in theory, is the true aim of warfare.... If one side uses force without compunction, undeterred by the bloodshed it involves, while the other side refrains, the first will gain the upper hand.... This is how the matter must be seen.

To achieve the means for compelling the enemy to do one's will, Clausewitz advocated that the state "equip itself with the inventions of art and science," viewing all elements of social and economic policy through the lens of its future needs in war.[39]

As chief of the General Staff, Moltke pushed to modernize the military and developed a new concept of war, centered on Clausewitz and the proposition that technology and superior organization could enable Prussia to gain mastery of time in a conflict. In the opening phases of a war, Moltke advocated the aggressive employment of Prussia's railways, using timetables developed by a special railway section of the General Staff, to achieve a rapid mobilization, deployment (*Aufmarsch*), and concentration against an enemy.

Once his concept was in motion, Moltke envisioned large-scale offensives in which Prussia's armies would move on multiple, converging paths toward a single theater of battle, using the railway and telegraph to avoid becoming entangled through stacking units on muddy roads as had so often occurred in the Napoleonic era. After arriving at the scene, Prussian troops would use their concentric angles of attack to create a *kessel* (cauldron) in which the still-concentrating enemy was encircled and annihilated using superior small arms technology and tactics, thereby avoiding a prolonged war of the kind that would bring logistical constraints and other disadvantages to bear against Prussia.

AUSTRIAN MILITARY EXPANSION AND STASIS

Habsburg statesmen and generals were aware of the Prussian threat. Tensions had brewed intermittently since the Vormärz period. As early as 1828, Radetzky warned in a memo that Prussia had not "renounced enlargement in Germany" and argued that Austria should see Berlin as its primary long-range rival due to the unfulfilled demands that it held, unlike Russia, on the central European status quo.[40] In 1850, the two states almost came to military blows, and in the years that followed Austrian military men came to view an eventual clash with the northern kingdom as inevitable. As Francis Joseph would later comment on the eve of the Austro-Prussian War, "How can one avoid war when the other side wants it?"[41]

The traditional Habsburg method for dealing with Prussia had been to use alliances, especially with Russia, to compel it to divide its forces, and either avoid war altogether or ensure that the conflict was fought on Austria's terms. This was how Austria dealt with Frederick II in the second Prussian war, how Radetzky advised containing Austria throughout his lifetime, and ultimately what had deterred Prussia from launching an offensive war in 1850.

With the demise of the Austro-Russian alliance, the monarchy had lost its main means for pursuing such a strategy. This left two others tools of past Austrian strategy: terrain (the empire's natural topographic advantages) and technology (fortresses and client state armies). Both had traditionally been means of preventing the full burden of survival from falling on the army's back. The fragility of this instrument—its polyglot makeup, tactical limitations, and the typically constrained Austrian military budget—had usually prevented Habsburg rulers from staking too much on its abilities alone. For this reason, as we have seen, the army frequently played a secondary role in Austrian security strategies. While cultivating the army and its cosmopolitan officer corps as a bastion of loyal support for the dynasty, Austrian monarchs had usually seen it as a last line of defense as opposed to a policy tool of first choice.

If it did come to war, the army typically rarely attempted the insuperable task of achieving dominance on multiple frontiers, seeking instead to avoid defeat until other favorable factors could come into play. Against a militarily stronger foe, it usually had not tried to compete toe-to-toe but rather used defensive terrain to slow down the contest until the monarchy's latent resources could be brought into play. This often resulted in long conflicts in which a string of limited wars was interspersed with periods of recuperation. The ability to draw out contests in this way had allowed Austria to absorb defeats—sometimes even catastrophic ones—until its own armies had been able to catch up in areas in which the monarchy may have fallen behind prior to the war. This ability to modulate the length of wars provided resiliency for the Habsburg Monarchy as a Great Power. While the results of such protracted contests could be ruinous for the economy in the short term, the long-term prize had been survival.

Moltke's new warfare methods posed a challenge to this traditional Austrian template for managing time in conflict. In the event of a war, Prussia was likely to be able to mobilize larger forces, more quickly, than either Frederick or Napoleon, and achieve a degree of lethality that would make it difficult to apply techniques of attrition and delay. Austria would make itself more susceptible to defeat by its own actions in three ways: by failing to keep pace with technological change, embracing offensive military doctrines not matched to Austria's needs or infrastructure, and neglecting the empire's natural defensive advantages.

FAILURE TO MODERNIZE

Paradoxically, Austria would fall behind in military capabilities at a moment when its army was larger and better funded than at any prior point in history. The expansion of the army occurred from the 1850s onward as a result of the 1848 revolution. The scale of the uprisings, involving not only Italy and Hungary but also areas of the monarchy's heartland normally considered reliable, came as a shock to the Habsburg elite. The army's role in suppressing the revolt had underscored its indispensability to the dynasty at the same time that its relatively feeble capabilities highlighted the deleterious effects of decades of low defense spending under the Metternich system.

The dynasty had responded to the revolution with a fundamental reappraisal of the methods for its self-preservation. Emperor Ferdinand I, a harmless epileptic, abdicated in favor of his nephew, the eighteen-year-old Francis Joseph I (1830–1916).[42] Later in life, Francis Joseph would become eponymous with the traits of weary devotion, bureaucratic tedium, and resignation to fate that characterized the late phases of the monarchy. But in his youth, he seemed to embody rejuvenation for the empire. Handsome and athletic, he possessed a combination of military interests, social charm, and good looks rare in a Habsburg ruler. Beneath this youthful exterior, however, lay a rigid ruler motivated by deep-seated insecurities about the future of his family. As emperor, Francis Joseph's highest aspiration would be to place the dynasty—and with it, Austria's prospects as a Great Power—on a more secure footing. Distrustful of decentralization, he sought a more stable domestic political order, supported by military autocracy and centralism of the kind that had occasionally tempted earlier Habsburg monarchs but had never been obtainable. In the years after 1848, Francis Joseph steered Austria onto a neoabsolutist path, forming a reactionary government under Schwarzenberg that revoked earlier constitutional concessions, suspended parliament, and eliminated the Council of Ministers to place himself in direct control of domestic and military affairs.

An integral component of Francis Joseph's vision for the empire was an expansion of the Habsburg military establishment (see figure 9.2). After decades of low spending, Habsburg defense budgets increased dramatically, from an annual outlay of about fifty million florins in the Vormärz to more than two hundred million in 1855.[43] Altogether between 1850 and 1861, Austria would

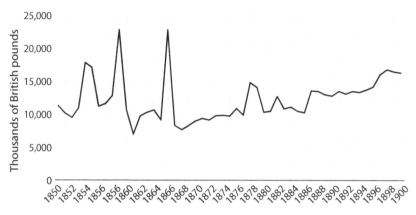

FIG. 9.2. Austrian Military Expenditure, 1850–1900. *Source:* C. A. Macartney,
The Habsburg Empire, 1790–1918 (New York: Macmillan, 1969).
Graph: Center for European Policy Analysis, 2017.

spend two billion florins on the army.[44] By the early 1860s, its military spending was twice that of Prussia, on par with that of France, and only slightly lower than Russia (see figure 9.3).[45] Historically one of the lowest defense spenders in Europe, Austria was now, in both total amounts and on a proportional basis according to state revenue, one of the highest.

With this growth came an increased role for the military in the state. Francis Joseph assumed personal command of the army—something not attempted by any prior ruler except for Joseph II. He gutted the Quartermaster's office and General Staff, abolished the War Ministry, expanded the imperial military chancery into a new Militärzentralkanzlei, and created a supreme military command with himself at its apex.[46] In place of Austria's long custom of a military dominated by civilians, he accumulated oversight in matters large and small to himself and a small circle of army advisers. A starker contrast with Metternich's system could hardly be imagined; within the space of a few years, the Habsburg Monarchy went from having the most diplomatically intensive security system in Europe to one of its most militarily intensive.

Expansion in size, though, did not mean that the army was increasing in fighting capabilities relative to its rivals. Even as Francis Joseph laid the foundations for a larger military machine, the army failed to keep pace with the military-technological revolution under way in other parts of Europe. Despite the devastating effects that new forms of warfare were beginning to show in places like Crimea, the army was slow to upgrade its weapons platforms. A committee to examine lessons from the 1854 war rejected breech-loading artillery on the grounds that muzzleloading cannons were "superior to breech-loaders in simplicity of construction and compare favorably in their efficiency

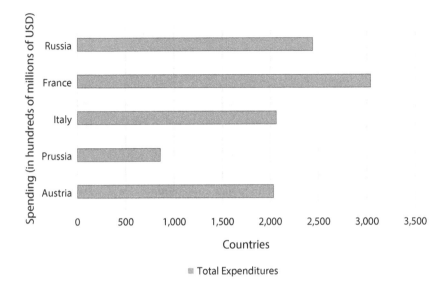

FIG. 9.3. Military Spending of European Land Powers, ca. 1862. *Source:* Geoffrey Wawro, "Inside the Whale: The Tangled Finances of the Austrian Army, 1848–1866," *War in History* 3, no. 1 (1996): 42–65. Graph: Center for European Policy Analysis, 2017.

for active service."[47] A similar commission rejected the Dreyse due to concerns that its rapid rate of fire would lead troops to waste ammunition in combat. Instead, Austria retained the muzzleloader, adopting the Infanteriegewehr M 1854, or "Lorenz" rifle—a percussion-cap rifle that while accurate at long ranges, fired at about a fifth the speed of a needle-gun.[48]

There were some structural reasons for retaining what was, by this point, increasingly outdated technology, but none were serious enough to explain why Austria fell behind. Financially, its increased budgets provided more than sufficient funds to purchase new weapons. Nor did the monarchy lack the native know-how to produce such technologies on its own, had it chosen to do so. Technical innovations flowed from Austria's proliferating polytechnical institutes throughout the Vormärz period, providing a vibrant link between science and industry with funding from Viennese banks.[49] Austrian firearms makers had experimented with various breech-loading rifles since the early 1800s, and native firms like that of Josef Werndl were capable of producing them.[50]

A more serious obstacle was the Habsburg military's human makeup. Some officers viewed the army's multilingual soldiers as intrinsically unfit for mastering the drill and marksmanship required for faster-shooting and more accurate firearms.[51] Certainly these factors made training a more complicated process than in most militaries. But from a purely technical standpoint, there was no reason why the Habsburg Army could not have mastered breech-loaders. With its three- to four-step loading process, the Dreyse needle-gun was easier to operate than muzzleloaders, which involve numerous, complex motions, are more prone to fouling and hang fires, more difficult to maintain in the field, and in the Lorenz's case, required complicated site adjustments.[52] With proper investment, even the least educationally advanced infantry could handle breech-loaders, as Britain demonstrated with the introduction of breech-loaders to the multiethnic armies of the Indian Raj.

The main reason Austria's military did not adapt technologically was not financial or technical but rather political. Only a portion of the outlays on defense was devoted to the maintenance and equipment of the army; at least as much was spent on shoring up the dynasty's position among key domestic constituencies. For not the first or last time in history, the government of a Great Power used resources set aside for the defense of the state to operate a jobs program. The impetus for doing so came from the 1848 revolution, which prompted the dynasty to look for new ways to cement the loyalty of the empire's political elite. Habsburg monarchs had long used gifts of various kinds to cultivate a base of support among the nobility. What made Francis Joseph different was the scale of state resources that he employed for this technique. Where Maria Theresa had given jobs in the imperial bureaucracy to a handful of Czech nobles to regain their loyalty after the Prussian wars, Francis Joseph gave jobs to *hundreds* of aging officers. In 1864, there were 1,203 such officers, the combined salaries of which were "roughly equal to the annual maintenance costs of Austria's eighty line infantry regiments."[53]

Spending on fighting forces—military hardware, modernization, research and development, and the fighting forces—as a proportion of the Austrian defense budget had remained relatively static for most of the period prior to Francis Joseph's reign. Even at the high point of Maria Theresa's expansion of bureaucracy, the amount spent on essentially political functions—pensions and salaries for senior officers—had constituted between a quarter and a third of the defense budget.[54] Under Francis Joseph, such expenses swelled to become higher as a proportion of defense spending than in any other European army. Out of a defense budget of 138 million florins, only half went to the fighting forces while the rest went to pensions, salaries, and various categories of supernumerary (see figure 9.4).[55] Of the half formally marked as spending on the regiments, a large portion was in fact diverted to nonmilitary purposes, including large numbers of *ad latus* officers falsely listed as "active duty" to hide the costs from parliament.[56]

The expansion of bureaucracy crowded out resources for combat troops. In order to support the increase in supernumeraries, fighting units were decommissioned, while procurement of new technologies became one of the

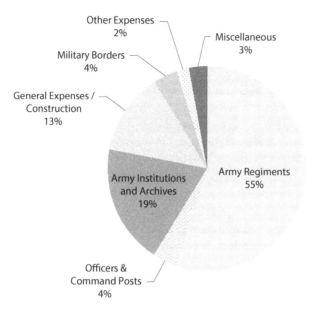

FIG. 9.4. Habsburg Military Spending, ca. 1862. *Source:* Geoffrey
Wawro, "Inside the Whale: The Tangled Finances of the Austrian
Army, 1848–1866," *War in History* 3, no. 1 (1996): 42–65.
Graph: Center for European Policy Analysis, 2017.

army's lowest priorities. Throughout the 1850s and early 1860s, the Habsburg
military devoted a trickle of money to equipment maintenance and munitions while continuing to add *ad lati.* In 1865, spending on overhead for provincial commands alone would have been enough to arm eight infantry regiments, while the army's top six supernumeraries earned enough to kit out a
regiment and a half of riflemen with Dreyse needle-guns.[57]

EMBRACING THE OFFENSIVE

At the same time that it was beginning to lag behind rivals in key technologies, the army gravitated toward offensive war-fighting doctrines. There were
precedents for this in Habsburg military history; at the tactical level, the Austrian infantry had favored the bayonet over firepower since the eighteenth
century, while the campaigns of Eugene and Laudon and Burcell's writings
had all to varying degrees emphasized mobility and aggression. But for the
most part, Habsburg strategic thinking and the military-diplomatic culture
underlying it had been defensive in nature, with a prevailing stress on logistics
and attrition over annihilation, and on survival over the proactive elimination
of rivals. Such proclivities had been rooted in an awareness of the fragility of

available military power, and corresponding political aversion to unnecessary risks or gambles. Thus Austria's desire for revenge for Prussia's seizure of Silesia, which was unmistakably a driving emotional force in Habsburg calculations from Maria Theresa onward, had been dampened by military constraints. Similarly, while the temptation to seize larger Balkan territories in the time of Joseph II had been real, Austria's actions in the 1788 war were essentially defensive in nature, allowing Kaunitz to boast of the "justice" of "our cause in a war that we had certainly not started."[58]

The transition to what would become a more offensive strategic outlook began at the tactical level in the Napoleonic Wars, when the ability of fast-moving French armies to quickly appear on the monarchy's frontiers and smash Habsburg forces to achieve rapid political decisions made a lasting impression on the younger generation of Austrian officers who served in this conflict. At the tactical level, an obsession with audaciously offensive battlefield movements took root in the ensuing decades, as army orthodoxy settled on the column as the main formation of deployment even as other militaries began to embrace firepower as the main determinant of battle. Radetzky summed up the conventional attitude when he observed that "modern infantry can trust only in the cold steel [bayonets] for ensuring victory on the battlefield."[59] Under Radetzky's guidance, Austria's generals created offensive war plans, often modeled on the successful 1814 campaign, for operations against France in the 1830s, Prussia in 1850, and Russia during the Crimean crisis.[60]

The shift toward offensive thinking was not, as in Prussia, the result of intellectual study but instead came in the form of a studied preference for audacity and animal vigor over intellectual contemplation in matters of war. As Francis Joseph built up the army in the period after the 1848 revolution, he had discouraged intellectual currents in the military leadership. "The quality of my army," the emperor said, "does not depend on learned officers, but on brave and chivalrous men."[61] Senior officers were chosen on the basis of their offensive spirit and loyalty to the emperor. Ludwig von Benedek (1804–81), who would serve as commander of Austrian forces in the 1866 war against Prussia, summed up the pervasive attitude when he said, "I conduct the business of war according to simple rules and I am not impressed by complicated calculations."[62]

The reasons for this anti-intellectual tilt were primarily dynastic in nature. While Austria had not developed philosophical writings on war in the period after 1815 on the scale of Prussia's Clausewitz or France's Jomini, it did possess a tradition of thinking defensively about war that was reflected in Archduke Charles's treatises. And while most Habsburg monarchs had distrusted military talent, the monarchy had since the period of Maria Theresa developed habits of extensive planning, including on the conceptual level, under men like

Lacy. In Francis Joseph's army, by contrast, the officer corps came to "not merely to disregard learning but to distrust it."[63] Coming to power at a young age and moment of chaos, Francis Joseph associated intellectualism with revolutionaries and liberals in parliament. The men who had saved his empire in 1848 were doers—"thrusters"—such as Windischgrätz and Radetzky, who were veteran campaigners and practitioners with little interest in formal war theorizing.

NEGLECTING CORE ADVANTAGES

Anti-intellectualism in the army went hand in hand with a de-emphasis on many of the traditional focal points of Habsburg military thinking. Nowhere was this more apparent than in the reduced study of terrain. As the century wore on, the extensive requirements for staff training in cartography that had begun under Maria Theresa lapsed. When a member of the Austrian General Staff's Geographic Bureau was tasked with creating a study of the military geography of Germany in 1864, he was told by his superior to go buy Baedeker travel guides.[64] And when the Prussian military attaché to Vienna invited Austrian colleagues to play the war game that the Prussian Army used for training officers, they were not interested because no gambling was involved.[65] As the French military attaché noted at the time, the Austrians "pay no attention to variable factors like terrain"—a dramatic shift for an army that had once lived by the maxim "terrain is everything."[66]

The same mind-set that rated offensive power above terrain deprioritized other aids that the monarchy had traditionally used to enhance its defensive power. One was fixed defenses. While forts were playing a diminished role in warfare by the mid-nineteenth century, they were by no means obsolete.[67] Modernized forts employing networks of diffuse, hardened positions were difficult to bypass and hard even for rifled artillery to reduce except by long siege. The quadrilateral, with its network of eighty forts across an almost 386-square-mile area, demonstrated the effectiveness of such defenses in both the 1848 and 1866 campaigns.[68] Forts like Verona and Olmütz, conceived as *places d'armes* and capable of hosting corps-size troop formations, continued to have a practical use, particularly for large land powers, as sites to house concentrations of force in situ near the frontier. Forts in the Vauban style, by contrast, which were relatively compact, and usually sited on terrain that had been chosen on the assumption of shorter and less powerful offensive weaponry, were at best useful as forward depots.

A majority of Austria's twenty-two forts were of the latter variety—most notably in Bohemia, where the eighteenth-century fortresses at Josephstadt, Theresienstadt, and Königgrätz remained largely unchanged from their original state.[69] Years earlier, Radetzky had warned the army to review the usefulness of such sites in light of technological change:

> It can happen, and indeed happens a lot, that a fortress which was highly necessary in one era becomes completely useless in another.... Advances in military science, fortification techniques and siege-craft, improvement in gunnery and weaponry, new inventions for strengthening powder and the like—all have an effect on the utility of a fortress as it relates to a specific defense purpose. From all of these considerations it follows that, in assessing the value of an existing fortress one must examine: the purpose for which it was originally constructed; whether this purpose still exists; if so, how the fortress serves that purpose; if not, the nature of that change and the implications that follow from it; how the fortress may serve the altered purpose; ... [and] in the event that a given fortress is of no more use as instrument of defense against any foreseeable enemy, to remove it and use its building materials for other military purposes.[70]

Some debate on the matter did occur. "In modern times," the leader of the Liberal Party, Karl Giskra, complained in 1865, "when artillery systems have evolved, the construction of fortifications should be carried out with greater caution [since] fortresses, which were considered impregnable because of their physical layout on the old system now lie in range of new cannons so that the works can be bombarded and razed in very short time."[71] Only after the catastrophic defeat the following year, however, did Austria seriously reexamine the utility of its Vauban forts. Had it done so earlier, it might have concluded, as Prussia did at the time, that some forts were worth retaining as garrisons while others were demolished in favor of railway development, or that outdated structures should be replaced by a handful of large defensive clusters on the Verona model, to be used in coordination with rail and field armies.

Instead, the Austrian military kept its old forts. In the 1850s, Austria invested 100 million florins in strengthening the quadrilateral forts.[72] And in 1861, the emperor initiated a 140 million florins project to "close the gaps" in frontier defenses.[73] But for most of the era, the story of Austria's forts is one of neglect. In 1865, on the eve of its conflict with Prussia, the empire spent a paltry 0.9 percent (2.1 million florins) on fortresses—about half the amount that went to supernumerary salaries, and a tenth of what it spent on annual travel.[74] The monarchy did not overemphasize fortresses, as some authors have claimed.[75] As a proportion of the defense budget, its spending on forts in this period was actually about the same as Prussia's.[76] But neither did it consciously upgrade them for new roles. Rather, Austria continued making blanket investments

TABLE 9.1. Comparison of Habsburg and Prussian Railways (in Miles)

Year	Habsburg Monarchy	Prussia
1841	218	233
1847	651	1,445
1850	843 +122	1,844
1860	1,819 +1,616	3,580
1865	2,298 +2,160	4,284
1870	3,798 +3,477	7,121

+ denotes track laid in Hungary.

Source: John Breuilly, *Austria, Prussia and the Making of Germany, 1806–1871* (London: Longman, 2011).

in legacy structures at levels too low to modernize them but high enough to detract from other uses. Little was done to conceptualize how forts should be used in conjunction either with the Habsburg field army or the monarchy's numerous client state armies and territories.

While neglecting the fixed defenses that had been its time management tool for warfare of the eighteenth century, Austria was also disregarding the time management tool of warfare in the nineteenth: railroads. Development in travel infrastructure had always represented a cost-effective investment for enhancing the interior lines of communication of the Danubian Basin. To this end, Maria Teresa and Joseph II had made road construction a strategic priority. As with weaponry, there was no intrinsic reason why Austria should not have been able to keep pace in railway construction at levels capable of supporting a modern defensive capacity (see table 9.1). Steam travel made an early appearance in the Austrian lands, and Vienna was quick to grasp its military potential. In 1841, an imperial decree laid the basis for trunk lines, one to each of the monarchy's major frontiers, producing more than 1,008 miles of track over the following seven years.[77]

But railways would fail to spread in Austria at the pace that they did in other western European states in the early years of Francis Joseph's reign. The reason lay in the nature of neoabsolutism and the disproportionate role that it gave to the state in controlling railway development. By midcentury, 68 percent of railways in Austria and 99 percent in Hungary were state owned. Only after government lines were privatized in 1854 (a concession to the financial pressures created by the Crimean War) did the empire's rail net begin to expand, increasing from 1,122 miles of track to 15,697 in nineteen years.[78] At the time that Austria entered into its contest with Prussia—though this process had just started, and the monarchy would enter the wars of 1866 with only one major line of track to each of the main war theaters.

ISOLATION AND DEFEAT

By the late 1850s, therefore, the Habsburg Monarchy's security position can be summarized as consisting of a degree of diplomatic loneliness uncharacteristic for Austria, married to a concomitant reliance on the army as guardian of the empire's Great Power status and as yet undetected lag in its forces' actual war-fighting capabilities. The first indication of the catastrophic results that this mixture could produce came four years after Crimea, when the monarchy became embroiled in its first military clash with a major rival since the end of the Napoleonic Wars.

The war with Italy in 1859 vividly demonstrated how severely the loss of Austria's traditional tools limited its options for effective security competition in general and its ability to manage the element of time in the new wars of the nineteenth century in particular. As always, the monarchy's cardinal need was to be able to avoid fighting two powers at once. It lost this ability by a continuation of the inflexible diplomacy it had showed over Crimea and overconfidence in its offensive military capabilities. Defying Metternich's dictum that "before Austria enters a war it must secure not only its military but its moral position," Vienna allowed itself to be baited into striking first and ceding the moral high ground.[79] With the Russian alliance defunct, there was nothing to dissuade Napoleon III from entering on Sardinia's side. Austria's sole option for support, Prussia, was estranged by Francis Joseph's unwillingness to concede to requests for leadership of federalist forces in Germany. Even when Britain succeeded in an eleventh-hour bid at Sardinian disarmament, Francis Joseph rejected the deal; trusting in the abilities of the army he had spent the past decade building, he presented an ultimatum to Sardinia *in hopes of triggering* war.[80]

Austria needed a quick victory of the kind Radetzky had achieved in 1849 to mitigate pressure on its finances. Yet without an ally to preoccupy France, it was unable to bring superior force to bear against the weaker of its two enemies. Promising to "treat Austria as Austria had treated him during the Crimean war," the Russian czar sought to pin down as many Austrian troops as possible in the east.[81] Trusting in his army's offensive power, Francis Joseph left the protection of the quadrilateral and sought out the Franco-Sardinian Army, ceding decades of built-up defensive advantages. Changes in technology quickly told against Austria. Using railways, French troops arrived at the combat scene faster than anticipated while Habsburg forces labored forward from scattered posts around the empire. On the field at Solferino, Austria's unwieldy columns were outmaneuvered by smaller French formations and mauled by rifled artillery. A plan to use the quadrilateral in the traditional defensive fashion, to "offer prolonged resistance so that the greater part of our army has the time to concentrate and rally," forced a halt to the French campaign.[82] But from a financial standpoint, continuing the conflict was not a viable option for the monarchy. At Villafranca, less than a month after the Solferino, Austria surrendered the majority of Lombardy along with the capital Milan to France, which in turn transferred them to Sardinia, thus relinquishing territories that Habsburg monarchs had held in almost-unbroken succession for nearly a century and a half.

The strategic consequences of Austria's defeat in Italy were far-reaching. In military terms, the monarchy salvaged the situation to some extent by retaining the fortresses at Mantua and Legnago. Together with the territory of Venetia, these positions provided a defensible salient beyond the Alps up to the Mincio, which with the addition of rearward fortifications could technically sustain Austria's Italian position in the event of renewed war. In broader diplomatic terms, however, the war diminished Austria's status as a Great Power, raising serious questions about its ability to defend its position against a determined opponent. While doubts along these lines had existed for some time, they had been allayed by the Austrian Army's reputation as a veteran fighting force—a reputation that Radetzky's successes in the campaign of 1848–49 had strengthened. The defeat of this force in battle, despite a decade's worth of significant financial investments and the personal presence of Francis Joseph as *Kriegsherr* on the field of battle, gave pause to Austria's allies and encouragement to its enemies.

THE ROAD TO RUIN

The lessons and implications of Austria's defeat were closely studied in Berlin. Since Frederick the Great, Austria's northern neighbor had chafed at the privileged position that Habsburg monarchs enjoyed in the affairs of the German Reich. In the immediate post-1815 period, these tensions had been submerged within the redesigned structures of the Bund and kept in check by mutual fears of revolution. Prussian cooperation, but also subordination, had been to essential Metternich's grand strategic vision of a stable European center organized under Habsburg leadership. In pursuit of this goal, Metternich envisioned an eventual economic framework to accompany the political organization of the Bund, in which the Federal Diet would be given legislative oversight of economic policy throughout Germany.[83] From the 1830s onward, he sought to encourage free trade within the Bund as a means of diminishing Prussia's industrial power.[84] While these plans failed to materialize, in part because of a notoriously prohibitive Austrian tariff system erected to obtain revenue from tax-exempt Hungary, Metternich succeeded in promoting a high degree of economic integration between Austria and southern Germany. By midcentury, Austria had more extensive commercial, investment, and infrastructure linkages to the Bund than to the rest of the Habsburg Monarchy.

Throughout the Vormärz period, a number of ambitious schemes were put forward for German economic integration. These evolved into two distinct and competing visions, one for a Germany organized under Prussian leadership, and the other under Habsburg leadership. The first was an outgrowth of the various customs unions that had been formed among German states in the period after the Congress of Vienna. In 1834, a German Zollverein (Customs Union) was created excluding Austria, which with Prussian encouragement, would quickly expand to include more than half of the Bund's members.[85] In addition to fueling intra-German commerce, the Zollverein acted as a buttress to the growth of Prussian economic power by using low tariffs to hobble emerging industry in other parts of Germany. An attempt to align Prussia and Austria into a common Middle European tariff union in the 1840s failed, further enhancing Prussia's status and reinforcing Habsburg exclusion from northern German commercial coordination.

A second blueprint for German integration emerged in the work of Baron Bruck, who served as Austrian commerce minister in the conservative government of Prince Schwarzenberg. Bruck envisioned nothing short of the unification of the lands of the German Bund and the Habsburg Monarchy into an economic Mitteleuropa—a massive bloc extending from the North Sea to the Danube. To this end, Bruck labored to remove the obstacles that had hindered Metternich's efforts of the 1830s–40s. In 1852, Austria's tariff walls were reduced; in 1853, a trade agreement was formed between the monarchy and Zollverein; Austria was brought into the German Postal and Telegraph Associations; a common trade and maritime code was developed; intra-German railway linkages were expanded; and in 1857, the relationship between the thaler currency of north Germany to the florin used in south Germany and Austria was stabilized.[86]

Bruck's efforts progressed in parallel with Francis Joseph's attempts at political centralization and expansion of the Habsburg military establishment. While economic in nature, Bruck's Mitteleuropa program pursued a geopolitical aim: the creation of an "empire of seventy millions" that would put a heretofore-unimaginable scale of resources under the aegis of Habsburg primacy. If successful, the resulting conglomeration would not only place Prussia in a permanent sidecar to Austria but also extend Germany's combined influence over the entire space between the frontiers of France and Russia, and to the southeast, down the Danube valley, into the Balkans, and eventually to the shores of the Black Sea.[87]

Bruck's plans, together with the broader effort to resolidify Habsburg leadership of Germany in the post-1848 period, brought Austria itself into increasing conflict with Prussia, whose burgeoning military and economic torque was intensifying during this period. In 1850, as we have seen, a narrowly averted Austro-Prussian military confrontation ended in Prussia's humiliation. Tensions continued to simmer in the years that followed as the two powers jostled for influence within the structures of the Bund. In these contests, Austria faced a forceful new opponent who, from the early 1850s onward, would gradually emerge as the monarchy's most dangerous one since the time of Napoleon: Bismarck.

A member of the Prussia's Junker gentry, Bismarck was, like Metternich, a political conservative with a magnetic personality and an instinctive grasp for people, intrigue, and diplomacy.[88] Unlike Metternich, he detested the mundane aspects of bureaucracy, was mercurial and forceful in manner, and not shy about using brute force to obtain his objectives. In outlook and proclivities, Bismarck bore the stamp of the Junker class, hating Catholic Austria, distrusting German nationalism as a potentially disruptive force, and sharing the reactionary orientation and anti-Polish hostility of czarist Russia.[89] In the Metternichian system, Bismarck saw an arrangement, as he wrote in 1854, "tying our neat seaworthy [Prussian] frigate to Austria's worm-eaten old battleship."[90] In Bruck's plans for a Mitteleuropa under Austrian leadership, Bismarck saw an exit ramp to permanent second-rank status for Prussia and recipe for future conflict with Russia.

Bismarck's meteoric rise as a Prussian statesman placed him on a collision course with the Habsburg Monarchy. As a Prussian delegate to the German Diet, Bismarck clashed violently with his Austrian counterpart, Count Friedrich von Thun, with whom he sought the trappings of equality to draw attention to Prussia's growing clout and power in German affairs.[91] As Austria's geopolitical difficulties intensified throughout the 1850s, Bismarck saw opportunities to confront the monarchy on terms favorable to Prussia. During the Crimea crisis, he lobbied the Prussian king, Frederick William IV, to place two hundred thousand troops in Silesia, not to assist Austria, but to pressure it into relinquishing its position in Germany. As Prussian ambassador to Russia, he went further, urging the king to launch a war of opportunity against the monarchy in Bohemia to take advantage of its distraction to the south.

For Bismarck, Austria's weakness following the Italian crisis, coming so soon after the debacle of Crimea, presented an opening of historic magnitude—an opportunity that as foreign minister from 1862 on, he was determined to exploit as a means of catapulting Prussia into the status of German primus inter pares and central Europe's most powerful state. For this contest, Prussia possessed certain advantages, not least its growing economy and Moltke's carefully calibrated military machine. But Bismarck faced a dilemma. While strong, Prussia was, like Austria, an interstitial power, flanked to the east and west by Great Powers. Even with Austria seemingly on the ropes, Prussia ran the risk of triggering a wider war in which it faced threats on other flanks—which indeed had been Austria's method for containing Prussian aggression in the past.

Bismarck handled these challenges by developing what would evolve into a time-based grand strategy of Prussia's own, matched to the northern kingdom's circumstances and the military and diplomatic tools at its disposal. Where Austria had used largely defensive and delay-based methods of time management in its past wars, Bismarck turned to the offensive as a means of securing the best diplomatic and military circumstances for Prussia. Like Austria in earlier decades, Bismarck used creative treaty diplomacy to gain control over the sequencing of Prussia's wars. To avoid the *cauchemar des coalitions* that had foiled Frederick, he broke his conquests into manageable chunks, first on an opportunistic basis and then more calculatedly, betting on the ability to secure and consolidate victories on an incremental basis that would not trigger a unified reaction from Europe's Great Powers.

Bismarck's first opportunity came in the north, where in 1863, a long-simmering dispute with the kingdom of Denmark over the duchies of Schleswig-Holstein boiled over with the promulgation of a new Danish Constitution attempting to incorporate the territories into the Danish state.[92] In response, the diet in Frankfurt appealed to Prussia and Austria for military intervention. The military campaign that followed was short, with Danish forces being defeated after only a few months of fighting. But the postwar negotiations opened a wide rift over the future of the duchies, with Austria preferring to see them united under a German prince and Bismarck angling to annex them in order to improve Prussia's window onto the Baltic. The concluding Gastein Convention of 1865 did little to resolve the issue, instead merely assigning Schleswig and Holstein to Prussia and Austria, respectively, and leaving the underlying questions of the duchies' fate and German leadership to be determined in the future.

As a bellwether for future Austro-Prussian relations, the Danish War highlighted the growing tension between the two powers. At the same time, it provided an extended opportunity for the two military establishments to observe one another in a combat setting. For Prussia, the war was the first major military campaign since 1815, and the first test for the army's new needle-guns and fire tactics. While the results were mixed, mainly due to the absence of large battles from which to extrapolate, several incidents from the campaign demonstrated conclusively the superiority of Prussia weapons against Danish units employing Habsburg-style columns and shock tactics.[93] For Austria, by contrast, on the basis of highly selective observations, the war was seen as confirming the value of shock tactics, with an analysis by the General Staff after the war concluding that Austria's victories in the campaign had validated the practice of headlong rushes by bayonet-wielding infantry while showing that the needle-gun's prowess was "purely theoretical."

KÖNIGGRÄTZ

Together with the Italian War of 1859, the Danish War acted as a proving ground for assessing the diplomatic and military characteristics of an eventual Austro-Prussian military conflict. When that war came, less than a year later, many of the prerequisites for a decisive Prussian military victory were already firmly in place. The alliance with Russia that had served to deter Prussia in 1850 lay in ruins as a result of the Crimean War. Relations with France remained frosty, coming so soon as they did after the two powers had been locked in mortal combat in Italy. A belated bid to entice France into friendship through a promise to cede Venetia yielded little, complicated in part by Bismarck's own overtures toward Paris. Reviewing the monarchy's constrained diplomatic options as the inevitable clash approached, Austrian foreign minister Count Mensdorff lamented, "I do not understand what we can offer France! Am I alone so incapable or will nothing come of the miserable basis on which our foreign policy stands?"[94]

Austria's diplomacy inside the Bund was complicated as well. Its German allies faced a strategic dilemma. Most were determined to resist Prussian expansion—to, as one observer put it, "construct a geographically consistent line of defense ... through Germany against Prussian arrogance."[95] But in the absence of large Austrian forces on their soil, most assumed they would succumb quickly to Prussian offensives. As a Württemburg report noted of its neighbors Hannover and Saxony, "Because of their geographic location, [these Austrian allies are] first of all, wedged between Prussian fortresses and garrisons, [and thus] cannot move, [so] will either be immediately occupied militarily by Prussia or forced to declare neutrality."[96] The Bavarian outlook was similarly bleak. "Our generals have low trust in the chances of our weapons against Prussia," one contemporary observed. "By all calculations, along with all of southern Germany, we would barely match Prussia's power."[97]

Before the war even broke out, the Habsburg Monarchy had lost control of the factor of time in the contest. Unlike in previous wars, Austria now needed to keep forces in the east to monitor Russia. Easily recruiting Sardinia as an ally, which used the crisis as an opportunity to advance its army on the quadrilateral forts, Bismarck was able to force the Austrians to further divide their troops to cover the possibility of operations in both Bohemia and Lombardy. At the same time, he worked assiduously to stir domestic crises inside the empire itself, putting out feelers to the Hungarians and other recalcitrant nationality movements in hopes of fomenting diversionary uprisings to pin down Austrian regiments in the Habsburg interior.[98]

Bismarck's determination to force a confrontation foreclosed even the most expansive of appeasement options. "Bismarck searches for a pretext," one Bund report lamented, "to either provoke or portray submission on our side, thereby to force a decision either through our weakness or the insulted honor of Prussia."[99] Commenting on an interview at the Austrian Foreign Ministry, the Bavarian ambassador in Vienna wrote to his king, "Count Mensdorff expressed several times the belief that Count Bismarck wants the war and admitted to me by telegraph later that Austria has not even armed yet."[100]

By the time Austria finally began to mobilize, virtually all its strategic options were bad. "I only see three alternatives," a prominent German politician of the time wrote.

> Austria fights on both fronts [Germany and Italy], uncertain about the ultimate intentions of the other German states. This is good and heroic, but I fear that it would exceed the strengths of the empire and is a risky choice. Or Austria sacrifices its interests in Germany and everything subsequent that is tied to our Reich will quickly fall as it may, in line with Prussia, as Austria shifts its entire strength toward Italy. Or finally, Austria will do the opposite: sacrifice its stance on Italy, join Italy, and together turn their entire strength against Prussia, not without the intention of winning there what it gave up on the other side. This shift at the front would, I believe, immediately tear away most German states and would, especially if Prussia attacks, elicit other threats in Europe.[101]

In the end, Austria chose the first option, and attempted to bear the brunt of a full-fledged two-front war on the Elbe and Po. From the outset, the technological investments that Austria's foes had made in the foregoing decade told to an even greater degree than they had in the 1859 war. Using abundant train lines and telegraphs, Moltke mobilized Prussia's forces in three weeks while Austria's took eight. Habsburg efforts were impeded by the wide geographic dispersal of its regiments in their far-flung imperial posts, a side effect of the empire's internal policing needs. As late as April 3, less than three months before the outbreak of hostilities, the Bavarian ambassador wrote despondently about Austrian military preparations:

> Until now, no man has been called to flags; on the north railway, no more than three battalions have been transported northward, two battalions from Pest, and one battalion to the Pruchna station in Austria-Silesia. Additional battalions reached Bohemia following other paths ... [but] the military was not pushed forward to the Prussian border.... What has been

done is limited to the standing up of regiments in distant areas that are far from railway stations, especially the cavalry in Transylvania, which have [been] placed at the center of the empire to be available to move in any direction.... All regiments, except those permanently stationed in eastern territory, were announced as march ready, so they could then be prepared in such a way that they were available to move without incurring unreasonable costs for the army.[102]

The Austrian military's wide geographic dispersal created both a logistical and financial strain in requiring regiments to be brought to full strength, and then shipped to the distant Saxon and Prussian borders. The opening of an Italian front made both problems worse. At a Council of Ministers meeting in late April, the emperor reacted to ominous telegraphs from the General Command in Verona by ordering preparations for the defense of Italy, which inevitably entailed new expenditures. "Above all," the war minister noted, "it will be necessary that the funds be made available for stepped-up mobilization measures," the costs of which would come "to 1.5 million florins, from which 1.14 million florins are recurring monthly expenses, and 400,000 florins a onetime expense. Until now, the Ministry of War has taken a loan of approximately 8.5 million for war preparations."[103]

MILITARY DEFEAT

As Austria's regiments mustered and lumbered into place, Prussian forces launched a Frederickian-style attack, cutting a quick path through the territory of its south German allies, most of which chose to withdraw their main forces and attempt to effect an allied concentration with Habsburg forces massing around the Elbe. Converging on the Austrian frontier on five rail lines while Habsburg forces slogged up to Bohemia by road and the monarchy's sole northward railway track, Moltke's forces were able to quickly concentrate a large force in the north while the Italians siphoned off Habsburg strength to the south.[104] Faced with the long-dreaded two-front war, Austria's generals detached three corps to Italy, leaving only seven corps for Bohemia—245,000 Austrians against 254,000 Prussians.[105]

On the battlefield, Moltke's effort to secure a quick victory and deny Austria the possibility of mobilizing its greater internal resources was aided by Vienna's neglect of traditional Habsburg advantages. The commander of Austria's Northern Army, Field Marshal Ludwig von Benedek (1804–81), made virtually no effective use of the terrain. Initially, he had planned to take the offensive against Prussia, but then switched to a plan modeled on the methods that Daun had used to confound Frederick: defending prepared positions, protected by the Elbe and flanked by hills, from which they could conduct a fighting retreat into the empire's interior if necessary. This was classic Austrian defensive strategy, rooted in denial, logistics, and terrain. The problem was that such a strategy made no sense in the context of Austria's isolated diplomatic posture or the offensive tactical doctrines now espoused by its soldiers. The point of delay in Austria's wars had always been to buy time— but in 1866, there was nothing to buy time *for*. There were no allied military interventions waiting on the horizon, as there had been in 1758, 1805, and 1848. Russia was not coming, Britain was not coming, and the one friendly neutral—France—was a long shot at best.

A terrain-based defensive strategy was also incongruous with the offensive doctrines and infrastructure investments that Austria had developed in the preceding decades. A US military study of the war would later conclude that "Benedek might have found a Metz in Königgrätz or Josephstadt," referring to the two-month Prussian siege of the French fortress at Metz in 1871.[106] But Metz was a modernized fortress on the Verona model, and the nearest of these that Austria possessed in the north was Olmütz, 87 miles east of the war zone. Instead of fighting defensively, Benedek repeated Austria's offensive behavior at Solferino, and took the army out beyond the protection of its forts and defensive terrain. Where Eugene and Charles had all made use of rivers as defensive barriers, Benedek deployed for battle in recessed ground north of the Elbe, with the river at his *back*. And where Daun at Kolin had occupied the heights to amplify the effects of Austria's one superior asset over the Prussians—artillery—Benedek, despite also possessing better artillery, largely forsook the protection of the abundant nearby hills. As one Habsburg officer commented after the battle, "We were standing in a hole ... a flat, uncovered plateau ... completely dominated by heights with excellent gun positions only 2,000 paces distant."[107]

Austria's forces would never have had the chance to attempt a Fabian campaign even if they had wanted. Prussian infantry units armed with the Dreyse took up defensive positions on the terrain and peppered Austria's exposed shock columns until Frederick, the main Prussian Army could arrive, achieving a classic *Kesselschlacht* at Königgrätz along the lines envisioned by Moltke. Trapped by the river behind them, the Austrian forces were bottled up, beaten, and routed, with a loss of nearly 43,000 troops and 641 guns.[108]

The extent to which Benedek deviated from classic Habsburg military strategy can be seen by comparing the northern campaign of 1866 with events in the south, where Archduke Albrecht inflicted defeat on the Italians at Custoza. Like Radetzky in 1848, Albrecht conducted a largely defensive campaign, using the forts of the quadrilateral to force the larger Italian Army—120,000 to Albrecht's 72,000—to fight on grounds of his choosing. It is noteworthy that

Radetzky and Albrecht, both of whom professed skepticism about defensive warfare, ended up achieving the greatest Habsburg victories of the era in strategic positions within Austria's lines of forts, while Francis Joseph and Benedek in 1859 and 1866, respectively, eschewed defensive terrain, took the strategic offensive out beyond the forts, and lost.[109] Albrecht's victory enabled Austria to shift troops northward, which might have had a significant impact on the course of the war if Benedek had managed to hold out longer. In a war council after Königgrätz, some of the emperor's advisers argued for doing just that.[110] But the scale of the battlefield defeat forced a capitulation.

Aftermath: Loss of Buffers

Austria might have lost the war in 1866 in any event. But the manner in which it lost—quickly, decisively, alone, and without any viable options for continuing the contest—effectively deprived it of the options that former generations of Habsburg leaders had used to recover from even the worst military defeats. Where Austria had fought Prussia to a standstill in a war that lasted seven *years* a century earlier, it now lost to Prussia in seven *weeks* (see figure 9.5). Where it had been able spread its defeats by revolutionary and Napoleonic France across a twenty-year period, always managing to mobilize Great Power alliances with which to recoup its losses, it now lost to two land-hungry revisionists while the rest of Europe stood idly by—indeed, with one of the onlookers (France) participating indirectly in the predation.

Königgrätz marked the end of the Habsburg Monarchy as a Great Power in any meaningful sense of the term. In its earlier wars, Austria had often been able to lose battles but win either the war or resulting peace through adroit diplomacy. This did not happen in 1866. What made the new postwar order different from those of the past was the permanent change that occurred in Austria's buffer regions. Where treaty rights and legitimacy had formerly provided a basis for preserving bands of smaller polities around the monarchy's borders, the force of nationalism now held greater moral authority for determining territorial configurations.

On every side, the mosaics of smaller client states that had surrounded Austria's borders for centuries were replaced by congealing nation-states. In the southwest, the monarchy was forced out of its remaining redoubts in Lombardy, ceding Venetia and the forts of the quadrilateral to Napoleon III, who gave them to Sardinia, which in turn quickly formed a new Great Power on the map of Europe: the nation of Italy. In the southeast, the Danubian Principalities over which Austria had fought the Crimean War morphed, with the substantial help of Austria's rivals, into the Kingdom of Romania under Prussian military tutelage. To this would be added, in the decades after 1866,

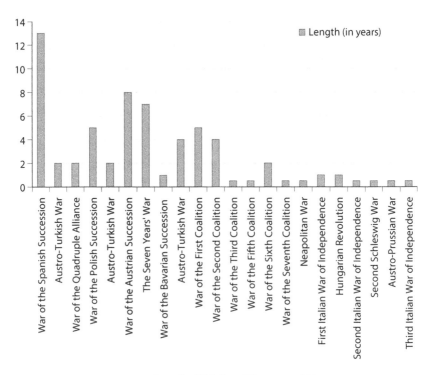

FIG. 9.5. Length of Habsburg Wars, 1700–1866.
Source: Center for European Policy Analysis, 2017.

a welter of Balkan nation-states, all clamoring for some degree of ethnic-based sovereignty, the fulfillment of which was antithetical to stable yet unthreatening buffers in the image of their now-decrepit Ottoman forebears.

The biggest change for Austria, however, came in Germany, its seat of strength as a Great Power. After Königgrätz, Bismarck fulfilled the longstanding Prussian ambition of kicking Austria out of Germany, abolishing the Austrian-led Bund that had been Metternich's great accomplishment after the last systemic European war and erecting in its place the Prussian-led North German Confederation. The new configuration was an expedient meant to speed the path to German unification under Prussian leadership. Foreseeing where Bismarck's ambition would lead, an Austrian official wrote amid the postwar negotiations,

> Prussia will have at its disposal the full strength of the northern German states, the complete unification of which is only a question of time, and a short one at that.... The imperial state will thus experience the humiliation of entering a smaller stage with weakened authority and less power.... An abundance of power and status cannot be brought back from the bat-

tles of the previous weeks. We will only suffer new victims, we will only incur a new element of weakness. If, for the time being, no German confederation and no Germany should continue to exist, we will better serve the future of Austria, if we temporarily stay out of an international connection with a Germany in shambles.[111]

Austria's eviction from Germany, it turned out, would not be "temporary." Together with changes in Italy and the Balkans, Bismarck's formation of a new German state marked a final, permanent defeat to what had been the overarching objective of Habsburg diplomacy for the preceding two centuries: the maintenance of stable buffer zones around the empire's borders.

With the extinction of these intermediate spaces, the Habsburg Monarchy lost the primary means by which it had managed time in strategic competition for more than a century and a half. In its place, it was surrounded by militarized frontiers that placed it in direct physical contact with major rivals. The army was forced to fall back from its forward positions to the frontier, and stripped of the insulating effects of buffer-state terrain, client armies, and tutelary fortresses, its range of responsibilities was drastically increased. In the decades after 1866, the monarchy would launch new rounds of fortress construction, attempting to compensate for the loss of space in buffers with steel and cement.[112] While many of these structures would show the application of lessons learned in 1866, they nevertheless represented capital investments in a form of warfare that had been bypassed by the Napoleonic and Moltkean military-technological revolutions. They were also expensive, requiring the equivalent of miniature Maginot-style structures on four sides to cover a four-thousand-mile security perimeter.

DOMESTIC POWER SHARING

The loss of buffers had ripple effects inside the empire, in the tone and structure of relations between the imperial center and periphery. Coming as the third crisis in a little more than a decade, the 1866 war had placed a catastrophic drain on public resources while significantly expanding the monarchy's debts. Already the mobilizations of 1854 and 1859 had brought the monarchy to the brink of bankruptcy and undermined its international credit. This string of wars caused wild fluctuations in the money supply, foiling repeated attempts at monetary reform and silver convertibility.[113] The empire's foreign policy effectively derailed the positive economic performance of the Vormärz period, crowding out investment and slowing overall growth.[114]

Straitened economic circumstances put the dynasty at a disadvantage for fending off the inevitable postwar efforts to restructure the empire. Such pressure, always from the Hungarians, had been a perennial feature of Habsburg wars that Austria had been able to largely resist. But now Vienna was forced to contemplate a fundamental renegotiation of its relationship with the Hungarians. In answering the demands that the Magyars brought forward, Francis Joseph was weakened by the state of Austrian public finances, which together with the loss of Italian revenues and emergence of Germany as a competing economic bloc, increased Austria's economic dependence on Hungary. Francis Joseph was further undercut by interference from Bismarck, who in the ultimate act of foreign meddling in the Habsburg Empire's internal affairs, connived with Magyar moderates to suggest an eastward shift in the empire's center of gravity, whereby Budapest would replace Vienna as the Habsburg capital. In responding to this pressure, the emperor reaped a bitter harvest from the intransigence he had shown in earlier years; where previous Habsburg rulers had often extended concessions to the Magyars preemptively ahead of conflicts, Francis Joseph's attempts at heavy-handed centralization after the 1848 revolutions restricted his options for resisting Hungarian demands for cohabitation once Austria had lost its allies and faced defeat in a major war.

The resulting compromise—the Ausgleich of 1867—brought an end to the Habsburg Empire as a unitary structure and introduced a dualist structure whereby Austria would share power with a formally coequal Hungary (see figure 9.6). Under the compromise, two political units were created that shared a common foreign policy but possessed separate governments, parliaments, and fiscal policies. Critically, the new arrangement granted the Hungarians considerable power in shaping the monarchy's behavior as a security actor. While the emperor remained commander in chief, three armies now formed, including a semiautonomous Hungarian defense force that would eventually obtain its own artillery. The Hungarian Parliament exercised influence over the annual defense budget and the financial terms of the compromise, subject to renegotiation at ten-year intervals. As a result, the Habsburg state would face a greater political contestation of defense resources than in the past. More broadly, the Ausgleich would intensify the problem of equivocal loyalties that had stalked the monarchy from its earliest days. The dynasty's historically loyal ethnicities—Croats, Slovaks, and Romanians—were subjected to culturally assimilationist rule from Budapest. Inspired by the Hungarian example, the empire's largest ethnicity, the Slavs, would seek a similar deal.

Forced domestic cohabitation and loss of external buffers worked in tandem to weaken Habsburg security. The presence of unifying nation-states in what had previously been fragmented buffer zones exerted a new and powerful magnetic pull on Habsburg ethnicities, many of which shared linguistic

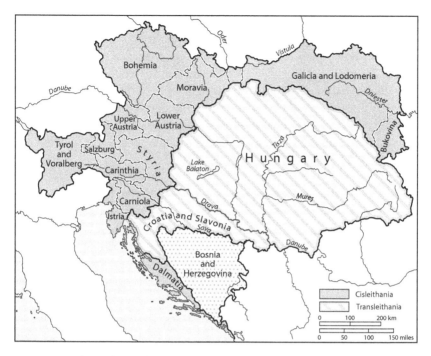

FIG. 9.6. The Hyphenated Empire: Austria-Hungary, ca. 1867. *Source:* Public domain.

and cultural ties with their neighbors. The Slavs looked to Russia, the Italians to national Italy, and the Romanians to national Romania. Most dangerously, Austrian Germans now saw in Bismarck and the German Empire a vehicle for fulfilling the aspiration of regional dominance on a more efficient national basis than had been possible via the arcane structures of the monarchy.

The Habsburg Monarchy would retain its role as a major, though not necessarily great, power for another half century. But in grand strategic terms, the game was up. Ironically, Austria would experience greater economic dynamism in the decades after 1866, as the turbulence of the midcentury wars gave way to a period of stability in the money supply and unprecedented growth. The ability to seize the opportunities created by this growth, though, was constrained by the monarchy's geopolitical circumstances, which effectively narrowed its options for steering an independent foreign policy course.

No amount of economic growth could have equipped Austria with the size of military required to permanently man a fortified, four-sided defensive position surrounded by rivals that were at least as economically strong, and in many cases stronger. As Kaunitz had worried would someday happen if the monarchy lost its buffers, the new Austria-Hungary gravitated toward greater geopolitical dependence on its strongest neighbor as a means of ameliorating

its 360-degree defense burden. With Russia more or less permanently estranged, Italy seeking to gain yet more Habsburg territory, and the Ottoman
Empire in Europe replaced by a belt of nettlesome statelets, the inevitable
pull in Austrian foreign policy was toward a closer relationship with Germany. In its final conflict, Austria would fight a war on three fronts, allied with
Europe's most revisionist power, without either the moral high ground or
meaningful alliance options among the other Great Powers. The Habsburg
Monarchy ran out of time in both a narrow military sense and, with the war
lost, broader geopolitical sense as a state.

There was nothing inevitable about the Habsburg Monarchy's demise as a
Great Power. That it faced growing ethnic pressure, intermittent economic
crisis, and rising rivals cannot be denied. But it had faced these things in the
past and survived. What made the crises of the mid-nineteenth century different was the extent to which Austria met them without possessing *any* of its
traditional tools for managing time in a geopolitical competition. These tools
had helped to ensure that Austria could bring its limited power to bear on
limited problems, usually with the help of a major portion of the international
system behind it. While Austria had frequently faced conflicts in which one
or more of these tools had failed, the failure of all three simultaneously
brought catastrophic defeat at a moment when rapid social and technological
change made it far less possible to recuperate from mistakes than it had been
in the past.

Certainly, the inordinate advantages that Austria had enjoyed under the
Metternich system were bound to come to an end eventually. Yet the manner
in which this system eroded and degree of Austria's geopolitical downgrading
were not foreordained. The loss of *all* options for Great Power support proved
especially crucial. With the possible example of Joseph II's brief Bavarian succession war, Habsburg monarchs had always adhered to one tenet of statecraft above all others: avoid isolation. With the support of at least one Great
Power, both the 1859 and 1866 crises might have gone quite differently. With
Prussian or Russian backing, 1859 would probably have looked more like the
crises of the 1830s or 1848, when Austria performed a localized military action
without French intervention. With Russian support, 1866 may well not have
happened at all or else turned out like the standoff in 1850, with Prussia ultimately backing down.

The fact that Austria lost its traditional strategic tools is attributable as
much to the decisions of individual leaders as to any structural changes beyond their control. In particular, the loss of the alliance with Russia, which
more than any single factor provided the foundation for the monarchy's security, appears in retrospect to have been an unforced error. Choices in the east

had always been tough, but it is hard to escape the impression that Austria made the wrong decision in choosing military escalation in Crimea at a moment when Austria's wider position depended on Russia, and when Austria knew from hard experience that the maritime powers could not take Russia's place in long-term Austrian security needs. The lost opportunities for Prussian support too, in 1848 but especially 1859, when it would likely have prevented France from entering the conflict, seem unwise, especially since they involved a price—Prussian leadership of the armies of the Bund—far more affordable than the loss of Italy. The same can be said of Austria's choice to shun the peace brokered by Britain with Sardinia 1859 and opt voluntarily for war.

A common thread running through all these choices is that they rested on greater estimations of military force as a policy tool than was usual for Austrian rulers and statesmen. Francis Joseph's development of the neoabsolutist state, with its heavy investment in the military, represented a departure from past Habsburg strategy. The self-sufficiency that the expanded army seemed to indicate possible is inextricably linked to the inflexibility of Habsburg diplomacy of this period. Trusting in the army, the monarchy neglected a central tenet of interstitial statecraft—that a surrounded empire cannot be strong everywhere, all the time. Austria had always needed to be flexible on at least one frontier—usually two—in order to achieve its objectives on a particular front; in Francis Joseph's time, it showed inflexibility on all four sides and lost.

In the end, Austria succumbed to another interstitial empire, Prussia, which had developed its own time management techniques better attuned to the technological realities of the day. While the rival in question was possessed of significant advantages and led by an unusually gifted strategist in the person of Bismarck, its ability to concentrate force and achieve victory was possible only because Austria had ceded key advantages—in mismanaged alliances and neglected technologies in the years leading up to the war, but also, once the war broke out, in the defensive use of terrain. Austria's traditional grand strategy had never been particularly glamorous militarily—a reality that frustrated centralizing and martial-minded rulers like Joseph II and Francis Joseph. But the formula had generally worked, allowing Austria to cultivate a high degree of influence over the European center. Its success had required, above all, recognition of limits. This is perhaps what Austria lacked most in the hour of crisis under Francis Joseph; coming at a moment when social and technological change made mistakes less recoverable than they had been in the past, the results were fatal.

10

The Habsburg Legacy

TAMING CHAOS

ALL GREAT POWERS need a grand strategy to survive. This book has argued that the Habsburg Empire had an especially pressing need to engage in the pursuit of grand strategy because of its vulnerable location and the unavailability of effective offensive military instruments with which to subdue the threats around its frontiers. Weakness is provocative, and apathy is rarely rewarded in even the most forgiving of strategic environments. For an impecunious power in the vortex of east-central European geopolitics, these traits, if permitted to coexist for long, would lead to the extinction of the state. This was the signal lesson from the wars of the eighteenth century, which had culminated in a succession struggle that saw a militarily weak Austria dangerously bereft of allies invaded from three directions and almost destroyed. These experiences spurred Habsburg leaders to conceptualize and formalize the matching of means to large ends in anticipation of future threats. The result was a conservative grand strategy that used alliances, buffer states, and a defensive army to manage multifront dynamics, avoid strains beyond Austria's ability to bear, and preserve an independent European center under Habsburg leadership.

Habsburg grand strategy was both necessitated and defined by the limits imposed by Austria's environment along with its internal makeup. Geography pointed to the tool of national excellence that a Great Power in Austria's position would ideally possess: a large land army, primed for offensive warfare, along the lines retained by other continental powers. The desire to create such a force and mobilize the resources needed to support it on a standing basis would continually resurface in Habsburg history, usually at the end of a lost or close-run war. Joseph II's attempt to expand and streamline the army after the Seven Years' War, the attempts to maximize Habsburg fighting capabilities after the 1805 catastrophe, and most notably, Francis Joseph's push to expand the army after the harrowing experiences of 1848–49 are all examples. Such efforts often bore fruit, at times placing Austria a close second to Prussia and France in size of fighting force. But the strains entailed by these exertions, both in economic and social terms, prevented them being sustained at the level that would have been needed to make the Habsburg Monarchy a first-rank land power on a permanent basis. "When one looks at the wars that Austria has waged," Radetzky wrote:

One notices constantly recurring events, namely the desire to improve and an equally large aversion to use the means to that end.... [O]ne observes at the start of each war an imbalance of the means and the end; the armies ... are either not strong enough or not adequately equipped.... [A]fter each battle that increases the bravery of the troops, the army is too weak to seize the fruits of victory.... [A]fter each defeat, they must search for their well-being while on the run or during truce ... an equal urgency at the start of war, in order to patch together an army.[1]

Even if it had possessed greater offensive military capabilities, Austria's surroundings presented no easy options for increasing Habsburg security through expansion. At least in theory, the location of the Danubian Basin and large heartland that it provided on Europe's Alpine-Adriatic fringe presented options for organizing sufficient resources to become an apex continental power. In the southwest lay the prospect of expansion into the Mediterranean Basin, along the axis of Trieste, the Adriatic, and northern Italy; to the northwest, there was the possibility of eventually harnessing the energies of Germany; and to the east, there was the allure of following the axis of expansion indicated by the river that made up the empire's aorta to renovate the Danubian Basin and the eastern expanses that lay beyond.

None of these was ever a realistic possibility for Austria. The Mediterranean was too limited as a resource base, too nettlesome in local politics, and too tenuous in its lines of communication to Alpine Austria to ever become a Habsburg hinterland. The German option would have required Austria to either co-opt or beat Prussia into permanent subordinate status—tasks that were consistently beyond Habsburg abilities. A scheme along the lines envisioned by Bruck would have committed Austria to a revisionist course, undermining the status of guardian of the status quo on which Austria's alliances rested. The Balkan option was neither a feasible nor particularly healthy enterprise for Austria; the lands in question were of dubious economic worth and caused much vexation to manage. Those to the east, forming the crucible of what the famous early twentieth-century British geopolitical writer Sir Harold Mackinder identified as the all-important eastern European resource zone, would have required a sustained contest with Russia, for which the Habsburg would have needed, at a bare minimum, a suspension of the contests on its western frontiers along with a scale of military capabilities that as events of the twentieth century would show, were well beyond the means of even the largest and technologically most advanced western industrial powers.

Inherent in Austria's inability to pursue any of these axes of expansion was the inescapable reality of the Habsburg military weakness. Whether in the west, north, east, or south, Austria could not use offensive power to build an enlarged resource base on the model of classical land empires of the magnitude that would have been needed to transform its prospects as a Great Power vis-à-vis other large, expanding states. When the monarchy did expand, the process often backfired by importing new administrative and ethnic challenges, bringing Austria into conflict with stronger rivals and prompting alignments of the balance of power against it. Yet at the same time, Austria could not ignore the dangers around its borders. Its position in the tectonic zone between Europe and Russia exposed the monarchy to an incessant flow of security crises of varying degrees of severity. The geographic gift of encircling mountain ranges was significant but not in itself sufficient to shelter Austria from these dynamics, making it impossible to ride out the storm of geopolitics like a giant Switzerland.[2]

The Logic of Habsburg Grand Strategy

It was in attempting to cope with this dilemma—the inability to expand, and the impossibility of hiding—that Habsburg grand strategy was defined. Understood as the calculated matching of means to large ends, the development of grand strategy was, for Austria, an extended exercise in attempting to use the tools of rationality to manage complexity and compensate for deficiencies in military power. As an abstract characterization of grand strategy, it would be hard to imagine a purer (or more thoroughly modern) definition than Kaunitz's statement that "the main purpose of a solid judgment of important state affairs consists of essentially a true and pure conception of the end purpose, because one must imagine the means that lead to this end purpose."[3] Kaunitz's immediate preoccupation may have been achieving an alliance with Russia, but writ large, the ends sought for Austria could be stated in negative terms as avoiding multifront wars. The paramount threat that such occurrences represented to the Austrian state was first shown by the War of the Spanish Succession, and then in a far more demonstrative form, by the War of the Austrian Succession. The need to avoid a recurrence of these supreme emergencies translated into a positive near-term military goal: achieving concentration of effort against the supreme security threat—initially Prussia, and later France. This in turn naturally evolved into a broader vision: the creation of structures to obviate the need for recurrent cycles of concentration against hegemons du jour by making security of the European center a shared responsibility of Austria's Great Power rivals.

In seeking these ends, Habsburg grand strategy came to be dominated by considerations of time, and specifically, the search for tools with which to influence the sequencing and duration of contests. The ends sought in Habsburg grand strategy—from the Danubian Monarchy's formative wars against the Spanish and Turks until its demise—were almost invariably framed in terms of time. This was true on the level of theater strategy, in the need to monitor how long a conflict lasted in order to regulate its strains (or opportunities for recueillement), and so to avoid exposing the empire to vulnerabilities on other frontiers. But it was also true in empire-wide grand strategy, in the need to set clear priorities among competing threats, get ahead of conflicts, and stagger the emergence of dangers.

The centrality of time to Habsburg grand strategy shaped how Austria's leaders thought about and employed the means at their disposal as a Great Power. These can be understood as a kind of layer cake, in descending order of magnitude of usefulness in influencing the time factor in strategy. At the top was the European balance of power, which held out the greatest hope, by way of balancing coalitions, of controlling the "whether" and "when" of conflicts as well as limiting the number of Habsburg frontiers that would be involved. The second layer was the Habsburg buffer zones in Italy, the German Reich, Poland, and the Danubian Principalities, which kept rivals at a distance, and bought time for Austria to rally its far-flung regiments and concentrate on the site of conflict. Behind these stood the Habsburg Army and, eventually, rings of forts around the monarchy's borders, as the dynasty's ultimate guarantor and last line of defense.

Together, these components comprised Habsburg grand strategy in its classic form from the time of Maria Theresa until the beginning of the reign of Francis Joseph. Many of the foundational elements for such a grand strategy had been in place in previous Habsburg wars. The need to manage two-front wars was a familiar preoccupation of Austrian strategy throughout the seventeenth-century contests with Bourbon France and the Ottoman Empire. Habsburg strategy under Leopold I, Joseph I, and Charles VI showed patterns in reliance on western allies and efforts to retain buffer zones that would find continuity under Maria Theresa and her successors. It was the supreme emergency of the Prussian wars that brought the increasing formalization of this grand strategy, not only in requiring a more deliberate, forward-looking matching of means to ends, but in clarifying the Austrian "way of war" and requiring the refinement of key institutions—the diplomatic corps, army, and so on—to conceive and execute grand strategy in future crises.

Viewed as a system, Austria's alliance networks, buffer states, and defensive army worked in combination to maximize its range of strategic options, avoid multifront war, and reduce the burdens for defending a 360-degree security position. Hard power played a secondary role in this architecture. At its high point under Metternich, Austrian grand strategy sought to tilt the playing field toward the Habsburgs' competitive advantage as Europe's most ancient dynasty: legitimacy, rules-based diplomacy, and treaty rights. The balance of power provided a means of doing so, but was also dangerous for Austria because of its tendency to devolve into cycles of conquest in which Austria, with its sprawling appendages in every corner of Europe, was chief victim.[4] The efforts of successive Habsburg statesmen to transcend the balance of power by creating systems or frameworks for mediating conflict was a calculated response to this problem.[5] To paraphrase the historian John Darwin's comment about the British Empire, imposing a system of this magnitude may have been beyond the physical power of the imperial government in Vienna, but a system emerged nonetheless.[6]

How conscious were Austrian leaders of this system? One historian may be close to the mark when he writes that even when reacting to events, "the state and extent of [Habsburg officials'] awareness ... cannot confute the course of their actions, nor the compelling strategic structures that predetermined the path they chose. Rather like actors reading a new script for the first time, they simply stumbled through their lines without benefiting from the perspective that comes from familiarity with the plot."[7] More than that, this book has argued that the "plot" itself became more familiar over time, that the stage props and screenplays stayed largely the same even as the actors shifted from one generation to the next. Certainly, both Kaunitz and Metternich engaged in extensive conceptualizations of grand strategy at the empire-wide level. The memorandums penned by Kaunitz late in his career on the Russia problem and documents such as "Reflections on the Concept of the Balance of Power" share a symmetry of thought on the ends to which Habsburg policy should be addressed and how these ends should be achieved with Metternich's memorandums on reorganizing the empire within a restructured balance of power at the end of the Napoleonic Wars. Developed over careers spanning more than a century of Habsburg foreign policy from the 1740s to the 1840s, these documents could be viewed as a kind of codex outlining the tenets of a conservative, risk-averse grand strategy in which Austria's problem of multiple azimuth threats would be alleviated by co-opting and ensnaring the powers that were the sources of this insecurity.

Central to this grand strategic template was the idea of placing Austria in a category apart from other Great Powers—an interstitial empire uniquely capable of performing a specialized functional role that would be hard for other powers to duplicate or replace.[8] Metternich's concept of Austria as the leader of an independent European center encased by weaker client states and buttressed by the support of Europe's flanking powers marked the high point of this concept. In this position, the Habsburg Monarchy's chief liability— its central geography and proximity to virtually all of Europe's security hot spots—to a certain extent became an asset to be leveraged in attracting and retaining the voluntary support of Austria's rivals. For the western powers, the monarchy was the key to restraining Russia and delaying the demise of Turkey; for Russia and Prussia, it was the bulwark against revolutionary nationalism; for the small states around its borders, it was the source of a benign hegemony preferable to the more efficient centralizing predators; and for everyone, it was the makeweight at the heart of Europe whose removal would open a vacuum of power competition capable of enflaming the continent. In all these cases, Austria's "necessity" status was not something that could be taken for granted; it required active tending and conscious cultivation by its diplomats.

Efforts at specialization and transcending the balance of power worked in tandem with Habsburg military force. The maintenance of a defensive army was essential both in its cultural and infrastructural dimensions for lending credibility to Austria's status as a stabilizing force in central Europe. The restraint that characterized Habsburg military thinking from the late seventeenth to early nineteenth centuries was rooted in tactical and political necessity, reflecting the need to preserve an army that was often smaller or weaker than its foes, and on whose shoulders rested the dynasty's fate. This restraint also furthered Austria's grand strategic objectives by ensuring that its neighbors would not feel threatened and form defensive coalitions against it. It is a notable characteristic of Habsburg war theories of the late eighteenth and early nineteenth centuries that virtually all agree on the definition of war as a means by which to achieve a favorable peace—in other words, not as a destructive force in its own right by which to annihilate or subjugate an enemy on the Prussian model.[9] This definition implied brakes on Austrian military behavior even in times of victory and a certain equanimity when an opponent has been defeated. The foremost example is the victory against Napoleon, when Austria labored to retain France as a future ally in the balance of power even as its armies joined with Russia and Prussia in the campaigns of 1813–14. Such restraint aided Habsburg diplomacy by avoiding the punitive warfare that tended so often in European history to produce permanent estrangement with other powers—the one thing that a central empire could never afford.

The positioning of forces in peacetime also reflected Habsburg grand strategic objectives. Austrian defense thinking shows a consistent tendency to
view the buffer territories around the Habsburg Monarchy as a common security space. From early concepts of the *Reichsbarriere* to federal fortresses
in the Metternich era, the Austrian Army understood the need to project military force at points beyond the Danubian heartland as a core requirement of
Habsburg security. Fortresses were an integral component of Austrian military and diplomatic strategy. They provided a means of anchoring the client
states of the periphery in the Habsburg imperium and resisting encroachments of influence by outside powers. Fortress networks incorporating positions at and beyond the frontier aided in the military objective of avoiding or
managing multifront wars by providing deterrence, and in wartime, the ability to pin down an enemy on one frontier with minimal force while shifting
units from distant posts to the point of crisis. At its height, fortresses allowed
Austria to exploit the interior lines that constituted its chief military advantage and police a space from the Middle Rhine to the Danube Delta with an
economy of force that did not strain its finances.

There were of course deviations from the standard Habsburg grand strategy.
It is possible to discern a running tension, intermittently surfacing throughout the period covered by this book, between the largely defensive template
outlined above and a secondary strand or "pole" in Austrian thinking that
aspired to achieve security through greater reliance on the army.[10] This was a
logical consequence of the empire's size along with the natural urge that its
leaders often felt both to develop a tool of national excellence corresponding
to their chief needs and adopt the trappings of a large centralized land power.
The tendency in this direction can be seen, for example, in Joseph II's desire
to reorganize the monarchy into a more centralized military machine along
the lines of Prussia, his debate with Kaunitz about the incorporation of Poland into the empire's administrative core, and the similar debate between
Francis and Metternich about Italy. It can be seen, too, in the more aggressive
military line of Eugene, Laudon, and especially Radetzky and other post-
Napoleonic military thinkers who became enamored with the idea of defeating enemies through offensives modeled on Schwarzenberg's 1813–14 campaign against France.

It is this secondary strand in the Habsburg grand strategic DNA that would
ultimately form the basis of Austrian military doctrine and tactics in the early
phase of Francis Joseph's reign. Even after the defeats of 1859 and 1866, the
allure of achieving security through reliance on the army would continue on
in various forms to become the dominant force in Habsburg military thinking
in the lead-up to World War I.[11] The curbing of this approach in favor of Austria's more traditional, defensive grand strategy for so many decades can be

attributed not to any inherent wisdom or passivity in the Habsburg elite but rather the constraints of Austria's position and the necessities they imposed for economy of force, alliances, and defensive military planning. The harsh reality of a *tous azimuts* threat environment, together with unremitting resource limitations, ruled out any but the most conservative of strategic options. Anything more acquisitive in nature had a tendency to outstrip Habsburg capabilities, fueling spiraling security dilemmas beyond Austria's ability to manage and requiring it to write checks it could not cash.

By contrast, the conservative approach of Kaunitz and Metternich, while certainly not awe inspiring from a military standpoint, tended to meet the basic requirements for Habsburg security without requiring a scale of effort beyond the monarchy's limited means to endure. As an intellectual framework, this defensive strand in Habsburg grand strategy was rooted in a homegrown, distinctively Austrian approach to war and statecraft to a greater extent than the military-offensive option. Where the latter found inspiration in France and above all Prussia, the former was more an outgrowth of the local characteristics and imperatives of the Danubian Basin. The geography of this region, with its encircling mountains and riparian heartland, encouraged a defensive mind-set in which an ordered imperium, grounded in reason and capable of withstanding the buffering outside forces of war and time, was obtainable.

This quest to impose order, tame the chaos of geopolitics, and construct a durable edifice made both possible and necessary by nature forms a major leitmotif of Habsburg strategic statecraft. It resurfaces repeatedly in the thinking of Austrian rulers, generals, and diplomats, who so frequently referred to their work in terms of building structures of various kinds—Metternich's "barricades of time," Charles's "dams" to steer the currents of time, and Radetzky's "common haven" and "protecting wall."[12] Integral to this quest for order was the idea of developing systems or frameworks to govern the entropic tendencies of war and unchecked balance-of-power competition. The concept of "systems" abounds in Habsburg culture and thought of the eighteenth and nineteenth centuries—systems of geometric precision and maneuver to render war a "tamed Bellona," systems of forts and "strategic points" to keep aggressive enemies at bay, and the apotheosis of Habsburg statecraft: systems of European congresses to regulate the storms sweeping over Europe's central empire from so many directions.

Attempts at creating systems to bring order to Austria's internal and external environment were part of the warp and woof of Habsburg grand strategy. As both a mental construct and process, systems thinking concerned itself chiefly with the matching of means to ends and creation of a "logic" to manage complexity. Such thinking was consistent with the cultural outlook and influences of the Habsburg elite, finding an undergirding in the classicist, Renaissance, Catholic just war and eventually Enlightenment traditions, each of which was shaped by Habsburg dynastic influences to form a uniquely Austrian strategic culture. The ideas that formed its currency were transmitted within a relatively small elite of perhaps two hundred families with close ties of marriage, class, and religion possessing a shared moral and political worldview.[13] Habsburg institutions—the diplomatic corps, army, and imperial decision-making bodies—formed structures of continuity that conveyed Habsburg strategic culture, experiences, and concepts from one generation to the next.

Prerequisites of Habsburg Success

The intellectual framework that emerged in Habsburg grand strategy, while showing elements of variation from one generation to the next, operated on a coherent logic distinct from the grand strategies of Europe's other Great Powers. It sought to spare Austria unbearable burdens by giving it breathing room, or space, in both a physical and temporal sense. Its aim was not just security narrowly contrived, though this was certainly the end goal, but rather to establish the foundations on which any such security, to be durable, would ultimately have to be based: a stable central Europe organized under Habsburg leadership. To exist at all, such a configuration required the perpetuation of a set of specific geopolitical conditions that collectively constituted the prerequisites to Habsburg survival and success. These included:

1. A benign Russia, allied to Austria or, at a minimum, not actively hostile to it
2. A supine Germany to garrison Austria's wars
3. A tributary Prussia
4. An intact but nonthreatening Ottoman Empire
5. A sequestered France, confined behind the Rhine

With little variation, these would constitute the main objects of Austrian grand strategy for most of the period covered by this book. As long as these conditions could be maintained, the Habsburg Monarchy held a considerable degree of influence over the middle mass of the European continent at a sustainable expense in resources. This preponderance rested on the ability to vouchsafe the continued independence of the numerous intermediary bodies, or buffer states, around its borders. Austria's buffers underwrote its status as a Great Power. Militarily, they interposed a physical distance between it and its principal rivals, obviating the monarchy's susceptibility to multifront war. The military reservoir provided by the German states represented a force multiplier for Austrian military power similar in extent to the impact that the forces of the Indian Raj had in extending British power in the nineteenth century. To this must be added the alliance with Russia, which in its infusion of support for Habsburg interests in the west and second-order effect in freeing up Habsburg resources from defending the eastern frontier, was tantamount to a subsidization of Austrian security.

Economically, Austria's preeminent, if not altogether dominant, position in Europe's center allowed it to reap many of the benefits of exposure to, and to some extent integration within, western Europe without paying the full military-administrative price for this privilege. Even when the retardant effects of Habsburg tariff walls are taken into account, Austria's access to what, in the absence of a rival power's control of this space, amounted to an extension of its economic heartland was a substantial boon to Austria's geostrategic position. Even without the realization of grander visions along the lines of Bruck's empire of seventy million, intermittent access to German capital and markets buttressed what would otherwise have been a largely agrarian polity mired in the middle-income gradient as economic power flowed to the Atlantic. This allowed Austria to persist as a Great Power in the gap between the European rimlands and Eurasian landmass without having to attempt to mobilize a commanding portion of the capital and technology of the former, or the natural resources of the latter—either of which would have been well beyond its ability to achieve.

In both a military and economic sense, therefore, Austria's success was intimately tied to its ability to maintain a set of intermediate spaces between itself and its rivals. This distance also aided in the management of Austria's complex internal dynamics. While the empire's rivals would attempt to exploit its ethnic cleavages, and above all Hungarian intransigence, as a geopolitical advantage during times of war, these dynamics were kept in check as long as a hostile Great Power did not control the spaces immediately adjacent to Habsburg borders. Maintaining these critical breathing spaces in the era of emergent nationalism depended on Austria's military capabilities and approach to administration, but above all on the commitment of Europe's major powers to treaty rights as taking precedent over ethnonationalist claims as a determinant of outcomes in international diplomacy.

When these geopolitical conditions changed or, more to the point, Austria ceased to influence outcomes in European diplomacy to a sufficient degree to maintain the prerequisites for an independent European middle zone, Austria's prospects as a Great Power diminished rapidly. It is a truism to say that the tectonic shifts that occurred in the European system in the mid-nineteenth century were beyond Austria's ability to steer or control. But this had to some extent always been the case; even in the era before the rise of ethnonationalism,

Austria had possessed few viable options for maintaining its position. The downgrading of its prospects and status in the mid-nineteenth century cannot fully be explained by structural changes; the decisions of Austrian leaders also accelerated the unraveling of the conditions that had allowed for the monarchy's past success by abandoning key tenets of traditional Habsburg grand strategy in favor of more aggressive and risk-acceptant strategic behavior. The inauguration of a military-intensive foreign policy under Francis Joseph marked an unmistakable deviation from Austria's defensive ways and heralded a new era of reliance on the army to secure Austria's place as a Great Power. The army's failure to evolve technologically at a time of rapid innovation gave Austria the worst of both worlds: a military equipped for defensive warfare yet trained and employed as an offensive instrument.

Austria's diplomatic failings in this period cannot be divorced from Francis Joseph's attempts at introducing neoabsolutism along with militarization of the Habsburg state and foreign policy. The monarchy's diplomatic options in the 1850s to 1860s were narrowing, to be sure. But Austria's aggressive handling of the rapid sequence of crises in this period must be viewed as unforced errors that accelerated Austria's isolation in European diplomacy at precisely the moment when it most needed the support of the rest of the system. The loss of the alliance with Russia in 1854 represented a permanent dislocation of the keystone in the arch of Habsburg grand strategy, which in turn made possible and indeed prompted the tectonic movements that followed in Austria's central European security environment. The clashes that followed in Italy in 1859 and against Prussia in 1866 had been brewing for decades, but had always been kept in bounds by Russian military support. By overplaying its hand against Russia in what was ultimately a matter of secondary importance to Habsburg security (the Danubian Principalities), Austria lost the ability to maintain its position in the two regions of primary significance to its security: Italy and Germany.

Austria's losses in this series of crises might have been survivable in a more permissive strategic environment. But coming at a time of rapid technological and political change, they positioned it for decisive military defeats that permanently ejected it from the buffer zones around its borders. The replacement of centuries-old intermediary bodies in Germany, Italy, and the east with unified nation-states, all within a period of little more than a decade after the 1866 war, sealed Austria's fate as a Great Power. This had always been predicated on the ability to prevent these spaces from falling under the control of military rivals. From a military standpoint, the solidification of the space around Austria's borders into new, unified actors possessing the size and military strength to threaten the monarchy required a degree of securitization on Austria's frontiers that it had never before faced and could not, on a long-term basis, afford. The fact that all three of these new actors—Germany, Italy, and Romania—shared ethnic ties to significant portions of the Habsburg population meant that henceforth, Austrian foreign policy would be intertwined with its domestic policy to a far greater and more dangerous extent than it had ever been before.

The Habsburg Monarchy may have continued on as a physically large state after 1866, but it is difficult to refer to it as a Great Power as Austria's options for conducting an independent foreign policy became tightly constrained. The array of intermediary bodies over which the monarchy had held sway, and from which it had derived significant diplomatic and military support, were not just gone but now also formed parts of large units with which Austrian power would have to contend as rivals. Nothing demonstrated the downward adjustment this would force in Austria's status more than the dominating influence that Prussia and later a unified Germany would exercise in the direction of Austrian foreign and indeed domestic policy, beginning with the Austro-Hungarian power-sharing agreement of 1867, by which the Habsburg Monarchy would lose many of the characteristics of a unitary actor.

It is a notable and telling feature of Austria in the post-1866 period that its economy continued to grow even as its geostrategic prospects dimmed. In fact, if anything, the monarchy's economic strength increased in the lead-up to the First World War, as the fiscal pressure that had been exerted by Francis Joseph's military buildup abated, and the fluctuations in Austrian money supply and credit standing caused by the series of foreign policy crises between 1848 and 1866 gave way to an economic boom.[14] An additional factor was the continuing de facto integration of many parts of the Austrian economy and infrastructure with the rest of Germany even as the monarchy found itself increasingly excluded by Prussia from Germany's political affairs.

The fact that Austria continued to experience economic growth amid a downturn in its military-strategic position defies the standard explanation that Great Powers decline when they lose access to their principal resource areas.[15] In Austria's case, the opposite is true: the empire's access to its main economic arteries in the west was expanding even as it declined geopolitically. Yet with the German territories increasingly becoming a formal part of the economic hinterland of a rival Great Power, this economic growth did little to fundamentally alter Austria's geopolitical prospects. The Habsburg case shows that control of space matters at least as much as economic performance in determining the strategic success of empires; without the former, the latter will be obviated to some extent by the increased resources needed to sustain the militarization of previously quiescent frontiers.

Whatever the virtues or failures of Habsburg foreign and security policy in the period after 1866, it is a central contention of this book that Austria was not in any way able to continue operating the main strands of the grand strategy by which it had navigated previous centuries. Austria's traditional, terrain-based defensive military culture gave way to the cult of the offensive, the empire's old buffer states were gone, and the networks of Great Power alliances that Austrian diplomats had assiduously nurtured rapidly for generations evaporated along with its foreign policy options, as Britain and France joined Russia to become an anti-Austrian bloc in European diplomacy.[16] By the time war came in 1914, the preconditions for Austrian success that previous Habsburg grand strategy had sought to promote were not only gone; they were a distant memory that even the most stupendous military victories or brilliant diplomacy would never have been able to resurrect.

Viewed in this light, the decisions of Austrian military and diplomatic officials in the months leading up to 1914 take on much less significance from the standpoint of Austria's ultimate fate than they are often accorded. By this point in the monarchy's history, Austria's ability to decisively influence European-level events was more or less gone; every new international flash point held the potential to devolve into a crisis for its existence. The lack of viable strategic options after the loss of Austria's buffers removes much of the onus of responsibility for the events that followed on the generation at hand at the same time that it underscores the scale of accomplishment of generations of Habsburg diplomats in playing the game as well as they had. If, as Austrian historian Otto Bruner wrote of Austria's foreign policy in the lead-up to 1914, "one [who] has a weak heart should not go mountaineering," then the success of prior Habsburg grand strategy lay in eschewing attempts at scaling impossible peaks while still maintaining Austria's Great Power status.[17] Tellingly, the war that ultimately destroyed Austria-Hungary saw it attacked on three sides—precisely the kind of conflict that Habsburg grand strategy since the Austrian succession sought, largely successfully, to avoid.

Epilogue

HABSBURG LESSONS

CAN WE LEARN anything from the Habsburg Monarchy? All states are different, and every time period has rhythms and constraints that are not easily relatable to any other period. Nevertheless, many of the problems that the Habsburgs faced are present in our own time. Geopolitics remains with us as a persistent and reintensifying force in which Great Powers seek to survive in competition with other large, purposeful actors. In this contest, geography remains both a key determinant of success and its ultimate prize. Advances in technology have only partially mitigated the effects of geography; even in the era of nuclear weapons, the search for security comes down to a battle for space in which finite resources must be arrayed in time to deal with virtually infinite challenges.

As in the Habsburg period, the threats arrayed against today's West are multidirectional in nature and vary widely in form, ranging from revisionist Great Powers with large conventional armies to economically backward but numerous and religiously motivated enemies employing asymmetrical weapons and tactics. In confronting these challenges, the West faces constraints in mobilizing and employing military force that would be perhaps more recognizable to the Habsburgs than to the leaders of an effectively centralized military power like Prussia. As for the Habsburgs, decisive battlefield victory is hard to achieve in the twenty-first century. The Clausewitzian model of the industrialized nation-state mobilizing its full population and resource base to resoundingly defeat an enemy has become less rather than more attainable in the modern era. The nature of modern war is murkier, involving often-nebulous opponents that seek limited aims with nontraditional means.

From the chapters above, a few broad principles of Habsburg strategic statecraft stand out as potentially relevant in any era.

You can't be strong everywhere. An overriding lesson from Habsburg strategic history is that a Great Power is unlikely to be able to sustainably match the strength of all its enemies on all its frontiers at all times. Awareness of this limitation, and attempts to cope with its various implications, forms a red thread through the annals of Austrian grand strategy, from Eugene's dictum that "two wars cannot be waged with one army," to Daun's observation that it is impossible to "be everywhere at once and anticipate the enemy."[1] The temptation to try to be strong everywhere is often great, since states naturally seek security against all threats, however numerous. It is especially pronounced at moments of relative economic or military strength. Survival for a Great Power beset by foes is a by-product of the ability to find ways of dealing with each threat without becoming exposed to inordinate opportunity costs elsewhere. Since power is finite, it has to be used in a way that allows for effective action against the threat at hand without losing the ability to manage other threats that could materialize simultaneously.

Avoid war when possible. War is bad for any state—in Archduke Charles's words, "The greatest evil that can happen to a state or nation."[2] But it is especially dangerous for an interstitial power, for two reasons. First, it drains resources that are already stretched by the need to maintain numerous frontiers. Second, it sets in motion interaction dynamics—what Clausewitz called "friction"—that are inherently more complex for the surrounded state because of the number of threats. In both cases, risk for an interstitial empire can be measured in time. The longer a war lasts, the greater the financial burden taken onto the state, and the greater the likelihood that other enemies will use your diversion as an opportunity to attack.

This implies a different relationship with risk for an interstitial empire compared to Great Powers with less numerous threat environments. Since war, once it is launched, takes on a dynamic all its own that is inherently hard to control, the encircled power must be more concerned with limiting risk rather than with maximizing gains. Limiting risk involves avoiding war altogether if possible, and if not, then making it as short as possible. Paradoxically, this places a higher premium on the ability to conduct offensive or even preemptive wars—*if they are likely to be decisive.* If they are tried and fail, the risks become far greater than if they had never been attempted, both because of the scarce resources that were ventured and lost, and because of the encouragement and opening that failure may provide for other enemies to act.

In Austria's case, early strikes were frequently attempted but rarely successful because of the limited offensive capabilities of the Habsburg Army. As a result, defensive warfare was the safest bet for the state since it reserved the greatest range of options for managing risk as the conflict unfolded. And in the pursuit of defensive war, Austria often faced incentives not to shorten a conflict but rather to draw it out in installments.

Delay engagement until the terms are favorable to you. Since war cannot always be avoided, the state should strive to avoid specifically those wars that are likely to occur on terms unfavorable to itself in order, as Joseph II put it, to ensure that "our great-grandchildren can defend themselves with dignity."[3] Those Habsburg rulers who succeeded most in securing their realm for a season were the ones who were clear in identifying wars that the monarchy could not win and deliberately delaying decisive engagement until they had built up sufficient strength.

The task of outlasting a stronger opponent always involves some combination of mobilizing domestic strength (internal balancing) and outside allies (external balancing). The way in which this is accomplished depends on the circumstances of war—that is, whether it is foreseen and prepared for in advance, or thrust on the defender and thus requiring preparation while the war is under way.

The latter is the greatest danger that an interstitial empire can face. Unpreparedness in war is costly for any state, but especially for one facing multiple enemies that are able to attack on their own preferred timing and terms, as the Habsburg Monarchy found in the War of the Austrian Succession. Gaining control of the time factor of competition well before war begins is the most important strategic task that the leaders of an encircled power can undertake since the onset of battle will only introduce new variables that act to its disadvantage. Succeeding in this task requires a high degree of unity in the national security elite about the identity of the main threat and a corresponding willingness to deprioritize others, even if these happen to involve a traditional foe against which the defender nurses a historic grudge.

"Turn off" secondary problems first. Delay can run counter to perceived political imperatives but can be helpful if it is used to gain an advantage for the main struggle. One of the most consistent traits of Habsburg strategic behavior was the effort to sequence contests, which often meant proactively addressing lesser threats in order to have a freer hand for dealing effectively with the main challenge.

This can take both a diplomatic and military form. Joseph II placated the Turks to prioritize war in the west before returning to deal with the Ottoman Empire from a position of strength. Maria Teresa employed a similar technique throughout the wars with Frederick II, and during the Austrian succession struggle, used a truce with Prussia to knock out the Bavarians before turning its attention back to the north. Joseph II sought, largely unsuccessfully, to deal swiftly with the Turks in 1788–91 before diverting attention back to Prussia; his failure to do so required large, simultaneous, and expensive force concentrations on two fronts.

Dealing with secondary threats first, when it can be achieved, is advantageous for an interstitial state for the obvious reason that it aids in the concentration of effort against the more serious threat. But it is also advantageous because it creates a positive demonstration effect of the state's ability to achieve victory, which can help to both reassure allies and deter other predators from bandwagoning.

Complexity is harder to manage during a conflict than before it. Interaction dynamics are by definition more intense for a surrounded power. Even in peacetime, it must exist in a state of complexity; once a war begins, this complexity increases dramatically. A move by one rival creates openings for others to exploit. It matters little whether this occurs by design or opportunity; for the interstitial state, the effect is the same: spiraling and increasingly uncontrollable "friction," in numerous places simultaneously, beyond the defender's ability to anticipate or manage, much less control.

Austria's most dangerous moments came when it failed to anticipate geopolitical shifts and found itself reacting to a multifront war that had already broken out. The wars of the first half of the eighteenth century, and particularly the Austrian succession war, show that pure crisis management is inherently more dangerous for an empire with multiple frontiers; to perhaps a greater extent than most states, they have an existential need to foresee and "get ahead" of conflicts. The greatest accomplishments of Habsburg statecraft came in later wars, when Austrian leaders had absorbed the lessons of the past and worked successfully to arrange their alliances so that by the time war broke out, they could concentrate scarce resources on one, main threat rather than three or four.

The need for a similar transition to anticipatory strategy in today's world has, if anything, been made more pressing by modern technology, which brings significantly higher stakes to even the smallest war than those of the eighteenth and nineteenth centuries. The nature of modern weapons adds to this effect, with both enhanced conventional lethality and the shrinking threshold for tactical nuclear exchanges likely to increase the escalatory dynamics of future conflicts. Once set in motion, the options for managing them shrink dramatically.

If possible, force the enemy to fight on their territory rather than yours. While Austria's wars tended to be defensive in nature, Habsburg strategy frequently sought to deflect the brunt of offensive war by forcing the enemy to fight on or near their own territory. This is valuable for any state to achieve in war but especially so for one confronting multiple rivals because it shifts the burden of fighting to the main aggressor, lessens the likelihood of attack on other frontiers, and buys the defender time to mobilize for the struggle.

The goal of what would today be called "preclusion" was reflected in Austrian defense infrastructure and alliance policy. The forts of the Rhine sought to hem France within its own frontiers, and the forts of the Elbe sought to contain Prussian attacks to a narrow sliver of frontier territory outside the economically vital Bohemian hinterland. The monarchy formed alliances with the maritime powers to attack Louis XIV's seaward flank, used an alliance with former rival France to open a second front against Frederick II, used an alliance with former rival Prussia to open a second front against revolutionary France, and used alliances with Russia to threaten Prussia's eastern frontier well into the nineteenth century.

Twenty-first century technologies both ease and complicate the goal of preclusion. They allow armies to cross great distances quickly and threaten a rival in their home territory, but by the same token, expose the defender to rapid threats from afar. Nevertheless, conventional wars continue to be fought for territory, and the spaces nearest the point of conflict bear the brunt of the human and economic costs. For this reason, the same basic methods used by the Habsburgs—forward infrastructure and frontier alliances—remain assets to be husbanded in today's landscape for the utility they offer in power projection.

Maintain smaller states between yourself and your main rivals. As time management tools, forts and allies have limitations. Walls are static and, at best, detain an opponent for a short period. Allies are fickle and may change sides from one war to the next. What provides the greatest aid in coping with multidirectional threats is physical space—territory around the frontiers that impose distance between oneself and a rival.

For most of its history the Habsburg Monarchy sought as a first object of grand strategy the maintenance of belts of weaker states around its borders. For a centrally located empire, these spaces are existentially important. As long as they are intact, enemies do not share direct, border-on-border contact with the defender. In peacetime, this reduces the need for expensive round-the-clock defense preparations; in wartime, it provides a shock absorber in the form of the territory and armies of the smaller states, through which enemy armies must pass to reach home soil.

In the contemporary strategic debate, the notion is gaining ground that modern technology and in particular long-range airpower can insulate a Great Power from attacks to such a degree as to eliminate the need for onshore engagement in difficult environments.[4] But even in the twenty-first century, intermediary spaces retain strategic utility. As a rule, passive objects like mountains or oceans are less valuable than space that is actively defended. Small, independent states are motivated to offer their own resistance to aggression before it reaches the soil of their Great Power sponsor. As in Austria's time, they offer perhaps the single most important tool for an interstitial empire to manage by both holding down one rival to deal with another and providing points d'appui for concentrating force quickly at the frontier to take the fight to the enemy when needed.

Prioritize regions that give long-term economic or strategic benefit. In a multifront war, Great Powers must choose what to prioritize and what to deprioritize. To some extent, the enemy makes this decision, since the greatest threat will usually receive the greatest attention. But to the degree that an option exists, it is prudent to prioritize places that are likely to bring the greatest benefit to the state in long-term strategic competition.

Habsburg diplomacy frequently put the most resource-rich regions at the top of the list for receiving military attention, even if it came at the expense of the ostensible "main" war theater and thus lengthened the war. In the War of the Spanish Succession, Joseph I went so far as to drain troops away from the Habsburg heartland and area around the imperial capital itself, despite persistent raids by Hungarian rebels, and even chose to relinquish the Spanish inheritance in order to secure the dynasty's rich holdings in Italy. On a similar logic, Metternich slowed down the 1813–14 campaign to ensure that the Austrian Army, and not its allies, was the first to reach and occupy Italy. In both cases, the monarchy leaned heavily on those allies closest to the threat to bear the brunt of the main effort while Austria concentrated its own military resources on securing long-term advantages to itself.

In not losing sight of the highest-value regions, Austria's leaders had a long-range objective in mind. This ruthless prioritization, while often requiring difficult resource trade-offs and sacrifices at the time, ensured that when the war ended, the dynasty would be left standing with the most valuable possessions, which in turn would put it at an advantage when the next war broke out.

Use local solutions for local problems. An interstitial power needs to be able to manage multiple threat vectors, each with its own intermediate spaces, strategic imperatives, and local actors. Yet trying to do so through the extension of formal empire runs the risk of accumulating costs in administration beyond the empire's ability to sustain. The most effective solution is for the states that inhabit these spaces to provide the bulk of security voluntarily, at minimal outside prompting or expense.

At its height, the Habsburg Monarchy was able to effectively outsource a major share of the task of its own defense to scores of client states, each with its own army and tutelary fortresses, in the territories around its borders: in the west, the lesser German states; in the east, Poland; and in the southwest, the northern Italian kingdoms and city-states. In the south, where it lacked the possibility of independent clients until the late nineteenth century, Austria instead attracted soldier-settlers from enemy territory to pacify the frontier and provide security to volatile territories. Relying on local actors in this way spared Austria the full costs of defending its long security perimeter and supplied a means of pinning down the local rival to free up Austria's own armies to deploy to the site of greatest danger at any given moment.

In all these cases, Austria eschewed the extension of more formal, centralized control over the frontier and worked with the momentum of local efforts to contain a common enemy. At the heart of this method of frontier management lay recognition of the natural tendency of powerful states to spark fear in smaller neighbors. Attempting to be excessively "present" in these spaces would drain Austria's own strength while leading locals to fear it rather than the adjacent rival; being too absent could ease the rival's job of spreading its own influence.

Instead, the Habsburgs often positioned themselves as powerful yet distant, not capable of threatening domination, but strong enough to help locals retain the thing they prized most—a continued independent existence. This typically took one of two forms. First, with those states that tended most to fear the outside enemy—usually those that sat closest to its borders—the Habsburgs encouraged this dynamic by providing preferential political relationships and other incentives to resist to the utmost. Two notable examples were the anti-French states of the Nördlingen Association and anti-Ottoman Grenzer communities of the Military Border. Second, with those small states or groups that tended to side *with* Austria's enemies in war—Bavaria being perhaps the prime illustration, and the Hungarians another—Habsburg monarchs usually mixed brutality and leniency, crushing resistance ruthlessly to show the futility of opposing Austria, but being quick to extend clemency after the war to avoid stoking the embers of future resistance.

Appease a rival to buy time, not to outsource a problem. Appeasement was a frequent tool of Habsburg statecraft. The Austrians often placated enemies that were either too strong to conquer or with whom a fight at a particular moment would have detracted from the task to concentrate elsewhere. Doing so aided in time management by offering a means of demilitarizing a given theater for a definable period of time and allowing for a concentration of resources to strike the crucial blow in another theater.

Habsburg appeasement took many forms. It frequently involved the calculated deprioritization of disputes with bitter enemies either to concentrate resources against a greater threat, or temporarily avoid war and thereby build up resources for the next round of conflict. Joseph's deal with the Bavarians at the Ilbesheim Convention in 1704 and with Charles XII at Altranstädt in 1706, and Maria Theresa's momentary peace with Frederick under the Convention of Kleinschnellendorf in 1742, are prominent examples. Others include Kaunitz's French and Turkish alliances to deal with Prussia and Russia, respectively, Maria Theresa's acceptance of Hungarian demands ahead of the Seven Years' War, Austria's alliance with Prussia on the eve of the Napoleonic Wars, and Metternich's policy of self-abasement toward Napoleon after the failed war of 1809. Perhaps the best example, however, is the various Habsburg treaties of restraint with Russia, which brought peace to the eastern frontier for nearly a century and a half, and allowed for a sustained focus of attention and resources to the west.

These instances fit within the context of strategies aimed at gaining time for the monarchy. For such efforts not to backfire, they had to come at an acceptable cost. Détente with France was not about ceding Italy to a rival but instead about leveraging French fear of Prussia to augment Austrian defenses. Respites with the Hungarians were not about yielding permanent claims or advantages but rather withholding prosecution of Habsburg rights to the fullest extent in order to avoid ill-timed uprisings. Treaties with Russia did not outsource management of the east but rather sought to keep pace with their gains and, if possible, push the burdens of Turkish wars to the Russians.

In this sense, it is important to distinguish between these forms of appeasement and the term as it is usually used today.[5] Appeasement for the Habsburgs was not capitulation to a rival in order to avoid war at "any cost." Instead, it was a stratagem, often deceptive and manipulative in nature, used to get something that the state would otherwise have lacked in the near term—time—without ceding crucial advantages vis-à-vis that rival in the long term.[6] It was about diverting one enemy, either by going along temporarily with its wishes or focusing on a shared threat, in order to concentrate greater attention on another enemy.

For an interstitial Great Power, diplomacy that hands away too many concessions to rivals can ultimately be as dangerous as military overstretch, since it runs the risk of whittling away at the independent spaces whose continued functioning the state relies on most for long-term security.

Beware of enemies using internal divisions against you. Foreign and domestic policies were inextricably intertwined for the Habsburg Monarchy. Even in the era before nationalism, the presence of a large and politically recalcitrant Hungarian nobility created opportunities for rivals to exploit in geopolitical competition. The prospect of Magyar uprisings creating internal distractions to tie down Habsburg forces in the interior and ease an invader's task at the frontier was a powerful lure for the Bourbon kings, the Swedes, Napoleon, his nephew, and Bismarck. The emergence of stronger ethnic identity among the empire's various nationalities from the mid-nineteenth century onward only heightened the danger. To a greater extent than their counterparts in western European states or even the Russian Empire, Habsburg rulers had to be cognizant in the crafting of grand strategy of both the political-administrative and military-logistic demands for managing what amounted to an ever-present potential fifth column inside the monarchy.

While vastly different in constitutional construction, modern Western states in many ways bear a closer resemblance to the supranational Habsburg Monarchy, with its patchwork of premodern political identities, than to the twentieth-century European nation-state, with its modern political foundations and largely homogeneous population. In addition to its intrinsic virtues, democracy as a political system carries important advantages in geopolitical competition against authoritarian rivals. Popular legitimacy provides a framework for long-term strategic resilience by facilitating successive, predictable, peaceful transfers of power and creating an unequaled basis for market-based economic growth.

Nevertheless, democracy also entails a high degree of complexity in both process and composition of the polity. As such, democracies are not immune to attempts at internal manipulation by rivals. One takeaway from Habsburg history is the importance of anticipating and dealing with sources of domestic friction before a major conflict rather than attempting to manage them once a war is under way. More important, it demonstrates the indispensability for a heterogeneous state of possessing a central mission as a Great Power that bridges strategic interests with a unifying source of identity among its people—in Austria's case, Catholicism. To an even greater extent than for the traditional nation-state, it is incumbent on the political elite of such a power to consciously cultivate and nourish the sense of civilizational purpose that animates its international role.

The most dangerous frontier is financial. War is a permanent feature of geopolitical competition, but it is a particularly persistent fact of life for a sprawling empire with multiple security frontiers. Geographic encirclement makes threats more numerous; the scale of security commitments means that some source of tension is likely to exist at every moment in at least one place with one or more enemies. War is usually imminent, under way, or on the horizon.

This places an encircled power in almost constant preparation for war, which in turn creates potentially inexhaustible demands on defense resources. Money is time, in the sense that the scale of available economic resources

determines how large the military resources will be for resisting many enemies at once. In the quest for time, interstitial empires have a greater propen-
sity than perhaps most states to be drawn into debt spirals. This creates two
disadvantages in geopolitical competition.

First, it makes it easier for enemies to pursue cost-imposition strategies.
The presence of mounting debt, and with it the costs of debt servicing, means
that rivals have the ability to exacerbate the defender's difficulties through
sustained military buildups. They need only be strong on the one front to
both gain a military edge and place stress on the defender's financial system,
and thus their position as a whole.

Second, untamed debt gives enemies greater control over the time parameters of war once it breaks out. In 1866, Austria was defeated by a rival that
while nominally weaker than itself in most metrics of power, had a stronger
financial position from which to prevent the Habsburgs from engaging in its
accustomed method of drawing out a struggle to bring its greater military and
human resources to bear, and hence beat back a militarily more advanced
attacker.

The time pressures created by debt were heightened for the Habsburg
Monarchy by its internal complexities. At the time of its final contest with
Prussia, Austria had for some time been prioritizing defense spending (which
eventually constituted 100 percent of state expenditures) to the exclusion of
virtually all other spending, at considerable long-term expense to the development of its economy.

Austria's experience suggests that this balancing act will become harder to
maintain in future decades without either encountering significant constraints
in military capabilities or social-foreign policy trade-offs. In its severest form,
multihorizon geopolitical competition can generate simultaneous foreign
policy crises on every side that tip debt beyond the point of sustainability
and force a downward adjustment in the state's relative power position. The
growth of debt, for the encircled power, imposes "financial-political frontiers"
on the state's actions and is as great an enemy as any foreign power.[7]

It's not enough to be a "necessity." Much of the Habsburg Monarchy's durability
as a Great Power can be attributed to the view among other powers and even
its rivals that it was a necessity—an entity whose existence rendered a net
benefit to the wider international system, the absence of which would present
insoluble problems to Europe. Austria was no less a necessity in the last decades of its existence; indeed, as later events would show, it was more essential than ever to possess a stabilizing force at the center of Europe. And yet
this reality did not prevent most of Europe's powers, including many of its
former allies, from turning against it and eventually presiding over its dismantlement as a state.

The fact that a state is a necessity implies that a certain degree of passivity is possible on its part, since other states benefit from its continued existence and will voluntarily work to prop it up. In Austria's case, the leaders who succeeded Metternich embraced what was an essentially isolationist diplomatic course as a Great Power. For the first time in its history, Austria looked more or less exclusively to its own strength to conquer the challenges of its surrounding environment. It neglected traditional alliances, ceded the moral high ground, and allowed itself to become embroiled on unfavorable terms in crises on three sides in which it was inflexible, became isolated, and lost.

Austria's experience shows that holding together a stable international order is more a matter of choice than inexorable structural forces. It casts a negative light on the idea that a Great Power must possess a preponderance of resources in order to decisively shape its environment. Even at its high point, Metternich's Austria was far weaker in relative terms than its main rivals and yet exercised a commanding influence over the affairs of Europe. It also shows, however, the speed with which such influence can be lost and the security of the state imperiled, when leaders choose to neglect the sources of strength that have sustained the state's position in the past. Above all, Austria's experience suggests that self-isolation is the greatest danger facing a centrally located power. Even the strongest power needs allies, especially in regions between its frontiers and the territory of its rivals, in order to manage the factor of time on which both the security of its multisided position and stability of the overall system rest.

The Final Ledger

How does the Habsburg Monarchy stack up as an empire? Despite the challenges arrayed against it after the death of Charles II and loss of the Spanish inheritance in 1700, the Danubian realm endured for a little more than two centuries until the dissolution of Austria-Hungary in 1919. If the dynasty's wider European résumé is taken into account, the Habsburg imperium in its assorted forms existed for more than six hundred years—two and a half centuries longer than that of the British Empire, two centuries longer than the Roman Empire, and three and a half centuries longer than the American republic to date.

One way of measuring Austria's performance as a strategic actor would be to compare the outcomes that it achieved against the cost required in money and effort. Between the beginning of the eighteenth century and mid-nineteenth, the Habsburg Monarchy was involved in twenty-two wars of various shapes and sizes.[8] Of these, it suffered outright defeat in perhaps four and was on the side with the greater number of allies in nineteen. Only in the final part of the period covered by this book, when Austria strayed from its traditional grand strategy, did it find itself irrevocably alone in a conflict, and even then it usually enjoyed the support of numerous smaller client states. Austria compiled its record of survival while maintaining an army that with the exception of a few periods of sustained buildup, tended to typically be smaller than the armies of its main rivals. The Austrian Army undoubtedly lost a majority of the major battles it fought, and debacles like 1741 and 1809 must be placed on the scales when assessing the Habsburg strategic ledger. But the tarnish of these defeats is diminished when viewed within the context of the wider conflicts of which they were part, and the resilience that the monarchy showed in recouping lost ground through persistence, the nursing of core advantages, and recueillement.

Another frame of reference for assessing Austria's strategic performance would be to compare it to that of the other Germanic Great Power inhabiting a central position on the European chessboard—Prussia. After 1871, the new German Empire would pass through three separate forms in rapid succession. The time-based strategies devised by Bismarck and Moltke, with their emphasis on rapid military strikes, would be used in modified form in 1914 and 1939. These methods continue to hold a mesmerizing effect in the modern military and national security communities. And yet judged by the outcomes they produced, Germany's offensive strategies compare unfavorably with the defensive strategies employed by Austria. After Bismarck's victory over France, Germany would participate in two colossal multisided wars ending in catastrophic defeat. The state that emerged in 1871 would last in altered form until 1945—a fraction of the life span of the Habsburg Empire.

Perhaps the best way to assess the Habsburg strategic legacy, however, would be to compare its impact in central and eastern Europe to what came afterward. All three of the twentieth century's global wars, two hot and one cold, had their origins in the interstitial spaces that the Habsburg Monarchy once managed. The monarchy's collapse paved the way for profound geopolitical turbulence, as far more aggressive military empires from both east and west tussled to fill the vacuum. If, as Kennan wrote, Austria-Hungary's collapse was "unfortunate for all concerned," its chief victims were the dynasty's former subjects: the scattered peoples of the Danubian Basin.[9] Or as Winston Churchill put it, "There is not one of the peoples or provinces that constituted the Empire of the Habsburgs to whom gaining their independence has not brought forth the tortures which ancient poets and theologians reserved for the damned."[10]

In the big sweep of history, the loss of the Habsburg imperium can be seen as the removal of an indigenous stabilizer that had steadied Europe's central mass and, with it, broader European order. Once this was gone, a contest for control of the resource-rich seams between the Eurasian rimland and heartland was inevitable, as a unified Germany quickly dominated Europe's ancient Great Powers and cast its weight eastward, triggering Russia's own counter expansion and the United States' intervention to restore the European balance. The cost of the resulting struggle can be measured in megadeaths: sixty million lives in the Second World War and further tens of millions in the Soviet dominion that followed.[11] A testament to Habsburg strategic statecraft can be seen in the fact that it took four distinct security orders, following in rapid succession from 1919 to 1989, to eventually find a durable template for organizing the "lands between." Neither the democratic *saisonstaats* of central Europe, with their promise of national determination at the expense of minority freedoms, nor the German Reich, with its sterile efficiency and quest for racial dominion at the expense of human decency, nor yet the Soviet empire, with its promise of a hollow proletarian equality at the expense of the gulags, delivered the degree of geopolitical stability and relative prosperity that had been achieved by the Habsburgs.

The United States' own path to superpower status is intimately intertwined with the attempts to fill the vacuum left by Habsburg Austria's demise. After presiding over the creation of independent nation-states in the Danubian Basin following the empire's collapse, the United States retreated from Europe, contributing to the conditions for the eventual renewal of conflict in 1939. Only with a second, cataclysmic European war, a permanent military presence on the European continent, and a protracted contest with the Soviet Union did the United States and its western allies succeed in constructing, with the eastern enlargement of NATO, a security order for east-central Europe attaining and exceeding the stability and prosperity the region had enjoyed under the old empire.

It is against the backdrop of attempts by other, larger, and militarily stronger powers to govern Europe's interstitial spaces that the true strategic accomplishment of the Habsburg Empire comes into focus. The methods by which Austria accomplished the task may, in today's age of instant communication, remote-controlled warfare, and quests for definitive victory, seem quaintly dilatory. In the end, Metternich may have been right that Austria's rulers were only "propping up moldering buildings" destined to decay and collapse. But perhaps this in itself is the greatest lesson that the Habsburgs can impart: an acute sense of the transience and fragility of all human accomplishment. Herein is a weary wisdom anchored in the humility that comes from the realization that geopolitical problems rarely can be solved, only managed. And with that comes an acceptance that the task of enlightened statecraft in all generations is to build the sturdiest bulwarks that we can against the old chaos of war and geopolitics, even if they last only for a season.

NOTES

Chapter 1. The Habsburg Puzzle

1. Quoted in Charles W. Ingrao, *In Quest and Crisis: Emperor Joseph I and the Habsburg Monarchy* (West Lafayette, IN: Purdue University Press, 1979), 163.

2. Austrian military effectiveness is a subject of historiographical debate. A critical tradition, anchored in the negative assessments of German military writers after the First World War, has been balanced in recent years by more positive assessments stressing the Habsburg Army's cohesion, political role as guarantor of the dynasty, and effectiveness as a defensive force. The most prolific representative of the latter tradition is Gunther Rothenberg; see, for example, Gunther E. Rothenberg, *The Army of Francis Joseph* (Lafayette, IN: Purdue University Press, 1999); Gunther E. Rothenberg, "The Shield and the Dynasty: Reflections on the Habsburg Army," *Austrian History Yearbook* 32 (2001): 169–208. For an excellent recent contribution in this tradition, see Richard Bassett, *For God and Kaiser: The Imperial Austrian Army, 1619–1918* (New Haven, CT: Yale University Press, 2015). Other historians taking a positive view are Lawrence Sondhaus, István Deák, Archer Jones, and Christopher Duffy. Hans Delbrück, Alan Sked, A. J. P. Taylor, and most notably Geoffrey Wawro are more critical. For older critiques, see Moriz Edler von Angeli, *Wien nach 1848* (Vienna: Braumüller, 1905); Eduard Bartels von Bartberg, *Der Krieg im Jahre 1866* (Leipzig: Verlag Otto Wigand, 1866). For a summary of the modern Habsburg military debates, see Lawrence Sondhaus, "The Strategic Culture of the Habsburg Army," *Austrian History Yearbook* 32 (2001): 225–34; Charles W. Ingrao, "Query: The Habsburg Military: Why Mediocrity?," H-Diplo-Net@H-Net.msu.edu, August 17, 1999. See also Manfried Rauchensteiner, "Die Militärgeschichtsschreibung in Österreich nach 1945," *Vorträge zur Militärgeschichte, vol. 6: Militärgeschichte in Deutschland und Österreich vom 18. Jahrhundert bis in die Gegenwart* (Berlin: Mittler, 1985), 134–61; Laurence Cole, Christa Hämmerle, and Martin Scheutz, eds., *Glanz-Gewalt-Gehorsam: Militär und Gesellschaft in der Habsburgermonarchie 1800 bis 1918* (Essen: Klartext Verlag, 2011).

3. Charles W. Ingrao, Nikola Samardžić, and Jovan Pešalj, eds., *The Peace of Passarowitz, 1718* (West Lafayette, IN: Purdue University Press, 2011), 6; Christopher Duffy, *The Army of Maria Theresa: The Armed Forces of Imperial Austria, 1740–1780* (New York: Hippocrene Books, 1977), 144.

4. The empire's economic picture was improving by the late nineteenth century and stronger than previously held. See David F. Good, *The Economic Rise of the Habsburg Empire, 1750–1914* (Berkeley: University of California Press, 1984).

5. Quoted in Harvey L. Dyck, "Pondering the Russian Fact: Kaunitz and the Catherinian Empire in the 1770s," *Canadian Slavonic Papers / Revue Canadienne des Slavistes* 22, no. 4 (December 1980): 469.

6. Frederick's comment was literally, "*f...-vous les Austrichiens.*" Friedrick to Podewils, September 1, 1741, quoted in *Politische Correspondenz Friedrich's des Großen* (Berlin: Geheimes Staatsarchiv Preussischer Kulturbesitz, 1879), 1:323. Fleury is quoted in Oskar Criste, *Kriege unter Kaiser Josef II. Nach den Feldakten und anderen authentischen Quellen bearbeitet in der kriegsgeschichtlichen Abteilung des k. und k. Kriegsarchivs* (Vienna: Verlag von L. W. Seidel und Sohn, 1904), 1.

7. Quoted in Sir Richard Lodge, *A History of Modern Europe* (New York: Harper and Brothers, 1886), 386. See also Reed Browning, *The War of the Austrian Succession* (New York: St. Martin's Press, 1995), 64.

8. There is an extensive literature on the foreign policy of the eighteenth- and nineteenth-century Habsburg Empire—too numerous to cover here in detail. For a good starting point on the eighteenth century, see Charles W. Ingrao, *The Habsburg Monarchy, 1618–1815* (New York: Cambridge University Press, 2000). In addition to covering the major security issues facing Austria in this period, it provides a helpful bibliography on major themes. For a panoramic view of Habsburg foreign policy priorities, see Charles W. Ingrao, "Habsburg Strategy and Geopolitics during the Eighteenth Century," in *East Central European Society and War in the Pre-Revolutionary Eighteenth Century*, ed. Gunther E. Rothenberg, Béla K. Király, and Peter F. Sugar (New York: Columbia University Press, 1982). Another highly useful work on the eighteenth century, and one that is cited frequently throughout this book, is Michael Hochedlinger, *Austria's Wars of Emergence, 1683–1797* (New York: Routledge, 2013). A researcher at the Austrian archives, Hochedlinger is perhaps the most gifted modern historian on eighteenth-century Habsburg. *Austria's Wars of Emergence* has broken significant ground in elucidating Austrian military and diplomatic behavior in the late seventeenth and eighteenth centuries for English-speaking audiences, and the book provides a thorough bibliographic note at the end of each chapter reviewing English- and German-language sources. Additional introductory sources for the eighteenth century include the various works by Christopher Duffy, Karl A. Roider Jr., and Franz Szabo, to name perhaps the most important. For the nineteenth century, alongside the works cited in the chapters that follow, the indispensable sources are Paul W. Schroeder and F. R. Bridge. Schroeder deals brilliantly and persuasively with vital aspects of Austrian diplomatic strategy from the late eighteenth century through the mid-nineteenth century in his numerous books and articles. See, in particular, Paul W. Schroeder, *The Transformation of European Politics, 1763–1848* (Oxford: Oxford University Press, 1994). For various essays by Schroeder on Metternich era Austrian diplomacy, see David Wetzel, Robert Jervis, and Jack S. Levy, eds., *Systems, Stability, and Statecraft: Essays on the International History of Modern Europe* (New York: Palgrave Macmillan, 2004). For Bridge's most important works, see F. R. Bridge, *The Habsburg Monarchy among the Great Powers, 1815–1918* (Oxford: Berg Publishers, 1990); F. R. Bridge, *From Sadowa to Sarajevo: The Foreign Policy of Austria-Hungary, 1866–1914* (London: Routledge and K. Paul, 1972); F. R. Bridge with Roger Bullen, *The Great Powers and the European States System, 1815–1914* (London: Longman, 1980).

9. A few historians have used the term "grand strategy" to characterize the policies of individual Habsburg monarchs, but their interest is usually confined to a specific war or campaign.

Matthew Z. Mayer describes a grand strategy under Joseph II to "confront the seemingly insoluble problem of how to match Russia's conquests while denying Prussian compensation in Poland." See Matthew Z. Mayer, "The Price for Austria's Security: Part II. Leopold II, the Prussian Threat, and the Peace of Sistova, 1790–1791," *International History Review* 26, no. 2 (September 2004): 482, 508; Matthew Z. Mayer, "The Price for Austria's Security: Part I. Joseph II, the Russian Alliance, and the Ottoman War, 1787–1789," *International History Review* 26, no. 2 (June 2004): 283. Gunther Rothenberg writes of Austria possessing a grand strategy under Emperor Francis and Archduke Charles: "Of course, ever since the days of Maria Theresa, Austrian chancellors had exercised considerable influence on grand strategy. This had been true of Kaunitz and would remain so under Stadion and Metternich. Thugut was no exception but for the range of his activities." And Michael Leggiere has written compellingly that Metternich and Emperor Francis pursued a largely successful grand strategy. See Michael V. Leggiere, "Austrian Grand Strategy and the Invasion of France in 1814," in *Selected Papers of the Consortium on the Revolutionary Era, 1750–1850*, ed. Frederick C. Schneid and Jack Richard Censer (High Point, NC: High Point University, 2007), 322–31. For a well-written account of Spain's Phillip II—the only book-length treatment of the grand strategy of a Habsburg ruler—see Geoffrey Parker, *The Grand Strategy of Philip II* (London: Redwood, 2000).

10. Ingrao, "Habsburg Strategy and Geopolitics," 50, 63.

11. Hochedlinger, *Wars of Emergence*, 60–61.

12. Rauchensteiner describes a trickle of Austrian military-theoretical writings paling in comparison to those of Prussia or France. See Manfried Rauchensteiner, "The Development of War Theories in Austria at the End of the Eighteenth Century," in *East Central European Society and War in the Pre-Revolutionary Eighteenth Century*, ed. Gunther E. Rothenberg, Béla K. Király, and Peter F. Sugar (New York: Columbia University Press, 1982), 75–82. For a detailed compendium that includes minor and less studied Austrian military writers from the late eighteenth to the mid-nineteenth century, see Günter Brüning, "Militär-Strategie Österreichs in der Zeit Kaiser Franz II (I)" (PhD diss., Westfälische Wilhelms-Universität Münster, 1983).

13. For the classic formulation of this argument, see Paul M. Kennedy, *The Rise and Fall of the Great Powers: Economic Change and Military Conflict from 1500 to 2000* (New York: Random House, 1987).

14. See the discussion in Spencer Bakich, "#Reviewing the Evolution of Modern Grand Strategic Thought," *Strategy Bridge*, September 21, 2016.

15. For an important corrective to this tendency, see Luttwak, *Grand Strategy of the Byzantine Empire*. Luttwak outlines a largely defensive grand strategy in the Eastern Roman Empire rooted in deceptive diplomacy, intelligence, and limited force.

16. Napoleon quoted in Alistair Horne, *How Far from Austerlitz? Napoleon, 1805–1815* (New York: St. Martin's Press, 1996), 9. Bismarck quoted in A. J. P. Taylor, *Bismarck: The Man and the Statesman* (London: Hamish Hamilton, 1955), 38.

17. For prominent postwar German military critics, see Max Hoffman, *War Diaries and Other Papers*, 2 vols. (London, 1929); Erich Ludendorff, *Meine Kriegserinnerungen, 1914–1918* (Berlin: Ernst Siegfried Mittler und Sohn, 1919). The German historian Hans Delbrück was critical of Austrian strategic and military performance in his 1920 history of warfare, juxtaposing it negatively alongside that of Prussia. See Hans Delbrück, *The Dawn of Modern Warfare: History of the Art of War*, trans. Walter J. Renfroe Jr., vol. 4 (Lincoln: University of Nebraska Press, 1990).

18. Schroeder, a famous diplomatic historian, while sympathetic to the Habsburg Monarchy and recognizing its valuable role in the European system, has written that Austria was "inextricably involved … in a game whose rules made it almost impossible for [it] to win, and guaranteed that even a victory would finally prove counterproductive…. The Habsburg Empire could not hide; more than any other Great Power, it was forced to play the balance of power game, and to lose." See Schroeder, *The Transformation of European Politics*, 33. For similar arguments, see A. J. P. Taylor, *The Habsburg Monarchy, 1809–1918: A History of the Austrian Empire and Austria-Hungary* (Harmondsworth, UK: Penguin Books, 1948); C. A. Macartney, *The Habsburg Empire, 1790–1918* (New York: Macmillan, 1969); Steven Beller, *A Concise History of Austria* (Cambridge: Cambridge University Press, 2007). Some historians argue against the inevitability of Habsburg decline. See, for example, Robert A. Kann, *A History of the Habsburg Empire, 1526–1918* (Berkeley: University of California Press, 1974); Dominic Lieven, *Empire: The Russian Empire and Its Rivals* (New Haven, CT: Yale University Press, 2002); Alan Sked, *Decline and Fall of the Habsburg Empire, 1815–1918* (New York: Routledge, 2001); Pieter M. Judson, *The Habsburg Empire: A New History* (Cambridge, MA: Belknap Press of Harvard University, 2016).

19. Quoted in Henry A. Kissinger, *A World Restored: Metternich, Castlereagh, and the Problems of Peace, 1812–22* (Boston: Houghton Mifflin, 1957), 26.

20. For the first major historical case study in grand strategy, see Edward N. Luttwak, *The Grand Strategy of the Roman Empire: From the First Century A.D. to the Third* (Baltimore: Johns Hopkins University Press, 1976). For other book-length cases, see Aaron L. Friedberg, *The Weary Titan: Britain and the Experience of Relative Decline, 1895–1905* (Princeton, NJ: Princeton University Press, 1988); John P. LeDonne, *The Russian Empire and the World, 1700–1917: The Geopolitics of Expansion and Containment* (Oxford: Oxford University Press, 1997); Parker, *Grand Strategy of Philip II*; Aaron L. Friedberg, *In the Shadow of the Garrison State: America's Anti-Statism and Its Cold War Grand Strategy* (Princeton, NJ: Princeton University Press, 2000); John P. LeDonne, *The Grand Strategy of the Russian Empire, 1650–1831* (Oxford: Oxford University Press, 2003); Luttwak, *Grand Strategy of the Byzantine Empire*; Dominic Lieven, *Russia against Napoleon: The True Story of the Campaigns of War and Peace* (New York: Penguin Books, 2009); Paul Anthony Rahe, *The Grand Strategy of Classical Sparta: The Persian Challenge* (New Haven, CT: Yale University Press, 2015); John Darwin, *The Empire Project: The Rise and Fall of the British World-System, 1830–1970* (Cambridge: Cambridge University Press, 2011).

21. As Luttwak writes, "All states have a grand strategy, whether they know it or not. That is inevitable because grand strategy is simply the level at which knowledge and persuasion, or in modern terms intelligence and diplomacy, interact with military strength to determine outcomes in a world of other states, with their own 'grand strategies.' All states must have a grand strategy, but not all grand strategies are equal." Luttwak, *Grand Strategy of the Byzantine Empire*, 410.

22. The concept of grand strategy has its origins in twentieth-century debates about British imperial defense. While coined in the 1830s, it was Sir Julian Stafford Corbett who fully developed the notion in lectures at the Royal Naval War College between 1904 and 1906, and the so-called Green Pamphlet, which was reproduced in part in the 1988 edition of Julian Stafford Corbett, *Some Principles of Maritime Strategy* (London: Hutchinson, 1923). The term was popularized first by J. F. C. Fuller in his book *The Reformation of War* (London: Hutchison, 1923) and then by B. H. Liddell Hart in his books and lectures from the mid-1920s onward, including

most notably *Strategy* (New York: Meridian, 1991). All three British authors emphasize naval warfare, the use of peripheries to strike land-based enemies, and the incorporation of commercial and economic means to limit warfare. In the United States, the term surfaced during the Second World War in H. A. Sargeaunt and Geoffrey West, *Grand Strategy* (New York: Thomas Y. Crowell Company, 1941); Nicholas John Spykman, *America's Strategy in World Politics: The United States and the Balance of Power* (New York: Harcourt, Brace and Company, 1942); Edward Mead Earle, *Makers of Modern Strategy: Military Thought from Machiavelli to Hitler* (Princeton, NJ: Princeton University Press, 1943). The advent of nuclear weapons brought a hiatus in the term's use, but the end of the Cold War has seen renewed interest in the topic by major scholars such as Paul Kennedy, Barry Posen, and John Lewis Gaddis. Among the most important sources dealing with grand strategy, see Colin S. Gray, "Geography and Grand Strategy," *Comparative Strategy* 10, no. 4 (1991): 311–29; Paul M. Kennedy, *Grand Strategies in War and Peace* (New Haven, CT: Yale University Press, 1992); Williamson Murray, MacGregor Knox, and Alvin Bernstein, eds., *The Making of Strategy: Rulers, States, and War* (Cambridge: Cambridge University Press, 1994); John Lewis Gaddis, *Surprise, Security, and the American Experience* (Cambridge, MA: Harvard University Press, 2004); Charles Hill, *Grand Strategies: Literature, Statecraft, and World Order* (New Haven, CT: Yale University Press, 2010); Williamson Murray, Richard Hart Sinnreich, and James Lacey, eds., *The Shaping of Grand Strategy: Policy, Diplomacy, and War* (Cambridge: Cambridge University Press, 2011); Thomas Mahnken, *Competitive Strategies for the 21st Century: Theory, History, and Practice* (Stanford, CA: Stanford University Press, 2012); Lawrence Freedman, *Strategy: A History* (Oxford: Oxford University Press, 2013); Barry R. Posen, *Restraint: A New Foundation for U.S. Grand Strategy* (Ithaca, NY: Cornell University Press, 2014); Hal Brands, *What Good Is Grand Strategy? Power and Purpose in American Statecraft from Harry S. Truman to George W. Bush* (Ithaca, NY: Cornell University Press, 2014); Williamson Murray and Richard Hart Sinnreich, eds., *Successful Strategies: Triumphing in War and Peace from Antiquity to the Present* (Cambridge: Cambridge University Press, 2014); William C. Martel, *Grand Strategy in Theory and Practice: The Need for an Effective American Foreign Policy* (Cambridge: Cambridge University Press, 2015); Colin Dueck *The Obama Doctrine: American Grand Strategy Today* (Oxford: Oxford University Press, 2015); Peter Mansoor and Williamson Murray, eds., *Grand Strategy and Military Alliances* (Cambridge: Cambridge University Press, 2016).

23. For a good introduction to the modern debate about the term "grand strategy," see Lukas Milevski, *The Evolution of Modern Grand Strategic Thought* (Oxford: Oxford University Press, 2006). Milevski traces the origins of the concept, asserting that its meaning is lacking in theoretical grounding and instead contingent on the times in which it is used. Criticisms of the term tend to revolve around two issues: nomenclature—doubts about the term "grand" and on what basis higher-level planning can be differentiated from any other kind of strategy—and rationality—the idea that leaders can formulate a coherent concept and transmit it with a high degree of fidelity within and across generations. The challenge facing detractors is to describe the strategy that occurs above the battlefield level. As one author wrote, it is not enough to merely find shortcomings in the terminology; one must offer an alternative answer to the question, "What does *strategy* look like at the highest levels?" See the review of Milevski's book in Bakich, "#Reviewing the Evolution of Modern Grand Strategic Thought." For a defense of the term, see Murray and Sinnreich, *Successful Strategies*.

24. John Lewis Gaddis, "What Is Grand Strategy?: American Grand Strategy after War" (lecture at the Triangle Institute for Security Studies and Duke University Program on American Grand Strategy, February 26, 2009), 7. Gaddis's definition is, among modern variants, the most consistent with the term as it was employed by its originator, Corbett, who sought to differentiate the process by which leaders direct the combined military resources of the state to obtain a political object in war from generalship, or the strategy that occurs in directing forces on the battlefield. Corbett's definition, as derived from his lecture notes, is that "first there is Grand Strategy, dealing with whole theater of war, with planning the war. It looks on war as a continuation of foreign policy. It regards the object of the war and the means of attaining it. It handles all the national resources together, Navy, Army, Diplomacy and Finance. It is the province of the Council of Defense. Handles Army, Navy, as divisions of one force." Quoted in Milevski, *Evolution of Modern Grand Strategic Thought*, 38. Interwar British military writers Fuller and Liddell Hart developed Corbett's definition further to encompass all the elements of national power rather than just military force. Fuller defined grand strategy as "the transmission of power in all its forms, in order to maintain policy." Ibid., 47. Liddell Hart wrote, "The role of grand strategy or higher strategy is to coordinate and direct all the resources of a nation, or band of nations, towards the attainment of the political object of the war goal defined by fundamental policy." Liddell Hart, *Strategy*, 321–22. Gaddis's definition builds on this lineage of thought while avoiding the two extremes of an overly narrow focus on wartime planning and more elastic, modern understandings that attempt to encompass everything from ideology to literature and art under the grand-strategic rubric. See Hill, *Grand Strategies*.

25. Brands, *What Good Is Grand Strategy?*, 1, 3. This "logic" may or may not be written down. Luttwak describes the leaders of the Byzantine Empire as adhering to an "operational code," which can be "imputed on the basis of observed behavior as well as the diverse recommendations of the Byzantine guidebooks and field manuals." Similarly, Rahe characterizes Sparta's grand strategy as emerging through a trial-and-error process that derived from a "clear-cut orientation" along with a "coherence that made her a *kósmos* and endowed her with *eunomía*," firing the need to "safeguard the *politeía*." See Luttwak, *Grand Strategy of the Byzantine Empire*, 416; Rahe, *Grand Strategy of Classical Sparta*, 2.

26. Liddell Hart was the first to recognize this dimension when he wrote that "grand strategy looks beyond the war to the subsequent peace. It should not only combine the various instruments, but so regulate their use as to avoid the future state of peace for its security and prosperity." Liddell Hart, *Strategy*, 322.

27. Murray, Sinnreich, and Lacey, *Shaping of Grand Strategy*, 2, 5.

28. Gray, "Geography and Grand Strategy."

29. Marvin Swartz, *Politics of British Foreign Policy in the Era of Disraeli and Gladstone* (London: Palgrave Macmillan, 1985), 56. Even in this extreme case, it is debatable to what extent Britain was as reactive to events as Salisbury suggested; a grand strategy of continental engagement to manage the Near East is discernible. See A. J. P. Taylor, *The Struggle for Mastery in Europe, 1848–1918* (Harmondsworth, UK: Penguin Books, 1954), 346; E. David Steele, *Lord Salisbury* (New York: Routledge, 2002), 320.

30. Luttwak, *Grand Strategy of the Byzantine Empire*, 410.

31. See the foreword to Carl von Clausewitz, *Vom Kriege* (Berlin: Ferd. Dümmlers Verlagsbuchhandlung, 1911).

32. William Fuller writes of this tendency in early twentieth-century imperial Russia, which came to view strategy as an almost "magical" substance by which to remedy, through hidden strengths of culture and native guile, what the state lacked technologically against stronger Western adversaries. See William C. Fuller, *Power and Strategy in Russia, 1600–1914* (New York: Macmillan, 1998), xvii–xviii.

33. For the first application of the term "interstitial" to political geography, see William Hardy McNeill, *Europe's Steppe Frontier, 1500–1800* (Chicago: University of Chicago Press, 1964). I define an interstitial Great Power as a state possessing major military potential that inhabits the space between two or more other power centers capable of threatening its existence. I distinguish interstitial Great Powers from so-called middle powers—a term that typically refers to small or midsize states. There is a substantial literature on middle powers. See, for example, Joshua B. Spero, *Bridging the European Divide: Middle Power Politics and Regional Security Dilemmas* (Lanham, MD: Rowman and Littlefield, 2004); Carsten Holbraad, *Middle Powers in International Politics* (London: Macmillan, 1984); David A. Cooper, "Somewhere between Great and Small: Disentangling the Conceptual Jumble of Middle, Regional, and 'Niche' Powers," *Journal of Diplomacy and International Relations* (Summer–Fall 2013): 25–35; Eduard Jordaan, "The Concept of a Middle Power in International Relations: Distinguishing between Emerging and Traditional Middle Powers," *South African Journal of Political Studies* 30, no. 1 (2003): 165–81; Bernard Wood, "Middle Powers in the International System: A Preliminary Assessment of Potential," North-South Institute Working Paper 11 (June 1987); Robert L. Rothstein, *Alliances and Small Powers* (New York: Columbia University Press, 1968); Paul W. Schroeder, "The Lost Intermediaries: The Impact of 1870 on the European System," in *Systems, Stability, and Statecraft: Essays on the International History of Modern Europe*, ed. David Wetzel, Robert Jervis, and Jack S. Levy (New York: Palgrave Macmillan, 2004).

34. Some modern Austrian historians have challenged the idea that the monarchy was a primarily defensive power as part of a larger "Habsburg myth" constructed in an effort to distinguish it from the military history of Prussia. See Michael Hochedlinger, "The Habsburg Monarchy: From 'Military-Fiscal State' to 'Militarization,'" in *The Fiscal-Military State in Eighteenth Century Europe: Essays in Honour of P.G.M. Dickson*, ed. Christopher Storrs (Farnham, UK: Ashgate Publishing Company, 2009), especially 58–61; Laurence Cole, "Der Habsburger-Mythos," in *Memorial Austritte I. Menschen, Mythen, Zeiten*, ed. Emil Prix et al. (Vienna: Oldenbourg Wissenschaftsverlag, 2004).

35. The subject of time has not received extensive attention in strategic studies. Perhaps the most fully developed discussion can be found in the literature on strategic surprise as it relates to technological adaptation, though as with the broader field, the bias is toward strategies of the offensive. See, for example, Colin S. Gray, "Transformation and Strategic Surprise" (Carlisle, PA: Strategic Studies Institute, 2005); L. B. Kirkpatrick, "Book Review of Pearl Harbor: Warning and Decision by Roberta Wohlstetter" (Langley, VA: CIA Historical Review Program, 1993); Jack Davis, "Strategic Warning: If Surprise Is Inevitable, What Role for Analysis?" (Reston, VA: Sherman Kent Center for Intelligence Analysis Occasional Papers 2, no. 1, 2003).

36. Ingrao, *Quest and Crisis*, 4.

37. See Parker, *Grand Strategy of Philip II*.

38. The final years of Austria-Hungary's existence and the lead-up to the World War I period have been a subject of interest among historians in recent years. For a small sample, see

Geoffrey Wawro, *A Mad Catastrophe: The Outbreak of World War I and the Collapse of the Habsburg Empire* (New York: Basic Books, 2014); Mark Cornwall, *The Last Years of Austria-Hungary: A Multi-National Experiment in Early Twentieth-Century Europe* (Exeter: University of Exeter Press, 2002); Prit Buttar, *Collision of Empires: The War on the Eastern Front in 1914* (Oxford: Osprey Publishing, 2016); John R. Schindler, *Fall of the Double Eagle: The Battle for Galicia and the Demise of Austria-Hungary* (Omaha: University of Nebraska Press, 2015); Christopher Clark, *The Sleepwalkers: How Europe Went to War in 1914* (New York: HarperCollins, 2014); Margaret MacMillan, *The War That Ended Peace: The Road to 1914* (New York: Random House, 2014).

39. In these regards, the Austrians compare favorably with the Roman and Byzantine empires, both of which possessed minimal structures or written records, and yet developed coherent grand strategies. See Lacey, "Grand Strategy of the Roman Empire," 38–41; Luttwak, *Grand Strategy of the Byzantine Empire*, 1–49.

40. For some of the best general accounts of the post-1700 Habsburg Empire in English, see Macartney, *Habsburg Empire*; Kann, *History of the Habsburg Empire*; Jean Bérenger, *A History of the Habsburg Empire, 1700–1918* (New York: Routledge, 1968); Andrew Wheatcroft, *The Habsburgs: Embodying Empire* (London: Penguin Books, 1995); Judson, *Habsburg Empire*. Hochedlinger provides an extensive review of German- and English-language secondary literature on the eighteenth-century monarchy in *Austria's Wars of Emergence*. For a valuable but somewhat dated review of historiographical debates, see Sked, *Decline and Fall of the Habsburg Empire*.

41. Most notable among these are the works of Oskar Regele, Kurt Peball, Rauchensteiner, and Hochedlinger. Rauchensteiner's 1974 essay "Zum operativen Denken in Österreich 1814–1914" was among the earliest modern attempts to tackle the question of Austrian military behavior, albeit from a primarily practical standpoint. Valuable works on the Austrian military of the nineteenth century include Joachim Niemeyer's 1979 *Das österreichische Militärwesen im Umbruch* and Walter Wagner's 1978 *Von Austerlitz bis Königgrätz. Österreichische Kampftaktik im Spiegel der Reglements 1805–1864*. Perhaps the most thorough and deliberative treatment on the theoretical aspects of Habsburg military thinking in this period can be found in the unpublished doctoral dissertation of Günter Brüning, "Militär-Strategie Österreichs in der Zeit Kaiser Franz II (I)." See the short historiographical note in his introduction and appendixes. For a short overview of Austrian historiography contrasted with that of Prussia, see Hochedlinger, "The Habsburg Monarchy," especially 58–61.

42. Friedberg has argued convincingly that single historical cases, as opposed to comparative analysis, hold special advantages for developing analogies. See Friedberg, *Weary Titan*, 17n54. For a thoughtful discussion of the broader complexities of using history to inform foreign policy making, see Richard E. Neustadt and Ernest R. May, *Thinking in Time: The Uses of History for Decision-Makers* (New York: Free Press, 1988).

Chapter 2. Empire of the Danube: The Geography of Habsburg Power

1. Nicholas John Spykman, *America's Strategy in World Politics: The United States and the Balance of Power* (New York: Harcourt, Brace and Company, 1942), 42.

2. For emphasis on these two requirements, see ibid. (navigable rivers and mountains); Edward N. Luttwak, *The Grand Strategy of the Roman Empire: From the First Century A.D. to the*

Third (Baltimore: Johns Hopkins University Press, 1976), 1 ("providing adequate security and a sound material base").

3. Paul Robert Magocsi, *Historical Atlas of East Central Europe* (Seattle: University of Washington Press, 1993), 2.

4. William Hardy McNeill, *Europe's Steppe Frontier, 1500–1800* (Chicago: University of Chicago Press, 1964), 2.

5. Hugh Seton-Watson, *Eastern Europe between the Wars, 1918–1941* (Hamden, CT: Archon Books, 1962), 3.

6. In the words of McNeill, the place "where the transcontinental gallop intersected the interregional river boat." McNeill, *Europe's Steppe Frontier*, 2.

7. William O. Blake and Thomas H. Prescott, *The Volume of the World: Embracing the Geography, History, and Statistics* (Columbus: J. and H. Miller, 1855), 584.

8. Figures calculated using the US Army's *Field Manual Number 21–18: Foot Marches*. The march time could increase dramatically with inclement weather, bad roads, and so on.

9. For a discussion of the power gradient problem as it relates to land versus sea empires, see, for example, Colin S. Gray, *The Geopolitics of Super Power* (Louisville: University of Kentucky Press, 1988), 50–51.

10. Seton-Watson, *Eastern Europe between the Wars*, 9.

11. Brian Campbell, *Rivers and the Power of Ancient Rome* (Chapel Hill: University of North Carolina Press, 2012), 292.

12. Dietrich Heinrich von Bülow, *The Spirit of the Modern System of War*, ed. and trans. C. Malorti de Martemont (1806; repr., Cambridge: Cambridge University Press, 2013), 283.

13. Robert Strausz-Hupé, *Geopolitics: The Struggle for Space and Power* (New York: G. P. Putnam's Sons, 1942), 16.

14. A. T. Mahan, *The Influence of Sea Power upon History: 1660–1783* (New York: Dover Publications, 1987), 21.

15. For a discussion of the Danube, see Guy Arnold, *World Strategic Highways* (London: Fitzroy Dearborn Publishers, 2000), 68–73.

16. Blake and Prescott, *Volume of the World*, 587.

17. Henry Hajnal, *The Danube: Its Historical, Political, and Economic Importance* (The Hague: Martinus Nijhoff, 1920), 132–34.

18. Johann Joseph Wenzel Radetzky von Radetz, "Militärische Betrachtung der Lage Österreichs" (1828), in *Denkschriften militärisch-politischen Inhalts aus dem Handschriftlichen Nachlass des k.k. österreichischen Feldmarschalls Grafen Radetzky* (Stuttgart: J. G. Cotta'scher Verlag, 1858), 423.

19. Ibid.

20. Carl von Clausewitz, *On War*, trans. Michael Eliot Howard and Peter Paret (Princeton, NJ: Princeton University Press, 1989), 437.

21. Archduke Charles von Habsburg, *Principles of War*, trans. Daniel I. Radakovich (Ann Arbor, MI: Nimble Books, 2009), 37.

22. Blake and Prescott, *Volume of the World*, 587.

23. Reed Browning, *The War of the Austrian Succession* (New York: St. Martin's Press, 1995), 97.

24. Ibid., 168.

25. Clausewitz, *War*, 424, 428, 432.

26. Archduke Charles, "Von dem Einfluss der Kultur auf die Kriegskunst," in *Erzherzog Karl: Ausgewählte Militärische Schriften*, ed. Freiherr von Waldstätten (Berlin: Richard Wilhelmi, 1882), 117–18.

27. James Fairgrieve, *Geography and World Power* (London: University of London Press, 1915), 329–30.

28. See Colin S. Gray, "Seapower and Landpower," in *Seapower and Strategy*, ed. Roger W. Barnett and Colin S. Gray (Annapolis: Naval Institute Press, 1989); Colin S. Gray, "Geography and Grand Strategy," *Comparative Strategy* 10, no. 4 (1991): 311–29.

29. For more on Habsburg cartography, see Oskar Regele, *Beiträge zur Geschichte der staatlichen Landesaufnahme und Kartographie in Österreich bis zum Jahre 1918* (Vienna: Notringes der wissenschaftlichen Verbände Österreichs, 1955); Johannes Dörflinger, *Die Österreichische Kartographie*, vol. 1 (Vienna: Österreichischen Akademie der Wissenschaften, 1984); David Buisseret, *Monarchs, Ministers, and Maps: The Emergence of Cartography as a Tool of Government in Early Modern Europe* (Chicago: University of Chicago Press, 1992); Madalina Valeria Veres, "Constructing Imperial Spaces: Habsburg Cartography in the Age of Enlightenment" (PhD diss., University of Pittsburgh, 2015). See also Larry Wolff, *Inventing Eastern Europe: The Map of Civilization on the Mind of the Enlightenment* (Stanford, CA: Stanford University Press, 1994); Jeremy Black, "Change in Ancien Régime International Relations: Diplomacy and Cartography, 1650–1800," *Diplomacy and Statecraft* 20, no. 1 (2009): 20–29; Jeremy Black, "A Revolution in Military Cartography?: Europe, 1650–1815," *Journal of Military History* 73, no. 1 (2009): 49–68. A number of the Habsburg maps referenced on this and subsequent pages have been reproduced in full or part in modern editions.

30. This map can be viewed in the Library of Congress Geography and Map Division, Washington, DC.

31. Veres, "Constructing Imperial Spaces," 7.

32. Ibid., 18–19.

33. Ibid., 107.

34. C. A. Macartney, ed., *The Habsburg and Hohenzollern Dynasties in the Seventeenth and Eighteenth Centuries* (London: Macmillan, 1970), 126.

35. Veres, "Constructing Imperial Spaces," 18–19.

36. Buisseret, *Monarchs, Ministers, and Maps*, 163.

37. Veres, "Constructing Imperial Spaces," 30; Buisseret, *Monarchs, Ministers, and Maps*, 164.

38. Veres, "Constructing Imperial Spaces," 53, 426.

39. Ibid., 439. See also John Brian Harley, "Silences and Secrecy: The Hidden Agenda of Cartography in Early Modern Europe," *Imago Mundi: The International Journal for the History of Cartography* 40, no. 1 (1988): 57–76.

40. Veres, "Constructing Imperial Spaces," 7.

41. Quoted in Buisseret, *Monarchs, Ministers, and Maps*, 165.

42. Owen Lattimore, *Studies in Frontier History: Collected Papers, 1928–1958* (London: Oxford University Press, 1962), 110–11.

43. Black, "Change in Ancien Régime International Relations," 23.

44. Michael Hochedlinger, *Austria's Wars of Emergence, 1683–1797* (New York: Routledge, 2013), 125, 308.

45. Buisseret, *Monarchs, Ministers, and Maps*, 166.

46. Veres, "Constructing Imperial Spaces," 151.

47. Ibid., 104–7.

48. For Maria Theresa's correspondence with Joseph II during the 1778 Bavarian succession crisis, see Karl Schneider, "Aus dem Briefwechsel Maria Theresias mit Josef II," in *Aus Österreichs Vergangenheit: Quellenbücher zur österreichischen Geschichte No. 11*, ed. Karl Schneider (Vienna: Schulwissenschaftlicher Verlag, 1917).

49. Quoted in Larry Wolfe, " 'Kennst du das Land?' The Uncertainty of Galicia in the Age of Metternich and Fredo," *Slavic Review* 67, no. 2 (2008): 277.

50. Veres, "Constructing Imperial Spaces," 107–8.

51. Prince Eugene of Savoy, "Memoirs of Prince Eugene of Savoy," in *Eugene of Savoy: Marlborough's Great Military Partner*, ed. Alexander Innes Shand, trans. William Mudford (London: Leonaur Ltd., 2014), 96.

52. Alfred Ritter von Arneth, *Correspondance secrète du comte de Mercy Argenteau avec l'empereur Joseph II et le prince de Kaunitz* (Paris: Imprimerie Nationale, 1877), 1:34–35.

53. Veres, "Constructing Imperial Spaces," 105.

54. Zbigniew Brzezinski, *Game Plan: A Geostrategic Framework for the Conduct of the U.S.-Soviet Contest* (New York: Atlantic Monthly Press, 1986), 6–7.

55. Claudio Magris, *Danube: A Sentimental Journey from the Source to the Black Sea*, trans. Patrick Creagh (New York: Farrar, Straus Giroux, 1989), 155.

Chapter 3. *Damnosa Hereditas:* Habsburg People and State

1. Anonymous, "Notary of King Béla: The Deeds of the Hungarians," ed. and trans. Martyn Rady and László Veszprémy, in *Central European Medieval Texts Series*, ed. János M. Bak, Urszula Borkowska, Giles Constable, and Gábor Klaniczay (Budapest: Central European University Press, 2010), 5:27; C. A. Macartney, *The Medieval Hungarian Historians: A Critical and Analytical Guide* (Cambridge: Cambridge University Press, 1953), 70–80.

2. Robert Strausz-Hupé, *Geopolitics: The Struggle for Space and Power* (New York: G. P. Putnam's Sons, 1942), 16.

3. Hugh Seton-Watson, *Eastern Europe between the Wars, 1918–1941* (Hamden, CT: Archon Books, 1962), 30.

4. David F. Good, *The Economic Rise of the Habsburg Empire, 1750–1914* (Berkeley: University of California Press, 1984), 20–21.

5. Ibid., 23.

6. Charles W. Ingrao, *The Habsburg Monarchy, 1618–1815* (New York: Cambridge University Press, 2000), 7–9.

7. Ibid., 64.

8. Michael Hochedlinger, *Austria's Wars of Emergence, 1683–1797* (New York: Routledge, 2013), 19.

9. For a challenge to the long-standing belief that the native Czech nobility were eradicated at the Battle of White Mountain in 1620, see R. J. W. Evans, *The Making of the Habsburg Monarch, 1550–1700: An Interpretation* (Oxford: Oxford University Press, 1984). For further discussion of this issue, see Jaroslav Pánek, "The Religious Question and the Political System

of Bohemia before and after the Battle of White Mountain," in *Crown, Church, and Estates: Central European Politics in the Sixteenth and Seventeenth Centuries*, ed. R. J. W. Evans and T. V. Thomas (New York: St. Martin's Press, 1991), 129–48.

10. Ingrao, *Habsburg Monarchy*, 11–12.

11. Good, *Economic Rise of the Habsburg Empire*, 23.

12. Ingrao, *Habsburg Monarchy*, 161.

13. Quoted in Reed Browning, *The War of the Austrian Succession* (New York: St. Martin's Press, 1995), 42, 108.

14. Ingrao, *Habsburg Monarchy*, 132, 164.

15. Good, *Economic Rise of the Habsburg Empire*, 25.

16. Ingrao, *Habsburg Monarchy*, 160.

17. Good, *Economic Rise of the Habsburg Empire*, 32.

18. William Hardy McNeill, *Europe's Steppe Frontier, 1500–1800* (Chicago: University of Chicago Press, 1964), 216.

19. Good, *Economic Rise of the Habsburg Empire*, 228.

20. In the words of Charles Tilly, "War made the state, and the state made war." Charles Tilly, *The Formation of National States in Western Europe* (Princeton, NJ: Princeton University Press, 1975), 42.

21. Good, *Economic Rise of the Habsburg Empire*, 25.

22. Ingrao, *Habsburg Monarchy*, 7–10.

23. Franz A. J. Szabo, *Kaunitz and Enlightened Absolutism, 1753–1780* (Cambridge: Cambridge University Press, 1994), 3. For a better understanding of the ambiguous nature of Austrian identity, see Greta Klingenstein, "The Meanings of 'Austria' and 'Austrian' in the Eighteenth Century," in *Royal and Republican Sovereignty in Early Modern Europe*, ed. Robert Oresko, G. C. Gibbs, and H. M. Scott (Cambridge: Cambridge University Press, 1997), 423–78; Richard G. Plaschka, Gerald Stourzh, and Jan P. Niederkorn, eds., *Was heisst Österreich? Inhalt und Umfang des Österreichbegriffs vom 10. Jahrhundert bis heute* (Vienna: Österreichischen Akademie der Wissenschaften, 1995).

24. The following section draws extensively on Hochedlinger, *Wars of Emergence*.

25. R. J. W. Evans, *Making of the Habsburg Monarchy*, 447. There are extensive secondary sources on early modern Austria. For an introduction, see ibid.; Hochedlinger, *Wars of Emergence*; Charles W. Ingrao, *State and Society in Early Modern Austria* (West Lafayette, IN: Purdue University Press, 1994); Karl Vocelka, *Österreichische Geschichte 1699–1815: Glanz und Untergang der höfischen Welt: Repräsentation, Reform und Reaktion im habsburgischen Vielvölkerstaat* (Vienna: Überreuter, 2001); Erich Zollner, *Geschichte Österreichs* (Vienna: Oldenbourg Wissenschaftsverlag, 1990); Ernst Bruckmüller, "Die habsburgische Monarchie im Zeitalter des Prinzen Eugen zwischen 1683 und 1740," in *Österreich und die Osmanen—Prinz Eugen und siene Zeit*, ed. Erich Zöllner and Karl Gutkas (Vienna: Österreichischer Bundesverlag, 1988).

26. Hochedlinger, *Wars of Emergence*, 27; Szabo, *Kaunitz and Enlightened Absolutism*, 3.

27. Prince Eugene of Savoy, "Memoirs of Prince Eugene of Savoy," in *Eugene of Savoy: Marlborough's Great Military Partner*, ed. Alexander Innes Shand, trans. William Mudford (London: Leonaur Ltd., 2014), 77.

28. In the words of Hochedlinger, "The Austrian Habsburgs did not so much rule through the Estates but rather jointly with them." Hochedlinger, *Wars of Emergence*, 268.

29. Ibid., 37.

30. Charles W. Ingrao, *In Quest and Crisis: Emperor Joseph I and the Habsburg Monarchy* (West Lafayette, IN: Purdue University Press, 1979), 28; Hochedlinger, *Wars of Emergence*, 37.

31. Richard Bassett, *For God and Kaiser: The Imperial Austrian Army from 1619 to 1918* (New Haven, CT: Yale University Press, 2015), 85–86.

32. Hochedlinger, *Wars of Emergence*, 285.

33. Quoted in P. G. M. Dickson, *Finance and Government under Maria Theresia, 1740–1780* (Oxford: Clarendon Press, 1987), 2:223.

34. Hochedlinger, *Wars of Emergence*, 29.

35. Even in the mid-nineteenth century, at the high point of Habsburg military spending, one historian notes, "Austrian forces were always 20 to 25 percent smaller than was generally admitted." See Gordon Alexander Craig, *The Battle of Königgrätz: Prussia's Victory over Austria, 1866* (Philadelphia: Lippincott Press, 1964), 29.

36. For the eighteenth century, see Hochedlinger, *Wars of Emergence*, 281; Dickson, *Finance and Government*, 2:344–52, appendix A; Lawrence Sondhaus, "The Strategic Culture of the Habsburg Army," *Austrian History Yearbook* 32 (2001): 225–34. For the nineteenth century, the figures above were calculated using Gunther E. Rothenberg, *The Army of Francis Joseph* (Lafayette, IN: Purdue University Press, 1999), 61: "128,286 Germans, 96,300 Czechs and Slovaks, 52,700 Italians, 22,700 Slovenes, 20,700 Romanians, 19,000 Serbs, 50,100 Ruthenes, 37,700 Poles, 32,500 Magyars, 27,600 Croats, and 5,100 other nationalities."

37. Hochedlinger, *Wars of Emergence*, 37–39.

38. See Michael Pammer, "Public Finance in Austria-Hungary, 1820–1913," in *Paying for the Liberal State: The Rise of Public Finance in Nineteenth Century Europe*, ed. Jose Luis Cardoso and Pedro Lains (Cambridge: Cambridge University Press, 2010), 156; Hochedlinger, *Wars of Emergence*, 78–79.

39. Dickson, *Finance and Government*, 2:47. The sections that follow draw extensively on ibid.; Hamish Scott, "The Fiscal-Military State and International Rivalry during the Long Eighteenth Century," in *The Fiscal-Military State in Eighteenth-Century Europe: Essays in Honour of P. G. M. Dickson*, ed. Christopher Storrs (Farnham, UK: Ashgate Publishing Company, 2009), 23–54; Michael Hochedlinger, "The Habsburg Monarchy: From 'Military-Fiscal State' to 'Militarization,'" in *The Fiscal-Military State in Eighteenth-Century Europe: Essays in Honour of P. G. M. Dickson*, ed. Christopher Storrs (Farnham, UK: Ashgate Publishing Company, 2009), 55–94.

40. Scott, "Fiscal-Military State," 51; Hochedlinger, "Habsburg Monarchy," 79.

41. Scott, "Fiscal-Military State," 48–49.

42. Eugene, "Memoirs," 43. Frederick II quoted in Browning, *War of the Austrian Succession*, 102.

43. For detailed accounts of Habsburg war financing in this period, see Thomas Charles Banfield, "The Austrian Empire: Her Population and Resources," *British and Foreign Review of European Quarterly Journal* 27 (1842): 218–87; Pammer, "Public Finance in Austria-Hungary."

44. Pammer, "Public Finance in Austria-Hungary," 144–46; William O. Blake and Thomas H. Prescott, *The Volume of the World: Embracing the Geography, History, and Statistics* (Columbus: J. and H. Miller, 1855), 587.

45. Karl Marx, "Austrian Bankruptcy," *New York Daily Tribune*, March 22, 1854, accessed May 19, 2016, http://chroniclingamerica.loc.gov/lccn/sn83030213/1854-03-22/ed-1/seq-4/.

46. Peter H. Wilson, *German Armies: War and German Politics, 1648–1806* (London: UCL Press, 1998), 112, 235.

47. Ibid., 235; Dickson, *Finance and Government*, 2:119, table 4.1; Dickson, *Finance and Government*, 2:388, table 4.4.

48. Hochedlinger, *Wars of Emergence*, 425.

49. Leopold Kolowrat, Nota, December 29, 1789, Kabinettsarchiv, Nachlässe der Kabinettskanzlei, 17, No. 1097–1174, LK 1146, HHSA, Vienna. See also Dickson, *Finance and Government*, 2:52–53, table 6.

50. Dominic Lieven, *Empire: The Russian Empire and Its Rivals* (New Haven, CT: Yale University Press, 2002), 140.

51. Maria Theresa to Joseph II, September 5, 1778, in Karl Schneider, "Aus dem Briefwechsel Maria Theresias mit Josef II," in *Aus Österreichs Vergangenheit: Quellenbücher zur österreichischen Geschichte No. 11*, ed. Karl Schneider (Vienna: Schulwissenschaftlicher Verlag, 1917), 90.

52. Eugene, "Memoirs," 99; Browning, *War of the Austrian Succession*, 351.

53. Alan Palmer, *Metternich* (London: History Book Club, 1972), 208.

54. Hochedlinger, "Habsburg Monarchy," 84.

55. Gunther E. Rothenberg, *Napoleon's Great Adversary: Archduke Charles and the Austrian Army, 1792–1814* (Boston: De Capo Press, 1995), 221.

56. Maria Theresa to Joseph II, August 2, 1778, in Schneider, "Aus dem Briefwechsel Maria Theresias," 77–78.

57. Leopold Kolowrat, Summarischer Ausweis, Kabinettsarchiv, Nachlässe der Kabinettskanzlei 17, No. 1097–1174, LK 1168, HHSA, Vienna; Leopold Kolowrat, Nota, December 29, 1789, Kabinettsarchiv, Nachlässe der Kabinettskanzlei, 17, No. 1097–1174, LK 1146, HHSA, Vienna.

58. Quoted in Alan Sked, *Radetzky: Imperial Victor and Military Genius* (London: I. B. Tauris and Co., 2011), 30.

59. Palmer, *Metternich*, 200; F. R. Bridge, *The Habsburg Monarchy among the Great Powers, 1815–1918* (Oxford: Berg Publishers, 1990), 33.

60. Palmer, *Metternich*, 241, 249.

61. Quoted in Sked, *Radetzky*, 126–27.

62. See, for example, Eugene, "Memoirs," 135.

63. Charles to Francis, March 3, 1804, in Alfred Kraus, *Supplement to 1805: Der Feldzug von Ulm* (Vienna: L. W. Seidel und Sohn, K. u. K. Hofbuchhändler, 1912), 3.

64. Johann Joseph Wenzel Radetzky von Radetz, "Wie Kann Man Gute und Grosse Herre mit Wenig Kosten Erhalten" (December 1834), in *Denkschriften militärisch-politischen Inhalts aus dem Handschriftlichen Nachlass des k.k. österreichischen Feldmarschalls Grafen Radetzky* (Stuttgart: J. G. Cotta'scher Verlag, 1858), 534–52.

65. R. J. W. Evans, "Maria Theresa and Hungary," in *Austria, Hungary, and the Habsburgs. Central Europe c. 1683–1867* (Oxford: Oxford University Press, 2006), 17–20.

66. G. E. Mitton, *Austria-Hungary* (London: Adam and Charles Black, 1914), 7.

67. McNeil, *Europe's Steppe Frontier*, 213. More recent literature has refuted the thesis that ethnic as opposed to economic motivations drove these efforts. See, for example, Ulrich Niggemann, "'Peuplierung' als merkantilistisches Instrument: Privilegierung von Einwanderern

und staatlich gelenkte Ansiedlungen," in *Handbuch Staat und Migration in Deutschland seit dem 17. Jahrhundert*, ed. Jochen Oltmer (Berlin: de Gruyter, 2016), 171–98; Márta Fata, *Migration im kameralistischen Staat Josephs II.: Theorie und Praxis der Ansiedlungspolitik in Ungarn, Siebenbürgen, Galizien und der Bukowina von 1768 bis 1790* (Münster: Aschendorff Verlag, 2014).

68. McNeil, *Europe's Steppe Frontier*, 215.

69. Ibid., 217.

70. Owen Lattimore, *Studies in Frontier History: Collected Papers, 1928–1958* (London: Oxford University Press, 1962), 167–68.

71. Palmer, *Metternich*, 249.

72. Claudio Magris, *Danube: A Sentimental Journey from the Source to the Black Sea*, trans. Patrick Creagh (New York: Farrar, Straus Giroux, 1989), 243–44.

73. Ibid.

74. As Schroeder writes, "The Habsburg monarchy was not a normal great power, and could not become one by expanding its military power or reforming itself internally in the directions of modernization and unity. Either of these kinds of reform might have been wise for Austria to pursue; no matter how vigorously pursued, they would not have solved its security dilemma, and could have made it worse. The only alternatives which could conceivably have given Austria security and independence were either imperialist conquest and expansion on a massive scale, embracing all of Central Europe and beyond—a course impossible and unthinkable, never attempted by any Austrian leader before Hitler—or a European international system which somehow transcended the limits of normal balance-of-power politics. For Austria to become independent and secure, Europe as a whole, and especially the whole European center, had to become independent and secure." See Schroeder, *Transformation*, 527.

75. Ibid.

Chapter 4. "Si Vis Pacem": Habsburg War and Strategy

1. Colin S. Gray, "Geography and Grand Strategy," *Comparative Strategy* 10, no. 4 (1991): 311–29.

2. Kaunitz to Maria Theresa, in Alfred Ritter von Arneth, *Geschichte Maria Theresia's* (Vienna: W. Braumüller, 1877), 7:530.

3. See the discussion about the historical debate regarding the Habsburg Army in the early footnotes of the introduction. For an indispensable source for the early period, see Jürg Zimmermann, *Militärverwaltung und Heeresaufbringung Österreich bis 1806*, vol. 3, *Handbuch zur deutschen Militärgeschichte, 1648–1939* (Frankfurt: Bernard und Graefe Verlag, 1965). The Austrian officer corps has not received much attention in English. For a notable exception, see Thomas Mack Barker, "Military Nobility: The Daun Family and the Evolution of the Austrian Officer Corps," in *East Central European Society and War in the Pre-Revolutionary Eighteenth Century*, ed. Gunther E. Rothenberg, Béla K. Király, and Peter F. Sugar (New York: Columbia University Press, 1982); Thomas Mack Barker, "Absolutism and Military Entrepreneurship: Habsburg Models," in *Journal of European Studies* 4, no. 1 (1974): 19–42. See also Robert A. Kann, "The Social Prestige of the Officer Corps in the Habsburg Empire from the Eighteenth Century to 1918," in *War and Society in East Central Europe*, ed. Béla Király and Gunther E.

Rothenberg, vol. 1 (New York: Brooklyn College Press, 1979). For the later period, see István Deák, *Beyond Nationalism: A Social and Political History of the Habsburg Officer Corps, 1848–1918* (New York: Oxford University Press, 1990).

4. There is a small literature on the subject of multiethnic armies, most of which centers on the nineteenth century. For an optimistic appraisal, see István Deák, "The Ethnic Question in the Multinational Habsburg Army: 1848–1918," in *Ethnic Armies: Polyethnic Armed Forces from the Time of the Habsburgs to the Age of the Superpowers*, ed. N. F. Dreisziger (Waterloo, ON: Wilfrid Laurier University Press, 1990). For a more negative assessment, see Geoffrey Wawro, "An 'Army of Pigs': The Technical, Social, and Political Bases of Austrian Shock Tactics, 1859–1866," *Journal of Military History* 59, no. 3 (1995): 407–33.

5. Archduke Charles von Habsburg, *Principles of War*, trans. Daniel I. Radakovich (Ann Arbor, MI: Nimble Books, 2009), 1.

6. Quoted in Günter Brüning, "Militär-Strategie Österreichs in der Zeit Kaiser Franz II (I)" (PhD diss., Westfälische Wilhelms-Universität Münster, 1983), 141.

7. Archduke Carl, "Betrachtungen über das Evangelium Matthaei, Cap. XXII, Vers 35–46, am siebzehnten Sonntag nach Pfingsten," quoted in ibid., 153–54.

8. Maria Theresa to Joseph II, May 29, 1778, in Karl Schneider, "Aus dem Briefwechsel Maria Theresias mit Josef II," in *Aus Österreichs Vergangenheit: Quellenbücher zur österreichischen Geschichte No. 11*, ed. Karl Schneider (Vienna: Schulwissenschaftlicher Verlag, 1917), 49.

9. Quoted in Brüning, "Militär-Strategie Österreichs," 125.

10. Ibid., 39–41.

11. J. W. Bourscheid, *Kaisers Leo des Philosophen: Strategie und Taktik* (Vienna: Joh. Thomas Ehlen v. Trattenern, kaiserlich-königlichen Hof- und Staatsdruckerei, 1777).

12. Niccolò Machiavelli, *Discourses on Livy*, trans. Harvey Mansfield and Nathan Tarcov (Chicago: University of Chicago Press, 1996), book I, chapter 33, 71–72.

13. Quoted in Brüning, "Militär-Strategie Österreichs," 132. For a discussion of the philosophical influences on Charles's military thought, see Lee W. Eysturlid, *The Formative Influences, Theories, and Campaigns of the Archduke Carl* (Westport, CT: Greenwood Press, 2000), 23.

14. Raimondo Montecuccoli, *Sulle Battaglie*, translated in Thomas M. Barker, *The Military Intellectual and Battle: Raimondo Montecuccoli and the Thirty Years War* (Albany: State University of New York Press, 1975).

15. Habsburg, *Principles of War*, 1.

16. For a discussion of the term "tamed Bellona," see Brüning, "Militär-Strategie Österreichs," 24–26; Mark Hewitson, *Absolute War: Violence and Mass Warfare in the German Lands, 1792–1820* (Oxford: Oxford University Press, 2017).

17. Prince Eugene of Savoy, "Memoirs of Prince Eugene of Savoy," in *Eugene of Savoy: Marlborough's Great Military Partner*, ed. Alexander Innes Shand, trans. William Mudford (London: Leonaur Ltd., 2014), 43; Gunther E. Rothenberg, "The Shield of the Dynasty: Reflections on the Habsburg Army, 1649–1918," *Austrian History Yearbook* 32 (2001): 182.

18. Quoted in Brüning, "Militär-Strategie Österreichs," 35, 37.

19. Ibid., 39–41.

20. Quoted in Christopher Duffy, "The Seven Years' War as a Limited War," in *East Central European Society and War in the Pre-Revolutionary Eighteenth Century*, ed. Gunther E. Rothenberg, Béla K. Király, and Peter F. Sugar (New York: Columbus University Press, 1982), 73–74.

21. Maria Theresa to Joseph II, September 26, 1778, in Schneider, "Aus dem Briefwechsel Maria Theresias," 95.

22. Maria Theresa to Joseph II, March 14, 1778, in ibid., 38.

23. Quoted in Brüning, "Militär-Strategie Österreichs," 328–39.

24. Maria Theresa to Joseph II, September 26, 1778, in Schneider, "Aus dem Briefwechsel Maria Theresias," 95.

25. Barker, *Military Intellectual and Battle*, 58.

26. Carl von Clausewitz, *On War*, trans. Michael Eliot Howard and Peter Paret (Princeton, NJ: Princeton University Press, 1989), 246.

27. For an elaboration on this point, see Rothenberg, "Shield of the Dynasty," 169–206.

28. Lawrence Sondhaus, "The Strategic Culture of the Habsburg Army," *Austrian History Yearbook* 32 (2001): 228.

29. Interestingly, the general staff of the Confederacy closely studied Charles's campaigns and writings. See Major D. Jonathan White, *Confederate Strategy in 1863: Was a Strategic Concentration Possible?* (Fort Leavenworth, KS: Penny Hill Press, 2000).

30. Gray, "Geography and Grand Strategy," 311–29.

31. Quoted in Barker, *Military Intellectual and Battle*, 117.

32. General von Lloyd, *Abhandlung über die allgemeinen Grundsätze der Kriegskunst* (Frankfurt: Philipp Heinrich Perrenon, 1783), xxvii.

33. G. Venturini, *Mathematisches System der angewandten Taktik oder eigentlichen Kriegswissenschaft* (Schleswig: J. Rohtz, 1800), 12.

34. Ibid., 12.

35. Jos. Auracher von Aurach, *Vorlesungen über die angewandte Taktik, oder eigentliche Kriegswissenschaft: Für die K. K. österreichische Armee bearbeitet nach dem systematischen Lehrbuche des G. Venturini* (Vienna: Anton Strauss, 1812), vol. 1, part. 1, 6.

36. G. Venturini, *Beschreibung und Regeln eines neuen Krieges-Spiels, zum Nutzen und Vergnügen, besonders aber zum Gebrauch in Militär-Schulen* (Schleswig: bey J. G. Röhß, 1797), xvi.

37. Auracher, *Vorlesungen*, 6.

38. Quoted in Brüning, "Militär-Strategie Österreichs," 270.

39. Auracher, *Vorlesungen*, 105–7.

40. Archduke Charles, "Geist des Kriegswesens," in *Erzherzog Karl: Ausgewählte Militärische Schriften*, ed. Freiherr von Waldstätten (Berlin: Richard Wilhelmi, 1882), 90.

41. Venturini, *Mathematisches System*, 1, 85.

42. Madalina Valeria Veres, "Constructing Imperial Spaces: Habsburg Cartography in the Age of Enlightenment" (PhD diss., University of Pittsburgh, 2015), 145.

43. Brüning, "Militär-Strategie Österreichs," 66.

44. Auracher, *Vorlesungen*, 6.

45. Heinrich Blasek, *Beiträge zur Geschichte der K. U. K. Genie-waffe: Nach den vom K. U. K. Obersten des Genie-Stabes, Im Auftrage des K. U. K. Reichs-Kriegs-Ministeriums zusammengestellt und bearbeitet* (Vienna: L. W. Seidel und Sohn, 1898), vol. 1, part 2, 737.

46. Franz Kinsky, *Über Emplacement der Festungen: Erster Nachtrag zu den Elementar Begriffen* (Vienna: Adam und Kompagnie, 1790), 3.

47. Eugene, "Memoirs," 43.

48. Kinsky, *Emplacement der Festungen*, 3–4.

49. Archduke Charles, "Grundsätze der Strategie," in *Erzherzog Karl: Ausgewählte Militärische Schriften*, ed. Freiherr von Waldstätten (Berlin: Richard Wilhelmi, 1882), 61.

50. Johann Joseph Wenzel Radetzky von Radetz, "Gedanken über Festungen" (1827), in *Denkschriften militärisch-politischen Inhalts aus dem Handschriftlichen Nachlass des k.k. österreichischen Feldmarschalls Grafen Radetzky* (Stuttgart: J. G. Cotta'scher Verlag, 1858), 423.

51. Eugene, "Memoirs," 95, 99.

52. Kinsky, *Emplacement der Festungen*, 6–7, 19.

53. Habsburg, *Principles of War*, 10–11.

54. Kinsky, *Emplacement der Festungen*, 5; Radetzky, "Gedanken über Festungen," 401–4.

55. Habsburg, *Principles of War*, 10.

56. Quoted in Barker, *Military Intellectual and Battle*, 172.

57. "Si vis pacem para bellum," Mem. 2/20, KA, Vienna.

58. Kinsky, *Emplacement der Festungen*, 12–14, 18.

59. G. Venturini, *Kritische Übersicht des letzten und merkwürdigsten Feldzugs im achtzehnten Jahrhundert* (Leipzig: Johann Conrad Hinrichs, 1802), 1.

60. Ibid., 3–4.

61. See Nicholas John Spykman, *America's Strategy in World Politics: The United States and the Balance of Power* (New York: Harcourt, Brace and Company, 1942), xiv, 19–20. See also Robert Strausz-Hupé, *Geopolitics: The Struggle for Space and Power* (New York: G. P. Putnam's Sons, 1942), 196–217.

62. Memorandum from Kaunitz, *Memoire über die Räthlichkeit, Nützlichkeit und Nothwendigkeit, das zwischen uns und Russland nun zu Ende gehende Allianzsystem nicht nur unverzüglich zu erneuern, sondern auch auf alle mögliche Art fortan bestens zu cultiviren*, May 10, 1789, Staatskanzlei Vorträge Kart. 146, Vorträge 1789, HHSA, Vienna.

63. Eugene, "Memoirs," 26.

64. Venturini, *Kritische Übersicht*, 8, 10.

65. Bradford A. Lee, "Strategic Interaction: Theory and History for Practitioners," in *Competitive Strategies for the 21st Century: Theory, History, and Practice*, ed. Thomas G. Mahnken (Stanford, CA: Stanford University Press, 2012), 28.

66. Ibid., 29.

67. Clausewitz, *War*, 139.

68. *Denkschrift über die Reichsbefestigung der ehemaligen Österreichisch-Ungarische Monarchie*, undated, 38, KA, Vienna.

69. Eugene, "Memoirs," 36.

70. For an excellent summary of the trade-offs facing Habsburg strategy in the War of the Spanish Succession, see Lothar Höbelt, "The Impact of the Rakoczi Rebellion on Habsburg Strategy: Incentives and Opportunity Costs," *War in History* 13, no. 1 (2006): 2–15. For a longer treatment, see Charles W. Ingrao, *In Quest and Crisis: Emperor Joseph I and the Habsburg Monarchy* (West Lafayette, IN: Purdue University Press, 1979).

71. Lee, "Strategic Interaction," 28–29.

72. Clausewitz, *War*, 92.

73. For a concise but detailed account of the evolution of Habsburg foreign policy decision-making processes, see Franz A. J. Szabo, *Kaunitz and Enlightened Absolutism, 1753–1780* (Cambridge: Cambridge University Press, 1994), 38–45. The paragraphs that follow draw

extensively on ibid.; Hubert Zeinar, *Geschichte des österreichischen Generalstabes* (Vienna: Böhlau, 2006); Thomas Fellner, *Veröffentlichungen der Kommission für Neuere Geschichte Österreichs: Die Österreichische Zentralverwaltung* (Vienna: Adolf Holzhausen, 1907); P. G. M. Dickson, *Finance and Government under Maria Theresia, 1740–1780*, 2 vols. (Oxford: Clarendon Press, 1987).

74. Szabo, *Kaunitz and Enlightened Absolutism*, 38.

75. Ibid., 48.

76. Zeinar, *Geschichte des österreichischen Generalstabes*, 47.

77. Ibid., 46; Richard Holmes, Charles Singleton, and Spencer Jones, "Hofkriegsrat," in *The Oxford Companion to Military History*, ed. Richard Holmes (Oxford: Oxford University Press, 2001); Dickson, *Finance and Government*, 2:215.

78. Oskar Regele, *Der österreichische Hofkriegsrat, 1556–1848* (Vienna: Österreichischen Staatsdruckerei), 15–16; Fellner, *Veröffentlichungen der Kommission für Neuere Geschichte Österreichs*, 277.

79. Regele, *Der österreichische Hofkriegsrat*, 15.

80. Zeinar, *Geschichte des österreichischen Generalstabes*, 49.

81. "The bad composition of the whole machine," Joseph II complained, "overwhelm[s officials] with muddles, and reduce[s] them to the point when they don't know what's to be done." See Derek Beales, *Joseph II*, vol. 1, *In the Shadow of Maria Theresa, 1741–1780* (Cambridge: Cambridge University Press, 1987), 184. The army tended to resent the preponderance of civilian "quill drivers" at the Hofkriegsrat, with their bickering and predilection for voluminous paperwork. Radetzky famously described the Hofkriegsrat as instituting a "civil and not military despotism, but one under which the Army would be entirely neglected." See Zeinar, *Geschichte des österreichischen Generalstabes*, 51.

82. Until the eighteenth century, a second Hofkriegsrat in Graz was responsible for military planning in the southeast; diplomatic relations with Russia and Turkey fell under overlapping management until institutionalized by Kaunitz; the Obrist-Proviantamt was also responsible for military supplies, the Department of Trade and Commerce tussled with the Hofkriegsrat over who would finance the navy; and so on. See Szabo, *Kaunitz and Enlightened Absolutism*, 40, 49, 298; Richard Bassett, *For God and Kaiser: The Imperial Austrian Army, 1619–1918* (New Haven, CT: Yale University Press, 2015), 122.

83. Zeinar, *Geschichte des österreichischen Generalstabes*, 42–43; Bassett, *God and Kaiser*, 122.

84. The record on Habsburg intelligence is partial, due to the fact that the Austrians destroyed documents from the Evidenzbüro after World War I, for the sensible reason that they "did not want the past to be explored by unfriendly governments such as the socialists or national ones." See Norman Stone, "Austria-Hungary," in *Knowing One's Enemies*, ed. Ernest R. May (Princeton, NJ: Princeton University Press, 1986), 41.

85. Siegfried Beer and Marianna Walle, *Les Services du Renseignement Habsbourgeois ont-ils échoué? La défaite des services du renseignement Austro-Hongrois dans la première guerre mondiale* (Paris: Presses Universitaires de France, 2008), 74.

86. Ibid.; Pieter M. Judson, *The Habsburg Empire: A New History* (Cambridge, MA: Belknap Press of Harvard University, 2016), 17.

87. Beer and Walle, *Les Services*, 74.

88. Eugene, "Memoirs," 95, 112.

89. "Si vis pacem para bellum," Mem. 2/20, KA, Vienna.

90. Quoted in Arneth, *Geschichte Maria Theresia's*, 7:222–23.

91. The memo was written in French and titled "Si vis pacem para bellum ou Memoire sur les preparatifs de guerre indispensablement necessaires pour la Conservation de la paix." It can be found in the Austrian Kriegsarchiv as Mem. 2/20 and is also reprinted in full in Graf R. Khevenhüller-Metsch and H. Schlitte, eds., *Aus der Zeit Maria Theresias. Tagebuch des Fürsten Johann Josef Khevenhüller-Metsch, kaiserlichen Obersthofmeisters, 1742–1776* (Vienna: Adolf Holzhausen, 1907), 6:458–67. For a discussion of this memorandum, see Beales, *Joseph II*, 185–86, 273.

92. "Si vis pacem para bellum," Mem. 2/20, KA, Vienna.

93. Niccolò Machiavelli, *The Prince and the Art of War* (London: CRW Publishing, 2004), 416.

94. For a discussion on Joseph's memorandum, see "The General Picture of the Affairs of the Monarchy" ("*Tableau Général*"), in Beales, *Joseph II*, 182–91.

95. Manfried Rauchensteiner, "The Development of War Theories in Austria at the End of the Eighteenth Century," in *East Central European Society and War in the Pre-Revolutionary Eighteenth Century*, ed. Gunther E. Rothenberg, Béla K. Király, and Peter F. Sugar (New York: Columbia University Press, 1982), 78.

96. "Organization of a Reliable Defense Strategy," Minutes of the Conferences of March 7, 10, and 14, 1767, KA, Vienna.

97. See, for example, Mem. 1/7, 1/8, 1/9, Kriegsarchiv, Vienna; "Combined Defense Plan for the Kingdom of Bohemia," in Oskar Criste, *Kriege unter Kaiser Josef II. Nach den Feldakten und anderen authentischen Quellen bearbeitet in der kriegsgeschichtlichen Abteilung des k. und k. Kriegsarchivs* (Vienna: Verlag von L. W. Seidel und Sohn, 1904), 260–62; Charles to Francis, March 3, 1804, in Alfred Kraus, *Supplement to 1805: Der Feldzug von Ulm* (Vienna: L. W. Seidel und Sohn, K. u. K. Hofbuchhändler, 1912), 1–17; "Operationsplan," in Alfred Kraus, *Supplement to 1805: Der Feldzug von Ulm* (Vienna: L. W. Seidel und Sohn, K. u. K. Hofbuchhändler, 1912), 1–6.

98. Hal Brands, *What Good Is Grand Strategy? Power and Purpose in American Statecraft from Harry S. Truman to George W. Bush* (Ithaca, NY: Cornell University Press, 2014), 1, 3.

99. Szabo, *Kaunitz and Enlightened Absolutism*, 286. For greater detail on the debates between Joseph and Kaunitz, see ibid., 286–87; Beales, *Joseph II*, 182–91.

100. Clausewitz, *War*, 139.

101. Habsburg, *Principles of War*, 1, 7, 10.

102. Maria Theresa to Joseph II, March 14, 1778, in Schneider, "Aus dem Briefwechsel Maria Theresias," 35.

103. Alan Sked, *Metternich and Austria: An Evaluation* (London: Palgrave Macmillan, 2008), 190.

104. For the foundational book on systems-level analysis, see Robert Jervis, *System Effects: Complexity in Political and Social Life* (Princeton, NJ: Princeton University Press, 1997).

105. Edward N. Luttwak, *The Grand Strategy of the Roman Empire from the First Century A.D. to the Third* (Baltimore: Johns Hopkins University Press, 1976), 6–7.

106. Claudio Magris, *Danube: A Sentimental Journey from the Source to the Black Sea*, trans. Patrick Creagh (New York: Farrar, Straus Giroux, 1989), 138–39.

107. Bourscheid, *Kaisers Leo des Philosophen*, 21.

108. Erzherzog Karl, *Militärische Werke*, vol. 1 (Vienna: kaiserlich-königlichen Hof- und Staatsdruckerei, 1862). There is some indication that Charles's thinking was derivative in a few important regards of Venturini in particular. See Manfried Rauchensteiner, "Zum operativen Denken in Österreich 1814–1914," *Österreichische Militärische Zeitschrift* 2, part 1 (1974).

109. Johann Joseph Wenzel Radetzky von Radetz, "Militärische Betrachtung der Lage Österreichs" (1828), in *Denkschriften militärisch-politischen Inhalts aus dem Handschriftlichen Nachlass des k.k. österreichischen Feldmarschalls Grafen Radetzky* (Stuttgart: J. G. Cotta'scher Verlag, 1858), 427.

110. Brüning, "Militär-Strategie Österreichs," 69.

111. "Si vis pacem para bellum," Mem. 2/20, KA, Vienna.

112. Archduke Charles, "Von dem Einfluss der Kultur auf die Kriegskunst," in *Erzherzog Karl: Ausgewählte Militärische Schriften*, ed. Freiherr von Waldstätten (Berlin: Richard Wilhelmi, 1882), 125.

113. Quoted in Duffy, "Seven Years' War," 73–74.

114. Habsburg, *Principles of War*, 6.

Chapter 5. Harvest of Briars:
Turks, Russians, and the Southeastern Frontier

1. Several good English-language accounts exist of the eighteenth-century security competition on the Habsburg Monarchy's southern and eastern frontiers. In addition to the sources on the Ottoman and Russian Empires listed in the notes below, this chapter draws extensively on Karl A. Roider Jr., *Austria's Eastern Question, 1700–1790* (Princeton, NJ: Princeton University Press, 1982); H. M. Scott, *The Emergence of the Eastern Powers, 1756–1775* (Cambridge: Cambridge University Press, 2001); Plamen Mitev, Ivan Parvev, Maria Baramova, and Vania Racheva, eds., *Empires and Peninsulas: Southeastern Europe between Karlowitz and the Peace of Adrianople, 1699–1829* (New Brunswick, NJ: Transaction Publishers, 2010); Charles W. Ingrao, Nikola Samardžić, and Jovan Pešalj, eds., *The Peace of Passarowitz, 1718* (West Lafayette, IN: Purdue University Press, 2011).

2. Paul Robert Magocsi, *Historical Atlas of East Central Europe* (Seattle: University of Washington Press, 1993), 63.

3. Ibid.

4. William Hardy McNeill, *Europe's Steppe Frontier, 1500–1800* (Chicago: University of Chicago Press, 1964), 215–16.

5. Ibid., 217.

6. Michael Hochedlinger, *Austria's Wars of Emergence, 1683–1797* (New York: Routledge, 2013), 24. Under the Treaty of Karlowitz, the Ottomans committed themselves for the first time to a political-linear border that technically required eschewal of continued raiding. See Rifa'at A. Abou-el-Haj, "The Formal Closure of the Ottoman Frontier in Europe, 1699–1703," *Journal of the American Oriental Society* 89, no. 3 (1969): 467–75.

7. Eugene to Charles, June 20, 1718, in Kriegsarchiv, *Feldzüge des Prinzen Eugen von Savoyen, Nach den Feldakten und anderen authentischen Quellen herausgegeben von der Abtheilung für Kriegsgeschichte des K. K. Kriegs-Archives* (Vienna: Verlag des K.K. Generalstabes, 1876), vol. 17, appendix 238.

8. There is a large and extensive literature on Ottoman military and economic power in this period. Here and elsewhere, this chapter draws on Virginia H. Aksan, *Ottoman Wars, 1700–1870: An Empire Besieged* (London: Pearson Education Limited, 2007); Rhoads Murphey, *Ottoman Warfare, 1500–1700* (New Brunswick, NJ: Rutgers University, 1999); Gábor Ágoston, "Firearms and Military Adaptation: The Ottomans and the European Military Revolution, 1450–1800," *Journal of World History* 25, no. 1 (2014): 85–124; Kaushik Roy, "Horses, Guns, and Governments: A Comparative Study of the Military Transition in the Manchu, Mughal, Ottoman, and Safavid Empires, circa 1400 to circa 1750," *International Area Studies Review* 15, no. 2 (2012): 99–121; Murat Çinar Büyükakça, "Ottoman Army in the Eighteenth Century: War and Military Reform in the Eastern European Context" (PhD diss., Middle East Technical University, 2007); Gábor Ágoston, *Guns for the Sultan: Military Power and the Weapons Industry in the Ottoman Empire* (New York: Cambridge University Press, 2005); Jonathan A. Grant, "Rethinking the Ottoman 'Decline': Military Technology Diffusion in the Ottoman Empire, Fifteenth to Eighteenth Centuries," *Journal of World History* 10, no. 1 (1999): 179–201; Mark L. Stein, *Guarding the Frontier: Ottoman Border Forts and Garrisons in Europe* (London: Tauris Academic Studies, 2007); Muhammed Fatih Calisir, "A Long March: The Ottoman Campaign in Hungary, 1663" (PhD diss., Central European University, 2009).

9. For characterizations of Russian strategy during this period, two works are especially helpful. John P. LeDonne's *The Grand Strategy of the Russian Empire, 1650–1831* (Oxford: Oxford University Press, 2003) examines the geographic pressures and opportunities that led to Russia's leaders to pursue policies of expansion beginning in the late seventeenth century. His analytic framework describing Russia's preference for client states and spurts of concentric expansion is particularly valuable, and his portrayals of military "deep strikes" draw on the work of twentieth-century Russian military writers such as General Mikhail Tukhachevsky. Carol B. Stevens's *Russia's Wars of Emergence, 1460–1730* (New York: Routledge, 2007) is a recent, valuable contribution to the subject; especially notable are her sections detailing Peter the Great's initial collisions with the Turks (ibid., 187–90) and the effects produced by Russian defeats at the hands of the Turks (ibid., 265–66).

10. LeDonne, *Grand Strategy*, 1–37.

11. Ibid., 85–93.

12. Harvey L. Dyck, "New Serbia and the Origins of the Eastern Question, 1751–55: A Habsburg Perspective," *Russian Review* 40, no. 1 (1981): 1–19.

13. Conference Protocol, February 23, 1711, quoted in Roider, *Austria's Eastern Question*, 33.

14. Ibid., 6.

15. Grant, "Rethinking the Ottoman 'Decline,'" 179–201; Ágoston, "Firearms and Military Adaptation," 102, 108.

16. McNeill, *Europe's Steppe Frontier*, 131.

17. Dominic Lieven, *Empire: The Russian Empire and Its Rivals* (New Haven, CT: Yale University Press, 2002), 140.

18. Erich Gabriel, *Die Hand- und Faustfeuerwaffen der habsburgischen Heere* (Vienna: Österreichischer Bundesverlag, 1990), 23–29.

19. Ágoston, "Firearms and Military Adaptation."

20. Gábor Ágoston, "Military Transformation in the Ottoman Empire and Russia, 1500–1800," *Kritika: Explorations in Russian and Eurasian History* 12, no. 2 (2011): 281–319.

21. "Janitscharen," 1787, in Oskar Criste, *Kriege unter Kaiser Josef II. Nach den Feldakten und anderen authentischen Quellen bearbeitet in der kriegsgeschichtlichen Abteilung des k. und k. Kriegsarchivs* (Vienna: Verlag von L. W. Seidel und Sohn, 1904), 272.

22. Archduke Charles von Habsburg, *Principles of War*, trans. Daniel I. Radakovich (Ann Arbor, MI: Nimble Books, 2009), 59.

23. Prince Eugene of Savoy, "Memoirs of Prince Eugene of Savoy," in *Eugene of Savoy: Marlborough's Great Military Partner*, ed. Alexander Innes Shand, trans. William Mudford (London: Leonaur Ltd., 2014), 78.

24. "Janitscharen," 273.

25. Eugene, "Memoirs," 78.

26. Ibid.

27. Habsburg, *Principles of War*, 60.

28. Ibid., 59.

29. Thomas M. Barker, *The Military Intellectual and Battle: Raimondo Montecuccoli and the Thirty Years War* (Albany: State University of New York Press, 1975), 61, 116.

30. McNeill, *Europe's Steppe Frontier*, 160.

31. Habsburg, *Principles of War*, 60–61.

32. Hochedlinger, *Wars of Emergence*, 126–27, 140.

33. Eugene, "Memoirs," 41.

34. Charles to Eugene, September 25, 1717, in Kriegsarchiv, *Feldzüge des Prinzen Eugen von Savoyen*, 17:438–39.

35. Roider, *Austria's Eastern Question*, 50.

36. Charles W. Ingrao, *In Quest and Crisis: Emperor Joseph I and the Habsburg Monarchy* (West Lafayette, IN: Purdue University Press, 1979), 57–67.

37. For an extended description of the crisis, see Roider, *Austria's Eastern Question*, 29–30.

38. Ingrao, *Quest and Crisis*, 153–55.

39. The word derives from the Latin for "crusader." The plural in Magyar is *kurucok*, but for simplicity's sake I will follow the conventional practice of kuruc for both singular and plural. See Lothar Höbelt, "The Impact of the Rakoczi Rebellion on Habsburg Strategy: Incentives and Opportunity Costs," *War in History* 13, no. 1 (2006): 2–15.

40. Ibid.

41. Quoted in ibid., 11.

42. Charles to Eugene, September 25, 1717, in Kriegsarchiv, *Feldzüge des Prinzen Eugen von Savoyen*, 17:438–39.

43. Nikola Samardžić, "The Peace of Passarowitz, 1718: An Introduction," in *The Peace of Passarowitz, 1718*, ed. Charles W. Ingrao, Nikola Samardžić, and Jovan Pešalj (West Lafayette, IN: Purdue University Press, 2011), 18. The terms of the treaty along with its military, economic, and cultural impacts on the Habsburg Monarchy and Ottoman Empire are extensively analyzed in this book.

44. Charles to Eugene, July 28, 1718, in Kriegsarchiv, *Feldzüge des Prinzen Eugen von Savoyen*, 17:385.

45. Samuel Whatley, *A General Collection of Treatys of Peace and Commerce, Manifestos, Declarations of War, and Other Publick Papers* (London: J. J. and P. Knapton, 1732), 4:402.

46. See Carl A. Roider Jr., *The Reluctant Ally: Austria's Policy in the Austro-Turkish War, 1737–1739* (Baton Rouge: Louisiana State University Press, 1972).

47. Roider, *Austria's Eastern Question*, 73.

48. Ibid., 76.

49. See ibid., 106.

50. Ibid.

51. Ibid., 95.

52. Ibid., 107.

53. For a description of these defenses, see Manfried Rauchensteiner, *Vom Limes zum "Ostwall,"* vol. 21, *Militärhistorische Schriftenreihe* (Vienna: Militärwissenschaftliches Institut Österreichischer Bundesverlag, 1972), 19–23.

54. Reed Browning, *The War of the Austrian Succession* (New York: St. Martin's Press, 1995), 65–67.

55. Géza David and Pál Fodor, eds. *Ottomans, Hungarians, and Habsburgs in Central Europe: The Military Confines in the Era of Ottoman Conquest* (Leiden: Brill, 2000).

56. Quoted in Géza Pállfy, "The Origins of the Border Defense System against the Ottoman Empire in Hungary (Up to the Eighteenth Century), in *Ottomans, Hungarians, and Habsburgs in Central Europe: The Military Confines in the Era of Ottoman Conquest*, ed. Géza David and Pál Fodor (Leiden: Brill, 2000), 3.

57. Gunther E. Rothenberg, *The Military Border in Croatia, 1740–1881: A Study of an Imperial Institution* (Chicago: University of Chicago Press, 1966), 1–40.

58. Quoted in ibid., 112.

59. Hochedlinger, *Wars of Emergence*, 241.

60. Richard Bassett, *For God and Kaiser: The Imperial Austrian Army, 1619–1918* (New Haven, CT: Yale University Press, 2015), 60; Hochedlinger, *Wars of Emergence*, 323.

61. See Rauchensteiner, *Vom Limes*, 19–23.

62. For a full discussion of these structures, see Josip Kljajić, *Vojnokrajiški Čardaci u Slavonsko-Srijemskom Posavlju u 18. i 19. Stoljeću* (Zagreb: Hrvatski Institut za Povijest, 2002), 35; Fritz Posch, *Flammende Grenze: Die Steiermark in den Kuruzzenstürmen* (Graz: Styria, 1968).

63. J. G. Kohl, *Austria: Vienna, Prague, Hungary, Bohemia, and the Danube; Galicia, Styria, Moravia, Bukovina, and the Military Frontier* (London: Chapman and Hall, 1842), 267.

64. Estimates of exact spacing distances vary but generally agree on thirty-minute walk times. The figure used here is based on an eyewitness account from the nineteenth century as well as spacing observed between *Chartaques* marked on the first and second military surveys using the time = distance / speed formula.

65. Kohl, *Austria*, 270.

66. Minutes of the Conferences of March 7, 10, and 14, 1767, KA, Vienna.

67. Anton Lešić, *Das Entstehen der Militärgrenze und die Geschichte der Stadt und Festung Brod* (Zagreb: Königliche Landesdruckerei, 1914), KA, Vienna, 15. See also Gunther E. Rothenberg, "The Origins of the Austrian Military Frontier in Croatia and the Alleged Treaty of 22 December 1522," *Slavonic and East European Review* 38, no. 91 (1960): 493–98.

68. David and Fodor, *Ottomans, Hungarians, and Habsburgs*, 62.

69. See Imre Berki, *A magyar határvédelem története* [History of border protection in Hungary], Múlt-Kor, September 29, 2010.

70. Hochedlinger, *Wars of Emergence*, 243, 323.

71. Whatley, *General Collection*, 291–92.

72. Kaunitz, "Memoire über die Räthlichkeit, Nützlichkeit und Nothwendigkeit ... Russland," May 10, 1789, Staatskanzlei Vorträge Kart. 146, Vorträge 1789, HHSA, Vienna.

73. Roider, *Austria's Eastern Question*, 120.

74. Memorandum from Maria Theresa, in Karl Schneider, "Aus dem Briefwechsel Maria Theresias mit Josef II," in *Aus Österreichs Vergangenheit: Quellenbücher zur österreichischen Geschichte No. 11*, ed. Karl Schneider (Vienna: Schulwissenschaftlicher Verlag, 1917), 20. Elsewhere, Maria Theresa bemoaned alignment with "the perpetual enemy of the Christians" and the Catholic monarchy's "natural enemy." See Saul K. Padover, "Prince Kaunitz' Résumé of His Eastern Policy, 1763–71," *Journal of Modern History* 5, no. 3 (1933): 352–65.

75. See Roider, *Austria's Eastern Question*, 117–18.

76. For a history of the Polish partitions, see Scott, *Emergence of the Eastern Powers*; Jerzy Lukowski, *The Partitions of Poland, 1772, 1793, 1795* (London: Routledge, 1999); Michael Muller, *Die Teilungen Polens* (Munich: C. H. Beck, 1984).

77. Lukowski, *Partitions of Poland*, 11.

78. For nuances in the positions taken on the partition among Habsburg officials, see Scott, *Emergence of the Eastern Powers*, 217–18.

79. Magocsi, *Historical Atlas of East Central Europe*, 70.

80. Franz A. J. Szabo, "Prince Kaunitz and the Balance of Power," *International History Review* 1, no. 3 (1979): 380.

81. For a detailed account of the challenges facing Austria in this period, and the deliberations that shaped Kaunitz's Russian policies, see Harvey L. Dyck, "Pondering the Russian Fact: Kaunitz and the Catherinian Empire in the 1770s," *Canadian Slavonic Papers / Revue Canadienne des Slavistes* 22, no. 4 (1980): 451–69.

82. Ibid., 453.

83. For a reproduction of this memorandum in full (in German), see Padover, "Prince Kaunitz' Résumé," 352.

84. There is a well-developed literature on the use of alliances as instruments of control. For foundational works, see George Liska, *Nations in Alliance: The Limits of Interdependence* (Baltimore: Johns Hopkins University Press, 1962); Robert E. Osgood, *Alliances and American Foreign Policy* (Baltimore: Johns Hopkins University Press, 1968). For an especially valuable analysis, see Paul W. Schroeder, "Alliances, 1815–1945: Weapons of Power and Tools of Management," in *Systems, Stability and Statecraft: Essays on the International History of Modern Europe*, ed. David Wetzel, Robert Jervis, and Jack S. Levy, (New York: Palgrave Macmillan, 2004), 195–222.

85. Matthew Z. Mayer, "The Price for Austria's Security: Part I. Joseph II, the Russian Alliance, and the Ottoman War, 1787–1789," *International History Review* 26, no. 2 (June 2004): 257–99.

86. Kaunitz, "Memoire über die Räthlichkeit, Nützlichkeit und Nothwendigkeit."

87. Dyck, "Pondering the Russian Fact," 438.

88. Kaunitz, "Memoire über die Räthlichkeit, Nützlichkeit und Nothwendigkeit."

89. Maria Theresa to Mercy, July 31, 1777, in Alfred Ritter von Arneth, *Geschichte Maria Theresia's* (Vienna: W. Braumüller, 1877), 3:99–100.

90. For good sources on Joseph II's Turkish war, see Mayer, "Price for Austria's Security: Part I"; Michael Hochelinger, *Krise und Wiederherstellung, Österreichische Großmachtpolitik zwischen Türkenkrieg und "Zweiter Diplomatischer Revolution," 1787–1791* (Berlin: Duncker and Humblot, 2000); Karl A. Roider Jr., "Kaunitz, Joseph II, and the Turkish War," *Slavonic and East European Review* 54, no. 4 (1976): 538–56.

91. Mayer, "Price for Austria's Security: Part I," 290.

92. Ibid., 270.

93. Mem. 1/7, 1/8, 1/9, KA, Vienna.

94. Ibid.

95. Mayer, "Price for Austria's Security: Part I," 293.

96. Ibid., 280.

97. Extract from a dispatch of Prince Kaunitz, July 12, 1788, SV 145 (Vorträge 1788), HHSA, Vienna.

98. Ibid., 299.

99. R. J. W. Evans, "The Habsburgs and the Hungarian Problem, 1790–1848," in *Transactions of the Royal Historical Society* 39 (1989): 41–62.

100. Matthew Z. Mayer, "The Price for Austria's Security: Part II. Leopold II, the Prussian Threat, and the Peace of Sistova, 1790–1791," *International History Review* 26, no. 2 (September 2004): 473–514.

101. Kaunitz offered his thoughts on the possibility of a two-sided war in the context of an exchange with Joseph about a French dispatch that was intercepted revealing France's intent to interpose itself as a mediator in the conflict. Joseph to Kaunitz, August 26, 1788, SV/145; Kaunitz comments on Dickwan to Joseph, August 26, 1788, SV 145 (Vorträge 1788), HHSA, Vienna.

102. Mayer, "Price for Austria's Security: Part II," 512.

103. Owen Lattimore, *Studies in Frontier History: Collected Papers, 1928–1958* (London: Oxford University Press, 1962), 147.

Chapter 6. "The Monster": Prussia and the Northwestern Frontier

1. For a concise account of the exceptional circumstances that set Brandenburg-Prussia apart from other states of the early modern period, see Brian M. Downing, *The Military Revolution and Political Change: Origins of Democracy and Autocracy in Early Modern Europe* (Princeton, NJ: Princeton University Press, 1992), 84–112. See also H. M. Scott, *The Emergence of the Eastern Powers, 1756–1775* (Cambridge: Cambridge University Press, 2001), 20–23. The paragraphs that follow draw on Downing, *Military Revolution*; Scott, *Emergence of the Eastern Powers*; Christopher M. Clark, *Iron Kingdom: The Rise and Downfall of Prussia, 1600–1947* (Cambridge, MA: Belknap Press of Harvard University, 2006); Philip G. Dwyer, ed., *The Rise of Prussia, 1700–1830* (London: Routledge, 2000); Sidney B. Fay and Klaus Epstein, *The Rise of Brandenburg-Prussia to 1786* (New York: Holt, Rinehart and Winston, 1964).

2. Downing, *Military Revolution*, 112.

3. While the degree to which Prussia was militarized in the eighteenth century has become a subject of historical debate, "the figures," as one historian puts it, "speak for themselves." See Dwyer, *Rise of Prussia*; Rodney Gothelf, "Frederick William I and the Beginnings of Prussian

Absolutism, 1713–1740," in *The Rise of Prussia 1700–1830*, ed. Philip G. Dwyer (London: Routledge, 2000).

4. Reed Browning, *The War of the Austrian Succession* (New York: St. Martin's Press, 1995), 24.

5. See Michael Hochedlinger, "The Habsburg Monarchy: From 'Military-Fiscal State' to 'Militarization,'" in *The Fiscal Military State in Eighteenth-Century Europe: Essays in Honour of P.G.M. Dickson*, ed. Christopher Storrs (Farnham, UK: Ashgate Publishing Company, 2009), 63–65.

6. Gothelf, "Frederick William I," 35.

7. Scott, *Emergence of the Eastern Powers*, 20.

8. Browning, *War of the Austrian Succession*, 20.

9. Alfred Ritter von Arneth, *Geschichte Maria Theresia's* (Vienna: W. Braumüller, 1877), 2:137; Browning, *War of the Austrian Succession*, 42.

10. Michael Hochedlinger, *Austria's Wars of Emergence, 1683–1797* (New York: Routledge, 2013), 125.

11. Clark, *Iron Kingdom*, 191.

12. Charles W. Ingrao, *In Quest and Crisis: Emperor Joseph I and the Habsburg Monarchy* (West Lafayette, IN: Purdue University Press, 1979), 38.

13. For a modern biographical treatment of Frederick II, see Tim C. W. Blanning, *Frederick the Great: King of Prussia* (New York: Random House, 2016).

14. Ibid., 401.

15. Browning, *War of the Austrian Succession*, 20.

16. For English-language accounts of Maria Theresa's life and reign, see Edward Crankshaw, *Maria Theresa* (London: Longman, 1969); Derek Beales, *Joseph II*, vol. 1, *In the Shadow of Maria Theresa, 1741–1780* (Cambridge: Cambridge University Press, 1987); P. G. M. Dickson, *Finance and Government under Maria Theresia, 1740–1780*, 2 vols. (Oxford: Clarendon Press, 1987); Christopher Duffy, *The Army of Maria Theresa: The Armed Forces of Imperial Austria, 1740–1780* (New York: Hippocrene Books, 1977); Karl A. Roider Jr., *Maria Theresa* (Upper Saddle River, NJ: Prentice Hall, 1973).

17. Beales, *Joseph II*, 24.

18. This was technically a series of separate wars, the First and Second Silesian Wars, and the fighting that followed the latter in Italy. For the sake of simplicity, I will refer to them collectively as the War of the Austrian Succession.

19. Quoted in Richard Bassett, *For God and Kaiser: The Imperial Austrian Army, 1619–1918* (New Haven, CT: Yale University Press, 2015), 85.

20. Browning, *War of the Austrian Succession*, 66–67.

21. Some modern historians have challenged the long-established notion that the Hungarian nobility succumbed to Maria Theresa's requests through chivalry and romantic charm as opposed to political self-interest. See, for example, László Kontler, *A History of Hungary: Millennium in Central Europe* (Basingstoke, UK: Palgrave Macmillan, 2002), 201–2.

22. Hochedlinger, *Wars of Emergence*, 243, 323.

23. Browning, *War of the Austrian Succession*, 73.

24. Lothar Höbelt, "The Impact of the Rakoczi Rebellion on Habsburg Strategy: Incentives and Opportunity Costs," *War in History* 13, no. 1 (2006): 5.

25. Browning, *War of the Austrian Succession*, 92.

26. Bassett, *God and Kaiser*, 95–100.

27. And. Henderson, *Memoirs of Field Marshal Leopold Count Daun, Translated from a French Manuscript, and Interspersed with Many Curious Anecdotes; Among Which Is a Full and Particular Account of Field Marshal Keith* (London: R. Withy and J. Ryall, 1757), 61.

28. Hans Delbrück, *The Dawn of Modern Warfare: History of the Art of War*, trans. Walter J. Renfroe Jr. (Lincoln: University of Nebraska Press, 1990), 4:281.

29. Quoted in Duffy, *Army of Maria Theresa*, 82.

30. Quoted in Browning, *War of the Austrian Succession*, 95.

31. Arneth, *Geschichte Maria Theresia's*, 2:46.

32. Browning, *War of the Austrian Succession*, 97

33. Quoted in Arneth, *Geschichte Maria Theresia's*, 2:429.

34. Ibid., 429–30.

35. Thomas M. Barker, *The Military Intellectual and Battle: Raimondo Montecuccoli and the Thirty Years War* (Albany: State University of New York Press, 1975), 61.

36. Archer Jones, *The Art of War in the Western World* (Champaign: University of Illinois Press, 1987), 676–77.

37. Hochedlinger, *Wars of Emergence*, 281.

38. Kaunitz was given the title of *Reichsfürst* in 1764 and *Erbländischer Fürst* in 1776. His career has been the subject of several books and articles in English. The sections that follow draw on Franz A. J. Szabo, *Kaunitz and Enlightened Absolutism, 1753–1780* (Cambridge: Cambridge University Press, 1994); Scott, *Emergence of the Eastern Powers*. See also Harvey L. Dyck, "Pondering the Russian Fact: Kaunitz and the Catherinian Empire in the 1770s," *Canadian Slavonic Papers / Revue Canadienne des Slavistes* 22, no. 4 (1980): 451–69; Saul K. Padover, "'Prince Kaunitz' Résumé of His Eastern Policy, 1763–71," *Journal of Modern History* 5, no. 3 (1933): 352–65. In German, and especially for the earlier phases of Kaunitz's life up to 1753, see Grete Klingenstein, *Der Aufstieg des Hauses Kaunitz: Studien zur Herkunft und Bildung des Staatskanzlers Wenzel Anton* (Göttingen: Vandenhoeck and Ruprecht, 1975).

39. Franz A. J. Szabo, "Prince Kaunitz and the Balance of Power," *International History Review* 1, no. 3 (1979): 400.

40. Duffy, *Army of Maria Theresa*, 20.

41. Browning, *War of the Austrian Succession*, 257.

42. Herbert H. Kaplan, *Russia and the Outbreak of the Seven Years' War* (Berkeley: University of California Press, 1968), 122.

43. Browning, *War of the Austrian Succession*, 203–4.

44. Ibid., 227.

45. The reforms undertaken by Maria Theresa and expanded on by Joseph II are too numerous to be properly dealt with here. For the authoritative source, see Dickson, *Finance and Government*. For a good primer on the domestic aspects of these reforms, see Szabo, *Kaunitz and Enlightened Absolutism*.

46. Pieter M. Judson, *The Habsburg Empire: A New History* (Cambridge, MA: Belknap Press of Harvard University, 2016), 28.

47. Ibid., 35–36.

48. Hochedlinger, "Habsburg Monarchy," 55–56.

49. For a detailed look at Maria Theresa's military reforms, see Duffy, *Army of Maria Theresa*. For a more recent, well-researched, and enjoyably readable account, see Bassett, *God and Kaiser*, 110–22; Franz A. J. Szabo, *The Seven Years War in Europe, 1756–1763* (London: Routledge, 2007), 25–29.

50. See Bassett, *God and Kaiser*, 122; Hochedlinger, *Wars of Emergence*, 272.

51. Judson, *Habsburg Empire*, 46.

52. Duffy, *Army of Maria Theresa*, 84.

53. Szabo, *Seven Years War*, 25; Bassett, *God and Kaiser*, 110.

54. Duffy, *Army of Maria Theresa*, 76–77.

55. Ibid., 80.

56. Ibid., 105–6.

57. Ibid., 24.

58. Ibid., 108; Bassett, *God and Kaiser*, 110.

59. Bassett, *God and Kaiser*, 105.

60. Quoted in ibid., 147.

61. Arneth, *Geschichte Maria Theresia's*, 5:170–72.

62. There has been considerable debate about whether Frederick's opening moves, while operationally offensive, were motivated by the defensive strategic calculation of forestalling an imminent attack by Austria or merely was a continuation of Prussian territorial aggression from the previous war. For the best modern English-language source for navigating these questions and understanding the Seven Years' War more generally, see Szabo, *Seven Years War*.

63. Ibid., 36–37.

64. Blanning, *Frederick the Great*, 224.

65. Quoted in Duffy, *Army of Maria Theresa*, 173.

66. Ibid., 193.

67. Delbrück, *Dawn of Modern Warfare*, 284–85.

68. Quoted in ibid., 353–54.

69. Austrian decision-making bodies of this period are often confused in the secondary literature. For an impressively lucid description, see Szabo, *Kaunitz and Enlightened Absolutism*, 51–52.

70. Szabo, *Seven Years War*, 28; Bassett, *God and Kaiser*, 143.

71. See Hubert Zeinar, *Geschichte des österreichischen Generalstabes* (Vienna: Böhlau, 2006), 180–81; Duffy, *Army of Maria Theresa*, 135.

72. E. Schröder, *Friedrich der Grosse in Seinen Schriften* (Leipzig: Johann Friedrich Hartknoch, 1875), 1:271–72. See also Zeinar, *Geschichte des österreichischen Generalstabes*, 137–39.

73. For a discussion of the military service of the Daun family, see Thomas Mack Barker, "Military Nobility: The Daun Family and the Evolution of the Austrian Officer Corps," in *East Central European Society and War in the Pre-Revolutionary Eighteenth Century*, ed. Gunther E. Rothenberg, Béla K. Király, and Peter F. Sugar (New York: Columbia University Press, 1982).

74. Henderson, *Memoirs of Field Marshal Leopold Count Daun*, 6, 7.

75. For a description of Kolin, see Szabo, *Seven Years War*, 64–67.

76. Ibid., 201.

77. Quoted in Duffy, *Army of Maria Theresa*, 144.

78. Quoted in Christopher Duffy, "The Seven Years' War as a Limited War," in *East Central European Society and War in the Pre-Revolutionary Eighteenth Century*, ed. Gunther E. Rothenberg, Béla K. Király, and Peter F. Sugar (New York: Columbus University Press, 1982), 73–74.

79. Delbrück, *Dawn of Modern Warfare*, 357.

80. Quoted in bid., 310.

81. For the best sources on Joseph II in English, see Tim C. W. Blanning, *Joseph II* (London: Pearson Educational Limited, 1994); Tim C. W. Blanning, *Joseph II and Enlightened Despotism* (Upper Saddle River, NJ: Prentice Hall, 1970); Beales, *Joseph II*.

82. "Si vis pacem para bellum," Mem. 2/20, KA, Vienna.

83. Heinrich Blasek, *Beiträge zur Geschichte der K. U. K. Genie-waffe: Nach den vom K. U. K. Obersten des Genie-Stabes, Im Auftrage des K. U. K. Reichs-Kriegs-Ministeriums zusammengestellt und bearbeitet* (Vienna: L. W. Seidel und Sohn, 1898), vol. 1, part 2, 737.

84. Minutes of the Conferences of March 7, 10, and 14, 1767, KA, Vienna.

85. Beales, *Joseph II*, 189.

86. Quoted in ibid.

87. Maria Theresa to Joseph II, March 14, 1778, in Karl Schneider, "Aus dem Briefwechsel Maria Theresias mit Josef II," in *Aus Österreichs Vergangenheit: Quellenbücher zur österreichischen Geschichte No. 11*, ed. Karl Schneider (Vienna: Schulwissenschaftlicher Verlag, 1917), 34–35.

88. Matthew Z. Mayer, "The Price for Austria's Security: Part II. Leopold II, the Prussian Threat, and the Peace of Sistova, 1790–1791," *International History Review* 26, no. 2 (September 2004): 493.

89. Maria Theresa to Joseph II, September 26, 1778, in Schneider, "Aus dem Briefwechsel Maria Theresias," 95.

90. Lacy memorandum on forts, attached to Minutes of the Conferences of March 7, 10 and 14, 1767, KA, Vienna.

91. "Si vis pacem para bellum," Mem. 2/20, KA, Vienna.

92. "Organization of a Reliable Defense Strategy," Minutes of the Conferences of March 7, 10, and 14, 1767, KA, Vienna.

93. Christopher Duffy, *The Fortress in the Age of Vauban and Frederick the Great, 1660–1789* (London: Routledge and Kegan Paul, 1985), 132–33.

94. Quoted in Duffy, *Fortress*, 134.

95. Ibid., 132.

96. See, for example, Gunther E. Rothenberg, *Napoleon's Great Adversary: Archduke Charles and the Austrian Army, 1792–1814* (Boston: De Capo Press, 1995), 36; Manfried Rauchensteiner, "The Development of War Theories in Austria at the End of the Eighteenth Century," in *East Central European Society and War in the Pre-Revolutionary Eighteenth Century*, ed. Gunther E. Rothenberg, Béla K. Király, and Peter F. Sugar (New York: Columbia University Press, 1982), 75–82.

97. Carl von Clausewitz, *On War*, trans. Michael Eliot Howard and Peter Paret (Princeton, NJ: Princeton University Press, 1989), 432.

98. Günter Brüning, "Militär-Strategie Österreichs in der Zeit Kaiser Franz II (I)" (PhD diss., Westfälische Wilhelms-Universität Münster, 1983), 273.

99. Duffy, *Army of Maria Theresa*, 144; Lacy memorandum on forts.

100. "Organization of a Reliable Defense Strategy."

101. Franz Kinsky, *Über Emplacement der Festungen: Erster Nachtrag zu den Elementar Begriffen* (Vienna: Adam und Kompagnie, 1790), 19–20.

102. "Organization of a Reliable Defense Strategy."

103. Blasek, *Beiträge zur Geschichte der K. U. K. Genie-waffe*, 724, 737.

104. Lacy, "Combined Defense Plan for the Kingdom of Bohemia," in Oskar Criste, *Kriege unter Kaiser Josef II. Nach den Feldakten und anderen authentischen Quellen bearbeitet in der kriegsgeschichtlichen Abteilung des k. und k. Kriegsarchivs* (Vienna: Verlag von L. W. Seidel und Sohn, 1904), 260–62.

105. Ibid.

106. J. Nosinich and L. Wiener, *Kaiser Josef II. als Staatsmann und Feldherr. Österreichs Politik und Kriege in den Jahren 1763 bis 1790*, compiled in the K. K. Kriegs-Archive (Vienna: L. W. Seidel und Sohn, 1885), 129.

107. Delbrück, *Dawn of Modern Warfare*, 362–63.

Chapter 7. *Teufelfranzosen:* France and the Western Frontier

1. For a description of the early fruits of the military revolution in France compared to other European states, see Brian M. Downing, *The Military Revolution and Political Change: Origins of Democracy and Autocracy in Early Modern Europe* (Princeton, NJ: Princeton University Press, 1992), 113–39.

2. There is an abundant secondary literature detailing the rise of France as a Great Power and its early competitive advantages vis-à-vis other European states. See, for example, John A. Lynn, *The Wars of Louis XIV, 1667–1714* (London: Routledge, 1999).

3. Charles W. Ingrao, *In Quest and Crisis: Emperor Joseph I and the Habsburg Monarchy* (West Lafayette, IN: Purdue University Press, 1979), 28.

4. Von Aresin, *Festungsviereck von Ober-Italien, seine Bedeutung für Deutschland, die Schweiz und das Machtgleichgewicht von Europa* (Vienna: kaiserlich-königlichen Hof- und Staatsdruckerei, 1860), 3.

5. G. Venturini, *Kritische Übersicht des letzten und merkwürdigsten Feldzugs im achtzehnten Jahrhundert* (Leipzig: Johann Conrad Hinrichs, 1802), 1, 5.

6. J. E. Kaufmann and H. E. Kaufmann, *The Forts and Fortifications of Europe, 1815–1945: The Central States: Germany, Austria-Hungary, and Czechoslovakia* (Barnsley, UK: Pen and Sword Military, 2014), 177.

7. Ingrao, *Quest and Crisis*, 31.

8. Joachim Whaley, *Germany and the Holy Roman Empire* (Oxford: Oxford University Press, 2011), 118.

9. Ingrao, *Quest and Crisis*, 32.

10. Ludwig Bittner, *Chronologisches Verzeichnis der Österreichischen Staatsverträge* (Vienna: A Holzhausen, 1970), 119–20. See also Whaley, *Germany*, 114; Michael Hochedlinger, *Austria's Wars of Emergence, 1683–1797* (New York: Routledge, 2013), 52.

11. Winfried Dotzauer, *Die deutschen Reichskreise, 1383–1806: Geschichte und Aktenedition* (Stuttgart: F. Steiner, 1998), 286–87.

12. Reed Browning, *The War of the Austrian Succession* (New York: St. Martin's Press, 1995), 99.

13. Ingrao, *Quest and Crisis*, 55.

14. Prince Eugene of Savoy, "Memoirs of Prince Eugene of Savoy," in *Eugene of Savoy: Marlborough's Great Military Partner*, ed. Alexander Innes Shand, trans. William Mudford (London: Leonaur Ltd., 2014), 26.

15. Hochedlinger, *Wars of Emergence*, 50, 72.

16. Ibid., 55.

17. Eugene, "Memoirs," 95, 99. See also Christopher Duffy, *The Fortress in the Age of Vauban and Frederick the Great, 1660–1789* (London: Routledge and Kegan Paul, 1985), 24.

18. Ingrao, *Quest and Crisis*, 65.

19. Duffy, *Fortress*, 45.

20. Ibid., 19–24.

21. Heinrich Blasek, *Beiträge zur Geschichte der K. U. K. Genie-waffe: Nach den vom K. U. K. Obersten des Genie-Stabes, Im Auftrage des K. U. K. Reichs-Kriegs-Ministeriums zusammengestellt und bearbeitet* (Vienna: L. W. Seidel und Sohn, 1898), vol. 1, part 2, 714–15, 731.

22. Duffy, *Fortress*, 19–20.

23. Ibid.

24. Quoted in Alan Palmer, *Metternich* (London: History Book Club, 1972), 155–56.

25. Ingrao, *Quest and Crisis*, 4.

26. Hans Delbrück, *The Dawn of Modern Warfare: History of the Art of War*, trans. Walter J. Renfroe Jr., vol. 4 (Lincoln: University of Nebraska Press, 1990), 396.

27. Ibid., 423.

28. B. H. Liddell Hart, *Strategy* (New York: Meridian, 1991), 99.

29. For an account of events in the German states during this period, see Enno E. Kraehe, *Metternich's German Policy, Volume I: The Contest with Napoleon, 1799–1814* (Princeton, NJ: Princeton University Press, 1963).

30. Gunther E. Rothenberg, *Napoleon's Great Adversary: Archduke Charles and the Austrian Army, 1792–1814* (Boston: De Capo Press, 1995), 65.

31. Clemens Wenzel Lothar Metternich, *Memoirs of Prince Metternich*, ed. Prince Richard Metternich (1880; repr., London: Forgotten Books, 2012), 74.

32. Rothenberg, *Napoleon's Great Adversary*, 132.

33. Palmer, *Metternich*, 57.

34. Quoted in ibid., 56.

35. Alfred Kraus, supplement to *1805: Der Feldzug von Ulm* (Vienna: L. W. Seidel und Sohn, 1912), 9.

36. Ibid., 16–17.

37. Rothenberg, *Napoleon's Great Adversary*, 91.

38. Ibid., 132.

39. Eberhard Mayerhoffer von Vedropolje, *Krieg 1809* (Vienna: L. W. Seidel und Sohn, 1907), 61.

40. Ibid.

41. For a reproduction in full of the memorandum, see Adolf Beer, *Zehn Jahre Österreichischer Politik, 1801–1810* (Leipzig: F. A. Brockhaus, 1877), 527.

42. For a reproduction in full of the memorandum, see Richard Clemens Wenzel Lothar Metternich, ed., *Memoirs of Prince Metternich, 1773–1815* (New York: H. Fertig, 1880), 2:301–8. With the benefit of hindsight, Metternich would later imply in his memoirs that he had reser-

vations about the timing of the 1809 campaign on the grounds that Russia would be slow to help and any popular spirit once stoked would "turn, not against Napoleon but against Austria." Metternich, *Memoirs*, 390.

43. This figure includes 300,000 regulars and 250,000 militia. See Palmer, *Metternich*, 64.

44. From 1822 on, Charles would also carry the title Duke of Teschen. Outside occasional references in the military-strategic literature, Charles has not received much attention in English-language sources. For the best guide to his military career, see Rothenberg, *Napoleon's Great Adversary*. See also Lee W. Eysturlid, *The Formative Influences, Theories, and Campaigns of the Archduke Carl* (Westport, CT: Greenwood Press, 2000). In German, see Helmut Hertenberger and Franz Wiltschek, *Erzherzog Karl: der Sieger von Aspern* (Graz: Styria, 1983); Oskar Criste, *Erzherzog Carl von Österreich*, 3 vols. (Vienna: W. Braumüller, 1912).

45. Rothenberg, *Napoleon's Great Adversary*, 162–63.

46. AFA Deutschland, Hauptarmee XIII, F13, KA, Vienna For a discussion of this memo, see Rothenburg, *Napoleon's Greatest Enemy*, 189.

47. AFA Deutschland.

48. Memorandum from Wimpffen, 1469 AFA Deutschland, Hauptarmee XIII (A) (1–46), F/13–17, KA, Vienna.

49. Quoted in Rothenberg, *Napoleon's Great Adversary*, 188–89.

50. Delbrück, *Dawn of Modern Warfare*, 435.

51. Quoted in Harold Nicolson, *The Congress of Vienna: A Study in Allied Unity, 1812–1822* (New York: Harcourt, Brace and Company, 1946), 41.

52. For a superbly written recent account of the 1813–14 campaign, see Michael V. Leggiere, *The Fall of Napoleon: Volume 1, The Allied Invasion of France, 1813–1814* (New York: Cambridge University Press, 2007).

53. Rothenberg, *Napoleon's Great Adversary*, 227–28.

54. As Francis directed Charles, "From now on, this directorate with all its branches will be your responsibility entirely. You answer only to me, and we will decide all issues between us. I further expect from you a comprehensive plan for the reorganization and improvement of the military order of the entire monarchy." Quoted in Moritz Elder von Angeli, *Erzherzog Carl von Österreich als Feldherr und Heeresorganisator* 2 (Vienna: Braumüller, 1896), 92–93.

55. Michael V. Leggiere, "Austrian Grand Strategy and the Invasion of France in 1814," in *The Consortium on the Revolutionary Era, 1750–1850*, ed. Frederick C. Schneid and Jack Richard Censer (High Point, NC: High Point University, 2007), 322–31. Leggiere argues persuasively that Habsburg strategy of this period was preoccupied with time management.

56. Metternich, *Memoirs*, 167.

57. Paul W. Schroeder, *The Transformation of European Politics, 1763–1848* (Oxford: Oxford University Press, 1994), 472.

58. Rothenberg, *Napoleon's Great Adversary*, 229.

59. Johann Joseph Wenzel Radetzky von Radetz, *Operationsentwurf* (October 5, 1813), in *Denkschriften militärisch-politischen Inhalts aus dem Handschriftlichen Nachlass des k.k. österreichischen Feldmarschalls Grafen Radetzky* (Stuttgart: J. G. Cotta'scher Verlag, 1858), 214–25.

60. Delbrück, *Dawn of Modern Warfare*, 438.

61. Quoted in Henry A. Kissinger, *A World Restored: Metternich, Castlereagh, and the Problems of Peace, 1812–22* (Boston: Houghton Mifflin, 1957), 18.

62. Leggiere argues that Metternich's and Schwarzenberg's strategies delayed the invasion for two months, and by giving Napoleon time to regroup, an additional ten weeks—a total of four and half months. See Leggiere, "Austrian Grand Strategy," 330–31.

63. Barbara Jelavich, *The Habsburg Empire in European Affairs, 1814–1918* (Hamden, CT: Archon Books, 1975), 18.

64. For the best source for Metternich's German diplomacy and creation of the Bund, and how it differed from Prussia's plans, see Enno E. Kraehe, *Metternich's German Policy, Volume II: The Congress of Vienna, 1814–1815* (Princeton, NJ: Princeton University Press, 1963). See also Schroeder, *Transformation of European Politics,* 567.

65. Adalbert Daniel Hermann, *Deutschland nach seinen physischen und politischen Verhältnissen* (Leipzig: Fues, 1870), 2:57.

66. Christian Gottfried Daniel Stein, *Handbuch der Geographie und Statistik nach den neuesten Ansichten für die gebildeten Stände, Gymnasien und Schulen* (Leipzig: J. C. Hinrichs, 1820), 262.

67. See Jürgen Angelow, *Von Wien nach Königgrätz: Die Sicherheitspolitk des Deutschen Bundes im europäischen Gleichgewicht 1815–1866* (Munich: De Gruyter Oldenbourg, 1996); Carl Wenceslaus von Rotteck and Carl Theodor Welcker, *Staats-Lexikon oder Encyklopädie der Staatswissenschaften in Verbindung mit vielen der angesehensten Publicisten Deutschlands* (Altona: Johann Friedrich Hammerlich, 1856), 3:507–20.

68. Angelow, *Von Wien nach Königgrätz,* 65–71.

Chapter 8. Barricades of Time: Metternich and the Habsburg System at Its Peak

1. The definitive source on the Metternich system is Paul Schroeder, on whose work this chapter draws extensively. For the lead-up to negotiations, major issues at the Congress of Vienna itself, and developments that followed in detail, see Paul W. Schroeder, *The Transformation of European Politics, 1763–1848* (Oxford: Oxford University Press, 1994), chapters 11–13. See also Paul W. Schroeder, *Metternich's Diplomacy at Its Zenith, 1820–1823: Austria and the Congresses of Troppau, Laibach, and Verona* (Austin: University of Texas Press, 1962); Paul W. Schroeder, "Did the Vienna Settlement Rest on a Balance of Power?," in *Systems, Stability, and Statecraft: Essays on the International History of Modern Europe,* ed. David Wetzel, Robert Jervis, and Jack S. Levy (New York: Palgrave Macmillan, 2004), 37–57. For an unsurpassed portrait of the personalities of Metternich and his major negotiating counterparts at the Congress of Vienna, see Henry A. Kissinger, *A World Restored: Metternich, Castlereagh, and the Problems of Peace, 1812–22* (Boston: Houghton Mifflin, 1957). For an incisive analysis of the Metternich system, see Henry A. Kissinger, *Diplomacy* (New York: Simon and Schuster, 1994), 78–102. For a contrast to the work of Bismarck, see Henry A. Kissinger, *World Order* (New York: Penguin Books, 2015), 73–75. For an older and more anecdotal but still highly valuable account, see Harold Nicolson, *The Congress of Vienna: A Study in Allied Unity, 1812–1822* (New York: Harcourt, Brace and Company, 1946). For recent contributions, see David King, *Vienna, 1814: How the Conquerors of Napoleon Made Love, War, and Peace at the Congress of Vienna* (New York: Random House, 2008); Adam Zamoyski, *Rites of Peace: The Fall of Napoleon and the Congress of Vienna* (New York: HarperCollins, 2008).

2. Clemens Wenzel Lothar Metternich, *Memoirs of Prince Metternich*, ed. Prince Richard Metternich (1880; repr., London: Forgotten Books, 2012), 71.

3. Metternich was elevated to the status of prince in 1813. There is a relatively large literature on his life and diplomacy. For primary documents, this chapter draws mainly on Metternich, *Memoirs*. Secondary sources on Metternich are abundant; this chapter utilizes Alan Palmer, *Metternich* (London: History Book Club, 1972); Mack Walker, *Metternich's Europe* (London: Palgrave Macmillan, 1968); Desmond Seward, *Metternich: The First European* (New York: Viking, 1991). Schroeder's various books and articles, many cited above and below, deal with various aspects of Metternich's career.

4. Kaunitz quoted in Richard Bassett, *For God and Kaiser: The Imperial Austrian Army, 1619–1918* (New Haven, CT: Yale University Press, 2015), 146–47; Metternich quoted in ibid., 249–50.

5. Quoted in Kissinger, *World Restored*, 160.

6. Ibid., 156; Christopher Hibbert, *Waterloo: Napoleon's Last Campaign* (Hertfordshire: Wordsworth Editions, 1998), 61–62.

7. Metternich, *Memoirs*, 264; Kaunitz, "Memoire über die Räthlichkeit, Nützlichkeit und Nothwendigkeit ... Russland," HHSA, Vienna.

8. Schroeder, *Transformation*, 578.

9. Metternich, *Memoirs*, 264

10. Schroeder, *Transformation*, 528.

11. Kissinger, *World Restored*, 158.

12. Schroeder, *Transformation*, 578.

13. Metternich, *Memoirs*, 207.

14. Schroeder, *Transformation*, 542.

15. Ibid., 527.

16. Kaunitz, "Reflections on the Concept of the Balance of Power in Europe or: Thoughts on What We Call 'the Balance of Power' in Europe," reproduced in full (in French) in Franz A. J. Szabo, "Prince Kaunitz and the Balance of Power," *International History Review* 1, no. 3 (1979): 399–408.

17. Metternich, *Memoirs*, 37.

18. Palmer, *Metternich*, 200.

19. Schroeder, *Transformation*, 591.

20. Archduke Charles, "Grundsätze der Strategie," in *Erzherzog Karl: Ausgewählte Militärische Schriften*, ed. Freiherr von Waldstätten (Berlin: Richard Wilhelmi, 1882), 61.

21. G. Venturini, *Kritische Übersicht des letzten und merkwürdigsten Feldzugs im achtzehnten Jahrhundert* (Leipzig: Johann Conrad Hinrichs, 1802), 7–8.

22. Alan Sked, *Radetzky: Imperial Victor and Military Genius* (London: I. B. Tauris and Co., 2011), 89.

23. Johann Joseph Wenzel Radetzky von Radetz, "Militärische Betrachtung der Lage Österreichs" (1828), in *Denkschriften militärisch-politischen Inhalts aus dem Handschriftlichen Nachlass des k.k. österreichischen Feldmarschalls Grafen Radetzky* (Stuttgart: J. G. Cotta'scher Verlag, 1858), 423–24, 427.

24. Ibid., 428.

25. Johann Joseph Wenzel Radetzky von Radetz, "Operationen der verbündeten Heere gegen Frankreich, mit besonderer Rücksicht auf die Armee des Oberrheins" (1832), in *Denkschriften militärisch-politischen Inhalts aus dem Handschriftlichen Nachlass des k.k. österreichischen Feldmarschalls Grafen Radetzky* (Stuttgart: J. G. Cotta'scher Verlag, 1858), 479–81. For further indications of his thinking on topography in strategy, see Johann Joseph Wenzel Radetzky von Radetz, "Betrachtungen über die defensiv Fähigkeit Österreichs mit Rücksicht auf seine topographische Lage," Nachlass Radetsky B/1151, 69 (a), 1850, Kriegsarchiv.

26. Radetzky, "Militärische Betrachtung der Lage Österreichs," 423.

27. Sked, *Radetzky*, 92–93.

28. Radetzky, "Militärische Betrachtung der Lage Österreichs," 424.

29. Johnn Joseph Wenzel Radetzky von Radetz, "Gedanken über Festungen" (1827), in *Denkschriften militärisch-politischen Inhalts aus dem Handschriftlichen Nachlass des k.k. österreichischen Feldmarschalls Grafen Radetzky* (Stuttgart: J. G. Cotta'scher Verlag, 1858), 401–4.

30. Antoine-Vincent Arnault, *Memoirs of the Public and Private Life of Napoleon Bonaparte*, trans. W. Hamilton Reid (London: Sherwood, Gilbert and Piper, 1826), 215.

31. Archduke Charles von Habsburg, *Principles of War*, trans. Daniel I. Radakovich (Ann Arbor, MI: Nimble Books, 2009), 10–13.

32. Charles, "Grundsätze der Strategie," 61.

33. Ibid., 10.

34. Habsburg, *Principles of War*, 10.

35. Radetzky, "Gedanken über Festungen," 401.

36. Günter Brüning, "Militär-Strategie Österreichs in der Zeit Kaiser Franz II (I)" (PhD diss., Westfälische Wilhelms-Universität Münster, 1983), 318.

37. Habsburg, *Principles of War*, 12.

38. Radetzky, "Gedanken über Festungen," 402–4.

39. Radetzky, "Militärische Betrachtung der Lage Österreichs," 428.

40. Sked, *Radetzky*, 118.

41. See, for example, Charles, "Verteidigungssystem des Kriegsschauplatzes," in *Militärische Werke* (Vienna: kaiserlich-königlichen Hof- und Staatsdruckerei, 1862); Charles, "Versuch eines Kriegssystems des österreichischen Kaiserstaates" (1855), in *Maximilian Joseph von Österreich-Este, Erzherzog, Festungsplaner, Hochmeister*, ed. Erich Hillbrand and Willibald Rosner (Linz: Wagner, 2013), 36–37.

42. Hillbrand and Rosner, *Maximilian Joseph*, 36–37.

43. Georg von Alten and Hans von Albert, *Handbuch für Heer und Flotte: Enzyklopädie der Kriegswissenschaften und Verwandter Gebiete*, vol. 4 (Vienna: Deutsches Verlangshaus Bong & Co., 1912).

44. J. E. Kaufmann and H. E. Kaufmann, *The Forts and Fortifications of Europe, 1815–1945: The Central States: Germany, Austria-Hungary, and Czechoslovakia* (Barnsley, UK: Pen and Sword Military, 2014), 136.

45. *Denkschrift über die Reichsbefestigung der ehemalige Österreichisch-Ungarische Monarchie*, undated, 55–60, KA, Vienna.

46. Adalbert Daniel Hermann, *Deutschland nach seinen physischen und politischen Verhältnissen* (Leipzig: Fues, 1870), 2:57; Hugo Franz von Brachelli, *Handbuch der Geographie und Statistik für die gebildeten Stände* (Leipzig: Hinrichs, 1861), 262.

47. M. Massari, *Sulla Necessitá delle Fortificazioni per la Difesa Degli Stati in Generale E Dell'Italia in Particolare* (Palermo: Rivista Sicula, 1871), 56.

48. Bartolomeo Malfatti, "Il Quadrilatero, la Valle del Po ed il Trentino," in *Biblioteca Utile* (Milan: Tipografia Internazionale, 1866), 37:9–72.

49. Michael Pammer, "Public Finance in Austria-Hungary, 1820–1913," in *Paying for the Liberal State: The Rise of Public Finance in Nineteenth Century Europe*, ed. Jose Luis Cardoso and Pedro Lains (Cambridge: Cambridge University Press, 2010), 167.

50. Gunther E. Rothenberg, "The Austrian Army in the Age of Metternich," *Journal of Modern History* 40, no. 2 (1968): 156.

51. Archer Jones, *The Art of War in the Western World* (Champaign: University of Illinois Press, 1987), 693–94.

52. Ibid.

53. Rothenberg, "Austrian Army," 163; Geoffrey Wawro, *The Austro-Prussian War: Austria's War with Prussia and Italy in 1866* (Cambridge: Cambridge University Press, 1966), 47.

54. Palmer, *Metternich*, 201.

55. The statistics and quotation in this paragraph are from David F. Good, *The Economic Rise of the Habsburg Empire, 1750–1914* (Berkeley: University of California Press, 1984), 45–50.

56. Gunther E. Rothenberg, *The Army of Francis Joseph* (Lafayette, IN: Purdue University Press, 1999), 48.

57. As one Austrian diplomat was instructed by Vienna, "It is absolutely necessary for us to bring the Italian problem to a speedy end.... We lack the means to wage a war in a sufficiently effective manner and even a battle won would not solve the problem." See Sked, *Radetzky*, 142–43.

58. See István Deák, *The Lawful Revolution: Louis Kossuth and the Hungarians, 1848–1849* (New York: Columbia University Press, 1979).

59. Schroeder, *Transformation*, 77.

60. Quoted in David Wetzel, Robert Jervis, and Jack S. Levy., eds., *Systems, Stability, and Statecraft: Essays on the International History of Modern Europe* (New York: Palgrave Macmillan, 2004), 5–6.

61. Kissinger, *World Restored*, 174.

62. Metternich, *Memoirs*, 253.

Chapter 9. Between Hammer and Anvil: Eclipse of the Habsburg Monarchy

1. See Robert Gilpin, *War and Change in World Politics* (Cambridge: Cambridge University Press, 1981); Paul M. Kennedy, *The Rise and Fall of the Great Powers: Economic Change and Military Conflict from 1500 to 2000* (New York: Random House, 1987).

2. David Good has challenged the standard picture of late nineteenth-century Habsburg economic decline. See David F. Good, *The Economic Rise of the Habsburg Empire, 1750–1914* (Berkeley: University of California Press, 1984).

3. In 1830, Austria ranked fifth in economic strength among Europe's top powers (fourth if Germany is not counted as a whole), and eighty-three years later, on the eve of World War I, it held roughly the same position. See Paul Bairoch, "European Gross National Product, 1800–1975," *Journal of European Economic History* 5 (1976): 282.

4. See Aviel Roshwald, *Ethnic Nationalism and the Fall of Empires: Central Europe, Russia, and the Middle East, 1914–1923* (London: Routledge, 2001).

5. Timothy Snyder has argued persuasively that the Habsburg Monarchy's multiethnic identity was not in itself the key determinant of its collapse and that German as opposed to Slav nationalism played a greater role than is commonly ascribed. See, for example, Timothy Snyder, "Integration, Counter-Integration, Disintegration," in Robert Cooper and Timothy Snyder, "Learning from the Habsburg Experience," *Magazine of the Institut für die Wissenschaften vom Menschen / Institute for Human Sciences* 111 (September 2012–April 2013): 3–4.

6. There is an extensive secondary literature dealing with nineteenth-century Italian political history and Habsburg-Italian relations. For two excellent German-language sources, see Heinrich Benedikt, *Kaiseradler über dem Apennin: Die Österreicher in Italien 1700 bis 1866* (Vienna: Herold, 1964); Hans Kramer, *Österreich und das Risorgimento* (Vienna: Bergland, 1963). For English-language sources that were consulted for this chapter, see Lucy Riall, *Risorgimento: The History of Italy from Napoleon to Nation State* (New York: Palgrave, 2009); Lucy Riall, *The Italian Risorgimento* (London: Routledge, 1994); Derek Beales and Eugenio F. Biagini, *The Risorgimento and the Unification of Italy*, 2nd ed. (London: Routledge, 2002); William A. Jenkins, *Francis Joseph and the Italians, 1849–1859* (Charlottesville: University of Virginia Press, 1978); Geoffrey Wawro, "Austria versus the Risorgimento: A New Look at Austria's Italian Strategy in the 1860s," *European History Quarterly* 26 (1996): 7–29; John Gooch, *Army, State, and Society in Italy, 1870–1915* (London: Macmillan, 1989); Frank J. Coppa, *The Origins of the Wars of Italian Independence* (London: Longman, 1992); Denis Mack Smith, *Vittorio Emanuele, Cavour, and the Risorgimento* (London: Oxford University Press, 1971).

7. Paul W. Schroeder, *The Transformation of European Politics, 1763–1848* (Oxford: Oxford University Press, 1994), 566.

8. Alan Palmer, *Metternich* (London: History Book Club, 1972), 155–56.

9. Metternich to Emperor Francis, December 29, 1815, quoted in ibid., 157.

10. Schroeder, *Transformation*, 567.

11. Geoffrey Wawro, *The Austro-Prussian War: Austria's War with Prussia and Italy in 1866* (Cambridge: Cambridge University Press, 1966), 47.

12. Antonio Gallenga, *Storia Del Piemonte Dai Primi Tempi Alla pace Di Parigi*, Vol. 2 (Turin: Eredi Botta, 1856).

13. He was president of France from 1848 to 1852, and emperor from 1852 to 1870.

14. "Report of Dr. Beda Dudik regarding His Audience by King Wilhelm I of Wurttemberg on October 4, 1859," in *Quellen zur deutschen Politik Österreichs: 1859–1866, Vol. 1—July 1859–November 1861* (Oldenburg: Gerhard Stalling, 1934), 43.

15. A. J. P. Taylor, *The Struggle for Mastery in Europe, 1848–1918* (Harmondsworth, UK: Penguin Books, 1954), 12.

16. Schroeder, *Transformation*, 526.

17. Ibid., 661.

18. For a detailed analysis of the evolution of the Eastern Question from the 1820s to the 1850s, see ibid., 655–61.

19. F. R. Bridge, *The Habsburg Monarchy among the Great Powers, 1815–1918* (Oxford: Berg Publishers, 1994), 52.

20. Paul W. Schroeder, "Bruck versus Buol: The Dispute over Austrian Policy, 1853–55," in *Systems, Stability, and Statecraft: Essays on the International History of Modern Europe*, ed. David Wetzel, Robert Jervis, and Jack S. Levy (New York: Palgrave Macmillan, 2004), 59–76; Taylor, *Struggle for Mastery*, 59.

21. Heinrich Friedjung, *Der Krimkrieg und die Österreichische Politik* (Stuttgart: J. G. Cotta'sche Buchhandlung Nachfolger, 1907), 77. Radetzky in particular was worried that a movement of major troop formations to the east to defend against Russia would expose Italy, the monarchy's most valuable and vulnerable possession, and his life's work (*lebensaufgabe*), to attack by France.

22. Quoted in Schroeder, *Transformation*, 62.

23. Ibid.

24. Norman Rich, *Why the Crimean War?: A Cautionary Tale* (Hanover, NH: University Press of New England, 1985), 120.

25. Friedjung, *Der Krimkrieg*, 98; Gunther E. Rothenberg, *The Army of Francis Joseph* (Lafayette, IN: Purdue University Press, 1999), 50.

26. Rothenberg, *Army of Francis Joseph*, 51.

27. For the finest source on this debate, see Schroeder, "Bruck versus Buol," 59–76. Schroeder argues convincingly that Buol was acting in the best traditions of Austrian eastern policy and had few realistic alternatives to the course he chose. See also Paul W. Schroeder, *Austria, Great Britain, and the Crimean War: The Destruction of the European Concert* (Ithaca, NY: Cornell University Press, 1972). Schroeder's views align with those in Friedjung, *Der Krimkrieg*; Richard Charmatz, *Minister Freiherr von Bruck, der Vorkämpfer Mitteleuropas* (Leipzig: S. Hirzel, 1916). For less favorable appraisals, see Bridge, *Habsburg Monarchy*; Taylor, *Struggle for Mastery*; Rothenberg, *Army of Francis Joseph*.

28. Bridge, *Habsburg Monarchy*, 55.

29. Palmer, *Metternich*, 334–35.

30. The main argument, advanced by Schroeder, is that Russia could no longer "be trusted in a crisis" (*Systems, Stability and Statecraft*, 66). But this is not entirely satisfactory; repeated Russian concessions to Austria in the Crimea crisis, including not least the evacuation of the Danubian Principalities (thus addressing Vienna's chief demand) suggest otherwise. Indeed, the principalities had been occupied intermittently by Russia, with Austrian consent, since 1829, and Russia was willing to compromise over their future status. As Taylor contends, of the four main demands made of Russia by the allies, all those concerning Austria's demands had been met. See Taylor, *Struggle for Mastery*, 65–66.

31. Schroeder, "Bruck versus Buol," 73.

32. Bridge, *Habsburg Monarchy*, 57.

33. Ibid., 58.

34. The Austrians had already begun to give thought to eastern defense during the partitions with Poland, after which the monarchy started to keep larger permanent troop formations here, using Olmütz as a staging post to monitor both Prussian and Russian movements. These preparations, however, paled in comparison to the consideration that Habsburg military planners would have to devote to the Russian theater over the half century following the Crimean War.

35. "Report of Dr. Beda Dudik," 44.

36. Jean Bérenger, *A History of the Habsburg Empire, 1700–1918* (New York: Routledge, 1968), 194.

37. For a discussion of Moltke's career along with the outsize impact he exerted on both Prussia's wars of this period and the development of the modern German military, see Arden Bucholz, *Moltke and the German Wars, 1864–1871* (New York: Palgrave Macmillan, 2001). See also Quintin Barry, *Moltke and His Generals: A Study in Leadership* (Solihull, UK: Helion and Company, 2015); Daniel J. Hughes, ed., *Moltke on the Art of War: Selected Writings* (Toronto: Presidio Press, 1993).

38. Max Boot, *War Made New: Technology, Warfare, and the Course of History, 1500 to Today* (New York: Gotham Books, 2006), 123.

39. Carl von Clausewitz, *On War*, trans. Michael Eliot Howard and Peter Paret (Princeton, NJ: Princeton University Press, 1989), 75–76.

40. Johann Joseph Wenzel Radetzky von Radetz, "Militärische Betrachtung der Lage Österreichs" (1828), in *Denkschriften militärisch-politischen Inhalts aus dem Handschriftlichen Nachlass des k.k. österreichischen Feldmarschalls Grafen Radetzky* (Stuttgart: J. G. Cotta'scher Verlag, 1858), 432.

41. Gordon Alexander Craig, *The Battle of Königgrätz: Prussia's Victory over Austria, 1866* (Philadelphia: Lippincott, 1964), 6.

42. Francis Joseph's life has received surprisingly little attention in English. See John Van der Kiste, *Emperor Francis Joseph: Life, Death, and the Fall of the Hapsburg Empire* (Stroud, UK: Sutton Publishers, 2005); Alan Palmer, *Twilight of the Habsburgs: The Life and Times of Emperor Francis Joseph* (New York: Atlantic Monthly Press, 1998).

43. Michael Pammer, "Public Finance in Austria-Hungary, 1820–1913," in *Paying for the Liberal State: The Rise of Public Finance in Nineteenth Century Europe*, ed. Jose Luis Cardoso and Pedro Lains (Cambridge: Cambridge University Press, 2010), 41.

44. *Stenographische Protokolle des Hauses der Abgeordneten des Reichsrathes*, 61; Sitzung der 2. Session, December 11, 1863, 1396; Pammer, "Public Finance in Austria-Hungary," 142.

45. Geoffrey Wawro, "Inside the Whale: The Tangled Finances of the Austrian Army, 1848–1866," *War in History* 3, no. 1 (1996): 42–65.

46. Rothenberg, *Army of Francis Joseph*, 39.

47. Quoted in ibid., 44.

48. Erich Gabriel, *Die Hand- und Faustfeuerwaffen der habsburgischen Heere* (Vienna: Österreichischer Bundesverlag, 1990), 316. For an excellent series of analyses on the Austrian military of this period, the reasons for its resistance to technological change, and the results of this conservatism on the battlefield, see Wawro's work. See, for example, Geoffrey Wawrow, "An 'Army of Pigs': The Technical, Social, and Political Bases of Austrian Shock Tactics, 1859–1866," *Journal of Military History* 59, no. 3 (1995): 407–33; Wawro, "Inside the Whale."

49. Good, *Economic Rise of the Habsburg Empire*, 63.

50. Gabriel, *Die Hand- und Faustfeuerwaffen*, 356.

51. Wawro, "Army of Pigs," 409, 410, 415.

52. Major-General George McClellan, *The Armies of Europe* (Philadelphia: Lippincott and Co., 1861), 65.

53. Wawro, "Inside the Whale," 46.

54. European State Finance Database; P. G. M. Dickson, *Finance and Government under Maria Theresia, 1740–1780* (Oxford: Clarendon Press, 1987), vol. 2.

55. Wawro, "Inside the Whale," 48.

56. Ibid.

57. Ibid., 46, 51.

58. Extract from a dispatch by Prince Kaunitz, July 12, 1788, SV 145 (Vorträge 1788), HHSA, Vienna.

59. Wawro, "Army of Pigs," 410.

60. Johann Joseph Wenzel Radetzky von Radetz, "Operationen der verbündeten Heere gegen Frankreich, mit besonderer Rücksicht auf die Armee des Oberrheins" (1832), in *Denkschriften militärisch-politischen Inhalts aus dem Handschriftlichen Nachlass des k.k. österreichischen Feldmarschalls Grafen Radetzky* (Stuttgart: J. G. Cotta'scher Verlag, 1858), 479–81; Rothenberg, *Army of Francis Joseph*, 48.

61. Taylor, *Struggle for Mastery*, 38–39.

62. Quoted in Rothenberg, *Army of Francis Joseph*, 60.

63. Ibid., 41.

64. Craig, *Battle of Königgrätz*, 11.

65. Ibid., 11.

66. Quoted in Wawro, "Army of Pigs," 418.

67. Similar structures would be used effectively throughout the twentieth century—in Saint Petersberg (1864), Belfort (1871), Plevna (1877), Port Arthur (1904), Przemyśl (1915), and Verdun (1916).

68. Bartolomeo Malfatti, "Il Quadrilatero, la Valle del Po ed il Trentino," in *Biblioteca Utile* (Milan: Tipografia Internazionale, 1866), 37:57. See also Reports of Committees of the House of Representatives, Second Session of the Thirty-Seventh Congress, vol. 4, no. 86 (1861–62), 320.

69. Heinrich Blasek, *Beiträge zur Geschichte der K. U. K. Genie-waffe: Nach den vom K. U. K. Obersten des Genie-Stabes, Im Auftrage des K. U. K. Reichs-Kriegs-Ministeriums zusammengestellt und bearbeitet* (Vienna: L. W. Seidel und Sohn, 1898), vol. 1, part 2, 737; Christopher Duffy, *The Fortress in the Age of Vauban and Frederick the Great, 1660–1789* (London: Routledge and Kegan Paul, 1985), 131.

70. Johann Joseph Wenzel Radetzky von Radetz, "Über Festungen," in *Denkschriften militärisch-politischen Inhalts aus dem Handschriftlichen Nachlass des k.k. österreichischen Feldmarschalls Grafen Radetzky* (Stuttgart: J. G. Cotta'scher Verlag, 1858), 398–402.

71. *Stenographische Protokolle des Hauses der Abgeordneten des Reichsrathes*, 54. Sitzung der 3. Session, May 3, 1865, 1461.

72. Von Aresin, *Festungsviereck von Ober-Italien, seine Bedeutung für Deutschland, die Schweiz und das Machtgleichgewicht von Europa* (Vienna: kaiserlich-königlichen Hof- und Staatsdruckerei, 1860), 8.

73. Wawro, *Austro-Prussian War*, 30–31.

74. *Stenographische Protokolle des Hauses der Abgeordneten des Reichsrathes*, 53. Sitzung der 3. Session, May 2, 1865, 1445. See also Wawro, "Inside the Whale," 55.

75. John Dredger argues in a well-reasoned analysis that the Austrians placed too much emphasis on fortifications in their planning of this period and spent too much on them, along with the navy, relative to other possible uses. See John Anthony Dredger, "Offensive Spending:

Tactics and Procurement in the Habsburg Military, 1866–1918" (PhD diss., Kansas State University, 2013), 18, 20, 23.

76. In 1865, Austria spent 1.2 million florins (about 0.9 percent) of a 138 million florins defense budget on twenty-two fortresses. Prussia spent 370,000 talers (about 0.85 percent) of a 43 million taler defense budget on twenty-seven fortresses. See Robert Millward, *The State and Business in the Major Powers: An Economic History, 1815–1939* (London: Routledge, 2013), 32; *Stenographische Protokolle des Hauses der Abgeordneten des Reichsrathes*, 53, 1445; Wawro, "Inside the Whale," 55.

77. Good, *Economic Rise of the Habsburg Empire*, 66.

78. Ibid., 99–100.

79. Henry A. Kissinger, *A World Restored: Metternich, Castlereagh, and the Problems of Peace, 1812–22* (Boston: Houghton Mifflin, 1957), 25.

80. Taylor, *Struggle for Mastery*, 111.

81. Ibid., 104.

82. Ramming, "Strategische Begründung der Dispositionen für die auf Verona gestütze k. k. Armee," June 4, 1859, in Supplement 17, *Der Krieg in Italien 1859* (Vienna: Verlag des k. k. Generalstabes, 1876), 63.

83. The work of Bascom Barry Hayes is the best English-language source for understanding the various German political and economic integration schemes of the nineteenth century. The paragraphs that follow are based on Bascom Barry Hayes, *Bismarck and Mitteleuropa* (Madison, NJ: Fairleigh Dickinson University Press, 1994), especially 63–67. See also Good, *Economic Rise of the Habsburg Empire*, 74–95.

84. Good, *Economic Rise of the Habsburg Empire*, 80.

85. Hayes, *Bismarck and Mitteleuropa*, 63.

86. Good, *Economic Rise of the Habsburg Empire*, 80–81; Hayes, *Bismarck and Mitteleuropa*, 64–65.

87. See Taylor, *Struggle for Mastery*, 26; Schroeder, "Bruck versus Buol," 73–74.

88. There is an extensive secondary literature on Bismarck's career. For a riveting, if unabashedly antagonistic, biography, see A. J. P. Taylor, *Bismarck: The Man and the Statesman* (London: Hamish Hamilton, 1955). See also Lothar Gall, *Bismarck: The White Revolutionary, 1871–1898*, 2 vols. (London: Routledge, 1990); Jonathan Steinberg, *Bismarck: A Life* (Oxford: Oxford University Press, 2011); Christopher M. Clark, *Iron Kingdom: The Rise and Downfall of Prussia, 1600–1947* (Cambridge, MA: Belknap Press of Harvard University, 2006).

89. Taylor, *Struggle for Mastery*, 26.

90. Quoted in Taylor, *Bismarck*, 38.

91. Bismarck's political views went through several phases during this period, becoming gradually more comfortable with the idea of German unification, on a national basis, in exclusion of Austria.

92. Much has been written about the short Danish War of 1864. For detailed coverage of the political background and military campaign, see Michael Embree, *Bismarck's First War: The Campaign of Schleswig and Jutland, 1864* (Solihull, UK: Helicon and Company, 2005). See also William Carr, *The Origins of the Wars of German Unification* (London: Longman, 1991); J. C. Clardy, "Austrian Foreign Policy during the Schleswig-Holstein Crisis of 1864," *Diplomacy and Statecraft* 2, no. 2 (1991): 254–69; Taylor, *Struggle for Mastery*, 142–55.

93. For an analysis of the differing lessons learned by the Austrian and Prussian militaries in the Danish War, see Wawro, "Army of Pigs," especially 424–31.

94. Private Message from Count Mensdorff to Count Moritz Esterhazy, September 13, 1865, in *Quellen zur deutschen Politik Österreichs: 1859–1866, Vol. 5—August 1865–August 1866* (Oldenburg: Gerhard Stalling, 1934), 52.

95. Report of Freiherrn von Werner, Gastein, September 1, 1865, in *Quellen zur deutschen Politik Österreichs: 1859–1866, Vol. 5—August 1865–August 1866* (Oldenburg: Gerhard Stalling, 1934), 43.

96. Report of Legation Council's Proceedings, Karlsruhe, February 7, 1866, in *Quellen zur deutschen Politik Österreichs: 1859–1866, Vol. 5—August 1865–August 1866* (Oldenburg: Gerhard Stalling, 1934), 183–84.

97. Report of Count Blome, Munich, March 26, 1866, in in *Quellen zur deutschen Politik Österreichs: 1859–1866, Vol. 5—August 1865–August 1866* (Oldenburg: Gerhard Stalling, 1934), 366.

98. Hayes, *Bismarck and Mitteleuropa*, 113–14.

99. Report of Legation Council's Proceedings," Karlsruhe, March 29, 1866, in *Quellen zur deutschen Politik Österreichs: 1859–1866, Vol. 5—August 1865–August 1866* (Oldenburg: Gerhard Stalling, 1934), 385–86.

100. Report of Count Bray to the Freiherrn von der Pfordten, Vienna, April 18, 1866, in *Quellen zur deutschen Politik Österreichs: 1859–1866, Vol. 5—August 1865–August 1866* (Oldenburg: Gerhard Stalling, 1934), 505.

101. Private letter from Mr. von Wydenburgk to Freiherrn von Biegeleben, Munich, May 5, 1866, in *Quellen zur deutschen Politik Österreichs: 1859–1866, Vol. 5—August 1865–August 1866* (Oldenburg: Gerhard Stalling, 1934), 607.

102. Report of Count Bray to King Ludwig II of Bavaria, Vienna, April 3, 1866, in *Quellen zur deutschen Politik Österreichs: 1859–1866, Vol. 5—August 1865–August 1866* (Oldenburg: Gerhard Stalling, 1934), 419.

103. Protocol of the Council of Ministers, Vienna, April 21, 1866, in *Quellen zur deutschen Politik Österreichs: 1859–1866, Vol. 5—August 1865–August 1866*, 524.

104. There were actually two, Vienna via Breslau to Dresden, and Vienna via Prague and Olmütz, but the proximity of the former to the war zone made it unusable. See Arthur L. Wagner, *The Campaign of Königgrätz: A Study of the Austro-Prussian Conflict in the Light of the American Civil War* (Kansas City: Hudson-Kimberly, 1899), 36–37.

105. Craig, *Battle of Königgrätz*, 17.

106. Wagner, *Campaign of Königgrätz*, 62.

107. Quoted in Wawro, *Austro-Prussian War*, 208.

108. *Österreichs Kämpfe Im Jahre 1866* (Vienna: Kriegsarchiv, 1868), 3:385.

109. Unit-level tactics under Radetzky and Albrecht were offensive and column based; the emphasis here is theater-level strategy.

110. Jean Bérenger, *A History of the Habsburg Empire, 1700–1918* (New York: Routledge, 1968), 207.

111. Report of Freiherrn von Kübeck," Augsburg, July 25, 1866, in *Quellen zur deutschen Politik Österreichs: 1859–1866, Vol. 5—August 1865–August 1866* (Oldenburg: Gerhard Stalling, 1934), 979.

112. J. E. Kaufmann and H. E. Kaufmann, *The Forts and Fortifications of Europe, 1815–1945: The Central States: Germany, Austria-Hungary, and Czechoslovakia* (Barnsley, UK: Pen and Sword Military, 2014), 140–71.

113. Good, *Economic Rise of the Habsburg Empire*, 88–89.

114. Thomas Francis Huertas, *Economic Growth and Economic Policy in a Multinational Setting: The Habsburg Monarchy, 1841–1865* (Chicago: University of Chicago, 1977), 45.

Chapter 10. The Habsburg Legacy: Taming Chaos

1. Quoted in Oskar Regele, *Der Österreichische Hofkriegsrat, 1556–1848* (Vienna: Österreichischen Staatsdruckerei, 1949), 66.

2. Such an option was occasionally considered. See F. R. Bridge, *The Habsburg Monarchy among the Great Powers, 1815–1918* (Oxford: Berg Publishers, 1994), 2.

3. The statement is surprisingly close to Gaddis's "calculated relationship between means and large ends." Quoted in Saul K. Padover, "Prince Kaunitz' Résumé of His Eastern Policy, 1763–71," *Journal of Modern History* 5, no. 3 (1933): 352.

4. See the discussion in Paul W. Schroeder, *The Transformation of European Politics, 1763–1848* (Oxford: Oxford University Press, 1994), 33.

5. There is a substantial theoretical literature and debate on the options of "hiding," "transcending," and "balancing." See, for example, Thomas Christensen and Jack Snyder, "Chain Gangs and Passed Bucks: Predicting Alliance Patterns in Multipolarity," *International Organization* 44, no. 2 (1990): 137–68; Randall Schweller, *Deadly Imbalances: Tripolarity and Hitler's Strategy of World Conquest* (New York: Columbia University Press, 1998); Joshua B. Spero, *Bridging the European Divide: Middle Power Politics and Regional Security Dilemmas* (Lanham, MD: Rowman and Littlefield, 2004), 20–24; Schroeder, *Transformation*, 32–35.

6. John Darwin, *The Empire Project: The Rise and Fall of the British World-System, 1830–1970* (Cambridge: Cambridge University Press, 2011), 3.

7. Charles W. Ingrao, "Habsburg Strategy and Geopolitics during the Eighteenth Century," in *East Central European Society and War in the Pre-Revolutionary Eighteenth Century*, ed. Gunther E. Rothenberg, Béla K. Király, and Peter F. Sugar (New York: Columbia University Press, 1982), 63.

8. See Paul W. Schroeder, "Historical Reality vs. Neo-realist Theory," *International Security* 19, no. 1 (1994): 108–48.

9. Günter Brüning, "Militär-Strategie Österreichs in der Zeit Kaiser Franz II (I)" (PhD diss., Westfälische Wilhelms-Universität Münster, 1983), 355.

10. As Brüning argues in "Militär-Strategie Österreichs," "The thinking of [Austrian] strategists moved between two poles: One, a more or less extensive adoption of the fundamental ideas of the Prussian school and the second, an almost complete alignment with Austrian tradition that was modified to a large extent through the thinking of the Archduke Charles" (355).

11. See Geoffrey Wawro, *A Mad Catastrophe: The Outbreak of World War I and the Collapse of the Habsburg Empire* (New York: Basic Books, 2014).

12. Henry A. Kissinger, *A World Restored: Metternich, Castlereagh, and the Problems of Peace, 1812–22* (Boston: Houghton Mifflin, 1957), 156; Brüning, "Militär-Strategie Österreichs," 159; Alan Sked, *Radetzky: Imperial Victor and Military Genius* (London: I. B. Tauris and Co., 2011), 118.

13. Franz A. J. Szabo, *Kaunitz and Enlightened Absolutism, 1753–1780* (Cambridge: Cambridge University Press, 1994), 3.

14. David F. Good, *The Economic Rise of the Habsburg Empire, 1750–1914* (Berkeley: University of California Press, 1984), 89–90.

15. For the best rendering of this argument, see Jakub J. Grygiel, *Great Powers and Geopolitical Change* (Baltimore: Johns Hopkins University Press, 2006).

16. See Paul W. Schroeder, "World War I as Galloping Gertie: A Reply to Joachim Remak," in *Systems, Stability, and Statecraft: Essays on the International History of Modern Europe*, ed. David Wetzel, Robert Jervis, and Jack S. Levy (New York: Palgrave Macmillan, 2004), 137–56.

17. Quoted in Bridge, *Habsburg Monarchy*, 2.

Epilogue. Habsburg Lessons

1. Eugene quoted in Nikola Samardžić, "The Peace of Passarowitz, 1718: An Introduction," in *The Peace of Passarowitz, 1718*, ed. Charles W. Ingrao, Nikola Samardžić, and Jovan Pešalj (West Lafayette, IN: Purdue University Press, 2011), 18. Daun quoted in Christopher Duffy, "The Seven Years' War as a Limited War," in *East Central European Society and War in the Pre-Revolutionary Eighteenth Century*, ed. Gunther E. Rothenberg, Béla K. Király, and Peter F. Sugar (New York: Columbus University Press, 1982), 73–74.

2. Archduke Charles von Habsburg, *Principles of War*, trans. Daniel I. Radakovich (Ann Arbor, MI: Nimble Books, 2009), 1.

3. "Si vis pacem para bellum," Mem. 2/20, KA, Vienna.

4. See Kent E. Calder, *Embattled Garrisons: Comparative Base Politics and American Globalism* (Princeton, NJ: Princeton University Press, 2007), 215.

5. For a discussion of the altered meaning of the term "appeasement" since the Second World War, see Paul Kennedy, "The Tradition of Appeasement in British Foreign Policy, 1865–1939," *British Journal of International Studies* 2, no. 3 (1976): 195–215. See also Michael Howard, *The Continental Commitment: The Dilemma of British Defence Policy in the Era of the Two World Wars* (London: Penguin Books, 1972), 79.

6. This aspect of appeasement places it within the literature on strategic deception. See, for example, John Gooch and Amos Perlmutter, eds., *Military Deception and Strategic Surprise!* (New York: Frank Cass and Company, 1982).

7. Ignaz Plener, quoted in Geoffrey Wawro, "Inside the Whale: The Tangled Finances of the Austrian Army, 1848–1866," *War in History* 3, no. 1 (1996): 45.

8. This number includes both wars with external powers and uprisings inside the monarchy or adjacent lands. It counts the War of the Austrian Succession as one conflict, and the revolutionary and Napoleonic Wars as another.

9. George F. Kennan, *Memoirs, 1925–1950* (Boston: Atlantic Monthly Press, 1983), 95.

10. Winston S. Churchill, *The Second World War, Volume 1: The Gathering Storm* (New York: Houghton Mifflin, 1948), 9.

11. For a proper sense of the scale of human tragedy that occurred in central and eastern Europe in the decades following Austria-Hungary's collapse, see Timothy Snyder, *Bloodlands: Europe between Hitler and Stalin* (New York: Basic Books, 2010).

SELECT SOURCES AND BIBLIOGRAPHY

Abbreviations

HHSA   Haus-Hof-und Staatsarchiv, Vienna
KA   Kriegsarchiv, Vienna
AFA   Alte Feldakten

Manuscripts and Archival Document Collections

Kriegsarchiv (KA) Vienna:
  FM Radetzky, *Nachlass,* 1850
  Alte Feldakten (AFA) for 1809
  Memoires (Mem.)—occasional memorandums, 1766, 1767, 1769
Haus-Hof-und Staatsarchiv (HHSA) Vienna:
  Staatskanzlei Vorträge, 1788, 1789, 1791
  Kolowrat Nachlass, 1789
Kriegsarchiv. *Denkschrift über die Reichsbefestigung der ehemalige Österreichisch-Ungarische Monarchie,* n.d.

———. *Feldzüge des Prinzen Eugen von Savoyen, Nach den Feldakten und anderen authentischen Quellen herausgegeben von der Abtheilung für Kriegsgeschichte des K. K. Kriegs-Archives.* Vols. 1–22. Vienna: Verlag des K.K. Generalstabes, 1876.

———. *Der Krieg in Italien 1859. Nach den Feldakten und anderen authentischen Quellen bearbeitet durch das k. k. Generalstabs-Bureau für Kriegsgeschichte.* Vols. 1–2. Vienna: Verlag des k. k. Generalstabs, 1876.

———. *Kriege unter der Regierung des Kaiser Franz. Im Aufträge des k. u. k. Chefs des Generalstabes herausgegeben von der Direktion des k. und k. Kriegsarchivs.* Vols. 1–2. Vienna: L. W. Seidel und Sohn k. u. k. Hofbuchhandler, 1904.

———. *Kriege unter Kaiser Josef II. Nach den Feldakten und anderen authentischen Quellen bearbeitet in der kriegsgeschichtlichen Abteilung des K. und K. Kriegsarchivs.* Vienna: L. W. Seidel und Sohn k. u. k. Hofbuchhandler, 1904.

———. *Österreichischer Erfolge-krieg 1740–1748. Nach den Feldakten und anderen authentischen Quellen herausgegeben von der Abtheilung für Kriegsgeschichte des K. K. Kriegs-Archives.* Vol. 1. Part 1. Vienna: L. W. Seidel und Sohn k. u. k. Hofbuchhandler, 1901.

———. *Österreichs Kämpfe Im Jahre 1866. Nach Feldakten bearbeitet durch das k. k. Generalstabs-Bureau für Kriegsgeschichte.* Vols. 1–3. Vienna: Verlag des k. k. Generalstabs, 1868.

Kriegsarchiv. *Sechzig Jahre Wehrmacht 1848–1908. Bearbeitet im k. u. k. Kriegsarchiv.* Vienna: Verlage des k. u. k. Kriegsarchivs, 1908.

Nosinich, J., and L. Wiener. *Kaiser Josef II. als Staatsmann und Feldherr. Österreichs Politik und Kriege in den Jahren 1763 bis 1790.* Compiled in the K. K. Kriegs-Archive. Vienna: L. W. Seidel und Sohn k. u. k. Hofbuchhandler, 1885.

Contemporary Memoirs, Letters, and Other Works

Arneth, Alfred Ritter von. *Correspondance secrète du comte de Mercy Argenteau avec l'empereur Joseph II et le prince de Kaunitz.* Vol. 1. Paris: Imprimerie Nationale, 1877.

———. *Geschichte Maria Theresia's.* Vols. 1–5. Vienna: W. Braumüller, 1877.

Auracher von Aurach, Joseph. *Vorlesungen über die angewandte Taktik, oder eigentliche Kriegswissenschaft. Für die k.k. österreichische Armee bearbeitet nach dem systematischen Lehrbuche des G. Venturini.* Vol. 1. Part 1. Vienna: Anton Strauss, 1812.

Beer, Adolf. *Zehn Jahre Österreichischer Politik, 1801–1810.* Leipzig: F. A. Brockhaus, 1877.

Blasek, Heinrich. *Beiträge zur Geschichte der K. U. K. Genie-waffe: Nach den vom K. U. K. Obersten des Genie-Stabes, Im Auftrage des K. U. K. Reichs-Kriegs-Ministeriums zusammengestellt und bearbeitet.* Vol. 1. Part 2. Vienna: L. W. Seidel und Sohn, 1898.

Bourscheid, J. W. *Kaisers Leo des Philosophen: Strategie und Taktik.* Vienna: Joh. Thomas Ehlen v. Trattenern, kaiserlich-königlichen Hof- und Staatsdruckerei, 1777.

Habsburg, Archduke Charles von. *Principles of War.* Translated by Daniel I. Radakovich. Ann Arbor, MI: Nimble Books, 2009.

Henderson, And. *Memoirs of Field Marshal Leopold Count Daun, Translated from a French Manuscript, and Interspersed with Many Curious Anecdotes; Among Which Is a Full and Particular Account of Field Marshal Keith.* London: R. Withy and J. Ryall, 1757.

Karl, Erzherzog. *Militärische Werke.* Vol. 1. Vienna: kaiserlich-königlichen Hof- und Staatsdruckerei, 1862.

Kinsky, Franz. *Über Emplacement der Festungen: Erster Nachtrag zu den Elementar Begriffen.* Vienna: Adam und Kompagnie, 1790.

Kraus, Alfred. *Supplement to 1805: Der Feldzug von Ulm.* Vienna: L. W. Seidel und Sohn, K. u. K. Hofbuchhändler, 1912.

Lesic, Anton. *Das Entstehen der Militärgrenze und die Geschichte der Stadt und Festung Brod A./S. Kriegsarchiv.* Zagreb: Koynigliche Landesdruckerei, 1914.

Lloyd, General von. *Abhandlung über die allgemeinen Grundsätze der Kriegskunst.* Frankfurt: Philipp Heinrich Perrenon, 1783.

Metternich, Clemens Wenzel Lothar. *Memoirs of Prince Metternich.* Edited by Prince Richard Metternich. London: Forgotten Books, 2012. First published 1880.

Politische Correspondenz Friedrichs des Grossen. Vol. 1. Berlin: Geheimes Staatsarchiv Preussischer Kulturbesitz, 1879.

Radetzky von Radetz, Johann Joseph Wenzel. *Denkschriften militärisch-politischen Inhalts aus dem Handschriftlichen Nachlass des k.k. österreichischen Feldmarschalls Grafen Radetzky.* Stuttgart: J. G. Cotta'scher, 1858.

Savoy, Prince Eugene of. "Memoirs of Prince Eugene of Savoy." In *Eugene of Savoy: Marlborough's Great Military Partner,* edited by Alexander Innes Shand, translated by William Mudford. London: Leonaur Ltd., 2014.

Schneider, Karl. "Aus dem Briefwechsel Maria Theresias mit Josef II." In *Aus Österreichs Vergangenheit: Quellenbücher zur österreichischen Geschichte No. 11*, edited by Karl Schneider. Vienna: Schulwissenschaftlicher Verlag, 1917.

Stenographische Protokolle des Hauses der Abgeordneten des Reichsrathes, 61. Sitzung der 2. Und 3. Session. May 11–December 1863.

Venturini, G. *Beschreibung und Regeln eines neuen Krieges-Spiels, zum Nutzen und Vergnügen, besonders aber zum Gebrauch in Militär-Schulen*. Schleswig: Bey J. G. Röhß, 1797.

———. *Kritische Übersicht des letzten und merkwürdigsten Feldzugs im achtzehnten Jahrhundert*. Leipzig: Johann Conrad Hinrichs, 1802.

———. *Mathematisches System der angewandten Taktik oder eigentlichen Kriegswissenschaft*. Schleswig: J. Rohtz, 1800.

Von Aresin. 1860. *Das Festungsviereck von Ober-Italien, seine Bedeutung für Deutschland, die Schweiz und das Machtgleichgewicht von Europa*. Vienna: kaiserlich-königlichen Hof- und Staatsdruckerei, 1860.

Whatley, Samuel. *A General Collection of Treatys of Peace and Commerce, Manifestos, Declarations of War, and Other Publick Papers*. Vol. 4. London: J. J. and P. Knapton, 1732.

Xylander, Max Ritter von. *Das Heer-Wesen der Staaten des Deutschen Bundes*. Augsburg: Karl Kollman'schen Buchhandlung, 1846.

Secondary Sources

Abbott, John S. C. *The Empire of Austria: Its Rise and Present Power*. Middlesex, UK: Echo Library, 2006.

Abou-el-Haj, Rifa'at A. "The Formal Closure of the Ottoman Frontier in Europe, 1699–1703." *Journal of the American Oriental Society* 89, no. 3 (1969): 467–75.

Ágoston, Gábor. "Firearms and Military Adaptation: The Ottomans and the European Military Revolution, 1450–1800." *Journal of World History* 25, no. 1 (2014): 85–124.

———. *Guns for the Sultan: Military Power and the Weapons Industry in the Ottoman Empire*. New York: Cambridge University Press, 2005.

———. "Habsburgs and Ottomans: Defense, Military Change, and Shifts in Power." *Turkish Studies Association Bulletin* 22, no. 1 (1998): 126–41.

Aksan, Virginia H. *Ottoman Wars, 1700–1870: An Empire Besieged*. London: Pearson Education Limited, 2007.

———. "Whatever Happened to the Janissaries? Mobilization for the 1768–1774 Russo-Ottoman War." *War in History* 5, no. 1 (1998): 23–36.

Anderson, R. C. *Naval Wars in the Levant, 1559–1853*. Princeton, NJ: Princeton University Press, 1952.

Andrássy, Gyula. *Bismarck, Andrássy, and Their Successors*. Boston: Houghton Mifflin, 1927.

Anonymous. "Notary of King Béla: The Deeds of the Hungarians." Edited and and Translated by Martyn Rady and László Veszprémy. In *Central European Medieval Texts Series*, edited by János M. Bak, Urszula Borkowska, Giles Constable, and Gábor Klaniczay. Vol. 5. Budapest: Central European University Press, 2010.

Badem, Candan. *The Ottoman Crimean War, 1853–1856*. Leiden: Brill, 2010.

Bairoch, Paul. "European Gross National Product, 1800–1975." *Journal of European Economic History* 5 (1976): 273–340.

Balbi, Francesco. *The Siege of Malta, 1565*. London: Folio Society, 1965.

Banfield, Thomas Charles. "The Austrian Empire: Her Population and Resources." *British and Foreign Review of European Quarterly Journal* 27 (1842): 218–87.

Barkey, Karen, and Mark von Hagen. *After Empire: Multiethnic Societies and Nation-Building: The Soviet Union and the Russian, Ottoman, and Habsburg Empires*. Boulder, CO: Westview Press, 1997.

Bassett, Richard. *For God and Kaiser: The Imperial Austrian Army, 1619–1918*. New Haven, CT: Yale University Press, 2015.

Beales, Derek. *Joseph II*. Vol. 1, *In the Shadow of Maria Theresa, 1741–1780*. Cambridge: Cambridge University Press, 1987.

———. "Review of R.J.W. Evans' Austria, Hungary, and the Habsburgs: Central Europe c. 1683–1867." *English Historical Review* 122, no. 499 (December 2007): 1423–25.

Beller, Steven. *A Concise History of Austria*. Cambridge: Cambridge University Press, 2006.

Benedikt, Heinrich. *Kaiseradler über dem Appenin; die Österreicher in Italien 1700 bis 1866*. Vienna: Herold, 1964.

Bérenger, Jean. *A History of the Habsburg Empire, 1700–1918*. New York: Routledge, 1968.

Berki, Imre. *A magyar határvédelem története* [History of border protection in Hungary]. Múlt-Kor, September 29, 2010.

Bittner, Ludwig. *Chronologisches Verzeichnis der Österreichischen Staatsverträge*. Vienna: Holzhausen, 1970.

Black, Jeremy. "Change in Ancien Régime International Relations: Diplomacy and Cartography, 1650–1800." *Diplomacy and Statecraft* 20, no. 1 (2009): 20–29.

———. *European Warfare, 1660–1815*. New Haven, CT: Yale University Press, 1994.

———. "A Revolution in Military Cartography?: Europe, 1650–1815." *Journal of Military History* 73, no. 1 (2009): 49–68.

Blake, William O., and Thomas H. Prescott. *The Volume of the World: Embracing the Geography, History, and Statistics*. Columbus: J. and H. Miller, 1855.

Blanning, Tim C. W. *Frederick the Great: King of Prussia*. New York: Random House, 2016.

———. "Paul W. Schroeder's Concert of Europe." *International History Review* 16, no. 4 (1994): 701–14.

Boot, Max. *War Made New: Technology, Warfare, and the Course of History, 1500 to Today*. New York: Gotham Books, 2006.

Börekçi, Günhan. "A Contribution to the Military Revolution Debate: The Janissaries' Use of Volley Fire during the Long Ottoman-Habsburg War of 1593–1606 and the Problem of Origins." *Acta Orientalia Academiae Scientarium Hungaricae* 59, no. 4 (2006): 407–38.

Brachelli, Hugo Franz von. *Handbuch der Geographie und Statistik für die gebildeten Stände*. Leipzig: Hinrichs, 1861.

Bridge, F. R. *The Habsburg Monarchy among the Great Powers, 1815–1918*. Oxford: Berg Publishers, 1994.

Brook-Shepherd, Gordon. *The Austrians: A Thousand-Year Odyssey*. New York: Carroll and Graf Publishers, 1998.

Browning, Reed. "Review of Hochedlinger, Michael, Austria's Wars of Emergence: War, State, and Society in the Habsburg Monarchy, 1683–1797." HABSBURG, H-Net Reviews, August 2003.

————. *The War of the Austrian Succession*. New York: St. Martin's Press, 1995.

Brüning, Günter. "Militär-Strategie Österreichs in der Zeit Kaiser Francis II (I)." PhD diss., Westfälische Wilhelms-Universität Münster, 1983.

Brzezinski, Zbigniew. *Game Plan: A Geostrategic Framework for the Conduct of the U.S.-Soviet Contest*. New York: Atlantic Monthly Press, 1986.

Buisseret, David. *Monarchs, Ministers, and Maps: The Emergence of Cartography as a Tool of Government in Early Modern Europe*. Chicago: University of Chicago Press, 1992.

Bülow, Dietrich Heinrich von. *The Spirit of the Modern System of War*. London: Whitehall, 1806.

Bushell, Anthony. *Polemical Austria: The Rhetorics of National Identity from Empire to the Second Republic*. Cardiff: University of Wales Press, 2013.

Büyükakça, Murat Çinar. "Ottoman Army in the Eighteenth Century: War and Military Reform in the Eastern European Context." PhD diss., Middle East Technical University, 2007.

Calder, Kent E. *Embattled Garrisons: Comparative Base Politics and American Globalism*. Princeton, NJ: Princeton University Press, 2007.

Calisir, M. Fatih. "A Long March: The Ottoman Campaign in Hungary, 1663." PhD diss., Central European University, 2009.

Campbell, Brian. *Rivers and the Power of Ancient Rome*. Chapel Hill: University of North Carolina Press, 2012.

Cardoso, José Luís, and Pedro Lains. *Paying for the Liberal State: The Rise of Public Finance in Nineteenth-Century Europe*. New York: Cambridge University Press, 2010.

Clark, Christopher M. *Iron Kingdom: The Rise and Downfall of Prussia, 1600–1947*. Cambridge, MA: Belknap Press of Harvard University, 2006.

Clausewitz, Carl von. *On War*. Translated by Michael Eliot Howard and Peter Paret. Princeton, NJ: Princeton University Press, 1989.

Cornwall, Mark. *The Last Years of Austria-Hungary: A Multi-National Experiment in Early Twentieth-Century Europe*. Exeter: University of Exeter Press, 2002.

Craig, Gordon Alexander. *The Battle of Königgrätz: Prussia's Victory over Austria, 1866*. Philadelphia: Lippincott Press, 1964.

Crankshaw, Edward. *The Fall of the House of Habsburg*. New York: Penguin, 1983.

Daniel, Hermann Adalbert. *Deutschland nach seinen physischen und politischen Verhältnissen*. Leipzig: Fues, 1874.

Darwin, John. *The Empire Project: The Rise and Fall of the British World-System, 1830–1970*. Cambridge: Cambridge University Press, 2011.

David, Geza, and Pal Fodor. "Ottomans, Hungarians, and Habsburgs in Central Europe: The Military Confines in the Era of Ottoman Conquest." In *The Ottoman Empire and Its Heritage*, edited by Suraiya Faroqhi and Halil Inalzik. Vol. 20. Leiden: Brill, 2000.

Deák, István. "Comparing Apples and Pears: Centralization, Decentralization, and Ethnic Policy in the Habsburg and Soviet Armies." In *Nationalism and Empire: The Habsburg Empire and the Soviet Union*, edited by Richard L. Rudolph and David F. Good. New York: St. Martin's Press, 1992.

————. "The Ethnic Question in the Multinational Habsburg Army: 1848–1918." In *Ethnic Armies: Polyethnic Armed Forces from the Time of the Habsburgs to the Age of the Superpowers*, edited by N. F. Dreisziger. Waterloo, ON: Wilfrid Laurier University Press, 1990.

Deák, István. "Imperial Armies: Sources of Regional Unity or Regional Chaos." PhD diss., Columbia University, 2000.

———. *Beyond Nationalism: A Social and Political History of the Habsburg Officer Corps, 1848–1918*. New York: Oxford University Press, 1990.

Deák, John. *Forging a Multinational State: State Making in Imperial Austria from the Enlightenment to the First World War*. Stanford, CA: Stanford University Press, 2015.

Delbrück, Hans. *The Dawn of Modern Warfare: History of the Art of War*. Translated by Walter J. Renfroe Jr. Vol. 4. Lincoln: University of Nebraska Press, 1990.

Dickson, P. G. M. *Finance and Government under Maria Theresa, 1740–1780*. 2 vols. Oxford: Clarendon Press, 1987.

Dörflinger, Johannes. *Die Österreichische Kartographie*. Vol. 1. Vienna: Österreichischen Akademie der Wissenschaften, 1984.

Dotzauer, Winfried. *Die deutschen Reichskreise, 1383–1806: Geschichte und Aktenedition*. Stuttgart: F. Steiner, 1998.

Downing, Brian M. *The Military Revolution and Political Change: Origins of Democracy and Autocracy in Early Modern Europe*. Princeton, NJ: Princeton University Press, 1992.

Dredger, John Anthony. "Offensive Spending: Tactics and Procurement in the Habsburg Military, 1866–1918." PhD diss., Kansas State University, 2013.

Dreisziger, N. F. *Ethnic Armies: Polyethnic Armed Forces from the Time of the Habsburgs to the Age of the Superpowers*. Waterloo, ON: Wilfrid Laurier University Press, 1990.

Duffy, Christopher. *The Army of Maria Theresa: The Armed Forces of Imperial Austria, 1740–1780*. New York: Hippocrene Books, 1977.

———. *The Fortress in the Age of Vauban and Frederick the Great, 1660–1789*. London: Routledge and Kegan Paul, 1985.

———. *The Fortress in the Early Modern World, 1494–1660*. London: Routledge and Kegan Paul, 1979.

———. "The Seven Years' War as a Limited War." In *East Central European Society and War in the Pre-Revolutionary Eighteenth Century*, edited by Gunther E. Rothenberg, Béla K. Király, and Peter F. Sugar. New York: Columbia University Press, 1982.

Dyck, Harvey L. "New Serbia and the Origins of the Eastern Question, 1751–55: A Habsburg Perspective." *Russian Review* 40, no. 1 (1981): 1–19.

Evans, R. J. W. "Communicating Empire: The Habsburgs and Their Critics, 1700–1919: The Prothero Lecture." *Transactions of the Royal Historical Society* 19 (2009): 117–38.

———. "The Habsburgs and the Hungarian Problem, 1790–1848." *Transactions of the Royal Historical Society* 39 (1989): 41–62.

Eysturlid, Lee W. *The Formative Influences, Theories, and Campaigns of the Archduke Carl of Austria*. Westport, CT: Greenwood Press, 2000.

Fairgrieve, James. *Geography and World Power*. London: University of London Press, 1915.

Friedjung, Heinrich. *Der Krimkrieg und die Österreichische Politik*. Stuttgart: J. G. Cotta'sche Buchhandlung Nachfolger, 1907.

Gabriel, Erich. *Die Hand- und Faustfeuerwaffen der habsburgischen Heere*. Vienna: Österreichischer Bundesverlag, 1990.

Gaddis, John Lewis. "What Is Grand Strategy?: American Grand Strategy after War." Lecture at the Triangle Institute for Security Studies and Duke University Program on American Grand Strategy, February 26, 2009.

Gady, Franz-Stefan. "The Genius of Metternich: Austria's Resurrection through 'Active Neutrality.'" *National Interest*, December 3, 2014.

Gallenga, Antonio. *Storia Del Piemonte Dai Primi Tempi Alla pace Di Parigi*. Vol. 2. Turin: Eredi Botta, 1856.

Giurescu, Dinu C. *Istoria Ilustrată a Românilor*. Bucharest: Sport-Tourism, 1981.

Good, David F. *The Economic Rise of the Habsburg Empire, 1750–1914*. Berkeley: University of California Press, 1984.

Gordon, Harold J., and Nancy M. Gordon. *The Austrian Empire: Abortive Federation?* Lexington, MA: D. C. Heath and Company, 1974.

Gottsmann, Andreas. *The Diet of Kromeriz and the Government of Schwarzenberg: The Constitutional Debate of 1848 between the Poles on the National Question and Response*. Vienna: Verl, 1995.

Grant, Jonathan. "Rethinking the Ottoman 'Decline': Military Technology Diffusion in the Ottoman Empire, Fifteenth to Eighteenth Centuries." *Journal of World History* 10, no. 1 (1999): 179–201.

Gray, Colin S. "Geography and Grand Strategy." *Comparative Strategy* 10, no. 4 (1991): 311–29.

———. *The Geopolitics of Super Power*. Louisville: University of Kentucky Press, 1988.

———. "Seapower and Landpower." In *Seapower and Strategy*, edited by Colin S. Gray and Roger W. Barnett. Annapolis: Naval Institute Press, 1989.

Griffith, Paddy. *Battle Tactics of the Civil War*. New Haven, CT: Yale University Press, 2001.

Gustav, Kolmer. *Parlament und Verfassung in Österreich 1. 1*. Graz: Akademische Druck-u. Verl.-Anst, 1972.

Hajnal, Henry. *The Danube: Its Historical, Political, and Economic Importance*. The Hague: Martinus Nijhoff, 1920.

Harley, John Brian. "Silences and Secrecy: The Hidden Agenda of Cartography in Early Modern Europe." *Imago Mundi: The International Journal for the History of Cartography* 40, no. 1 (1988): 57–76.

Hartley, Janet M. *Russia, 1762–1825: Military Power, the State, and the People*. Westport, CT: Praeger, 2008.

Hicock, Michael Robert. *Ottoman Military Administration in Eighteenth Century Bosnia*. Leiden: Brill, 1997.

Hill, Charles. *Grand Strategies: Literature, Statecraft, and World Order*. New Haven, CT: Yale University Press, 2010.

Himka, John-Paul. "Nationality Problems in the Habsburg and the Soviet Union." In *Nationalism and Empire: The Habsburg Empire and the Soviet Union*, edited by Richard L. Rudolph and David F. Good. New York: St. Martin's Press, 1992.

Höbelt, Lothar. "The Impact of the Rákóczi Rebellion on Habsburg Strategy: Incentives and Opportunity Costs." *War in History* 13, no. 1 (2006): 2–15.

Hochedlinger, Michael. *Austria's Wars of Emergence, 1683–1797*. New York: Routledge, 2013.

———. "The Habsburg Monarchy: From 'Military-Fiscal State' to 'Militarization.'" In *The Fiscal Military State in Eighteenth-Century Europe: Essays in Honour of P.G.M. Dickson*, edited by Christopher Storrs. Farnham, UK: Ashgate Publishing Company, 2009.

———. "Who's Afraid of the French Revolution? Austrian Foreign Policy and the European Crisis, 1787–1797." *German History* 21, no. 3 (2003): 293–318.

Howard, Michael. *The Continental Commitment: The Dilemma of British Defense Policy in the Era of the Two World Wars*. London: Maurice Temple Smith Ltd., 1972.

Hroch, Miroslav. "Language and National Identity." In *Nationalism and Empire: The Habsburg Empire and the Soviet Union*, edited by Richard L. Rudolph and David F. Good. New York: St. Martin's Press, 1992.

Huertas, Thomas Francis. *Economic Growth and Economic Policy in a Multinational Setting: The Habsburg Monarchy, 1841–1865*. Chicago: University of Chicago, 1977.

Hughes, Michael. *Law and Politics in the Eighteenth Century Germany: The Imperial Aulic Council in the Reign of Charles VI*. Woodbridge, UK: Royal Historical Society, 1988.

Hupchick, Dennis P., Harold E. Cox., and Dennis P. Hupchick. *The Palgrave Concise Historical Atlas of Eastern Europe*. New York: Palgrave, 2001.

Ingrao, Charles W. *The Habsburg Monarchy, 1618–1815*. New York: Cambridge University Press, 2000.

———. "Habsburg Strategy and Geopolitics during the Eighteenth Century." In *War and Society in East Central Europe*, edited by Gunther E. Rothenberg, Béla K. Király, and Peter F. Sugar. Vol. 2. New York: Brooklyn College Press, 1982.

———. *In Quest and Crisis: Emperor Joseph I and the Habsburg Monarchy*. West Lafayette, IN: Purdue University Press, 1979.

Ingrao, Charles W., and Yasir Yilmaz. "Ottoman vs. Habsburg: Motives and Priorities." In *Empires and Peninsulas: Southeastern Europe between Karlowitz and the Peace of Adrianople, 1699–1829*, edited by Plamen Mitev, Ivan Parvev, Maria Baramova, and Vania Racheva. New Brunswick, NJ: Transaction Publishers, 2010.

Jászi, Oszkár. *The Dissolution of the Habsburg Monarchy*. Chicago: University of Chicago Press, 1929.

Jelavich, Barbara. *The Habsburg Empire in European Affairs, 1814–1918*. Hamden, CT: Archon Books, 1975.

Jones, Archer. *The Art of War in the Western World*. Champaign: University of Illinois Press, 1987.

Judson, Pieter M. *The Habsburg Empire: A New History*. Cambridge, MA: Belknap Press of Harvard University, 2016.

Kagan, Robert. *The World America Made*. New York: Vintage Books, 2013.

Kahan, Arcadius, and Richard Hellie. *The Plow, the Hammer, and the Knout: An Economic History of Eighteenth-Century Russia*. Chicago: University of Chicago Press, 1985.

Kann, Robert A. *A History of the Habsburg Empire, 1526–1918*. Berkeley: University of California Press, 1974.

———. *The Multinational Empire: Nationalism and National Reform in the Habsburg Monarchy, 1848–1918*. Vols. 1–2. New York: Octagon Books, 1964.

———. "The Social Prestige of the Officer Corps in the Habsburg Empire from the Eighteenth Century to 1918." In *War and Society in East Central Europe*, edited by Béla Király and Gunther E. Rothenberg. Vol. 1. New York: Brooklyn College Press, 1979.

Kann, Robert A., Béla K. Király, and Paula S. Fichtner. *The Habsburg Empire in World War I: Essays on the Intellectual, Military, Political, and Economic Aspects of the Habsburg War Effort*. Boulder, CO: East European Quarterly, 1977.

Kaplan, Herbert H. *Russia and the Outbreak of the Seven Years' War*. Berkeley: University of California Press, 1968.

Kaufmann, J. E., and H. E. Kaufmann. *The Forts and Fortifications of Europe, 1815–1945: The Central States: Germany, Austria-Hungary, and Czechoslovakia*. Barnsley, UK: Pen and Sword Military, 2014.

Keegan, John. *A History of Warfare*. New York: Vintage Books, 1993.

Kennedy, Paul M. *The Rise and Fall of the Great Powers: Economic Change and Military Conflict from 1500 to 2000*. New York: Random House, 1987.

———. "The Tradition of Appeasement in British Foreign Policy, 1865–1939." *British Journal of International Studies* 2, no. 3 (1976): 195–215.

Kinder, Hermann, and Werner Hilgemann. *The Anchor Atlas of World History: Volume I: From the Stone Age to the Eve of the French Revolution*. Garden City, NY: Anchor Books, 1978.

———. *The Anchor Atlas of World History: Volume II: From the French Revolution to the American Bicentennial*. Garden City, NY: Anchor Books, 1978.

Kissinger, Henry A. *Diplomacy*. New York: Simon and Schuster, 1994.

———. *World Order*. New York: Penguin Books, 2015.

———. *A World Restored: Metternich, Castlereagh, and the Problems of Peace, 1812–22*. Boston: Houghton Mifflin, 1957.

Kljajić, Josip. *Vojnokrajiški Čardaci u Slavonsko-Srijemskom Posavlju u 18. i 19. Stoljeću*. Zagreb: Hrvatski Institut za Povijest, 2002.

Kohl, J. G. *Austria: Vienna, Prague, Hungary, Bohemia, and the Danube; Galicia, Styria, Moravia, Bukovina, and the Military Frontier*. London: Chapman and Hall, 1842.

Kontler, László. *A History of Hungary: Millennium in Central Europe*. Basingstoke, UK: Palgrave Macmillan, 2002.

Kramar, Laszlo. "The Military Ethos of the Hungarian Nobility." In *War and Society in East Central Europe*, edited by Béla K. Király and Gunther E. Rothenberg. Vol. 1 New York: Brooklyn College Press, 1979.

Kramer, Hans. *Österreich und das Risorgimento*. Vienna: Bergland, 1963.

Lacey, James. "The Grand Strategy of the Roman Empire." In *Successful Strategies: Triumphing in War and Peace from Antiquity to the Present*, edited by Murray Williamson and Richard Hart Sinnreich. Cambridge: Cambridge University Press, 2014.

Lackey, Scott W. *The Rebirth of the Habsburg Army: Friedrich Beck and the Rise of the General Staff*. Westport, CT: Greenwood Press, 1995.

Lattimore, Owen. *Studies in Frontier History: Collected Papers, 1928–1958*. London: Oxford University Press, 1962.

LeDonne, John P. *The Grand Strategy of the Russian Empire, 1650–1831*. Oxford: Oxford University Press, 2003.

Lee, Bradford A. "Strategic Interaction: Theory and History for Practitioners." In *Competitive Strategies for the 21st Century: Theory, History, and Practice*, edited by Thomas G. Mahnken. Stanford, CA: Stanford University Press, 2012.

Leggiere, Michael V. "Austrian Grand Strategy and the Invasion of France in 1814." In *The Consortium on the Revolutionary Era, 1750–1850*, edited by Frederick C. Schneid and Jack Richard Censer. High Point, NC: High Point University, 2007.

Liddell Hart, B. H. 1991. *Strategy*. New York: Meridian, 1991.

Lieven, Dominic. *Empire: The Russian Empire and Its Rivals*. New Haven, CT: Yale University Press, 2002.

Loraine, Peter F. *Napoleon and the Archduke Charles: A History of the Franco-Austrian Campaign in the Valley of the Danube in 1809*. London: Greenhill Books, 1991.

Lucas, James Sidney. *Fighting Troops of the Austro-Hungarian Army, 1868–1914*. New York: Hippocrene Books, 1987.

Luttwak, Edward N. *The Grand Strategy of the Byzantine Empire.* Cambridge, MA: Belknap Press of Harvard University, 2009.

———. *The Grand Strategy of the Roman Empire from the First Century A.D. to the Third.* Baltimore: Johns Hopkins University Press, 1976.

Macartney, C. A. 1953. *The Medieval Hungarian Historians: A Critical and Analytical Guide.* Cambridge: Cambridge University Press.

Macartney, C. A. *The Habsburg and Hohenzollern Dynasties in the Seventeenth and Eighteenth Centuries.* London: Macmillan, 1970.

———. *The Habsburg Empire, 1790–1918.* New York: Macmillan, 1969.

Machiavelli, Niccolò. 1996. *Discourses on Livy.* Translated by Harvey Mansfield and Nathan Tarcov. Chicago: University of Chicago Press, 1996.

———. *The Prince and the Art of War.* London: CRW Publishing, 2004.

Magocsi, Paul Robert. *Historical Atlas of East Central Europe.* Seattle: University of Washington Press, 1993.

Magris, Claudio. *Danube: A Sentimental Journey from the Source to the Black Sea.* Translated by Patrick Creagh. New York: Farrar, Straus Giroux, 1989.

Mahan, A. T. *The Influence of Sea Power upon History: 1660–1783.* New York: Dover Publications, 1987.

Mahnken, Thomas G. *Competitive Strategies for the 21st Century: Theory, History, and Practice.* Stanford, CA: Stanford University Press, 2012.

Malfatti, Bartolomeo. "Il Quadrilatero, La Valle Del Po Ed Il Trentino." Vol. 37, *Biblioteca Utile.* Milan: Tipografia Internazionale, 1866.

Marx, Karl. "Austrian Bankruptcy." *New York Daily Tribune*, March 22, 1854.

Massari, M. *Sulla Necessitá Delle Fortificazioni Per La Difesa Degli Stati in Generale E Dell'Italia in Particolare.* Palermo: Rivista Sicula, 1871.

May, Arthur J. *The Hapsburg Monarchy, 1867–1914.* Cambridge, MA: Harvard University Press, 1951.

Mayer, Matthew Z. "Joseph II and the Campaign of 1788 Against the Ottoman Turks." Master's thesis, McGill University, 1997.

———. "The Price for Austria's Security: Part I. Joseph II, the Russian Alliance, and the Ottoman War, 1787–1789." *International History Review* 26, no. 2 (June 2004): 257–99.

———. "The Price for Austria's Security: Part II. Leopold II, the Prussian Threat, and the Peace of Sistova, 1790–1791." *International History Review* 26, no. 2 (September 2004): 473–514.

Mazower, Mark. *The Balkans: A Short History.* New York: Modern Library, 2002.

McClellan, George B. *The Armies of Europe: Comprising Descriptions in Detail of the Military Systems of England, France, Russia, Prussia, Austria, and Sardinia; Adapting Their Advantages to All Arms of the United States Service and Embodying the Report of Observations in Europe during the Crimean War, as Military Commissioner from the United States Government, in 1855–56.* Philadelphia: J. B. Lippincott and Co., 1861.

McFall, Kelly. "Ethnicity as a Problem for Grand Strategy: Conrad Von Hotzendorf, Nationalism, and the Habsburg Imperial Army at War, 1914–1916." PhD diss., Ohio State University, 1998.

McGuigan, Dorothy Gies. *The Habsburgs.* Garden City, NY: Doubleday, 1966.

McNeill, William Hardy. *Europe's Steppe Frontier, 1500–1800*. Chicago: University of Chicago Press, 1964.

Milevski, Lukas. *The Evolution of Modern Grand Strategic Thought*. Oxford: Oxford University Press, 2006.

Millward, Robert. *The State and Business in the Major Powers: An Economic History, 1815–1939*. London: Routledge, 2013.

Mitton, G. E. *Austria-Hungary*. London: Adam and Charles Black, 1914.

Montecuccoli, Raimondo. "Sulle Battaglie." Translated by Thomas M. Barker. In *The Military Intellectual and Battle: Raimondo Montecuccoli and the Thirty Years War*. Albany: State University of New York Press, 1975.

Münkler, Herfried. *Empires: The Logic of World Domination from Ancient Rome to the United States*. Cambridge, UK: Polity, 2007.

Murphey, Rhoads. *Ottoman Warfare, 1500–1700*. New Brunswick, NJ: Rutgers University Press, 1999.

Murray, Williamson, Richard Hart Sinnreich, and Jim Lacey. 2011. *The Shaping of Grand Strategy: Policy, Diplomacy, and War*. Cambridge: Cambridge University Press, 2011.

Neustadt, Richard E., and Ernest R. May. *Thinking in Time: The Uses of History for Decision-Makers*. New York: Free Press, 1988.

Nicolle, David, and Angus McBride. *Armies of the Ottoman Turks, 1300–1774*. London: Osprey Publishing, 1983.

Nicolson, Harold. *The Congress of Vienna, A Study in Allied Unity, 1812–1822*. New York: Harcourt, Brace and Company, 1946.

Nosworthy, Brent. *Battle Tactics of Napoleon and His Enemies*. London: Constable and Company Ltd., 1995

Pálffy, Géza. "The Origins of the Border Defense System against the Ottoman Empire in Hungary (Up to the Eighteenth Century)." In *Ottomans, Hungarians, and Habsburgs in Central Europe: The Military Confines in the Era of Ottoman Conquest*, edited by Géza David and Pál Fodor. Leiden: Brill, 2000.

Palmer, Alan. *Metternich*. London: History Book Club, 1972.

———. *Twilight of the Habsburgs: The Life and Times of Emperor Francis Joseph*. New York: Atlantic Monthly Press, 1998.

Pammer, Michael. "Public Finance in Austria-Hungary, 1820–1913." In *Paying for the Liberal State: The Rise of Public Finance in Nineteenth Century Europe*, edited by Jose Luis Cardoso and Pedro Lains. Cambridge: Cambridge University Press, 2010.

Parker, Geoffrey. *The Grand Strategy of Philip II*. London: Redwood, 2000.

Posch, Fritz. *Flammende Grenze: Die Steiermark in den Kuruzzenstürmen*. Graz: Styria, 1968.

Rahe, Paul Anthony. *The Grand Strategy of Classical Sparta: The Persian Challenge*. New Haven, CT: Yale University Press, 2015.

Rauchensteiner, Manfried. "The Development of War Theories in Austria at the End of the Eighteenth Century." In *East Central European Society and War in the Pre-Revolutionary Eighteenth Century*, edited by Gunther E. Rothenberg, Béla K. Király, and Peter F. Sugar. New York: Columbia University Press, 1982.

———. *Vom Limes zum "Ostwall."* Vol. 21, *Militärhistorische Schriftenreihe*. Vienna: Militärwissenschaftliches Institut Österreichischer Bundesverlag, 1972.

Regele, Oskar. *Beiträge zur Geschichte der staatlichen Landesaufnahme und Kartographie in Österreich bis zum Jahre 1918*. Vienna: Notringes der wissenschaftlichen Verbände Österreichs, 1995.

Reports of Committees of the House of Representatives, Second Session of the Thirty-Seventh Congress, vol. 4, no. 86 (1861–62).

Rich, Norman. *Why the Crimean War?: A Cautionary Tale*. Hanover, NH: University Press of New England, 1985.

Ritter, Gerhard. *The Sword and the Scepter*. Vol. 1, *The Prussian Tradition, 1740–1890*. London: Penguin Allen Lane, 1972.

Roider, Karl A., Jr. *Austria's Eastern Question, 1700–1790*. Princeton, NJ: Princeton University Press, 1982.

———. *The Reluctant Ally: Austria's Policy in the Austro-Turkish War, 1737–1739*. Baton Rouge: Louisiana State University Press, 1972.

Romsics, Ignác, and Béla K. Király. *Geopolitics in the Danube Region: Hungarian Reconciliation Efforts, 1848–1998*. Budapest: Central European University Press, 1999.

Roshwald, Aviel. *Ethnic Nationalism and the Fall of Empires: Central Europe, Russia, and the Middle East, 1914–1923*. London: Routledge, 2001.

Rothenberg, Gunther E. *The Army of Francis Joseph*. West Lafayette, IN: Purdue University Press, 1976.

———. "The Austrian Army in the Age of Metternich." *Journal of Modern History* 40, no. 2 (1968): 156–65.

———. *The Austrian Military Border in Croatia, 1522–1747*. Chicago: University of Illinois Press, 1960.

———. *East Central European Society and War in the Pre-Revolutionary Eighteenth Century*. New York: Columbia University Press, 1982.

———. "The Habsburg Military Border System: Some Reconsiderations." In *War and Society in East Central Europe*, edited by Béla K. Király and Gunther E. Rothenberg. Vol. 1. New York: Brooklyn College Press, 1979.

———. *The Military Border in Croatia, 1740–1881: A Study of an Imperial Institution*. Chicago: University of Chicago Press, 1966.

———. *Napoleon's Great Adversary: Archduke Charles and the Austrian Army, 1792–1814*. Boston: De Capo Press, 1995.

———. "The Origins of the Austrian Military Frontier in Croatia and the Alleged Treaty of 22 December 1522." *Slavonic and East European Review* 38, no. 91 (1960): 493–98.

———. "The Shield of the Dynasty: Reflections on the Habsburg Army, 1649–1918." *Austrian History Yearbook* 32 (2001): 169–206.

Roy, Kaushik. "Horses, Guns, and Governments: A Comparative Study of the Military Transition in the Manchu, Mughal, Ottoman, and Safavid Empires, circa 1400 to circa 1750." *International Area Studies Review* 15, no. 2 (2012): 99–121.

Rudolph, Richard L., and David F. Good. *Nationalism and Empire: The Habsburg Empire and the Soviet Union*. New York: St. Martin's Press, 1992.

Rumpler, Helmut, and Peter Urbanitsch. "Review of The Habsburg Monarchy, 1848–1918, and the Habsburgermonarchie Project." *English Historic Review* 122, no. 498 (2007): 1016–22.

Rusinow, Dennison. "Ethnic Politics in the Habsburg Monarchy and Successor States." In *Nationalism and Empire: The Habsburg Empire and the Soviet Union*, edited by Richard L. Rudolph and David F. Good. New York: St. Martin's Press, 1992.

Rycaut, Paul, and Richard Knolles. *The History of the Turkish Empire from the Year 1623 to the Year 1677; Containing the Reigns of the Three Last Emperours*. London: Printed by J. M. for J. Starkey, 1680.

Sanchez J. J. "Military Expenditure, Spending Capacity, and Budget Constraint in Eighteenth-Century Spain and Britain." *Revista De Historia Economica: Journal of Iberian and Latin American Economic History* 27, no. 1 (2009): 141–74.

Schroeder, Paul W. "Bruck versus Buol: The Dispute over Austrian Eastern Policy, 1853–55." In *Systems, Stability, and Statecraft: Essays on the International History of Modern Europe*, edited by David Wetzel, Robert Jervis, and Jack S. Levy. New York: Palgrave Macmillan, 2004.

———. *The Transformation of European Politics, 1763–1848*. Oxford: Oxford University Press, 1994.

Scott, Hamish. "A Habsburg Emperor for the Next Century." *Historical Journal* 53, no. 1 (2010): 97–216.

Seton-Watson, Hugh. *Eastern Europe between the Wars, 1918–1941*. Hamden, CT: Archon Books, 1962.

Seward, Desmond. *Metternich: The First European*. New York: Viking, 1991.

Sked, Alan. *Decline and Fall of the Habsburg Empire, 1815–1918*. London: Pearson Education, 2001.

———. *Radetzky: Imperial Victor and Military Genius*. London: I. B. Tauris and Co., 2011.

Sondhaus, Lawrence. "The Strategic Culture of the Habsburg Army." *Austrian History Yearbook* 32 (2001): 225–34.

Sperber, Jonathan. *The European Revolutions, 1848–1851*. Cambridge: Cambridge University Press, 1994.

Spykman, Nicholas John. *America's Strategy in World Politics: The United States and the Balance of Power*. New York: Harcourt, Brace and Company, 1942.

Stein, Mark L. *Guarding the Frontier: Ottoman Border Forts and Garrisons in Europe*. London: Tauris Academic Studies, 2007.

Stone, David R. *A Military History of Russia: From Ivan the Terrible to the War in Chechnya*. Westport, CT: Praeger Security International, 2006.

Storrs, Christopher. *The Fiscal-Military State in Eighteenth-Century Europe: Essays in Honour of P. G. M. Dickson*. Farnham, UK: Ashgate Publishing Company, 2009.

Stoye, John. *The Siege of Vienna: The Last Great Trial between Cross and Crescent*. New York: Pegasus Books, 2006.

Strausz-Hupé, Robert. *Geopolitics: The Struggle for Space and Power*. New York: G. P. Putnam's Sons, 1942.

Sugar, Peter F. *Southeastern Europe under Ottoman Rule, 1354–1804*. Seattle: University of Washington Press, 1977.

Szabo, Franz A. J. *The Seven Years War in Europe, 1756–1763*. London: Routledge, 2007.

Taylor, A. J. P. *The Habsburg Monarchy, 1809–1918; A History of the Austrian Empire and Austria-Hungary*. Harmondsworth, UK: Penguin Books, 1948.

Taylor, A. J. P. *The Struggle for Mastery in Europe, 1848–1918*. Harmondsworth, UK: Penguin Books, 1954.

Tilly, Charles. *The Formation of National States in Western Europe*. Princeton, NJ: Princeton University Press, 1975.

Tott, François de. *Memoirs of Baron de Tott: Volumes I and II*. New York: Arno Press, 1973.

Tuck, Christopher. "'All Innovation Leads to Hellfire': Military Reform and the Ottoman Empire in the Eighteenth Century." *Journal of Strategic Studies* 31, no. 3 (2008): 467–502.

Tunstall, Graydon A. *Planning for War against Russia and Serbia: Austro-Hungarian and German Military Strategies, 1871–1914*. Boulder, CO: Social Science Monographs, 1993.

Turhan, Fatma Sel. *The Ottoman Empire and the Bosnian Uprising: Janissaries, Modernisation, and Rebellion in the Nineteenth Century*. London: I. B. Tauris, 2014.

US Army. *Field Manual Number 21–18: Foot Marches*. Washington, DC: Department of the Army, 1990.

Van der Kiste, John. *Emperor Francis Joseph: Life, Death, and the Fall of the Hapsburg Empire*. Stroud, UK: Sutton Publishers, 2005.

Vann, James. "Mapping under the Austrian Habsburgs." In *Monarchs, Ministers, and Maps: The Emergence of Cartography as a Tool of Government in Early Modern Europe*, edited by David Buisseret. Chicago: University of Chicago Press, 1992.

Veres, Madalina Valeria. "Constructing Imperial Spaces: Habsburg Cartography in the Age of Enlightenment." PhD diss., University of Pittsburgh, 2015.

Voges, Dietmar-H. *Nördlingen seit der Reformation: Aus dem Leben einer Stadt*. Munich: C. H. Beck, 1998.

Wagner, Arthur L. *The Campaign of Königgrätz: A Study of the Austro-Prussian Conflict in the Light of the American Civil War*. Kansas City: Hudson-Kimberly, 1899.

Walker, Mack. *Metternich's Europe*. London: Palgrave Macmillan, 1968.

Wank, Solomon. "The Habsburg Empire." In *After Empire: Multiethnic Societies and Nation-Building: The Soviet Union and the Russian, Ottoman, and Habsburg Empires*, edited by Karen Barkey and Mark Von Hagen. Boulder, CO: Westview Press, 1997.

Wawro, Geoffrey. "An 'Army of Pigs:' The Technical, Social, and Political Bases of Austrian Shock Tactics, 1859–1866." *Journal of Military History* 59, no. 3 (1995): 407–33.

———. *The Austro-Prussian War: Austria's War with Prussia and Italy in 1866*. Cambridge: Cambridge University Press, 1966.

———. "Inside the Whale: The Tangled Finances of the Austrian Army, 1848–1866." *War in History* 3, no. 1 (1996): 42–65.

———. *A Mad Catastrophe: The Outbreak of World War I and the Collapse of the Habsburg Empire*. New York: Basic Books, 2014.

Wessely, Kurt. "The Development of the Hungarian Military Frontier until the Middle of the Eighteenth Century." *Austrian History Yearbook* 9 (1973): 55–110.

Whaley, Joachim. *Germany and the Holy Roman Empire*. Oxford: Oxford University Press, 2011.

Wheatcroft, Andrew. *The Habsburgs: Embodying Empire*. London: Penguin Books, 1995.

White, Major D. Jonathan. *Confederate Strategy in 1863: Was a Strategic Concentration Possible?* Fort Leavenworth, KS: Penny Hill Press, 2000.

Wilson, Peter H. *German Armies: War and German Society, 1648–1806*. London: UCL Press, 1998.

————. "Prussia's Relations with the Holy Roman Empire, 1740–1786." *Historical Journal* 51, no. 2 (2008): 337–71.

Winder, Simon. *Danubia: A Personal History of Habsburg Europe*. London: Picador, 2013.

Wohlforth, William C. "The Stability of a Unipolar World." *International Security* 24, no. 1 (1999): 5–41.

Wolfe, Larry. "'Kennst du das Land?' The Uncertainty of Galicia in the Age of Metternich and Fredo." *Slavic Review* 67, no. 2 (2008): 277–300.

Woods, Kyle. "Indivisible and Inseparable: The Austro-Hungarian Army and the Question of Decline and Fall." PhD diss., Claremont McKenna College, 2003.

Zeinar, Hubert. *Geschichte des österreichischen Generalstabes*. Vienna: Böhlau, 2006.

INDEX

Note: Page numbers in italic type refer to figures or tables.

A NOTE ON THE TYPE

This book has been composed in Arno, an Old-style serif typeface in the
classic Venetian tradition, designed by Robert Slimbach at Adobe.

Printed in the USA
CPSIA information can be obtained
at www.ICGtesting.com
JSHW022111221223
54242JS00002B/51

9 780691 196442